BACKGROUND PAPERS
Volume I

HUMAN DEVELOPMENT REPORT 1999

GLOBALIZATION WITH A HUMAN FACE

Human Development Report Office,
The United Nations Development Programme,
New York

ISBN 92-1-126116-3
U.N. Sales Number E.99III.B.40

Distribution and Sales: United Nations Publications
New York, New York 10017

Printed on recycled paper

Foreword

The theme for Human Development Report 1999 is Globalization with a Human Face. From a human development perspective, globalization is not only about trade, capital or financial markets, but fundamentally about people and all the things that encompass their lives—technology, environment, culture, care, etc. Global markets, global technology, global ideas and global solidarity can enrich the lives of people everywhere. The challenge from a human development perspective, argues the Report, is to ensure that the benefits of globalization are shared equitably and that the increasing interdependence works for people—not just for profits.

Human Development Report 1999 also highlights key defining characteristics of present-day globalization: shrinking space, shrinking time and disappearing borders, with new markets, new actors, new rules and new tools. Globalization—driven by competitive global markets—has swung open doors to opportunities, but these are not equitably distributed among nations or people. Equally important, the Report argues, efficient but inequitable markets can put squeezes on non-market activities vital for human development. The Report recommends a three-tiered agenda for action: reforms within global governing institutions and rules to ensure greater equity; new regional approaches for collective action; and national and local policies to capture global opportunities and translate them more equitably into human advance.

This Report, as in the previous nine editions, has drawn on a number of independent research papers by distinguished academics and policymakers. This volume brings together fifteen of the background papers prepared for Human Development Report 1999, covering such areas as trade and capital flows, poverty and inequality, culture, environment, care, and national and global policy issues. Collectively, they represent a diverse but detailed analysis of globalization with a human face.

Papers by John Whalley, Martin Khor Kok Peng, and Stephany Griffith-Jones with J. Kimmis constitute the trade and capital flows cluster. Whalley's paper outlines emerging trade issues, particularly labour and environmental standards, that developing countries will face in future trade negotiations, and provides recommendations. Griffith-Jones and Kimmis argue that volatility in domestic economies can be causally linked to short-term speculative capital flows, by drawing on data from the East Asian and Mexican crises of the past decade. The paper offers both long- and short-term measures to cure and prevent such crises. Martin Khor Kok Peng's paper presents a detailed account of how various provisions of the Multilateral Agreement on Investment can curtail the scope of independent domestic policies for foreign investment, emphasising the impact such agreements can have on human development.

Jong-Wha Lee and Changyong Rhee's paper on the East Asian Crisis points to increased unemployment, inequality and poverty as the crisis' most distressing impacts, and it defines the groups that have borne the brunt—women, youth, the less experienced and the less educated. The paper stresses that social recovery takes longer than economic reversals. It examines the programmes of the International Monetary Fund within the context of social impacts, and offers important policy recommendations for creating social safety nets.

Three papers focus on globalization and links with poverty and inequality. Mohan Rao's paper on Openness, Poverty and Inequality is an attempt from cross-sectional country experiences to examine the relationship between the opening up of an economy and impacts on poverty and inequality. The quantitative analysis does not show any particular pattern and the paper argues that the outcome, to a large extent, depends on policy-matrices. Pablo Rodas-Martini's paper re-examines the literature on income inequality in both developed and in developing countries, with two key findings: the roots of inequality differ between the developing and the developed world, and the degree of inequality is widening in many parts of the world, both within nations and between nations. Focusing on the Latin American labour market, Victor Tokman and Emilio Klein argue that economic reforms stemming from structural adjustment policies led to more inequality and impoverishment, resulting in deeper social stratification.

Süle Özler, Lourdes Arizpe and Alejandro Ramirez Magaña covered employment, gender and culture. Looking at survey results from Turkey and Colombia, Özler's paper analyzes the impacts of globalization on women's work. The links, Özler concludes, are not gender-neutral, whether in the context of the formal labour market, the informal economy, or at home. In Culture, Globalization and International Trade, Lourdes Arizpe argues that culture is rapidly becoming one of globalizations' most contentious issues because it provides the images—and thus the underlying values—with which people construct their view of the world. Her paper reviews trends in three areas: cultural heritage and cultural rights, cultural effects of multimedia and cultural goods in trade agreements. Magaña's paper on the film industry in a globalized world focuses on three phenomena: declines of various national film industries and American leadership in world film markets; support schemes by governments to revive their domestic industries; and consumer preferences and the globalization of movies.

Globalization as the HDR 1999 defines it can put three squeezes: a time squeeze reducing the supply and quality of caring labour, a fiscal squeeze constraining the provisioning of social services, and an incentive squeeze harming the environment. Nancy Folbre's paper maintains that the relentless pressures of global competition are squeezing out care, the invisible heart of human development. In Globalization and the Fiscal Autonomy of the State, Mohan Rao argues that the revenue-generating capability of the state has been constrained, resulting in erosion of provision of social services. Finally, the fact that prices of natural resources do not reflect their full cost provides an incentive for environmental degradation. Theodore Panayotou's paper describes this process within the context of globalization's increased production, trade and capital flows. It also raises the issue of environmental standards being used for trade sanctions, but argues that it is an inefficient and inequitable instrument.

Finally, two papers that explore global governance. Philip Alston looks at the normative areas of global governance for the protection and promotion of human rights, offering both short- and long-term proposals for a reform programme in this field. The developing world's unequal participation in global negotiations and in global economic governance is the main theme of Gerry Helleiner and Ademola Oyejide's paper. The authors document the nature of this participation, providing innovative measures to redress under-representation.

These papers are presented with the objective of contributing more to the debate on how globalization can enhance human development. The opinions expressed in these papers do not represent the views of the United Nations Development Programme, or of the Human Development Report Office. We do, however, welcome all comments to contribute to the lively debate on human development.

Richard Jolly
Special Adviser to the Administrator
United Nations Development Programme

Sakiko Fukuda-Parr
Director
Human Development Report Office

Contents

International Governance in the Normative Areas

Philip Alston

One of the most noteworthy developments of the 1990s has been the realisation on the part of policymakers that efforts to promote and ensure human rights not only can, but should, be an integral part of a wide range of other activities. During the years of the Cold War, efforts to inject human rights considerations into areas such as development, trade, aid or security were regularly dismissed as being ideologically motivated and thus inappropriate. In fact, they were indeed sometimes partly driven by such calculations, although this should not necessarily have been permitted to determine definitively whether or not they were valid concerns. But throughout the 1970s and 1980s, the allegation, whether justified or not, that human rights-based approaches carried excessive ideological baggage was seized upon with alacrity by those who had other reasons to downplay their importance. Very often those other reasons were essentially political in nature. Many politicians and military leaders had good reason to avoid human rights discussions, and they were ever ready to shine the spotlight on other priorities such as national security, economic growth, or avoiding domestic instability. But politics was not the only factor in the downgrading of rights. There were also jurisdictional reasons within international organisations and elsewhere: human rights belonged on a separate part of the organizational chart and should not be injected into areas where they did not belong. There were professional reasons: human rights just got in the way of serious economic or security analysis. And there were philosophical and cultural reasons for questioning the extent to which human rights were truly universal.

As the year 2000 approaches, these concerns have not been entirely pushed aside, let alone forgotten. Nor should they be, since there are legitimate aspects of some of them that deserve to be taken into account. But they are no longer able to block appropriate initiatives and they must now, as a result of various developments, be seen in a very different perspective. Those developments include 1) the waning of the cultural relativism debate in the wake of the 1989 ratification of the single most comprehensive international human rights treaty—the Convention on the Rights of the Child—by 191 States; 2) greater recognition on the part of economists and other policymakers that governance and the rule of law (human rights by other names) are indispensable elements of strategies for growth and development; 3) the transformation of the ideological debate, which can now be located within the framework of human rights discussions rather than outside it; and 4) the maturing of the human rights framework itself.

These factors have opened up important opportunities for policymakers to begin to reflect much more openly on the possible relevance of human rights within the broader array of activities undertaken by the international community. They have also highlighted the need to re-examine institutional and procedural arrangements that were somewhat reluctantly put in place during the Cold War era, so as to take account of the new context and of the greatly expanded opportunities and expectations which now exist in the field of human rights.

This paper constitutes an attempt to examine some of these issues, although it leaves many important questions to be taken up elsewhere. The paper is in three principal parts: a review of the current institutional arrangements of global governance; an assessment of the need for global governance in the normative areas, for the protection and promotion of human rights; and proposals for a programme of reform. For purposes of the analysis, the human rights component of global governance is referred to, using the terminology of political science, as the international human rights regime. It consists of those international norms, processes, and institutional arrangements, as well as the activities of domestic and international pressure groups, that are directly related to promoting respect for human rights. The latter term, however, is now increasingly being taken to include international humanitarian law, despite the very different assumptions on which the two bodies of standards are grounded. Another area, which is becoming increasingly closer, but still remains quite distinct, is refugee law. The latter two areas are not dealt with in detail in this analysis.

A. Review of the current institutional arrangements of global governance, the institutions, their roles and mandates, their overall functioning and impact

Although it is the main focus of what follows, the United Nations is only one part of the broader international regime. By any definition, that regime must also embrace at least: the authentically human rights-conscious United Nations agencies such as the International Labour Organization (ILO) and the United Nations Children's Fund (UNICEF). The United Nations Development Programme (UNDP) and the United Nations Population Fund (UNFPA) are in the next rank along with the United Nations Educational, Scientific and Cultural Organization (UNESCO) and the United Nations High Commissioner for Refugees (UNHCR). Regional mechanisms such as the Organization for Security and Cooperation in Europe (OSCE), the Council of Europe, the Organization of American States and the Organization of African Unity also have important human rights activities which contribute, albeit in varying degrees, to global governance in this field.

1. An overview of the evolution of the UN regime

Before reviewing these arrangements, it is useful to identify the proper place of today's international human rights law in historical terms. The fiftieth anniversary of the Universal Declaration of Human Rights, celebrated in 1998, served to remind us of both how young and how mature UN efforts are in this field. Human rights advocates also sometimes seek to downplay the novelty inherent in these developments by insisting that international efforts are little more than the rightful heirs of a tradition which is now many centuries old and whose roots are geographically and philosophically diverse. Within limits, a strong case of this type can be made. But by the same token, it is important to acknowledge just how recent are the developments which have made it possible to suggest that the international community can, and indeed must, be guided in its principal activities by respect for the norms of human rights.

While scattered norms (dealing with slavery, protection of aliens, a limited range of labour rights, etc.) existed within international law prior to the adoption of the Universal Declaration, these were generally of very limited significance in the overall scheme of things, and their application was greatly hampered by a range of jurisdictional limitations and an absence of arrangements for institutional follow-up (the ILO being the notable exception). Thus, for example, the complex arrangements for the protection of minority rights within Europe, developed during the inter-war years under the auspices of the League of Nations, had come to little. Initially, the principal practical impact of the Universal Declaration was to set in motion a flurry of standard-setting activities which, in the course of the next forty years or so, generated a plethora of treaties and softer standard-setting instruments at both the global and regional levels. But it was not until the 1970s that the United Nations began to respond even to massive human rights violations other than those occurring in relation to *apartheid* or the Occupied Palestinian Territories. Indeed it was not until the 1980s that the Commission on Human Rights began to develop techniques for monitoring particular types of violations on an across-the-board basis (through the so-called thematic mechanisms dealing with issues like disappearances, summary executions and torture). Not until 1994 (with the creation of the post of High Commissioner for Human Rights) was responsibility for human rights within the UN secretariat entrusted to a senior official with the status and clout (although still not the resources) necessary to ensure that the issue would be prominently on the institutional agenda. And finally, it was not until Kofi Annan took office in 1997 that the UN had a Secretary General who was prepared to see human rights as an integral part of the activities of the organization as a whole.

This very brief historical overview is designed to demonstrate that the human rights regime, at least within the UN context, is of remarkably recent provenance and is still in the relatively early phases of its evolution.

2. Institutional development within the UN

The years since the Commission on Human Rights was set up in 1946, and particularly since 1966, have seen a dramatic increase in the number of UN 'organs' devoted primarily to dealing with human rights matters, as well as a major increase in the time devoted by some of the existing organs to the human rights part of their mandates. Any depiction of this growth as being systematic, gradual or even rational is largely unwarranted. The system has grown 'like Topsy' and the boundaries between the different organs are often only poorly delineated. For the most part, this pattern has hardly been accidental. Rather, it is the inevitable result of a variety of actors seeking to achieve diverse, and perhaps sometimes even irreconcilable, objectives within the same overall institutional framework. If an existing body could not do a particular job, whether because of some intrinsic defects, sheer incompetence or, more likely, political intransigence, the preferred response was to set up yet another. In a very short space of time, states and individual actors would develop a vested interest in the maintenance of the new body in the same form. This pattern simply repeated itself when a new policy agenda, to which none of the existing bodies were sufficiently responsive, emerged.

In general then, the evolution of the regime has reflected specific political developments. Its expansion has depended upon the effective exploitation of the opportunities that have arisen in any given situation from the prevailing mix of public pressures, the cohesiveness or disarray of the key geopolitical blocks, the power and number of the offending state(s) and the international standing of their current governments, and a variety of other, often rather specific and ephemeral, factors. For that reason, efforts to identify and describe steady and principled patterns in the evolution of the various procedures are generally misplaced. Pragmatism, rather than principle has been the touchstone of the UN's evolution. This is especially apparent in almost any aspect of the activities of the Charter-based organs. Examples include: the reticence of those organs to spell out the normative basis on which they are acting in specific cases in condemning violations, especially in relation to states that are not parties to relevant treaty regimes; their failure to adopt any particular framework designed to enhance the integrity and perceived objectivity of fact-finding activities; and their reluctance to identify principles which would assist in determining the circumstances under which technical assistance (advisory services) should be offered to states, as well as the kind of assistance that might appropriately be provided when violations are involved. In each case, the main organs have tended to adopt ad hoc approaches from which lessons might or might not be drawn for application in subsequent cases.

It is tempting to speak of this evolution in unstintingly critical terms and to rue the lack of coordination, of a rational division of labour, or of any clear institutional blueprint. While there is indeed much to criticize, it must also be borne in mind that this unstated preference for 'letting a hundred flowers bloom' was largely responsible for whatever (albeit limited) capacity that the system exhibited for responding to new circumstances and taking advantage of new opportunities. But, the bottom line is that the UN human rights system consists of a wide range of disparate, and often only formally related, bodies with overlapping mandates and different, perhaps sometimes even inconsistent, approaches. There has been no grand design, there is a built-in resistance to institutional and procedural reform, and there is a reluctance to professionalise combined with a preference for relying upon diplomats or part-time 'experts'.

In certain respects the post-Cold-War era has been dominated by the need to respond to massive violations committed in the context of predominantly internal conflicts, whether in the former Yugoslavia, Chechnya, Rwanda, Burundi, Zaire/Democratic Republic of the Congo, Liberia, Sierra Leone, Angola, etc. As a consequence, there has been a preoccupation with the development of new approaches designed to establish human rights components of field operations and to develop mechanisms for the criminalization of gross violations (the courts established for the former Yugoslavia and Rwanda and the Rome International Criminal Court (ICC) Statute). While crucial in themselves, these efforts have tended to distract attention and especially resources away from the need to develop and refine the mainstream mechanisms.

3. The UN 'system' in a nutshell

The standard distinction for analytical purposes is between those organs whose establishment may be justified by reference to the provisions of the UN Charter (Charter-based organs) and those whose creation is justified by reference to the provisions of specific treaties (treaty-based organs). This distinction was, of course, unavailable—or at least meaningless—until 1970 when the first of the UN's human rights treaty bodies met for its inaugural session. Since that time a clearly discernible two-track approach to institutional arrangements has emerged.

Put succinctly, the essential role of each of the treaty bodies is to monitor and encourage compliance with a specific treaty regime, while the political organs have a much broader mandate to promote awareness, to foster respect and to respond to violations of human rights standards. Each treaty-based organ has been established either pursuant to the terms of a specific treaty or for the specific purpose of monitoring compliance with such a treaty. The Charter-based organs on the other hand derive their legitimacy and their mandate, in the broadest sense, from the human rights-related provisions of the Charter.

Within that overall framework, the treaty-based organs are distinguished by: a limited clientele, consisting only of states that are parties to the treaty in question; a clearly delineated set of concerns reflecting the terms of the treaty; a particular concern with developing the normative understanding of the relevant rights; a limited range of procedural options for dealing with matters of concern; caution in terms of setting precedents; consensus-based decision-making to the greatest extent possible; and a non-adversarial relationship with State Parties based on the concept of a 'constructive dialogue'.

By contrast, the political organs generally: focus on a diverse range of issues; insist that every state is an actual or potential client (or respondent), regardless of its specific treaty obligations; work on the basis of a constantly expanding mandate, which should be capable of responding to crises as they emerge; engage, as a last resort, in adversarial actions vis-à-vis states; rely more heavily upon the inputs of NGOs (non-governmental organizations) and public opinion generally to ensure the effectiveness of their work; take decisions by often strongly-contested majority voting; pay comparatively little attention to normative issues; and are very wary about establishing specific procedural frameworks within which to work, preferring a more ad hoc approach in most situations.

It is, of course, easy to overstate the differences between the two types of organ and to underestimate the ability of one type to emulate certain characteristics of the other. Thus a Charter-based organ might choose to play down its political character and devote some of its efforts to a systematic clarification of the normative content of a specific right, while a treaty-based organ might play down its constructive-dialogue approach in order to indicate its strong disapproval of a state's behaviour. Nevertheless, the differences of mandate, content, and style between the two types of organs are sufficiently clear and consistent as to justify using this as the principal distinction for purposes of the present analysis.

(a) The charter-based organs

The formal hierarchy of United Nations Charter-based organs consists of the General Assembly and the Economic and Social Council (ECOSOC) as principal organs and, underneath them as 'functional commissions', the Commission on Human Rights and the Commission on the Status of Women. This is as far as the system goes in terms of specific Charter authorization. However, each of these organs is entitled to create whatever subsidiary mechanisms it considers necessary to enable them to carry out its own responsibilities and functions under the Charter. It is at this point that the proliferation begins. The only such body to which specific attention need be drawn in this context is the Sub-Commission on Prevention of Discrimination and Protection of Minorities. It has long stood out because of its flexible agenda and working methods, its preparedness to act as a pressure group vis-à-vis its parent body (the Commission on Human Rights) and its ambiguous and often antagonistic relationship with that parent.

While in principle the lines of authority are reasonably clear-cut and obvious, in practice they are much less so. The ECOSOC, which once played a major role as an intermediary between the Assembly and the Commission, had become little more than a rubber stamp by the mid-1970s. With the recent emphasis on mainstreaming human rights into a much broader range of UN activities, the Council might, however, find a more substantive coordinating role for itself. The Assembly, on the other hand, has come to play an important initiating role in a number of areas while at the same time deferring (in substance, although not in form) to the Commission in many respects. Similarly, any analysis that portrayed the Sub-Commission as little more than a subsidiary organ to advise the Commission and do its bidding (and no more) might be an accurate reflection of the initial design as seen by some of its creators, but would otherwise be singularly out of touch with today's reality. The result of these various evolutionary trends is a much more complex inter-relationship among the group of bodies than any diagram or flow-chart could ever convey. The other principal organ which has become far more relevant in the course of the 1990s, but whose position on human rights still remains ambivalent, is the Security Council. Until 1991, the Council had a long history of refusing to consider itself as an organ for the promotion of respect for human rights, except insofar as a given situation constituted a threat to international peace and security, usually defined rather narrowly. In recent years, however, there have been many examples of the Council taking up human rights issues both in country-specific terms and more thematically. Thus it has met with South Africa's Graca Machel and subsequently Olara Otunnu, in their respective capacities as the Representative of the UN Secretary General for Children in Armed Conflict. To a large extent, however, the Council remains reticent and the great majority of its work has been based on international humanitarian law.

In such a setting, the latter body of law has a number of advantages in the eyes of states. It is more confined in scope than human rights law; it applies only in conflict situations, which usually implies a higher threshold; questions of interference in external affairs are generally less sensitive; the basic provisions are unquestionably part of customary law; it applies to both/all sides to any conflict and not just the government; and it is seen as a sufficient basis to enable governments to respond to the most pressing concerns of the public, such as genocide, mass rape, and other crimes against humanity.

(b) The Treaty-Based Organs or 'Treaty Bodies'

Since the Committee on the Elimination of Racial Discrimination (CERD) first met in January 1970, the treaty-based system has expanded at a rate that is without precedent in the field of international organization. By September 1991, when the Committee on the Rights of the Child (CRC) began its first session, there were six treaty bodies, and another one might eventuate when (if?) the International Convention on the Protection of the Rights of All Migrant Workers and Members of Their Families enters into force. Of these six, five are almost identical in form and basic mandate. They are, in addition to the two already mentioned, the Human Rights Committee (HRC) (which first met in 1976), the Committee on the Elimination of Discrimination against Women (CEDAW) (1982) and the Committee against Torture (CAT) (1988).

The other treaty body is the Committee on Economic, Social and Cultural Rights (CESCR), which first met in 1987. It is a curious hybrid in that it has been established by a Charter-based organ (ECOSOC), ostensibly to advise it on the implementation of the relevant treaty (the Covenant on Economic, Social and Cultural Rights), but in reality to perform virtually all of the Council's relevant treaty-based functions on its behalf. While the Committee can thus be abolished at any moment by the Council, it has been given a quasi-independent existence by being authorized by the latter to imitate in every significant way the role and working methods of the five other bodies that operate pursuant to specific treaty provisions.

In brief, each of the treaty bodies performs the task of monitoring State Parties' compliance with their obligations under the relevant treaty. Each of them does so through a dialogue with the representatives of each of the State Parties on the basis of a detailed report (an 'initial' report, followed by 'periodic' reports at approximately four- or five-year intervals). The principal outcome of this process is the 'concluding observations' adopted by the Committee, along with the summary records of the dialogue between the Committee and the Government concerned. The concluding observations indicate the extent to which, in the view of the Committee, the State party is, or is not, complying with its treaty obligations. Each of the Committees also adopts carefully drafted statements in the form of 'General Comments' (or some comparable terminology), which purport to be based directly on the Committees' work in examining reports, and which seek to elaborate upon the normative content of specific rights or to address specific issues that have arisen.

Three of the six Committees also deal with complaints from individuals alleging violations of their rights under the treaty concerned. The exceptions are CEDAW, CRC and CESCR. The latter has proposed a procedure to enable it to respond to individual petitions, but the Commission on Human Rights has yet to respond to the proposal. In contrast, a comparable proposal endorsed by CEDAW has led to the drafting of a complaints procedure which is now nearing completion (in the Commission on the Status of Women). Finally, there is an inter-state complaints mechanism which can be invoked before three of the treaty bodies (HRC, CERD, and CAT). The latter mechanism has attracted no attention from states and seems unlikely to generate any 'business' in the foreseeable future, despite the fact that there would seem to be a good number of disputes over minority rights and related issues which might be appropriately referred to such mechanisms.

There is no formal hierarchy among the treaty bodies, although the Human Rights Committee tends to have the potentially most significant mandate and to have attracted the most competent membership. The CRC, however, has made rapid strides and is now the best-resourced of all of the committees, thanks mainly to UNICEF and a not unrelated degree of attention on the part of NGOs, both at the national and international levels. The relationship among the treaty bodies and the need for measures to promote better coordination, to reduce overlapping and to rationalize the burden imposed on states that are parties to many of the treaties, have only recently begun to be addressed by UN organs. The main opportunity to do so is in the Meeting of the Chairpersons of the Human Rights Treaty Bodies, which was first convened in 1984, and now meets annually.

4. The Secretariat

In technical terms, the Secretary General and his staff also constitute a principal organ. The establishment of the Office of High Commissioner for Human Rights (HCHR) in December 1993 created the potential for an authentic human rights persona within the system.[1] Because of a lack of support by the previous Secretary General and bureaucratic infighting, it was only with the arrival of the second HCHR, in September 1997, that this potential has begun to be realised.

The principal development since 1993 has been the creation of a large number of 'field presences'. The origins of the first of these dates back to 6 April 1994, just one day after the first HCHR took office. The situation in Rwanda erupted after the shooting down of the President's plane and the ensuing genocide demanded a UN response. An emergency session of the Commission on Human Rights (only its third ever) was held and a Special Rapporteur was appointed. At High Commissioner Ayala-Lasso's suggestion, the Commission also agreed to send six human rights monitors, a number that reached well over a hundred by the time the mission was finally withdrawn in July 1998, after a dispute over whether it should continue to monitor or simply provide technical assistance.

Since 1994 field activities have proliferated. The development has been reactive and ad hoc, and little attempt has been made so far to 'rationalise' the situation. Some of these presences fall at the promotional end of the spectrum and emphasise the development of national capacities such as the creation of national human rights institutions and education programmes. Others are located directly within situations of 'deadly conflict', to use the Carnegie Commission's terminology. The human rights component in such situations can aim at prevention, protection, or capacity building, depending on the stage the conflict has reached and the attitude of the parties. A rough typology of activities undertaken to date includes:

- human rights missions linked to UN peace processes (the first of which was brokered by former Secretary General Perez de Cuellar in El Salvador) and similar missions function today in Haiti and Guatemala;
- human rights components of peacekeeping operations (the first was Cambodia, and Angola is a current example);
- human rights field operations run by the Office of the High Commissioner for Human Rights (OHCHR) with widely varying, but extensive mandates (Rwanda was in this category, and Burundi, Cambodia and Colombia still are). By way of illustration, the stated objectives of the latter are to: 'provide technical assistance; monitor the human rights situation in the country; receive complaints and allegations of human rights violations and other abuses, including breaches of humanitarian norms...; follow up the complaints and allegations received with the national authorities and appropriate international human rights bodies and mechanisms in Geneva; and report periodically to the High Commissioner, who will report to the Commission on Human Rights;[2]
- small-scale OHCHR field offices supporting monitoring by special rapporteurs and implementing technical cooperation programmes (Zaire/Democratic Republic of the Congo); and
- on-site technical cooperation missions, such as in Malawi and Gaza.

The OHCHR also has a significant technical cooperation programme, whose activities are not entirely separate from those noted above. They are, however, much more in the way of carrots rather than sticks. Under the programme, assistance is provided with the drafting of legislation, the development of new national institutions to protect human rights, the provision of human rights training and education and other such activities. In 1997, the first HCHR said that he had sought to expand the programme 'to the maximum degree', resulting in there being 'more than 400 technical cooperation activities' in 1996 alone.[3] Critics have questioned whether this should be a priority concern, whether such assistance should be provided by the Centre for Human Rights as opposed, for example, to the United Nations Development Programme; whether clear enough guidelines exist to prevent the blurring of the line between assistance and political reinforcement; and whether the enthusiasm of governments for such activities derives mainly from a concern to divert UN attention away from their continuing violations.

5. International Criminal Tribunals

The other major development since 1993 has been the establishment of the Ad Hoc Criminal Tribunals for the former Yugoslavia in 1993 and for Rwanda in 1995, and the adoption of the Statute of the International Criminal Court in July 1998. These developments have had enormous significance in terms of reinforcing the notion of individual criminal responsibility at the international level and breaking down the shield of sovereignty. Recent events in relation to former Chilean President Pinochet are another manifestation of this trend towards universal criminal jurisdiction for certain crimes.

6. Towards an evaluation

The UN's effectiveness in this domain has been the subject of much casual comment but remarkably little systematic evaluation. This is because of the difficulty in reaching agreement on an appropriate set of criteria. One explanation for this failure is the unquestioning acceptance of the assumption that the UN's central function is to respond effectively to violations of human rights wherever they occur. What constitutes an 'effective' response is usually not spelled out. Thus some critics might be satisfied with a focused discussion in an international forum of any relevant situation; others might insist upon a formal condemnation or at least the establishment of a fact-finding and reporting mechanism wherever appropriate; still others might be unsatisfied with anything less than the imposition of sanctions or even the mounting of a military exercise designed to restore respect for human rights.

In other words, some evaluators might start with a very strong 'world order' set of assumptions, while others might be firmly convinced of the need to protect 'state sovereignty' and the principle of non-intervention (as narrowly defined). Many will see the mobilization and pursuit of international pressures, primarily by or through the UN, as the key component in any global endeavour to protect human rights, while others will relegate UN action to a secondary role, perhaps at best. All of these factors will have a major and direct influence on the outcome of an evaluation exercise.

The question of causality also presents major difficulties in evaluation in general, and in this domain in particular. It is difficult enough to measure significant long-term impacts (even an immediate change in government or a direct reversal of offending policies may have little to do with UN measures) on issues such as the treatment of detainees, police harassment, freedom of the press, the fairness of the political system, freedom of association, etc. But it is even more difficult to attribute such impacts, even in part, to the actions taken by the UN or other international organizations.

Within the UN itself, there has tended to be an emphasis upon what might be termed bureaucratic indicators, such as the number of pages of documents 'processed' by the Centre for Human Rights, the number of meetings serviced, the number of trips undertaken, or the number of observers and NGOs at meetings. From a global governance perspective, these are hardly very useful.

Academics have varied greatly in their evaluations. One of the most negative has been Allott, who argues that after 1945 the 'idea of human rights quickly became perverted by the self-misconceiving of international society. Human rights were quickly appropriated by governments, embodied in treaties, made part of the stuff of primitive international relations, swept up into the maw of an international bureaucracy.' In sum, he concludes that 'the deterrent effect of bureaucratized human rights is negligible.' This is too negative, however.

Non-governmental groups have, de facto, been supportive of UN efforts if one judges by the amount of time and money they put into lobbying, observing and assisting with a wide range of activities. Nonetheless, they remain highly critical. It is worth briefly noting some of those criticisms.

- Some serious situations have been given very little attention by United Nations bodies; moreover, a few powerful countries seem to enjoy a degree of de facto immunity from sustained scrutiny;
- The mandates given to different 'investigative' and 'humanitarian' procedures remain subject to a complex array of restraints of both a substantive and procedural nature;
- The techniques available to thematic and country rapporteurs to mobilize the shame which might help to put an end to specific violations remain singularly under-developed;
- The follow-up measures accompanying these procedures are too often ineffectual, and many of the targeted governments have succeeded in ignoring them, or making only token gestures in response;
- The United Nations system, broadly defined, continues to overly compartmentalise human rights concerns, although this is now changing significantly;
- Very little progress has been made in relation to certain issues, including most notably economic, social and cultural rights, and minority rights;
- The financial and human resources available to carry out the various United Nations mandates are clearly inadequate;
- Many field agencies remain very reluctant to cooperate openly with human rights missions, although this is changing slowly.

Overall, however, fifty years after the adoption of the Universal Declaration, very significant progress has been made. The standards contained in the Universal Declaration are, in practice, applicable to every state, whatever its formal attitude to their legal status. The view that human rights violations are essentially domestic matters, while still put forward in an almost ritual manner from time to time, receives very little credence from the international community. The Universal Declaration has been supplemented by a vast array of international standards, the most important of which are the six 'core' human rights treaties. In addition to the six treaty bodies, regional human rights conventions, and implementing machinery, have been set up in Europe, the Americas and Africa, and the United Nations has created a complex array of other, additional monitoring mechanisms.

In the mid-1960s, the Commission on Human Rights began responding to human rights violations, albeit in a very limited number of situations. Since 1979, when the magnitude of unanswered atrocities forced it to go beyond the 'unholy trinity' of South Africa, Israel and Chile, it has gradually and persistently expanded both the number and diversity of countries subjected to public monitoring and the range and intrusiveness of the procedures it has been prepared to apply. NGOs and the victims of human rights violations now participate in ever-increasing numbers in the work of one or more of the bodies set up by the Commission or its Sub-Commission. Governments attest to the growing potential of the United Nations to be effective by the lengths to which they go in order to achieve membership of the Commission and to influence its deliberations, as well as by the occasional harshness of their denunciations of its actions.

Most recently, the United Nations has become heavily involved in the administration of human rights programmes of unprecedented scope and importance in countries such as Angola, El Salvador, Cambodia and Haiti. Electoral assistance has developed into a major United Nations activity and technical assistance in the human rights field has been provided to a significant number of countries.

In brief, the international human rights system has developed to an extent that would have been considered inconceivable by the vast majority of observers in 1945. At the time of the first World Conference on Human Rights, held in Teheran in 1968, not a single treaty-monitoring body was in existence, and there were absolutely no procedures for the investigation of violations (other than for Southern Africa and the Occupied Territories in the Middle East). States were simply not held accountable (except when egregious violations coincided with the short-term political interest of at least two of the three geopolitical blocs). In the space of twenty-five years, the United Nations system has made immense progress. As noted at the outset of this paper, however, there is still a very long way to go before we can conclude that an effective and reliable international system for the protection of human rights is in place.

7. Reluctance to reform

There is a rather curious reluctance on the part of governments to embark upon significant reforms of the UN human rights programme, despite the many criticisms which they themselves have levelled at it. For example, while international human rights standard-setting efforts have sometimes been duplicative, imprecise or incomplete, there is a reluctance to acknowledge this problem, as a prelude to tackling it, for fear that the status of international standards in general would be undermined. Similarly, while the dire need to rationalize some of the procedural and institutional arrangements in the human rights field is acknowledged, there is considered to be too great a risk that any attempt to do so will be hijacked by those who wish to reduce, rather than enhance, the effectiveness of the bodies or procedures concerned. As a result, a patchwork quilt of considerable complexity serves to confuse or deter many potential 'consumers' of these procedures and to diminish the pressures to develop procedures that will be truly effective.

In essence, the devil you know is better than the one you don't. But, in the longer term it will not be sustainable to treat all of these issues as a Pandora's box which must forever remain closed for fear that, if ever opened, it will wreak havoc upon those who dared to do so. Such an approach only delays the constructive consideration of complex but crucial issues, which ultimately will need to be addressed if progress is to be made towards a truly effective global governance regime in the human rights field.

8. A Framework for Analysis

The present paper cannot possibly be comprehensive in scope. It is important, however, to emphasize that a focus on the human rights dimensions of international governance must not be concerned solely with responding to gross violations. The following analytical framework provides an indication of the nature and extent of the human rights regime and points to some of the elements that are of greatest relevance for the purposes of the *Human Development Report* (HDR). The regime is treated as consisting of three major parts: standards, promotion, and the development of accountability mechanisms.[4]

Standards

(a) Setting standards
(b) Promoting universality
(c) Implementing indivisibility
(d) Deepening normative understanding
(e) Issue analysis (studies, etc.)

Promotion

(a) Promoting rights-consciousness, expertise and the use of rights discourse
(b) Encouraging and facilitating the acceptance of international standards and promoting their translation into domestic legal systems
(c) Encouraging and facilitating monitoring and institution building at the national level
(d) Promoting a supportive international environment: the right to development, aid, technical cooperation and conditionality
(e) Strengthening the international institutional regime through mainstreaming and cooperation with other international and regional human rights bodies

Establishing accountability

(a) Development of an accepted international legal framework
(b) Ensuring an appropriate role for NGOs and civil society
(c) Monitoring respect for obligations by means of authoritative, regular reviews
(d) Enhancing the accountability of non-State actors
(e) Anticipating and seeking to prevent violations through early-warning systems, mediation, conciliation, publicity, pressure, etc. as appropriate
(f) Responding to violations through, *inter alia,* effective fact-finding; mobilization of shame, and, as a last resort, enforcement through sanctions, etc.
(g) Securing relief and redress for victims of violations
(h) Deterrence and punishment for violators

This framework has several significant features: (1) it treats both the Charter-based and treaty-based organs as though they are both parts of a single integrated programme; (2) the 'protection' mandate, which often tends to become an exclusive feature of the criteria applied (often only implicitly) by many observers, is but one part of the overall set of criteria; and (3) the work of the UN is seen in its wider context, in terms of the need to reach out beyond the UN's own human rights programme to take full account of the opportunities offered for collaboration and coordination with other extant regimes, and to reach out to those agencies and activities that traditionally have not been part of the core human rights framework.

B. The Need for Global Governance in the Normative Areas, for the Protection and Promotion of Human Rights[5]

Globalisation is a phenomenon preoccupying the international community, even though the term is capable of multiple and diverse definitions. Leaving aside the developments in science, technology, communications and information processing that have made the world smaller and more interdependent in so many ways, globalisation has also come to be closely associated with a variety of trends and policies, including an increasing reliance upon the free market; a significant growth in the influence of international financial markets in determining the viability of national policy priorities; a diminution in the role of the state and the size of its budget; the privatization of various functions previously considered to be the exclusive domain of the state; the deregulation of a range of activities designed to facilitate investment and reward individual initiative; and a corresponding increase in the role and even responsibilities attributed to private actors both in the corporate sector and in civil society.

None of these developments in itself is necessarily incompatible with human rights principles or the specific obligations of governments. Taken together, however, and if not complemented by appropriate additional policies, globalisation risks downgrading the central place in world affairs accorded to human rights by the United Nations Charter and the Universal Declaration. Because there often seems to be little that can be done to change its course or slow its development, there has been a tendency to assume that the two issues of human rights and globalisation can, indeed should, be kept separate. This also reflects in part the preoccupation of human rights proponents with the maintenance of the *status quo*, in the name of preserving the continuity that is essential in the human rights area. But if taken to the extreme, that preoccupation can blind us to the equally important need for change in order to adapt to new challenges.

Globalisation is by no means a one-way street in terms of human rights. There are clear benefits resulting from it. The freer flow of information has many positive ramifications. Similarly, there is much to be said in favour of the pressures upon governments generated by financial institutions and markets to respond to concerns about good governance and the rule of law, through the elimination of corruption and cronyism and the upholding of a free and independent judicial system. But the principal concern in the present analysis is the risks inherent in the enterprise in the form in which it is currently being pursued. One indication of those risks comes from a recent analysis of what the authors perceive to be among the benefits of globalization. The technological revolution will

> *liberate individuals at the expense of the twentieth-century nation state. ...The shift from an industrial to an information-based society will result in the collapse of the Welfare State and of the capacity for big employers to supply regular jobs. Economic responsibility will be shifted to individuals who will become completely responsible for their own destinies.*[6]

In relation to civil and political rights, the process of globalisation has called into question the sustainability of the traditional divide between governmental accountability for human rights violations and the non-accountability of private actors. As corporations assume an ever greater role in managing or even establishing prisons, hospitals, public parks, and shopping and recreation areas, and for providing much of the security available to citizens, so too must new and innovative ways be found to ensure respect for civil and political rights. The new political 'consensus' that has developed since the end of the Cold War has also seen a tendency to restrict international concern to a certain core of rights, while giving governments a far greater benefit of the doubt to experiment with 'new' policies to combat crime, drug abuse, terrorist threats and anti-social behaviour in general. But many of these policies seem to be little more than throwbacks to an inhumane past, and little consideration is given to their compatibility with the notion of 'human dignity'. Yet, it is probably the single most important principle underpinning the Universal Declaration, from the assertion in Article 1 that '[a]ll human beings are born free and equal in dignity and rights', through the affirmation in Article 22 of 'economic, social and cultural rights [which are] indispensable for [the individual's] dignity and the free development of his personality', to the reference in Article 23 to 'the right to ... remuneration ensuring ... an existence worthy of human dignity.'

The actual or potential impact of globalisation—and the values and approaches associated with it—is especially significant in relation to economic, social and cultural rights. Thus, for example, respect for the right to work, and the right to just and favourable conditions of work, is threatened by an exclusive emphasis upon competitiveness, to the detriment of respect for the labour standards recognised in the principal human rights treaties. The right to form and join trade unions may be threatened by restrictions upon freedom of association that are claimed to be 'necessary' in a global economy, by the effective exclusion of possibilities for collective bargaining, and by the closing off of the right to strike for various occupational and other groups. The right of everyone to social security might not be ensured by arrangements relying entirely upon private contributions and private schemes. While workfare policies might be effective in many circumstances, they can be no substitute for the panoply of measures inevitably required to ensure respect for the right to an adequate standard of living.

Similarly, respect for the family and for the rights of parents to be with their children in an era of expanded global labour markets for certain individual occupations might require new and innovative policies rather than a mere laissez-faire approach. The introduction of user fees, or cost-recovery policies, when applied to basic health and educational services for the poor, can easily result in significantly reduced access to services that are essential for the enjoyment of the rights recognised in the Universal Declaration, the Covenant on Economic, Social and Cultural Rights and various regional treaties. An insistence upon payment for access to artistic, cultural and heritage-related activities risks undermining the right to participate in cultural life for a significant proportion of any community.

Most, although perhaps not all, of these risks can be guarded against, or compensated for, if appropriate policies are put in place. But it is clear that while much energy and many resources have been expended by governments on promoting the trends and policies that are associated with globalisation, insufficient efforts are being made to devise new or complementary approaches to enhance the compatibility of those trends and policies with full respect for human rights. A fascination with simplistic one-shot policies (the social equivalents of the 'three strikes and you are out' approach to dealing with criminal recidivism) must not be permitted to wipe clean the slate of governmental responsibilities in relation to human rights.

C. Key issues and reforms required

In the following analysis, an attempt is made to identify a select range of key issues and to suggest some of the reforms that should be considered. The issues addressed are considered in more or less the order in which they arise in the analytical framework proposed above.

Is there a need for new standards?

Standard-setting is likely to be considerably less important in the decade ahead than it has been throughout the period since 1948. Apart from two proposed protocols to the Convention on the Rights of the Child (dealing with the age of participation in armed conflicts and child sexual exploitation), the principal current standard-setting initiative is a proposal, currently under consideration, that the General Assembly should adopt a draft Universal Declaration of Human Responsibilities.[7] The draft was drawn up in September 1997 by the InterAction Council, a group of former government leaders, led by Helmut Schmidt of Germany and Malcolm Fraser of Australia. It is modelled on the Universal Declaration of Human Rights (UDHR), follows the framework of the biblical Ten Commandments, and consists of nineteen articles stating 'norms of good behaviour, including honest dealing, speaking and acting truthfully, commends non-violence and generally showing respect to others.'

The preamble states its guiding philosophy, which is that 'the exclusive insistence on rights can result in conflict, division and endless dispute, and the neglect of human responsibilities can lead to lawlessness and chaos.' It then proceeds to proclaim notions such as 'sensible' family planning, 'inhumane behaviour', and the responsibility not 'to injure' people, without reference to the formulations contained in existing international human rights law. The section on the responsibilities of the media is open to especially draconian interpretation. Similarly, economic and social rights are reduced to a responsibility to 'make serious efforts to overcome poverty, malnutrition, ignorance and inequality' provided people are 'given the necessary tools'. This entirely undermines the rights dimension reflected in the UDHR.

As Amnesty International has noted,[8] there are parts of the draft declaration with which no one would argue. For the most part, these are essentially reiterations of provisions of the UDHR. The remainder, however, is often expressed in very vague and open-ended terminology which is potentially confusing and certainly leaves open significant potential for misuse.

Duties are in fact recognised in the UDHR. Article 29 provides as follows:

1. Everyone has duties to the community in which alone the free and full development of his personality is possible.
2. In the exercise of his rights and freedoms, everyone shall be subject only to such limitations as are determined by law solely for the purpose of securing due recognition and respect for the rights and freedoms of others and of meeting the just requirements of morality, public order and the general welfare in a democratic society.
3. These rights and freedoms may in no case be exercised contrary to the purposes and principles of the United Nations.

This was criticised at the time of drafting (in June 1948) by the Soviet representative. He insisted that 'the declaration on human rights should define not only the rights but also the obligations of citizens towards their country, their people and their State.' He also lamented 'the failure to include in the declaration any concrete obligations whatsoever on the part of the individual towards his native land, the people to which he belongs and the State...'.[9] But the counterarguments, still valid today, were clearly laid out by Lauterpacht:

> *The Bill of Rights is not the proper occasion for affirming the obligations of the individual to the State. This is not so because it is based on a distinctively individualistic philosophy. The reason why a Bill of Rights need not concern itself with the duties of man to society is that its object is limited to the protection of his rights against the State. History has shown that there is a need for such protection. There is no imperative necessity to safeguard the State against man. Too much has been heard of his duty to the State and too much has been done to give effect to it. But it is consonant with the dignity and the proper understanding of the Bill of Rights to emphasise that the rights to be protected are conceived as a means to enable man to do his duty, in freedom, to man and society.*[10]

Recommendation: Standard-setting should not be a priority concern for the international community in the years ahead. While duties or responsibilities are an important part of the overall human rights framework, they are not appropriately promoted by means of a new international instrument. In future, priority in standard-setting efforts should be accorded to economic, social and cultural rights, which have so far been largely neglected in this respect. The rights to health and education could usefully be the subject of new instruments.

Universality

Neither the general principle of the universality of human rights, nor specific efforts to promote universal participation in the international human rights treaty regime, should be considered to conflict in any way with recognition of the relevance of different cultural, philosophical, social and religious factors in relation to the application and interpretation of human rights norms. Sensitivity and flexibility are necessary, albeit within certain clear limits. There is a need to take account of cultural diversity. Once we move beyond the core rights of physical integrity, the nature of the society, its traditions and culture and other such factors become highly pertinent to any efforts to promote and protect respect for the rights concerned. We must recognize that the reflexive, often dogmatic, admonitory and homogeneous approach that is appropriate in relation to such core violations, will simply be less productive, and achieve far less enduring results than a more sensitive, open and flexible approach that situates the goals sought within the society in question. The precise requirements of what is often termed the right to democracy is a case in point. Human rights efforts will be enriched, not compromised, by an approach that is, in appropriate respects, more probing, more self-conscious and more eclectic than that which many countries have achieved to date.

A related need is to recognize the fact that there are conflicts among rights, and that the resolution of such conflicts requires greater openness about the difficulties involved and a more concerted attempt to accommodate the different values involved. The human rights movement must move beyond the metaphor of rights as 'trumps' that simply override all competing considerations, and acknowledge that the actual equation is rather more complicated. Religious rights and women's rights are a case in point, although there are many others as well.[11] It should be noted, however, that this is by no means to suggest that the non-human-rights dimensions of a problem should be put on a par with those that clearly are covered by universal norms.

Claims of relativism must be scrutinised more carefully and systematically in terms of their foundations within the cultural, philosophical or religious traditions of societies. Many of the claims made have no foundation whatsoever in such traditions. Instead they reflect no more than the age-old tendency of governments to justify the cynical and self-interested proposition that their own citizens neither want nor need the protection of human rights.

The introduction of greater complexity, and the abandonment of absoluteness where it is not justified, will be seen by some human rights activists as a step backwards. It is, in fact, the opposite. It reflects the growing importance, maturity and sophistication of the international debate, and signifies the fact that international human rights principles are at last starting to infiltrate themselves into the more deeply-rooted social, cultural and legal norms of diverse societies. Until that process begins to succeed, the human rights revolution will remain little more than an aspiration, however noble.

In many respects, the best way to ensure that different cultural and other perspectives are taken into account is to ensure that all such views can be adequately represented and debated within the principal forums set up to monitor human rights. This should include in particular the six treaty bodies. The virtually universal level of ratification achieved by the Convention on the Rights of the Child points to both the appropriateness and feasibility of this objective, as well as making it very difficult to sustain many of the more extreme versions of cultural relativism that some governments have sought to promote.

Similarly, it is necessary to take those governments that insist on the fundamental importance of economic and social rights at their word. Those that have not ratified the relevant Covenant must immediately be urged to do so. It must be said, without equivocation or reticence, that advocacy of these rights, coupled with a failure to accept any legal obligations to respect them, does not demonstrate a genuine commitment. Thus, for example, the record of Asian governments is particularly poor in relation to the Covenant on Economic, Social and Cultural Rights.

In a 1997 study submitted to the Commission on Human Rights and the General Assembly, the following recommendation was made:

> *The goal of achieving universal ratification of the six core treaties has been affirmed frequently. Concrete measures aimed at making it a reality are needed. They should include: (a) consultations with the leading international agencies to explore their potential involvement in a ratification campaign (para. 32); (b) the appointment of special advisers on ratification and reporting and the earmarking of funds for those purposes (paras. 33-34); (c) special measures should be explored to streamline the reporting process for states with small populations (para. 35); and (d) particular attention should be paid to other substantial categories of non-parties.*[12]

Recommendation: Universality should be actively promoted, including in the ways suggested above. In this way, it need not come at the expense of appropriate cultural sensitivity and diversity in the interpretation and application of the standards.

Implementing indivisibility

The principle of indivisibility, according to which the two sets of rights—economic, social and cultural rights, and civil and political rights—are of equal importance, is central to an examination of the place of human rights in global governance. For a variety of compelling reasons, the United Nations recognized from the outset—in the Universal Declaration in particular—that neither set of rights could be accorded priority over the other. But that has not deterred various governments, NGOs and others from arguing, when it suits them, that one set of rights is, in practice, a prerequisite to enjoyment of the other.

Renewed attention is now being accorded to these rights. This is partly as a result of the attention being given to the social consequences of the financial crises in Asia, Latin America and Russia, and partly because those and other developments are beginning to highlight the inadequacy of an approach to human rights that is limited to the promotion of democracy and respect for a core range of civil and political rights. In addition, since becoming UN High Commissioner for Human Rights in September 1997, Mary Robinson has attached considerable emphasis to economic and social rights in her work. This in turn has compelled governments and the human rights community to follow suit. It is not coincidental that the most recent annual report of Amnesty International devoted a major section to economic rights, the first time it has ever done so. It began by noting the importance of these rights:

> *Addressing the imbalance between economic rights and other human rights is vital at a time when the debate over human rights is increasingly being played out in the economic sphere. When governments fail to protect their citizens from the negative consequences of globalization, the need to protect and enhance economic rights becomes evident. The parallel imperative of ensuring that economic rights are not divorced from other human rights is shown each time that people are harassed, tortured and killed in the name of economic progress.*[13]

The report goes on to acknowledge that Amnesty International itself 'has been a part of this imbalance' and notes that 'this side of its work has remained relatively underdeveloped'. The organisation has committed itself to seeking to remedy this deficiency.

Recommendation: Acceptance of the principle that all of the recognised human rights form part of an indivisible package is a prerequisite to a balanced, viable and acceptable approach. If this principle is to be upheld, the main challenge is to accord more emphasis to economic, social and cultural rights.

Economic, social and cultural rights

The most useful approach to overcoming the lack of national-level action in relation to these rights is that of benchmarking. Extensive work has been done in recent years on the elaboration of a wide range of economic and social 'indicators' of development. This is attested to by the recent publication of the second edition of the World Bank's valuable study of *World Development Indicators* and by the important sectoral analyses produced by agencies such as the Food and Agriculture Organization (FAO), ILO, UNESCO, UNICEF and the World Health Organization (WHO), among others. But indicators differ in very significant ways from the benchmarks, which are the focus of current attention in relation to efforts to promote economic, social and cultural rights. Without entering into a technical debate, it is useful to highlight some of the characteristics of indicators. For the most part, they are essentially statistical in nature. That, in turn, means that their subject matter must be potentially quantifiable, not only in a technical sense but in practical terms as well. Indicators draw strength from the objectivity of both the data and the manner in which it is compiled and used. The need for objectivity, quantifiability and accuracy point in turn to the technical expertise required in order to compile indicators. The same applies to their subsequent interpretation, which should take account of the known weaknesses of the process, and compensate for any likely biases or other suspected shortcomings. Accordingly, a significant number of caveats or qualifications will usually be attached to the use of any given indicator. Finally, the capacity to gather, analyze and make use of the data required for indicators is heavily dependent upon the availability of the appropriate technical expertise and resources.

In contrast, benchmarks are potentially very different. They are, in essence, targets established by governments, on the basis of appropriately consultative processes, in relation to each of the economic, social and cultural rights obligations that apply in the state concerned. Those targets will be partly quantitative (and thus more closely assimilated to indicators) and partly qualitative. They will be linked to specific time frames. And they will provide a basis upon which the reality of 'progressive realization', contained in both the International Covenant on Economic, Social and Cultural Rights and the Convention on the Rights of the Child (with respect to the economic, social and cultural rights recognized therein), can be measured. Benchmarks will initially differ significantly from one country to another, reflecting both the 'available resources' and the priority concerns in each country. Over time, however, one would expect a gradual coming together of the approaches without necessarily ever leading to a formal systematization or uniformity.

Benchmarks are thus different from indicators because they take specific human rights standards as their starting point. Thus, the setting of a benchmark, and the identification of the criteria by which it is to be measured, is not dependent upon, or limited by, the availability of a technically accepted indicator or of detailed statistical data linked to that indicator. Benchmarks can be more subjective and more tailored to a specific context than indicators because they are firmly rooted in the human rights framework. The manner in which they are set should be consultative rather than technocratic, and opportunities should be available for the social partners and civil society in general to make inputs into their design and evaluation.

Also unlike indicators, benchmarks should be linked to mechanisms of accountability in the sense that failure to reach a given benchmark should trigger an appropriate remedial response. Both the nature of the trigger and of the relevant remedies are matters to be determined in lights of domestic considerations, provided only that the human rights framework is borne constantly in mind. This dimension also serves to underline the essentially domestic nature of the benchmark process, thus reflecting the principle that implementation and monitoring of respect for economic, social and cultural rights is preeminently a matter for domestic action.

There is no inevitable place for economic, social and cultural rights within a dominant discourse of market-driven economic decision-making, competitiveness and flexibility, and a global marketplace without borders for goods, services and capital. Without the deliberate and systematic injection of those rights, and the values that attach to them, into the overall equation, there is no natural or obvious, let alone effective, constraint upon a race to the bottom in terms of salaries, working conditions, social security and forms of insurance against emergencies. In the absence of this element, governmental functions, community programs, and corporate priorities are inevitably assessed primarily and perhaps exclusively in terms of economic efficiency and profitability.

The concept of establishing benchmarks for the realization of economic, social and cultural rights serves to emphasise some aspects of the inter-relationship that exists between these rights on the one hand and civil and political rights on the other. The conclusion to be drawn is that a program to begin moving towards the realization of, for example, the right to food or the right to education or the right to housing cannot usefully be seen solely in terms of technical, bureaucratic or even economic solutions. The civil and political dimensions are vital. Individuals must be empowered to participate in decisions relating to the steps to be taken towards meeting those rights and be given the opportunity to contribute to monitoring and evaluation processes. In this sense, civil and political rights can be seen not only as ends in themselves, but also as a vital means by which to facilitate the realization of economic, social and cultural rights.

While governments might be reluctant to involve individuals and groups in this way in the broader political process relating to these rights, it is clear that there are significant potential advantages, particularly in situations in which resources are scarce and difficult decisions must be made as to priorities. Community involvement carries with it the potential to make such decisions more palatable, more equitable and more sustainable.

One of the major concerns that arises from the current emphasis upon the role of civil and political rights within the development process is the extent to which economic, social and cultural rights objectives are excluded from the equation. Concepts such as the rule of law and good governance are extremely important but, when they are defined in ways which give them a narrow civil and political rights focus, they can potentially reinforce the unacceptable message that economic, social and cultural rights should be viewed as little more than secondary, coincidental or residual policy objectives, which might or might not be met once the specific civil and political rights concerns have been satisfied. By including benchmarks for economic, social and cultural rights as a dimension in any basic conception of good governance, this objection is overcome, and we can begin to move to policies that authentically reflect the fundamental principle of the equal importance of the two sets of human rights.

Relating human rights benchmarking to broader monitoring efforts

No theme has been more consistently reflected in the outcomes of the major United Nations international conferences in the 1990s—whether on environment, human rights, women, population, housing, food, etc.—than the need for adequate domestic monitoring to ensure the targeting of particularly vulnerable individuals and groups, and to ensure the systematic promotion of the agreed goals. A great many of the specific objectives identified at these conferences relate directly and unequivocally to the various economic, social and cultural rights to which all governments are committed on the basis of the United Nations Charter, the Universal Declaration, and a range of subsequent international instruments.

It is surprising, however, that so few efforts have been made to bring these endeavours together under the umbrella of human rights and of economic, social and cultural rights in particular. The idea of benchmarks provides an ideal means by which these diverse, sometimes competing and too often uncoordinated monitoring processes could be brought together and given particular meaning. Such an approach would have far more resonance in terms of the populations addressed than any of the often complex, bureaucratic and essentially diplomatic monitoring exercises that are currently underway in various United Nations fora. In many respects, the bases upon which national HDR reports have been prepared might constitute an example of the use of benchmarks. What remains to be done, however, is to bring such exercises closer to the human rights framework, and to make more effective use of those reports in the context of developing authentic human rights accountability at the national level, closely linked to the international human rights framework.

Recommendation: Various actors could take the lead in developing an effective system of benchmarking, including the following:

(a) national human rights institutions, which should systematically adopt a benchmark-based approach in relation to economic, social and cultural rights;

(b) other national-level government agencies that are involved either in sectoral or general oversight of areas covered by economic, social and cultural rights;

(c) the Office of the High Commissioner for Human Rights, which should develop a targeted and well-financed technical cooperation project to assist in the development of national approaches to benchmarks;

(d) the agencies of the United Nations that are engaged in the formulation of a coherent United Nations Development Assistance Framework (UNDAF), which must be expanded to include benchmarks for these rights;

(e) the specialised agencies and other parts of the United Nations system working in specific sectoral areas, such as health, labour, education, culture, food, etc., as well as more broadly, which should contribute to the development of methodologies for the identification and monitoring of benchmarks and their incorporation into related activities; and

(f) the Committee on Economic, Social and Cultural Rights, which should emphasise to reporting governments that these rights cannot be effectively and fully promoted at the national level in the absence of a mechanism for the identification, monitoring and evaluation of benchmarks.

The need for greater technical expertise in the human rights area

One of the most obvious elements that is missing within the UN's human rights programme is professional expertise in various key areas. It is an issue that has rarely been examined, but it deserves attention because of the negative consequences that flow from it.

Participants in the UN human rights system are essentially divided up into five groups: (a) government representatives, whose role is openly political: (b) 'independent experts', who compose the treaty bodies, the Sub-Commission on Prevention of Discrimination and Protection of Minorities, and the so-called thematic and country mechanisms of the Commission on Human Rights; (c) experts from other international agencies or from official or semi-official governmental human rights bodies; (d) non-governmental groups, or in some cases, civil society; and (e) the secretariat, including special representatives and others appointed by the Secretary General.

Government representatives bring political, not technical, expertise; they cannot reasonably be expected to bring the latter. They do, however, tend to resist proposals that such expert inputs are necessary. It is striking to note that human-rights standard-setting exercises in the UN are preceded by almost no sustained, expert and systematic analyses of the issues. The drafting is left very largely at the mercy of political inputs. This is in dramatic contrast to the approach reflected in the great majority of other areas, such as in the work of the International Law Commission, the International Labour Organization, or the Hague Conference on Private International Law.

The expertise of the independent experts is as variable as their independence. On the Sub-Commission, it is widely accepted that political considerations have all but overwhelmed pretensions to independence, even though there is clearly some expertise present. The individuals who are appointed to the thematic and country mechanisms of the Commission are generally much more independent and have much more obvious expertise. One problem is that many of them are required to work on subjects in which their specialist expertise is limited. This could be overcome if they had the time to do the required research, but they are entirely unpaid and very few of them are able to devote the necessary time. The same applies, perhaps even more strongly, to the experts who make up the treaty bodies. A member of the Human Rights Committee or the Committee on the Rights of the Child, for example, receives an honorarium of $3,000 per year plus daily expenses, in return for nine weeks in Committee sessions and up to another three weeks in Working Groups. Other, related, representational activities can also be very time-consuming.

Many experts therefore depend, to some extent, on outside inputs. Sometimes these are excellent, but they are neither systematic nor necessarily balanced. NGOs are advocacy organizations, rather than think tanks or research outfits. They should not reasonably be expected to produce even-handed analyses of controversial issues. Academic institutions often lack the involvement to know what is required and what might be useful within the system.

Since the early 1950s the vast majority of expert 'studies' generated within the UN human rights framework have been prepared by experts from the Sub-Commission. Originally, these studies were in fact prepared on the basis of detailed expert inputs, case studies, and extensive secretariat research. By the early 1970s this system no longer worked due to a lack of resources and a lack of political will to generate serious studies. The Sub-Commission continues to churn out studies at a great rate, and it considers that one of the 'three relatively unique [*sic*] contributions [it makes] to the human rights field [is] undertaking comprehensive studies that contribute to the work of the human rights bodies, particularly to the United Nations treaty-monitoring bodies.'[14] A few of them have made a major contribution and would have warranted publication in a competitive or refereed environment. The great majority, however, are either compilations of information that remains largely unprocessed or are strongly partisan analyses unsupported by serious research. This would not be such a bad thing if it meant only that the reports were filed and forgotten. The problem is that there are various negative effects as well: poor quality research becomes the basis for the political debates; the studies are treated as official UN analyses, regardless of their content, because they are printed and disseminated as UN books; and these studies make it difficult for the secretariat or other experts to justify undertaking serious studies of the same issues.

The third group consists mainly of experts from other international agencies. Almost by definition, these experts are present to inform, 'coordinate' and observe but not to assist in any significant way with original inputs of an expert character. This would not be so problematic if their own agencies were producing high quality studies on human rights issues. In fact, however, such studies are extremely rare.

This leaves the secretariat. It is the source that one would 'normally' expect to be responsible for generating the detailed, thoroughly researched, analyses to form the basis for that part of the work of the experts which they are unable to undertake themselves and would provide the starting point for the political debates. Unlike the situation in most secretariats, however, the OHCHR is sadly lacking in the necessary resources and expertise. While there are a handful of highly qualified individuals within the Office who would easily qualify for jobs as analysts in high-powered contexts, they are both overworked and almost entirely preoccupied with routine administrative responsibilities. The great majority of the staff has little specialist expertise and has been given no research or analytical training. Similarly, the Office has very little money available for the employment of consultants, and the great majority of those who are employed are called upon to perform quasi-administrative functions rather than to generate or pull together new thinking in the field.

One caveat is in order. The call for expertise should not be interpreted as overstating the gap between the technical and the political. I accept March and Olsen's conclusion that, despite certain characteristics that are usually associated with each approach, 'a sharp division of labor between specialists and policy-makers is impossible to sustain, either conceptually or behaviorally.'[15] Similarly, on the basis of an examination of the very early work of the Sub-Commission on Prevention of Discrimination and Protection of Minorities, Inis Claude rejected 'the notion that every participant in the work of international organization can be stuffed into one of two categories—"governmental representative" or "uninstructed expert"—without doing Procrustean violence to the facts.'[16] Nevertheless, it is important for expertise to be available and for an effort to be made to separate the two dimensions of analytical work on human rights within the UN system.

There is therefore a very large gap that needs to be filled. The result is especially problematic given the intrinsically interdisciplinary nature of good human-rights research and the types of challenges that are now emerging. Three factors will make the need particularly great in the years ahead: (1) the basic research has been done (in many respects, it was the easiest phase and the more complex issues remain); (2) the growing universality of the system as a whole make it all the more important to undertake wide-ranging and innovative research reflecting different legal, cultural, religious and other traditions; and (3) the challenges provoked by globalisation are especially complex in economic and sociological terms and require both empirical and highly specialised research. To take but one example, in August 1998 the Sub-Commission decided to create a sessional working group on 'the effects on human rights of the activities and working methods of transnational corporations'. (UN Press Release HR/SC/98/32, 28 Aug 1998). The potential for such an exercise, if badly done, to muddy the waters and set back the cause of reform is considerable.

Recommendation: Possibilities include: systematic commissioning of human rights-related studies by other UN agencies; the allocation of adequate funding to the OHCHR specifically to support high-quality research, both within and outside the house; the development of UN-focused research programs in think-tank contexts.

Promoting the use of rights language

It is often suggested that a human rights approach to issues can be pursued without actually referring to any specific norms, and without making any use of the language of rights. The World Bank, for example, has very often insisted that virtually all of its activities are human rights-promoting, by definition. But, in fact, a commitment to human rights cannot be given effect solely by reference to surrogate terms such as poverty reduction, social exclusion, basic needs, human security and so on. While these all describe important issues and responses, they lack the indispensable elements of a human rights framework. Simply expressed, those elements are: normative specificity, an accepted legal obligation, a commitment to the use of all appropriate means, the provision of forms of redress in response to violations and the establishment of mechanisms of accountability at the national and international levels. And, most important of all, the use of rights language is inherently empowering. To recognise that a girl living in a remote village has a right to education is very different from affirming that bureaucratically framed and administered programs will endeavour, in the course of time and depending upon resource availability and overall governmental priorities, to increase educational opportunities in the village concerned. The former approach empowers the girl *vis-à-vis* her own family, empowers that family *vis-à-vis* the local community and so on. It opens up a vast array of potentially effective solutions, rather than simply relying upon governmental action. The use of the terminology of economic, social and cultural rights is thus essential.

The same point can be made in relation to notions such as 'good governance', 'the rule of law' (or 'the Rule of Law'), 'human security', or 'sustainable development'. These are all capable of being developed in a way that makes human rights an authentic and integral part of the relevant framework, or in ways that purport to invoke a human rights dimension, but in fact assiduously avoid one by not using the language or framework of human rights.

For example, World Bank President James Wolfensohn, in an address to the Board of Governors,[17] noted, in speaking of the need for a new development framework, that it would first 'outline the essentials of good governance – transparency, voice, the free flow of information – a commitment to fight corruption, and a well trained, properly remunerated, civil service.' But an accompanying story in the *New York Times* spelled out what he was said to have had in mind. The headline was 'A Free Press is Encouraged as a Watchdog Against Graft'. The author then quoted World Bank officials as saying that 'freer, more aggressive and more critical news media in the region would have put a brake on the governmental corruption and the so-called crony capitalism ...'.[18] The human rights content of such a notion of good governance appears minimal, despite the congruity of the objectives sought.

Recommendation: A concerted effort should be made to encourage the use of specific human rights terminology, especially in relation to human development issues.

Encouraging and facilitating human rights monitoring and institution building at the national level

Once formal international obligations have been accepted, the next task is to encourage governments to establish appropriate domestic arrangements to monitor the enjoyment of these rights, and to provide at least some means by which they can be formally vindicated (whether by individuals or groups) at the national level. The great majority of governments have not yet taken either of these steps, and NGOs have permitted many of them the luxury of ratifying the Covenant and doing very little by way of follow-up. A campaign should be launched to hold governments accountable in this regard.

In December 1998, the UN Committee on Economic, Social and Cultural Rights took up this issue in relation to 'the role of national human rights institutions in the protection of economic, social and cultural rights'.[19] It noted that, in recent years, there has been a proliferation of these institutions, and the trend has been strongly encouraged by the General Assembly and the Commission on Human

Rights. The Office of the High Commissioner for Human Rights has established a major programme to assist and encourage states in relation to national institutions. These institutions range from national human rights commissions through ombudsman offices, public interest or other human rights 'advocates', to *defenseurs du peuple* and *defensores del pueblo*. In many cases, the institution has been established by the government, enjoys an important degree of autonomy from the executive and the legislature, takes full account of international human rights standards which are applicable to the country concerned, and is mandated to perform various activities designed to promote and protect human rights. The Committee observed, however, that although such national institutions have a potentially crucial role to play in relation to economic, social and cultural rights, that role has too often either not been accorded to them or has been neglected or given a low priority. It suggested the following types of activities that could be, and in some instances already have been, undertaken by national institutions in relation to these rights:

(a) the promotion of educational and informational programmes designed to enhance awareness and understanding of economic, social and cultural rights both within the population at large and among particular groups such as the public service, the judiciary, the private sector and the labour movement;
(b) the scrutinising of existing laws and administrative acts as well as draft bills and other proposals to ensure that they are consistent with the requirements of the Covenant on Economic, Social and Cultural Rights;
(c) providing technical advice, or undertaking surveys in relation to economic, social and cultural rights, including when requested by the public authorities or other appropriate agencies;
(d) the identification of national level benchmarks against which the realization of Covenant obligations can be measured;
(e) conducting research and inquiries designed to ascertain the extent to which particular economic, social and cultural rights are being realised, either within the State as a whole or in areas or in relation to communities of particular vulnerability;
(f) monitoring compliance with specific rights recognised under the Covenant and providing reports thereon to the public authorities and civil society; and
(g) examining complaints alleging violations of applicable economic, social and cultural rights standards within the State.

Recommendation: The role of national human rights institutions in relation to the promotion of human development goals, and the monitoring of progress in that regard, should be enhanced.

Promoting a supportive international environment: the right to development, aid, technical cooperation and conditionality

The North-South dimension of the human rights debate is of fundamental importance but it continues to be pursued largely by means of exercises in shadow boxing. The rhetoric of both sides has often been quite similar—as has been their failure to focus on specifics. Thus, for example, the North sometimes identifies 'solidarity' as the key element in the Declaration on the Right to Development—'solidarity between industrialised countries and their developing partners, solidarity in every country with the most disadvantaged'[20]—while the South calls the right to development 'universal and inalienable' and argues that the main obstacles to its realisation 'lie at the international macroeconomic level'.[21] But neither side has been prepared to go beyond such generalities and render the debate meaningful in human rights terms.

Similarly, debates over economic and social rights and conditionality serve to highlight one of the dimensions of economic, social and cultural rights that is conveniently overlooked by most governments. Developing country governments insist that conditionality is unacceptable but that international assistance is indispensable. Their developed country counterparts reply that obligatory international assistance is unacceptable but that minimum standards of conduct by actual or potential aid recipient countries is indispensable. In essence, we find a mirror image of refusal to accept responsibility. Neither side loses the high ground in the rhetorical debate. The only mutually assured loser is the principle that, by whatever means are appropriate and available, respect for economic, social and cultural rights should be promoted.

The benchmarks approach, explored above, provides a potential way out of this impasse. Benchmarks are in every respect a domestic matter. They flow from the voluntarily accepted obligations of governments. They are set through appropriate domestic political processes and they are tailored to meet the circumstances and needs of each individual country, provided only that the satisfaction of the relevant human rights obligations is their *leitmotif*. In situations where governments have set reasonable minimum benchmarks but are clearly unable on the basis of all their available resources to meet those standards, the obligation of the international community to assist must come into play. This is not to say that any specific government must assume any particular burden or obligation, but that the totality of aid donors and international agencies must ensure that, one way or another, measures are taken which are consistent with the balanced and holistic conception of human rights enshrined in the Universal Declaration.

Recommendation: More creative efforts should be made to link levels of development assistance to specific programmes aimed at meeting the economic, social and cultural rights of the people in developing countries.

Institutional reforms: confining human rights debates to the good guys

Two important issues of institutional reform within the UN's human rights machinery are: (1) whether governments that commit gross violations of human rights should be able to participate in debates over human rights policy within the UN: and (2) whether individuals elected as 'independent experts' should be permitted to participate in discussions concerning the human rights situation in countries of which they are nationals.

In relation to the first issue, Professor Anne Bayefsky has written that one of the major problems with the treaty monitoring system is that it 'includes many states that share no common democratic aspirations'. Resistance to reform, she states, 'comes from nondemocratic states'. In her view, this gives rise to two further questions:

(1) What is the best method for securing democratic reform? Through the equal participation of nondemocracies within the treaty system? Or through alternative venues for interchange outside the treaty system, such as the marketplace – that is, economic pressure for reform?

(2) Who is the system for? Is it aimed at assisting democracies, or aspiring democracies, to adjust and calibrate their laws and practices? Or is it aimed at the unrepentant social deviant, and intended to expose the depravity and provide a tool for critics everywhere?

Her conclusion, in effect, is that 'nondemocracies' should be excluded from the treaty system by one means or another.[22]

A rather more limited proposal, but one nevertheless going in the same direction, has been put forward by the NGO Human Rights Watch. In its view, it is 'time to end the charade that permits abusive governments to join the U.N.'s highest human rights body [the Commission] for the principal purpose of shielding their human rights conduct from criticism and enfeebling the U.N.'s capacity to defend human rights.'[23] Unlike Bayefsky's radical solution, this approach could, in practice, be promoted informally by urging that votes not be cast in favour of 'abusive governments' in the relevant elections, thus leaving each government free to make its own determination in that regard rather than requiring the system to do so.

It is not at all clear, however, that either of these proposals is consistent with the principle of inclusiveness upon which the UN system has been constructed, nor even with human rights principles, unless any punitive measures were directly and proportionately linked to a specific finding in relation to the state concerned. Moreover, it is by no means clear that it would help to make the inter-state human rights regime more effective or improve global governance as a whole.

The second practice that has been questioned seems to be more clearly problematic. In relation to the human-rights treaty bodies and several other similar bodies (including the Sub-Commission on the Prevention of Discrimination and the Protection of Minorities), individuals are elected in their individual capacities as 'independent experts' and not as representatives of their countries, although the latter must nominate them for election. The question then is whether such experts should be permitted to participate in discussions concerning the human rights situation in the countries of which they are nationals. In this regard, there is an increasingly clear trend towards insisting upon an approach that is more transparently independent. Thus the Sub-Commission agreed in 1998 that '[w]hen examining a situation which appears to reveal a pattern of gross and consistent violations of human rights in a country of which an expert of the Sub-Commission is a national, it would be desirable that the expert concerned not participate in the debates.' Rather than enforcing such a rule, however, the Sub-Commission left an element of discretion by adding that '[t]he ultimate decision on whether or not such expert will intervene in the public discussion remains the responsibility of the expert concerned.'[24]

A stronger approach was taken by the Meeting of Chairpersons of the UN human rights treaty bodies in 1997 when it adopted the following statement on the 'independence of experts':

> *The chairpersons recommended that members of treaty bodies refrain from participating in any aspect of the consideration of the reports of the States of which they were nationals, or communications or inquiries concerning those States, in order to maintain the highest standards of impartiality, both in substance and in appearance.*
>
> *... States parties to human rights treaties should refrain from nominating or electing to the treaty bodies persons performing political functions or occupying positions which were not readily reconcilable with the obligations of independent experts under the given treaty. The chairpersons also urged that consideration be given to the importance of expertise in areas related to the mandate of the treaty body, the need for balanced geographical composition, the desirability of an appropriate gender balance and the nominee's availability in terms of time to discharge the responsibilities of an expert member of a treaty body.* [25]

Recommendation: Greater efforts should be made to emphasise the need for transparently independent behaviour on the part of those individual experts participating in the work of UN human rights bodies composed of experts.

Reform proposals relating to the treaty bodies

The role played by the six treaty bodies is of great importance, as noted in the introductory part of this paper. Many recommendations have already been made with a view to enabling those bodies to function more effectively. For present purposes, it is sufficient to recall the principal recommendations contained in a study submitted to the UN in 1997:[26]

- Non-reporting has reached chronic proportions. In addition to considering reforms to the overall system (noted below), a new specially tailored project for the provision of advisory services should be implemented. In responding to cases of persistent delinquency, all treaty bodies should be urged to adopt procedures which lead eventually to the examination of situations even in the absence of a report (paras. 37-45). Such an approach should reflect thorough research and lead to detailed, accurate and comprehensive "concluding observations" (para. 47).

- The present reporting system functions only because of the large-scale delinquency of States which either do not report at all, or report long after the due date. If many were to report, significant existing backlogs would be exacerbated, and major reforms would be needed even more urgently (paras. 48-52).
- The public information materials relating to the work of the treaty bodies are highly inadequate. The treaty bodies should be given a direct input into future decision-making in this regard. A public information budget should be made available to support grassroots initiatives designed to disseminate information about the treaty bodies in culturally appropriate and more popular formats and media. Partnerships with academic and other external institutions should be explored in order to enhance the publications programme. An external advisory group should be asked to review the human rights-related publications programme and make recommendations (paras. 66-70). The Secretary General should report on the actual availability of treaty body-related materials at United Nations information centres (para. 71).
- The advisory services programme has not provided sufficient support for surveys required prior to ratification of a human rights treaty or for the preparation of reports by States in need of assistance. Regional and sub-regional training courses in relation to reporting are unlikely to produce results commensurate with their cost. A specially designed programme should be devised to address the needs in this area and it should be accorded priority (paras. 72-77).
- The effectiveness of "special reports" and "urgent procedures" should be carefully evaluated by the committees concerned. At present, the value they add seems low. In general, the division of labour between the treaty bodies and special mechanisms should be maintained (paras. 78-79).
- In light of current trends the existing reporting system is unsustainable (paras. 81-84). Four options are available to States: (1) to dismiss the concern as alarmist and take no action; (2) to urge the treaty bodies to undertake far-reaching reforms and adapt to cope with existing and new demands from within existing resources; (3) to provide greatly enhanced budgetary resources to sustain the status quo; (4) to combine some elements of (2) and (3) with the adoption of some far-reaching reforms (paras. 85-89). The latter could include: the preparation of "consolidated reports" (para. 90); elimination of comprehensive periodic reports in their present form and replacement by reporting guidelines tailored to each State's individual situation (paras. 91-93); and a consolidation (reduction) of the number of treaty bodies (para. 94). If the political will exists in relation to the latter, a small expert group should be convened to examine modalities. Pro-active measures should also be considered, including amending the Migrant Workers Convention to entrust the supervisory functions to an existing committee and giving more systematic consideration to the institutional implications of the proposed optional protocol to the Convention against Torture (paras. 96-98).
- The procedural provisions of human rights treaties need to be made more susceptible to amendment. Various recommendations are suggested (para. 101). Constructive attention needs to be given to the taboo subject of working languages (paras. 102-06). Existing arrangements for cooperation with the specialised agencies and other bodies have been improved in some respects but remain very inadequate. The HCHR should convene a high level meeting to explore better means of cooperation with the treaty bodies (para. 108).
- Treaty bodies must strive to further improve the quality of their "concluding observations", in terms of their clarity, degree of detail, level of accuracy and specificity (para. 109).

A major reform issue concerning the treaty bodies is the fact that it is complicated, confusing and expensive for governments, NGOs and the UN itself to have to deal with six separate committees engaging in very similar types of work and performing overlapping functions. One option is to consolidate the six committees into one or perhaps two new treaty bodies.[27] Such a system would: standardize the various procedures to be followed; reduce the overall volume of documentation; eliminate the need for multiple reports and accordingly reduce the overall reporting burden imposed on states; eliminate overlapping competencies; greatly reduce the likelihood of inconsistent interpretations; and facilitate the emergence of an extremely competent supervisory committee potentially enjoying both considerable credibility and high visibility.

Of course, some of these advantages can equally well be portrayed as disadvantages, and vice-versa, depending on the assumptions and perspectives of the observer. This may be illustrated by several examples. It can be argued that the single consolidated committee would, by virtue of its extensive purview and probably almost permanent sessions, develop enormous expertise. The counterargument is that the variety of expertise represented on the existing range of committees is greater than could ever be captured on a single committee. Or, it can be argued that a single report would enable all dimensions of a given problem to be presented, but the counterargument is that the single report might still be superficial, and would probably be presented by one or two representatives of the State concerned who would have little, if any, detailed knowledge of some of the relevant fields. Or, it can be argued that a single committee would facilitate the effective integration of different concerns such as racial and sex-based discrimination, children's and migrant workers' rights, and economic, social and cultural rights. The counterargument is that some of those concerns might simply be glossed over, and that the supervisory process would no longer serve to galvanize those sectors of the government and of the community dealing with, or interested in, a specific issue.

A comparably radical reform undertaken by the Council of Europe resulted in the elimination of the European Commission on Human Rights and the creation of a greatly enlarged European Court of Human Rights. It came into effect on 1 November 1998. While it also faced considerable initial opposition, the turning point came when the difficulties confronting the system became so great that less dramatic solutions appeared pale and ineffective.

A second option for reform is the preparation of a single 'global' report by each State, which would then be submitted to each of the relevant treaty bodies to which that State is legally required to report.[28] There could be many advantages to such a system: a global report would give effect to the doctrine of the equality of the various rights; each committee would be presented with a truly comprehensive picture of the overall situation in the State party and be enabled to appreciate more fully the context in which particular issues are situated; a global report would resolve the otherwise unavoidably complex question of how different committees could avoid overlapping in terms of the issues dealt with. From the perspective of the State party, the main advantage would be in the need to produce only one report in a five-year period. The State would also have a much stronger incentive to produce a detailed and thorough stock-taking of the human rights situation than is currently the case, where none of the six reports that might be required over a five-year reporting cycle is seen to be especially definitive or comprehensive. From the perspective of the most important constituency of all—the local community in the State concerned—it is much easier to focus upon a single report on the state of human rights in that country than to make sense of a bewildering array of reports, each with a different emphasis, each submitted to a different international body at different times, subject to significantly different procedures when being considered, and so on. The possibilities for developing a genuine national dialogue would seem far greater in relation to one such report than to a series of them. Finally, the preparation of a global report would be more likely to involve high-level policymakers and to constitute a process in relation to which advisory services would be both more relevant and more sought after.

There are, however, some potential disadvantages. The State would only be required to report once every five years which, in human rights terms, is a long time, but this concern is less compelling in light of the increasingly common practice of committees to call for special or supplementary reports when circumstances so warrant. Another disadvantage is that the global report would be very lengthy.

A third reform option is to replace the existing approach whereby a State party is required to submit a periodic report covering the entire gamut of issues covered in the relevant treaty, with a report that addresses only a limited range of specific issues identified in advance by the responsible committee. ' Apart from concern at the excessive burden of comprehensive reporting, the main rationale is that existing reporting requirements are so extensive that it is difficult at best, and impossible at worst, for some States to satisfy them entirely. The example of the Committee on Economic, Social and Cultural Rights is instructive in this regard. When it first met, in 1987, its work was based on existing guidelines that had been drawn up a decade earlier. Their approach is best illustrated by taking an example. Article 7 (b) relates to the relatively minor issue of 'safe and healthy working conditions'. The guidelines requested each State to submit, *inter alia*, all of its 'principal laws, administrative regulations, collective agreements and court decisions' along with details of the 'principal arrangements and procedures (including inspection services and various bodies at the national, industry, local, or undertaking level entrusted with the promotion or supervision of health and safety at work) to ensure that these provisions are effectively respected in individual work-places' (E/C.12/1987/2). Yet only the arrival of tractor-trailer loads of documents at the Palais des Nations in Geneva could have signified that a medium-sized industrialized State was taking such a reporting requirement seriously.

How then might an alternative approach work? In effect, the existing system would be reversed. Instead of beginning with a State report and then drawing up a list of specific issues to be the principal focus of the Committee's examination, the process would begin with the identification by a Committee (or its designated Working Group) of the key issues in relation to which the State party is requested to report. The Committee would determine these issues on the basis of all information available to it and would not generally require information on matters in relation to which there appeared to be no significant problems or difficulties. This would mean that a State party would not have to present a comprehensive report but would be expected to report in detail only on the issues identified. Thus, the overall reporting burden would, in most cases, be greatly reduced but the specificity and timeliness of information provided would be specifically enhanced.

This approach would also enable State Parties to choose the composition of the delegation to appear before the Committee with much more attention to the specialist expertise required. A dialogue with such experts would, at least potentially, be far more productive than are many of the dialogues taking place under the existing arrangements. Such an approach would not, of course, apply to initial reports due under any of the treaties since a comprehensive initial review of the situation is an important dimension of the process as a whole.

Recommendation: My own preference, which is shared by the U.S. expert on the Human Rights Committee, Professor Thomas Buergenthal, along with many other commentators, is that the six committees be consolidated into two bodies: 'one with power to review country reports under all six treaties, the other to deal with individual communications [complaints]'. He justifies the need for two committees by noting that the expertise required is very different for each of the functions.[29] He has also proposed the creation of a UN Human Rights Court. Such proposals have been around since the mid-1940s and have periodically been revived, although to no avail. Almost all such proposals have been modelled on the work of the European Court of Human Rights. Buergenthal acknowledges however that any such model 'could not possibly get the support of states within the foreseeable future'. For that reason, his proposal is limited to a court which, initially at least, would have 'advisory jurisdiction only to interpret the six treaties at the request of' the two consolidated treaty bodies and the member states.

Enhancing the accountability of non-state actors: the case of transnational corporations

The impact of private actors on the enjoyment of human rights is growing rapidly in a global economy. Privatization, deregulation, and the diminishing regulatory capacities of national governments have all contributed to enhancing the importance of corporations and other private entities in terms of human rights.

Globalisation is itself highly conducive to the growing power of transnational corporations (TNCs). In some respects, the essence of the phenomenon is to make business across borders easier in a great many ways, as well as more profitable. Improved mobility, economies of scale and a greater ability to communicate and manage across long distances, have all contributed to an enhancement of the role of TNCs. Many of the principal legal and political initiatives associated with globalisation have been designed specifically to improve the capacity for TNCs to do business. Partly as a result, foreign direct investment flows are at record levels. In 1997 they were nearly double what they had been in 1990 and seven times 1980 levels. They are expected to continue growing despite the financial crises afflicting many countries.[30] Indeed TNCs have been the principal conduit for globalisation. This fact alone would be sufficient to warrant a sustained focus on the relationship between the role of TNCs and efforts to ensure the promotion and protection of human rights.

In addition, several other phenomena closely associated with globalisation have further increased the importance of TNCs. Privatisation, for example, in the case of certain industries is significantly more likely to create opportunities for TNCs than for local corporations which lack the scale or expertise to bid successfully. The same is often true even for activities such as prison management, some aspects of law enforcement and even aspects of military security. Deregulation reinforces the same trend. At the same time, pressure on the state to reduce its own expenditures will often lead it to downgrade its efforts to enforce those regulatory arrangements that are left in place. Labour inspection is a simple example in this regard. This combination of factors has led many commentators and groups in civil society to focus on the responsibilities of corporations. In addition, a range of widely publicised instances in which major corporations have been implicated in situations involving either significant violations of human rights or of environmental standards have generated consumer and other pressures upon corporations to demonstrate their responsibility. Shell Oil, Nike, Levi Strauss and many other firms have responded to strong criticism by adopting codes of behaviours designed to insulate themselves from such criticism and to build an image of good corporate citizenship.[31]

Governments have been supportive of such efforts while at the same time remaining unwilling to take regulatory measures of their own. There has been strong resentment over certain exercises of extra-territorial jurisdiction, including especially some purportedly aimed at upholding human rights. Most notable have been the actions by the US Congress in the Helms-Burton and D'Amato Acts, which seek to punish foreign corporations investing in Cuba, Iran and other countries considered to be *non grata*. The result is that the same governments which successfully insisted upon corporate codes of conduct in relation to South Africa at the time of *apartheid* are not prepared to act in relation to TNCs in general.

There are various reasons for the reticence to use human rights standards, but the most important by far is simply the fact that TNCs, as private or non-State actors, are not bound by human rights standards as such. Human rights obligations are assumed by governments pursuant to international law (either through treaty ratification or by virtue of the application of principles of customary international law) and are thus not formally or directly opposable to TNCs.[32]

Much of the literature talks of social responsibility, corporate good citizenship, social audits, etc., but generally does not talk in terms of human rights. The result is a diverse range of standards, varying significantly in scope and focus. Many human rights issues are not addressed at all. Others are, but not in a manner that matches the formulation or even the approach reflected in international human rights standards. But some of the issues in relation to which the performance of corporations is being evaluated actually go well beyond human rights issues per se. They include, for example, the firm's contribution to employment creation, the amount of revenue it earns per worker, and the percentage of its pre-tax profits that is devoted to philanthropic activities. There is much to be said, however, for focusing on a more limited range of issues in relation to which the standards are clear, and accountable public authorities rather than corporate officials make the key decisions.

Human Rights Watch, while expressing concern about the lack of human rights accountability of TNCs and the strong reluctance of governments to take an interest in corporate responsibility issues, has nevertheless been encouraged by the trend towards the adoption of voluntary codes of conduct in the footwear, apparel and other sectors. 'While governments are unwilling to insist that corporations not profit from repression, a vibrant and burgeoning NGO movement is leading this campaign.'[33] However, existing arrangements for monitoring compliance with human rights standards are ill-equipped to respond to these developments.[34] In response to growing corporate awareness and increasing consumer pressure, there has been a significant expansion in the number of voluntary codes of conduct and the like that have been adopted within different business sectors. In principle, these developments are to be welcomed, but they are insufficient. They are not necessarily based squarely on international standards, their monitoring is uneven, they are mostly overseen by the corporations themselves, and they remain entirely optional.[35]

Ultimately, however, as Human Rights Watch acknowledges, such matters cannot be based on voluntary undertakings. The standards thus set are excessively flexible, and their conformity with international human rights norms is by no means assured. The element of accountability is lacking, insofar as firms 'police' their own behaviour and the international mechanisms, as well as the representatives of civil society, are often excluded.

Some governmental efforts exist but they are neither comprehensive nor consistent. The European Union (EU) is an example in this regard. In 1977 the Council of the European Union adopted a Code of Conduct for businesses operating in South Africa[36] and in May 1998 it adopted an EU Code of Conduct on Arms Exports.[37] While there are significant differences in

the scope and approach of these codes, it is difficult to accept as the last word a recent statement by the European Commission to the effect that existing Community law makes it impossible to develop a code of conduct to oblige EU-based companies operating in third countries to observe human rights norms.[38] The Commission should evaluate existing voluntary codes of conduct and prepare a study on the ways in which an official EU code of conduct for corporations could be formulated, promoted and monitored.[39]

Recommendation: While voluntary arrangements, such as the 'global compact of shared values and principles' proposed at Davos, Switzerland by UN Secretary General Kofi Annan,[40] should be developed, mechanisms also need to be set up to review the conformity of these various codes etc. with human rights standards. Means must be devised by which to enhance the accountability and responsibility of TNCs in relation to human rights.

A Treaty-Based Petitions System to Secure Relief and Redress for Victims of Violations of Economic, Social and Cultural Rights

There is a need to begin the process of drafting an Optional Protocol to the Covenant on Economic, Social and Cultural Rights to permit the submission of complaints alleging serious violations of these rights. This exercise will: (a) fill the existing vacuum, as a result of which international procedures effectively exclude these rights from their purview; (b) bring the debate over these rights to bear upon real-life situations and to move beyond the determinedly abstract character of past debates; and (c) provide the specificity of focus which is required to enable the development of meaningful jurisprudence in this area.[41] While the Vienna Programme of Action encouraged 'the Commission on Human Rights, in cooperation with the Committee on Economic, Social and Cultural Rights, to continue the examination of optional protocols', nothing has been done in response to the Committee's completion of its work.

The Possibility of Introducing a Universal Petition Procedure

Sir Hersch Lauterpacht, the most incisive of all the early international legal commentators on human rights, wrote in 1950 that '[t]he effective right of petition must be deemed to be an irreducible right of the individual not only in relation to his own nation but also in relation to the United Nations.'[42] Reports published in 1994 and 1995 called for the establishment of an international right of petition.[43] It is significant that these proposals came not from human rights experts or groups but from international relations practitioners in the context of examining overall reforms required within the United Nations system.

There are, in fact, various petition procedures in place, under the auspices of the UN, the ILO, UNESCO and the regional human rights commissions. But for the most part, these are limited in scope or require that the government concerned has accepted a treaty-based procedure, such as that contained in the Optional Protocol to the International Covenant on Civil and Political Rights (ICCPR). The only comprehensive procedure, theoretically open to all, is that established almost 30 years ago and known as the '1503 procedure', after the resolution by which the Economic and Social Council (ECOSOC) established it.[44] The procedure authorizes action to be taken by the Council and the Commission on Human Rights in response to 'particular situations which appear to reveal a consistent pattern of gross and reliably attested violations of human rights'.[45] While it constituted a historic breakthrough at the time of its adoption in 1970, the procedure has failed to evolve in any of the ways that its proponents had reasonably anticipated.

In assessments of its first decade, the line taken by virtually all commentators was that only time would tell whether or not it could be effective. But as the year 2000 approaches, the procedure is no longer in its infancy and surely it must be judged as a mature adult. Indeed, a United Nations official responsible for the processing of complaints has recently estimated that 'millions of petitions have been received and examined' under the 1503 procedure.[46] If that is accurate, then it is high time that a careful evaluation is undertaken of a procedure that has consumed an enormous amount of time and energy not only on the part of victims and their representatives, but of UN officials, diplomats, national governments and human rights non-governmental organizations.

My own assessment is that time has now rendered its verdict and it is, on balance, a damning one. Indeed, in the absence of a radical overhaul of the way in which the procedure functions, it would be better to disband it than to maintain the existing masquerade. If such reforms are considered politically unacceptable, the procedure should be abolished so that a proper debate can develop over the need for, and more importantly the modalities of, establishing procedures to give effect to such a right. Ironically, one of the major obstacles hindering such a development is the reluctance of many actors within the human rights domain to tamper with a wholly inadequate and unsatisfactory petition procedure.

The lack of an authentic international petition procedure to enable complaints to be lodged in response to alleged violations constitutes a major deficiency in the international human rights regime. The omission is all the more curious given the central importance accorded to the right of petition in the seventeenth- and eighteenth-century conceptions that were so influential in shaping existing international approaches. Not only is the right reflected in a great many national constitutions and bills of rights, ranging from the United States Bill of Rights to the Constitution of the Peoples' Republic of China, but most of the early visions of a desirable United Nations human rights framework assumed it would be included from the outset.[47]

Recommendation: Work should begin on the design of an authentic and effective international petition procedure to enable complaints to be lodged in response to alleged violations of all human rights.

The role and responsibilities of international organizations in the face of globalization

While governments bear the principal responsibility for ensuring respect for human rights, international organizations are an important instrument of policies that can either be conducive to human rights or can directly or indirectly undermine them. Those organizations, as well as the governments that have created and manage them, have a strong and continuous responsibility to take whatever measures they can to assist governments to act in ways that are compatible with their human rights obligations and to seek to devise policies and prescriptions that promote respect for those rights. It is particularly important to emphasise that the realms of trade, finance and investment are in no way exempt from these general principles, and that the international organizations with specific responsibilities in those areas should play a positive and constructive role in relation to human rights.

In 1997, the UN Committee on Economic, Social and Cultural Rights sought to highlight this responsibility in one of its 'General Comments' when it insisted that even the Security Council, and even when it was acting on the basis of the draconian powers entrusted to it under Chapter VII of the UN Charter, was still subject to human rights requirements. In an important analysis the Committee wrote that these rights:

> *cannot be considered to be inoperative, or in any way inapplicable, solely because a decision has been taken that considerations of international peace and security warrant the imposition of sanctions. Just as the international community insists that any targeted State must respect the civil and political rights of its citizens, so too must that State and the international community itself do everything possible to protect at least the core content of the economic, social and cultural rights of the affected peoples of that State (General Comment 8 (1997), para. 7).*

This analysis has clear parallels in relation to the activities of those international organizations that are in the frontline of dealing with issues put in the spotlight by developments associated with globalisation.

Recommendations: The International Monetary Fund and the World Bank should pay careful attention to the human rights impact of their policies, albeit within reasonable bounds in light of their mandates and responsibilities. While the Managing Director of the Fund observed in May 1998 that 'human rights violations can never be accepted and are never a good thing for economic progress', neither the Fund nor the Bank has a clear, let alone comprehensive, policy relating to human rights. This includes policies designed to promote respect for economic, social and cultural rights, which should include explicit recognition of those rights, the identification of country-specific benchmarks to facilitate their promotion, and the development of appropriate remedies for responding to violations. Social safety nets should be defined by reference to these rights, and enhanced attention should be accorded to such programs for the poor and vulnerable in the context of structural adjustment programs. Effective social monitoring should go hand in hand with the enhanced financial surveillance and monitoring policies accompanying loans and credits for adjustment purposes.

Similarly, the World Trade Organization should devise appropriate methods to facilitate more systematic consideration of the impact upon human rights of particular trade and investment policies. Regardless of whether such policies should focus on the adoption of a 'social clause' linked to sanctions against non-complying countries, there are many other options that should be explored to enable the WTO to be a responsible partner in the international community's quest to give the fullest possible meaning to the commitments contained in the Universal Declaration of Human Rights.

As we enter the twenty-first century, it is imperative that we acknowledge that human rights are the only bulwark that remains against a world whose 'values' are defined solely by reference to economic determinism, by the notoriously and in many ways appropriately selfish and narrow preferences of the market. We must therefore redouble our efforts to ensure that the real values enshrined in the Universal Declaration of Human Rights move closer to realization in the second half-century of its existence than they have in the first.

The Importance of Instrumentalist Approaches

One of the most hopeful signs in terms both of reform and of the systematic acceptance of the relevance of human rights is a move towards a greater recognition of instrumentalist justifications for human rights. Human rights are a reflection of ethical or moral values. They can be grounded in different philosophical or religious traditions, in natural law or natural rights theory, or in positive law (an option that has only become fully convincing in recent years). They cannot systematically be justified through the application of economic or efficiency criteria and instrumentalist approaches will have major shortcomings. Nevertheless, for pragmatic and operational reasons, it is important to develop instrumentalist reasoning as far as possible, as a complement to the basic ethical and normative grounding of human rights. This is, in a number of respects, the path followed in relation to gender-in-development endeavours, many of which relied far more heavily upon arguments based on the beneficial economic consequences of inclusion rather than the ethical imperative to end discrimination and exclusion.

UN Secretary General Kofi Annan has systematically repeated the statement that 'human rights are part of human security'. This is a partly ethical statement but its principal significance is instrumentalist. In other words, the assertion is being made that those who care about human security (whether defined in traditional or in more enlightened 1990s terms)[48] have practical, or authentically 'strategic', reasons to seek to factor human rights considerations into their analyses.

Various other examples can be mentioned, although they will not be systematically developed in the present paper:

- Peace and security: the Security Council is prepared to act in response to some violations and to condone the creation of war crimes tribunals primarily on the assumption that there will be a direct benefit in terms of the restoration or maintenance of peace.
- Democratic peace theories: democratic nations are much less likely to go to war (against each other).[49]
- Economic policies: human rights-related measures have been embraced insofar as they appear to contribute directly to the effective functioning of free markets. The clearest example is the concept of good governance, which is generally defined by economic agencies to include the free flow of information, anti-corruption measures, a functioning legal system, an effective civil service, etc.
- Good neighbourliness: Chinese expressions of concern over the May 1998 riots in Indonesia, combined with Indonesian and Filipino expressions of concern over developments in Malaysia, amounted to an affirmation of the view that human rights violations in a neighbouring country have sufficiently negative implications as to justify 'intercession' (to use a more neutral term) by other countries.
- TNCs: codes of conduct are increasingly popular, as are calls for capitalism with a human face, etc., primarily because of a perception that aspects of globalization will be unsustainable in the absence of attention to certain undesirable side-effects of the process. This is dealt with below.

Ensuring an Appropriate Role for NGOs and Civil Society

The work of international and domestic NGOs can make an enormous difference to the positions taken by governments and can create conditions in which international organizations are able to become more effective. In addition, developments in relation to communications technology are rapidly creating the conditions in which it will be ever more difficult for governments to stem the vitally important flow of information from local groups to international 'umbrella' human rights groups and inter-governmental monitoring bodies. These developments relate less to the impact of CNN-type media coverage of 'horror' situations than to the impact being achieved by the development of wireless technologies that eliminate the dependence upon governmentally-controlled lines of communication. Because of their diminishing cost, their relative ease of use and the difficulty of impeding or preventing their use, these technologies have the potential to offer small groups, even in remote and somewhat inaccessible areas, a degree of direct access to the international community that had previously been available only to well-resourced groups, in large urban areas, with established international links.

History shows that recognition of human rights is not volunteered by governments but is rather extracted from them by popular movements and what are now known as NGOs. No well-informed observer would doubt that NGOs have been instrumental in contributing to many of the breakthroughs that have been achieved in the international human rights regime.

One of the challenges confronting international NGOs is to encourage and assist the work of domestic NGOs. Any such help must be non-paternalistic and be provided on terms set in consultation with the grassroots groups. Far too little attention has been paid in the past to what might be done to build up indigenous capacity. Too many Western NGOs act as though they believe that respect for human rights in the world will be won or lost in a handful of Western capitals. In the same vein, it is necessary not to overstate the importance for domestic groups to be actively engaged vis-à-vis international forums. The work in such forums is undoubtedly important but it does not require the direct involvement of every small domestic group, many of whose scarce resources would be better spent at home.

NGOs active at the international level need to become both better coordinated and more systematically critical. Both challenges are difficult in practice. Better coordination will be required in forums such as the Commission on Human Rights and its Sub-Commission if NGOs, because of their sheer numbers and diversity, are not to risk being relegated to a mere sideshow role which can safely be ignored by the governmental representatives and the press to whom their efforts should be directed. There is a clear need for more effective strategies to be worked out to pool resources, reduce unhelpful repetition, enable better targeting and encourage greater specialization. In the absence of such strategies, governments which are looking for excuses to hobble NGOs will not find the task as difficult as it should be. An encouraging development in this respect is the increase in the number of joint statements being put forward.[50]

It must be said in conclusion, however, that the need to enhance the role and effectiveness on NGOs vis-à-vis the United Nations programme is by no means a one-way street in which all of the responsibility lies with the NGOs themselves. The United Nations must begin to address in a constructive and systematic fashion the need to accord NGOs the status and rights which they deserve as full partners in a common endeavour. It makes no sense, for example, that local and national NGOs are, virtually by definition, excluded from consultative status with the Economic and Social Council, especially at a time when they are coming to be seen as vital partners in a genuine dialogue with governments. ■

Notes

[1] See P. Alston, 'Neither Fish nor Fowl: The Quest to Define the Role of the UN High Commissioner for Human Rights', 8 *European Journal of International Law* (1997) pp. 321-335.

[2] *HCHR News*, vol. 1, no. 9, Dec. 1996–Jan. 1997, at 2. The initiative was based on a statement of 23 April 1996 by the Chairman of the Commission on Human Rights. UN Doc. E/1996/23 (1996), at 297.

[3] *Supra* note 15, at 3.

[4] This framework is a significantly adapted version of one put forward in P. Alston, 'Critical Appraisal of the UN Human Rights Regime', in Alston (ed.), *The United Nations and Human Rights: A Critical Appraisal* (Oxford, Clarendon Press, 1992).

[5] This analysis draws heavily upon P. Alston, 'The Universal Declaration in an Era of Globalisation', in Barend van der Heijden and Bahia Tahzib-Lie (eds.), *Reflections on the Universal Declaration of Human Rights: A Fiftieth Anniversary Anthology* (The Hague, Martinus Nijhoff, 1998).

[6] J.D. Davidson and W. Rees-Mogg, *The Sovereign Individual* (London, Pan Books, 1997).

[7] UN doc. A/C.3/53/L.5 (1998).

[8] Amnesty International - Report - IOR 40/02/98, April 1998 'Muddying the Waters: The Draft ' Universal Declaration of Human Responsibilities': No Complement to Human Rights.

[9] Report of the third session of the Commission on Human Rights, 7 ESCOR, UN doc. E/800 (1948), Appendix, pp. 30-31.

[10] H. Lauterpacht, *International Law and Human Rights* (Steven & Sons Limited, USA, 1950, reprinted 1968), pp. 326-327.

[11] See generally D. Sullivan, 'Gender Equality and Religious Freedom: Toward a Framework for Conflict Resolution', 24 *New York University Journal of International Law and Politics* 795 (1992); and A. An-Na'im, 'Human Rights in the Muslim World: Socio-Political Considerations and Scriptural Imperatives', 3 *Harvard Human Rights Journal* 13 (1990).

[12] P. Alston, 'Final report on enhancing the long-term effectiveness of the United Nations human rights treaty system', UN doc. E/CN.4/1997/74 (27 Mar. 1997). The references that follow refer to the paragraph numbers in the report in which the relevant issue has been examined.

[13] See: http://www.amnesty.org/ailib/aireport/ar98/intro2.html, p. 3 of 6.

[14] 'Enhancing the effectiveness of the Sub-Commission: Note by the Chairman', UN doc. E/CN.4/Sub.2/1998/38, para. 9.

[15] March, J. and J. Olsen, *Rediscovering Institutions: The Organizational Basis of Politics* (New York, Free Press, 1989), p. 30.

[16] Claude, I., 'The Nature and Status of the Subcommission on Prevention of Discrimination and Protection of Minorities', 5 *International Organization* 300 (1951).

[17] Washington DC, 6 Oct 1998, p.13.

[18] Paul Lewis, International Herald Tribune, 12 October 1998, p.2.

[19] Committee on Economic, Social and Cultural Rights, General Comment 10 (Nineteenth session, 1998) – Adopted on 1 December 1998.

[20] World Conference on Human Rights: Position Paper by the European Community and its Member States, April 1993, para. 10.

[21] Bangkok Declaration of 1993, adopted by the Asian Regional Meeting preceding the World Conference on Human Rights, paras. 17-18.

[22] A. Bayefsky, Remarks in panel on 'The UN Human Rights Regime: Is It Effective?', in 91 *Proceedings of the Annual Meeting of the American Society of International Law* (1997) 466 at 471-72.

[23] Human Rights Watch World Report 1998, p. xxix.

[24] 'Enhancing the effectiveness of the Sub-Commission: Note by the Chairman', UN doc. E/CN.4/Sub.2/1998/38 (13 Aug. 1998), para. 28.

[25] UN doc. A/52/507, (21 Oct. 1997), paras. 67-68.

[26] Note 12 above. The paragraph numbers in parentheses refer to those paragraphs in the report in which the relevant issue has been examined.

[27] This was first put forward in P. Alston, 'Study on long-term approaches to human rights treaty supervision', UN doc. A/44/668 (1989).

[28] This option was canvassed in P. Alston, 'Interim report on study on enhancing the long-term effectiveness of the United Nations human rights treaty régime', study prepared for the World Conference on Human Rights, Vienna 1993, UN doc. A/CONF.157/PC/ 62/Add.11/Rev.1 (1993),

[29] T. Buergenthal, Remarks in panel on 'The UN Human Rights Regime: Is It Effective?', in 91 *Proceedings of the Annual Meeting of the American Society of International Law* (1997) 482 at 483.

[30] *World Investment Report 1998: Trends and Determinants* (UNCTAD, 1998) p. 8.

[31] See e.g. *Visions of Ethical Business* (London, Financial Times Management, 1998).

[32] See generally *Multilateral Enterprises and Human Rights*, A Report by the Dutch Section of Amnesty International and Pax Christi International (Utrecht, Nov. 1998).

[33] Human Rights Watch World Report 1998, p. xvii.

[34] See Amnesty International, Human Rights Principles for Companies, AI Report 70/01/98, Jan. 1998.

[35] Kamminga, 'Holding Multinational Corporations Accountable for Human Rights Abuses: A Challenge for the European Community', in P. Alston (ed.), *The EU and Human Rights* (forthcoming 1999, Oxford University Press).

[36] Code of Conduct for companies from the European Community with subsidiaries, branches or representation in South Africa as revised by the Ministers for Foreign Affairs of the ten countries of the European Community and Spain and Portugal, 1977, revised in 1985. For an assessment see M. Holland, *The European Community and South Africa: European Political Co-operation Under Strain* (1988) 74.

[37] Council of the European Union, 2097th meeting, Brussels, 25 May 1998, Press Release 8687/98 (Presse 162), p. 16.

[38] Letter of 14 November 1997 to the Chairman of the European Parliament's Committee on Foreign Affairs, Security and Defence Policy.

[39] P. Alston and J.H.H. Weiler, 'An 'Ever Closer Union' in Need of a Human Rights Policy', 9 *European Journal of International Law* (1998) forthcoming.

[40] UN Press Release SG/SM/6881, 1 Feb. 1999.

[41] See generally P. Alston, 'No Right to Complain About Being Poor: The Need for an Optional Protocol to the Economic Rights Covenant', in Eide and Helgesen (eds.), *The Future of Human Rights Protection in a Changing World* (Oslo, Norwegian University Press, 1991) 79.

[42] Hersch Lauterpacht, *International Law and Human Rights* (1950) 231.

[43] See notes XXX.

[44] ECOSOC Res. 1503 (XLVIII)(1970)

[45] *Id.* at para. 5.

[46] Alfred-Maurice de Zayas, 'Petitioning the United Nations', in Rosa da Costa (ed.), *The European Convention on Human Rights and Other International Protection Mechanisms* (1997) 59.

[47] Breugel, 'The Right to Petition an International Authority', 2 *International and Comparative Law Quarterly* 542 (1953).

[48] For a fascinating analysis of such developments in more traditional security thinking, see M. Alagappa (ed.), *Asian Security Practice: Material and Ideational Influences* (Stanford, Stanford University Press, 1998).

[49] E. Gartzke, 'Kant We All Just Get Along?: Opportunity, Willingness, and the Origins of the Democratic Peace', 42 *American Journal of Political Science* (1998) 1.

[50] See the joint NGO submission to the October 1998 session of the UNHCR Executive Committee entitled 'Sharing the Responsibility to Protect Refugees', which was coordinated by the International Coalition of Voluntary Agencies (ICVA).

References

Alagappa, M. (ed.), *Asian Security Practice: Material and Ideational Influences* (Stanford, Stanford University Press, 1998).

Allott, P., *Eunomia: New Order for a New World* (Oxford, Clarendon Press, 1990), 288.

Alston, P., 'The Myopia of the Handmaidens: International Lawyers and Globalization', 8 *European Journal of International Law* (1997) 435.

Bauer, J. and D. Bell (eds.), *The East Asian Challenge to Human Rights* (Cambridge, Cambridge University Press, 1998).

Clark, I., *Globalization and Fragmentation: International Relations in the Twentieth Century* (Oxford, Oxford University Press, 1997).

Claude, I., 'The Nature and Status of the Subcommission on Prevention of Discrimation and Protection of Minorities', 5 *International Organization* 300 (1951).

Cook, R., 'Effectiveness of the Beijing Conference: Advancing International Law Regarding Women', in 91 *Proceedings of the Annual Meeting of the American Society of International Law* (1997) 310.

Davidson, J.D. and W. Rees-Mogg, *The Sovereign Individual: The Coming Economic Revolution, How to Survive and Prosper in It* (London, Pan Books, 1997).

DeBary, W.T., *Asian Values and Human Rights: A Confucian Communitarian Perspective* (Cambridge, Harvard University Press, 1998).

Donnelly, J., 'Human Rights at the United Nations 1955-85: The Question of Bias', 32 *International Studies Quarterly* 275 at 278 (1988).

Donnelly, J., 'International Human Rights: A Regime Analysis', 40 *International Organization* 599 (1986).

Elazar, D., *Constitutionalizing Globalization: The Postmodern Revival of Confederal Arrangements* (Lanham, Rowman and Littlefield, 1998).

Forsythe, D., 'The United Nations and Human Rights, 1945-1985', in *The Internationalization of Human Rights* (Omaha, University of Nebraska Press, 1991), chap. 3.

Keck, M.E. and K. Sikkink, *Activists Beyond Borders: Advocacy Networks in International Politics* (Ithaca, Cornell University Press, 1998).

Kelly, D. and A. Reid (eds.), *Asian Freedoms: The Idea of Freedom in East and Southeast Asia* (Cambridge, Cambridge University Press, 1998).

Krasner, S., 'Structural Causes and Regime Consequences: Regimes as Intervening Variables', 36 *International Organization* 185 (1982).

March, J. and J. Olsen, *Rediscovering Institutions: The Organizational Basis of Politics* (New York, Free Press, 1989).

Neier, A., *War Crimes: Brutality, Genocide, Terror, and the Struggle for Justice* (New York, Times Books, 1998).

Orford, A. and J. Beard, 'Making the State Safe for Market: The World Bank's *World Development Report 1997*', 22 *Melbourne University Law Review* (1998) 195.

Posner, M., 'Reflections on the Vienna Conference on Human Rights' in 91 *Proceedings of the Annual Meeting of the American Society of International Law* (1997) 317.

Ratner, S.R. and J.S. Abrams, *Accountability for Human Rights Atrocities in International Law: Beyond the Nuremburg Legacy* (Oxford, Clarendon Press, 1997).

Teubner, G. (ed.), *Global Law Without a State* (Aldershot, Dartmouth, 1997).

CULTURE, GLOBALIZATION AND INTERNATIONAL TRADE

*Lourdes Arizpe and Guiomar Alonso**

This paper argues that culture is rapidly becoming one of the major issues in globalization because it provides the images—and the underlying values—with which people construct their view of the world. While economic goods are slowly reaching more and more remote places in all countries of the world, they have been preceded by the sounds and images of telecommunications. Radios and televisions had already invaded a majority of households. Film audiences are counted by the millions and phonographic records have crossed all political borders to reach listeners who are now attuned to music from all cultures of the world. To this must now be added planetary telephony and the Internet. This daily confrontation with other cultures is exciting for the young, disquieting for a majority of people trying to keep the best of their traditions, and risky for governments aware that they must reposition their nation-states and cultural groups in a new global map.

The perspective from which culture and globalization—both wide-ranging terms as analyzed further on—are examined in this paper, is development policies. We will be using the term 'globalization' to refer to the process of increased exchanges and interdependence occurring in the world today; and 'globality' to the permanent structures slowly being built in which positions, actions and values are embedded in a single matrix. Within this framework, the liberalization of trade and financial markets and the environmental challenge have been intensely surveyed, dissected and debated. The accompanying cultural processes, however, have not been given systematic attention. This has do to partly with the polysemic nature of the term culture, which can be extended to touch practically all anthropogenic phenomena.

The topics, however, that have surfaced in the international development agenda may be clustered around three kinds of issues. First, there are cultural heritage, identity politics, and cultural rights issues. Second, there are the cultural effects of television, multimedia and now teleinformatics, especially in relation to linguistic and cultural pluralism on the Internet. Finally, there is the issue of cultural goods in international trade agreements, particularly in terms of the 'cultural exemption' as discussed in the negotiations on the General Agreement on Trade and Tariffs (GATT), and at the Organisation for Economic Co-operation and Development (OECD) and World Trade Organization (WTO). This essay is a rapid review of the most important trends in relation to these issues, with as much updated information as possible.

Trade-offs that have caught people's minds

These issues are directly related to recent phenomena associated with globalization, although some are effects of latter and others are a reaction to it. The end of the Cold War brought about the breakdown of traditional political discourses which provided both a vision of the future and a set of values that cemented political and social unity. To fill the gap left by this discursive shift, people have turned to, resurrected or, indeed, invented 'traditional culture' to rebuild their sense of belonging, place and purpose. As a result, cultural movements which were dormant or only involved in minority groups or indigenous militancies are now overrunning traditional political boundaries and platforms. In many cases, however, these movements take a cultural form yet their basic demands have more to do with governance realignments than with culture.

The most visible set of phenomena related to culture and globalization is that of the unimagined new spaces for cultural dialogue, exchange, invasion or confrontation that have been created by the multimedia and telecommunications. Needless to say, all these spaces are now sites of intense cultural contestation.

* We are indebted to Elizabeth Jelin, Mark Jamieson and Nestor Garcia Canclini for suggestions for this essay.

Additionally, the virtual space recently created by the Internet is creating practices which are running much faster than our ability to develop concepts and frameworks to think about them.

Finally, current international political economy is characterized by changing patterns of production, consumption and trade of goods, services and assets. In this changing landscape, cultural goods are no exception. The pre-eminence of the market in driving development has accelerated the commoditization of cultural objects and services that hitherto were considered as following a non-economic rationality. For example, copyright is now being sought for Inuit art and for Australian aboriginal designs to protect their creativity; shamanic services in many indigenous communities are now remunerated as meta-medical therapeutic services.

Yet the greatest concern everywhere about culture is that the flooding of commodities with a different cultural content will lead not only to changes in the style of living of individuals and societies, but also in their philosophical, ethical and relational values. The UN World Commission on Culture and Development[1] —of which I [Lourdes Arizpe] had the honour to be a member—was able to attest to this in the nine consultations it held between 1992-1995 in Paris, Stockholm, San Jose Costa Rica, Manila, Oman, Moscow, Tokyo and South Africa. This has led to questions about cultural goods, especially films, videos, cultural heritage objects, art by certain national artists and so on: Should they be treated as any other commodity, or should special clauses apply to them in general trade and investment agreements?

This debate will grow more heated with the next round of trade negotiations in 2000. Already in October 1992, the *Economist* had stated that in worldwide long-term economic growth, the culture sector would remain at about 10% per year, ahead of many other industrial and commercial segments. This forecast has proved to be true for many countries. Thus, the issue of culture and trade has now acquired prime strategic significance: Cultural products convey specific cultural contents and values, but are at the same time, a crucial "free factor of production" in the emerging knowledge economy. Treatment of culture in the upcoming round of multilateral negotiations on trade and investment will have decisive consequences on the economic hegemony of the markets in the culture sector as well as on cultural diversity and innovation at the global level. So far there has been a strong polarization of governmental positions with regard to culture and trade, expressing both sides of the public interest vs. market forces ideological debate—and of a market positioning strategy on how to ensure control of the emerging markets of cultural goods and services.

David Throsby makes a useful distinction in the *World Culture Report* between 'internationalization' and 'globalization' as a way of understanding culture and globalization. The internationalization of economies and cultures refers to the opening of frontiers to commodities and cultural content from other countries. Globalization, however, "is marked by functional interaction between different economic activities and cultures, generated by a system with many centres, where speed in reaching other parts of the world and strategies for attracting audiences are more decisive than the inertia of local traditions."[2] This new functionality is altering the traditional relationships of every culture to 'other' cultures.

As a result of all these phenomena, culture has been firmly placed in the international agenda on development. One indication of this has been the strong interest, both enthusiastic and critical, shown to *Our Creative Diversity*, the report by the World Commission on Culture and Development. Since its presentation in 1995, it has been translated into 14 languages, including Arab and Japanese; it has been the subject of presentations or seminars in 70 countries; and it has become a text for courses in many schools and universities.

Since its publication, the debate on culture and development has evolved very rapidly. The report by the Council of Europe, *In from the Margins* gave a different perspective and added very valuable insights into precisely many of the areas not covered by *Our Creative Diversity* that should be pursued further.

At the Intergovernmental Conference on Cultural Policies organized by UNESCO, which took place in Stockholm in March, 1998, one of the major debates touched on the issue that as a result of globalization, cultural policies must now take into account events and trends happening outside national borders. It was recognized that production in the arts, crafts and cultural industries engage national concerns of cultural identity and solidarity. It was further noted that an increasingly larger sector of cultural consumption comes from the international market, circulates in transnational communication networks and is creating "audiences of deterritorialized messages," as Nestor Garcia Canclini has called them.

In the words of Ulf Hannerz, a specialist on culture and globalization, we are now living in "a global ecumene of persistent cultural interaction and exchanges."[3] This global ecumene is one in which, in our view, *it is the perception of cultural interaction that becomes important in political terms.* Witness the strange political bedfellows such perceptions sometimes make, as the following examples show. Sendero Luminoso, the radical left-wing guerrilla movement in Peru, fought to "reinstate the authentic culture to Peru" that is, the culture stemming from the pre-Hispanic Inca civilization, so as to "reindigenize" the country. Then, the regime of Slobodan Milosevic in Yugoslavia, which identifies itself as a socialist regime, is responsible for some of the most brutal "ethnic cleansing" in recent history. Finally, on the other extreme of the political spectrum, M. Bruno Megret, the main ideologue of the right-wing Front National of France, stated in February 1998 that: "Politics must no longer be seen as divided between right and left but between identity and globalization." His party—subdivided now—advocates identity and the closing of cultural borders.

All three positions are based on an essentialist perspective of ethnicity that finds its mirror image in fundamentalist views in religions. Such positions cut across traditional political alignments and are altering the electoral maps in many countries. In the May 1999 Prime Ministerial elections in Israel, the comment was made that voters from the main political parties were allied in defending the secular nature of the state of Israel, rather than specific political platforms.

Globalization, positionality and the politics of difference

The recent emergence or revitalization of cultural movements, overlapping with communal and religious fundamentalist mobilizations, can be seen in one way or another as reactive movements to globalization.[4] Thus, the whole discussion on the consequences of the interaction of culture and globalization hinges on understanding what possible directions these movements may take.

Some authors, among them, Alaine Touraine, argue that the building of identity by individuals will lead to their constructing themselves as *subjects* who will transform societies to reach new collective and holistic meanings. These new meanings would build new forms of shared governance. Some authors, Laclau, for example, take this to mean that a "relative universalization of values" will emerge. He argues that "this universalization and its open character certainly condemn all identity to an unavoidable hybridization, but hybridization does not necessarily mean decline through the loss of identity: it can also mean empowering existing identities through the opening of new possibilities. Only a conservative identity, closed on itself, could experience hybridization as a loss..."

For other authors, on the contrary, identity politics will have primacy in the network society. Manuel Castels believes that "...subjects, if and when constructed, are not built any longer on the basis of civil societies that are in the process of disintegration, but as prolongation of communal resistance..."[5] This implies that in the near future, intense negotiations will continue among actors mobilizing from the smallest village or tribe to large regional units over who gets to define cultural canons, and over the control and use of cultural heritage.

A "third way" is advocated by Anthony Giddens and has been taken up as the basis for a "third way" political positioning by Tony Blair and Romano Prodi, among others. Giddens' key concept: "The more tradition loses its hold, and the more daily life is reconstituted in terms of the dialectical interplay of the local and the global, the more individuals are forced to negotiate lifestyle choices among a diversity of options... Reflexively organized life-planning...becomes a central feature of the structuring of self-identity"[6]. He argues that "reflexivity is using information to learn to live in the world...we no longer live our lives as fate" and he gives gender as the main example of how tradition can no longer be justified in a traditional way.[7] The future, in his view, is a world of *global cosmopolitan dialogue based on a decentered globalization.*

It is interesting that the role of culture in all three scenarios is seen as reflecting autonomy, reflexivity and decenteredness. In fact, it could be said that culture has been reactivated precisely because it allows self-reflexivity based on difference, and such difference is crucial today since it provides actors with distinctive insignia to reposition themselves in a globalized setting. The insignia may be local but these are used to reposition the actors at the meso-, macro-, regional and global levels.

In some countries, the above issues are discussed in terms of the *politics of difference*. In some cases it is seen with suspicion by national governments as a disruptive element of traditional centralized politics, but welcomed by leaders of subaltern groups to foster internal cohesion to reposition themselves vis-à-vis these traditional structures. In others, it is used to reinforce traditional domination, or to impose religious fundamentalist regimes, as in the case of the Taliban. Radovan Karadzic, who led the "ethnic cleansing" by Serbs in Bosnia, has been quoted as saying "ethnic borders are drawn in blood." It is all the more significant that this has been said in an era in which air wave broadcasts, fibre-optic networks, cable and satellite transmissions, trade and finance exchanges, travel, tourism and migrations *all* work against essentialist, solid, unmoveable cultural borders.

Does globalization lead to cultural homogenization?

At one point, Alain Touraine, among many others, raised the issue that globalization can be perceived as an ideological process to impose a given "global culture" on the rest of the world. As mentioned earlier, this perception comes from real villages around the world as people express their concern over the risk of cultural homogenization implied in the image of the "global village." It is popularly argued that our common exposure to American ways of life, images and ideas, transmitted mainly through global telecommunications, television and the Internet, are making people around the world more alike.

Although this view is widely held, it has not been confirmed in surveys or research. In fact, there is considerable disagreement on the effects of globalization on culture, for against this view there are a number of other authors and certainly many governments who convincingly contend that global processes are producing new and qualitatively distinct forms of difference. Actually, the term "cultural globalization" is sometimes used to refer to a single process, yet because of the inclusiveness of the term culture, very diverse processes get thrown in together which in fact have separate dynamics of their own. In general terms, as Paul Streeten has argued for economics, where the perception of globalization and integration is of a greater degree than has in fact occurred, the same could be said of cultural processes.

In studies of World System Theory, Immanuel Wallerstein contends that global processes operate according to the logic of global capitalism. Some authors extend this theory to culture, implying that one single culture is in the making worldwide. Most authors, however, argue that globalization operates according to several different dynamics and see many new cultures being constructed. Featherstone fuelled the debate by noting that "the varieties of response to the globalization process clearly suggest that there is little prospect of a unified global culture, rather there are several global cultures in the plural." Some authors differentiate, on the one hand, according to locally specified patterns of consumption,[8] and others, by the fact that commodities, ideas, media images, technologies, and so on, circulate according to quite different criteria.[9]

Appadurai, in particular, has insisted that "the new global cultural economy has to be understood as a complex, overlapping, disjunctive order, which cannot any longer be understood in terms of existing center-periphery models" (1990: 296), a state of affairs, he contends, which is producing increasingly significant disjunctions between the logic of cultural 'flows' in a number of global 'landscapes': in particular, ethnicity ('ethnoscapes'), the media ('mediascapes'), technology ('technoscapes'), finance ('finanscapes') and other aspects of culture ('ideoscapes').

The inconclusive nature of this debate is probably related to the scarcity of empirical data on such cultural processes. Few countries collect cultural statistics and even fewer social science studies relate cultural processes to development issues. *The World Culture Report*, in fact, has been created to fill this need by promoting the collection of data and research in this field.

Are production and consumption related to different cultural effects?

As Mark Jamieson has noted, few people writing on cultural homogenization advance the simplistic proposition that contact between peoples and goods produces imitative practices in itself.[10] Yet this has given rise to widespread alarm, especially from many governments, as well as in public opinion all over the world. Seeing youth watching American films, dancing to rock music, drinking Coca-Cola and now glued to the Internet is causing reactions from governments, as in Singapore, where access to the Internet is strictly government controlled. In Iran, parabolic antennas have been forbidden by the government.

It is not imitative practices, then, some authors argue, but rather the common relationship shared by various people to the global productive process that produces cultural homogenization. And as the world's inhabitants become increasingly incorporated into the global labour market and people become more dependent on forces that only see them in terms of the competitively cheap labour power they are able to provide, the more they come to organize their actions around the realization that this is the case.[11] Hannerz argues that the apparent disjunctions between the cultural 'flows' operating in different landscapes are mystifications of underlying realities.[12] According to this line of argument, different logics of 'finanscapes' and 'ethnoscapes,' for example, are to be understood in terms of a common logic of 'conjugated oppression' that emphasizes apparent difference while at the same time veiling important relations of underlying connectedness, particularly to the means of production.

The view that seems to bridge the two positions is that of Barrie Ashford. He believes it "...highly unlikely that these flows and signs, whether in mass communications or in tourism, will produce 'a' global culture, given the diversity of their reception and use by local audiences. However, because they permit forms of social interaction not tied to place or limited in time, it is proper to see them as contexts or frames of reference with which new identities may be formed, and new understandings of the world fashioned."[13]

To summarize, the debate is inconclusive. Mark Jamieson emphasizes, though, that the position that the effects of globalization are making all cultures of the world more alike is taken mainly by those who see culture as a direct or indirect outcome of the productive process. The opposing view, that it is allowing greater cultural differentiation, comes from authors focussing mainly on patterns of consumption.

The Culture Sector in International Trade: the GATT and the MAI

At present, one of the most important international debates on culture is related to 'cultural content commodities.' Trade in cultural goods has grown exponentially in the last two decades. Between 1980 and 1991, world trade of printed matter, literature, music, visual arts, cinema, photographic, radio and television equipment almost tripled from $US 67 billion to $US 200 billion.[14] International sales of software and entertainment products in the US totalled $US 60.2 billion in 1996.[15] Also, cultural industries provide jobs and are an important source of revenue from international trade. For example, Statistics Canada estimates that in 1994-1995, the entire culture sector in Canada accounted for over Can$ 20 billion or 3% of Canada's GDP, providing direct and full and part time jobs for 610,000 people – almost 5% of Canada's labour force. According to the newly-created British Creative Industries Task Force, cultural industries employ directly and indirectly, some 1.4 million people. Employment in the sector is growing at 5% a year—twice the national average. Exports are valued at £7.5 billion.[16]

During that decade, a few countries enjoyed most of the exports and imports in cultural goods. 1990 figures show that Japan, USA and Germany were the three big exporters (comprising 46% of total exports), followed by the United Kingdom, Korea, France, Singapore, and The Netherlands. The United States, Germany, and the United Kingdom were the three major importers (40% of total imports), followed by France, Japan, Hong Kong, Italy and Canada (See Tables 1 & 2). A series of articles beguilingly entitled "The World Welcomes America's Cultural Invasion" in the 26 October 1998 *International Herald Tribune* started with the phrase: "America's biggest export is no longer the fruit of its fields or the output of its factories, but the mass-produced products of its popular culture—movies and music, television programs, books and computer software." Further on it adds: "Since 1991, when the collapse of the Soviet Union opened new markets around the world to the United States, total exports of intellectual property from the United States have risen nearly 94 percent in dollar terms."

Although we lack updated and consolidated statistics of global cultural trade, it is very likely that trade volume of cultural products has dramatically increased since 1991. The above figures on cultural flows do not reflect the boom during the 90s of multimedia and audiovisual industries, which can be grasped by the US$118 billion total turnover of the 50 largest audiovisual companies worldwide during in 1993.[17]

Cultural, entertainment, content or creative industries—however we call them—have become the most important export sectors in the United States. According to the United States Commerce Department in 1996, international sales of mass produced cultural products (i.e. computer software products, movies, music, television programmes and books) totalled US$602 million above any other American industry. Its film industry reaches every market. In less than a year, *Titanic* grossed almost $US 1.8 billion worldwide. Hollywood today gets half of its revenues from overseas, compared to just 30% in 1980.

As far as the direction of audiovisual trade flows is concerned, the world average for imported films between 1990-93 was 79%. The US share of foreign films was only 22%. By contrast, Canada imported 1,115 films, which represents 98% of the total films shown in the country in that period. Similarly high percentages of imported films are found in countries such as Belgium, Malaysia, and Peru, among many others.[18]

The whole dimension of this imbalance is reflected in Europe's audiovisual trade deficit, which grew from $US 4.8 billion to $US 5.6 billion between 1995-1996.[19] Although it is true that audiovisual businesses, especially television conglomerates, are becoming increasingly multinational, the scale of North America's role in global media, both as exporter and investor, remains unique. Indeed, other countries are big producers of cultural products: India, for instance, makes more films each year than the US. But North American-based multinational companies (Time Warner/Turner Broadcasting, Walt Disney/Capital Cities/ABC and Viacom/Paramount), dominate cultural export markets and lead joint ventures which are creating new television businesses around the world.

Finally, and taking into consideration trends in the consumption of cultural goods, there is certainly an increasing demand for cultural products and services. For instance, in EU countries, the level of expenditure on audiovisual and multimedia goods and services has been growing in the 90s at a faster rate than GDP and overall consumption expenditures. These somehow scattered figures speak eloquently of how culture industries are taking over the traditional forms of production and circulation of culture, turning the culture sector into one of the most promising emerging markets within the knowledge economy.

The economic aspects of culture have now come forcefully into national and international agendas and are becoming a key issue in global, regional and bilateral trade fora such as the WTO, NAFTA, OECD or APEC.

a. The debate on cultural products and services in trade agreements.

The issue of culture and trade was first raised during the Uruguay Round GATT (1986-1994), which represented a fundamental change in the multilateral approach to some cultural products. First signed in 1947, GATT was designed to provide an international forum that encouraged free trade between member states by regulating and reducing tariffs on traded goods and by providing a common mechanism for resolving trade disputes.

The Uruguay Round broke the 1947 status quo, which acknowledged the 'special nature' of cultural goods. Substantial negotiations were required before limited forms of exemptions or exclusions for cultural products were adopted. In 1993, France demanded that audiovisual materials be exempted from trade agreements. Backed up by the EU, some exceptions were included with regard to the application of the "Most Favoured Nation" clause and a special provision related to Cinematographic Films was included then as Article IV of Part II of the General Agreement. A general exception for measures designed to protect "national treasures of artistic, historic or achaeological value" was also adopted. Any other cultural goods remained subject to the GATT rules (i.e. Most Favoured Clause and National Treatment).

The general regime of preferences granted to developing countries (3/4 of GATT Member States), allowed them a flexible use of tariff protection in all cultural goods by not applying GATT rules and enabling them to create custom zones or zones for free exchange of goods among themselves. Intellectual property and copyright were incorporated into the GATT under a separate agreement on Trade-Related Intellectual Property Rights (TRIPs), shifting the forum of debate from the World Intellectual Property Organization (WIPO) to the WTO.

Developed countries had to conform to the TRIPs provisions by 1 January 1996.[20] Developing countries were given an extra four years, until 1 January 2000, to comply. Least developed countries received a longer transition period that lasts, in general, until 1 January 2006.

This first clash of positions during the GATT, in which the United States gave in for the sake of finalizing the agreement, was shortly reopened on a different front—that of the Multilateral Agreement on Investments (MAI). This global trade pact started to be quietly negotiated at the OECD in September 1995, and came to the open with a big public opinion splash after two and a half years of negotiations.

The words of former French Minister of Culture Jack Lang— *"The MAI is the enemy"*[21]—captures the strong anti-American, anti-uniformization wave of public opinion and media movement that convulsed France at the beginning of 1998. Others have described the MAI as a "sort of coup d'etat of multinationals" (J. Estefania, Opinion Chief Editor, *El Pais)* or as a "multi-lever lock system of legal constraints for States" (N. Albala, lawyer and member of the Observatoire de la mondialisation, Paris), or as "turning copyright works into commodities and investments" (J. Ralite, President of the French Etats Généreux de la Culture) or bluntly as "the end of democracy" (Ontario Public Interest Research Group).

The campaign to oppose the MAI has allied many other movements. Mobilizations have also taken place within the US, claiming that the MAI is "a treaty of corporate rights and government obligations which ignores the concerns of citizens" (Lori Wallach, Director of Public Citizen's Global Trade Watch); or "a step backwards in international human rights" (Harvard Law School, Human Rights Clinical Project Program and Robert F. Kennedy Memorial Center for Human Rights). Diverse interest groups have actively rallied against the MAI, which "elevates the rights of investors far above those of governments, local communities, citizens, workers and the environment." Similar movements have been active in other countries such as New Zealand, Australia or Canada, using the Internet as a prime mechanism for getting their messages across, reaching their political representatives (Senators, Members of Parliament) and the printed media.

Opposition to the treaty led negotiators in April 1998 to decide on a six-month delay to allow countries to seek domestic support and carry out consultations between countries.

b. What is at stake?

What is so explosive about the MAI which has generated such strong resistance? Furthermore, how does it affect culture, understood in the French sense of *"oeuvres de l'esprit,"* or in the Anglo-Saxon one of "citizenship" as embodying civil rights, workers rights, and other rights citizens have as members of a society?

According to the OECD, multilateral investment rules are aimed to enhance investors' confidence by providing a stable framework of clear and transparent rules applicable to all participants. Such a framework would have high standards for the liberalisation of investment regimes and protection, with an effective dispute settlement procedure. The MAI proposal would apply the principle of "National Treatment," which imposes governments to grant foreign investors the same benefits granted to domestic ones. It would also apply the principle of "Most Favoured Nation" to investment rules, requiring equal treatment among all foreign investor and target countries. Finally, it would also include a ban on "performance requirements," so governments would not be able to impose performance measures on investors.

The overall goal was to apply the deregulatory agenda of the GATT-WTO in the area of investments by creating a set of global rules that would replace a patchwork of 1,600 or so bilateral investment treaties.[22]

The MAI would set the stage for eliminating remaining barriers against foreign investors, just as global talks have gradually lowered trade barriers.[23]

Opening barriers to foreign corporations and investors from member countries is at the core of the controversy and the tip of the iceberg of a much more complex issue connected to technological change and the liberalization of international trade and investment. This is reopening old questions raised many years ago, by the Frankfurt School among others, related to culture and the role of the State, the notion of public service, as well as the balance between public interest and market forces. New questions are being formulated: How are governments dealing with the way business is reorganizing the market at the global level, thus remodelling the "public space" by subordinating the social order to their own private interests? Have national, regional and international political bodies the right to intervene in the public sphere in the same way multinational companies do? [24]

Some negotiating countries in the MAI believe that a reference to public 'interest' is necessary to allow governments to take exceptional measures based on this principle. Advocates of the MAI claim that 'exceptions' or 'reservations' may be made to protect culture, public health, the environment and social rights. Pages and pages of proposed exceptions from the general rules have been put forward. One of the most controversial is the French Exception Clause for Cultural Industries.[25]

c. The debate on the "exceptions" and the free market

So far, there is a strong polarization of government positions with regard to culture and trade that expresses not only an ideological debate, but also positioning in the market.

As the herald of free market principles and with strong economic interests in the culture sectors' exports, the US strategy is to place cultural and economic goods and services in the same playing field as other exports, therefore deserving exactly the same treatment. Culture is viewed as an industry like any other, subject to market laws and benefiting from all advantages of free trade. As M. Marando, spokesperson for the California Trade and Commerce Agency said, "We do not see it as cultural imperialism. We see it as a marketplace issue." Closely aligned with them are countries like Japan, the United Kingdom or Germany, which are precisely the biggest exporters and importers of cultural goods.

At the opposite end of the spectrum, we find the French Cultural Exception doctrine, based on the principle that cultural goods have an intrinsic value on their own[26] that is essential to maintain and protect, not only for artistic production and diversity, but also for national identity and cultural sovereignty. As French Ministry of Culture Catherine Trautmann stated in February 1998, "Pluralism and openness are at the core of the principle of cultural exception...necessary for keeping our sovereignty in the area of culture, both nationally and at the European level...Culture touches upon what is most essential for an individual: access to knowledge, to a plural vision of the world...it is linked to identity and citizenship; what makes a group of people to decide to live together in a same territory with common rules. I am against culture dissolving in an international economic system leading to uniformization."[27]

Some authors interpret French exception as an acknowledgement of the country's history and the wealth of its literary, philosophical, artistic and scientific culture.[28] Others see it as an attempt to protect its culture and domestic market against what it is seen as 'cultural dumping' practised by those who dominate world export markets of cultural products. However, this position cannot be explained only in terms of French interest.

In fact, the US first invoked the cultural exception in the early 50s when negotiating the very first multilateral trade agreement for cultural goods at UNESCO, the so-called Florence Agreement on the Importation of Educational, Scientific and Cultural Materials. The United States' reservation was published as an annexe of the agreement. The French approach is founded on a strong regulatory framework to protect and subsidize the content industries and calls for a differential treatment of cultural goods and services.

Close to the French position is Canada, with less emphasis on public subsidies, but supporting measures "to help domestic companies to remain an element of choice in their cultural markets." Canada also claims a special treatment for cultural products and services in trade fora in order to ensure respect for cultural concerns of equality of access, diversity of content, and the rights of the creator within the global information society. Other European governments are divided. Italy, Belgium, Greece as well as New Zealand and Australia tend to adhere to French positions, whilst some Nordic countries like Denmark are closer to non-protectionist approaches.

Whereas it is relatively easy to understand the market positioning arguments, i.e. to counter trade imbalances on audiovisual products between the US and Canada as well as the US and the EU, it is far more complex to establish the fault lines of the ideological debate. They do not necessarily correspond to traditional political divisions. For example, Spain's conservative government has been sympathetic to the French-Canadian position in the MAI; so has the right-wing French party *Front National* in calling for a crusade against globalization. Finally, Britain's Labour government has been much closer to the American position than to the French socialist one. In other words, the 'cultural exception' ideological debate is not politically bounded but rather is related to different ways of understanding property rights, the role of the state, and how citizens relate to their governments.

The view that globalization makes it harder for governments to govern has come to be widely accepted and is based on the idea that globalization expands the reach and power of the market. Governments, then, as well as firms and people, must comply with the rules of worldwide competition. With the liberalization of their economies in the 1980s, governments were left with more restricted margins for economic decision-making than they had expected. Front-edge technology adds to the sense of lack of control: they are unable to control the global communications system, which transcends physical and regulatory barriers. Things that governments could once forbid or restrict—foreign borrowing, imports of computer software, pornography, or political ideas—are now harder to control because modern communications have eroded the boundaries between nations.

When technology and liberalisation come together, governments can be taken by surprise. To a certain extent, this is what is happening with the issue of culture and trade in the sense that the new rules of the game are being written now. Governments interested in protecting their national and regional cultural industries and the intellectual property rights of their citizens enter in conflict with multinational companies that insist on the free circulation of cultural products. It is also a clash that goes beyond confrontation between countries or between governments and the private sector, to include global investors, artists, creators and the public.

This may explain why the internal controversy on the MAI, which could not be solved between negotiating delegations, was handed out in early1998 to the world's public opinion, which took it up with great interest. This interpretation is underscored by the public statement of WTO Director-General Renato Ruggerio in describing the MAI as the process of *"writing the constitution for a single global economy."*

It may also explain the decision of France to pull out of the negotiations, as was solemnly announced by Prime Minister Lionel Jospin, days before MAI talks were to resume on 20 October 1998. Canada's Minister of Culture, Sheila Copps, supported France's decision by saying, "It gives strength to the argument that there are some legitimate national concerns around cultural sovereignty. We have not pulled out of the negotiations as a country.... But we are solidly in favour of the position that we need a cultural exemption. The world is more than a market place."

d. What is next?

In the absence of the French delegation, MAI talks have had only an informal character. However, there are quite a number of new free trade agreements down the road. Some of them are taking place at a regional level, like APEC and the projected Free Trade Area of the Americas, but also in the EU, SELA, ALADI, and SICA. Such negotiations are consolidating economic blocs which are developing their own trade rules and redefining the 'geography' of economic competence and national culture in the groupings of countries and regions.

The kick-off meeting for the next round of multilateral negotiations is now set for 30 November to 3 December 1999. Seattle has been selected as the host city for the WTO Ministerial meeting, which will define the scope and objectives of what some call the "Millennium Round." Although the agenda and the trade disciplines to be negotiated are not yet clear, it seems that transparency will have to be a major feature of this round. As President Clinton said in his 1999 State of the Union Address, "We must insist that international trade organizations be more open to public scrutiny, instead of mysterious secret things subject to wild criticism."

Internal discussions about culture and free investment rules within OECD's closed rooms in the context of the Multilateral Agreement on Investments have had far less importance than the effects they have created and the process they have set in motion. In other words, the MAI negotiations have operated like a pent-up mechanism, releasing to the outside world what it could not resolve internally. Indeed there were many conflicting areas of which culture was just one, i.e. labour rights, national sovereignty, environment, etc. However, culture became the ultimate argument, the bottom line of the confrontation. And indeed, it was in the name of culture that France blocked the negotiations.

Unlike the aftermath of the GATT, a new dynamics around culture has unfolded from the MAI. What we are currently seeing is a repositioning of actors in the new scene. Different actors, from the private, public, and third sectors, as well as NGOs are repositioning themselves, building alliances, devising and applying new strategies. Treatment of culture in the upcoming round of multilateral negotiations on trade and investment will have decisive consequences on the economic hegemony of the markets and culture at the global level. To take the expression used by some leading world newspapers, we are in the threshold of a 'cultural war.' The MAI just set the stage. At stake is not only the huge economic potential of 'content' or 'cultural' industries, but also and not less important, the power to define and impose meanings about how we see the world and what really matters in life. In short, culture has become a 'War Room' and a site of contestation over the power to define both the contents and messages.

Table 1. Major exporters of cultural goods between 1980 and 1990. Percentages as of total countries available (values in $US millions)

Countries	Cultural Goods TOTAL Value	1980 %	Cultural Goods TOTAL Value	1985 %	Cultural Goods TOTAL Value	1990 %
Japan	12,417	31	20,235	42.7	23,405	22.3
USA	5,209	13	3,757	7.9	13,253	12.6
Germany	4,647	11.6	4,619	9.8	11,547	11
UK	2,964	7.4	3,289	6.9	9,996	9.5
Korea	1,075	2.7	2,045	4.3	6,084	5.8
France	2,108	5.3	1,815	3.8	5,484	5.2
Singapore	1,222	3.1	1,225	2.6	4,957	4.7
Netherlands	1,505	3.8	1,433	3	3,644	3.5
Benelux	1,940	4.8	1,574	3.3	3,533	3.4
China	not ranked		not ranked		2,721	2.6
Italy	1,333	3.3	1,045	2.2	2,449	2.3
Switzerland	683	1.7	682	1.4	2,361	2.2

Table 1 cont'd

Malaysia	not ranked		not ranked		2,307	2.2
Austria	760	1.9	703	1.5	2,306	2.2
Hong Kong	1,483	3.7	1,156	2.4	1,560	1.5

Source: *Study on International Flows of Cultural Goods for the 1980-91.* UNESCO, 1994

Countries ranked according to the percentages of their exports of cultural goods in relation to the total countries available for 1990. Exports are calculated according to the UNESCO framework of statistics: PRINTED MATTER AND LITERATURE (books, newspapers and periodicals, other printed matters), MUSIC (phonographic equipment, records and tapes, music instruments), VISUAL ARTS (paintings, drawings and pastels, engravings, prints and lithographs, sculpture and statutary) CINEMA AND PHOTOGRAPHY (photographic and cinematographic cameras and supplies), RADIO AND TELELVISION (television and radio receivers), GAMES AND SPORTING GOODS.

Table 2. Major importers of cultural goods between 1980 and 1990. Percentages as of total countries available (values in $US millions)

Countries	Cultural Goods TOTAL Value	1980 %	Cultural Goods TOTAL Value	1985 %	Cultural Goods TOTAL Value	1990 %
USA	7,447	190	17,413	336	25,102	211
Germany	4,500	115	4,007	77	11,816	99
UK	3,711	95	4,381	85	10,737	90
France	3,209	82	2,724	53	8,314	70
Japan	1,220	31	1,398	27	8,063	68
Hong Kong	923	2.4	1,562	30	5,800	49
Italy	1,787	4.6	1,685	33	5,157	43
Canada	1,934	49	2,765	53	4,902	41
Netherlands	2,012	5.1	1,681	32	4,801	40
Singapore	Not ranked		956	18	3,731	31
Switzerland	1,410	26	1,297	25	3,441	29

Table 2 cont'd

Spain	Not ranked		Not ranked		3,026	25
Benelux	1,316	34	1,029	20	2,998	25
Australia	1,017	26	1,323	26	2,085	18
Austria	813	21	Not ranked		2,027	17

Source: *Study on International Flows of Cultural Goods for the 1980-91*. UNESCO, 1994

Countries ranked according to the percentages of their imports of cultural goods in relation to the total countries available for 1990. Imports are calculated according to the UNESCO framework of statistics: PRINTED MATTER AND LITERATURE (books, newspapers and periodicals, other printed matters), MUSIC (phonographic equipment, records and tapes, music instruments), VISUAL ARTS (paintings, drawings and pastels, engravings, prints and lithographs, sculpture and statutary) CINEMA AND PHOTOGRAPHY (photographic and cinematographic cameras and supplies), RADIO AND TELELVISION (television and radio receivers), GAMES AND SPORTING GOODS.

One example of a cultural product in international trade: music

Phonographic records, films or printed music are tradeable goods but they are different from cars or carrots because they have a type of content which is not present in other kinds of commodities. On the one hand, they may represent an original creation of an author, i.e., books, which are thus subject to specific copyright—or 'copyleft', pertaining to the public domain, rights. On the other hand, they may represent a 'culture' in the sense that they convey, explicitly or implicitly a set of symbols, values or styles that identify the way of life of a group of people.

These 'content industries', as they are called to distinguish them from other industries, have rocketed in international trade.[29]

A major issue in the international debate on cultural products that will not be taken up here is copyright. The rapid expansion of world trade in the content industries has created the need for international standards dealing with services and intellectual property rights. Accordingly, international programs focusing on authors' rights and neighbouring rights such as UNESCO's program have gained considerable attention. A specific body, the WIPO, has been created to work closely with the WTO on these issues. A summary of such issues and programs can be reviewed in the chapter by Milagros Del Corral and Salah Abada in the *1998 World Culture Report*.

To illustrate the way in which globalization is restructuring international imports and exports of such products, we will look at the case of international trade in the music industry, as examined by David Throsby.[30] He begins by explaining that as happens with most cultural industries, the definition itself of the 'music industry' is difficult, since it deals with music reproduced and disseminated in different ways. These include recordings, live performances, broadcasts, rentals, transmissions via cable or satellite, and so on. Its primary participants are composers, songwriters and musical performers. They also include agents, managers, promoters, music publishers, record companies, copyright collecting societies and a variety of other service providers such as studio owners as well as users of music and individual consumers.

According to a survey of the US National Music Publishers' Association, total reported music revenues in 58 major world markets was $5.8 billion in 1994. This revenue was shared primarily by the US, which took 21% of total music revenues; Japan, 16%; Germany, 15%; France, 11% and the UK, 9%.[31]

Data from the International Federation of Phonographic Industry indicates that the global value of reported retail sales in 1996 was almost $40 billion. However, more than 80% of the world market is controlled by the so-called "Big Six" transnational corporations: Sony (Japan), Polygram (Netherlands), Warner (United States), BMG (Germany), Thorn-EMI (UK) and MCA (Japan). The dominance of Europe, Japan and the United States in the world market of music is readily apparent.[32]

Interestingly, data shows a shift in the demand of music in different continents, with relatively slower growth in the traditional markets of the US and Western Europe, and more rapid growth rates in Eastern Europe, Latin America, Asia, Africa and the Middle East.[33] Analysis of per capita demand for music in different countries indicates that it is consumer incomes that principally determine the amounts spent on music recordings, as shown by a simple demand equation estimated for data from 35 countries in 1994.[34]

How has globalization shifted the structure of the world music industry?

Throsby explains that "...the expansion of music markets in developing countries themselves has primarily arisen from a growing consumption of European and American music in those countries; that is, the main flow in international trade in music has been from the developed to the developing world, not the other way around". He cites Negus in stating: "The dominance of world markets by Anglo-American music and artists is reinforced by the way in which the American and British sales charts decisively influence the local policies of record companies and the decisions of radio programmers throughout the world..."[35]

In spite of this trend, the category known as "World Music" has emerged over the last decade as a small segment of the world market, representing a range of specific musical genres or styles originating in various parts of the world. The list includes such music as salsa from Cuba and Puerto Rico, zouk from the French Antilles, rembetika from Greece, rai from Algeria, qawwali from Pakistan and India and many more.[36]

In some such cases, as Martin Roberts explains in describing the expansion of Indonesian gamelan music on the world market, "...what is striking here is how...global capitalism and its associated culture industries depend on the construction of a cultural otherness that can be presented as the 'authentic' instance of a culture to consumers...(Yet) if gamelan music does exist in this traditional form, it also exists, as noted above, in increasingly modernized, hybridized and global forms. It is this global hybridized dimension of gamelan music that is ignored (perhaps even denied) by World Music through its exclusive focus on gamelan in its traditional, local forms—all the more ironic, given that the emergence of World Music itself is symptomatic of this process of globalization."[37]

Finally, globalization has encouraged piracy, a major concern of producer countries, as non-legitimate pirate sales have amounted to over $2.1 billion worldwide. It is estimated that a 10% increase in a country's level of piracy reduces the value of legitimate sales per head by about 1.2%, other things being equal.[38]

Culture and telecommunications

The expansion of telecommunications worldwide and the circulation of films and audiovisuals are bringing about basic shifts in communication but also in intercultural knowledge, perceptions of the world and cognitive outlooks. The number of televisions per thousand people in the world almost doubled from 126 in 1980 to 204 in 1995. Significantly, there has been a higher annual rate of change for the developing world —from 26 in 1980 to 115 in 1995—while the developed world had corresponding figures of 424 to 527.[39] Economic growth contributed in the case of East Asia and South Central Asia to annual rates of change for televisions per 1,000 people of 21.9% and 24.4%, the highest in developing regions. In Arab States it was only 7.0%, lower than that for Africa, which had a 12.5% annual rate of change.[40] In the latter region, some countries had an extremely high annual rate of change in televisions during this same period. In Senegal, for example, it jumped 201.1%; in Mozambique 126.9%; in Ghana, 125.8%. In Asia the highest annual rate of change was 145.2% in China, followed by 135% in Sri Lanka and 61.5% in Thailand.[41]

As already mentioned, most films and audiovisuals in the international market originate in the US or Europe. Data are insufficient to aggregate by regions but the trends may be discerned for specific countries. For example, Chile, Malaysia, Belgium, Canada and Peru imported 98% or more of total distribution of films during the period 1990-93; Egypt, which has a big cinema industry of its own, Italy, and Russia import around 70%. The world average for imported films is 79%.[42]

The US film industry dominates the world market. In some developing countries, however, a domestic film industry continues to enjoy a large share of the home market, as in India, which produced 840 films while importing only 140 during this same period.[43]

The new planetary reach of telecommunications through fiber-optics, satellites, parabolic antennas and now the integration of informatics and telephony systems carry these images to the ends of the world. Not only do these images have greater planetary reach every day, but the time people spend watching them is also increasing. In the US, on average, people spend seven hours daily watching television. This almost matches the time they spend at work, an average of eight hours for most people. Moreover, images have a way of occupying mental space and becoming cultural referents that make them even more pervasive. Thus, Latin American television soap operas are watched in India, for example, while designs from Australian beer bottles find new meaning as images on Melanesian war shields.

Is this globalization of images through television and films positive or negative for development? Hundreds of studies could be quoted arguing for or against, with no conclusive results. The following study, in our view, summarizes some of the primary cultural effects brought by television to rural villages around the world.

Philip Carl Salzman calls television an "electronic Trojan horse." He analyzed the cultural impact of television though ethnographic examples in Italy, Egypt, and Sudan, as well as his own fieldwork data from Sardinia. He describes the following major effects from the introduction of television:

- elites are bypassed in the flow of information;
- consumption is adopted as an appropriate orientation;
- urban, metropolitan and cosmopolitan models are legitimated for living and working;
- establishment scientific and state ideologies are authoritatively advocated; and
- certain languages, dialects, concepts and terms become privileged.

Salzman concludes that "television radically if selectively expands the terms of reference from which local viewers may choose, and the vividness of its offerings stimulates the creative reconstruction of societies and selves." [44]

Culture and the Internet: interactivity

It is interesting to contrast the above effects of television with those now being discussed for the Internet. Based on discussions of projects on culture in the new media at UNESCO and our own observations, the Internet will accentuate two of the effects mentioned above. First, certain languages, dialects, concepts and terms will not only become privileged, but a basic cyberlanguage which creates specific cultural cognitive structures is at present being put into place. This is the reason why linguistic and cultural pluralism in telecommunications, films and the Internet is the concern most strongly advocated by many governments in international debates.

As mentioned in previous pages, the problem of content has been expressed in its simplest terms as "the invasion of American culture."[45] One American response to this already mentioned were the series of articles entitled "The World Welcomes America's Cultural Invasion" in the 26-27 October *Washington Post Service*. As a broader issue in international fora, it is taken up as a question of linguistic and cultural pluralism. In the Plan of Action of the Stockholm Intergovernmental Conference on Cultural Policies for Development, advocating such pluralism is one of the priorities in relation to information technologies.[46]

Secondly, in comparison to television, the Internet does seem to intensify the bypassing of elites, whether political or religious, as recent attempts at controlling its use has shown in Iran, Singapore and other countries where previous authoritative state and scientific ideologies are being undermined. In a 26 October 1998 article in the *International Herald Tribune*, the Chinese head of the Shanghai Police Department's Computer Security Supervision office, Mr. Qing Guang, is quoted as saying: "No one is allowed to release harmful information on the Internet.... You cannot send out harmful information which attacks our nation's territorial integrity, attacks our nation's independence or attacks our socialist system."

In contrast, orientations towards consumption and towards urban, metropolitan and cosmopolitan models are not as strongly imposed by the Internet as by television and films because of the key element in the latter, namely, the seemingly unending possibility of choice. Already, choice has expanded through television and cable companies which offer 500 channels, 'dial-a-movie', video-by-demand and other such new services. But this is being dwarfed by the permanent accretion of Internet sites offering just about everything the human imagination can come up with – and some things, which it would have been better to leave inside it. This choice, if anything, will continue to expand as the world telephony system and technological convergence make it even easier to place this creative diversity online.

Cyberculture, however, must be examined in the wider framework of the multimedia and hypermedia revolution, which gives prolongation to the new communication technologies through off-line products—CD-ROMs and DVD-ROMs.[47] As Isabelle Vinson notes, the 'edutainment industry' opens unprecedented opportunities to develop 'rings of knowledge' as a new means of sharing knowledge for the preservation and enhancement of cultural diversity in the information society.[48]The problem, in Philippe Queau's view, is "one of knowing how the new culture can contribute to the creation of a new global forum for public, democratic debate on new ethical values—or 'Infoethics.'[49]

The major upheaval introduced by the Internet is well summarized by Arturo Escobar in his report on the meeting on Women and Cyberculture at the 1997 Society for International Development Conference: "What shifted was the way to think about the agency of women in ways that go well beyond the slogan of participation of an earlier period. To use a metaphor of communications, the development age could be likened to the era of television, that is, passive consumers and a 'programme' designed by experts. The new technologies, by contrast, demand interactivity, communication of many different types and in many different directions. People interact from their own positions, culturally and socially defined. In this way interactivity and positionality define another form of relating which helps people develop a consistent picture of the world in a more autonomous fashion. *Can it be said that interactivity and cultural positionality exemplify the new way of being, doing and knowing in times of globalization?*" [50]

Globalization and international standards for culture: the case of the World Heritage List

Negotiations between national governments to set up international standards and agreements in the context of globalization, which are now at centre stage in economic affairs, have in fact been preceded by important initiatives already taken by UNESCO in the field of culture since the 1950s. The best known international convention that created the World Heritage List is worth reviewing here because it is ratified by the highest number of countries in UNESCO and it has the highest consensus on international standards.

The Convention Concerning the Protection of the World Cultural and Natural Heritage developed out of the success of the 1959 UNESCO campaign to save the Philae and Abu Simbel temples, jewels of ancient Egyptian civilization, from flooding by the Aswan High Dam. After a White House Conference in 1965 which called for a "World Heritage Trust" and the proposal by the Stockholm Conference on Human Environment for the conservation of nature, the Convention was adopted at the General Conference of UNESCO in 1972. The aim of the convention is to ensure national and international cooperation to safeguard "the masterpieces of human creative genius."

It seems highly significant that at a time when globalization is having the ambiguous effect of pushing people to realign themselves with local cultural identities, the one value on which everyone seems to agree is that these human-made masterpieces must be saved.

Why is there such consensus on this value? On one of my trips as Assistant Director General for Culture at UNESCO [Lourdes Arizpe], I was given many indications why such heritage is valued. Once, in Manila, the point was explicitly made as I was taken around on a visit to the local Baroque Churches on the World Heritage List. The guide had been beaming with pride, all throughout the visit, about the artwork. At one point I asked him "If you are so proud of this, why do you need the UNESCO plaque for it, then?" And he answered: "Ah, Madam, because then we will know it is not only our pride, but that of all of humanity and that makes us even more proud." What has been created, then, is a metonymy, that is, an implicit assessment matrix providing a hidden sense that makes recognition on the List all the more significant in global terms.

While the main purpose driving the World Heritage Program is to urgently save or protect such heritage, it is significant that given that the World Heritage List is negotiated between national governments, it inevitably has been taken to imply an assessment of cultural achievement in nation-states or regions. As a consequence, questions emerged as to the number of sites on the List by country and by region. In response to this and other concerns, a group of experts in 1994 was commissioned to report on the representativity of the World Heritage List. They concluded that there was an overrepresentation of European heritage; of historic cities and religious buildings, especially Christian; of 'elite' architecture, in contrast to more 'popular' architecture; and of historic sites in comparison to prehistoric and twentieth century sites.

Already, one can see a background metonymy emerging, on the basis of which new criteria have been negotiated. For example, a broader notion of 'authenticity' was proposed by Japan, which now allows for the inclusion of cultural heritage buildings which follow ancient designs yet have been constantly rebuilt in recent centuries. The inclusion of Brasilia as a world heritage site opened up the possibility for developing countries to include present-day future-heritage achievements. Many other sharp edges related to the issues mentioned by the group of experts are at present being worked on to find solutions. For example, a new category of site, that of 'cultural landscape' was created, and non-physical heritage is receiving greater attention.[51] This is a positive development in that the cultural criteria behind the selection can be given a richer texture by adding those criteria of other cultures that will make the List more truly representative in cultural and historical terms.

For the purposes of this essay, however, we would like to emphasize that the value of the World Heritage List in relation to globalization lies obviously on the actual progress made in preserving cultural and natural heritage but also in the international standard-setting it has achieved. Even if slow, progress has been impressive in creating *global* standards to describe and examine cultural heritage and in setting up mechanisms for cooperation at the national and international level for its safeguarding.

Given the increased interest in international conventions related to cultural heritage and goods, international cultural standards will certainly constitute some of the main axes on which globality will continue to be built.

Policy Implications

The policy implications related to culture and globalization must apply at both national and international levels since the phenomena they influence are interrelated in such a way that shifts at one level will have immediate repercussions at other levels.

The following policy implications may be proposed, in schematic form:

1. While advocating cultural pluralism in all fields of cultural activities and cultural content, it is not enough only to insist on diversity. More cultural diversity does not ensure more development. In fact, the recognition of greater cultural diversity may lead to problems of governance as it questions political and social hierarchies, economic privileges and property rights. This will be positive only if democratic institutions and practices make it possible to accommodate such questions while continuing to develop the economy. If democracy is not present, they may also create conflicts that erode a group or a country's ability to cope with the new pressures from liberalization and globalization.

2. In relation to the concerns over the global reach of American and European cultural products, a balance must be found between protection of national artists and producers during a certain period to develop the know-how, organisation and connections necessary to profit from world market opportunities, while allowing quality assessments which are increasingly referents of international standards. Truly creative artists and groups interested in developing traditional cultural activities or products must be strongly supported by cultural policies of the State together with self-financing, cooperative or voluntary schemes and funding from foundations and private enterprises. This means encouraging creators and performers wanting to produce new cultural content goods that will appeal to new publics in their own country and "world" music,

painting and other art markets. This seems to be in the long run a more effective policy to counter "cultural invasion" from the outside than policies of cultural protectionism.

3. Where formal or informal mechanisms are in place which discriminate against cultural producers and artists from cultural minorities or developing countries—or in some cases, industrialized countries—by skewing international and national markets, they must be opposed. This applies especially to the circulation and distribution of cultural goods, as was seen in the case study on music in international trade. Policies of governments in this respect must be accompanied by advocacy from cultural producers and artists associations, particularly when mechanisms of exclusion are informal rather than formal.

4. Policies must now give full attention to the development of linguistic and cultural pluralism in relation to the new technologies: Internet, CD-ROMs and DVDs. Initiatives by local artists, especially women artists, must be supported financially, and assistance must be given to provide them with openings both to national and international markets. Only by providing appropriate conditions for cultural creation nationally will governments be able to prevent the brain drain of creative people, which ends up reinforcing the dominance of American and European cultural goods in the world market.

5. Policies for international development must continue to emphasize international standards for the whole range of cultural activities, from the safeguarding of cultural heritage to cultural tourism. Illegal trafficking of art objects, piracy and art theft must be strongly combatted. Those countries that have not ratified international conventions in the field of culture must be convinced to do so.

6. Cultural diversity may be positively correlated to expanding exports of cultural products in the international market, when it strengthens a cultural group or country's comparative advantages. Therefore, policies should promote cultural industries, art and performance, and crafts that provide original designs and culturally diverse content for cultural goods.

7. Culture must be recognized as a domain with special connotations in discussions and analyses of economic globalization, global governance and sustainability. The absence of this recognition has meant that governments have neglected the standardization and collection of data on culture. Without adequate data, indicators on culture and development cannot be created and analysis of the interaction of culture and globalization, for example, cannot be based on reliable quantitative data. Research must be strengthened, both in developing new conceptual analysis, as well as in establishing methodologies to categorize and aggregate cultural data.

Finally, it is important to end by saying that culture has now been firmly inserted in the international agenda on globalization. John Naisbit had defined "the global paradox" in which "the larger system (is) in service to the smallest player," that is, the individual consumer.[52] Yet we have found, in this brief review of the issues on culture and globalization, that one of the most interesting phenomena today are signs that individual consumers do not want to be adrift in a sea of several million people glued to the television or wired to the Internet. As noted above, self-organizing trends are evident in every cultural sphere, from world music" to cyberculture, in which individuals are reaching out to some kind of community, either ethnic or national, or gender, or by thematic interests, or hobbies. So it could be said that the smallest players are busy building or adhering to intermediate structures that replace those that globalization itself has undermined by giving them access, seemingly, to the whole world. Men and women seek in these new intermediate structures, rekindled ethnic ties, historical allegiances or virtual communities, a sense of place, of purpose and of companionship. This, in our view, is the real "global paradox"—the fact that the boundlessness of global horizons created by the new telecommunications and audiovisual technologies are fostering new boundings by individual consumers wanting new forms of communities. The term I have been using in other places to describe such self-organizing trends is that of 'conviviability'[53] in the sense of the building of new social structures that allow people to live together and cooperate in response to the new challenges of globality and sustainability. And culture seems to be the best stuff, malleable and heart-felt, to build these new ways to live together.■

Notes

[1] The U.N. World Commission on Culture and Development was created at UNESCO in 1993 and presented its report, Our Creative Diversity in 1995. Headed by Mr. Javier Perez de Cuellar, it included 19 social scientists, artists, and practitioners in all fields of culture.

[2] Garcia Canclini, N. "Cultural Policy Options in the context of Globalization" in World Culture Report, no. 1, June 1998:159. See also Appadurai, A. 1990. "Disjuncture and Difference in the Global Cultural Economy" In: Featherstone (ed) Global culture, Nationalism, Globalization and Modernity. London: Sage Publications; and Arizpe, L. (Ed.). 1996. The Cultural Dimensions of Global Change: and Anthropological Approach. Paris: UNESCO.

[3] Hannerz, Ulf. 1991: 107.

[4] For an excellent overview of social movements related to this issue, see Castels, Manuel. 1997. *The Power of Identity*. (Volume II of The Information Age: Economy, Society and Culture) Blackwell: London.

[5] Castels, Manuel. 1997:11.

[6] Cited in Manuel Castels, op.cit.:...

[7] Giddens, Anthony. Conference at the Culture Sector of UNESCO, May 12, 1998.

[8] Sahlins, 1985; Featherstone, 1990; Miller 1995; Barber and Waterman 1995.

[9] Appadurai 1990, 1991; Hannerz 1992.

[10] Jamieson, M. "Values and Globalization". Paper written for the World Commission on Culture and Development. 1996.

[11] For a world-historical account of this process, see Wolf (1982).

[12] Hannerz, Ulf. 1992.

[13] Ashford, Barrie. 1995. The Global System: economics, politics and culture. Cambridge: Polity Press:157.

[14] World Culture Report, UNESCO 1998:432.

[15].International Herald Tribune, " The World Welcomes America's Cultural Invasion", October 26, 1998, cover page.

[16] Statistics Canada.1997. Canada's Culture, Heritage and Identity: A Statistical Perspective. Ministry of Industry: Canada.

[17] European Audiovisual Observatory, Statistical Yearbook 1995.

[18] World Culture Report, UNESCO 1998:168.

[19] These figures are even more striking compared to those of 1992, when the European Union of the twelve had an audiovisual trade deficit with the US of 860 million US$ in cinema 1,716 million US$ in television programmes and 1,153 million $US in video films. (In from the Margins, 1997:328). European broadcasters have become huge markets for imported television programmes. Some European governments therefore advocate quotas on the proportion of foreign programming that national channels can show. After a long debate, the European Union agreed in 1997 to a "Television without Frontiers: directive, aimed at setting quotas for domestic television programmes. However, intense opposition, led by Britain, added to the directive "where practicable," rendering the provision ineffectual.

[20] i.e. Bringing their laws on copyright, patents, trademarks and other areas of intellectual property into line with the agreement, and providing for effective enforcement of these laws in order to deal with piracy, and other forms of intellectual property infringements.

[21] "La machine infernales a destructurer le monde avance inexorablemente dans les coulisses des organisations internationales...L'AMI c'est l'ennemi de la diversity, l'ennemi de la creation, l'ennemi de la justice sociale", Jack Lang, Le Monde, 20 February 1998.

[22] Worldwide, foreign direct investment has been growing three times as fast as total investment. At the end of 1996, the total stock of foreign direct investment owned by companies outside their home countries were over US$3 trillion and OECD members are the source of 85% of all foreign direct investment, UN 1997 World Investment Report.

[23] In the original mandate, this free-standing international treaty would be open to al OECD Members and the European Communities, and to accession by non-OECD Member countries, which will be consulted as the negotiations progress.

[24] The position of the nationalist group Council of Canadians reflects well this concern: "Our government must acknowledge that the current model for trade and investment negotiations is wrong. We need a new approach -one that doesn't allow the power of citizens and their governments to be bartered away".

[25] Which reads as follows: "Nothing in this agreement shall be construed to prevent any Contracting Party to take any measure to regulate investment of foreign companies and the conditions of activity of these companies, in the framework of policies designed to preserve and promote cultural and linguistic diversity". Other countries have joined this approach: New Zealand has apparently advanced a proposal for a general exception of government procurement from the MAI's coverage. The European Union wants some of its investment-promotion agencies to be able to discriminate against foreigners and the US think their Federal States should continue to be able to limit foreigners purchases of farm land, etc.

[26] "Un livre n'es pas, pour l'auteur, une marchandise, un objet de commerce; c'est un usage de ses forces qui'il peut conceder a d'autres, mail qu'il ne peut jamais aliener".

[27] Debate on "L'exception generale pour la culture, l'audiovisuel et l'exclusion de la propriete litterarire artistique dans les accord AMI: une question de survie". Organized by the Societe des auteurs et compositeurs dramatiques (SACD).

[28] "...le veritable enjeu pour la France est de conserver la civilisation europeene dont notre culture est une composante", Guy Sorman, in "La Gauche nous enferme dans une logique de ligne Maginot", Figaro Magazine, September 1998.

[29] Corral, Milagros del, and Salah Abada. "Cultural and economic development through copyright in the information society" in World Culture Report, no. 1, June, 1998, 210-221:219.

[30] Cf. Throsby, David. "The Role of Music in International Trade and Economic Development" in World Culture Report, no. 1, June 1998: 193-203.

[31] Throsby, op.cit.:195.

[32] Op.cit.:196.

[33] Throsby, op.cit.:198.

[34] Op.cit.:199.

[35].Cited in Throsby, 1998:203.

[36].Broughton S. et al (eds.) 1994. World Music. The Rough Guide. London: the Rough Guides Ltd., cited in Throsby, 1998.

[37] Roberts, Martin. 1998. "World Music: the Relocation of Music" in World Culture Report, no. 1, June, 1998:205.

[38] Op.cit.:208.

[39] Table 13: Cultural Trends: Radio and Television in World Culture Report, op.cit.:420.

[40] Ibid.

[41] Ibid.

[42] World Culture Report, op.cit.:168.

[43] World Culture Report, op.cit.:168.

[44] Salzman, Philip. 1996. "The Electronic Trojan Horse:television in the globalization of paramodern cultures" in The Cultural Dimensions of Global Change, Arizpe, L. ed. Paris:Unesco:197-216.

[45] Cf. Barber, Benjamin. 1995. Jihad vs. McWorld. New York. Ballantine Books; Featherstone, Mike. 1990. Global Culture. London: Sage Publications.

[46] UNESCO.1998. Plan of Action of the Stockholm Intergovernmental Conference on Cultural Policies for Development. Paris: Unesco.

[47] Vinson, I. "Heritage and Cyberculture" in World Culture Report, op.cit.239.

[48] Vinson, op.cit.:247.

[49] Queau, P. "Cyberculture and Infoethics" in World Culture Report, op.cit.:244.

[50] Escobar, Arturo. "The Laughter of Culture" in Development, 40, no.4,Dec.1997, 21-24:24.

[51] Cf. Levi-Strauss, Laurent. "Conceptual issues on World Cultural Heritage". Working Paper, 1998.

[52] Naisbit, John. 1995. The Global Paradox. New York: Avon Books: 356.

[53] Arizpe, Lourdes. "Convivencia: the goal of conviviability" in World Culture Report, no. 1, June 1998:71.

Care and the Global Economy

*Nancy Folbre**

Once upon a time, the goddesses (the specifically feminine goddesses, you understand, not your ordinary gods) decided to sponsor a competition, a kind of Olympics, among the nations of the world. They agreed to award a wonderful prize—of health and prosperity for all—to the nation that could collectively run the greatest distance in a set period of time. This was not an ordinary race, in which the distance was determined, and the winner was the runner who took the shortest time, but rather a contest to see which society, acting as a team, could maximize the average number of miles run per person.

Each nation that decided to compete had a giant scoreboard placed in the sky to keep count. But the goddesses did not tell them how long the time period of the race would be—part of the game was that they had to guess. When the starting gun went off, one nation assumed that the race would not last long. They urged all their citizens to start running as quickly as possible. It was every person for themselves. Very soon, of course, the young children and the elderly were left behind, but none of the fast runners bothered to help them out, because it would have slowed them down.

At first, those who were out in front were exhilarated by their success. But as the race continued, some of them became tired, or hurt, and fell by the wayside. No one stopped to help them. And still the race continued. Gradually all the runners grew exhausted or sick, and there was no one to replace them. It became clear that this nation would not, after all, win the race.

Everyone's attention turned to a second nation, which adopted a slightly different strategy. They sent all their young men, the fastest runners, out ahead to compete, but required all the women to come along behind, carrying all the children, the sick, and the elderly, and caring for all the runners who needed help. They explained to the women that this was a natural and efficient arrangement from which everyone would benefit. They provided great incentives for the men to run fast, and gave them authority and power over the women.

At first this seemed to work. But then the women found out that they could run just as fast as the men, if they were not burdened with extra responsibilities. And they began to argue that the work they were doing—of caring for the runners—was just as important as the running itself, and deserved equal reward. The men, whose brains were perhaps impaired by years of mindless running, found this claim ridiculous and refused to make any changes. As a result, the nation began to argue and to fight and to waste a great deal of energy on bargaining and negotiation, which slowed its progress. Gradually, it became clear that this nation, too, was losing the race.

So attention turned to a third nation, which had started out moving quite slowly, but like the tortoise in competition with the hare, made steady and persistent progress. In this nation, everyone was required both to run and to take care of those who could not run. Both men and women were given incentives to compete, to run as fast as possible, but the rules required them all to carry a share of the weight of care. Running with this load, both men and women became strong as well as fast.

Having agreed to rules that rewarded both kinds of contribution to the collective effort, they left people free to choose their own speed, to find a balance between individual effort and collective

*This paper draws heavily from my joint work with Thomas Weisskopf and Paula England.

responsibility. This freedom and equality contributed to their solidarity. Of course they won the race. What did you expect? It was a race that goddesses, not gods, designed.

Perhaps you think this is a utopian fairy tale. And perhaps the ending is a bit too happy. But I want to remind you that the global economic system tells us that we are all in a race. It tells us all to hurry up. It tells us all to worry about our speed, but it does not tell us how long the race will last or what the best long-term strategy is. Nor does it tell us how victory will be defined. If we are going to compete, let it be in a game of our own choosing. This is, in a nutshell, the challenge of the new global order: how to define a world economy that preserves the advantages of market competition, but establishes strict limits and rules that prevent competition from taking a destructive form.

Criticisms of unlimited competition and unrestrained free markets as the primary means of creating a global economy have come from many directions. This paper emphasizes the contributions that feminist theory makes to this larger critique. It focuses on the economic importance of what some have called "the costs of social reproduction" and what I call the "caring labor" of providing for dependents—children, the sick, the elderly, and (let us not forget!) all the rest of us, exhausted from the daily demands of work in a competitive market place. I will argue that care is not only crucial to the development of human capabilities, but is itself a human capability. Furthermore, care can and should be conceptualized in economic terms as an indispensable public good that cannot be adequately supplied through competitive markets.

An economic analysis of care offers some important insights into the possible impacts of globalization for three reasons. First, the quantitative expansion of market participation, reflected in the ongoing reallocation of labor time from production for direct family use to production for exchange, has implications for the ways in which caring services are provided. Material needs once provided almost exclusively by family labor are now being purchased from the market or provided by the state. Second, increases in the scope and speed of transactions have implications for the qualitative nature of markets, which are becoming increasingly "disembedded" and disconnected from local communities. As market relationships become more impersonal, reliance on families as a source of emotional support tends to increase even as they are becoming less economically and demographically stable. Finally, and perhaps most important, the expansion of markets may reduce the supply of caring labor—both because it undermines traditional forms of patriarchal control over women (a good effect, from women's point of view!), and because markets tend to penalize altruism and care (a bad effect, from everyone's point of view!). Both individuals and institutions are tempted to free ride on the caring labor that women, in particular, provide. Whether women will continue to provide such labor without fair remuneration is another matter.

The first section of this paper provides a basic definition of care and explains its economic importance. The second section explores the interface between care and the concept of human capabilities, arguing that more attention needs to be devoted to ways in which capabilities are gendered and rewarded. The third section explains why caring capabilities are public goods undervalued by the market. The final section examines political responses to concerns about the effects of globalization on care and outlines some implications for policy.

Defining care

The family is the locale of transactions in which identity dominates; however, identity is also important in much of what we consider the "market," and, in fact, recent developments in economics can be interpreted as a departure from impersonal economics.

—Yoram Ben-Porath, "The F-Connection: Families, Friends, and Firms and the Organization of Exchange"

Care is a word that is used quite promiscuously in the feminist literature. Its meaning is often mediated by prepositions. To care *for* someone is different than to care *about*; "to care" is distinct from "take care" which in turn means less, somehow, than to "take care of." The *American Heritage Dictionary* (1992) gives two rather negative definitions of the noun care: "1. A burdened state of mind, as that arising from heavy responsibilities; worry. 2. Mental suffering; grief. As a verb, its first two meanings are positive: 1. To be concerned or interested. 2. To provide needed assistance or watchful supervision." The lesson may be that to be concerned or interested is to assume a burden.

But these meanings don't seem quite right. Feminist thinkers have begun to use the word care in a more specific way, to describe something more than a feeling—a responsibility. Care is not necessarily linked to trust (you can care for someone without trusting them at all). But it often involves trust. Emily Abel and Margaret Nelson (1990, 4) write that "caregiving is an activity encompassing both instrumental tasks and affective relations. Despite the classic Parsonian distinction between these two modes of behavior, caregivers are expected to provide love as well as labor, 'caring for,' while 'caring about' ". Similarly, Sara Ruddick (1983) defines "maternal thinking" as a "unity of reflection, judgement, and emotion."

It is useful to make a distinction between "care services," a type of work, and "caring motives," which are intrinsic to the worker. Care services are services that involve personal contact between provider and recipient. In activities such as teaching, nursing, and counseling, personal identity is important. The service provider generally learns the first name of the service recipient or client. However, the service provider does not necessarily have an emotional or social connection to the client and may work simply to be paid or to avoid being punished.

Many, though certainly not all, care services are motivated by motives more complex than pecuniary or instrumental concerns. They involve a sense of connection with the care recipient that may be based on affection, altruism, or social norms of obligation and respect. In this case, the delivery of the service includes an extra component, a sense of "being cared for" that may augment and enhance the delivery of the service itself. This extra component is often present even in wage employment. Individuals often choose caring jobs because they are a means of expressing caring motives, as well as earning a living. Even if they were not initially motivated by care, workers often come to acquire affection and/or a sense of responsibility for those they care for.

In the past I have simply termed this subset of care services infused with caring motives "caring labor" (Folbre 1995; Folbre and Weisskopf 1998; England and Folbre 1998). The disadvantage of this term is that it fails to immediately convey the distinctive quality intended. Perhaps a better term is the colloquial "tender loving care," or "tender labor of care," which we can abbreviate as TLC. This nomenclature is not terribly important, because the larger issue at stake is the quality of care services, and how these may be affected by different types of motivation and remuneration. What is important is the fact that the boundaries of care services and TLC cannot be mapped directly on to the boundaries of the market and the home. When I refer to care services, I am not referring not only to family labor, but to all services, paid and unpaid, that entail a personal relationship.

The intellectual traditions of European-American social science have traditionally romanticized family and community, contrasting them with the impersonal, self-interested world of the market. This romanticization has often come at women's expense. A key element of the emerging feminist reinterpretation of modernization is an emphasis on the weakening of forms of patriarchal control over women, with complex and contradictory consequences (Folbre 1994a). Therefore, it is especially important to emphasize here that not all family labor is TLC. Some is provided as a result of coercion, or in direct response to the possibility of pecuniary reward or punishment. Furthermore, many care services provided for pay are TLC. At issue here are the conditions that promote TLC both inside and outside the family.

A. Care is not just a preference

> *Unpaid domestic labor is not carried out entirely for love, disregarding the economic costs and benefits; but neither is it simply another economic activity. The process of the reproduction and maintenance of human resources is different from any other kind of production because human*

resources are treated as having an intrinsic value, not merely an instrumental value.
—Diane Elson, Male Bias in the Development Process

The Norwegian word for care is "omsorg." Originally, it designated the feeling of care, but was consciously appropriated by Kari Waerness (1987) to describe a type of work: caring for other people who can't take care of themselves: children, the sick, the needy elderly. There are advantages to this narrow definition. It emphasizes the necessity of care and calls attention to circumstances in which it is clear that care is not an exchange: it is being given to the recipient (even if paid for by a third party). But the image is incomplete, even misleading. It implies that dependency is merely a phase of the life cycle or the result of some malfunction. It implies that adults should not be dependent. Why not? Even the healthiest and happiest of adults require a certain amount of care. Their need for it may ebb and flow, but sometimes it comes in tidal waves. As the biologist Franz de Waal explains: Absorption of parental care into adult human relationships is evident from the widespread use of infantile names (such as "baby") for mates and lovers...The continuum of nurturance, attachment, and succorance may not be entirely understood; still, it is hard to argue with its existence. (de Waal 1996, 43)

Groups often refer to their members as symbolic kin. Feminists often appeal to a larger concept of "sisterhood." Trade union members, like fraternities and sororities, often refer to each other as "brothers and sisters." Patriots vow to love their mother country, and so on. Most adults need to be cared for in the emotional sense, even if not in the economic sense of relying on another to take responsibility for them.

Social connections have a positive impact on human life expectancy that is at least as significant as the negative effects of cigarette smoking, hypertension, and lack of physical exercise (Sapolsky 1998, 143). Married adults, in general, enjoy much better health than those who are single. Furthermore, a large amount of evidence suggests that economic inequality, which is associated with more social conflict, creates psychosocial stresses that lower overall levels of health (Wilkinson 1996).

Much of the literature on care (including my own previous work) treats the words "altruism," "care," and "nurturance" synonymously (England and Folbre 1997; Folbre 1995; Folbre and Weisskopf 1998; England 1992). However there are important distinctions among them. Altruism is a word commonly used in the literature of economics, game theory, and sociobiology. Economists generally interpret altruism as a feeling or a preference; it represents a parameter in a utility function. This interpretation implies that intrinsic rewards are always forthcoming. In the circular reasoning of utility maximization, no one would perform a selfless act unless they got a selfish pleasure from it.

"Care" and "nurturance" are more likely to be described as forms of obligation or reciprocity. Feminist economist Julie Nelson (1998) gives a compelling example. When a mother gets up for the fifth time in the middle of the night to soothe her crying child, it is not necessarily because she gets pleasure from doing so. In fact, she may feel quite cranky. Regardless of her feelings, however, she accepts a social obligation to care for her child, even at some cost to her own health or happiness. Commitment to care for others, including family members, may be partly God-given or genetically inscribed. But it is also socially constructed—which is exactly why it is fragile. Rather than accepting the traditional emphasis on either love or reciprocity, I will argue for a definition of care that includes elements of both.

B. Care Requires Reciprocity

A broad feminist literature criticizes the traditional dichotomies of Western thought, which often entail an elevation of the masculine as "rational" over the feminine as "emotional" (Nelson 1996). Reflecting this dichotomy, economists tend to pay more attention to informal exchanges that can be described in cognitive terms than to emotions of love and affection.[1] For instance, the growing literature on social capital tends to emphasize trust and reciprocity, rather than love and affection (Putnam 1995; Putnam et. al. 1993; Fukuyama 1995; World Bank 1997). Perhaps as counterbalance, the feminist literature on care tends to emphasize its emotional dimensions. But the dichotomy between reason and emotion, between reciprocity and altruism is simplistic, obscuring a complex continuum in between both extremes.

Traditional sociobiologists argue that altruism takes one of two extreme forms—either it is "hard-core altruism" that is unaffected by rewards and punishments, or it is "soft-core altruism," a form of reciprocity that is actually selfish (Wilson 1978, 155). This distinction is often mapped onto the difference between "kin-based altruism" and "reciprocal altruism" (Hamilton 1963; see also discussion in Sober and Wilson 1998). Kin-based altruism is generally described as a robust instinct, with obvious evolutionary advantages: if altruism is limited to those individuals who share substantial genetic material with the altruist, then self-sacrifice may actually increase the representation of one's own genes. Early studies of the social insects emphasized the fact that their cooperation was strongly related to their genetic relatedness.

Reciprocal altruism, on the other hand, is pictured as contingent and vulnerable. If an altruistic allocation is always reciprocated, it does not reduce the resources of the altruistic in the long run, but rather serves as a kind of insurance. Thus, reciprocal altruists, as cooperators, might be able to out-compete pure individualists, and these altruistic genes might increase their representation in the gene pool. But cheaters can take advantage of true cooperators by enjoying transfers from them but then skipping town and neglecting to repay their debt. If cheaters (or, we might call them opportunists) succeed, then their genes will increase representation. The question then becomes whether social animals can devise ways of discouraging such opportunism and of monitoring and punishing bad behavior? [2]

One implication of this analysis is that altruism is "hard-core" and "natural" among kin and "soft-core" or "unnatural" among non-kin. These extremes, however, may define a spectrum of motives and behavior that is usually somewhere in between. Kinship itself is a continuous rather than a binary variable. Human beings share a large amount of genetic material not only with one another, but also with other animals. But the sharpest challenge to the notion that these two forms of altruism generally take an extreme form comes from the growing evidence that group selection is an important mechanism of evolution. Groups that are successfully able to elicit "solidaristic" behavior from their members may be able to out-compete those that don't (Sober and Wilson 1998). This is the point of the parable of the feminist goddesses and their Olympiad.

The sharp distinction between "natural" or "emotional" or "instinctual" altruism and "social" or "rational" or "reciprocal" altruism is also challenged by much of what we know about the history of family life. Even relationships that we consider naturally altruistic are strongly reinforced by explicit or implicit contracts and expectations of reciprocity. Opportunism is not uncommon in families, and societies often monitor and punish bad behavior towards family members such as domestic violence and child neglect or abuse. Legal rules of monogamy are hypothesized to have emerged historically because they improved child survival rates (McDonald 1995). Social enforcement of paternal responsibilities, which varies widely across cultures and over time, has particularly salient implications for child welfare (Folbre 1994a). In the United States, for instance, widespread failure to pay child support can be interpreted in biological terms as paternal opportunism, and in social terms as a default on care responsibilities.

In practice, care and trust are closely related, as are love and reciprocity. Consider the two following Biblical prescriptions. "Love thy neighbor as thyself" is an emotional appeal, encouraging empathy with others. "Do unto others as you would have them do unto you" has no emotional content. It is a principle of behavior based on reciprocity and trust. The latter appeals more explicitly to self-interest than the former, suggesting that if you treat people well, they will treat you well. But love also requires some reciprocity. In economic terminology, we can call it an endogenous preference.

At first glance, it might seem that trust is more impersonal than altruism, because it requires only a cognitive assessment of someone else's behavior. Sometimes trust is impersonal, as when associated with the rule of law and respect for rules. But the literature on social capital suggests that some forms of trust are more likely to emerge in personal relationships and in close-knit communities (Putnam, Leonardi, and Nanetti 1993; Putnam 1995). Likewise, altruism and love are typically expressed towards people one has a close, almost physical attachment to. But altruism can be impersonal, even abstract. For instance, people give money for famine relief for victims they have never met.

Trust and altruism may be located in somewhat different places on a continuum from impersonal to personal, but both can be found at either end. Trust is perhaps more conditional than altruism. You trust someone if you think they are trustworthy. If they betray your trust, they may never regain it. Altruism is sometimes unconditional. We speak of unrequited love, but not of unrequited trust. But altruism is not always unconditional. Knowledge of other people's feelings may change our own. We don't always continue to love someone if they don't love us. Most of us would reject the notion that someone could "decide" to love someone else in the same way they could decide to cooperate with them. But we can often describe circumstances in which people are more likely or less likely to fall in love with someone, just as we can describe circumstances that encourage or discourage trust. Also, we are more likely to have and express altruistic feelings towards individuals who we believe are "deserving." For instance, people convinced that poor people are responsible for their own plight are less likely to support charitable transfers to them (Bowles and Gintis 1998c).

Think of a continuum of behavior ranging from the completely conditional ("I will love you only if you do x") to the completely unconditional ("I will love you no matter what"). Susan Rose-Ackerman's (1998) distinction between bribes and gifts helps illustrate this continuum. A bribe involves an explicit quid pro quo, while a gift does not. But a gift often generates implicit obligations. Indeed, the distinction between bribes and gifts is often unclear, as with campaign finance contributions. Yet this distinction is crucial to the way we think about payments for TLC.

Are they bribes, paid in anticipation of getting something in return? Or are they gifts that will be forthcoming no matter what? Probably payments for TLC are a little bit of both. If this is the case, then the supply of TLC, as well as care services in general, is at least partially determined by the relative reward given for it. And this implies that the economic organization of care shapes both the quantity and quality of care provided. At the same time, the emotional dimension of TLC means that it cannot be treated like any other good or service. It cannot be stripped of its personal characteristics and meaning.

C. Care requires (and creates) empathy

Traditional neoclassical economic theory postulates that individuals are largely self-interested in the market, and altruistic in the home. If this were the case, we would expect to find care services in one place, and TLC in the other. As pointed out earlier, however, this isn't necessarily the case. Instead, we find that self-interest, wherever it works, depends on definitions of the self that are often altered by caring motives that include empathy. In a kind of "social egoism" that echoes the presumptions of neoclassical economic theory, some psychologists assume that individuals care for one another only because they derive some personal satisfaction from such care, not because they experience true empathy. Other psychologists, however, argue that the role of selfishness in human behavior has been overestimated. For instance, some experiments show that subjects asked to predict how much the promise of monetary payment would modify other subjects' behavior (such as willingness to give blood or provide assistance) consistently overestimated the actual impact (Miller and Ratner 1996).

The notion that altruistic behavior is often motivated by empathy is consistent with the finding that individuals who have experienced damage to their frontal lobes may score normally on tests of cognitive functioning and memory, but exhibit a loss of emotion associated with an inability to maintain interpersonal relationships. At the same time, they are completely present-oriented, as if they lack the ability to empathize with their future selves (Loewenstein 1997).

If we care for others only in order to make ourselves feel better, our goal might be considered instrumental and egoistic. Edward O. Wilson (1978, 154) writes that "compassion is selective and often ultimately self-serving." But the consequences of selfishness are rather different for people whose concept of the self encompasses the welfare of others, and those whose concept of the self is narrowly bounded. In a sense, empathy with others renders selfishness unselfish, a point that Adam Smith actually made in his *Theory of the Moral Sentiments*. The effects of helping others are not diminished by getting some personal pleasure in the process.

Still, the sources of such pleasure may not be truly empathetic. One way to determine whether they are or not is to ask whether helping behavior is likely to take a different form if motivated by empathy than by some more superficial emotion. Psychologist Daniel Batson has constructed a number of experiments along these lines. For instance, suppose that people don't like to see other people in pain simply because this is uncomfortable; they act to help others primarily to relieve their own distress.

This can be tested by offering potential helpers an "easy out." For instance, one could conduct an experiment in which human subjects are confronted with a stylized dilemma. Another person is being subjected to pain (e.g., electric shock), and the test subject is offered the possibility of behaving in an altruistic way (e.g., agreeing to be shocked themselves in place of the other). If individuals offer to help only to relieve their own psychic distress, they should be less likely to help if they can easily exit from the experiment. However, the results show that ease of exit is less significant in explaining their actions than the degree of empathy they express with the person being shocked.

A number of other experiments have been designed to explicitly manipulate degrees of empathy and to vary other factors (such as reputation effects or social norms) that might also explain altruistic actions. In general, the results show that empathy has an extremely significant impact. Batson (1990, 344) does not argue that empathy is the only motive for altruism, nor that empathy always overrides self-interest. Rather, he suggests that empathy is a more powerful force than hitherto suspected, a suggestion with obvious implications for both economics and biology.

Some psychologists have suggested that our empathetic emotions and caring responses have a genetic base in the response of mammalian parents to their helpless offspring. If this is true, then it is apparently also true that we can cognitively "adopt" a wide range of nonkin, bringing them under the umbrella of care. Indeed, often it seems that we must take steps to avoid feeling empathy, whether for the homeless, those starving in Africa and Cambodia, or refugees from Central America. Lest we feel too much, we turn the corner, switch channels, flip the page, or think of something else. Could this apparent necessity to defend ourselves against feeling empathy be a clue to magnitude of our capacity to care?

Care is a siren song. Ulysses instructs his sailors to fill their ears with wax and bind him to the mast of the ship so he will be able to hear the music without jumping overboard. But perhaps he would be better off if he jumped overboard and swam towards the sirens.

Care as a capability

The human development approach emphasizes a completely different metric of progress than conventional emphasis on gross domestic product (GDP). Amartya Sen (1984, 497) defines capabilities as "what people can or cannot do, e.g. whether they can live long, escape avoidable morbidity, be well nourished, be able to read and write and communicate, take part in literary and scientific pursuits, and so forth." Framed in these terms, capabilities seem like a combination of opportunities and skills. The external environment determines opportunities for health, for cultural access, for the entire range of choices facing an individual. Individual characteristics play a role in the acquisition of skills such as literacy and forms of education that economists term "human capital."

The role that care plays in the production of human capabilities should be obvious. Without genuine care and nurturance, children cannot develop any capabilities at all, and adults have hard time maintaining or expanding the capabilities they have.[3] But the supply of caring labor is not merely an input into the process of development. It is also an output.

A. Capabilities and Economic Development

The complementaries between capabilities and care are highlighted by a brief comparison of standard approaches to development typically based on measures of GDP or measures of welfare or utility. Neither of these approaches puts much emphasis on what neoclassical economists might call the "human capital sector" of the economy, and what Marxian economists refer to as "social reproduction." A more appropriate term, I believe, is the "human capabilities sector." As Amartya Sen (1997) points out, many of our capabilities have intrinsic value beyond their economic rate of return. We can interpret human capital, or the accumulation of skills that may contribute to labor productivity, as a subset of capabilities.

Thinking about problems of care that include the elderly, as well as children and the sick or disabled, helps reveal the limitations of traditional economic approaches. It is difficult to construe expenditures on the retired elderly as an investment in human capital, and rather offensive to think of aging as depreciation. A welfare-based approach doesn't get us around this problem. Many elderly people would report a greater feeling of subjective well-being if they were high on heroin. Few would argue that we should maximize well-being this way. Most of us believe that our goal should be to live a good life, not merely a happy one. As Plato and Aristotle pointed out a while back, it behooves us to think about what a good life means.

Capabilities may encompass states of mind such as the ability to be happy, but they cannot be reduced to any purely eudaemonic measure. Capabilities include outputs that are quite objective, such as the probability that a child will graduate from high school or that an elderly person will enjoy good health. They also include some subjective feelings that are more difficult to measure, such as the capability to enjoy oneself, or to care for others. All forms of human capital, and perhaps even some of what economists call "social capital," fall into the category of capabilities, but not all capabilities offer transferable benefits to others.

Figure 1 illustrates the relationship between income, welfare or utility, and capabilities. Human capabilities are designated as H, and defined as a category that includes components of income (Y) and welfare (U), but cannot be reduced to these. Examples of human capabilities that seem more like components of welfare (U) include social skills and emotional health. Rather than thinking of these as different approaches to conceptualizing the economy, they can be seen as three interrelated dimensions of the economy. Production and welfare help produce capabilities and vice versa. The question is which dimension best reflects our primary goal.

In order to illustrate the difference between these three dimensions, compare three families, each consisting of two adults and two young children. In Family A, both adults work 40 hours a week for pay, and perform a combined total of ten hours a week in non-market work, a total of 90 hours of work. Their combined income after taxes is $51,000. In Family B, one adult works 40 hours a week for $50,000, and another adult devotes 60 hours a week to non-market work, for a total of 100 hours of work. In Family C, both adults work 20 hours a week for pay, with a combined market income of $50,000, and do 20 hours each of non-market work, for a total of 80 hours of work. Which family is better off?

By conventional market income measures, we would rank Family A first, because they have the highest market income. But we could construe "better off" in at least three other ways. By any measure that imputed the value of non-market work, we would probably rank Family B first, on the grounds that the extra 50 hours of non-market work per week provided in this family are surely worth more than the $1,000 a year difference in market income. The total sum of Y, or transferable benefits, seems largest in Family B.

A welfare-based approach requires us to impute some measures of subjective well being. There is no reason to believe, a priori, that Family B is happier. If we had no information on subjective well-being we would be required to make some imputations about the likely value of the extra 20 hours of leisure enjoyed by Family C.

Figure 1: Production, Welfare, and Human Capabilities

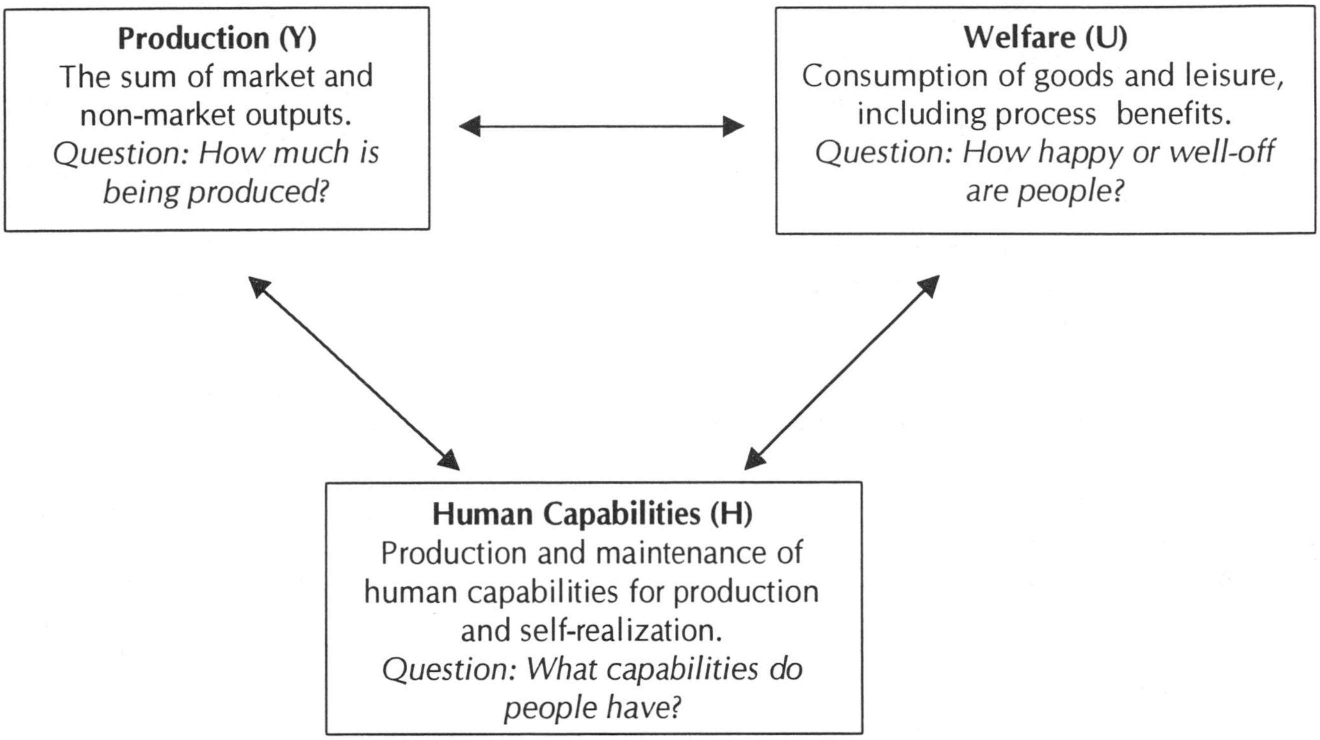

Production (Y)
The sum of market and non-market outputs.
Question: How much is being produced?

Welfare (U)
Consumption of goods and leisure, including process benefits.
Question: How happy or well-off are people?

Human Capabilities (H)
Production and maintenance of human capabilities for production and self-realization.
Question: What capabilities do people have?

A capabilities approach raises a different question, urging us to collect some information about how the capabilities of family members are being developed. In particular, we would want to know how these families organize the provision of care, and what the consequences are for both children and adults. However an emphasis on capabilities also points beyond the family to the larger production of care services that contribute to health, education, and welfare.

The constant reference to GDP in comparisons of international economic competition reflects what might generously be termed a childish perspective: The Country with the Most Toys at the End Wins. The alternative approach could be described as "People Are Our Most Important Product." Emphasizing the production of human capabilities is not the same as a traditional welfare-oriented approach, though it certainly urges consideration of welfare. Even those who want to stick to the "most toys at the end" goal must concede that many human capabilities are necessary to create and maintain human skills that are crucial factors of production. We do not have a very good understanding of the production of these skills, in part because economists have focused almost entirely on the contribution of formal schooling.

Indeed, a visitor from another planet reading the economic literature on human capital might conclude that our children are delivered ready-made to schools, where they are injected with a dose of knowledge, then fast-frozen and returned to a passive storage facility known as the family until the next treatment. In fact, families and communities play a crucial role not only in getting children ready for school but in enabling them to make good use of it (Klebanov et al. 1994; Duncan and Brooks-Gunn 1997). Families and communities are also central to adult development, which continues even after individuals retire from "productive" work.

B. Capabilities, Skills, and Preferences

Capabilities encompass preferences, as well as skills. Economists don't have much practice thinking about preferences, which are often taken as exogenously given. But they have always considered some preferences (such as self-control, a low rate of time discount, or willingness to take risks) better than others (such as a propensity towards impulsiveness, cruelty, or laziness). Adam Smith emphasized the importance of what he called the "moral sentiments." Irving Fisher (1907), one of the pioneers of human capital theory, emphasized preferences more than skills. In his most recent book, Gary Becker (1996) explains why parents try to instill "good" preferences in their children.

The provision of caring labor clearly requires skills. Often certain physical skills are relevant. Simple active touching is extremely important to the development of most mammals. Young mice separated from their mothers simply stop growing. Contact with an anesthetized mother generates some growth hormones. But if a scientist strokes the babies, mimicking active licking by the mother, growth completely normalizes. The famous monkey experiments conducted by Harry Harlow in the 1950s showed that young monkeys preferred a cuddly, terry-cloth "fake mother" to one constructed of wood and chicken wire, even when the latter provided a bottle of food and the former did not. Premature human infants who are regularly touched and stimulated thrive more successfully than those kept in isolation (Sapolsky 1998).

Cognitive skills are also relevant. A caregiver may need to know how to give an inoculation or bandage a wound. Nursing requires knowledge of biology, the teacher needs to know how to read to teach reading, and so forth. But caring labor is particularly likely to require emotional skills—the ability to understand and respond effectively to another person's emotional needs. The task of parenting, for instance, goes far beyond spooning food in a baby's mouth, changing diapers, and giving physical hugs. Virtually every advice book ever written for parents in the U.S. emphasizes the importance of loving nurture and emotional attachment (Hays 1996, 57). Put in more scientific terms, a preschool child's cognitive skills, as assessed by test scores, are positively affected by a mother's degree of warmth, even controlling for her educational attainment, cognitive test scores, and many sociodemographic variables (Klebanov et al. 1994). Note: psychologists have hardly begun to study the effects of *paternal* warmth on children!

An extreme example of the consequences of not being cared for is seen among children who have what is called "attachment disorder." This sometimes occurs for unknown physiological reasons, even with normal parenting. But it is disproportionate among children reared in orphanages with no consistent caretaker who regularly hugged them and expressed affection for them. One famous study of German orphanages after World War II even found that the personal warmth of the matron in charge had an impact on children's physical development (Sapolsky 1998, 85).

Emotional labor clearly requires skills. But it also requires a certain set of feelings or preferences of affection that are difficult (though not impossible) to fake. Once we start taking emotions seriously, the distinction between skills and preferences weakens. Psychologist Daniel Goleman (1995, xii) describes emotional intelligence as "self control, zeal and persistence, and the ability to motivate oneself." These factors are skills in the sense that they can be developed with instruction and practice. But they are preferences in the sense that they are themselves the outgrowth of loving care and healthy socialization. Learning empathy for others can also encourage empathy towards oneself, generating rich psychic rewards from caring relationships.

The development of caring capabilities is a relatively new area of developmental psychology. As Carol Gilligan (1982) points out, many of the influential founding fathers of psychology, including Freud, Jung, Erikson, Piaget, and Kohlberg, all viewed individuation as synonymous with maturation, but viewed emotional connection to others as developmentally regressive. The newer literature emphasizing that emotional connection is developmentally progressive needs to be integrated into a larger theory of human capabilities.

C. Conflicting capabilities

Expanding the domain of choice is probably a good thing. However, most of the literature on capabilities seems to take a rather simple more-is-better approach. What about either/or aspects? Some capabilities are at odds with others. For instance, the capability to be assertive and exert leadership may conflict to some extent with the capability to be supportive and nurturant. Capabilities most likely to enhance market earnings may not be those most likely to enhance the quality of family life. As these examples suggest, capabilities are highly gendered. We don't know the extent of innate differences between men and women, but we do know that social norms create strong pressures for differentiation of roles by gender.

Experimental studies of altruism show no significant overall differences between men and women (Kohn 1990). They also show that helping behaviors are highly context dependent. Men are more likely to help someone carry their laundry; women are more likely to help someone fold it. On a less banal level, men are far more likely to go to war and risk death and injury than women are. However, women are more likely to behave in helping and altruistic ways towards kin and community. Their altruism is more likely to find expression in caring labor.

Considerable recent research in developing countries supports the "good mother hypothesis." Mothers generally devote a significantly larger share of their income and earnings to family needs than fathers (Benería and Roldan 1987; Chant 1991). Income that is controlled by women is more likely to be spent on children's health and nutrition and less likely to be spend on alcohol (Dwyer and Bruce 1988; Hoddinott, Alderman, and Haddad 1998). In many countries, a large proportion of fathers provides little or no economic support for their children (Folbre 1994a). Women may be more risk-averse than men, with negative consequences for their income, but positive consequences for those dependent upon them (Daly and Wilson 1983). Such altruism is, obviously, good for children. But maternal altruism almost certainly increases women's vulnerability to poverty (Fuchs 1988). A large share of the difference in economic position between men and women seems related to women's greater assumption of care responsibilities.

Indeed, caring labor in general seems to be penalized, whether performed by men or women (England and Folbre 1998). A parent who devotes time and energy to "family-specific" activities typically experiences a significant reduction in lifetime earnings. Joshi (1990, 1991) and Waldfogel (1997) document substantial costs to mothers in Great Britain and the United States. The human capital that housewives and/or househusbands acquire is less transportable than that of a partner who specializes in market work, leaving them in a weaker bargaining position in the family, economically vulnerable in the event of separation or divorce (Weitzman 1985). Furthermore, employees in caring occupations are typically paid less than others, even controlling for a large list of other personal and job characteristics (England 1992; England et al. 1994; Kilbourne et al. 1994). Women are disproportionately concentrated in these jobs.

Why do women tend to devote more time and effort to care than men do? Sociobiologists emphasize the greater biological investment in each child made by females (Daly and Wilson 1983). But one can concede the importance of biology without dismissing the importance of culture. Even Edward O. Wilson (1978, 129), the most famous advocate of sociobiology, writes that divergence in male/female behavior is "almost always widened in later psychological development by cultural sanctions and training." Most societies reinforce female altruism towards family and children far more strongly than male altruism. If women "naturally" choose to specialize in care, why do societies develop coercive rules and practices that make it difficult for them to do otherwise? Women are far more likely than men to care for the infirm elderly, as well as children, hardly a pattern that can be explained by the fact that female eggs are few in number compared to male sperm.

Gender norms are increasingly coming under scrutiny as social constructions that often benefit men as a group. Most institutional economists describe norms and preferences simply as solutions to coordination problems (Schotter 1981). But groups often seek to enforce norms and preferences they find beneficial. As Edna Ullmann-Margalit (1977, 189) writes, a norm may be conceived of as a sophisticated tool of coercion, used by the favored party in a status quo of inequality to promote its interest in the maintenance of this status quo. It will be considered sophisticated to the extent that the air of impersonality remains intact and successfully disguises what really underlies the partiality of norms, vis. an exercise of power.

Men as a group have much to gain by encouraging women's caring propensities. Of course, the opposite is also true: women have much to gain by enforcing norms, and preferences of caring in men. But our constructs of gendered behavior emerged from societies in which men had far more cultural and economic power than women. The result can be described as "socially imposed altruism" or a gender-biased system of coercive socialization (Folbre and Weisskopf 1998). Another apt phrase is a system of "discriminatory obligation" (Ward 1993, 103).

Feminist theorist Joan Tronto (1987, 647, 650) points out that robbing individuals of opportunities to effectively pursue their own self-interest may encourage them to live through others, using caring as a substitute for more selfish gratification. Amartya Sen (1990) hints at a similar problem: women may not realize they are exploited when they lack a cultural conception of themselves as individuals with interests separate from those of their family members (see also Kabeer 1994). While neoclassical economists tend to avoid questions of how and why preferences are gendered, they suggest that parents may inculcate caring preferences in their children in order to ensure that they are cared for in old age (Becker 1996; Stark 1995). Men may try to inculcate caring preferences in women for similar reasons. Some sociologists argue that women's caregiving is rooted in the social structures of adult life rather than preferences formed in early life (Gerstel and Gallagher 1994).

If caring norms and preferences are constructed in these ways, they can be reconstructed. We could try to increase men's capabilities for care by increasing their responsibilities for it. One study of single fathers (none of whom had actively chosen their role) found that having responsibility for child care fostered nurturance and sympathy (Risman 1987). Some cross-cultural anthropological research shows that children who are given responsibility for other children become more caring adults (Monroe 1996, 176). Encouraging male participation in care could reduce gender inequality. As sociologist Scott Coltrane (1998, B8) points out:

> *Cross-cultural research shows that when men take an active role in the details of running a home and raising children, they develop emotional sensitivities, avoid boastful and threatening behavior, and include women in community decision making. Increasing men's involvement in family work thus has the potential to increase women's public status and reduce men's propensity for violence.*

Male participation in child care, insists sociologist David Popenoe (1996, 218), is good for men themselves, as well as for society. What these sociologists fail to fully acknowledge is that men may resist care responsibilities because they know they will be costly—especially if they learn to like them. Ulysses fears the sirens' song.

Human capabilities as a public good

> *The importance of women's unpaid care for kin and community, and the way in which responsibility for it puts women at a disadvantage in markets, is something which needs to be much more systematically addressed in thinking about human development.*
>
> **—Diane Elson, in Global Governance and Development Fifty Years After Bretton Woods: Essays in Honor of Gerald K. Helleiner**

There are a number of reasons why caring labor may not be remunerated very generously, especially in competitive markets (England and Folbre 1998). Of particular relevance to the issue of economic development and globalization is the claim that caring labor produces a public good that also has some of the characteristics of a common property resource, with a value that is difficult to measure but which benefits a large number of people beyond the person immediately cared for (England and Folbre 1999). As a non-priced public good/common resource, TLC will almost inevitably be underproduced and/or overexploited unless non-market institutions solve the coordination problems involved. The traditional patriarchal family offers one solution to this problem that is particularly costly to women. As this institution is destabilized, women may enjoy some gains that are at least partially neutralized by the difficulty of establishing another form of coordination that protects the well-being of mothers and children.

The notion that children are public goods has been widely articulated in the advanced industrial countries where welfare state institutions such as Social Security create rather obvious fiscal externalities (Demeny 1987; Lee 1990; Folbre 1994b; Burggraf 1993). A closer look at this argument, especially with reference to the developing world, leads away from an emphasis on number of children, and toward more attention to the capabilities embodied in both children and adults. TLC is the particular input into human capabilities that is most likely to be underproduced in a competitive market economy. It is also the input that is heavily penalized by many structural adjustment policies.

A. Public Goods and Common Property Resources

The classic commodity of economic theory is excludable in consumption and creates no positive or negative externalities. The terms of the exchange perfectly capture the effects of the exchange. Someone will sell something for ten dollars only if she benefits from doing so, and someone will buy something for ten dollars only if it is worth at least ten dollars to her. By assuming away any spillover effects, this approach eliminates any possible divergence between consequences for individuals and consequences for society as a whole. Textbooks in microeconomic theory devote relatively little attention to departures from this world of private transactions. They commonly include a chapter on the role of the state, which provides public goods such as national defense and education, and a chapter on the environment, describing the negative externalities created through degradation of common property resources such as air, water, and climate.

Public goods are underproduced by the market because individuals can enjoy the benefits without paying the costs. They can free-ride on the efforts of others. A classic example is national defense. If this were left up to voluntary purchases, individuals would avoid making expenditures, in the hope that others would pay up. This problem provides the traditional justification for taxation of private citizens. Education is commonly listed as another public good that requires taxation for public provision. Even though individuals clearly derive some private benefits from education, the value of these benefits depends in some ways on the opportunity to work with other educated individuals. Employers and fellow-workers, as well as citizens, capture some of the gains.

As pointed out in section II above, education cannot begin, continue, or succeed without the provision of family and community services of care. Yet the role of these services in the production of "human capital" is largely ignored. The implicit assumption seems to be that the optimal level of education requires state provision but that non-market services of care will be provided whether or not they are remunerated (as though they require no reciprocity or reward).

Family labor, as well as the qualitatively important aspects of market labor, are relegated to the world of nature, outside the realm of calculated exchange. This inconsistency reflects the traditional dichotomy between reciprocal altruism and kin altruism described in section I above.

In economic terms, the assumption seems to be that the supply of non-market care services is fixed by human nature and/or cultural norms. As Diane Elson (1992, 34) puts it, "Macromodels appear to treat human resources as a nonproduced means of production like land." If the supply of TLC were fixed, we could represent it by a vertical line in a supply/demand diagram: the same amount is supplied no matter what the "price." But some aspects of the social organization of care services are demonstrably responsive to changes in relative prices. It is difficult, otherwise, to explain the process of fertility decline that typically accompanies economic development (Caldwell 1982). In some countries, one concomitant of fertility decline is reduced paternal contributions, which are partially related to the increasing opportunity costs of time and resources devoted to children (Folbre 1994a).

However, even if the supply of non-market care services is somewhat affected by price, it is not very sensitive to price, especially in the short run. This is especially true of the component of care services that we have singled out, TLC, which is defined by the importance of intrinsic motives of affection and obligation. You cannot elicit more TLC from a partner or a parent by promising to pay them for it. In the long run, however, the norms and internalized preferences that generate TLC are probably influenced by large shifts in relative prices. Women who feel aggrieved that they have been penalized for specializing in TLC may encourage their daughters to behave differently. Children who enjoy complete economic independence from their parents may be less likely to care for them in their old age.

A more vivid analogy is that of an artesian well, a natural fountain of water. No pumps or pipes are needed to bring it to the surface. The water, like TLC, is a free good. Still, it will be affected by changes in the underground aquifer. If many holes are drilled into that aquifer, tapping into the same reservoir, the water pressure and rate of flow in the artesian well will be reduced. As this analogy suggests, it may be more helpful to think of TLC as a common property resource rather than as a pure public good.

Common property resources are resources (usually endowed by nature) that are difficult to price on an individual basis. Examples are fish in the sea, grass in an unfenced area, or underground water. Unlike public goods, they will be produced whether or not they are paid for. However, because they are costless, they will tend to be overexploited, perhaps to the point of non-replenishment, unless social institutions (such as laws or norms) control access to them.

Environmental economists are devoting increasing attention to the valuation of "natural capital" and pointing out that failure to estimate its rate of depreciation leads to overstatement of the rate of economic growth (Daly 1997). Sociologists and political scientists have persuaded economists to pay more attention to the production and maintenance of "social capital" (Coleman 1998; Putnam 1993, 1995). Yet most studies of this topic focus on trust and reciprocity, with little attention to the production or the exploitation of TLC within caring services in general or the family in particular. Economists have well-developed concepts of "market failure" and "state failure." We need to develop a better theory of "family failure" and "community failure."

B. Children and fiscal externalities

A more specific example of the public-goods/common-property-resource dimension of care lies in the fiscal externalities created by welfare state policies. In highly developed countries such as the United States, the working-age population as a whole transfers significant benefits to the elderly through taxation. Yet the individuals who invest time, money and care into the creation of the next generation of workers are not explicitly rewarded for their efforts. Parental efforts are considered socially important, but economically unproductive.

Perhaps the best way to explain the argument that children are a public good is to articulate the opposite argument, that children are nothing more than a source of pleasure to the individuals who raise them: the "children as pets" approach. If people spend a lot of money on their golden retriever, it must be because it makes them happy to do so. In utility terms, they are no worse off than those who simply put an equivalent amount of money in the bank. From this point of view, people who acquire pets but cannot maintain them at a decent level of health and well being are irresponsible, and should be punished. The innocent pets may suffer in the meantime, but if all else fails they can be removed to the animal shelter (also known as the orphanage or foster care).

As pointed out earlier, this approach is obviously inconsistent with an emphasis on the intrinsic importance of human capabilities. But one can also challenge the "children as pets" approach on its own terms by pointing out that children create far more significant positive externalities. Members of the working age population are taxed to help pay the debts accumulated by the previous generation, as well as the direct costs of old age provision through Social Security. As Kotlikoff (1992) emphasizes, differences in the relative size of cohorts (particularly the large bulge of the baby-boom generation in the United States) can lead to significant redistribution across age groups.

As a concrete illustration, consider two individuals who have the same marriage and employment history: they will receive exactly the same retirement benefits from Social Security, even if one of them raised three children who grew up to become productive members of society and to pay taxes on the income they earned, while the other raised none, and simply enjoyed higher levels of personal consumption. Current policies in the United States socialize many of the economic benefits of children while requiring parents, mothers in particular, to pay most of the costs (Folbre 1985, 1994b).

Women who put time and energy into children are investing in what is essentially a "family public good." They pay most of the costs, but other family members, including children and fathers, claim an equal share of the benefits (Lommerud 1997). This investment is far less fungible or transferable outside the family than investment in a career (England and Farkas 1986). The resulting loss of bargaining power may lead to a reduction of women's consumption and/or leisure time even if they remain married and enjoy a share of their husband's market income.

Individuals who devote time and energy to parenting often enjoy some economic as well as psychological benefits. Adult children seldom transfer much income to their parents, but they often provide care and assistance to those who are elderly. Partly as a result, elderly individuals with living children are less likely than others to require publicly subsidized nursing-home care (Wolf 1997). However, these private benefits are small compared to the transfers provided through taxation of the working age population, as well as the less tangible benefits enjoyed by the friends, spouses, and employers (Lee 1990; Folbre 1994b).

Public expenditures on children are modest, compared to those made by parents. Haveman and Wolfe (1995, 1829) estimate that the sum of public expenditures on children in the United States, comprised mostly of education, housing and income transfers, accounted for about 38% of the total cost, and their estimate of total cost is probably low. Public expenditures on children in the United States are far lower per child than those in countries which, like France, provide subsidized child care for all children at age three and beyond (Bergmann 1997). Over the last thirty years, the elderly in the United States have received far greater transfers per capita than the young (Preston 1984; Fuchs and Reklis 1992).

Analysis of the public goods aspect of childrearing has largely focused on the advanced industrial countries. Indeed, Ronald Lee (1990) argues that children may create negative externalities in developing countries, which could benefit from further fertility decline. Whether or not this is this case, it is important to make a distinction between number of children and the level of time, energy, and resources devoted to each child. (Neoclassical economists call this child quantity vs. child quality.) Even in an economic context in which additional numbers of children may create some negative externalities, parental and community investments in existing children create positive externalities. Indeed, the main advantage of fertility decline is that it frees up resources that may be spent on the capabilities of children already born.

C. Public Goods and Political Conflict

The public goods aspect of the production of human capabilities helps explain why both groups and individuals engage in forms of strategic behavior designed to help them enjoy the benefits without paying the costs. A rich historical record demonstrates many complex forms of collective conflict based on gender, race, class, age, and nation (Folbre 1994a). Examples of gender-based conflict range from men's opposition to strict specification and enforcement of child support responsibilities to the cultural claim that women "should" feel greater love and responsibility for children than men. The relevance to current policy debates is obvious.

Most of the policies promoted by international agencies such as the World Bank and the International Monetary Fund (IMF) are explicitly designed to increase the rate of growth of measured output. It is hardly surprising, then, that they often have an adverse effect on public goods such as care. The analogy with environmental degradation is quite clear. A country can speed up its rate of GDP growth by depleting a resource such as tropical hardwood at a non-sustainable rate. It can also speed up its rate of GDP growth by encouraging a shift from the production of unpaid services to tradeable goods. The lack of adequate measures of the value of non-market wealth or income makes it easier to pretend that progress is unambiguous.

The gender and development literature includes many examples of the deleterious effects of structural adjustment on family welfare. The direct effects of cutbacks in the provision of social services such as health, education, and child care are often compounded by increased demands on women's time. Mothers may be forced to withdraw from paid employment or to increase their demands on daughters to help with household chores. Increases in the intensity of women's work may have deleterious effects (Floro 1995a, 1995b). Families maintained by women alone are particularly susceptible to such pressures.

It is important to recognize the analogies between structural adjustment policies imposed on developing countries and political struggles within the developed countries over the organization of care services. There is a distinct gender gap in support for the provision of services such as child care, for the obvious reason that these services tend to benefit women more than men. Publicly subsidized child care tends to increase mother's labor force participation and reduce gender inequalities in both the workplace and in the home (Juster and Stafford 1991). Many more single women than single men take responsibility for the care of young children.

Much attention has been devoted to the difficulties of enforcing paternal child support obligations. One could think of public spending on education, child care, and health as a kind of collective child-support obligation which has been poorly specified and even more poorly enforced. Gender conflicts are overlaid by class inequalities. Affluent families who purchase high-quality services in the private market are particularly likely to oppose tax increases to finance public provision. Age-based conflict also comes into play. Elderly families, especially those who believe that they have already paid for the public benefits they are receiving, would prefer to pay less rather than more in taxes to care for "other people's children."

The emergence of welfare states represented an explicit effort to socialize many of the transfers of income and labor once located within the family, such as the education of the young and the support of the elderly. Many welfare state policies, influenced by women's increased political power, can be described as a victory for "maternalist" values (Skocpol 1993; Koven and Michel 1993). But race and class differences, as well as perceptions of national self-interest, have significantly shaped policy outcomes. In general, ethnically and religiously homogeneous countries who have lost population through out-migration and/or war have been particularly likely to provide public support for childrearing. In the United States, on the other hand, white apprehensions about the growth of the Black and Hispanic population discouraged policies that could be construed as pro-natalist, even when it became apparent that fertility rates were steadily declining (Folbre 1994a; Quadagno 1994).

It is important to locate an analysis of the effects of globalization within a larger picture of conflicts over the distribution of the costs of care. Consider the similarities between a mother who devotes considerable time and energy to enhancing her children's capabilities and a country that devotes a large portion of its national budget to family welfare. In the short run, both are at a competitive disadvantage, because they are devoting fewer resources to directly productive activities. In the long run, their position depends on their ability to claim some share of the economic benefits produced by the next generation, which is quite limited.

The following imaginary scenario illustrates the problem: A multinational corporation, tired of the frustrations of negotiating over taxation and regulation with host governments, buys a small Caribbean island, writes a constitution, and announces the formation of a new country. Its name is Corporation Nation. Anyone who is a citizen of the new country will automatically receive a highly paid job. However, the following restrictions apply to citizenship: Individuals must have advanced educational credentials, be physically and emotionally healthy, have no children, and be under the age of sixty. They do not have to physically emigrate, but can work from their home country over the Internet. However, they immediately lose their new citizenship and their job if they require retraining, become seriously ill, acquire children, or reach the age of sixty.

Corporation Nation can completely free-ride on the human capabilities of its citizen/workers without paying either for their production or their maintenance when ill or old. It can offer high wages to attract the very best childless and carefree workers in the world, without threatening its own profitability. As a result, it is likely to enjoy unprecedented success in global competition. This disturbing scenario is not as far-fetched as it might initially seem. Consider the words of Dow Chemical executive Carl A. Gerstaker:

I have long dreamed of buying an island owned by no nation and of establishing the World Headquarters of the Dow Company on the truly neutral ground of such an island, beholden to no nation or society (cited in Barnet and Müller 1974, 16).

Bits and pieces of the policies described above are already in effect in a number of countries. Canada has largely credential-based immigration criteria. Within the United States, the state of California refuses to provide any social services for illegal immigrants. Germany sends immigrant workers back to their home countries when unemployment goes up. As the result of the current East Asian economic crisis, non-native workers are being deported from Malaysia and other countries.

Family, state, and globalization

Economic development entails a transfer of economic activities from family and kin-based systems to larger, more complex social institutions. One stage in this process is the emergence of nation-states, which function in some ways like fictive families—our fatherlands, our mother countries. We speak of "national interests" much as we speak of "family interests," recognizing that individuals who often disagree are nonetheless willing, under certain circumstances, to act as one.

The movement of markets beyond national boundaries has always been part of the process of economic development. But for much of the last two hundred years, nations have exercised a great deal of control over social reproduction, organizing the production of care services such as education, health, and provision for dependents. The analogy between the family and the state is clear. On the positive side, both institutions demand commitment to the welfare of the collectivity, rather than the individual. On the negative side, both institutions can generate oppressive hierarchies that interfere with the full development of human capabilities.

Today, as we near the end of the twentieth century, it is easy to see that economic development has strengthened some aspects of family life even as it has weakened others. Yet we cannot help but feel a certain anxiety about the increasing relative costs of caring labor. Globalization, the rapid acceleration of market exchanges across national boundaries, creates a similar anxiety about the future of state-supported care services. One of the lessons of recent history seems to be that markets function effectively only within a matrix of effective non-market institutions. Ironically, market forces themselves often tend to undermine these institutions.

A. The contradictory effects of markets

Feminist theory warns against romanticization of precapitalist societies that were typically based on patriarchal control over women and children. The expansion of wage employment is associated with individuals' increased choice to enter into and exit from caring relationships, which almost certainly increases their quality. On the other hand, the market tends to reward individualism in ways that may ultimately weaken care (Folbre and Weisskopf 1998). Whether the positive or the negative effect of markets dominates probably depends on particular historical and cultural circumstances. In countries with high levels of income inequality and racial/ethnic conflict, economic development is associated with significant disruption of family ties, increases in the percentage of families maintained by women alone, and high levels of poverty among mothers and children. More egalitarian countries fare better (Folbre 1994a).

The growth of wage employment destabilizes patriarchal coercion partly because it modifies the economics of family life. Changes in relative prices, including increases in the cost of raising children, make traditional patriarchal forms of control over women less advantageous to men. A traditional housewife may have less bargaining power than a well-educated professional woman, but she also contributes less income to the family. Men eventually gain from increases in their wives' labor force participation, and a more egalitarian family begins to emerge, based on ideals of quid pro quo and reciprocity rather than coercion or internalized norms of maternal responsibility. Both men and women enjoy more freedom of entry and exit into families; the percentage of individuals living together out of wedlock tends to rise, along with divorce rates.

The benefits to women, however, are uneven. Single women benefit more than mothers, whose bargaining power is limited by their tendency to take primary responsibility for children. A more egalitarian family is almost inevitably a less stable one. It is easier for women to obtain rights over their own earnings than to enforce claims on men's income. Children suffer as a result. In the United States, poor enforcement of paternal child-support responsibilities, inadequate child care provision and decreasing levels of public assistance have contributed to increased rates of poverty among all individuals under eighteen.

The impact of wage employment on women's empowerment is blunted by the fact that they tend to specialize in jobs that have a large caring component. Employers prefer to hire them for such jobs, and, as a result of the socialization processes described in the preceding section, women themselves may prefer them. To the extent that care service labor is supplied for caring motives rather than for compensation, the supply curve of labor to care service jobs such as teaching, day care, and nursing will be lower, as will therefore the wages paid to those who are compensated for such labor. Thus, many workers in care service jobs are exploited in the sense that they are being paid less than they would be in a world entirely lacking in altruism, responsibility, or intrinsic enjoyment of helping others.

Economics textbooks portray markets as impersonal arenas in which homogeneous products are bought and sold. In the real world, however, markets often have a personal dimension (Nelson 1998). They are embedded in a social context that blunts the operation of competitive forces. Many individuals who work primarily for a wage also have intrinsic motives for choosing the kind of work they do. In many caring occupations, such as teaching and nursing, a powerful professional ethic reinforces standards of excellence even though these are costly to both workers and their employers. Long-term relationships lower transactions costs and lead to implicit contracts based on trust and reciprocity. Small businesses, in particular, often feel a responsibility to their employees as well as their share holders.

Karl Polanyi argued long ago that economic development tended to "disembed" companies from the communities in which they operate. Over the last twenty years it has become increasingly apparent that the intensification of global competition imposes harsher penalties on companies that are not strict profit-maximizers. Privatization of services previously provided by the public sector has a similar effect. The reorganization of the health care industry in the United States has significantly reduced the escalation of health costs. But there is a growing concern that the quality of care is threatened. As a recent *New York Times* article noted, critics say "hit and run" nursing has replaced Florence Nightingale.[4] Especially when defined in ways that include emotional well-being, quality of care is far more difficult to measure than out-of-pocket costs.

A process that can be termed "the commodification of care" is underway in virtually all countries. Clearly, this process has some good features, beyond the obvious possibilities for increases in efficiency. But we need to pay closer attention to the ways in which emphasis on "fee for service" may affect quality. As Clare Ungerson (1997, 377) puts it, "the social, political, and economic contexts in which payments for care operate and the way in which payments for care are themselves organized are just as likely to transform relationships as the existence of payments themselves."

Globalization is clearly a major aspect of this context. Robert Kuttner (1996, 62) describes two related dangers of extending the scope of market relationships:

The first is that market institutions drive out extra-market institutions. Faced with an onslaught of competitive pressure, nonmarket institutions, like charity hospitals or public television or "amateur" sport, begin looking and behaving more like profit-making ones. The second danger is that market norms drive out nonmarket norms. Market theory advises us to behave more like textbook economic man. When everything is for sale, the person who volunteers time, who helps a stranger, who agrees to work for a modest wage out of commitment to the public good, who desists from littering even when no one is looking, who forgoes an opportunity to free-ride, begins to feel like a sucker.

Jon Elster reaches similar conclusions in his book *The Cement of Society*.[5] Care services, and caring labor in particular, are especially vulnerable to these dangers. If globalization is associated with an increase in unregulated competition, it will almost certainly erode families and communities along with nation-states.

The rise of multinational corporations creates an international managerial class that has no roots in any specific geographic or cultural community. Therefore, it seems quite likely to increase corporate "disembeddedness" and reduce the space for care both inside and outside of market relationships. Childcare workers sometimes refer to a corporate chain of franchised day care centers as "Kentucky Fried Children." Benjamin Barber (1995, 29) predicts the ultimate victory of "McWorld," a nightmarish theme park of undifferentiated malls and fast food featuring an "unobstructed set of exchange relationships among individual consumers and individual producers." Barber also argues that it is precisely this threat that gives rise to a conservative backlash based on ethnic and religious absolutism, which he calls "jihad."

The contrast between "McWorld" and "jihad" summarizes the contradictions of markets. If we disagree with the ways in which some families, communities and states are organized, we might *like* the idea of destabilizing them. New opportunities for wage employment outside the home, for instance, empower women to challenge traditional patriarchal authority. Many women would prefer a poorly paid job in a factory to a forced marriage. But destabilizing existing social institutions that provide care services is easier than constructing new ones. Given a choice between a patriarchal versus more democratic and egalitarian provision of care services, it is easy to demand the latter. But some people may fear that the choice is between patriarchal provision and none at all.

B. Between the Devil and the Deep Blue Sea

The resurgence of religious fundamentalism around the world testifies to anxiety about the destabilization of traditional patriarchal relationships that have ensured a relatively cheap supply of caring labor. Some of this anxiety reflects political interests based on nation, race, class, and gender. But it also reflects a more generalized concern about the threat of "McWorld." Responses to patriarchal backlash highlight the tensions between a liberal feminism that emphasizes individual rights and a social feminism that emphasizes the obligations of care. The challenge to feminists is to find the right balance between these two.

Many conservatives believe that economic globalization fuels market-based individualism at the expense of family and community. Within the United States, Patrick Buchanan (1998, 106) is among the most eloquent: "Where does one's loyalty lie?" he asks. "That is the issue raised by the onset of the Global Economy and the rise of the transnational elite. To whom, to what do we owe allegiance and love?" Later (p. 325), he groans, "We are ceasing to be a band of brothers." The solution Buchanan proposes includes not only high tariffs, but also a return to the traditional family in which women stayed home and provided care. The policies implemented by the Taliban in Afghanistan represent a more extreme version of the same response—banning female employment outside the home, along with television.

Patriarchal authority over women provides men with an easy solution to "McWorld." In June 1998, the convention of Southern Baptists, the largest Protestant denomination in the United States, declared that a wife should "submit herself graciously" to her husband's leadership.[6] In Egypt, a 1985 Supreme Court decision struck down a law giving a woman the right to divorce her husband should he take a second wife. Sudan's military regime does not allow women to leave the country without permission from a father, husband, or brother.[7] But women do not find the "jihad solution" to the caring labor problem particularly attractive and tend to mobilize collectively against it. Furthermore, its seems likely that the quality of caring labor itself is diminished by such explicit forms of coercion.

At the same time, it is important to face the specter of "McWorld," a fast-care society in which individuals buy cheap, standardized, pre-packaged units of supervision, instruction, and therapy. In a world of spot markets and instantaneous transactions, there is little room for the development of solidarity or affection. If more and more individuals opt for an individualistic strategy that emphasizes autonomy over commitment, the costs and risks of commitment will increase. The result can be a bit like an arms race, in which individual efforts to gain strategic superiority lead to a tremendous waste of social resources and, ultimately, a destructive war of all against all.

Conservatives often castigate feminists as proponents of "Western" or "liberal" values of individualism.[8] This is inaccurate. To assert that women should have exactly the same individual rights as men leaves open the questions of how individual rights should be defined, and how they should be balanced against social responsibilities. Women have always been especially aware of the tensions between care and extreme individualism. As Sharon Hays (1996, 97) puts it, "The same society that disseminates an ideology urging mothers to give unselfishly of their time, money, and love on behalf of sacred children simultaneously valorizes a set of ideas that runs directly counter to it, one emphasizing impersonal relations between isolated individuals efficiently pursing their personal profit." Arlie Hochschild (1998, 533), among others, deplores what she describes as a growing "care deficit" in the United States:

We legitimate the care deficit by reducing the range of ideas about what a child, wife, husband, aged parent, or home "really needs" to thrive. Indeed, the words "thrive" and "happy" go out of fashion, replaced by thinner, more restrictive notions of human well-being.... Most advice books for men concern money and sex and say virtually nothing about caring for their elderly parents or small children. Books for women, such as Helen Gurley Brown's *Having it All* or Sonya Freeman's *Smart Cookies Don't Crumble*, now also glamorize a life for women that is relatively free of the burden of this care.

Hochschild is describing the arms-race aspect of changes in gender roles, the retaliatory logic of "what's good for the gander is good for the goose." In game-theoretic terms, it is easy to see why the two extreme alternatives of "jihad" and "McWorld" loom large. One represents a totalitarian response, the other an anarchistic one. Both responses require far less effort and negotiation than the democratic response, which demands serious thinking about how to collectively enforce responsibilities for care.

C. Sharing care

The "welfare state" does not offer a simple or easy solution. It represents a series of patchwork programs that emerged in response to a poorly understood series of family, community, and market failures. Most programs such as Social Security, family allowances, and maternity leave are based on an outdated homemaker/breadwinner model (Folbre 1994a; Fraser 1994). The emergence of such programs has made it possible to postpone basic changes in the structure of work both inside and outside the family. Furthermore, the welfare state defines social responsibility almost exclusively in monetary terms—the payment of taxes to help provide care services that are paid for by the state. Indeed, this emphasis on money transfers may help explain waning support for redistributionist policies. Taxpayers have little personal contact with those they are helping to provide for.

There is growing evidence of international feminist mobilization around care issues. A number of Women's Budget Initiatives call attention to the "care sector" (Bakker 1998). A recent report to the National Women's Council of Ireland concludes that state policies should be modified in ways that valorize caring work, that actively encourage sharing of this work between men and women, and that reward flexibility in career structures (Isis Research Group 1998).

Debates over the organization of care have become a major issue in the Netherlands. Marga Bruyn-Hundt (1996, 129) asks: "How can governments encourage the provision of unpaid care work without discouraging women's independence?" The report of a Dutch Expert Committee has called for elimination of breadwinner's subsidies in income tax and social security, expansion of subsidized child care and home care for sick and elderly people. Some Dutch policy makers argue that state support is not enough, because complete "outsourcing" of family care is undesirable. A clear alternative is a reduction in men's paid work time, and a concomitant increase in time devoted to family care, to help balance women's participation in market work (Brouwer and Wierda 1998).

The Scandinavian countries have a long tradition of public recognition and payment for care (Ungerson 1995). Public policies could, following the Scandinavian example, support and reward family commitments without reinforcing traditional gender roles. But the project of encouraging caring labor should not be limited to families. Citizens could be given tax credits for contributing care services that develop long term relationships between individuals. Many young adults benefit from public support for higher education. They could pay their fellow citizens back by engaging in a period of mandatory national service that would include taking some responsibility for children and other dependents in their community. The care services they could provide would be at least as valuable as the non-care services currently emphasized by the military.

Policies designed to foster a greater supply of caring labor appear "unproductive" or "costly" only to those who define economic efficiency in terms of misleadingly narrow measures such as contribution to GDP. The erosion of family and community solidarity imposes enormous costs that are reflected in inefficient and unsuccessful educational efforts, high crime rates, and a social atmosphere of anxiety and resentment. The care and nurturance of human capital has always been difficult and expensive. In the past, a sexual division of labor based upon the subordination of women helped minimize both the difficulties and the expense. Today, however, the costs of providing caring labor should be explicitly confronted and fairly distributed. ■

Notes

[1] A clear exception here is the work of Robert Frank (1988, 1990) on economics and emotions.

[2] Bowles and Gintis (1998a, 1998b, 1998c) make a persuasive argument for the evolutionary emergence of what they call "strong reciprocity."

[3] For a more detailed discussion of capabilities see England and Folbre (1998).

[4] Peter T. Kilborn, "Nurses Put on Fast Forward in Rush for Cost Efficiency," *New York Times*, April 9, 1998, A1.

[5] Elster writes, "Let me conclude with another speculative argument, to the effect that scientific, technical, economic and social development tends to erode the ability to make credible threats and promises, by undermining social norms and reducing the scope for long-term self-interest. This historical argument, taken together with the theoretical argument sketched in the preceding paragraph, suggests that modern societies are safer and bleaker than their traditional counterparts. They are safer because fewer threats are made and carried out, and bleaker because fewer promises are made and kept. People are less violent, but also less helpful and cooperative. In addition, bonds of altruism and solidarity may also be weaker" (1989, 284).

[6] *International Herald Tribune*, June 11, 1998, p.1.

[7] Lisa Beyer, "Life Behind the Veil," *Time*, November 8, 1990.

[8] For a quite systematic polemic on this point, see Fox-Genovese (1991).

References

Abel, Emily K., and Margaret K. Nelson, 1990. "Circles of Care: An Introductory Essay." In *Circles of Care. Work and Identity in Women's Lives*, ed. Emily K. Abel and Margaret K. Nelson. New York: State University of New York Press.

American Heritage Dictionary of the English Language, 1992. Third Edition. Boston: Houghton Mifflin Company.

Bakker, Isabella. 1998. "Globalization: A Different View from Feminist Economists." Paper presented at the Out of the Margin 2/IAFFE Conference, Amsterdam, The Netherlands, June.

Barber, Benjamin R. 1995. *Jihad vs. McWorld: How Globalism and Tribalism are Reshaping the World*. New York: Ballantine.

Barnet, Richard J. and Ronald E. Müller. 1974. *Global Reach: The Power of the Multinational Corporation*. New York: Simon and Schuster.

Batson, C. Daniel. 1990. "How Social an Animal?: The Human Capacity for Caring." *American Psychologist* 45(3): 336-346.

Becker, Gary. 1996. *Accounting for Tastes*. Cambridge: Harvard University Press.

Benería, Lourdes. 1992. "Accounting for Women's Work: Assessing the Progress of Two Decades." *World Development* 20 (11): 1547-60.

Benería, Lourdes, and Martha Roldan. 1987. *The Crossroads of Class and Gender*. Chicago: University of Chicago Press.

Ben-Porath, Yoram. 1980. "The F-Connection: Families, Friends, and Firms and the Organization of Exchange." *Population and Development Review* 6:1-30.

Bergmann, Barbara. 1997. *Saving Our Children from Poverty: What the United States Can Learn from France*. New York: Sage.

________.1981. "The Economic Risks of Being a Housewife." *American Economic Review* 7(2): 81-86.

Bowles, Samuel, and Herbert Gintis. 1998a. "The Evolution of Strong Reciprocity." Santa Fe Institute Working Paper #98-08-073E.

________. 1998b. "Is Equality Passe? Homo Reciprocans and the Future of Egalitarian Politics." *Boston Review*.

________.1998c."The Moral Economy of Community: Structured Populations and the Evolution of Prosocial Norms." *Evolution and Human Behavior* 19(1): 3-25

Brooks-Gunn, Jeanne. 1995. "Strategies for Altering the Outcomes of Poor Children and Their Families." Pp. 87-120 in *Escape from Poverty. What Makes a Difference for Children?* ed. P. Lindsay Chase-Lansdale and Jeanne Brooks-Gunn. New York: Cambridge University Press.

Brooks-Gunn, Jeanne, Greg J. Duncan, Pamela Kato Klebanov, Naomi Sealand. 1993. "Do Neighborhoods Influence Child and Adolescent Development?" *American Journal of Sociology* 99(2): 353-395.

Brouwer, Ina and Eelco Wiarda. 1998. "The Combination Model: Child Care and the Part Time Labour Supply of Men in the Dutch Welfare State?" In *Child Care and Female Labour Supply in the Netherlands: Facts, Analyses, Policies*, ed. J.J. Schippers, J.J. Siegers, J. De Jong-Gierveld. Amsterdam: Thesis Publishers

Bruyn-Hundt, Marga. 1996. "Scenarios for a Redistribution of Unpaid Work in the Netherlands." *Feminist Economics* 2(3): 129-133.

Buchanan, Patrick. 1998. *The Great Betrayal*. New York: Little, Brown and Company.

Burggraf, Shirley. 1993. "How Should the Cost of Child Rearing be Distributed?" *Challenge*, 37(5): 48-55.

________. 1997. *The Feminine Economy and Economic Man*. New York: Addison-Wesley.

Caldwell, John. 1982. *The Theory of Fertility Decline*. New York: Academic Press.

Chant, Sylvia. 1991. *Women and Survival in Mexican Cities: Perspectives on Gender, Labour Markets and Low-Income Households*. New York: Manchester University Press.

Chase-Lansdale, P. Lindsay, and Jeanne Brooks-Gunn, eds. 1995. *Escape from Poverty: What Makes a Difference for Children?* New York: Cambridge University Press.

Chase-Lansdale, P. Lindsay, Lauren S. Wakschlag, and Jeanne Brooks-Gunn. 1995. "A Psychological Perspective on the Development of Caring in Children and Youth: The Role of the Family." *Journal of Adolescence* 18:515-556.

Children's Defense Fund. 1994. *Wasting America's Future: The Children's Defense Fund Report on the Costs of Child Poverty*. Boston: Beacon Press.

Coleman, James. 1988. "Social Capital in the Creation of Human Capital." *American Journal of Sociology* 94 (Supplement): S95-S120.

Coltrane, Scott. 1998. "Fathers' Role at Home is Under Negotiation." *The Chronicle of Higher Education* (2 October).

________.1996. *Family Man*. New York: Oxford University Press.

Daly, Herman. 1997. *Beyond Growth: The Economics of Sustainable Development*. Boston: Beacon.

Daly, Martin, and Margo Wilson. 1983. *Sex, Evolution, and Behavior*. Belmont, CA: Wadsworth.

Demeny, Paul. 1987. "Re-Linking Fertility Behavior and Economic Security in Old Age: A Pronatalist Reform." *Population and Development Review* 13(1): 128-132.

de Waal, Frans. 1996. *Good Natured: The Origins of Right and Wrong in Humans and Other Animals*. Cambridge: Harvard University Press.

DiLeonardo, Micaela. 1987. "The Female World of Cards and Holidays. Women, Families, and the Work of Kinship." *Signs: Journal of Women in Culture and Society* 12(3): 440-53.

Duncan, Greg, and Jeanne Brooks-Gunn, eds. 1997. *Consequences of Growing Up Poor*. New York: Russell Sage Foundation.

Dwyer, Daisy, and Judith Bruce, eds. 1988. *A Home Divided: Women and Income in the Third World*. Stanford: Stanford University Press.

Elson, Diane. 1991. *Male Bias in the Development Process*. Manchester, U.K.: Manchester University Press.

________. 1992. "From Survival Strategies to Transformation Strategies: Women's Needs and Structural Adjustment." In *Unequal Burden: Economic Crises, Persistent Poverty, and Women's Work*, ed. Lourdes Benería and Shelly Feldman. Boulder, CO: Westview Press.

________.1997. "Economic Paradigms and Their Implications for Models of Development: The Case of Human Development." In *Global Governance and Development Fifty Years After Bretton Woods: Essays in Honour of Gerald K. Helleiner*, ed. R. Culpeper, A. Berry, F. Stewart.

Elster, Jon. 1989. *The Cement of Society: A Study of Social Order*. New York: Cambridge University Press.

England, Paula. 1992. *Comparable Worth: Theories and Evidence*. New York: Aldine de Gruyter.

England, Paula, and George Farkas. l986. *Households, Employment, and Gender: A Social, Economic, and Demographic View*. New York: Aldine Publishers.

England, Paula, and Nancy Folbre. 1997. "Reconceptualizing Human Capital." Paper presented at the Annual Meeting of the American Sociological Association.

________. 1998. "The Cost of Caring." *Annals of the American Academy of Political and Social Science*, forthcoming.

________. 1999. "Who Should Pay for the Kids?" *Annals of the American Academy of Political and Social Science*, forthcoming.

England, Paula, Melissa S. Herbert, Barbara Stanek Kilbourne, Lori L. Reid, and Lori McCreary Megdal. 1994. "The Gendered Valuation of Occupations and Skills: Earnings in 1980 Census Occupations." *Social Forces* 73(1): 65-100.

Ferguson, Ann. 1989. *Blood at the Root: Motherhood, Sexuality, and Male Dominance*. London: Pandora Press.

Fisher, Irving. 1907. *The Rate of Interest*. New York: Macmillan.

Floro, Maria. 1995a. "Women's Well-Being, Poverty, and Work Intensity." *Feminist Economics* 1(3): 1-25.

_______. 1995b. "Economic Restructuring, Gender, and the Allocation of Time." *World Development* 23(11): 1913-29.

Folbre, Nancy. 1985. "The Pauperization of Mothers: Patriarchy and Public Policy in the US." *Review of Radical Political Economics* 16(4):72-88.

_______. 1994a. *Who Pays for the Kids? Gender and the Structures of Constraint*. New York: Routledge.

_______.1994b. "Children as Public Goods." *American Economic Review* 84(2):86-90.

_______.1995. "Holding Hands at Midnight: The Paradox of Caring Labor." *Feminist Economics* 1(1):73-92.

_______. 1997a. "The Future of the Elephant Bird." *Population and Development Review* 23(3): 647-654.

Folbre, Nancy, and Thomas Weisskopf, 1998. "Did Father Know Best?: Families, Markets and the Supply of Caring Labor." In *Economics, Values and Organization*, ed. Avner Ben-Ner and Louis Putterman. Cambridge: Cambridge University Press.

Fox-Genovese, Elizabeth. 1991. *Feminism Without Illusions: A Critique of Individualism*. Chapel Hill: University of North Carolina Press.

Frank, Robert. l988. *Passions Within Reason: The Strategic Role of the Emotions*. New York: Norton.

Fraser, Nancy. 1994. "After the Family Wage: Gender Equity and the Welfare State." *Political Theory* 22(4):591-618.

Fuchs, Victor. 1988. *Women's Quest for Economic Equality*, Cambridge: Harvard University Press.

Fuchs, Victor, and Diane Reklis. 1992. "America's Children: Economic Perspectives and Policy Options." *Science* 255 (3 January): 5040.

Fukuyama, F. 1995. *Trust: The Social Values and the Creation of Prosperity*. New York: Free Press.

Gerstel, Naomi, and Sally Gallagher. 1994. "Caring for Kith and Kin: Gender, Employment, and the Privatization of Care." *Social Problems* 41(4): 519-539.

Gilligan, Carol. 1982. *In a Different Voice: Psychological Theory and Women's Development* Cambridge: Harvard University Press.

Goleman, Daniel. 1995. *Emotional Intelligence*. New York: Bantam.

Hamilton, W.D. 1963. "The Evolution of Altruistic Behavior." *American Naturalist* 97:354-356.

Haveman, Robert, and Barbara Wolfe. 1984. "Schooling and Economic Well-Being: The Role of Nonmarket Effects." *Journal of Human Resources* 19:378-407.

______. 1993. "Children's Prospects and Children's Policy." *Journal of Economic Perspectives* 7(4): 153-174.

_________. 1995. "The Determinants of Children's Attainments: A Review of Methods and Findings." *Journal of Economic Literature* 33 (December):1829-1878.

Hays, Sharon. 1996. *The Cultural Contradictions of Motherhood*. New Haven: Yale University Press.

Hochschild, Arlie. 1989. *The Second Shift*. New York: Viking.

_______. *The Time Bind*. 1997. New York: Henry Holt.

_______. 1998. "Ideals of Care: Traditional, Postmodem, Cold-Modem, and Warm-Modern." In *Families in the United States: Kinship and Domestic Politics*, ed. Karen V. Hansen and Anita Ilta Garey. Philadelphia: Temple University Press.

Hoddinott, John, Harold Alderman, and Lawrence Haddad, eds. 1998. *Intrahousehold Resource Allocation in Developing Countries: Methods, Models and Policy*. Baltimore: Johns Hopkins University Press.

Isis Research Group. 1998. "Caring for All Our Futures: Policy Recommendations for Establishing a National Child Care Strategy Based on Successful NOW-funded Models." Study conducted on behalf of the National Women's Council of Ireland, Centre for Women's Studies, Trinity College, Dublin.

Juster, F. Thomas, and Frank Stafford. 1991. "The Allocation of Time: Empirical Findings, Behavioral Models, and Problems of Measurement." *Journal of Economic Literature* 29 (June): 471-522.

Kabeer, Naila. 1994. *Reversed Realities: Gender Hierarchies in Development Thought*. New York: W.W. Norton.

________. 1992. "Beyond the Threshold: Intrahousehold Relations and Policy Perspectives." Paper prepared for the International Food Policy Research Institute/World Bank Conference on Intrahousehold Resource Allocation: Policy Issues and Research Methods, Washington, DC, 12-14 February.

Kilbourne, Barbara, Paula England, George Farkas, Kurt Beron, and Dorothea Weir. 1994. "Returns to Skill, Compensating Differentials and Gender Bias: Effects of Occupational Characteristics on the Wages of White Women and Men." *American Journal of Sociology* 100: 689-719.

Klebanov, Pamela Kato, Jeanne Brooks-Gunn, and Greg J. Duncan. 1994. "Does Neighborhood and Family Poverty Affect Mothers' Parenting, Mental Health and Social Support?" *Journal of Marriage and the Family* 56: 441-445.

Knack, S., and P. Keefer. 1995. "Institutions and Economic Performance: Cross-Country Tests Using Alternative Institutional Measures." *Economics and Politics* 7(3): 202-27.

________. 1996. "Does Social Capital Have an Economic Payoff?: A Cross-Country Investigation." Washington, DC: World Bank, Policy Research Department.

Kohn, Alfie. 1990. *The Brighter Side of Human Nature*. New York: Basic Books.

Kotlikoff, Laurence J. 1992. *Generational Accounting: Knowing Who Pays, and When, for What We Spend*. New York: The Free Press.

Koven, Seth, and Sonya Michel, eds. 1993. *Mothers of a New World: Maternalist Politics and the Origins of Welfare States*. New York: Routledge.

Kuttner, Robert. 1997. *Everything for Sale: The Virtues and Limits of Markets*. New York: Alfred Knopf.

Lee, Ronald D. 1990. "Population Policy and Externalities to Childbearing." *Annals of the American Academy of Political and Social Sciences* 510: 17-32.

Leira, Arnaud. 1994. "Concepts of Caring: Loving, Thinking, and Doing." *Social Service Review* 68(2): 185-201.

Loewenstein, George. 1997. "The Role of Emotions in Time Discounting." Research proposal to the MacArthur Research Network on Preferences.

Lommerud, Kjell Erik. 1997. "Battles of the Sexes: Non-Cooperative Games in the Theory of the Family." In *Economics of the Family and Family Policies*, ed. Inga Persson and Christina Jonung. New York: Routledge.

MacDonald, Kevin. 1995. "The Establishment and Maintenance of Socially Imposed Monogamy in Western Europe." *Politics and the Life Sciences* (February):3-23.

Miller, Dale T. and Rebecca K. Ratner. 1996. "The Power of the Myth of Self-Interest." Pp. 25-48 in *Current Social Concerns about Justice*, ed. Leo Montada and Melvin J. Lerner. New York: Plenum Press.

Monroe, Kristen Renwick. 1996. *The Heart of Altruism: Perceptions of a Common Humanity*. Princeton: Princeton University Press.

Moser, Caroline O.N. 1997. *Confronting Crisis: A Comparative Study of Household Responses to Poverty and Vulnerability in Four Poor Urban Communities*. Environmentally Sustainable Development Studies and Monographs Series No. 8. Washington D.C.: The World Bank.

________. 1992. "Adjustment from Below: Low-Income Women, Time, and the Triple Burden in Guayaquil, Ecuador." In *Women and Adjustment Policies in the Third World*, ed. H. Afshar and C. Dennis. New York: St. Martin's Press.

Nelson, Julie. 1993. "The Study of Choice or the Study of Provisioning? Gender and the Definition of Economics." Pp. 23-36 in *Beyond Economic Man*, ed. Marianne A. Ferber and Julie A. Nelson. Chicago: University of Chicago Press.

________. 1996. *Feminism, Objectivity, and Economics*. London: Routledge.

________. 1998. "For Love or Money or Both?" Manuscript, Department of Economics, Brandeis University, Waltham, MA.

Popenoe, David. 1996. *Life Without Father*. New York: The Free Press.

Preston, Samuel. 1984. "Children and the Elderly: Divergent Paths for America's Dependents." *Demography* 21: 435-57.

Putnam, Robert. 1993. "The Prosperous Community: Social Capital and Public Life." *American Prospect* 13: 35-42.

_______. 1995. "Bowling Alone: America's Declining Social Capital." *Journal of Democracy* 6(1): 65-78.

Putnam, Robert, with R. Leonardi and R. Nanetti. 1993. *Making Democracy Work: Civic Traditions in Modern Italy.* Princeton: Princeton University Press.

Quadagno, Jill. 1994. *The Color of Welfare: How Racism Undermined the War on Poverty*. New York: Oxford University Press.

Risman, Barbar J. 1987. "Intimate Relationships from a Microstructural Perspective: Men Who Mother." *Gender and Society* 1:6-32.

Rose-Ackerman, Susan. 1998. "Bribes and Gifts." In *Economics, Values and Organizations*, ed. Avner Ben-Ner and Louis Putterman. New York: Cambridge University Press.

Ruddick, Sara. 1983. "Maternal Thinking," Pp. 231-62 in *Mothering: Essays in Feminist Theory*, ed. Joyce Trebilcot.Totowa, NJ: Rowman and Allanheld.

Sapolsky, Robert M. 1998. *Why Zebras Don't Get Ulcers*. New York: W.H. Freeman and Company.

Schotter, Andrew. l981. *An Economic Theory of Social Institutions*. London: Cambridge University Press.

Sen, Amartya K. 1984. *Resources, Values and Development*. London: Blackwell.

_______. 1987. *On Ethics and Economics*. New York: Basil Blackwell.

_______.1990. "Gender and Cooperative Conflicts." Pp. 123-49 in *Persistent Inequalities: Women and World Development*. New York: Oxford University Press.

_______. 1993. "Capability and Well-Being." Pp. 30-53 in *The Quality of Life*, ed. Martha Nussbaum and Amartya Sen. Oxford: Clarendon Press.

_______. 1997. "Human Capital and Human Capability." *World Development*. Washington, DC: The World Bank.

Simon, Julian L. 1981. *The Ultimate Resource*. Princeton: Princeton University Press.

Skocpol, Theda. 1993. *Protecting Soldiers and Mothers: The Politics of Social Provision in the United States, 1870s-1920s*. Boston: Harvard University Press.

Sober, Elliot, and David Sloane Wilson. 1998. *Unto Others: The Evolution and Psychology of Unselfish Behavior*. Cambridge: Harvard University Press.

Stark, Oded. 1995. *Altruism and Beyond: An Economic Analysis of Transfers and Exchanges Within Families and Groups*. Cambridge: Cambridge University Press.

Tronto, Joan. 1987. "Beyond Gender Difference to a Theory of Care." *Signs: Journal of Women in Culture and Society* 12 (4): 644-63.

Ullmann-Margalit, Edna. l977. *The Emergence of Norms*. Oxford: Clarendon.

Ungerson, Clare. 1995. "Gender, Cash, and Informal Care: European Perspectives and Dilemmas." *Journal of Social Policy* 24(1): 31-52.

_______. 1997. "Social Politics and the Commodification of Care." *Social Politics* (Fall): 363-381.

Waerness, Kari. 1987. "On the Rationality of Caring." 207-34 in *Women and the State*, ed. A. S. Sassoon. London: Hutchinson.

Waldfogel, Jane. 1997. "The Effect of Children on Women's Wages." *American Sociological*

Review 62 (2): 209-217.

Ward, Deborah. 1993. "The Kin Care Trap: The Unpaid Labor of Long Term Care." *Socialist Review* 23(2): 83-106.

Weitzman, Lenore. 1985. *The Divorce Revolution: The Unexpected Social and Economic Consequences for Women and Children in America*. New York: The Free Press.

Wilkinson, Richard G. 1996. *Unhealthy Societies: The Afflictions of Inequality*. New York: Routledge.

Willis, Robert. 1982. "The Direction of Intergenerational Transfers and Demographic Transition: The Caldwell Hypothesis Reexamined." In *Income Distribution in the Family*, ed. Yoram Ben Porath. *Population and Development Review* 8 (Supplement):207-234.

Wilson, Edward O. 1978. *On Human Nature*. Cambridge: Harvard University Press.

Wolf, Douglas A. 1997. "Efficiency in the Allocation and Targeting of Community-Based Long-Term Care Resources." Syracuse, New York: Center for Policy Research, Syracuse University.

World Bank. 1997. *Expanding the Measure of Wealth. Indicators of Environmentally Sustainable Development.* Washington, D.C.: The World Bank.

Capital Flows: How To Curb Their Volatilities

S. Griffith-Jones with J. Kimmis

The deep integration of developing countries into the global economy has many advantages and positive effects. In particular, capital flows to developing countries have clear and important benefits. The benefits are especially clear for foreign direct investment, which is not only more stable but also brings technological know-how and access to markets. Other external flows also have important positive microeconomic effects, such as lowering the cost of capital for creditworthy firms. At a macroeconomic level, foreign capital flows can complement domestic savings, leading to higher investment and growth; this latter positive macroeconomic effect is very valuable for low-savings economies, but may be less clear for high-savings economies like those of East Asia.

However, large surges of short-term and potentially reversible capital flows to developing countries can also have very negative effects. Firstly, these surges pose complex policy dilemmas for macroeconomic management, as they can initially push key macroeconomic variables, such as exchange rates and prices of assets like property and shares, away from what could be considered their long-term equilibrium. Secondly, and more important, these flows pose the risk of very sharp reversals. These reversals—particularly if they lead to currency and financial crises—can result in very serious losses of output, investment and employment, as well as sharp increases in poverty. This has been dramatically illustrated by the impact of the current crisis in Asia, which has now spread to many other countries.

Asian-style currency crises—and their extremely high development costs—raise a very serious concern about the net development benefits for developing countries of large flows of potentially reversible short-term international capital. While the high costs of reversals of those flows are evident, the benefits are less clear. This is in sharp contrast with foreign direct investment (FDI) and trade flows, where the very large developmental benefits clearly outweigh the costs. As a result, volatile short-term capital flows emerge as a potential Achilles' heel for the globalised economy and for the market economy in developing countries. If the international community and national authorities do not learn to manage these flows better, there is a serious risk that such volatile flows could undermine the tremendous benefits that globalisation and free markets can otherwise bring.

Analysis of the East Asian Crisis

A year after the East Asian crisis started, its financial aspects have not yet been fully contained. Indeed other emerging economies—particularly in different regions—have increasingly been affected. Furthermore, the East Asian financial crisis has been transformed in the affected countries into a serious crisis in the real economy, with highly negative social and environmental effects, as well as problematic effects for political stability. The very rapid decline in output has implied the urgent need for policies to help reverse this decline, and restore growth.

It is noteworthy that the East Asian crisis itself, as well as its depth and length, had been almost totally unforeseen. The speed and extent of contagion was especially unexpected. It is therefore essential to understand both the causes that sparked off the East Asian crisis, as well as the causes that led to its deepening and spreading through contagion.

In examining the causes of the East Asian crisis, three key elements need to be noted. First, the roots of external imbalances were grounded in private sector deficits, as most East Asian economies were running budget surpluses. Second, the crisis was a consequence of over-investment (though some of it may have been misallocated, especially in the property and electronic sectors) and not of over-consumption. Third, an important cause of the crisis was a sharp deterioration in confidence throughout the region, spread through contagion effects, rather than significant changes in macroeconomic fundamentals, which were mostly strong. Indeed, the most disturbing element in the crisis was that it affected countries with long track records of good economic management that had been remarkably successful over extended periods, in terms of economic growth, dynamism of their export sectors, low rates of inflation and high rates of saving.

How were these economies suddenly shaken by such major currency and financial crises? Clearly there were serious problems in the countries themselves, including important weaknesses in their domestic financial systems and particularly in their banking systems, which were not appropriately regulated. There had been poor monitoring and regulation of short-term private debt, incurred both by banks and by corporate borrowers. Some mistakes also seem to have been made in the form in which the capital accounts were liberalised, as this was reportedly done in ways that particularly encouraged short-term flows. Furthermore, several of the East Asian countries had fixed exchange rate policies, with their currencies pegged to the US dollar; this policy became particularly problematic when the US dollar appreciated sharply vis-à-vis the Japanese yen.

There is another crucial causal factor, which relates more to the international dimension, and in particular to the behaviour of international capital flows. This aspect is linked to certain imperfections of international capital markets that have almost always featured in the financial panics of earlier times, but whose impact has increased significantly due to the speed with which markets, aided by highly sophisticated information technology, can react in today's global economy. Paradoxically, this impact appears to be strongest for economies that either are—or are perceived to be in the process of becoming—highly successful. In these situations, euphoria in international capital markets interacts perversely with complacency by governments in recipient countries.

Successful economies offer high returns by way of yields as well as capital gains. If international investors can find ways to enter these economies, or if their entrance is facilitated by capital account liberalisation, they tend to rush in, generating a surge of capital inflows that affects key economic variables. Exchange rates become over-valued; the prices of key assets—like shares or real estate—rise quickly and sharply. There is an increase in both real income and perceived wealth. Assuming that current trends will continue, banks tend to relax lending standards, lifting firms' liquidity constraints. The payments balance deteriorates, often quite rapidly, as both consumption and investment rise. Initially, this is not seen as a problem, as foreign lenders and investors are willing to continue lending/investing. Economic authorities delay necessary adjustment, confident that their previous success will be continued, and that crises happen elsewhere.

Then, something changes. The change may be domestic or international, economic or political, important or relatively small. This change triggers a sharp modification in perceptions, leading to a large fall in confidence in the economy among internationally mobile investors, including both foreign investors and nationals able to take their liquid assets out. The change of perception tends to be both large and quick. A country that was perceived as a successful economy or a successful reformer—for which no amount of praise was sufficient—suddenly is seen as fragile, risky and crisis-prone. The change of perception tends to be far larger than warranted by the magnitude of underlying change in fundamentals. Furthermore, any weakness in economic fundamentals is then discovered and magnified by markets. As in East Asia, there can be much overshooting. Exchange rates collapse; stock markets and property prices also fall sharply.

This pattern helps explain the currency and banking crises in the Southern Cone of Latin America in the early 1980s and the Mexican peso crisis. It also provides important elements to understand the 1997 East Asian crisis. There are significant differences between these crises and previous ones throughout the centuries, and amongst East Asian economies. But the boom-bust behaviour of short-term lenders and investors—driven not just by real trends, but by dramatic changes in perceptions—is a common denominator to these crises. So is the complacency of the economic authorities in recipient countries during the period of boom. The damage that can be done by sharp changes in capital flows is far larger when, as in East Asia, a high proportion of the inflows are short-term and easily reversible.

In the case of the East Asian crisis, the reversal of private capital flows has been quite dramatic. According to figures from the Institute of International Finance (IIF), the five East Asian countries hardest hit by the crisis (South Korea, Indonesia, Malaysia, Thailand and the Philippines) experienced in a single year a turnaround of US$105 billion—a shift from an inflow of US$93 billion in 1996 to an estimated outflow of US$12 billion in 1997, an outflow projected to continue in 1998. Most of this swing occurred in commercial bank lending, followed by short-term portfolio flows, whilst foreign direct investment remained constant. The turnaround of US$105 billion in the five Asian economies represents more than 10% of their combined gross domestic product (GDP); as a consequence, this shift is larger than the 8% shift that occurred in Latin America in the early 1980s.

Capital and financial markets are special, in that—though generally functioning well—they are prone to important imperfections. Asymmetric information and adverse selection play an important role in explaining these imperfections, as financial markets are particularly information-intensive. Furthermore, there are strong incentives for 'herding' in financial markets, as each individual short-term investor, lender or fund manager tries to choose the investment or loan that he/she thinks is most likely to be chosen by other investors or lenders. Herding seems strongly encouraged by the incentive systems (excessively short-term) with which financial market actors operate. Distortions are also caused by structures within private financial institutions, which give insufficient influence on decision-making to research departments concerned with analysis and risk assessment. Further investigation seems required on the 'microeconomics of speculation', by different categories of market actors. This could be helpful for designing measures, for example to be taken by the financial industry itself, to help inhibit excessive speculative behaviour, which would imply designing new systems of reward/punishment to help prevent crises.

The crises in Asia have had extremely negative economic and social effects on the worst affected countries. Indonesia's GDP is expected to fall by at least 15% in 1998, and the number of people living below the poverty line is expected to increase from 20 million to 80 million, reversing many years of successful poverty reduction. GDP in Thailand is expected to shrink by at least 8% in 1998. Other affected countries, like South Korea and Malaysia, will see somewhat smaller, but also very significant, declines in GDP, leading to sharp falls in employment and real incomes. Of particular concern is the fact that the poorer and more vulnerable groups in those countries will be the worst affected, even though they did not contribute to causing the problem. This is particularly unfair, given that those who caused the problem, are on the whole unaffected.

Also of relevance for understanding the East Asian crisis is the analysis of self-fulfilling attacks, that is crises arising without obvious current policy inconsistencies; in such cases, the attitude of speculators and investors is crucial to whether an attack occurs. The existence of self-fulfilling attacks and multiple equilibria for exchange rates, and for other key variables, implies that good macroeconomic fundamentals are a very important necessary but not sufficient condition for avoiding currency crises. There is at present limited understanding of what triggers self-fulfilling attacks. The main explanations given by market actors for different recent crises (e.g., the Mexican peso crisis, crises in different East Asian countries) tend to be rather different. As a result, developing country policymakers face the daunting task of 'playing to moving goal-posts', to avoid crises. However, there are conditions of vulnerability that can be identified (such as the ratio of short-term debt to foreign exchange reserves, or high current account deficits as a proportion of GDP). Further investigation is clearly required into conditions of vulnerability and the nature of triggering events, to be able to predict risk and, above all, improve prevention of currency crises.

Another important set of factors explaining the depth, length and geographical extension of the East Asian crisis relates to mistakes in the management of the Asian crisis; this partly reflects lack of experience with managing crises of this type. Capital account-led crises, which relate to expectations of private investors and lenders, may need different responses to traditional balance-of-payments crises, provoked by problems on the current account, and caused by public sector deficits. In the 'new style' of crisis, increasing confidence of private actors is absolutely central. In this new context, diagnosis and policy measures suggested by international institutions, which emphasise negative structural features of the crisis-hit countries and require sweeping structural reforms in short periods as a precondition for financial disbursements, may exacerbate crises to the extent that they further undermine confidence, rather than rebuilding it. This is particularly the case when such structural reforms are not central to stabilisation and crisis management. Furthermore, even necessary structural reforms may be unnecessarily costly to implement if done very fast and in the middle of a crisis.

A second problem has been that Asian—and other—countries initially tend to postpone as much as possible going to international institutions like the International Monetary Fund (IMF), partly because they fear that the IMF's required stabilisation measures will be too draconian and its structural adjustment requirements too intrusive. Countries come to the IMF only when the situation has already deteriorated sharply, and the margin of manoeuvre for policymaking has become very restricted; as a result, the IMF policy conditions on stabilisation are particularly draconian. Mutual recriminations follow, negotiations are long, and programmes are broken, which further undermines private sector confidence.

Clearly, new, more positive dynamics of interaction between crisis-prone countries and the IMF need to be urgently developed, and some suggestions are made below. Furthermore, policy conditionality—by the IMF and other institutions—needs to be designed primarily so as to restore confidence of both foreign and domestic actors. Though excessively loose monetary and fiscal policies would be counter-productive in this context, so are excessively tight monetary and fiscal policies, which will seriously undermine both confidence as well as economic activity and investment. A key objective in the design of macroeconomic policies also needs to be the protection of the most vulnerable and poorest groups of the society. Furthermore, it may be desirable that crisis management should be based on a two-tier approach, which implies first stabilising and then undertaking structural adjustment.

Another determinant of the protracted and deep nature of the East Asian crisis is the very weak evolution of the Japanese economy, which in 1998 deteriorated into recession, accompanied by a further sharp fall of the yen. Because Japan is such an important trading and investment partner for the East Asian countries, this negative evolution has been particularly damaging.

The Mexican and Asian Crises: A Comparative Analysis

The Mexican peso crisis of 1994-1995, and the international financial crisis which began in Asia in the summer of 1997, have raised important questions about the effects of increasing global economic integration, particularly on less developed countries, and the risks associated with fully free capital flows. This section will examine some of the key similarities and differences between these two major crises of the 1990s, both of which can be described as systemic: both have resulted in a sharp reduction or complete loss of access to international capital for the crisis countries; both have involved serious banking and currency crises in the affected countries; and both have set off a process of contagion, or spillover effects.

There are clearly important differences, as well as a number of striking similarities, between the Mexican crisis of 1994-95 and the international crisis that began in East Asia. Perhaps the most crucial difference has been in the length and depth of the crisis, and the extent of contagion. A full discussion of the reasons for this difference are beyond the confines of this paper, yet it is clear that the United States played a very important role in Mexico's more rapid recovery.[1] The US not only supported its partner in the North American Free Trade Agreement (NAFTA) with emergency financing, but its strong economy provided the market which allowed Mexico to export its way out of the crisis. The recession in Japan, together with the extent of contagion across Asia, have meant that this path out of crisis was not open to the East Asian economies.

On the nature of the crises, the Mexican peso crisis was one of over-consumption while the Asian crisis was one of over-investment. Moreover, while the Mexican crisis primarily involved a sovereign debtor and non-bank creditors, the Asian crisis has been mainly private sector debtors and bank creditors. However, the differentiation between sovereign and private sector debt crises can be over-emphasised, as loss of credibility appears to seep from one sector to the other. The Mexican private sector found it extremely difficult to access foreign capital immediately after the peso crisis. In Asia, the private sector crisis quickly spread to the public sector because the line between the two had been blurred by the explicit and implicit government guarantees to the private sector.

Examining some of the key similarities between the Mexican and Asian crises can highlight some common elements which further our understanding of how such crises arise. The broad areas of similarity identified below are: the international economic environment and emerging market countries' access to international capital, the surge of capital inflows to affected countries, and the sudden and deep nature of the market panic and capital reversals.

The global economic environment was favourable for emerging market countries wanting to access foreign capital throughout most of the 1990s, until the current crisis began. In industrialised countries, inflation rates were low and falling, there was a shortage of attractive investment opportunities, and interest rates were low. This encouraged investors to look to emerging markets for more exciting opportunities and higher yields. The 1990s also saw significant improvements in the terms and conditions under which emerging market economies could access international capital, principally because of economic policy reforms undertaken by many of these countries.

These factors, easy global liquidity and improved access to international capital, combined with newly liberalised emerging-market economies, helped create the conditions for a surge of capital inflows to many of these countries during the 1990s. Both the Mexican and Asian crises were preceded by large-scale capital inflows; private capital flows to emerging market economies reached US$155 billion in 1994, and a record US$304 billion in 1996. (In 1994, Latin America was receiving around 40% of these flows, while in 1996 Asia/Pacific was receiving over 50% of the total).[2]

It is in this sense that both these crises have been described as 'crises of economic success'. Mexico and East Asia, prior to difficulties that affected their economies, were 'victims' of a very positive perception by international markets; Mexico was the model reformer, the East Asian countries were 'tigers' that had built 'miracle economies'. The surge of capital inflows accompanying this positive perception presented problems of management for the receiving countries, with inflows magnifying existing domestic weaknesses (such as weak and inadequately supervised banking systems) and accentuating swings in the business cycle.

As Reisen (1998) has argued, factors often cited as causes of financial crises in emerging markets (such as large current account deficits, over-valued real exchange rates, over-investment, etc.) are actually the endogenous effects of massive capital inflows. In Asia, capital inflows were mainly channelled into short-term banking instruments while in Mexico they went into short-term government securities. In both cases, they led to a rapid accumulation of short-term foreign currency-denominated debt, which left the recipient countries extremely vulnerable to reversals of capital flows triggered by changing investor/creditor perceptions.

Both the Mexican peso crisis of 1994-95, and the crisis which began in East Asia in 1997, were largely unforeseen by market participants and governments. In the Mexican case, the year leading up to the peso devaluation in December 1994 had certainly seen political uncertainty and some market volatility, but there was no warning of the extent of the ensuing crisis. Similarly, in Asia, despite problems exhibited by some countries, no one could have anticipated the severity of the panic and crisis that hit the affected economies.

Despite the weaknesses that were undoubtedly present in both the Mexican economy and the economies of the East Asian crisis countries, neither crisis had to happen. In both cases, the countries were illiquid rather than insolvent. In Mexico, the devaluation of the peso caused panic among international investors, and the Mexican government was unable to roll over its short-term, dollar-denominated debts. In Asia, the devaluation in Thailand alerted markets to the high levels of short-term, foreign currency-denominated debt in some countries. This led to panic among international lenders and investors and a massive withdrawal of funds from Asian markets, which precipitated the crisis that they had feared.

Both crises also produced significant spillover effects. Contagion from the peso crisis sent shockwaves through Latin America and other emerging markets in the so-called 'tequila effect'. However, as pointed out above, the 'tequila effect' proved to be relatively short-lived and contained when compared with the contagion effect from the Asian crisis. The immediate effect of the devaluation of the Thai baht, in July 1997, was that significant pressure was placed on the currency and equity markets of other East Asian economies. However, the knock-on effects of the crisis which began in East Asia have been, and are continuing to be, felt around the world in an unprecedented case of contagion from emerging to more developed economies.

Lessons for Crisis Containment and Reversal, Future Crises Prevention and Better Crises Management

Within present arrangements, there is growing concern that the volatility and reversibility of some categories of capital flows, as dramatically illustrated by the East Asian crisis and their very negative effects, imply that the costs of these flows to countries' development may be higher than their benefits, at least during certain periods of time. As a consequence, there is growing consensus amongst leading policymakers—in developed and developing countries—and market actors that important changes need to be made urgently in the international monetary system as a whole and in recipient country policies, to avoid costly crises, or manage them better if they do occur. This will help limit the negative effects of volatile capital flows. Care must be taken, however, that the measures adopted contribute to broaden access by all developing countries to capital flows, particularly long-term ones. In this context, foreign direct investment is especially beneficial, as it contributes not only to a more stable source of capital flows, but also technological and managerial know-how as well as better access to markets.

It seems urgent to:

- Identify the possible changes required to achieve these aims;
- Evaluate carefully the potential economic effects of such changes and
- Adopt the required measures, including possible institutional developments where gaps exist for implementing such measures.

At the time of writing, the issue of better crisis containment and reversal was particularly urgent, due to the depth and width of the crises affecting East Asia, Russia and spreading into Latin America, and increasingly contributing to a slowing down of the developed economies. Especially important, in that respect, is that monetary authorities in the major developed countries (especially the US and Western Europe in the current context) are willing to relax monetary policy sufficiently and soon enough to help avoid widespread currency crises causing recessionary tendencies, not only in the affected countries, but also in the world economy.

In the measures outlined above, we can distinguish three levels:

a) measures that could be easily taken, within existing institutional arrangements. Two important examples are more expansionary monetary policy in the developed countries, which could be done by Central Banks of the US and Europe, and changes in the capital adequacy requirements for short-term and long-term lending (see below), which could be done in the context of the expanded Basel Committee.

b) measures requiring some development, expansion and adaptation of existing institutions, such as the IMF or the regulatory committees that meet under the aegis of the Bank for International Settlements (BIS). Examples would be new facilities within the IMF or adaptation of existing ones, to cope with capital account-caused currency crises (see below); another example would be filling international regulatory gaps, to include regulation of mutual funds and hedge funds, both nationally and their international co-ordination (see below).

c) measures requiring more institutional radicalism, in the sense of creating new institutions or drastically adapting existing ones. Though this is clearly desirable from the perspective of having institutions and mechanisms designed for the new needs of a globalised private financial system, it is significantly more difficult to achieve; the key problem is that new global institutions are needed to manage effectively a globalised private financial system, but there is no global government to create them, and the political process for national governments to create global institutions could be complex and slow. However, it seems, at the very least, highly desirable to develop a clear vision of an appropriate new international financial architecture that would allow an orderly global financial market to support the development process, and would avoid developmentally and financially costly crises like the current one. Such a vision should inform current debates on a new financial architecture.

In this context, there are three essential functions of global financial market management that are currently not properly met, and would best be met, at least in part, by new institutional developments. We sketch them out here, but discuss them in more detail below.

1. Firstly, the provision of appropriate surveillance and prudential regulation of financial intermediaries, in developed and developing countries, as well as globally. This could best be done by a World Financial Authority or World Financial Organisation.

2. The provision of international official liquidity to countries or financial markets, including in particular last-resort lending in distress conditions caused by currency crises originating in capital account problems. This could be done by existing international institutions (like the IMF and the BIS, with co-financing from the private sector), but with an important change to the concept of conditionality, and the timing of these facilities.

3. The provision of emergency standstill and orderly debt workout procedures that would allow suspension of payments during times of crisis without triggering default, and debt reduction where solvency problems exist, again without triggering default. Again here an optional institutional arrangement would require some new institutional developments; some of these, like the creation of an international bankruptcy court to apply an international chapter 11 may not be too feasible. However, an alternative procedure, suggested in the 1998 *Trade and Development Report* (produced by UNCTAD, the United Nations Conference on Trade and Development) could be more feasible. As discussed below, this would imply establishing an independent panel to determine whether the country concerned is justified in imposing exchange restrictions with the effect of debt standstills, in the context of the IMF Articles of Agreement.

In the areas of crises prevention, better crises management and containment as well as reversal, changes are required, both nationally and internationally. Both national and international aspects involve public and private actors (Table 1 provides a matrix of the categories of actions required and the actors that need to be involved).

TABLE 1

Actors	Capital-receiving Countries		Capital-supplying Countries		International Financial Institutions (IFIs)		
Types of Measures	Authorities	Markets	Authorities	Markets	IMF	BIS	IBRD*
Crisis Prevention	Restrict short-term inflows Improve prudential regulation and strengthen domestic financial sector Liberalise more carefully	Develop equity and forward markets Avoid uncovered foreign currency debt exposure	Risk weighted cash requirements on foreign investments for institutional investors Avoid regulatory bias towards short-term lending	Use available information more efficiently	Last-resort lending	Extend international regulation and supervision of bank loans and portfolio flows to emerging markets	
Better Crisis Management	Use interest rates policies with care Allocate rescue package to protect the poorest first	Participate in burden-sharing		Participate in burden-sharing	Make funds available faster Promote market confidence through conditionality Allow for orderly debt workouts		Contain the social impact of crises

*International Bank for Reconstruction and Development

A. Crisis prevention

As crises are so costly, particularly to developing countries, but also to the international financial community, utmost priority needs to be given to crisis prevention measures. *As in medicine, so in finance, prevention is much kinder, more efficient and cost-effective than cure.*

1. *Issues currently discussed*

A number of proposals aimed at preventing crises are currently being discussed in the international community. In response to the Asian crisis the G-22, which is composed of the G-7 countries and a range of emerging economies, was established with working groups looking at three areas: (i) Enhancing Transparency and Disclosure of Information; (ii) Strengthening Financial Systems, in National Economies and Globally; (iii) Appropriate Burden-sharing in International Financial Crises. This section will briefly discuss the first two areas, while the third will be discussed in the section on crisis management.

a) Enhancing Transparency and Disclosure of Information

The Asian crisis has provoked calls for improvements to information disclosure and data dissemination. Gaps in information certainly played a part in the genesis of the Asian crisis. However, it is equally important that the available information is used and analysed effectively. Markets and ratings agencies were initially slow to respond to certain danger signals in Asian economies and then overreacted once the crisis broke.

Firstly, it is important to establish how information could best be generated. In order to encourage transparency in emerging market economies it was proposed at the 1998 Spring meeting of the IMF and the World Bank that the Fund could delay the completion of its annual Article IV health check of a country's economy if it is not satisfied with the information being disclosed.

Secondly, there is the question of how increased transparency can improve the effectiveness of IMF and other bodies' (including regional ones) surveillance. In the aftermath of the peso crisis the Fund established the Special Data Dissemination Standard (SDDS) and the Dissemination Standard Bulletin Board (DSBB) on the IMF website. The IMF is currently looking at ways in which the SDDS could be broadened and strengthened. Though improved information on countries is useful, insufficient information clearly was not the main cause of the crisis, which was induced far more by the herd behaviour of lenders and investors, as they based their decisions on what they perceived 'the market' believed, rather than on a systematic analysis of economic fundamentals. Therefore, improved information is necessary, but clearly not sufficient, for crisis avoidance.

Furthermore, while the focus of the current call for improved transparency and surveillance is at the recipient country level, it is clear that there is also a need for better surveillance of the international financial markets; countries' efforts at improving financial market intelligence should be backed by support in this field by institutions like the BIS and the IMF. Particular help is required to understand fully the risks of some off-balance sheet instruments, like certain derivatives transactions, and the actions of large players, both of which can destabilise currency markets. During interviews carried out at the BIS, there was important support for the idea that the BIS could provide more analysis and information on international banking and market developments to developing country policymakers. This could include both analysis of structural changes in international markets, as well as timely information on recent trends. This would consist both of improvements and broadening in existing data gathering, and of systematically centralising very current information provided by different central banks (of developed and developing countries) and market actors, and making it accessible very rapidly to the economic authorities of developing countries. This could provide 'early warnings' to developing countries about changing perceptions in international markets and banks (not just as regards their own countries, but also towards other emerging countries), and thus facilitate early preventive policy measures to avoid crises. As identified in the October 1998 Ottawa Statement by Commonwealth Finance Ministers, priority areas for improved information would include greater disclosure of the activities of currency traders and hedge funds, given gaps in information there and the role they play in influencing currency and asset price movements in developing countries, often with large negative effects on growth and levels of employment and poverty.

b) Financial System Strengthening and Capital Account Liberalisation

The Asian crisis has highlighted the importance of strong financial systems in maintaining the stability of national economies, and international currency and capital markets. One of the working groups of the G-22, the ad hoc group of developing and industrialised countries assembled by the US to look at issues arising from the international crisis, looked at the strengthening of financial systems. The report emerging from the G-22 working group noted that the key to strengthening domestic financial systems was the implementation of sound practices, aided by close international co-operation.

International consensus has already been reached on what constitutes sound practices in many areas of banking supervision and securities regulation. The Basel Committee on Banking Supervision has produced the 'Core Principles for Effective Banking Supervision' and the International Organisation of Securities Commissions (IOSCO) has produced similar guidelines for the securities industry. However, the G-22 report also drew attention to a number of areas, including corporate governance, risk management, and safety net arrangements, where standards for sound practices need to be developed.

The G-22 report states that the implementation of sound practices is best achieved through market-based incentives, combined with official sector actions. The report sets out a number of mechanisms which can be employed to promote implementation including clear regulatory tools, such as the Basel Capital Accord, and oversight mechanisms, such as conditionality, surveillance, peer review, and technical assistance programmes. The G-22 report emphasises the importance of co-operation and co-ordination among national supervisors and regulators, as well as among international groups. Proposals to enhance co-operation on the international financial system are discussed below.

Turning to capital account liberalisation, it is clear that this should be carried out in a very careful and gradual way. There are a number of minimum standard pre-conditions that should be met by any country in the process of liberalising the capital account. These include: a sound macroeconomic policy framework; reforms to the financial system including adequate regulatory and supervisory arrangements; a phased opening of the capital account, taking account of the country's macroeconomic situation and the state of domestic reforms; and timely and accurate information disclosure. Recent events in Asia have confirmed the conventional wisdom that long-term flows should be liberalised first, and short-term flows should be liberalised last.

However, while more prudent capital account liberalisation in developing countries may be appropriate under certain conditions, the crisis in Asia has highlighted the problems that can result when fragile economies open their capital accounts. In this context, it is important that countries maintain the necessary flexibility to manage capital inflows according to the macroeconomic conditions they face, both at home and abroad. More broadly, a very careful assessment of the costs and benefits of capital account liberalisation needs to be undertaken before further liberalisation is carried out. It therefore follows that the proposed amendment to the IMF's Articles, which would give the Fund jurisdiction over the liberalisation of capital movements, would not be appropriate at the present time.

2. *Additional Issues For Crisis Prevention*

a) Capital-receiving countries

Though much of the focus of this study relates to changes in international financial arrangements, appropriate policies of capital-receiving countries clearly are also of great importance. An important part of the responsibility for discouraging excessive reversible inflows lies with recipient economics.

It is in the period of excessive surges of capital inflows that recipient countries have greater degrees of freedom for policymaking. The role of counter-cyclical monetary and fiscal policies is essential, to reduce excessive growth of domestic absorption and/or current account deficits. Recent experience and the literature indicate that a tightening of macroeconomic policies is particularly desirable when indicators of vulnerability to currency crisis start to deteriorate quickly or pass certain thresholds. This includes when current account deficits start to grow rapidly and exceed 4% of GDP, when the proportion of capital flows which are easily reversible in total flows is high and rising and, particularly, when short-term external liabilities grow rapidly and start approaching the same level or even exceed foreign exchange reserves. Thus, high levels of foreign exchange reserves and limits on the level of short-term external liabilities are crucial for avoiding currency crises.

An appropriate exchange rate regime is also essential for relatively small open economies, so as to make them less vulnerable to currency attacks. Though this is a complex issue, and the choice of the exchange rate regime should be linked to the country's specific circumstances, international evidence seems to show that exchange rate regimes featuring wide bands—with a possible crawling peg element—offer a good combination of flexibility with some desirable guidance to the market and anchor for monetary policy. Fixed exchange rates—though they have some advantages—offer apparently secure yields to very short-term investors, leading to surges of such inflows and can create fixed goalposts for hedge funds and others to attack, when the situation deteriorates. Furthermore, if domestic inflation exceeds international inflation, fixed exchange rates can lead to over-valuation, which encourages domestic corporations to borrow abroad.

A counter-cyclical approach should also be applied to supervision and regulation of the financial system, and particularly the banking system. In boom times, supervision and regulation of banks—as well as credit decisions by banks themselves—should not be based just on expectations of a continued growth scenario among borrowers. Potential downside risks, including if capital flows slow down or are reversed—and the economy slows down—need to be considered both in credit decisions and in supervisory evaluations of loans. This counter-cyclical approach would moderate booms of domestic bank lending which often exacerbate the impact of excessive surges of capital inflows.

Where these surges of potentially reversible capital are excessive, it may also be appropriate for recipient countries to take measures to discourage them temporarily. Indeed, some countries (e.g., Chile and Colombia) have implemented measures (such as taxes and non-remunerated reserve requirements on flows during a fixed period) with this objective. Their aim has been threefold: a) change the structure of capital inflows, to decrease the share of short-term and potentially reversible flows, by discouraging them. The lower level of short-term flows makes the country less vulnerable to currency crisis; b) increase the autonomy of domestic monetary policy; and c) help curb large over-valuation of the exchange rate.

There is growing evidence that measures to discourage excessive inflows—in Chile, Colombia and other countries—have contributed to relatively more successful management of capital inflows. Two attractive features of Chilean-style measures may be noted: a) they are market-based, rather than quantitative, and b) they apply to practically all short-term flows, thus simplifying administrative procedures and reducing (though not eliminating) possibilities of evasion. Other domestic measures can be useful to discourage excessive short-term borrowing, such as modifying withholding tax on companies' 'external' borrowing.

The major international financial institutions now explicitly recognise that—though having some limitations and minor microeconomic disadvantages—market measures taken by recipient governments to discourage excessive short-term capital flows can play a positive role, if they are part of a package of policy measures including sound macroeconomic fundamentals as well as a strong and well-regulated domestic financial system.

b) International measures

(i) Towards a world financial authority

Clearly an important part of the responsibility for discouraging excessive reversible inflows—as well as managing them—lies with the recipient countries. However, the large scale of international funds—compared to the small size of developing country markets—leads us to question whether measures to discourage excessive short-term capital inflows by recipient countries are enough to deal with capital surges and the risk of their reversal. Three strong reasons make complementary action by source countries and internationally necessary. Firstly, not all major recipient countries will be willing to discourage short-term capital inflows, and some may even encourage them. For instance, the tax and regulatory measures taken to encourage the Bangkok International Banking Facility, encouraged short-term borrowing. Secondly, even those recipient countries that have deployed a battery of measures to discourage short-term capital inflows have on occasions found these measures insufficient to stem very massive inflows. Thirdly, major emerging countries experiencing attacks on their currencies may find it difficult to service their debt, forcing them to seek large official funding. Thus, there is a clear need for international and/or source country regulation that will discourage excessive reversible capital inflows. If this is not developed, international private investors and creditors might continue to assume excessive risks, in the knowledge that they will be bailed out if the situation becomes critical. This is the classical problem of moral hazard.

A key issue arises here about how improvement and completion of global regulation should be carried out. A first approach, which we will develop more below, is to complete and improve national and global prudential supervision and regulation, basically using or developing existing institutional arrangements, such as the Basel Committee. A second, institutionally more radical approach, would be to create, for this purpose, a new international body—which could be called a World Financial Authority (Eatwell and Taylor 1998) or a Board of Overseers of Major International Institutions and Markets (Kaufman 1992). Such a body would have wide-ranging powers for global oversight and regulation, based for example on suitably defined risk-weighted capital or cash requirements on commercial banking, securities business and insurance. It would thus integrate and make compatible regulation between different financial sectors (to take account of growing integration in the markets of banking, securities and insurance, for example through financial conglomerates) and integrate regulation globally (to take account of the global nature of these markets). Though very desirable, as it would correspond to the new needs of the global economy, such an institution would be complex to establish, and it may be difficult to achieve international agreement, particularly if it required an international treaty to be approved by national Parliaments.

However, a very positive intermediate step that seems far more feasible to implement has been proposed by Gordon Brown and Clare Short in the October 1998 Development Committee, and reportedly is being further studied by the Governor of the German Central Bank, Hans Tietmeyer. The proposal is for 'a new and permanent Standing Committee for Global Financial Regulation, which would bring together not only the World Bank and the IMF, but also the Basel Committee and other regulatory groupings on a regular—perhaps monthly—basis.... The Committee would be charged with developing and implementing a mechanism to ensure that the necessary international standards for financial regulation and supervision are put in place and properly co-ordinated.'

Indeed, the infrastructure for such a Standing Committee, which could later evolve into a World Financial Authority, already exists, based on the advances for agreed co-ordination of regulation of the BIS—particularly in the context of the Basel Committee—and the co-operative work in the context of IOSCO (the International Organisation for Securities Commissions). What is needed is to deepen the co-operative framework developed, give it significantly greater powers, broaden the representation of developing countries in it, and—above all—fill regulatory gaps. It is to these regulatory gaps that we now turn.

(ii) Filling regulatory gaps

There are three categories of flows and institutions to emerging markets where additional international and/or source country regulation and supervision may be particularly necessary, as these flows seem insufficiently regulated and their surges, as well as outflows, have played a particularly prominent role in sparking off recent currency crisis; the latter would seem to occur particularly because they are reversible. One of these are short-term bank loans (particularly important in the Asian crisis); the second are easily reversible portfolio flows, made by institutional investors, such as hedge funds (especially important in the Mexican peso crisis but also important in East Asia); the third are activities by hedge funds, relating in particular to different types of derivatives.

International bank loans (including short-term loans) are already regulated by industrial countries' Central Banks; these national regulations are co-ordinated by the Basel Committee. However, existing regulations were not enough to discourage excessive short-term bank lending to several of the East Asian countries. A key reason was that, until just before the crisis, most of these East Asian countries (and particularly countries like South Korea) were seen by everybody, including regulators, as creditworthy. Another, important reason seems to have been current regulatory practice. For example, for non-OECD countries, loans of residual maturity of up to one year have a weighting of only 20% for capital adequacy purposes, whilst loans over one year have a weighting of 100% for capital adequacy purposes. This was done to reflect the fact that is easier for individual banks to pull out from renewing short-term loans. However, as a result of this rule, short-term lending is more profitable for international banks. Therefore, added to banks' economic preference for lending short-term, especially in situations of perceived increased risk, is a regulatory bias that also encourages short-term lending. An overall increase in short-term loans, however, makes countries more vulnerable to currency crises and paradoxically, makes banks more vulnerable as well, to risk of non-payment. The issue needs to be rapidly examined, therefore, whether the weighting differential for capital adequacy is too large in favour of short-term loans for non-OECD countries, resulting in excessive incentives for short-term lending. A narrowing of this differential may therefore be desirable.

As regards portfolio flows to emerging markets, there is an important regulatory gap, as at present there is no international regulatory framework, for taking account of market or credit risks on flows originating in institutional investors, such as mutual funds (and more broadly for flows originating in non-bank institutions). This important regulatory gap needs to be filled, both to protect retail investors in developed countries and developing countries from the negative effects of excessively large and potentially volatile portfolio flows (Griffith-Jones 1998).

However, the East Asian crisis confirms what was already clearly visible in the Mexican peso crisis. Given the very liquid nature of their investments, institutional investors, like mutual funds, can play an important role in contributing to currency crises. It seems important, therefore, to introduce some regulation to discourage excessive surges of portfolio flows. This could perhaps best be achieved by a variable risk-weighted cash requirement for institutional investors, such as mutual funds. These cash requirements would be placed as interest-bearing deposits in commercial banks. Introducing a dynamic risk-weighted cash requirement for mutual funds (and perhaps other institutional investors) is in the mainstream of current regulatory thinking, and would require that standards be provided by relevant regulatory authorities or agreed internationally. The guidelines for macroeconomic risk, which would determine the cash requirement, would take into account such vulnerability variables as the ratio of a country's current account deficit (or surplus) to GDP, the level of its short-term external liabilities to foreign exchange reserves, the fragility of the banking system, as well as other relevant country risk factors. It is important that quite sophisticated analysis is used, to avoid simplistic criteria stigmatising countries unnecessarily. The views of the national Central Bank and the Treasury in the source countries and of the IMF and the BIS should be helpful in this respect. The securities regulators in source countries would be the most appropriate institutions to implement such regulations, which could be co-ordinated internationally by IOSCO.

The fact that the level of required cash reserves would vary with the level of countries' perceived 'macroeconomic risk' would make it relatively more profitable to invest in countries with good fundamentals, and relatively less profitable to invest in countries with more problematic macroeconomic or financial sector fundamentals. If these fundamentals deteriorate, investment would decline gradually, which hopefully would force an early correction of policy, and a resumption of flows. Though the requirement for cash reserves on mutual funds' assets invested in emerging markets could increase somewhat the cost of raising foreign capital, this would be compensated by the benefit of a more stable supply of funds, at a more stable cost. Furthermore, this smoothing of flows would hopefully discourage the massive and sudden reversal of flows that sparked off both the Mexican and the Asian crises, making such developmentally costly crises less likely.

Given the dominant role and rapid growth of institutional investors in countries such as the US, the UK and France, this proposal—for a risk-weighted cash requirement on mutual funds—could be adopted first in those countries, without creating significant competitive disadvantages. However, once implemented in that type of country, efforts to harmonise such measures internationally would need to be given urgent priority for global discussions at IOSCO, so as to prevent investments by mutual funds being channelled through other countries, and especially off-shore centres, that did not impose these cash requirements (the latter point draws on communication with the Federal Reserve Board).

Such IOSCO international guidelines would be formulated through international consultations similar to those employed by the Basel Committee in developing the 'Core Principles for Effective Banking Supervision'. The guidelines could be developed by a working group consisting of representatives of the national securities' regulatory authorities in source countries, together with some representation from developing countries, in the context of IOSCO. Due account should be taken of relevant existing regulations, such as the European Commission's Capital Adequacy Directive.

Finally, it is important to stress that additional regulation of mutual funds should be consistent with regulation of other institutions (e.g., banks) and other potentially volatile flows.

Further urgent study is required to detect and cover any other existing monitoring and/or regulatory gaps, e.g., as relates to instruments (such as derivatives) and institutions (such as hedge funds). Careful analysis—both technical and institutional—is required on how hedge funds can best be regulated to reduce their impact on magnifying volatility of capital flows, exchange rates and stock markets in developing countries, and the negative effect that this volatility has on development and on poverty. One avenue is to regulate hedge funds directly; another is to regulate bank lending to hedge funds, as this could limit their ability to leverage their assets to such a large extent.

More generally, further work is required to gain a better understanding of recent changes in global credit and capital markets, and—more specifically—of the criteria used by different categories of market actors—including banks, mutual funds, hedge funds and others—to go in and out of countries. What are the incentives that encourage particular patterns of market actors' behaviour, contributing to speculative pressures on individual countries and to contagion to other countries? A better understanding of behavioural patterns and of trends in outflows would contribute to designing measures—to be taken by individual firms, by parts of the financial industry via self-regulation, by regulators and/or by governments (e.g., via tax measures)—to discourage market imperfections, like disaster myopia and herding, that contribute to currency crises.

It can be concluded that a package of measures needs to be adopted to make currency crises in emerging markets far less likely, and therefore ensure the efficient operation of the economy in emerging markets, which should be a basis for sustained development. The objective of crises avoidance seems to require some discouragement and/or regulation of excessive and potentially unsustainable short-term inflows. Such measures would be most effective 1) if they are applied both by source and recipient countries (though the main responsibility lies with recipient countries); 2) if these measures avoid discouraging more long-term flows—which on the contrary need to be encouraged; 3) if the rules designed are simple and clearly targeted at unsustainable flows; and, particularly 4) if they are complemented by good policies in the emerging economies.

B. CRISIS MANAGEMENT

Though prevention is far better than cure, if prevention fails and major currency crises do unfortunately occur, measures need to be in place to manage them as well as possible. Thus, measures for better crisis management—both nationally and internationally—are clearly complementary with measures for crisis prevention.

1. National measures

Once a currency crisis explodes, the domestic policy options are very narrow, and the trade-offs very problematic. The standard response required by the markets, includes sharp increases in interest rates and significant fiscal tightening, the latter even in countries with fiscal surpluses.

Rapid sharp rises in interest rates have been quite effective in some, but not in all, cases for preventing large currency depreciations. Interest rate increases seem to have been most effective when they are timely, sharp and temporary, and when other measures (e.g., fiscal ones) are taken simultaneously or were previously in place. The effect of increased interest rates depends on whether or not the increase restores confidence. If interest rates remain high for a significant period, they have very damaging and undesirable effects due to their recessionary impact on the real economy. This may contribute to second-round negative effects on exchange rates. Further work is required to understand the effect of increased interest rates on investor confidence during and after currency attacks, to clarify what the best monetary policy is in this context, and whether complementary or alternative policies to increasing interest rates could be adopted. Account also needs to be taken of the specific features of individual economies, including the high debt-to-equity ratios in East Asian companies. This high leverage implies that increases in interest rates in East Asia were more likely to lead to companies' insolvency than in other regions; as a consequence, the transmission mechanism of contagion between the financial sector to the real economy was greater in East Asia than in Latin America or Russia. As regards fiscal tightening, it seems important to evaluate its relevance in contexts when budget deficits are not large, or there are even budget surpluses.

2. International measures

a) Sufficient liquidity

(i) Improved and enhanced role for the IMF

The first response internationally when a large currency crisis starts unfolding in one or more countries is to activate quickly a sufficiently large financing package to provide stability, an important public good. The key institution in this has been, and is likely to continue to be in the short to medium-term, the International Monetary Fund, through its own resources and its catalytic role in attracting other resources, both public and private. In this context, it is a positive development that the IMF itself was given more resources, through an expansion of its quotas. Given the large scale of the resources required—and the limitation of IMF resources, even if those are expanded—complementary avenues for sufficient provision of early liquidity need to be explored. One possible modality is via enhanced central bank co-operative arrangements, through greatly enlarged swap arrangements, both within regions as well as particularly between G-10 members and non-members. Another possible avenue is via pre-committed stand-by arrangements with private banks, as Argentina and Mexico have recently done; however, these latter arrangements are still untested, and it is unclear how well they would operate in a severe crisis. The BIS could play an important role in co-ordinating the provision of liquidity by G-10 Central Banks and private banks (as discussed below). The problem is a crucial one: to be effective for restoring confidence, the liquidity provided needs to be large. It is important that in facing currency crises, an appropriate combination of adjustment, financing and, if necessary, debt workouts be adopted (for the latter, see below). Also, an appropriate combination of resources—provided for stabilisation by the IMF and for dealing with social effects of crisis by the World Bank—needs to be achieved.

A number of issues arise relating to the IMF's role of providing liquidity. Besides the crucial issue just discussed—of scale of resources—other issues include timing, conditionality and ways to avoid moral hazard.

The issue of timing is important, as currency crises happen so quickly. Though the IMF and the international financial community have made important efforts to develop emergency procedures to speed up significantly response to currency crises, the response is still not fast enough. A currency crisis may unfold for a couple of weeks before a financing package can be put in place. As markets move so fast and overreact, a great deal of damage can occur in that period, and due to contagion, the crisis can spread rapidly to other countries. A solution worth considering is to have increasing recourse to IMF-supported preventive programmes. This implies that a request for a country's right to borrow from the IMF could be made before a crisis happens, for example during the country's Article IV consultations. The country would only draw on this facility if a crisis occurred, but could do so immediately. This would imply that the Fund would have a 'shadow programme' with the country, including policy conditions that would make a currency crisis less likely; these would naturally be less stringent than would be called for in a crisis. Hopefully, the adoption of these measures would make the currency crisis less likely. However, if a currency crisis still occurred in a country that had such a 'shadow programme' with the IMF, there would be no further conditionality for immediate disbursement. This would be particularly appropriate as the crisis would have occurred in spite of the country following appropriate policies, as defined by the IMF; the crisis would be due to external factors, such as pure contagion in international capital markets.

An additional serious problem, particularly relevant for low-income countries, is that when such large volumes of IMF—as well as World Bank and regional development bank—funding is channelled towards middle-income countries in crisis, funding available from those institutions for low-income countries can fall drastically. Another related issue deserves enhanced attention. For example, how will the system respond to financial crises, including those originating within the private sector, in small and poor countries? Sharp reversals in private capital flows have already created serious instability in some low-income countries. It is important that official support from the IMF and others should also be provided to 'less important' countries in the same way as it is provided to 'systemic threats' when they face identical difficulties.

Two types of measures can help alleviate the pressure on the IMF to provide international liquidity. The first is to reduce the likelihood of currency crises, with preventive measures along the lines discussed above, which will limit moral hazard. The second is to attempt to have more equitable burden sharing between public and private contributions. This makes it very important to develop orderly workout procedures, which will reduce the required scale for international lending (see section b, below).

A final issue is the nature of IMF conditionality that should accompany the large financial packages linked to currency crises. A number of relevant criticisms have arisen of IMF conditionality in East Asia. Radelet and Sachs (1998) have argued that some of the IMF conditionality (e.g., on bank closures, excessive tightening of fiscal policy) not only were inappropriate, but actually added to, rather than ameliorated, panic in international financial markets. Furthermore, Feldstein (1998) has argued that IMF conditionality has been too intrusive and too comprehensive, trying to make dramatic changes in short periods. It is therefore, crucial that *IMF conditionality contributes to rebuild, and not undermine, markets' confidence in countries*. Also, as far as possible, IMF conditionality should focus on macroeconomic policies, and not be too intrusive and comprehensive. Only where more structural reforms are essential for building confidence, and can be effectively implemented in the short run, should they be included as part of policy conditionality. Other structural reforms could be undertaken later, once stabilisation had been achieved and growth restored.

(ii) Towards an international lender of last resort

As discussed above, global capital markets can be inherently unstable, at least under conditions of stress. To diminish their instability, as well as its serious negative impact on countries' growth and development, it would be highly desirable that significant improvements in global regulation be accompanied with steps towards the creation of an international lender of last resort. Just as the growth of domestic banking in the last century created the need for central banks to act as national lenders of last resort (to prevent frequent crises and their negative effects on output and employment), so at the end of the twentieth century the rapid growth of global credit and capital markets and their extreme volatility poses the urgent need to develop steps towards an international lender of last resort. This would play an essential role in helping to avoid currency and financial crises in individual developing countries, but would play a particularly valuable role in helping avoid the contagion of such crises, due to panic, to other countries, and therefore the highly negative cumulative effects on growth and development that widespread currency and financial crises can have.

To be able to stop the rise and spread of panic, a lender of last resort must have the discretion to create any level of necessary liquidity. At a national level, this has implied that central banks are the institutions that play this role, by providing as much liquidity as they consider necessary to private financial institutions—and especially banks—in trouble.

At an international level, there is at present no global institution that performs such a function, nor is such liquidity available internationally. National financial institutions have on occasion played bilaterally the role of an international lender of last resort, as in the 1992 German Central Bank support for the French franc during the European Exchange Rate Mechanism crisis, and in the 1995 US Treasury support to the Mexican government during the peso crisis. The IMF has increasingly become the main source of support to developing countries experiencing currency crises. However, the IMF—under its current mandate—is not a genuine international lender of last resort for several reasons. Firstly, and most important, the IMF cannot at present create unlimited liquidity. Secondly, the IMF lends to governments, linked to conditionality; an international lender of last resort would provide liquidity to countries in distress, at higher cost but without conditions.

As a consequence if a new international financial architecture were to be designed, as is highly desirable, two separate institutional mechanisms could be envisaged. One would be an expanded and improved IMF, along the lines discussed above. The other would be a complementary facility for unconditional official lending. At a later stage, when a global central bank develops, it could become institutionalised. In the meantime it could be based on G-10 Central Bank facilities, possibly combined with private sector lending. The BIS, which is and should play an increasing role in global financial regulation, would also be very well placed to play a key co-ordinating role for rapidly assembling financial packages by G-10 Central Banks, combined where feasible with private credit lines, to countries in currency crises, that have not been caused by countries' policy mistakes, and that are thus not required to have changes in policy.

Therefore, there would be three categories of situations. Firstly, would be those countries that, during Article IV consultations with the IMF, were deemed by the Fund to have good policies. If these countries had a run on their currency, and a crisis started to unfold, caused for example, by contagion, a non-conditional financial package would be assembled by the BIS, drawing possibly on its own resources, but mainly on those of G-10 Central Banks and, if feasible, on private lending. Secondly, there would be countries that during Article IV consultations with the IMF had agreed a 'shadow programme' of conditionality with the Fund (see above). If the economic authorities implemented the programme fully, and a crisis still broke out, the IMF would disburse automatically (without additional conditionality). If a bigger package was necessary, the BIS could help co-ordinate additional financing from G-10 Central Banks and private banks. Thirdly, there would be countries which, during Article IV consultations, did not want to accept a 'shadow programme' with the IMF, and did not improve their policies. If these countries were hit by a currency crisis, they would have to go as a first step to the Fund for conditional lending.

Such a structure would provide very strong incentives for countries to have good policies, either implemented on their own or under a Fund 'shadow programme', which should make crises less likely. If, nevertheless, crises did occur, then large lending facilities by the IMF and/or lending by Central Banks and commercial banks co-ordinated by the BIS would be disbursed quickly and without additional conditionality. The role of the IMF conditionality would be greater in the crisis-prevention phase, but smaller in the crisis-management phase. As a result, its conditionality could be less draconian (in terms of growth) and thus less controversial.

As pointed out above, the scale of liquidity required from official institutions could be very large, given the scale of private flows involved. Such operations also carry a certain level of risk for taxpayers in creditor countries, were they not to be paid back. Until global prudential regulation is developed and perfected further, there is the problem of moral hazard for the original private investors and lenders. Therefore, it is important to reduce the scale required of additional official financing, by creating mechanisms for standstills and orderly debt workout, along the lines discussed immediately below and in the 1998 Trade and Development Report.

b) Orderly debt workouts

The international financial crisis, which began in Asia in the summer of 1997, has lent a sense of urgency to the search for ways to manage financial crises more effectively. In April 1998, the United States assembled an ad hoc group of industrialised and developing countries, the Group of 22, to examine issues related to the stability of the international financial system. Three G-22 working groups were formed, looking at transparency, strengthening national financial systems, and international financial crises. The third group examined policies to help prevent crises and to help facilitate the orderly and co-operative resolution of crises. This section will look at proposals under discussion to facilitate orderly debt workouts, in the light of the G-22 working group report.

The larger scale of capital flows to emerging market countries in recent years means that official funds can no longer be relied upon to offset private outflows during a crisis. Moreover, the scale of recent IMF-led rescue packages in Asia and Mexico has led to increased concern about the issue of moral hazard. The perception that official resources will be made available should a country experience difficulty in meeting its financial obligations can distort incentives for both creditors and debtors. This moral hazard is particularly strong on the lenders' side, as lenders and investors are spared by IMF-led bailouts from bearing the full risks of their investment decisions.

The need to reduce moral hazard does not, however, imply that the official sector has no role in the resolution of financial crises. The problems involved in collective action, and the risk of contagion are justification for official intervention in crises. There is clearly a need for a system which can bring about the rapid resolution of crises, while limiting the problems of moral hazard. There is now a growing consensus that ways need to be found to encourage a greater assumption of risk by the private sector, as well as to involve the private sector at an early stage in crisis resolution in order to achieve equitable burden-sharing vis-à-vis the official sector.

The G-22 working group looking at crisis resolution reviewed some of the proposals appearing in a G-10 report—produced in the wake of the Mexican peso crisis—which examined ways to deal with sovereign liquidity crises.[3] One issue common to both reports is the importance of promoting orderly arrangements to co-ordinate debtors and creditors in the event of a crisis. Difficulties associated with creditor co-ordination, particularly the creditor 'grab race' in which actions taken by individual creditors in pursuit of their self-interest can disrupt orderly debt workouts, can reduce the resources potentially available to all creditors and help create a situation of panic. The greater diversity of recent capital flows to emerging market countries, with a more heterogeneous set of international creditors than in the past, has also added to the difficulties of co-ordinating debt workouts.

The G-22 group, mirroring the G-10 report, put forward the proposal that certain contractual clauses could be incorporated into sovereign bonds issued in foreign offerings. The three contractual clauses outlined in the G-22 report would (a) provide for the collective representation of debt holders in the event of a crisis; (b) allow for qualified majority voting to alter the terms and conditions of contracts; and (c) require the sharing among creditors of assets received from the debtor. Such clauses would encourage dialogue between debtors and creditors, as well as among creditors, and prevent a minority of dissident investors from holding up settlement. This would therefore facilitate a more orderly resolution of crises.

The G-22 report also examines alternative ways of achieving standstill-type arrangements, including ways in which the international community might be able to signal its approval for standstills in exceptional cases. Countries, the report states, should make every effort to meet the conditions of all debt contracts in full and on time. However, in certain cases, a temporary suspension of payments may be a necessary part of the crisis-resolution process. In such cases, a voluntary, co-operative and orderly restructuring, combined with a programme of reforms, constitutes the most efficient means of crisis resolution. Countries should avoid the kind of unilateral default or restructuring that Russia declared in the summer of 1998.

However, the report does recognise that there may be extreme cases when an orderly and co-operative restructuring process would be aided by *'an enhanced framework for future crisis management'*[4] that would allow the international community to signal its approval of a temporary suspension of payments by providing financial support to the crisis country. The G-22 therefore supported the IMF decision to extend its policy of lending to countries in arrears on payments to private creditors. This signal would only be provided where the international community believed the government's decision to suspend debt payments was the only reasonable course open to it, that the government is implementing a strong programme of policy reform, and that it is making every effort to reach agreement with creditors.

Lending in such circumstances provides the IMF with the opportunity to manage a crisis by signalling confidence in the debtor country's policies and longer-term prospects, and indicating to unpaid creditors that their interests would best be served by reaching agreement with the debtor quickly. Governments imposing a standstill as part of a process of co-operative and non-confrontational debt renegotiation, it is argued, would be unlikely to be penalised by creditors.

The series of proposals in the G-22 report constitute an effective means of promoting more orderly arrangements to achieve debt rescheduling (or reduction) in the event of a crisis. However, the fear is that, as was the case with similar proposals made by the G-10 after the Mexican peso crisis, the G-22 proposals may not be implemented.

The G-22 report stops short of supporting proposals to provide sovereign debtors with greater formal protection from legal action by creditors during a payments suspension. There has been some debate over the idea that a legal mechanism could be created which would protect sovereign debtors from legal action by private creditors, allowing space for an orderly and co-operative restructuring. One suggestion was that Article VIII 2 (b) of the IMF's Articles of Agreement could be amended to allow the Fund to protect countries that are initiating debt negotiations. The G-22, however, does not see this suggestion as feasible, and regards the general issue of protection from legal action as one requiring further consideration.

One important concern often raised is that any mechanisms which would make it easier for borrowers to default on their financial obligations, even with the support of the international community, could make it harder for borrowing countries, and possibly emerging markets generally, to access international capital in the long-term or, at least, increase their cost of borrowing. The counter-argument is that financial crises, like the one which began in Asia in the summer of 1997, drastically reduces the access of affected countries to international capital and, when they can borrow, sends their borrowing costs sky-high. Similarly, some argue that payment standstills may spark off contagion; if markets get wind of a payments suspension in one emerging market economy, they may well pull out of other markets perceived to be in some way 'similar'. This argument may well have validity, but the absence of declared payments suspensions during the early months of the Asian crisis did not stop contagion sweeping through East Asia.

Another objection voiced over orderly workout procedures designed to assist countries that are forced to declare a temporary payments standstill is based on moral hazard. If countries can default on their debts with an official-sector sanction, it is feared, false incentives will provided to borrow imprudently. However, moral hazard for borrowing countries would be limited by the painful experience of crises, and by the strict conditionality that the IMF currently imposes on lending in such circumstances. Furthermore, the possibility of a suspension of payments would reduce the moral hazard that encourages lenders to lend too much in the expectation that they will be bailed out by an IMF-led rescue should things go wrong.

The search for more effective ways to manage financial crises remains a priority as, although prevention is undoubtedly better than cure, crises will never be eliminated altogether. The standard crisis response, which concentrates on imposing tough stabilisation measures on debtors, has contributed to undermining growth, as well as dramatically increasing poverty, in the countries affected by the crisis. The lengthy negotiations to agree debt restructuring in Indonesia provides a potent example of the failings of the present arrangements. The absence of an adequate framework for crisis management has meant that valuable time was wasted in Asia, and crises which may well have been short-term liquidity crises at the outset became full blown economic, financial and social crises, reversing many of the achievements previously made in Asia towards poverty reduction.

Conclusions

The seriousness of the current crisis—which started in East Asia, spread to Russia, and is threatening to spread to Latin America and cause a decline in world growth—is a source of major concern. The depth of the crisis and the speed of contagion were not foreseen. It has implied that a sizeable proportion of the world economy is in recession. This is not only eroding impressive previous gains in poverty reduction in the most affected countries, but also leading to major increases in poverty.

Action is therefore urgently required to rapidly contain and reverse the current crisis, to prevent future crises and to manage them better, if unfortunately they do occur.

To contain and reverse the current crisis, sufficient and sufficiently timely loosening of monetary policy by the industrial countries is crucial, to provide a favourable environment for restoring growth, and to help avoid the spreading of crises to other countries.

Steps also urgently need to be taken to prevent future crises and manage them better if they do occur. Some of these can be done within existing institutional arrangements, or with some development, expansion and adaptation of existing international institutions.

These include *filling regulatory gaps* (in particular relating to mutual funds and hedge funds) and improving regulation of bank lending, to help prevent excessive surges of capital inflows. They would also include new mechanisms within the IMF, adapted to cope with balance-of-payments crises generated by problems in the capital account. 'Shadow programmes' with preventive conditionality established before crises explode, accompanied by rapid disbursement without additional conditionality if a crisis occurs, seem an appropriate avenue to explore. Expanding the IMF's ability to 'lend into arrears' is also important.

However, it is also important to develop a vision of—and start building—a new financial architecture that would meet the development needs in the context of the new globalised economy. This includes: a) developing steps towards a world financial authority, which would carry out prudential regulation of capital flows in a consistent way (across countries and financial sectors). Such a world financial authority could build on existing practice, as developed under the aegis of the BIS and IOSCO; b) expanding and perfecting mechanisms to provide more official liquidity, including last-resort lending to countries in distress. An expansion of available liquidity is required, as are a broadening of institutional mechanisms (possibly to include the BIS channelling funds from the G-10 Central Banks), and the tailoring of conditionality to the circumstances of the crisis. As regards the latter, additional conditionality in crises should only be imposed if the crisis is caused by mistaken policies of countries. Furthermore, conditionality in crises should be designed in ways that strengthen, and not undermine, market confidence. Last, but not least, it is necessary to develop methods and institutions for orderly debt workouts and standstills, which would avoid debtors having to carry all the burden of crises.

Though international actions are crucial, clearly countries must themselves adopt their own policies to prevent and better manage currency crises. This includes more counter-cyclical macroeconomic and domestic regulatory policies, strengthening of domestic financial systems, and more prudent opening of their capital account, accompanied where necessary by market-based measures to discourage excessive surges of capital inflows.■

Notes

[1] Clearly, factors such as similarities in domestic conditions and competition in trade were important in the contagion that affected Asia. It has also been stated that the asset price bubble was less severe in Mexico, and the country's problems (such as the bunching of Tesobono maturities) were seen as more temporary.

[2] Figures from the Institute of International Finance (1998).

[3] The Group of Ten, 1996, 'The Resolution of Sovereign Liquidity Crises', Bank for International Settlements, Basel and International Monetary Fund, Washington.

[4] See point 4.9 of the report of The Working Group on International Financial Crises.

References

Agosin M. 1996. 'El retorno de los capitales extranjeros a Chile'. *El Trimestre Economico*, Mexico.

Akyuz Y. 1998. 'The East Asian Financial Crisis: Back to the Future?' http://www.unicc.org/unctad/en/pressref/prasia98.htm

Bagehot W. 1873. *Lombard Street: A Description of the Money Market.* (London, reprinted John Murray, 1917).

Bank for International Settlements (BIS). 1995. *65th Annual Report.* (Basel, BIS).

Boorman J. 1998. 'Reflections on the Asian Crisis: Causes, Culprits, and Consequences', paper prepared for the FONDAD conference on 'Coping with financial crises in developing and transition countries: regulatory and supervisory challenges in a new era of global finance', March.

Budnevich C. and Le Fort G. 1997 'Capital account regulations and macro-economic policy: Two Latin American experiences' *Documento de Trabajo* 06 (March). (Santiago, Banco Central de Chile).

[i]Camdessus M. 1998a. 'Is the Asian Crisis Over?' Address by Michel Camdessus at the National Press Club, Washington DC, 2 April. http://www.imf.org/external/np/speeches/1998/040298.HTM

Camdessus M. 1998b. 'Capital Account Liberalization and the Role of the Fund'. Remarks by Michel Camdessus at the IMF Seminar on Capital Account Liberalization, Washington DC, 9 March. http://www.imf.org/external/np/speeches/1998/030998.HTM

Chote R.[ii] 1998. 'Crystal Balls in Washington'. *Financial Times*, 17 April, p19.

Corsetti G., Pesenti P. and Roubini N. 1998. 'What caused the Asian currency and financial crisis?' Asian Crisis Homepage, March. http://www.stern.nyu.edu/~nroubini/asia/AsianCrisis.pdf.

Eatwell J and Taylor L. 1998. 'Proposal for a new financial architecture', Cambridge, mimeo.

Eichengreen B and Portes R. 1995. *Crisis? What Crisis?: Orderly Workouts for Sovereign Debtors.* (London, CEPR).

Feldstein M. 1998, 'Refocusing the IMF'. *Foreign Affairs* 77(2):20-33.

French-Davis R. and Griffith-Jones S. (eds). 1995. *Surges in Capital Flows to Latin America.* (Boulder, Lynne Reinner).

Fischer S. 1997, 'Capital Account Liberalization and the Role of the IMF'. 19 September. http://www.imf.org/external/np/apd/asia/FISCHER.htm.

Fischer S. 1998. 'The IMF and the Asian Crisis', March 20 1998, Los Angleles. http://www.imf.org/external/np/speeches/1998/032098.HTM.

Greenspan, A. 1998. *Financial Times*, 28 February.

Griffith-Jones S. 1998 (forthcoming). *Global Capital Flows.* (London, MacMillan).

Griffith-Jones S. 1996. 'How can future currency crises be prevented or better managed?' in *Can Currency Crises Be Prevented or Better Managed?* ed. J Joost Teunissen. (The Hague, FONDAD).

Griffith-Jones S. and Lipton M. 1987. 'International lender of last resort:are changes required?'. in *International debt and central banking in the 1980s,* ed. Z Ros and S Motamen. (London, Macmillan).

Group of Ten. 1996. 'The Resolution of Sovereign Liquidity Crises'. A Report to the Ministers and Governors prepared under the auspices of the Deputies, May.

Institute of International Finance (IIF). 1998. *Private Capital Flows to Emerging Economies* (newsletter, April).

International Monetary Fund (IMF). 1998. *Toward a Framework for Financial Stability.* Prepared by a Staff Team led by D Folkerts-Landau and C Lindgren (Washington, International Monetary Fund).

IMF. 1997. *World Economic Outlook: Interim Assessment, December 1997.* (Washington, International Monetary Fund).

IMF 1995. *International Capital Markets: Developments, Prospects and Key Policy Issues*. Washington D.C.

Interim Committee of the Board of Governors of the IMF. 1998. Communiqué, 16 April. http://www.imf.org/external/np/cm/1998/041698a.htm.

Kaufman H. 1992. 'Proposal for a board of overseers', Paper presented at the annual conference of the International Organisation of Securities Commissions.

Kaul I., Grunberg I., and Ul Haq M. (eds). 1996. *The Tobin Tax: Coping with Financial Volatility* (New York, Oxford Univeristy Press).

Kenen P. 1996. 'The Feasibility of Taxing Foreign Exchange Transactions', in *The Tobin Tax: Coping with Financial Volatility*. (New York, Oxford University Press).

Keynes, J. 1936. *The General Theory of Employment, Interest and Money*. (Cambridge, Cambridge University Press).

Khan M. and Reinhart C. 1995. 'Macro-economic management in APEC economies: The response to capital flows'. in *Capital Flows in the APEC region,* ed. M Khan and C Reinhart. IMF Occasional paper 122 (March). (Washington DC, IMF).

Mishkin, F. 1996. 'Understanding financial crises: a developing country perspective'. *Proceedings of the World Bank Annual Conference on Development Economics*, pp 29-77.

McKinnon R. 1991. *The order of economic liberalisation: Financial control in the transition to a market economy*. (Baltimore, John Hopkins University Press).

Obstfeld M. 1995. 'International currency experience: new lessons and lessons relearned'. *Brookings Papers on Economic Activity*, No 2:119-220.

Phillips S. 1998. 'Risk weighted regulation'. Paper presented at FONDAD Conference, Holland. March.

Radelet S. and Sachs J. 1998. 'The Onset of the East Asian Financial Crisis'. First draft, 10 February. http://www.hiid.harvard.edu/pub/other/eaonset.pdf.

Rodrik D. 1998. 'Who Needs Capital Account Convertibility?' Harvard University http://www.nber.org/~drodrik/essay.PDF.

Soros G. 1997. 'Avoiding a Breakdown'. *Financial Times*, 31 December, p 12.

Stiglitz J. 1994. 'The role of the state in financial markets', *Proceedings of the World Bank Annual Conference on Development Economics*, pp19-61.

Stiglitz J. 1997. 'Statement to the Meeting of Finance Ministers of ASEAN *plus* 6 with the IMF and the World Bank, Kuala Lumpur', 1 December. http://www.worldbank.org/html/extdr/extme/jssp120197.htm.

Stiglitz J. 1998a. 'Boats, planes and capital flows', personal view in the *Financial Times*, 25 March, p32.

Stiglitz J. 1998b. 'The Role of International Financial Institutions in the Current Global Economy'. Address to the Council on Foreign Relations, Chicago, 27 February 27 1998. http://www.worldbank.org/html/extdr/extme/jssp022798.htm.

Strauss-Kahn D. 1998. 'A Fix, not a Fudge', personal view in the *Financial Times*, 17 April

Global Economic Governance, Global Negotiations and the Developing Countries

Gerry Helleiner and Ademola Oyejide

As a global economy emerges, there arises the same need for the performance of certain "public" functions at the global level as has long been recognized within individual national market economies. Global "public goods" (defined as those that are non-rival and non-excludable in consumption) are at present only weakly supplied, if they are supplied at all, in the global economy. These public goods include

- global macroeconomic management, so as to reduce the prospect of crisis and instability;
- the provision of "firefighting" responses to crises of every sort (not least within the global economy);
- the formulation and policing of rules for international exchange and investment;
- the provision of some elements of global infrastructure (those requiring a longer time- horizon for planning purposes than is typical within markets);
- research in such socially important spheres as public health and improved technology for poor farmers; and,
- management of the global commons (oceans, electromagnetic spectrum, etc.).

Beyond the supply of such public goods, governments are also usually expected to undertake efforts to set a floor for human living standards, and seek to achieve a reasonable degree of equity in the distribution of income and wealth.

There is virtually zero prospect of global "government" within any foreseeable future. Yet, as the full implications of a globalized economy become more apparent, many of the *functions* of government—in particular, the supply of public goods and the pursuit of social objectives—will somehow have to be undertaken at the global level. Institutions for this purpose will therefore need to be constructed; and international rules, laws and dispute settlement mechanisms will need to evolve. So, probably, will international private sector codes and standards, introduced on a voluntary basis, and, in some instances, "hybrid" private-public arrangements to achieve the same ends (Clapp 1998). Government is not the only instrument of economic governance.

Generally, the industrialized countries (i.e., the countries of the Organization for Economic Cooperation and Development, or OECD) entrust far more responsibility for economic "governance" activities to private market actors, working voluntarily in their perceived collective interest, than is typically the case in developing countries. The same is true of their approaches to the establishment of international regimes. For instance, in the International Organization for Standardization (ISO), founded in 1946 to promote global standardization and compatibility of products and technical specifications, most of the developing country members (only about half the developing countries are represented at all) are governmental standard-setting organizations, whereas OECD countries are mainly represented by organizations that are either private or have heavy private sector involvement (Clapp 1998, 301). Similarly, in the intergovernmental discussion of possible regimes for foreign investment, OECD governments have worked assiduously, under the pressure of heavy lobbying from the financial sector and transnational corporations (TNCs), to leave as much rule-setting as possible for market participants themselves. That they can seek to control and regulate in this sphere, if they really want to, is illustrated by the extraordinary lengths, including heavy pressure on developing countries to cooperate, to which OECD governments have gone to control money laundering (and the trade in drugs) at the international level.

OECD governments are also typically more responsive to the representations of non-governmental organizations (NGOs) and civil society than are the governments of developing countries. In the emerging discussions of global governance arrangements, Northern NGOs are likely to make their voices heard, whereas the interests of the people of the developing countries will be represented only by their governments (or, in some instances, by Northern NGOs purporting to speak for the disempowered in the developing countries). How (or whether) to involve non-governmental actors—profit-oriented or charitable—in future global governance is a large question, too large for this brief paper the focus of which is intergovernmental relations and governance arrangements.

On the basis of experience to date, there is reason to fear that the future evolution of governance arrangements for the global economy may be seriously biased in favour of the interests of industrial countries, particularly the G-7 countries, whose governments and private firms (and even, in some cases, NGOs) now exercise disproportionate influence over global economic affairs. Above all, there must be concern as to whether emerging global economic governance arrangements will grant sufficient weight to the imperative of global development and the struggle against human poverty (Culpeper and Pestieau 1995; Commission on Global Governance 1995, chapter 4).

It will be a major challenge not only substantively to envisage and design appropriate institutional and legal requirements for global economic governance, but also to develop effective and legitimate processes—processes that are participatory and fair—to move the world toward its required new governance system. If the global rules system is to be "harmonized" through deeper integration among national economies within an agreed overall framework, as most now forecast and many advocate, there must be full and reasonably democratic representation as the rules and framework are created and implemented. There can be "no harmonization without representation". Yet decision making on key global economic issues remains highly concentrated in the major industrial powers, and there still seems deep resistance to relinquishing much of their power.

In Sachs' words, "... developing countries are not trying to overturn Washington's vision of global capitalism, but rather to become productive players in it. Only if they are shut out might they change their minds. But the developed world should not fear dialogue with the developing world. It should join it urgently, for our mutual well-being" (1998a). Speaking of the G-7 Finance Ministers' end-October 1998 statement, he observes that "for all its advances [it] still reflects a haughty disregard for the rest of the world. There is no talk about negotiation with the poorer countries, no talk about finding a fairer voice for those countries in the new international system. The rest of the world is called on to support the G-7 declarations, not to meet for joint problem-solving. ... Until the poor are brought into the international financial system with real power, the global economy cannot be stable for long" (Sachs 1998b).

There are essentially two kinds of representational problems with respect to the development of appropriate global economic governance processes and arrangements:

1) The central intergovernmental institutions in today's global economy are still those of the major industrial powers (the G-7) and the international financial institutions (the International Monetary Fund, the World Bank group and the Bank for International Settlements) which they control. Although they account for over 85% of the world's population (and that percentage is rising) and nearly 50% of its gross output, the developing countries still have only limited influence in the key international economic institutions or in the development of reforms and improvements therein. If new processes and systems are to carry credibility and legitimacy (and therefore be sustainable), they must provide for greater collective influence and power for the developing countries.

2) The poorest people and smallest countries may be at particular risk within the emerging global economy; their problems and their potential marginalization therefore require focused consideration at the global level. In this case, the problem is not the system's failure democratically to respond to the needs of the majority so much as its potential failure to protect the rights and welfare of particular "minorities". These "minorities" should be thought of as including the poorest and most vulnerable within the larger and wealthier countries of the international system, as well as those in the poorest and smallest countries.

As developing countries increasingly realize their previously underutilized economic potential and thereby acquire increasing economic strength, they will grow in importance to the functioning of the industrial economies and to overall global welfare. Since their economic performance is typically subject to much greater volatility than that of the industrialized countries, the closer integration of developing (and transition) economies into the global system and their greater importance to it will also pose increasing risks—not only to themselves but also (systemically) to the entire global economy. There are bound to be more Mexican, East Asian and Russian-style crises in the years to come.

Thus the economic and political security of the G-7 countries now rests significantly and increasingly upon events in the rest of the world. From this will undoubtedly flow some efforts, on the part of the industrial countries, to accommodate the interests of the more economically significant non-G-7 countries, at least those whose problems may create systemic risks. Within the financial sphere, such efforts have already begun. It may prove much more difficult, however, to motivate, within the industrial countries, the full inclusion of the poorest and weakest, or effective protection of their interests, within efforts to reform the current system of global economic governance.

This paper on developing country roles and objectives in global economic governance is organized around themes in negotiation processes rather than the specific objectives of improved global governance themselves. These objectives are considered, of course, but within the context of a discussion of better process. Section II addresses the prospect for fairly short-term and modest reforms within the key current multilateral economic institutions—the International Monetary Fund (IMF), the World Bank and the World Trade Organization (WTO). Section III considers the particular problems of the smallest and poorest countries in the global economic system. In section IV, the potential for improved developing country cooperation within the existing system is addressed. Section V focuses upon the importance of the choice of forums and appropriate processes for moving toward longer-term and more fundamental reforms in the global economic governance system. There follows a brief conclusion.

Reforming Today's Key Institutions

In official perceptions, the weakest dimension of current global economic governance arrangements—and that which is therefore now receiving the most official attention—is in the realm of international finance. Difficulties created by volatile short-term private capital flows and financial crises in developing countries, the evident need for further supervision of private international financial institutions and markets, and the growing impact of turmoil in international financial markets upon national and global economic performance, have combined to elicit intense discussion of the governance requirements for a stable global financial system. This in turn has engendered widespread reconsideration of the roles of the existing multilateral institutions and intensified some turf struggles between the IMF, World Bank, WTO and Bank for International Settlements (BIS) for jurisdiction and influence. There is also more active discussion of the possible future role of stronger regional financial institutions—not only development banks but also monetary associations (Mistry 1998).

The central multilateral institutions concerned with the overall functioning of the global economy and the global monetary and financial system are the IMF and the World Bank Group. The representation of the majority of the world's population within these institutions is particularly weak. Whereas developed countries, as defined by the World Bank, account for only 17% of voting strength in the United Nations (and in the Global Environment Facility), 24% in the WTO, and 34% in the International Fund for Agricultural Development (IFAD), they account for 61–62% in the World Bank and IMF (Woods 1998). Decision making in international organizations is often done by "consensus" rather than via formal voting, but even then the underlying voting power influences outcomes profoundly. Moreover, key appointments and staffing decisions/practices, which are fundamental to effective governance, are also somewhat problematic. By custom, for instance, the President of the World Bank is appointed by the United States, and the Managing Director of the IMF has always been a European. Although there may have been a rationale for such disproportionate voting arrangements and undemocratic management selection procedures within these institutions at the time of their foundation, it is difficult to defend them today—particularly when both institutions press borrowing countries to improve their own governance via conditions on their lending.

Reforms in IMF and Bank governance are badly needed, but it is unlikely that those countries that now exercise disproportionate power and influence within these institutions will give them up lightly. In the medium term, there will have to be efforts at internal reforms *within* the current institutions and systems, and *within* the constraints of current power relationships. There is much that can and should be done in this respect.

Improvement of institutional accountability is an obvious priority in the reform of current international governance arrangements. Powerful international organizations are fallible. To ensure accountability (and effectiveness) they require a modicum of transparency, independent evaluation, and ombudsman-like mechanisms for protection of the weak against abuse of their power.

Within the World Bank, there is an independent Operations Evaluation Department (OED) which assesses performance of projects and programmes on a regular basis and publishes its reports. In 1993, the Bank also established an Inspection Panel, which is mandated to investigate (when agreed to by the Bank's Board) local citizens' complaints concerning harm done because of violations of Bank policies or procedures; thirteen cases have so far been filed from eight developing countries. The panel's operations have frequently been impeded by delay and politicization in the Bank's Board; clearly, it is not as independent as it needs to be to play its role effectively. The World Bank is also at present embarking, on a pilot basis, on a new form of "partnership" relationship with some of the countries to which it lends, with the borrowing countries more clearly "taking the lead". (Similar aspirations have long been agreed by bilateral donors in the Development Assistance Committee of the OECD, although their translation into altered practices has lagged.) This initiative receives firm support from developing countries. Its progress itself deserves careful and independent monitoring and evaluation.

In the IMF, however, purportedly for prudential and security reasons, there are traditions of greater secrecy, internal discipline and centralization of power. Transparency has increased somewhat in recent years, but there is still no permanent institution for independent evaluation of IMF performance. In 1997–98, an *ad hoc* Board initiative generated an independent external evaluation of its Enhanced Structural Adjustment Facility (ESAF) programmes which, tellingly, proved far more critical than a previous internal review had been. An independent assessment of IMF surveillance activities has also been commissioned for 1999. But these have only been modest first steps. A recent independent consideration of these issues by a committee of experienced Washington hands concluded that the IMF "should establish a permanent evaluation office and endow it with a maximum of independence" (Polak et al. 1998, 15).

As far as "partnership" initiatives are concerned, the IMF also lags behind the Bank. Defending its more heavy-handed approaches, it argues the need for speed in responding to crises and the continuing need for a "short leash" (i.e., stringent conditionality for its lending) on critical matters of monetary and fiscal discipline. At the same time, the IMF has increasingly been imposing conditions on its lending that relate to structural and longer-term developmental issues that have never previously been within its mandate, expertise or experience. Paradoxically, it emphasizes at the same time that the country stabilization and adjustment programmes it supports are their "own". When slippage and interruptions occur, IMF staff tend to attribute them to national-level deficiencies rather than to inappropriate programme design or limited local ownership. There are obviously profound differences of perception on these issues. Absent an ombudsman, independent evaluations, or a power structure more responsive to developing country concerns, the IMF seems doomed to continuing controversy, and hence probably declining influence and respect.

As a young and still small entity, the WTO is not, of itself, so powerful a player as the international financial institutions (Krueger 1998). It has been argued, for instance, that, even with respect to pressure to amend trade policies, African countries probably have less to fear from the WTO than from the IMF and Bank (Elbadawi and Helleiner 1998). Moreover, its formal voting structure and its dispute settlement system both allow, in principle, for greater input from its smaller and poorer members, and create the potential for more equitable outcomes for them—if *only* they can get their collective act sufficiently "together" to realize the opportunities.

In reality, however, the capacity of many, perhaps most, developing countries to participate effectively in the WTO system—to take advantage of their rights and to defend their interests, indeed even to meet their obligations in the WTO—is very much in doubt. The WTO is a member-driven organization in the sense that, since it has no permanent Executive Board, delegates from member countries are actively involved in its day-to-day activities. If they are not, their interests are ignored. A "continuous dialogue" takes place in the WTO. It is estimated, for instance, that the continuous WTO process involves at least 45 meetings per week in Geneva (Blackhurst 1997). The requirements for effective participation place an enormous strain on resource-constrained smaller and poorer countries.

Most of the smaller and poorer developing countries are either not represented at all or not adequately represented, and hence cannot be part of the consensus-building consultations that go on inside and outside the formal meetings. When they are represented, their staffing is weak and clearly inadequate for handling the ever-increasing complexity of issues and the rising number of meetings and obligations characterizing the WTO process. A recent study of this issue suggests that almost 60% of developing country members of the WTO suffer from one or more handicaps that render their participation suboptimal (Michalopoulos 1998).

At present, the WTO remains a fairly secretive institution with its major decisions, despite the formal structures, disproportionately influenced by the major industrial powers. The less than fully transparent nature of the negotiating process has also contributed to the disenfranchisement of developing countries. Often, the most critical issues are discussed between the Director-General and a limited group of the more powerful countries. As had been the case in most of the earlier rounds, decision-making in the Uruguay Round negotiations was "pyramidal" in structure in that the major trading countries (those at the "top") had implicit, but nonetheless effective, veto power over the negotiations' overall outcome (Winham 1998). Thus, through various informal consultations, the larger developed countries agreed among themselves with respect to the major issues and presented the results to other members, essentially for ratification. In particular, over the last two years of the Uruguay Round negotiations, the decisive voices were those of the United States and European Union (EU).

Because of the increasing "legalization" of trade and investment issues and disputes (Ostry 1998), WTO procedures are often extremely difficult for poorer countries to utilize effectively. As the WTO grows and its mandate expands to include investment, competition, and possibly environmental and labour issues, its role in the governance of the global economy is likely to increase in relative importance. Because of its basic structure, developing countries have a chance to influence its evolution—its governing structures, its rules, its financing, etc.—but such an outcome is obviously far from assured. Developing countries should urgently plan together how better to exercise their potential influence in the future of the WTO.

The Particular Problems of the Smallest and Poorest Countries

It is sometimes argued that small countries derive exceptional benefits from their interaction with the international economy and, to some degree, this is true. On the other hand, the smaller and poorer members of the international community are typically much more open to global influences and vulnerable to external bullying than larger countries. At the same time, they obviously have much less influence in overall global events. Their vulnerability to external shock and inability to influence the rules system or the manner in which it is implemented can involve them in severe costs. To portray them as disproportionate "winners" from international exchange within the global economy is therefore a gross oversimplification (Helleiner 1997; see also Commonwealth Secretariat 1997). Small and poor countries, like others, must and can find ways to interact with the global economy so as to maximize their gains and minimize their risks.

As they do so, they typically experience severe difficulties in making their voices heard within the international community. Their small size and limited incomes make it difficult for them to finance diplomatic and/or legal representation in international negotiations, conferences or other events. Their interests are therefore frequently defended only within larger constituencies. Even then, however, their interests inevitably tend to be relatively neglected. In the IMF and World Bank, for instance, one Executive Director seeks to represent 23 African countries. Within such large "constituencies", representatives of individual countries must patiently await their turn for actual representation in decision-making circles. In the WTO, as has been seen, most of the smallest and poorest are not represented at all.

In any case, the small professional cadre of a small, poor country is typically fully occupied in the management of national affairs and has little opportunity for detailed involvement in multilateral economic diplomacy. Those who represent the small and poor countries are typically working "on their own", without support or instruction from national capitals. These countries' roles in the negotiation of future rules, institutions and arrangements is therefore likely to be quite limited. Moreover, the attention and expertise directed by international institutions towards the problems of the smallest and poorest of their members, while perhaps showing some positive per capita "small country effects", tend to be by their most junior and least experienced staff.

Negotiations in the Uruguay Round of the General Agreement on Tariffs and Trade (GATT) illustrate well the enormous difficulties encountered by smaller and poorer countries, particularly the African ones. Only a limited number of these countries, those few able to maintain a permanent presence in Geneva, managed to play any role at all. Of the 29 "least developed countries" that belong to the WTO (out of a possible 48), only 12 had missions in Geneva, and these were required to service a number of other international organizations as well (Michalopoulos 1998, 9). Most African countries were unable to participate effectively in the negotiations. Constrained by inadequate understanding of the complex issues being negotiated and lacking access to in-depth analysis of how the various agreements might affect them, they could not effectively defend their national interests (Ohiorhenuan 1998).

Factors limiting the effective participation of African countries were not confined to those associated with their Geneva-based negotiators, but extended to their capitals as well. In particular, there were typically few, if any, effective interministerial consultative mechanisms in their national capitals for debating the issues, reaching agreement, and sending instructions to Geneva. Erratic and sporadic communication characterized the weak connections between national negotiators in Geneva and their principals in the capitals. The few instructions that came through often lacked specificity since they were usually not based on detailed analysis. The contrast between the weak backup for these countries' trade negotiators and the batteries of trade lawyers, economists, industry specialists and lobbyists surrounding OECD members' negotiators could hardly be more stark.

As indicated earlier, WTO's evolving mandate already covers a wide variety of complex issues. The results of the Uruguay Round clearly impose on the smaller and poorer developing countries more obligations than had previous rounds. In particular, these countries now have substantive obligations to fulfil with respect to a large number of agreements ranging from agriculture to intellectual property. In addition to these, they must also comply with approximately 160 notification requirements under the WTO agreements, the implementation of which in turn affects their substantive rights.

It is difficult to imagine that African governments, let alone civil society, would have any sense of "ownership" of the results of the Uruguay Round. Yet now the WTO is to offer technical assistance to these countries in implementing the rules system that they had no role in drafting!

To participate effectively in the WTO process, any country needs to have, in Geneva, officials with the requisite technical skills, knowledge and experience of how the WTO process works. These officials would also have to be supported by the provision of timely and adequate technical analysis, advice and directives from their country's capital. Furthermore, the country needs to have the institutional framework and administrative support structure for meeting its WTO obligations and, in particular, for carrying out its notification requirements. For virtually all the smaller and poorer WTO members, paucity of human and material resources and limited knowledge base constitute real constraints on their ability to be effective members. These are key areas in which technical and other assistance is required (Oyejide 1997; Ohiorhenuan 1998). In particular, many of the smaller and poorer countries badly need assistance for human resources training and for developing institutional support within their countries. They also need assistance in building negotiating capacity, including the provision of policy analysis and identification of national interests and policy options.

Failure adequately to involve all the parties in the Uruguay Round resulted in gross underestimation of the problems now being encountered in many developing countries that are short on relevant legal expertise, as they seek to implement the agreement. Dispatching teams of Northern lawyers to redraft the trade and intellectual property laws of African countries is hardly a realistic solution. What will now be required is a careful, deliberate and participatory reconsideration of many elements of the Marrakesh agreement, not least those relating to transition periods and the obligations of the least-developed countries. In particular, it already seems clear that, with minor exceptions, the "more favourable treatment" of developing country members promised at the launch of the Uruguay Round negotiations—and finding expression in the WTO agreements on transition periods, differences in threshold levels for certain obligations, and offers of technical assistance, rather than substantive exemptions—was too haphazardly and arbitrarily put together and will be ineffective. The length of these transition periods and the threshold levels for various obligations are not linked to specific and objective indicators of levels of development. Nor is there any considered assessment of what institution-building, strengthening of administrative capacity or other resources would be required to bring the relevant developing countries up to the point at which their "favourable" treatment might appropriately end.

The smallest and poorest countries (and firms) are also at an enormous disadvantage when they attempt to *play* by the agreed "rules of the game" for trade and investment, whatever these rules may be. In principle, rules systems and pre-agreed dispute settlement mechanisms should help to protect the weak against bullying by the strong. In practice, however, such protection is not always realized. Today's rules systems are complex and their implementation requires legal inputs that are expensive. The mere threat of US or European anti-dumping action, for instance, is enough to discourage small exporters without the wherewithal to launch a legal defence. Similarly, when large countries breach the agreed rules at the expense of the small and poor, the cost of a legal challenge may exceed the financial capacities of the latter (or, in some cases, even the relevant trade losses).

Within many national jurisdictions, the legal rights of those who are unable to afford legal costs are protected by publicly-funded provision of legal aid. Analogous international provisions are now required to permit international rules systems to function effectively and, in particular, to protect small and poor countries against bullying by the strong in the areas of international trade and investment.

In the context of the WTO and its dispute settlement mechanism, various options have been suggested more effectively to protect the interests of the smaller and poorer countries (Whalley 1989; Blackhurst 1997). One such option is for the WTO to have a larger and more activist Secretariat, in which the smaller and poorer countries are adequately represented, and in which the strengthened Secretariat is endowed with the power to monitor and investigate violations of WTO rules, and to initiate dispute settlement cases against offending members. A second option would be the establishment of an international legal advisory service to help the smaller and poorer members protect their interests in the WTO system. A third suggestion, recognizing the inability of this group of countries to support an adequate level and number of representatives in Geneva, is that the WTO should itself provide funding to enable each country keep a minimum number of professionals working full-time on WTO activities.

Conceivably, increased transparency and the use of the Internet could be disproportionately helpful to the smallest and poorest. Part of the problem might also be tackled by the poorer and smaller countries themselves seeking to compensate for their individual inadequacies by pooling resources through joint representation in the context of regional and sub-regional groupings or similar arrangements (Oyejide 1997; Yeo 1998).

Developing Country Cooperation in the Existing System

Whatever the formal structure of governance and decision making in international organizations, there is underutilized potential for increased influence on the part of the small and poor countries through increased cooperation with one another. Such cooperation can take many forms—ranging from merely *ad hoc* issue-specific collaboration to more institutionalized arrangements for information exchange and the development of common positions.

Developing countries have not as yet been very successful in efforts at collective action within the principal multilateral economic institutions—the IMF, the World Bank group and the WTO. They have had neither an effective equivalent of the G-7 Economic Summit nor anything remotely resembling the industrialized countries' Organisation for Economic Cooperation and Development (OECD). Such cooperative research and technical support operations as they have had have been quite weak. Developing country interests have therefore tended to be analysed at greatest length in the multilateral organizations themselves; such analyses are subject to obvious constraints (not least the influence of the industrialized countries within these bodies) from which more independent such work would be free.

For this weakness the developing countries have largely had themselves to blame. Their collective organizations (G-77, G-15, G-24, the fifteen developing-country members of the US-created G-22, etc.) are not only each weakly funded but they are also poorly coordinated one with another. Their research and analytical capacities have been and remain minimal. The South Centre in Geneva, the product of the South

Commission (1990), has only a tiny professional research staff. Nor do their purely regional organizations (e.g., SELA (Latin American Economic System) or the Organization of African Unity) function much more effectively. Developing countries have so far simply not devoted the financial or technical resources to the joint pursuit of their common interests that would be required to achieve real impact in global economic affairs. (Perhaps the poorest and smallest countries cannot be expected to devote significant resources to these "larger" international and global issues since, even if they banded together, their influence would probably still be too small to justify the opportunity costs.) Negotiation has often been left to ill-prepared, technically deficient and/or overworked diplomats, while lobbying and public positioning has frequently been done by unaccountable (often Northern) NGOs and academics.

In the critically important realm of international finance, the developing countries' interests are represented in the IMF and World Bank by the Intergovernmental Group of Twenty-Four on International Monetary Affairs (G-24). Only in 1998, after more than 25 years of its existence, did G-24 Finance Ministers agree to fund a (very small) permanent "liaison office" in Washington to maintain a collective "memory" and assist developing country Governors and Executive Directors in the IMF and Bank. Even now, its funding remains precarious. The G-24 research programme offers some support to developing country representatives and decision-makers, but it is still primarily donor-funded and it has no full-time or on-site staff. Its annual budget is about one-twentieth of the annual cost of the World Bank's *World Development Report*!

Collective representation of the developing countries in the WTO is, if anything, even worse. Whereas, as noted above, the WTO's formal voting structure allows for greater developing country power than in the international financial institutions, its governance does not incorporate a permanent Executive Board or equivalent body. If national interests are to be protected, member countries must each have permanent representatives in Geneva, but, of course, that is expensive and difficult for small and poor countries. (The Commonwealth Secretariat has therefore supplied a staff advisor to assist its smaller member countries in WTO matters.) There is as yet no equivalent of the G-24 (or its research programme) working in support of developing country interests in the WTO. The situation is sufficiently alarming to G-24 Finance Ministers that they have authorized research on WTO issues out of their own (very small) research budget. The staff of the United Nations Conference on Trade and Development (UNCTAD) have also been deployed to help provide background papers on the developing countries' interests in particular issues—including "fresh" issues not previously on the agenda as well as the "unfinished business" of earlier rounds of GATT bargaining—despite the potential for tension with industrial countries and with the WTO itself that such activities create. Developing countries have so far been unable effectively to develop and promote their own agendas in the WTO, leaving them forever searching merely for ways to respond to US and other initiatives.

Prior to the Uruguay Round negotiations, it was not unusual for the developing countries to operate through a blocwide approach using the G-77 framework. However, this approach appears not to have been seriously considered during the Uruguay Round, partly because the bargaining format made the blocwide approach unsuitable, and more fundamentally because the commonality of interests of the G-77 group has weakened over time, as different countries have developed in different ways (Whalley 1989; Oyejide 1990).

Forums for Discussion and Negotiation

The choice of the forum for discussion and negotiation of international economic issues is fundamentally important to the determination of outcomes. This has been shown repeatedly, e.g., in the case of investment and trade regimes, which we discuss below; it is likely to be the case in forthcoming discussions and negotiation of a new international financial architecture. In no sphere has this been more dramatically evident than in approaches to a global regime for investment, and, in particular, for transnational corporations and foreign direct investment. In the 1970s, when negotiations were based in the United Nations system, they focused on a "code of conduct" for TNCs, which was to set restraints on some of their activities. Parallel discussions took place in the UNCTAD on "rules and principles" governing restrictive business practices in the international arena, and on another code of conduct on the transfer of technology. In each case, developing countries' concerns were assiduously advanced. Industrial countries, on the defensive, worked to keep the proposed codes and rules legally non-binding and to limit their impact, and, of course, they succeeded.

The recent discussions of the proposed Multilateral Agreement on Investment (MAI), within the OECD, were utterly different—not so much, as some suggest, because of a global change of approach to TNCs as because of the common interests of OECD members as home bases for TNCs. The draft MAI set out to protect foreign owners of capital, in a wide variety of forms and activities (not just foreign direct investors), from the "distorting" policies of governments. It sought national treatment for *all* foreign "investment", even prior to establishment within a country. Yet it did *not* seek to impose any rules or limits on the degree to which national governments might favour or subsidize foreign investors. Its draft provisions proved too restrictive upon national sovereignty even for some OECD governments (notably that of France). They would never have been acceptable to most developing countries (Ganesan 1998; Agosin 1998). Investment issues (at least some of them) now seem likely to land within the jurisdiction of the WTO, where no doubt developing countries' concerns will have some influence. (In the meantime, UNCTAD has been asked to undertake research on developing countries' potential interests in a multilateral framework for foreign investment, and on the developmental implications of foreign direct investment.)

More fundamentally, the globalization of business activity will eventually require a globalized system of accounting, audit and disclosure standards; corporate taxation; competition laws and the like. Current disputes over transfer pricing, tax revenue-sharing, and the role of tax havens are a harbinger of the multilateral negotiations that will be required to usher in an agreed global corporate tax system. The problems created for tax authorities by mobile capital and globalized firms are already widely recognized and will soon have to be systematically addressed. No doubt they would be best addressed within the context of an overall assessment of the need for "global taxes" to finance global public goods and other global objectives (Mendez 1992), but they need not await such an overall approach and they probably will not. Similarly, current debates, within the WTO and elsewhere, over the appropriate use of anti-dumping duties and the link between trade and competition policies are a foretaste of the inevitable future negotiation of a global competition regime for transnational corporations. Where these matters are addressed will again influence the outcomes.

The story of the generalized system of preferences (GSP) illustrates a similar phenomenon in the trade area. In 1968, during UNCTAD II, the developed countries agreed to the establishment of the GSP as an automatic, unconditional, across-the-board preferential market access in the developed countries for *all* products of developing countries. This UNCTAD agreement then went over to the GATT for confirmation and implementation. In its decision of June 1971, the GATT provided legal backing for the agreement by waiving the provisions of its Article I for a period of ten years to enable its developed country members to offer trade preferences to developing countries. In the process, the GSP was converted from what was in principle a general, contractual and secure special market-access scheme for developing countries into today's caricature thereof—which is riven with exceptions, non-contractual and subject to unilateral modification or withdrawal at the pleasure of preference-granting countries (Oyejide 1998). Thus, the vision guiding the scheme's design in UNCTAD failed fully to carry over into the reality of its implementation by the GATT; the different outcome reflected the different forum.

The choice of forum will similarly be extremely important to current negotiations over a future architecture for the international financial system. Some indication of how important this choice may be can be gleaned from the major and substantive differences in approach to future capital account regimes, between the IMF and UNCTAD. Dominated by G-7 governments and financial interests, the IMF has consistently pressed for capital account liberalization not only via its technical advice but also through a proposed amendment to its Articles of Agreement that would add this objective to its basic purposes and expand its jurisdiction to this end. It has done so despite continued expressions of reservation and caution on the part of the G-24 and other developing country spokespersons (Helleiner 1998). In UNCTAD, on the other hand, where developing country interests are better represented, the risks of capital account liberalization and the potentially important role for capital account taxes and controls have always been highlighted (UNCTAD 1998, 1995). Only in the aftermath of the Asian crisis have IMF positions begun to converge toward UNCTAD and developing country ones, and, of course, significantly different orientations remain.

There are also significant longer-term jurisdictional issues to be resolved—between, for instance, the IMF, World Bank, WTO (in financial services), BIS, the International Organisation of Securities Commissions

(IOSCO), a possible new World Financial Authority (as suggested by Eatwell and Taylor 1998 and Kaufman 1998, among others), and even the UN itself. Most *immediate* is the question as to the appropriate *process* for moving the current global financial system towards some new agreed architecture.

Since the IMF and World Bank's voting and power structures are so unbalanced, they would certainly *not* be the developing countries' venue of first choice, nor would their Interim or Development Committees, which, in any case, have been discredited as serious negotiating or decision-making bodies. On the other hand, developing countries would not like to see the G-7 or the OECD or the BIS, in which their voices are scarcely heard at all, become the prime *loci* for key decisions on the future of the international monetary and financial system.

In 1998, the United States Government unilaterally initiated a discussion of international financial issues (notably increasing accountability and transparency, strengthening national financial systems, and managing international financial crises) among G-7 countries and a selection (by the US) of fifteen middle-income countries, together constituting the so-called Group of Twenty-Two. Apart from its limited aspirations and timetable, the G-22 is not fully representative—it totally excludes the poorest and smallest, not to speak of such "like-minded" or "middle powers" as the Scandinavians, Dutch and Australians. Moreover, the US Treasury wields disproportionate influence within the G-22. A more representative and legitimate forum for such negotiation and discussion is urgently required.

One possibility that has been discussed, indeed formally recommended by the G-24, is the recreation of some version of the *ad hoc* Committee of Twenty on "Reform of the International Monetary System and Related Issues" of the 1970s. This committee was made up of ten developing countries and ten industrial countries, reflecting the (then) constituencies of the IMF's Executive Board. It functioned through a Committee of Deputies (senior national officials), a supervisory Bureau, and seven Technical Groups on particular topics. (For a brief summary, see Mohammed 1996). In the current context, because of the breadth of its required mandate, it would not be appropriate for such a committee to function solely as a committee of the IMF's Board, as it did then. What is required is an intergovernmental task force answerable and reporting not only to the IMF but also to the World Bank, the BIS, IOSCO and the UN Economic and Social Council (ECOSOC). Now, as then, it could be helpful to have parallel unofficial research on and discussion of the key issues by academics and other knowledgeable persons, as was done in the so-called "Bellagio group" in the 1970s. Now, however, one would require much more input into such a group from the developing countries.

The terms of reference for such an intergovernmental task force and the objects of focus for its technical subcommittees are suggested by the current problems and issues in the international monetary, financial and trading systems. In broad terms, the mandate would be to find improved means for the governance of the newly globalized economy. More specifically, the task force would seek to provide an appropriate system for global macroeconomic management, including

- provision for adequate liquidity and emergency responses;
- a stable system of development finance for all developing countries and for development-related research;
- an agreed framework of rules and obligations for the conduct of international trade and investment (including provision for prudential regulation of international financial markets and institutions), with a capacity for their effective and equitable application; and,
- most important of all, provision of the key elements of human development for all of the world's population.

As suggested by the G-24, the topics the task force would most urgently need to address include the following:

- the capacities and modalities of the international monetary and development finance institutions to prevent—as well as to respond in a timely and effective manner to—crises induced by large-scale capital movements;
- the appropriateness of the conditions prescribed by these institutions to deal with such crises;
- the equitable sharing of the costs of post-crisis financial stabilization among private creditors, borrowers, and governments;
- the more effective surveillance of the policies of major industrialized countries affecting key international monetary and financial variables, including capital flows;

- the strengthening of social safety nets as integral elements of stabilization and adjustment programs to protect the most vulnerable segments of the population;
- the increased representation and participation of developing countries at the decision-making level of international financial institutions to properly reflect developing countries' growing role in the world economy, including through the revision of the bases determining the voting power in these institutions; and,
- the need to enhance the role of SDRs [Special Drawing Rights] in the international monetary system to achieve greater stability, particularly in view of the prospect of an emerging polarization around three major currencies.

(G-24 communiqués, October 3, 1998 and April 14, 1998;
Caracas Declaration, February 9, 1998)

To date, these seemingly quite reasonable and good-faith public proposals from the principal developing-country group within the international financial institutions have been greeted with a resounding silence from the G-7 members, the IMF and the World Bank. As noted above, the US has simply unilaterally pushed on with its own idea, its Group of Twenty-Two.

Conclusions

Governance is not simply a matter of designing an optimal system and then putting it in place through whatever mechanisms are available (including coercion if necessary). Rather, it should be thought of as a communicative and consultative process through which disputes are resolved, consensus is built and performance is continually reviewed. No less critical to its success than its policy instruments is the forum that a governance arrangement must provide for the expression of claims, review, and discussion of continuing reform. Above all, good governance is good process. To develop the required new arrangements for the effective governance of the global economy one must therefore *begin* with an effective and credible process—ideally a process involving civil society and business as well as governments and existing international organizations.

Current efforts to improve governance in the newly globalized economy are heavily biased towards the interests of the governments, firms and peoples of the wealthiest of the world. This bias will not easily be overcome. Whereas there are signs that larger and potentially more influential players in the global economy may eventually be admitted to global governance and decision-making councils, in the interest of their very effectiveness and efficiency, the smallest and poorest risk continuing exclusion.

The most realistic starting point in any attempt to move toward more effective global governance arrangements is reform in the key multilateral economic institutions—the IMF, the World Bank and the WTO. Each requires greater transparency, increased accountability, more independent evaluations, and ombudsman-like and/or legal-aid mechanisms to protect the weak against the strong. Particular effort will have to be made to protect the interests of the smallest and poorest countries, and the poorest peoples everywhere, in such reform efforts.

Transparency and evaluation procedures are ripest for reform in the IMF. In the Bank (as well as in the IMF), the key issue is the effective "ownership" of country programmes—an issue in which bilateral aid donors are also, of course, heavily involved—and the strengthening of ombudsman facilities. The WTO is still young enough to permit more "fundamental" debate as to its rules system, its decision-making systems, the role of its secretariat, and the capacity of all its current or prospective members to benefit from it; such debate should be fully participatory and transparent.

To provide a common framework, a common point of reference, and systemic monitoring for all of these discussions of reform—and thereby to improve the prospect of a coherent overall system of global economic governance—it might make sense to constitute a special committee of the United Nations or a subcommittee of its Economic and Social Council or even some high-level independent body to formulate agreed principles (e.g., full participation or representation, transparency, independent evaluation, ombudsman facilities, assistance to the weakest, mutual consistency, etc.) for the emerging governance arrangements and systematically monitor their translation into practice on a regular basis.

The most immediate need is for appropriate process and participation in the current and forthcoming discussion of a new international financial architecture. This discussion is the one to which economic policymakers in the North are now most committed. The US-initiated Group of Twenty-Two, originally seen as a one-off crisis-responsive affair, may be seen as a step in the right direction, but, as noted above, its representativeness is flawed, its processes inadequate to the task, and its future, in any case, uncertain. It is not the right forum for carrying these issues forward. The G-24, among others, has suggested the basis for a better one.

At present, proposals for change in the global financial system originate almost exclusively in G-7 governments, Northern businesses and Northern universities – and they are typically brought to the world in the pages of the *Financial Times (FT)*, the *Wall Street Journal* or the *International Herald Tribune*. (For instance, on November 27, 1998, the *FT* reported that G-7 officials were discussing a possible merger of the Bretton Woods institutions' two key committees, the Interim and Development Committees.) There does not yet appear to be any comparable detailed developing-country discussion of their own interests in international financial architectural issues. Where are the voices from the South in these critically important architectural discussions? (In the longer run, such discussions of Southern interests in the emerging trade regime will be no less important.)

Greater effort could be made by developing countries themselves, who have been fairly quiescent in recent years, to develop positions that are in their agreed collective interest and then press them energetically in the relevant multilateral fora. An essential early step is for an organized effort to be made, within the South, to exchange ideas and formulate their own agreed positions on international financial architecture, wherever such agreement is possible, *prior* to entering into detailed discussion and negotiation with the more powerful actors who still are accustomed to setting the terms for international policy debate. Negotiations toward improved arrangements for the governance of the global economy, if they are to be truly effective, require that the developing countries be better prepared for them, and that they take place in a mutually agreed and representative forum. Developed countries' long-term interest in effective global economic governance should lead them to assist in the development of such negotiation processes.■

References

Agosin, M., 1998, "Capital Account Convertibility and Multilateral Investment Agreements", *International Monetary and Financial Issues for the 1990s*, Vol. X (United Nations) (forthcoming).

Blackhurst, R., 1997, "The Capacity of the WTO to Fulfill Its Mandate", in Anne Krueger (ed.) *The WTO as an International Organization* (University of Chicago Press).

Clapp, Jennifer, 1998, "The Privatization of Global Environmental Governance: ISO 14000 and the Developing World", *Global Governance*, 4, pp. 295–316.

Commission on Global Governance, 1995, *Our Global Neighbourhood* (Oxford University Press).

Commonwealth Secretariat, 1997, *A Future for Small States: Overcoming Vulnerability* (London).

Culpeper, Roy and Pestieau, Caroline, 1995, (eds) *Development and Global Governance* (North-South Institute/International Development Research Centre, Ottawa).

Eatwell, John and Taylor, Lance, 1998, "International Capital Markets and the Future of Economic Policy", CEPA Working Paper Series III, Working Paper No. 9 (Centre for Economic Policy Analysis, New School for Social Research, New York).

Elbadawi, I. and Helleiner, G., 1998, "African Development in the Context of New World Trade and Financial Regimes: The Role of the WTO and Its Relationship to the World Bank and the IMF" (African Economic Research Consortium, Nairobi), mimeo.

Ganesan, A. V., 1998, "Strategic Options Available to Developing Countries with regard to a Multilateral Agreement on Investment", *International Monetary and Financial Issues for the 1990s*, Vol. X (United Nations) (forthcoming).

Helleiner, G. K., 1996, "Why Small Countries Worry: Neglected Issues in Current Analyses of the Benefits and Costs for Small Countries Integrating with Large Ones", *The World Economy*, 19, 6 (November).

——, 1998, (ed.) *Capital Account Regimes and the Developing Countries* (Macmillan).

Kaufman, Henry, 1998, address to G-24 Ministerial Meeting, Caracas.

Krueger, Anne, 1998, (ed.) *The WTO as an International Organization* (University of Chicago Press).

Mendez, Ruben P., 1992, *International Public Finance: A New Perspective on Global Relations* (Oxford University Press, New York and London).

Michalopoulous, C., 1998, "Developing Countries' Participation in the World Trade Organization", Policy Research Working Paper 1906 (World Bank and World Trade Organization, Washington and Geneva).

Mistry, Percy, 1998, "Coping with Financial Crises: Are Regional Arrangements the Missing Link?", *International Monetary and Financial Issues for the 1990s*, Vol. X (United Nations, forthcoming).

Mohammed, Aziz Ali, 1996, "Global Financial System Reform and the C-20 Process" in *International Monetary and Financial Issues for the 1990s*, Vol. VII (United Nations).

——, 1998, "The Future of the G-24", G-24 paper, mimeo.

Ohiorhenuan, John, 1998, "Capacity Building Implications of Enhanced African Participation in Global Rules-Making and Arrangements", Paper prepared for the African Economic Research Consortium's collaborative research project on "Africa and the World Trading System", (AERC, Nairobi), mimeo.

Ostry, Sylvia, 1998, "Reinforcing the WTO", Occasional Paper 56, Group of Thirty (Washington, DC).

Oyejide, T. A., 1990, "The Participation of Developing Countries in the Uruguay Round: An African Perspective", *The World Economy*, vol 13, no 3.

——, 1997, *Africa's Participation in the Post-Uruguay Round World Trading System*, Program for the Study of International Organizations (PSIO) Occasional Paper, WTO Series No 6, Geneva.

——, 1998, "Costs and Benefits of S and D Treatment for Developing Countries in the GATT/WTO: An African Perspective" (African Economic Research Consortium, Nairobi), mimeo.

Polak, J. et al., 1998, *IMF Study Group Report: Transparency and Evaluation* (Center of Concern, Washington).

Rodrik, Dani, 1999, *Making Openness Work: The New Global Economy and the Developing Countries* (Overseas Development Council, Washington).

Sachs, Jeffrey, 1998a, "Global Capitalism, Making It Work", *The Economist*, September 12.
——, 1998b, "Stop Preaching", *Financial Times*, November 5.

South Commission, 1990, *The Challenge to the South* (Oxford University Press).

UNCTAD, 1996, *Trade and Development Report*.
——, 1998, *Trade and Development Report*.

Whalley, J., 1989, *The Uruguay Round and Beyond* (Macmillan).

Winham, G. R., 1998, "Explanation of Developing Country Behaviour in the GATT Uruguay Round Negotiation", *World Competition*, vol 21 no 3.

Woods, Ngaire, 1998, "Governance in International Organizations: The Case for Reform in the Bretton Woods Institutions", *International Monetary and Financial Issues for the 1990s*, Vol. IX (United Nations).

Yeo, S., 1998, "Trade Policy in Sub-Saharan Africa: Lessons from the Uruguay Round Experience" (African Economic Research Consortium, Nairobi), mimeo

Foreign Investment Policy, The Multilateral Agreement On Investment And Development Issues

Martin Khor Kok Peng

Context And Background Of The Issues Surrounding The Multilateral Agreement On Investment (MAI)

The recent interest and controversy on the issue of investment has been sparked by the proposal of the developed countries to introduce a legally binding international regime on foreign investment.

Among the member countries of the Organization for Economic Cooperation and Development (OECD), a Multilateral Agreement on Investment (MAI) has been the subject of intense negotiations. The negotiations started in 1995 and were originally to be concluded in mid-1997, but by the end of 1998, they had been bogged down by disagreements, partly generated by public criticisms in many OECD countries. The negotiations produced a comprehensive text, which has gone through many drafts. It was the intention that the OECD countries would first sign the MAI and then the treaty would be opened to other countries to accede to. OECD officials have stressed that although the negotiations involve only OECD member countries, the MAI is not meant to be an "OECD treaty" (applying to OECD members only) but is a "multilateral agreement", which developing countries are expected to join.

On a separate track, in informal discussions in the World Trade Organization (WTO), some developed countries in 1995 also proposed negotiations towards a multilateral investment agreement (MIA). They had planned that the first WTO Ministerial Conference in Singapore in December 1996 would adopt a decision to set up a Working Group to discuss "trade and investment". A paper by the European Commission (EC), "A level playing field for direct investment worldwide", and speeches and articles by leading EC officials made it clear that the ultimate aim and design of this initiative was to establish an MIA within the WTO. In this context, WTO general principles relating to trade (including reduction and removal of cross-border barriers, national treatment, most-favoured nation treatment) as well as the integrated dispute settlement system (which enables retaliation and cross-sectoral retaliation) would now be applied also to investment.

Many developing countries had objected to the issue of investment per se being brought onto the agenda of the 1996 WTO Ministerial Conference. However, discussion did take place in Singapore, and a decision was taken to establish a working group to examine the relation between trade and investment. This was meant to be only an educative process for an initial two-year period, and any decision to have negotiations for an agreement would have to be taken only on the basis of explicit consensus. In 1997-98 the working group held several meetings. By early 1999, several developed countries led by the European Union were advocating that the investment issue be included in a proposed new round of multilateral trade negotiations, to be launched at the WTO Ministerial Conference in Seattle in November/December 1999.

With the MAI negotiations stalled (at least temporarily) at the OECD, the European Commission and several developed countries are apparently eager to pursue the investment issue in the WTO forum. They are likely to press for the trade and investment working group to upgrade its work from an educative process to negotiations for an investment agreement. However, some developing countries have voiced the view that the "study process" in the WTO working group should continue for some more years and that there should not be negotiations for an investment agreement, at least not at this stage.

A reading of the draft text of the MAI in the OECD and the European Commission's 1995 paper, "A level playing field", shows that the MAI and the EC vision of an investment agreement in the WTO are basically similar in objectives and content. Both are aimed at protecting and advancing the rights of international investors vis-à-vis host governments and countries. The main elements include the right of entry and establishment of foreign investors and investments; the right to full equity ownership; national treatment; the right to free transfer of funds and full profit repatriation; protection of property from expropriation; and other accompanying measures such as national treatment rights in privatisation. Whilst an agreement in the WTO would presumably be subjected to the WTO's dispute settlement system, the OECD's negotiating text proposes a state-to-state and investor-to-state dispute settlement system with a choice of international arbitration.

It is unclear at this point whether negotiations will resume on the MAI in the OECD, or whether there will be a decision in the WTO to begin negotiations for an investment agreement. In any case, it can be expected that there will continue to be strong pressures from some developed countries for an investment agreement like the MAI to be established, whether in the OECD, the WTO or some other forum. It is thus useful, especially for developing countries, to review the MAI, which is the most recent and advanced model of the kind of investment agreement that has been advocated by the developed countries. Such a review is important so that developing countries can prepare themselves to take a position on such a model of an investment agreement.

This paper begins with a brief review of the nature and effects of foreign investment, and the conditions for its successful use and management. The following section presents and analyses the content of the major aspects of the MAI, based on the latest available negotiating text. The next section makes some conclusions about the implications of the MAI from the perspective of human sustainable development. The following section gives a brief account of alternative approaches to regimes on foreign investment and investors, focusing on past international efforts. The final section provides some suggestions for an appropriate approach and action.

Foreign Investment, Its Effects, Management and Regulation

Introduction: There has been a significant increase in foreign investment, including to developing countries, in recent years. According to Nayyar (1995), annual foreign direct investment (FDI) outflows averaged close to $50 billion from 1981-85, rose to $243 billion in 1990, reduced to below $210 billion per annum in 1991-94, before climbing sharply to $318 billion in 1995. Much of FDI and its increase are due to flows among the advanced countries. However, since the early 1990s, FDI flows to developing countries have risen relative to flows to the developed countries, averaging 32% of total flows in 1991-95 compared with 17% in 1981-90. This coincides with the recent liberalisation of foreign investment policies in most developing countries. However, again, FDI flows to developing countries are highly concentrated: much of the FDI is centred in only a few countries. The least developed countries (LDCs) in particular are receiving only very small FDI flows, despite having liberalised their policies. Thus, FDI is insignificant as a source of external finance to most developing countries, and is likely to remain so in the next several years.

The last few decades have also witnessed a significant shift of perspective in many developing countries towards foreign investment. In the 1960s and 1970s there was considerable reservations and mistrust on the part of governments of many developing countries, as well as many development economists and other academics, towards foreign investment and transnational companies. Starting in the 1980s, however, there has been a growing tendency to view foreign investment more positively. This was partly due to the disillusionment with foreign loans, because many developing countries that had borrowed heavily in the 1970s and 1980s ended up with external debt crises. A new orthodoxy came into being, that as a form of foreign funds, foreign investment is superior to foreign loans because the investments (unlike loans) would not land the host country into a debt crisis. Indeed, in some quarters and for some countries, foreign investment has come to be seen almost as a panacea for removing the obstacles to development.

Just as originally the view of many may have been extremely unfavourable to foreign investment, the pendulum could now have swung to the other extreme, to the extent that some now view foreign investment as an unmixed blessing. In reality, there are benefits and costs accompanying foreign investment. The task for policymakers and analysts alike is to ascertain the determinants of the benefits and costs, and attempt to devise policies to increase the benefits and reduce the costs, with the aim of ensuring that there be net benefits.

Results of some recent studies on effects of FDI on developing countries

There are various categories of foreign investments. It is important that these be distinguished, because the MAI defines investments in a very broad way, including foreign direct investment (FDI), portfolio investment, loans, contracts, and many other forms of property owned by foreigners in the host country, including intellectual property.

This section deals only with FDI, which is usually considered the best component of foreign investment. The supposed benefits of portfolio investment and short-term capital flows (including loans) have now been called into question as a result of the series of financial crises starting with Thailand in mid-1997. However, there is a dominant assumption that FDI brings only benefits, and its costs are much less known generally. A balanced and objective perspective on FDI and on investment liberalisation is thus important, especially in view of the attempts to establish an international investment regime.

This is especially so when little seems to be known of the effects of investment liberalisation. At an OECD-organised workshop on FDI and the MAI in Hong Kong in March 1996, the keynote speaker, Dr Stephen Guisinger of University of Texas, said that, "Very little is known about repercussions of foreign direct investment liberalisation on host economies...The link between investment liberalisation and macroeconomic performance has received scant attention from researchers."

The following is a summary of some studies on the effects of foreign investment on developing countries that may throw some light on the issue.

1. Effects of FDI on Balance of Payments and Growth

A leading Malaysian economist, Dr. Ghazali Atan, has studied the effects of FDI on trade, balance of payments and growth in developing countries. His study (Ghazali 1996) examines the literature and empirical evidence on the subject. A detailed case study of Malaysia, one of the few developing countries that have received a large inflow of FDI in the past few decades, presents an interesting case for study on the effects of FDI. Whilst many studies deal with one aspect of FDI's effects, Dr. Ghazali's study empirically examines various facets (effects on savings, financial inflows and outflows, trade and growth). Using these, he constructed a model (see Figure 1) with equations on each aspect and a simultaneous equation to capture the total or combined effects of the various aspects.

Among the main conclusions of the study:

- Successful growth in developing countries is premised essentially on raising the domestic savings rate to a high level and productively investing the savings. This is more important than the role of foreign capital, including FDI. The East Asian growth success is based mainly on high domestic savings rather than FDI.
- Foreign capital can help to supplement domestic savings but this has its downside. There are three types of foreign capital inflow: aid, debt and FDI. FDI has many advantages: bringing in

Figure 1: Block Diagram Showing the Interlinkings Between the Economic Effects of FDI on GDP Growth as Captured by the Model Used:

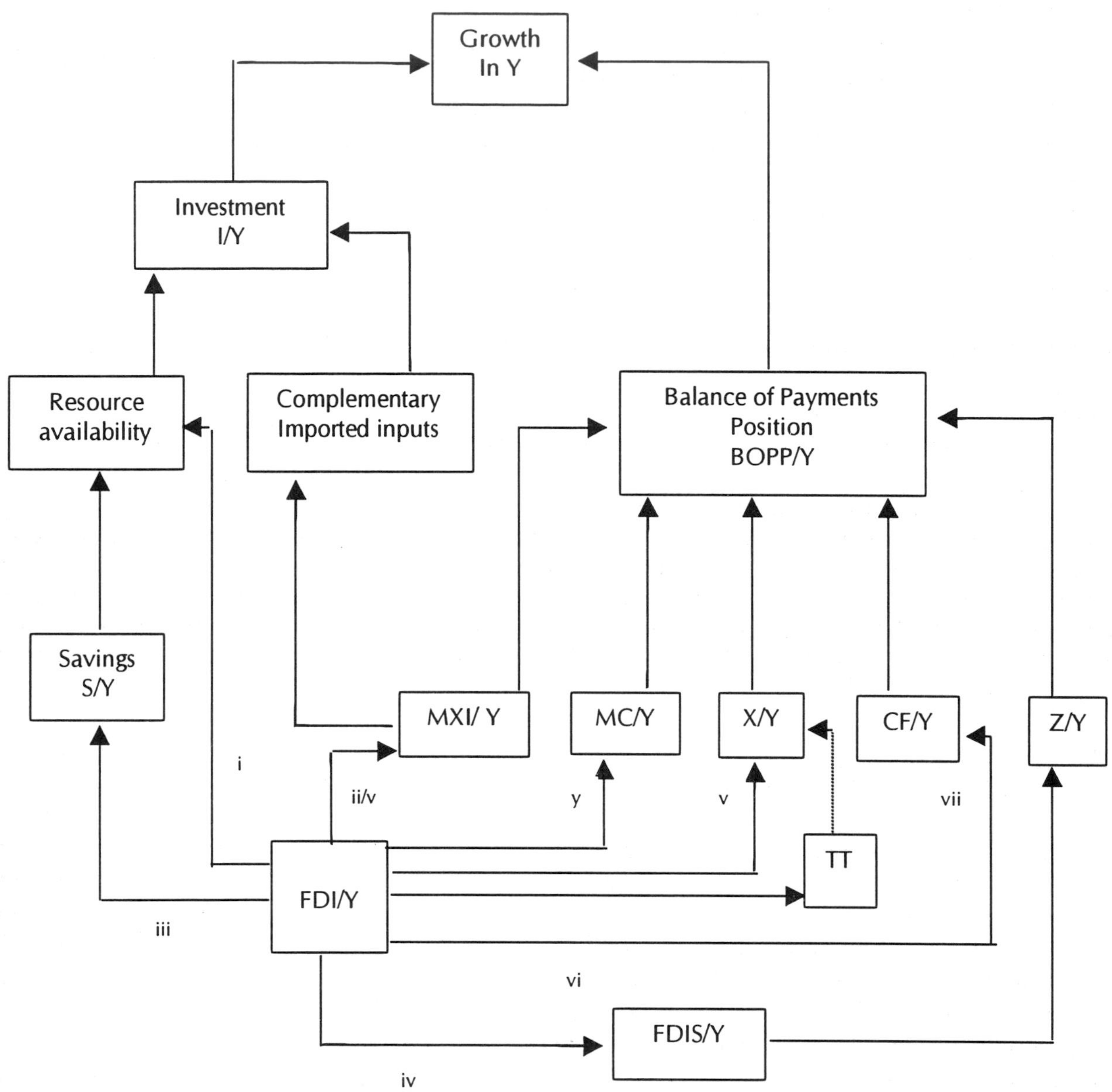

Notes:

MXI = Imports of capital and Intermediate goods
X = Exports
CF = Flight of capital abroad
Y = GDP
MC = Consumption imports
Z = Factor payments outflows
TT = Terms of trade
FDIS = Stocks of FDI

Source: Ghazali Atan (1996)

- productive capital, foreign expertise, brand names, market linkages, aiding in industrialisation, exports, employment.
- However, there are also disadvantages or costs to FDI. These impacts need to be managed to ensure a net positive outcome.
- The study found that FDI has a negative effect on domestic savings, as it gives room for the recipient country to increase its consumption.
- FDI generates positive and negative effects on the flow of foreign exchange on two accounts: financial and trade. The effects from these two accounts are summarised in Table 1.

Table 1: Summary of FDI Effects on Inflow/Outflow of Funds and Balance Of Payments

	Positive Effects	Negative Effects
Financial Flows	-Inflow of foreign capital	-Outflow of profit, royalties and revenue/ incomes
Trade Flows	-Increased export earnings -Savings from reduced imports	-Increased import of capital goods -Increased import of intermediate goods -Increased import of consumer goods

NOTE: The balance of financial flows will tend to be strongly negative over time, as the one-time inflow of capital would give rise to a stream of outflows of investment income. The larger the stock of foreign investment, the greater will be the outflows. To avoid balance of payments (BOP) difficulties, the balance of trade flows should be strongly positive to offset the deficit in financial flows. However this is not necessarily so. In some cases, the trade balance from FDI may be positive but weakly so; in other cases, it may even be negative, when the imports of foreign companies exceed their export earnings. In the latter case, a trade deficit is added to the finance deficit, which may cause BOP problems.

- On the financial side, FDI brings in capital, but also leads to a stream of outflows of profit and other investment income. This outflow increases through time as the stock of foreign capital rises. Thus, FDI has a tendency to lead to "decapitalisation".
- Comparing aid, debt and FDI, the study finds that because of the much higher rate of return of FDI compared to the rate of interest paid on aid or debt, the "decapitalisation" effect of FDI is greater than of aid or debt. For instance, in the illustrative case shown in Table 2, at 1.5% interest, the outflow due to *aid* would be less than inflow, even after 17 years; at 5% interest it would take 17 years for outflow to exceed inflow. At 10% interest on *debt*, it would take six years before outflow exceeds inflow. At 15% return on *FDI*, it would take only three years before outflow exceeds inflow. By year 17, the outflow of $6,300 far exceeds the new inflow of $2,000.
- On the trade side, FDI has a positive effect through higher export earnings and a savings on imports (for products locally produced), but a negative effect through higher imports of intermediate and capital goods (refer to Table 1). It may also have a negative effect in raising imports of consumption goods. In many cases, FDI is heavily reliant on large imports of capital and intermediate goods. The high import content reduces the positive trade effect. Ghazali's study shows that generally there is a weak positive trade effect from FDI, and in some cases a negative trade effect.

Table 2: The Net Financial Effect of FDI and Other Sources of Inflows

Year	Inflow	Stock	Stock-1	Outflow at 1.5%	Outflows at 5%	Outflows at 10%	Outflows at 15%
1	2000	12000	10000	150	500	1000	1500
2	2000	14000	12000	180	600	1200	1800
3	2000	16000	14000	210	700	1400	2100
4	2000	18000	16000	240	800	1600	2400
5	2000	20000	18000	270	900	1800	2700
6	2000	22000	20000	300	1000	2000	3000
7	2000	24000	22000	330	1100	2200	3300
8	2000	26000	24000	360	1200	2400	3600
9	2000	28000	26000	390	1300	2600	3900
10	2000	30000	28000	420	1400	2800	4200
11	2000	32000	30000	450	1500	3000	4500
12	2000	34000	32000	480	1600	3200	4800
13	2000	36000	34000	510	1700	3400	5100
14	2000	38000	36000	540	1800	3600	5400
15	2000	40000	38000	570	1900	3800	5700
16	2000	42000	40000	600	2000	4000	6000
17	2000	44000	42000	630	2100	4200	6300

Source: Ghazali Atan (1996)

- In order for FDI to have a positive effect on balance of payments, the trade effect must be positive and sufficiently strong to offset the negative decapitalisation effect. However, due to a weakly positive trade effect, or even a negative trade effect in some cases, there is a tendency for FDI to cause a negative overall effect on the balance of payments. Without careful policy planning, the negative effect could grow through time and be serious as profit outflow builds up.
- Too rapid a build-up of FDI could also lead to "de-nationalisation", where the foreign share of the nation's wealth stock increases relative to local share. To avoid economic or social problems that this may cause, Ghazali proposes obeying "Moffat's rule", that the rate of growth of domestic investment should exceed FDI growth.
- Regarding the effect of FDI on economic growth, there are direct effects (which are generally positive) and indirect effects (which are generally negative, due mainly to the decapitalisation effect). Whilst the inflow of new FDI exerts a positive effect, the outflow of investment income arising from the accumulated foreign capital stock exerts a negative effect.
- The general model (Figure 1) was applied to the case of Malaysia (1961-86). It estimated the impact of FDI on variables such as investment, savings, exports, imports and factor payments, and found that there was an overall negative impact on growth. Each increase of 1% in the ratio of FDI to gross domestic product (GDP) slowed growth by 0.03%. Looking at the long-term impact of FDI, debt and aid on growth, the study finds that, "For FDI the effect starts off from a negative position and worsens over time; for debt the effect starts off being positive but turns progressively negative in the longer term; the effect of aid shows the opposite tendency, i.e. negative on impact but turning more benign later. The key dynamic influence was found to be the factor payment effect (i.e., the decapitalisation effect)." (Ghazali 1996, 21)
- Given the various ways in which FDI affects the host economy, Ghazali (1996, 8-9) proposes that for FDI to be used successfully (with net overall benefit), the following conditions should be met:

(i) Availability of foreign capital does not detract from own savings effort.
(ii) The factor payment cost must be minimised and prudently managed.
(iii) Encourage or require joint ventures so that part of the returns accrues to locals and is retained by the local economy.
(iv) Get foreign firms to list themselves on local bourses.
(v) To enhance positive trade effects, DFI (direct foreign investment) must be concentrated in the tradable sector, especially in export-based activities.
(vi) Local content of output should be raised over time to improve trade effect.
(vii) Moffat's rule should be adhered to (growth of domestic investment should exceed FDI growth).
(viii) To avoid reliance on foreign capital, developing countries should increase their savings rate and maintain sound economic and political conditions.

Ghazali (1996, 9-10) concludes that:

> *The above are among preconditions for ensuring successful use of FDI. Countries using DFI without regard to the above conditions would do so at their own peril. Any moves designed to prevent host countries from instituting such policies, however they are couched, are moves designed to keep developing countries at the bottom of the global economic ladder...With the correct policies, DFI can be of great help to host countries. Without the correct policies, however, the use of DFI can lead to severe problems especially with regard to the long-term viability of the recipient's balance of payments.*

2) Benefits, Costs and Risks of Foreign Investment

The South Centre (1997) examines the benefits, costs and risks of FDI, as well as the issue of an appropriate policy towards foreign investment. From the viewpoint of host developing countries, there are both important benefits and potentially significant costs associated with FDI. The possible benefits include technology transfer; increased production efficiency due to competition from multinationals; improvement in quality of production factors such as management (including in other firms); benefits to the balance of payments through inflow of investment funds; increases in exports; increases in savings and investments and hence faster growth of output and employment.

The acknowledged costs include possible negative effects on the balance of payments due to increased use of imported inputs and repatriation of profits by foreign investors; non-competitive pricing (and resulting overall inefficiency in resource allocation) due to the large market power of multinationals; adverse impact on the competitive environment; discouragement of development of technical know-how by local firms. If it fails to generate adequate linkages with the local economy, FDI will have fewer spillover beneficial effects and may on balance be harmful if the other negative features above exist. Other costs are transfer pricing (which diminishes host government taxes); distortion of consumption patterns due to brand names of multinationals (with costly effects when expensive foreign foods from FDI supplant local and more nutritious foods in the diet of the urban poor); the net loss of jobs when capital-intensive FDI displaces labour-intensive local firms.

There are also environmental and natural resource costs associated with FDI, and FDI in the media risks facilitating Western cultural hegemony. Also, politico-strategic interests are at stake if FDI comprises a large component of total investment and involves loss of local control over strategic sectors, infrastructure and natural resources. Decisions made abroad can impact on the local economy and society, and sometimes even the country's sovereignty may be at stake.

These factors have to be taken into account in an overall net evaluation of the costs and benefits of FDI. Although there are arguments encouraging any kind or volume of FDI, the South Centre study concludes that an undiscerning policy towards FDI may cause serious long-run economic difficulties, harming a country's development prospects. In particular, the growing liberalisation of FDI and of financial markets poses significant new hazards to developing countries that can threaten their financial viability.

Among these risks are:

- Balance of payments. The current account position of developing countries is a critical variable deserving the utmost attention in a world of free capital movements, as shown in the Mexican and Asian financial crises. FDI gives rise to foreign exchange outflows due to profit payments and import costs; whether FDI generates sufficient foreign exchange earnings to cover these foreign exchange costs is of great relevance. For example, if FDI takes place in a non-tradable service industry (e.g., a supermarket, especially if it sells imported goods) and if profits are repatriated, the balance of payments implications are inimical to a country's future development.
- FDI volatility. FDI flows can be volatile, especially since financial liberalisation and new financial instruments such as derivatives have blurred the distinction between FDI and portfolio investment, so that the stock of FDI can easily be exported as capital. Also, the level and degree of profits that are retained (which is a key component of FDI flow) can be highly volatile especially in a crisis. The old presumption that FDI flows are less volatile than portfolio investment may no longer hold.
- Cyclical behaviours and surges in FDI. FDI surges pose macroeconomic problems as acute as those caused by surges in portfolio investment—as they lead to currency overvaluation and financial instability. In addition, pro-cyclical FDI flows may exacerbate economic fluctuations. If retained foreign profits are a large part of FDI inflows, these are likely to be pro-cyclical.
- Financial fragility. The impact of FDI depends on factors such as the steadiness or volatility of FDI inflows; the proportion of FDI accounted for by retained profits; the level of imports related to the FDI; the percentage of output exported. A situation can develop where a decision to increase just the rate of profit repatriation can lead to a foreign exchange crisis. A similar crisis can also occur if there is a reduction or interruption of FDI inflows, in a country using FDI inflows to finance current account deficits.

The South Centre study concludes that not all FDI is conducive to development, some kinds may do more harm than good, and a policy to accept any and all FDI may harbour trouble for future development prospects. To limit the risks and avoid undesirable effects, the study recommends that governments take a selective policy on FDI by 1) determining the composition of capital inflows and intervening to manage inflows of capital including FDI; 2) exercising discretion with respect to specific projects, e.g., confining FDI to priority sectors; and 3) prudence with respect to total FDI stock and flows to avoid more financial fragility. It concludes: "A global investment regime that took away a developing country's ability to select among FDI projects would hinder development and prejudice economic stability."

The Need for National Regulation and Policy Instruments/Options on Foreign Investments

The major issue concerning the desirability of a global investment regime is not whether foreign investment is good or bad, or should be welcomed. The issue is whether or not national governments should retain the right and powers to regulate FDI, including adequate authority and means to establish policy instruments and options concerning investment, including foreign investment.

Most countries presently accept the importance of foreign investment and are trying their best to attract foreign investments. However, as the previous sub-section showed, there is evidence that foreign investment can have both positive and negative effects. A major objective of development policy is to maximise the positive aspects whilst minimising the negative aspects, so that on balance there is a significant benefit.

Experience shows that for foreign investment to play a positive role, government must have the right and powers to regulate its entry, terms of conditions and operations.

1) Regulations on entry and establishment

Most developing countries now have policies that regulate the entry of foreign firms, and include various conditions and restrictions for foreign investors overall and on a sector-by-sector basis.

There are few developing countries (if any) that have adopted a policy of total right of entry. In some countries, foreign companies are not allowed to operate in certain sectors, for instance banking, insurance or telecommunications. In sectors where they are allowed, foreign companies have to apply for permission to establish themselves, and if approval is given, it often comes with conditions.

Of course the mix of conditions varies from country to country. They may include equity restrictions (for example, a foreign company cannot own more than a certain percentage of the equity of the company it would like to set up) and ownership restrictions (for instance, foreigners are not allowed to own land or to buy houses below a certain price).

In a recent study on how the MAI would affect the South, the Friends of the Earth-US (1997) compiled a list of existing regulations in developing countries that make foreign investment subject to conditions or restrictions. The following are examples of policies and regulations restricting entry and establishment:

- In China, investment guidelines were issued in June 1995 detailing sectors in which investment is encouraged, restricted or prohibited. China prohibits foreign investment for projects with objectives not in line with national economic development. Categories of restricted investment generally reflect the protection of domestic industries, such as the services sector, in which China fears its domestic market and companies would be quickly dominated by foreign firms. Restrictions also aim to limit imports of luxuries or enterprises requiring large imports of components and raw materials, as well as to avoid redundancy or excess capacity.
- In Taiwan, foreign investment is not allowed in agricultural production (including agricultural chemicals production); in Pakistan foreign investors are not allowed to own land for agriculture or irrigation; and in Brazil foreign ownership of land in rural areas and adjacent to international borders is prohibited.
- In the forestry sector, Bangladesh bars foreign investment in forest plantations and mechanical extraction in reserved forest areas; Taiwan forbids foreign investment in forestry; and China does not allow wholly foreign-owned investment in processing and export of raw wood.
- Malaysia has regulations limiting the degree of foreign equity ownership in some sectors; in manufacturing, the equity limit varies with the degree of exports in a firm's output.
- In India, proposals for foreign equity participation exceeding 51 percent and projects considered to be politically sensitive are screened by the Foreign Investment Promotion Board.

An international investment regime granting the right to establishment and national treatment to foreign investors would put pressure on developing countries to give up or phase out present policies regulating the entry and the degree and conditions of participation of foreign investors.

2) Policies favouring local firms and domestic economy

Many developing countries also have policies that favour the growth of local companies. For instance, there may be tax breaks for a local company not available to foreign companies; local banks may be given greater scope of business than foreign banks; only local institutions may be eligible for research and development grants; local firms may be given preference in government business or contracts.

Governments justify such policies and conditions on the grounds of sovereignty (that a country's population has to have control over at least a minimal but significant part of its own economy) or national development (that local firms need to be given a "handicap" or special treatment at least for some time so that they can be in a position to compete with more powerful and better endowed foreign companies).

Most developing countries would argue that during the colonial era, their economies were shaped to the advantage of foreign companies and financial institutions (belonging usually to the particular colonising country). Local people and enterprises were therefore at a disadvantage, and require a considerable time when special treatment is accorded to them, before they can compete on more balanced terms with the bigger foreign companies. This has been the central rationale for developing countries' policies in applying restrictions or imposing conditions on foreign investments.

A global investment regime that prohibits or severely restricts affirmative action by developing countries for local firms and the domestic economy would therefore have serious consequences. No longer will each government have the freedom to choose its own particular mixture of policies and conditions on foreign investments. The major policies would be already determined by the multilateral set of investment rules, and the choice available would be limited to more minor aspects.

Under the Services Agreement (GATS) in the WTO, establishment rights and national treatment are to be given to those services sectors that are put on offer by a country. The Services Agreement is not a catchall agreement and applies only to those sectors or activities that the country has put "on offer". The proposed MAI would in contrast be a catchall agreement, in which all sectors and activities are included, unless specifically excluded. Thus, any "affirmative action" measures promoting local industries or services (through subsidies, preferential tax treatment, specified conditions for investment, and even subsidies for research and development (R&D)) could be seen as "discriminatory" against foreigners and thus prohibited.

3) Measures to manage the balance of payments

As earlier shown, there is a general tendency for FDI to generate a net outflow of foreign exchange. Many developing countries have taken measures to try to ensure a more positive result from FDI on the balance of payments and on the domestic economy. These measures may aim at (a) increasing the share of export earnings (and thus foreign exchange) in the output of FDI (for example, incentives or permission for higher-equity ownership are given to firms that are more export-oriented in order to encourage export earnings; (b) reducing the imports of capital and intermediate goods by foreign firms through encouraging the use of local products; (c) reducing the amount of foreign profits through requirements that foreign firms form joint ventures with local partners, or allocate a part of the company's shares to locals, so that a portion of FDI profits accrue to locals; (d) requiring or encouraging a foreign firm to retain a significant part of their profits for reinvestment. The objectives are to generate spinoffs for and linkages to the domestic economy and thus boost growth, whilst also attempting to create a more positive impact of FDI on the balance of payments, by increasing the share of revenue and value-added that is retained in the economy.

Some of the traditional measures have already come under pressure from the WTO's Trade-Related Investment Measures (TRIMS) Agreement. For instance, governments have required that firms use specified local inputs, or a percentage of the output value must be locally sourced (local content policy). Another condition is that imported inputs of a firm must be restricted to only a certain percentage of that firm's export earnings (balancing of foreign exchange policy). Another policy may be to restrict a commodity or product from being exported (by imposing a ban or limiting export to a percentage). All these policy measures have been explicitly mentioned in an illustrative list and made illegal by the TRIMS Agreement, on the ground it discriminates against foreign products or foreign trade. The removal of these policy measures would make it more difficult to resolve balance-of-payments deficits. Developing countries have five years (from January 1995) to implement this.

The MAI's proposals to prohibit a wide range of "performance requirements" (including the above but expanding the list to many new items) would make the situation even more difficult.

Governments now are able to control the quantity and quality of foreign investment. As shown above, some countries limit the percentage of foreign equity, in some cases requiring the foreign firm to form joint ventures so that locals retain a share of the profits. Some countries limit the outflow of profits. If a global investment regime like the MAI were to prohibit these measures, then governments would lose these as instruments to protect the balance of payments. Inability to regulate entry will increase the foreign share of equity. Removal of joint-venture arrangements would further raise foreign equity. Together these would raise the foreign share of profits in the economy. In line with international trends, corporate tax rates are also being reduced in many countries, thus adding to the trend of higher net foreign profit. If foreign profit outflow is too high and threatens the BOP or reserves and financial stability, the option of limiting profit repatriation would not be available.

Conclusions: At present, most governments in developing countries have maintained systems of regulation of foreign investment, including policies and rules on entry, establishment, operations and requirements to fulfil certain obligations in line with national, development, social and environmental objectives. These policies and regulations reflect the recognition that the role of foreign investment should be placed in an appropriate context, and that it is the responsibility of government to ensure that the benefits of FDI accrue to the country, whilst the risks and costs are reduced or minimised, so that there will be net positive results. Thus, many of the existing policies and regulations have a logic and rationale within this overall context and framework. An appropriate international approach to investment should recognise and endorse this developmental framework. To do away with this carefully constructed policy framework and with the many kinds of regulations may well damage or destroy the opportunities and conditions for sustainable and human-oriented development.

Key Features of the Mai and their Development Implications

Introduction: The core objectives of the MAI are "to establish a broad multilateral framework for international investment with high standards for the liberalisation of investment regimes and investment protection and with effective dispute settlement procedures."

The MAI seeks to radically broaden the scope of freedom of movement and operation of foreign investors and their investments, and to provide more rights for them. Correspondingly, the MAI severely narrows and restricts the rights and powers of states to regulate the entry, establishment and operations of foreign companies and their investments. It also makes host developing countries greatly more susceptible to legal action by foreign investors and their home governments, due to the MAI's articles on expropriation (which is widely defined) and on dispute settlement.

The MAI has three key elements:

- Deregulating and liberalising foreign investments. Foreign investors will have rights to operate in all member countries, with minimal regulations, and be treated as well as or better than local firms or citizens. States will be forbidden to impose conditions such as technology transfer, local share equity, or the use of local materials, on foreign companies.
- Providing maximum rights to foreign investors, who will be protected from expropriation of their property, and from equivalent measures that could reduce their economic prospects. Investors must also be given total freedom to take money in and out of the host country.
- A dispute settlement system of enforcement, where a state or an investor can sue another state for not conforming to the MAI rules. The complaint can be brought before an international tribunal, which can direct the offending state to pay compensation or undertake other forms of relief. Foreign corporations will be able to sue governments for up to hundreds of millions of dollars in damages for claimed losses caused by non-compliance with the MAI.

The following is an outline of the main features of the MAI, and an analysis of their implications for developing countries. This account and analysis is based on a reading of "The Multilateral Agreement on Investment: Consolidated Text" dated 23 April 1998 (DAFFE/MAI/NM(98)2/REV1), issued by the OECD's Directorate for Financial, Fiscal and Enterprise Affairs. As far as is known, this is the latest text available, and given the stalemate in the negotiations (at least up to February 1998), it could be the final draft, unless negotiations resume. Reference was also made to "Commentary to Consolidated Text" issued by the OECD (DAFFE/MAI/NM(98)4) dated 6 March 1998. The 23 April 1998 text contains many sections and words which had been agreed upon by the negotiators, whilst several sections, paragraphs and words are within brackets, denoting that agreement had not been reached on these points or terms.

General Provisions and Scope of the MAI

The MAI's preamble affirms the decision of signatories "to create a free-standing Agreement open to accession by all countries." Among the agreed points are that the Members: 1) emphasise that fair, transparent and predictable investment regimes complement and benefit the world trading system; 2) wish to establish a broad multilateral framework for international investment with high standards for the liberalisation of investment regimes and investment protection and with effective dispute settlement procedures; and 3) recognise that the agreed treatment to be accorded to investors and investments will contribute to efficient use of economic resources, creation of employment opportunities and improving living standards.

This preamble lays out the basic assumptions that the MAI regime is fair and equitable for all parties, and that the targets of "high standards for liberalisation and protection", backed by an effective enforcement mechanism, will lead to the goals of efficient resource use, job creation and higher living standards. These are only assumptions and have to be assessed in line with existing knowledge of the investment-development nexus. For example, so-called "high standards" of liberalisation in countries where local firms are not yet able to compete could result in net loss of jobs.

As for the scope and application of the MAI, the text reveals a very broad definition of investors and investments. The term "investor" includes a natural person who is a national of or resident in a contracting party, and a legal person or entity constituted under the law of a contracting party, whether or not for profit, whether private or government-owned, and includes a corporation, trust, sole proprietorship, partnership, joint venture, association or organisation.

This is a very broad definition, which includes any commercial *or* non-commercial organisation, including non-profit groups and institutions. This has significant implications beyond economic considerations, as the broad definition can also include, for example, political, social, religious organisations of all types. The freedom granted to these non-commercial organisations would of course have significant social and political implications for developing countries, almost all of which regulate the establishment or operations of such groups.

The definition of "investment" is "every kind of asset owned or controlled, directly or indirectly, by an investor." Eight categories are specifically described, including an enterprise; shares, stocks and equity participation; bonds, loans and forms of debt; rights under contracts; claims to money and performance; intellectual property rights; rights conferred pursuant to law or contract (concessions, licenses, authorisations, permits); any other property and property rights (e.g., leases, mortgages, liens and pledges).

This is an extremely broad definition, deliberately chosen to go "beyond the traditional notion of FDI to cover virtually all tangible and intangible assets and which applies to both pre- and post-establishment." (OECD 1997a, 4). Significantly, its coverage includes intellectual property rights (IPRs) and "any portfolio investment that an investor has acquired or may wish to acquire."

The broad coverage has serious implications. It implies that the liberalisation and protection provisions, and the dispute settlement system (which includes the right of investors to sue states) extends to all these areas, and not only to FDI. This wide definition of investment has serious implications for most developing countries, which have regulations restricting FDI and especially portfolio investment, foreign loans and loan repayment, rights under contracts and other property rights. Since investment also covers the "pre-establishment" phase, rights are conferred by the MAI to foreigners intending to invest, even before their investment. The significance is that the MAI's developing-country members will have to recognise the rights of foreigners (from other member countries) to "invest" in their countries and participate in the broad range of activities defined as "investment". This may have serious effects on the ratio between foreigners and locals in the ownership of assets and in participation in many aspects of economic life. Moreover, as the scope is so broad, foreigners will have rights to freely take in and out funds in all forms (through loans, portfolio investment, FDI, etc.), with serious implications for money supply and financial policy, exchange rate and balance of payments (BOP).

"Treatment of Investors and Investments": MAI Provisions for Deregulation and Liberalisation of Foreign Investment

Introduction: The MAI text has a key section (Section III), entitled "Treatment of Investors and Investments", in which the main features are liberalisation and deregulation of policies relating to foreign investment. Under the liberalisation sections, the MAI aims at ultimately giving foreign investors the right to enter and establish enterprises with full equity ownership in all member countries. This is particularly significant since, as we have seen, a very broad definition is given to the terms "investors" and "investments".

Thus, governments would no longer have the authority to screen the entry of foreign investors (or even of non-commercial societies), nor to place limits on the degree of their participation in the national economy and society. (The MAI would however allow some general exceptions as well as country-specific reservations, including on a sectoral basis. However, countries will be under pressure for continuous liberalisation and any "rolling back" of domestic investment rules would be prohibited.)

1) National Treatment

The "national treatment" principle is one of the most important aspects of the MAI. The text states that: "Each contracting party shall accord to investors of another contracting party and to their investments, treatment no less favourable than the treatment it accords (in like circumstances) to its own investors and their investments with respect to the establishment, acquisition, expansion, operation, management, maintenance, use, enjoyment and sale or other disposition of investments."

This article has very serious implications for developing countries. The article makes it mandatory for member states to allow the entry and establishment of any foreign company or institution in all sectors (unless specifically covered by a "reservations list" submitted by the country), and the foreign investors must be treated at least as well as local investors.

At present, most developing countries have agencies or committees that screen foreign investment applications in line with certain criteria, national goals and development objectives. Many of these are aimed at protecting local enterprises from stronger foreign enterprises, until such time that the local firms are strong enough to compete on more equal standing. Some restrictions are for reasons of monetary and financial control and policy and for protection of the balance of payments. Certain strategic sectors are also protected or partially protected for social, cultural or political and strategic reasons: for example, in the food-producing agriculture sector, with a predominance of small farms, foreign ownership of land may be prohibited or restricted to protect the resources and livelihoods of a large and vulnerable segment of the population. The financial sector is protected because of its crucial economic role. In many countries, the media, health and educational sectors are protected for cultural and social reasons. In some countries, in some sectors where local enterprises already have the required technology and marketing channels (e.g., plantation export crops, mining), foreign investment may be restricted or not encouraged. These restrictions would be removed through the national treatment article, either immediately or in due course (for sectors included in a reservations list).

Moreover, most developing countries have policies and laws that promote or favour local enterprises. The rationale is that, partly due to the colonial experience, local farms and firms have not been given the full opportunity to develop to a level where they can compete with the large foreign enterprises. Also, the development of local enterprise capacity is important for national development, in terms of upgrading local technology and skills, retention of income within the economy, linkages within and between sectors in the economy, employment generation and for economic, social and political security. Therefore, most governments, whilst welcoming foreign investments, also take positive measures to promote local enterprises through general provisions (for example, equity requirements, research and development grants, preference to locals in government contracts and expenditure) or through specific sectoral policies (for example, subsidy to local farms, permission for local banks to open more branches, state financing or encouragement for local-owned or joint-venture industrial enterprises, etc.).

The national treatment principle that underlies the whole MAI would seek to deny the validity of past and present state policies and actions in developing countries in providing assistance to local enterprises to protect and promote their survival and growth. Such policies have been a fundamental assumption in much of development economics.

Countries will have to review the basic assumptions of their existing development strategies and plans and either reaffirm them or change them drastically, in the process of making a decision whether to join the MAI. The existing (explicit or implicit) policies that favour or assist local enterprises will have to be listed and re-examined for their desirability and validity, and the implications of changing the policies.

A developing country deciding to join the MAI, even with reservations on a list, would be obliged to accept the national treatment principle, and to have standstill in and rollback of the present restrictions on foreign investors and of the present policies that favour local enterprises. If a mistake is made, and reservations are not entered (or are entered but at a particular level that later proves inappropriate), it would not be possible to return to an earlier level of protection.

On the other hand, the national treatment principle would also make it easier for investors from a developing country to be established and compete on more equitable terms (vis-à-vis locals) in other countries. In reality, only a few existing big enterprises from developing countries will be able to take advantage of this, at the moment. The numbers could of course grow in time. However, the interests of outward-bound investors can also be protected through bilateral investment treaties; thus, the MAI is not the only instrument for investor protection.

Developing countries have to weigh the benefits and costs of joining the MAI in terms of the effects it will have on the domestic economy and on the position of local enterprises, and in terms of the benefits that may accrue to its outward-bound investors.

2) Most Favoured Nation (MFN) Treatment

The MAI text states that each contracting party shall accord to investors (and investments) of another contracting party treatment no less favourable than it accords to investors (and investments) of any other contracting party or of a non-contracting party. This is with respect to the same range of activities (establishment, operation, etc.) as in the national treatment article.

This MFN principle would prohibit a country from developing more favourable relations with certain other countries in relation to investment. This could be a drawback for policies by developing countries to establish closer links with other developing countries at the same stage of development, or in the same regional area. For example, a country that is a member of ASEAN and participates in preferential arrangements for investors and investments within the ASEAN region, would have to offer the same terms to investors from MAI member countries, should it join the MAI.

The article might also pose a problem for a developing country that has established special links with particular countries—for example some Asian developing countries have invested resources to develop special links with China or with African and Latin American countries—in promotion of South-South investments. Should those other countries join the MAI, the special relationships with these Asian countries could be called into question. For example, investors from other countries could challenge decisions made by a state to award contracts or projects to investors from "friendly countries", on the ground that they were more deserving. In general, the prospects for more special South-South or regional investment links would be made more difficult.

3) Rights of Key Foreign Personnel and Employment Requirements

According to the MAI text, member countries must grant temporary entry, stay and authorisation to work to a foreign investor and to key personnel (defined as executives, managers and specialists) of foreign firms. The spouse and children of these persons shall also be granted entry and stay. Entry and stay or work authorisation cannot be denied for reasons relating to labour market or other economic needs test or numerical restrictions in national laws or procedures. Foreign investors must be given the right of entry and work authorisation and their numbers cannot be restricted.

The MAI also forbids a member country from requiring a foreign investor to appoint individuals of any particular nationality as executives, managers and board members. Presumably this is to remove existing measures in countries that require foreign firms to hire locals in management or directorship posts. Also, member countries must permit foreign investors to employ anyone of their choice, regardless of nationality, provided the person holds a valid work permit.

These provisions on foreign key personnel, on management and choice of employees will seriously affect many developing countries. These countries have regulations restricting the number (and functions) of foreign staff a foreign investor can bring in. Also, they have policies, especially in joint-venture arrangements, that local citizens should occupy certain senior managerial positions as well as membership and positions on the Board of Directors. The aim of these policies is to ensure that there should not be a dominance of foreign personnel and that there be a transfer of managerial and professional skills to local people, as well that in joint-ventures, local citizens be able to occupy key leadership positions. The existing restrictions have created job opportunities for local managers and professionals in foreign and joint-venture firms.

The MAI provisions prevent or severely restrict governments from acting towards these goals. Instead, governments would be obliged to allow the entry of a large number of foreign personnel, since numerical restriction is specifically forbidden and since the definition of key personnel is broad. The opportunities for locals will likely be reduced.

4) Performance Requirements

One of the most important of the MAI's provisions is that contracting parties are prohibited from imposing or maintaining specified "performance requirements" on any investor, in connection with the establishment, acquisition, expansion, management, operation, use or sale of an investment.

The MAI text lists twelve performance requirements that are prohibited, including requirements on firms to achieve a given level or percentage of local content; to export a given level or percentage of goods and services; to buy, use or prefer locally-made goods and services; to transfer technology or a production process; to achieve a given level of research and development in the country; to relate the firm's value of imports or local sales to its export value; to establish a joint venture with domestic participation; to achieve a minimum level of local equity participation; or to hire a given level of nationals.

Many items on this prohibition list are seen by governments (especially in developing countries) as social obligations that foreign corporations should meet as a contribution to the host country's development goals. The MAI would ban governments from requiring any corporation (local as well as foreign) to meet these obligations.

The MAI, however, allows government to offer an advantage to investors to comply with some of the listed items as well as offer an advantage to comply with other commitments such as to locate production, provide particular services, train or employ workers, construct particular facilities, or carry out R&D.

This is a very significant article with serious implications for development. The coverage of the prohibited performance requirements is very broad: it includes not only foreign investors from MAI countries, but also from non-MAI countries, as well as local investors and firms. This means that the performance requirements are banned for all foreign and local firms.

Also, the MAI list goes far beyond the prohibited investment measures of the TRIMS (trade-related investment measures) Agreement in the WTO, which are only "trade-related" (such as the local content requirement). The MAI prohibited measures include many "non trade related" measures such as technology transfer, establishing joint ventures, and local equity participation.

Many countries have regulations or policies obliging foreign investors to follow many or most of the performance requirements specified as prohibited in the MAI. Most of the requirements are imposed so that foreign investors meet their obligations to help host countries fulfil their development or national goals, such as upgrading technology, stimulating the business of local enterprises and the domestic sector, establishing or strengthening linkages with the domestic sectors, and earning or saving foreign exchange so as to protect the balance of payments. Without fulfilment of these goals, development may not take place or be sustainable. The removal of the right of governments to impose these requirements would deprive host countries of key economic instruments to pursue macroeconomic policies as well as long-term industrial policy and development strategies.

The prohibition on requiring joint ventures and minimum local equity participation is also very significant. This implies that foreign firms (whether or not from MAI countries) must be allowed 100 percent equity ownership. Many countries now have regulations limiting the equity participation of foreign firms. This could be aimed at increasing local ownership, limiting foreign monopolisation, as well as retention of profits and revenues within the country so as to protect the balance of payments—objectives that are seen in many countries to be important for maintaining social and economic stability.

The prohibition on imposing these performance requirements could thus have serious adverse effects on the ability of a host country to reach development goals, and on the attainment or preservation of economic, social and political stability.

5) Privatisation

Under the MAI, governments must give "national treatment" and MFN treatment to foreign investors in all kinds of privatisation schemes and in subsequent transactions involving a privatised asset. Preference shown to local firms, or reservation of shares for local enterprises or citizens, during privatisation exercises, would be illegal. Special share arrangements (for example, retention of golden shares by a state in order to maintain policy control of the privatised entity) may also be banned. Contracting parties must publish features and procedures for participation in each privatisation.

The inclusion of privatisation considerably broadens the scope of the MAI since current investment rules (including in the OECD) do not cover this subject. The MAI does not oblige states to privatise, but once a publicly owned enterprise is offered to private investors, then national treatment and MFN applies. Foreign investors would have the same (or better) rights as local investors to acquire government-held assets.

The application of national treatment and MFN treatment has serious implications for developing countries. Many countries are in the process of privatisation. In this process, it is often the case that preference may be given to local investors, or a certain percentage of shares (or even all) may be reserved for locals. The protection of local interests is seen as needed in order that there be a retention of significant local participation in what are often key economic and social sectors or activities previously owned and controlled by government. In addition, if privatisation were opened up equally to foreigners, the stronger foreign investors would have an advantage by virtue of the resources they command. This section of the MAI prohibiting advantageous treatment to locals would open the road for significant foreign purchase of privatised assets, including what a country may consider its strategic sectors or industries.

Moreover, the additional restrictions placed by the MAI on special share arrangements would make it difficult or impossible for government to retain a fair amount of control over privatised or partially-privatised enterprises and activities (which it may now exercise through "golden shares"). These provisions may also prohibit (or at least make very difficult) the reservation of certain percentage of shares (or shares at preferential prices) for certain groups in the local society, or even reservation of shares for the management and staff of the privatised entity. These prohibitions have the potential to prevent the benefits of privatisation from accruing to broader sections (or selected sections) of the local population. Since privatisation is often a socially and politically sensitive topic, the sale of a lot of the "family silver" to foreigners or foreign firms (without the state having the ability to reserve some shares for locals) could generate controversy and discontent and increase the unpopularity of privatisation in general.

6) Monopolies/State Enterprises/Concessions

According to the MAI, a contracting party has the right to maintain, designate or eliminate a monopoly. However it shall accord non-discriminatory treatment when designating a monopoly.

The monopolies must provide non-discriminatory treatment to investors in their sales of the monopoly good or service, and provide non-discriminating treatment in its purchase of the monopoly good or service (with the exception of government procurement).

The MAI does not challenge the right of states to designate or maintain monopolies. It however insists that government-designated monopolies should not be allowed to treat foreign investors less favourably than local enterprises. These monopolies should act in line with the national treatment and MFN obligations when they exercise regulatory powers in connection with a monopoly good or service. The above provisions would prevent government monopolies from selling goods or services more cheaply to local enterprises, or to buy from them at favourable rates.

7) Investment Incentives

There was no consensus on how to treat investment incentives in the MAI text. Several delegations thought no additional text was needed. Many however wanted provisions on incentives but differed as to their nature and scope. Some proposed a built-in agenda for future work.

The discussion focused on a draft article on investment incentives containing four paragraphs. This draft article was regarded as a compromise text by those who preferred more far-reaching disciplines.

In an agreed paragraph 1, the contracting parties confirmed that the articles on national treatment, MFN and transparency apply to investment incentives.

There were differences on whether to have obligations on non-discriminatory investment incentives. This is reflected in the heavily bracketed (indicating lack of agreement) para 2. Some were concerned about the increasing use of incentives, with governments having to engage in costly competition with others to attract investments. Some delegations believed investment incentives "may have distorting effects on the flow of capital and investment decisions". Several however pointed out that not all investment incentives are bad, and that the distorting effects of incentives on investment decisions and capital flows should be balanced against their possible benefits in achieving legitimate social objectives. Some proposed that a contracting party whose investors are adversely affected by an incentive of another party and having a distorting effect may request consultations with that party, and may also bring the incentive before the Parties Group for its consideration.

The text has a bracketed para 3, stating that to avoid and minimise distorting effects and avoid undue competition to attract or retain investments, parties shall negotiate (within three years) to establish additional MAI disciplines after signature of the MAI. The negotiations would recognise the role of investment incentives with regard to the aims of policies (regional, structural, social, environmental or R&D policies), and other work of a similar nature in other fora. They shall in particular address issues of positive discrimination, transparency, standstill and rollback.

The immediate implication is that countries joining the MAI that are now providing investment incentives would have to provide them on a national treatment and MFN basis. Countries could still request reservations in order to continue discriminatory application of incentives. However the trend of thinking within the OECD members is clear: gradually (if not now), disciplines would be imposed to curb or limit non-discriminating incentives. The limitations or curbing of incentives, if not now then in the near future, could reduce the ability of countries to use incentives as an added attraction to foreign investments.

8) Not Lowering Labour and Environment Standards

Several delegations proposed an article on how to address the potential pressure to lower environment and labour standards to attract investments, but this was opposed by a few delegations. The April 1998 MAI text shows there is still considerable debate on how this issue should be approached. It lists four alternative texts under discussion, including an alternative 4 that only covers environment (reflecting the view of some that labour standards be left out).

Alternative 1, which is the oldest approach, states that the Parties recognise that it is inappropriate to encourage investment by lowering health, safety or environmental standards, or relaxing (domestic) (core) labour standards. Accordingly a Party should not waive or derogate from such standards to encourage investment. A Party that considers that another has offered such an encouragement may request consultations with a view to avoiding such encouragement.

Alternative 3 on the other hand proposes that a party shall accord to foreign investors treatment that is "no more favourable" than it accords to its own investors by waiving or derogating from domestic health, safety, environmental or labour measures.

This proposed article remains under intense discussion. There were attempts by some delegations to expand the article because the issues of environmental and labour standards have attracted much attention from civil society groups that have criticised the MAI for its potential effect in lowering these standards worldwide. The proposed article however does not appear to be legally binding and obliges a complained-against Party only to enter consultations with the complainant Party.

Greatly Expanded Protection to Foreign Investors

Introduction: The MAI seeks to give maximum protection to the interests of foreign investors. Under the MAI's Section IV on "investment protection", member states cannot expropriate or nationalise a foreign investor's assets (or take any measures having equivalent effect) except for a public purpose and accompanied by prompt and adequate compensation.

Since the definitions of expropriation and equivalent measures cover broad areas, compensation claims can be made against a state not only for clear instances (such as acquisition of land or factory), but also in such cases as when an investor feels he has been unfairly taxed, that his intellectual property rights are not adequately protected, or that his rights to resources or business opportunities have not been respected.

In another clause on "transfers", the MAI states that all payments relating to an investment may be freely transferred into and out of the host country without delay. This obliges host countries to have the most liberal policy towards capital inflows (including the entry of funds for portfolio investment) and outflows (including profits, proceeds for sale of shares or assets).

With this clause, countries would be prevented from having measures which they believe are needed to prevent the kind of hot-money flows that have recently caused financial havoc in the Southeast Asian countries, and led eventually to balance-of-payments difficulties.

1) General Treatment

The MAI text states that each Party shall accord to investments of investors of another Party "fair and equitable treatment and full and constant protection and security" and the treatment should not be less favourable than required by international law. Also, a Party shall not impair by (unreasonable and/or discriminatory) measures the operation, management, maintenance, use, enjoyment or disposal of investments of investors of another Party.

The general treatment article is sweeping in scope in that the host country may not take measures that impair the operations, use, enjoyment or disposal of investment of the foreign investor. An investor that feels his rights are violated under this article can take legal action against the host state. This puts the host country on the defensive in its creation or use of measures or policies that may cause the foreign investor to feel aggrieved.

2) Expropriation and Compensation

A Party shall not expropriate or nationalise directly or indirectly an investment of investors of another Party, or take any measure or measures having equivalent effect (hereinafter referred to as "expropriation"), except for a public-interest purpose, on a non-discriminatory basis, in accordance with due process of law, and accompanied by payment of prompt, adequate and effective compensation. Compensation shall be paid without delay, shall be equivalent to fair market value of the investment immediately before the expropriation, and shall be fully realisable and transferable. Compensation should include interest at a commercial rate from the date of expropriation until the date of actual payment. (In a footnote, the text says that an interpretive note could provide that the host country bear any exchange rate loss arising from delay in paying compensation).

The definition of the "expropriation" that is to be prohibited is very broad, going beyond the usual meaning as in expropriation of physical or monetary assets. The broad coverage is partly due to the MAI's broad definition of what constitutes "investment" in the first place, and partly to the definition of what constitutes "expropriation" itself.

The broad scope of "expropriation" is shown in the Commentary accompanying the text. The Commentary explains that in cases where the investment consists of shares, the rights of shareholders have to be defined if an expropriation takes place. Thus, "expropriation" will clearly cover portfolio investment, and an investor could argue that its definition includes some measures taken by a government to regulate, restrict or tax the exit (or profits made from) purchases of shares by foreigners. It might be argued that the definition might cover the kinds of measures taken by Malaysia in September 1998, originally to prevent the repatriation of foreign funds in portfolio investment for a period of twelve months, and subsequently changed to an imposition of an exit tax on either the capital or profits. The MAI could therefore constrain developing countries from taking measures to regulate the otherwise volatile flow of short-term funds in portfolio investment.

The Commentary also states that "expropriation in cases where the investment consists in total or in part of intellectual property rights was seen as critical." This makes clear that an investor that is dissatisfied with what he perceives as inadequate protection of intellectual property rights (IPRs) can seek recourse to the MAI and its enforcement system by claiming his investment or property is being expropriated.

The Commentary also says that "creeping expropriation" in general is covered by the words of Section IV, article 2: "measures or measures having equivalent effect." The inclusion of "creeping expropriation" greatly widens the scope of actions that can be taken by an investor against a state under the MAI. Investors can make use of a broad interpretation of the term "expropriation" in order to bring complaints to or against the host government for "measures" that the investor perceives to have caused him loss or damage. An investor who feels that he has been unfairly taxed, or that his IPRs have not been adequately protected, or even generally that his rights to resources or business opportunities have not been adequately respected, could charge that his investment has been expropriated.

In a related section (Section VIII) on taxation, the MAI text contains an article dealing with expropriation as it applies to taxation measures. An interpretative note states that imposition of taxes does not generally constitute expropriation. However, it also clarifies that "a taxation measure will not be considered to constitute expropriation where it is generally within the bounds of internationally recognised tax policies and practices", and that an analysis of whether this principle is satisfied should include whether and to what extent taxation measures of "a similar type and level" are used around the world. Also, expropriation may be constituted even by measures applying to all taxpayers, but measures that are aimed at particular nationalities or individual taxpayers are more likely to suggest an expropriation. From the above, it is clear that tax policies have been brought into the ambit of the MAI and its under its definition of expropriation, thus allowing foreign investors the right to take action against states for alleged unfair tax measures. Given the MAI Commentary, it appears that tax measures that especially relate to foreign investment (including its broad definition of investment) are especially susceptible to claims of expropriation. Thus, measures such as the Malaysian exit tax on either the principal funds or profits made by foreign portfolio investors purchasing shares in local companies, could well be subjected to claims of expropriation.

Under the MAI, the conditions for legitimate expropriation are limited. Also, the terms of compensation are strict and yield the maximum rate for the foreign investor. Compensation will be equivalent to "the fair market value" immediately before the expropriation occurred. It shall be fully realisable and freely transferable (which implies that it should be in hard currency and is allowed to be taken out of the country). Moreover, it should include interest at a commercial rate (for the currency of payment) for the period between expropriation and payment. The Commentary also makes clear the host state will bear the losses from currency fluctuations before the date of payment. It includes notes on the options on how compensation (including coverage of exchange loss) is to be calculated.

It is clear from the above that the host country will be liable to meet terms of compensation for expropriation that highly favour the foreign investor. This is especially significant since "expropriation" is so widely defined. Developing countries that join the MAI (or a similar agreement) could thus be burdened with a series of huge compensation claims and thus with potentially large losses and outflows of foreign exchange.

3) Protection from Strife

An investor that has suffered losses to its investments due to war, emergency, revolution, civil disturbance (or any other similar event) shall be accorded by the host party (as regards restitution, compensation or other settlement) treatment no less favourable than accorded to its own investors or any third State, whichever is most favourable to the investor. Notwithstanding this, an investor suffering a loss in the above situations resulting from the forces or authorities requisitioning its investments, or destruction of its investments which was not required by the necessity of the situation, shall be given restitution or compensation which is prompt, adequate and effective (similar to that for expropriation).

Whilst these clauses seem to recognise that the host state need not automatically compensate foreign investors for damage due to conditions of strife, they also make clear that if locals are compensated or if a locally owned property is "restituted", the foreign investor is also entitled to the same on similar or better terms. This seems to imply that, in the national reconstruction exercise in the aftermath of war or civil disturbance, the host state is also liable to compensate or subsidise foreigners for damage to their property, if it provides subsidies for restituting nationally owned property. This is potentially very costly to the host country. Moreover, the general clause that compensation be given to foreign investors for destruction "which was not required by the necessity of the situation" opens the door for potentially expensive claims, as whether and to what extent the damage done to particular properties during conditions of strife could have been avoided are often matters of subjective opinion.

4) Transfers

Each member state shall ensure that all payments relating to a foreign investment may be freely transferred into and out of its territory without delay. The specified transfers include: (a) initial capital and additional amounts to maintain/increase an investment; (b) returns; (c) payments made under contract, including a loan agreement; (d) proceeds from sale or liquidation of investment; (e) payments of compensation for expropriation and conditions of strife; (f) payments from settlement of a dispute; (g) earnings of personnel engaged from abroad.

Each party shall ensure the transfers may be made in a freely convertible currency, at the market rate of exchange on transfer date.

Exceptions are given to allow delay of prevention of transfer for measures to protect the rights of creditors; or in relation to ensuring compliance with laws on securities, futures and derivatives and laws concerning reports or records of transfers; or in connection with criminal offences. However these measures should not be used as a means to avoid commitments or obligations.

The articles on transfers are most significant, as they oblige host countries to have the most liberal policy towards capital inflows and outflows as regards foreign investors. Many developing countries have previously imposed or are presently imposing controls on the inflows of foreign funds either into banks or stock markets or other investments, as well as some limitations on funds repatriation. Countries that have liberalised may want the option to re-impose some controls if the situation requires it. The MAI would prohibit such restrictions, except during balance-of-payments or foreign exchange crises, in which case stringent IMF conditions and approvals would be necessary (see section on temporary safeguards). Thus, host countries would be prevented from having measures which they believe may be needed to prevent balance-of-payments or foreign exchange difficulties, but can ask for temporary suspension of obligations only when crises have occurred and can be proven to be prevailing.

5) Protecting Existing Investments

The text says the MAI shall apply to investments existing at the time of entry into force as well as to those established or acquired thereafter.

Thus, the MAI investment protection articles would apply not only to new investments after the host country has joined the agreement, but also apply retrospectively to all existing investments, thereby superseding the agreements or arrangements made previously between these investors and the state.

Dispute Settlement System

Introduction: In order to effectively enforce the investors' rights spelled out above, the MAI has a dispute settlement system that covers two types of action in the event of an alleged breach of the agreement: state-to-state and investor-to-state. Under this system, a state can take another state to an international arbitration court for not meeting its obligations, and an investor can likewise sue a state.

If found guilty, the offending state will have to pay financial compensation for the damage, or undertake restitution in kind, and other forms of relief.

State-to-state disputes are also heard in other fora, such as the World Trade Organisation. The MAI is, however, unique in that under its system, an investor can also sue a state. This would make it the first multilateral treaty providing such a privilege and legal standing to a private investor.

1) State-State Procedures

A Party may request another Party to enter consultations regarding any dispute between them. If the consultations and subsequent mediation efforts fail, the dispute can be submitted to an arbitration tribunal for decision. The tribunal may award the following forms of relief: (i) a declaration that a Party's action contravenes the agreement; (ii) a recommendation that a Party brings its actions into conformity with its obligations; (iii) pecuniary compensation for loss or damage to the requesting party's investor; (iv) any other form of relief, including restitution in kind to an investor. Tribunal awards are final and binding. Each party shall pay the cost of its representation in the proceedings. The costs of the tribunal shall be paid for equally by the Parties. Either party to the dispute can request the annulment of an award on one of five grounds, to be submitted to a tribunal.

Failure of a Party to comply with its obligations as determined in the award can lead to the other Party taking responsive measures or suspending the application of its obligations to the other Party. The effect of any such responsive action must be proportionate to the effect of the other Party's non-compliance.

2) Investor-State Procedures

Under this article, an investor can bring for arbitration a case against the host country for breaching its obligations under the agreement, or for violating any obligation the host country entered into for a specific investment of the investor.

The investor can choose to refer the dispute to the host country's courts; or to any dispute settlement procedure agreed upon prior to the dispute arising; or for arbitration under any of four international mechanisms mentioned (the International Centre for the Settlement of Investment Disputes (ICSID) Convention, the ICSID Additional Facility, the arbitration rules of the UNCITRAL (UN Commission on International Trade Law), or the arbitration rules of the International Chamber of Commerce.

The tribunal can provide the following forms of relief: (i) a declaration the Party failed to comply with its obligations; (ii) pecuniary compensation, including interest from the time the loss or damage was incurred until time of payment; (iii) restitution in kind in appropriate cases or pecuniary compensation in lieu; (iv) any other form of relief agreed to by the Parties. Awards will be final and binding and shall be carried out without delay.

3) General Comments

The dispute settlement system has very serious implications, especially for developing countries. Firstly, by enabling cases to be brought up against Parties, in which non-compliance can result in heavy monetary fines, the host governments will have to take the MAI seriously, as there is serious enforcement capability.

Second, the investor-to-state actions mandated by the MAI establish new rights for corporations and investors to sue governments for failure to comply with their MAI obligations. As the MAI obligations are so many and so broad, this can result in a developing host-country facing a long series of expensive legal cases brought on by many foreign companies on a wide variety of charges. This is especially so as the costs of representation are to be met by each Party whilst the costs of the tribunal are to be shared. Developing countries are at a great disadvantage as they have very little financial, human and technical resources to fight such international legal battles. This possibility alone would put the host government very much in the defensive in dealings or policies towards foreign companies, for fear that they could intimidate the host government with tribunal cases. The hands of the big corporations would be very much strengthened whereas the government would be in a much weakened position.

The investor-state dispute settlement system under the MAI system (which would be new in a multilateral context) will particularly be of concern to developing countries. A precedent for investor-to-state dispute settlement system in international commercial law is in one narrow provision of NAFTA (the North American Free Trade Agreement). Under this, in April 1997, a US company, Ethyl Corporation, sued the Canadian government for banning the import of a gasoline additive MMT, which is a dangerous toxin (Preamble 1997). Canada had banned MMT because its emissions pose a significant health risk. The US has banned its use in reformulated gasoline, whilst California has imposed a total ban on MMT. NAFTA requires member countries to compensate investors when their property is "expropriated" or when governments take measures "tantamount to expropriation". Ethyl claimed the ban would reduce the value of its MMT plant, hurt its future sales and harm its reputation. According to ICSID (International Centre for the Settlement of Investment Disputes), the $251 million in compensation sought by Ethyl is higher than any amount in an ICSID investor-to-state case.

As pointed out by Preamble (1997), the Ethyl case raises a host of issues: (i) It could set a precedent under which a government would have to compensate investors when it wishes to regulate them or their products for health or environmental reasons; (ii) effective limitations on the frequency and impact of lawsuits are removed when investors are granted the right to sue governments; (iii) if claims like Ethyl's are successful and proliferate, the costs to governments could be burdensome; (iv) the threat of suits like Ethyl's could be used to pressure governments or lawmakers who are considering new regulations; (v) in cases like Ethyl's, international panels, not domestic courts, will have ultimate legal authority; (vi) the Ethyl case suggests these agreements could pose a threat to national sovereignty.

In August 1998, Canada repealed its ban on MMT and agreed to pay Ethyl US$13 million in damages and to cover the company's legal costs. It would also proclaim publicly that MMT is safe, which is in contradiction of the view of its national environmental protection agency. According to Public Citizen, an American consumer advocacy group.

Trade negotiators in the US and Canada have generally dismissed concerns that trade and investment agreements would have a 'chilling effect' on public interest laws. The outcome of the Ethyl case demonstrates that corporations can and will use the rights granted to them under trade agreements to attack, and in some cases eliminate, public health and environmental laws. If a country with the economic standing of Canada can be forced to repeal its public health laws, the threat is obvious for environmental and health and safety protections worldwide, including in the US. Even before Ethyl forced Canada to dump its public health law, a more potent version of the NAFTA provision Ethyl employed had become one of the most controversial elements of the proposed MAI. (Public Citizen 1998a).

The Ethyl case in NAFTA is an example of the kind of suits governments could face before international tribunals under the MAI. Such court cases would create a condition in which governments would be fearful of having any policy or measure that displeases the corporations, for they could resort to the MAI enforcement system. Even the fear of the threat of a suit could put brakes on health, safety, environmental and social policies.

Other Aspects (Exceptions, Safeguards, Reservations, Accession, Withdrawal, Etc.)

Besides the three core aspects of investor treatment, investor protection and dispute settlement, the MAI text also covers several areas, the most important being exceptions and safeguards, reservations, and accession (especially by non-OECD members).

1) Exceptions and Safeguards

a. General exceptions

In its Article VI, the MAI allows for general exceptions to its meeting obligations, on the following grounds: to protect essential security interests; to protect information essential to security interests; to meet its obligations under the UN Charter for maintaining international peace and security; to maintain public order, provided the measures are not arbitrary or discriminatory or a disguised investment restriction. However this article on general exceptions shall not apply to the MAI's articles on expropriation and compensation, and protection from strife.

There are very few general exceptions, made only for security reasons and maintenance of public order. Moreover the general exceptions are not to apply to the key articles on expropriation and protection from strife. Thus, the coverage of the MAI is almost all-encompassing. For developing countries, a major weakness of the MAI is its lack of recognition that exceptions should be allowed on "development" grounds, i.e., that developing country obligations should be less strict because of their weaker position and thus their need to protect smaller local enterprises, or to impose performance requirements so that investors can be made to contribute to developmental and social objectives.

b. Transactions in pursuit of monetary and exchange rate policies

The articles on national treatment, MFN and transparency do not apply to transactions carried out by central banks in pursuance of monetary or exchange rate policies. However, such non-conforming transactions shall not be used as a means of avoiding the Party's MAI's commitments or obligations.

c. Temporary safeguards

The MAI recognises the following temporary safeguards. A Party can have measures inconsistent with obligations under Transfers and National Treatment for cross-border capital transactions: (a) in the event of a serious balance-of-payments and external financial difficulties or threat; (b) where capital movements cause serious difficulties for operation of monetary or exchange rate policies.

These measures shall be consistent with IMF articles, shall not exceed what is necessary, shall be temporary and be eliminated as soon as conditions permit, and shall be promptly notified. They shall be subject to review and approval within six months and every six months after. The IMF is to be given a key role in assessment of the necessity and adequacy of the measures.

Thus, temporary safeguards are allowed only on the ground of balance-of-payments and external financial difficulties. The temporary suspension of obligations can be considered only when the crisis has occurred, and when the IMF has certified that the situation is in compliance with IMF principles. Exception from the rules in order to take measures to avoid a crisis or to prevent a crisis from developing is not permitted. Moreover, a developing country that believes it has a legitimate case for temporary safeguards could come into conflict with the IMF's assessment, and it may have to submit (in some cases, even more) to IMF conditions which it may or may not think are appropriate for resolution of the crisis.

2) Taxation

The MAI draft text indicates that the following issues relating to taxation will be included: (i) The article on expropriation will apply to taxation measures. An interpretative note states that taxation measures may constitute an outright expropriation or may have the equivalent effect of an expropriation (so-called "creeping expropriation"); (ii) The article on transparency shall apply to tax measures, although the MAI does not require information to be disclosed that is covered by tax secrecy; (iii) In a dispute on issues regarding expropriation or transparency, certain parts of the MAI's article on dispute settlement will apply. Tax measures are defined as measures not only at federal level but also state and municipal levels; and taxes include direct and indirect taxes and social security contributions.

The above shows that the MAI also has implications for a host country's taxation laws and policies. Perhaps more importantly, the MAI opens the road for corporations to take legal cases against the host government, claiming the tax measures are equivalent to expropriation, or that the government is in violation of relevant general obligations.

3) Country-Specific Exceptions

Under this section, countries are allowed to make country-specific exceptions (a term the MAI negotiators decided to use rather than "reservations"). There are three paras in this section: para A (generally agreed to by negotiators) and paras B and C (which are not yet agreed to).

Para A states that the articles on national treatment and MFN (and other not yet specified articles) do not apply to any existing non-conforming measure by a Party as set out in its Schedule to Annex A of the agreement; and to amendments to any non-conforming measure to the extent the amendment does not increase the non-conformity of the measure with the articles on national treatment, MFN, etc. (A footnote says para A is needed as the core provision to "grandfather" existing non-conforming measures and prevent introduction of more restrictive measures ("standstill").

Para B states that various articles (to be specified later) do not apply to any measure that a Party adopts with respect to sectors, subsectors or activities set out in its schedule to Annex B of the agreement.

Para C states that no Party may, under any measure adopted after the MAI comes into force and covered by its schedule to Annex B, require an investor of another Party, by reason of its nationality, to sell or dispose of an investment existing at the time the measure becomes effective. (A footnote explains this is to protect existing rights of foreign investors against discriminatory treatment resulting from measures permitted under Para B).

The country-specific exceptions provision is very important as it allows parties to set out reservations (or country-specific exceptions) in a country's schedules to be annexed to the agreement. The lists are expected to have information on the sectors and activities that come under reservations, the extent of compliance and non-compliance, and indications on the expected future progress towards compliance with respect to each sector or activity. The exceptions do allow countries a degree of space and freedom to decide as to which sectors to protect and which existing domestic rules to maintain. However these will be subjected to "standstill", with no option to backtrack, and under the MAI, developing countries will come under intense pressure to continuously liberalise their investment rules.

4) Relationship to Other International Agreements

Under this heading the MAI text states that the MAI provisions do not alter the obligations undertaken by a Party to the IMF's articles of agreement. The text also deals with how the MAI relates to the OECD guidelines for multinational enterprises. The non-binding character of these guidelines (which cover information disclosure, competition, employment and industrial relations, environment) was notably mentioned.

5) Final Provisions

Among the significant "final provisions" are those pertaining to:

Accession—The agreement will be open for accession to any state, regional economic integration organisation or any separate customs territory, which is willing and able to undertake its obligations on terms agreed between it and the Parties Group.

Amendment—Any Party may propose to the Parties Group an amendment to the agreement. Any amendment will enter into force when all parties ratify the amendment.

Withdrawal—At any time after five years from the date of joining the MAI, a Party may withdraw from the agreement, the withdrawal to take effect six months after receipt of the notice of withdrawal. However, the provisions of the agreement shall continue to apply for 15 years after notice of withdrawal, to an investment existing at that date.

The above points have the following implications for developing countries. Non-OECD countries wishing to join will have to negotiate their terms of entry with the existing members.

Amendments to the agreement will be very difficult, as these require consensus. The withdrawal rules mean that an MAI country will have to wait for at least five years after joining before it can apply to withdraw from the agreement. And even after its withdrawal, a former member must continue meeting its obligations to already existing investments for a period of 15 years. Thus, joining the MAI would "lock" a country into being a member for at least five years, and then after withdrawal, that country is still "locked" into the MAI its rules, for at least 15 years after withdrawal. Thus, joining the MAI would mean that a country would have to observe MAI rules for at least 20 years and six months.

Implications and Possible Impacts of the MAI on Developing Countries

This section follows from the previous section (which analysed the main features of the MAI) by reviewing the likely impacts of the MAI from the perspective of sustainable human development. The question that this section seeks to answer is: assuming the MAI, or an investment agreement that has its main features, has come into being, and that a developing country were to join it, what would be the consequences?

Likelihood of Deriving Claimed Benefits

The MAI's preamble lists some of its key assumptions and goals: that international investment has assumed great importance to the world economy and considerably contributed to development; that a fair and predictable investment regime benefits the trading system; that a investment framework with "high standards" for investment liberalisation, investor protection and strong dispute settlement would contribute to efficient use of resources, create job opportunities and improve living standards.

Besides these assumptions in the preamble, the proponents of the MAI have also claimed that such an agreement would lead to a greater flow of foreign investments to developing countries joining it, and that this is an indispensable condition for their development as it would spur economic growth. It is this claim that has attracted the positive attention of some developing countries to the MAI model.

The MAI's main assumption is that foreign investment and its free movement generates only benefits for the host country, and does not result in costs, and that thus any increase will necessarily contribute to development. This assumption cannot stand the test of reality.

Firstly, since investment is defined in such a broad way, and no distinction is made for the possible differential effects of different kinds of "investment", there is the unsustainable case made out that all kinds of foreign investment, especially when controls and regulations are lifted, necessarily lead to benefits.

It is true that if the inflow of funds is well managed and the investment is used and implemented in the proper way, the benefits of increased capital, technology and market networking could more than offset the costs (which include the servicing of the investment and its possible eventual repatriation). However, the record shows that in the case of foreign loans (included as investment under the MAI), the lack of control over their inflow and the absence of a framework for ensuring their proper use often (or usually) lead to an external debt crisis that causes recession for many years. In the case of foreign portfolio investment, its free movement in and out of developing countries can cause great volatility and instability in the flow of funds, in the exchange rate, and in the real economy, as the current financial crisis in many Asian countries, Russia and Brazil has shown. Even in the case of FDI, as we have earlier seen, there are costs as well as benefits (in terms of savings, growth and balance of payments, and also in social and cultural terms) and only under certain conditions will the balance be positive.

Given these complex realities, it is obvious that foreign investment has to be prudently and well managed, so that the benefits are well brought out and the costs reduced, and that the former exceeds the latter. As this will happen only under certain conditions, the policymakers in the host developing countries need an array of policy instruments in an attempt to achieve net positive results. In the past and presently these instruments have included careful screening of investments and various conditions imposed on approved investments, a wide range of performance requirements (including technology transfer, establishment of joint ventures, local content), and controls on capital inflows and outflows (especially on loans and short-term capital). It is precisely these policy instruments that the MAI is aiming to dismantle and make illegal. By so doing, the MAI would deprive developing countries of the opportunity or even the possibility of ensuring net benefits from foreign investment, and ironically (despite its preamble) it would more than tilt the balance so that foreign investment would probably result in costs outweighing the benefits in many cases.

As for the argument that an MAI-like agreement, by ensuring greater rights and protection to investors, would lead to a greater increase of investments in developing countries, and thus to higher growth and development, once again this makes assumptions that do not stand the test of reality.

Even if an MAI-like agreement leads to increased investment in a country, this is not necessarily good, as the effects depend on the quality and type of investments and their management. Thus, especially under conditions of capital deregulation and liberalisation (which are the conditions championed by the MAI), it is possible (and even more likely) that the increased inflow will cause problems, even massive problems, as the current Asian crisis has demonstrated.

But even if a country is willing to take the risks of increased and unregulated inflows, there is no guarantee (and in many cases no likelihood) that there will be an increase in foreign investment. The flow of foreign investment is determined by many factors, of which the treatment and protection of investment is only one factor, and usually not the most significant. Other factors are the opportunities for sales and profits, the size of the market, the general level of development of a country, the state of the infrastructure and quality of labour skills, political and social stability, the availability of natural resources to exploit, and the location of the country. A developing country that joins the MAI but does not possess some or most of the above qualities is likely not to experience an increase in foreign investment. Many countries that liberalised their foreign investment regimes under structural adjustment programmes have not seen a rise in foreign investment inflow.

A case may be made that, all other things being equal, between two developing countries, the one that joins the MAI will have an additional factor to attract foreign investments. However, presumably the proponents of the MAI (or a similar agreement) would like as many countries as possible to join. Thus, should most developing countries be persuaded to be members, then there would be no advantage for any of them. The advantage would be to the foreign investor, whose treatment and protection is tremendously enhanced but whose obligations to the host country would be minimised. The developing countries as a whole would be at a disadvantage and lose both their policy options and their opportunity to maximise or increase their benefits from foreign investment.

Indeed, it is likely that the least developed countries (LDCs) would be the most disadvantaged. More advanced developing countries have more of the attractive qualities (profitable market, infrastructure, skilled labour). An LDC can offset its lack of attractiveness by offering better treatment, protection or incentives. But if most or all developing countries were to join the MAI, then the LDCs would lose this advantage.

Loss of Policy Autonomy

All OECD members are expected to be initial members of the MAI, but it will also be open to any other countries willing and able to undertake the MAI's obligations. The OECD Secretariat and some of its member countries are already actively persuading developing countries to join the MAI. It is possible that when the MAI is ready for signature, this persuasion exercise will intensify, in the form of pressures put on selected countries.

Whilst the implementation of the MAI will have serious implications for any country joining it, the developing nations will be particularly seriously affected. Most countries of the South welcome foreign investments for their role in fostering economic growth. However, many countries also have sophisticated regulatory frameworks that govern the entry and conditions of establishment and operations of foreign firms.

Restrictions are placed on foreign investments in certain sectors or in some ways (for example, requiring that a percentage of equity be reserved for locals). These are aimed at attaining a minimum level of participation of local people in the economy; at protecting and strengthening local firms and small farmers, which would otherwise not be able to face the onslaught of giant multinationals; and at protecting the balance of payments from too much financial outflows due to profit repatriation and high import bills of foreign companies.

Under the liberalisation sections, the MAI aims at ultimately giving foreign investors the right to enter and establish enterprises with full equity ownership in all member countries. This is particularly significant since, as we have seen, a very broad definition is given to the terms "investors" and "investments". Thus, governments would no longer have the authority to screen the entry of foreign investors (or even of non-commercial societies), nor to place limits on the degree of their participation in the national economy and society. (The MAI would however allow some general exceptions as well as country-specific reservations, including on a sectoral basis. However any "rolling back" of investment rules would be prohibited.)

The proposed MAI would prevent developing countries from having the policy instruments and options they require to attain economic and social development. A very major component of economic policymaking (that relating to investment mobilisation, strategy and use, and capital flows) would be removed from the jurisdiction of national authorities, affecting industrialisation, finance and development as a whole. The loss of policy autonomy in this crucial area will seriously and adversely affect the development prospects of developing countries.

By removing much of the regulatory authority of governments, and by allowing investors to sue governments in international courts, the MAI would also create the conditions where it would be difficult for member states to strengthen or even maintain environmental, safety, health and social standards.

Erosion of Sovereignty and Local Participation in the National Economy

The MAI or a similar agreement would seriously erode national sovereignty as well as local participation in the national economy.

States at present have national sovereignty over their natural resources. This was more recently reaffirmed in the Convention on Biological Diversity, where national sovereignty over biological and genetic resources was recognised as a primary principle. However, the extreme liberalisation model of the MAI would severely reduce and limit this sovereignty, as foreign investors would have the right of establishment and national treatment in all sectors, including land, forestry, mining and other natural resources, unless these sectors are specifically excluded in a country's exclusion schedule. Even if such resources are listed, there would be a "standstill" in that the existing policies cannot be altered in the direction of more regulation, and there will be continuous pressures for further liberalisation. In practice as well as in the rules, developing countries would find their sovereignty over resources eroded.

Several features of the MAI would result in erosion of sovereignty and of local participation in the economy. They include the following:

a. The broad definition of "investor" and "investment" to also include non-commercial organisations and activities would make it difficult for states to disallow or regulate the entry and operations of foreign political, social, cultural or even religious organisations.

b. The right to establishment (especially in the pre-establishment phase) would remove (or at least seriously erode) the state's crucial authority in approving, approving with conditions, or rejecting foreign direct investment applications as well as proposals for foreign operations in finance.

c. The national treatment principle implies that policies that favour local businesses, farmers or even consumers (for example in house and land purchases and ownership) would be prohibited. Small and medium-sized local firms and farms would not be able to enjoy "affirmative action" policies as these would be considered illegitimate acts of discrimination against foreign companies.

d. The prohibition of a long list of performance requirements would remove the state's right to impose obligations on foreign (and even local) investors to meet social and development objectives. Moreover, this would prevent several measures presently taken by many governments to increase local participation in the domestic economy. Besides the local-content requirement (which is already prohibited in the WTO), the prohibition of the requirements on technology transfer, establishing joint ventures with local partners, on minimum level of equity participation, hiring nationals and preference to purchase local products, will affect the ability of governments to boost local enterprises, the level of local skills and technology and the domestic economy in general.

e. The application of national treatment to privatisation exercises means that in many developing countries local investors would lose their present advantage, since privatisation policies often give preference to nationals or may require foreign investors to form partnerships with local investors (or to allow a certain level of local equity ownership). The erosion of local control is made worse by restrictions on "golden shares", which make it difficult for governments to retain some control over privatised concerns. As a result, a substantial part of privatised national assets is likely to come under foreign investor control.

f. The definition of "expropriation" and the dispute settlement system will be powerful devices that severely constrain a developing country from formulating economic, social and environmental policies, as revealed in the Ethyl Corporation case. The wide latitude given to states and investors to sue other states, and the high costs of defence and of compensation (in the event the case is lost) would act to exert great pressure on developing countries not to have any policies that could offend foreign investors, as the mere threat of action by them may cause the government to reverse its intended policies.

Possible Effects on National Financial Position

The deregulation and liberalisation of such a wide variety of foreign investments, credit and financial operations (through the MAI provisions on the right of establishment and on transfers of funds) is likely to result in conditions under which a host developing country faces deterioration in its financial position, or even a financial crisis.

Decontrol and deregulation of foreign loans and portfolio investment can lead to greatly increased volatility in inflows and outflows. As most developing countries (and even some developed countries) do not have the capacity to withstand the potential shocks caused by such volatility, the financial liberalisation process will create greater potential for financial crises of the type seen in recent years in Mexico, East Asia and Brazil. Needless to say, susceptibility to these crises would greatly affect the potential for development.

Even in the case of FDI, there is a tendency for its liberalisation to generate net outflows of foreign exchange and a deterioration in the balance of payments, which in the worst cases could also generate sharp currency depreciation and financial crisis. The MAI, by preventing host countries from taking measures to compensate for the negative balance-of-payments effects of FDI, could well contribute to this process. Given the increasing financial integration of the world, the risks of balance-of-payments deficits becoming financial crises that then develop into recession in the real economy have become much greater. It is really a case of bad timing that the MAI would prevent or seriously constrain governments from avoiding or reducing those risks.

Finally, developing countries could also find themselves facing a series of expensive legal suits from either other states or foreign investors. Bearing the costs of defence and of the tribunal proceedings can already be a heavy burden, whilst in the event of losing the cases the country may find itself with enormous compensation claims that have to be met in international foreign exchange. The potentially very high financial losses on this account should not be underestimated, given the Ethyl case.

Effects on Social Development

A key point in the MAI preamble is that the treatment given to investors will contribute to efficiency, employment and living standards. However this assumption should be tested against the possible effects of the MAI on aspects of social development.

The inclusion of short-term capital flows in the MAI, and its tendency to encourage member states to liberalise these flows, would in the light of present knowledge and experience more likely lead to financial instability and multiyear recession. The MAI would make developing countries more susceptible to the kind of crisis that befell East Asian countries in 1997-99. The crisis has caused not only unprecedented rates of declines in the GDP, but also sharp deterioration in social conditions, with dramatic increases in the rates of poverty, unemployment and living standards and deterioration in education and health standards.

Even without considering these negative effects of liberalising short-term capital flows, the liberalisation and national treatment of FDI through the MAI can also lead to negative effects on social development.

The treatment provided to FDI in the MAI could cause the displacement of local enterprises and also local farms, since the protection or favourable treatment accorded to them would be removed. This is especially so in the case of FDI that targets the home market, rather than the export market. In such cases, this will result in retrenchments as the local sector loses its share of business. It is true that FDI would also generate local employment and thus could offset some of these job losses. However, it is well known that per unit of capital employed, FDI generates far fewer jobs than local firms (which are more labour-intensive). Since the flow of FDI, including to developing countries, is limited, it would not be possible for FDI to generally be in such great quantities as to absorb the loss of jobs caused by displacement of local firms. There can of course be exceptions, in those few developing countries where much of the flow of FDI is concentrated and where FDI is predominantly export-oriented. However, for countries where there is a large population and high unemployment, it is unlikely that FDI can make a significant dent in reducing unemployment, and the overwhelming task of generating jobs will fall on local enterprises. The constraints placed on governments will make it much more difficult to assist in capacity building and operations in this local sector.

The MAI provisions on foreign key personnel, on management and choice of employees could also affect the employment opportunities of local professionals in many developing countries, since the governments would have to phase out or remove policies that reserve executive, managerial or professional positions for local people through restrictions on the entry of foreign personnel. Most developing countries now have regulations restricting the number (and functions) of foreign staff a foreign investor can bring in.

Implications for Human Rights

The NGO human rights community has also expressed concern over the implications of the MAI on the enjoyment of human rights. Partly through the efforts of human rights activists, the MAI was recently brought to the attention of the Human Rights Commission (Kothari and Prove 1999). In August 1998, the United Nations Sub-Commission on Prevention of Discrimination and Protection of Minorities adopted a resolution on "Human rights as the primary objective of trade, investment and financial policy." The resolution emphasised that the realisation of human rights and fundamental freedoms described in the international human rights instruments is the "first and most fundamental responsibility and objective of States in all areas of governance and development."

In this context, the Sub-Commission expressed concern about the human rights implications of the MAI and "particularly about the extent to which the Agreement might limit the capacity of States to take proactive steps to ensure the enjoyment of economic, social and cultural rights by all people, creating benefits for a small privileged minority at the expense of an increasingly disenfranchised majority." The resolution called on the OECD to "review the draft text of the Multilateral Agreement on Investment to ensure that all its provisions are fully consistent with their human rights obligations, and to keep these obligations in mind during any future negotiations on the Agreement" (Kothari and Prove 1999). The Sub-Commission also mandated the preparation of a working paper on ways by which the primacy of human rights norms could be better reflected in trade, investment and financial agreements and practices, and how the UN human rights system could play a central role in this regard. The paper is also to include "an analysis of the text of the MAI from a human rights perspective, and to consider ways to ensure that future negotiations on the MAI or analogous agreements or measures take place within a human rights framework."

In 1998, several human rights groups formed the International NGO Committee on Human Rights. The impetus to form the Committee came from the perceived threat to economic, social and cultural rights posed by the MAI (Kothari and Prove 1999). A policy statement by the Committee noted that the following four human rights principles are under threat:

a. The primacy of human rights. The promotion and protection of human rights must be accepted as the fundamental framework for and goal of all multilateral and bilateral investment, trade and financial agreements. Such agreements cannot exclude or ignore human rights principles and aims without losing their most fundamental claim to legitimacy.

b. Non-retrogression. All States have a duty to respect, protect, ensure and fulfil international human rights obligations and cannot derogate or limit them except as provided for in human rights treaties. "Rollback" and "standstill" requirements in the MAI are incompatible with the requirement that economic, social and cultural rights be realised progressively as stated in the International Covenant on Economic, Social and Cultural Rights. There is a specific duty on States to not take retrogressive measures that would jeopardise these rights.

c. The right to an effective remedy in the appropriate forum. The right to an effective remedy for anyone whose rights have been violated cannot be contracted away by the State nor denied by the operations of inter-governmental institutions. Investment or trade bodies should not adjudicate concerns that fall firmly into the human rights domain, as disputes between corporations and State actors, but these should be dealt with by appropriate domestic, regional and international human rights fora and enforcement mechanisms.

d. Rights of participation and recourse of affected individuals and groups. Human rights cannot be effectively realised unless the right of participation of the affected populations in planning, implementation and seeking redress for violations is respected. The participation of women in all these processes is particularly important.

Effects on the Environment and Community Rights

Investment liberalisation and increased rights of foreign investors could also result in adverse environmental effects.

Firstly, it would be more difficult for developing countries to restrict the participation or regulate the operations of transnational corporations (TNCs) and other foreign firms in the natural resources sector. As the large multinationals generally have greater technical capacity, their ability to exploit, damage, destroy or pollute the physical environment can be greater than that of smaller local firms. It is true that local firms are usually also do not have ecological practices, and that some TNCs could have more environmentally friendly technology. But by and large the large firms can do more damage due to their greater scale and speed of operations.

TNCs are the most important players and factors involved in many environmentally damaging activities. Their activities generate more than half of the greenhouse gases emitted by industrial sectors with the greatest impact on global warming. In mining, TNCs still dominate key industries and are intensifying their activities. In agriculture, TNCs control 80% of land worldwide cultivated for export crops, and 20 firms account for 90% of pesticide sales. TNCs manufacture most of the world's chlorine, the basis for some of the most toxic chemicals including PCBs, DDT and dioxins. TNCs are the main transmitters of environmentally unsound production systems, hazardous materials and products to the Third World (Khor 1997).

Case studies of the recent performance of 20 TNCs by Greer and Bruno (1996) show that, despite public relations exercises claiming greater environmental responsibility, and despite more and more voluntary codes of industry conduct, there has been little change and much "business as usual", with the corporations continuing with activities that are environmentally harmful.

Investment liberalisation and deregulation under the MAI will greatly facilitate the further spread of TNCs in the developing world. With their continuing use of unsustainable production systems (and promotion of wasteful lifestyles), and in many cases displacing more sustainable systems or lifestyles, more environmental degradation worldwide must be expected.

The case of investment liberalisation in the mining sector is illustrative. In recent years, there has been a worldwide escalation of mining projects by foreign companies, accompanied by social protests by affected communities, including in Venezuela, Ecuador, Ghana, Nigeria, Papua New Guinea, Myanmar, Borneo, and the Philippines.

Pressure on developing countries to open up to foreign investors have led to new or amended mining laws that threaten the environment and are resulting in widespread dislocation of communities and social chaos. In a study of recent trends in the global mining industry, Corpuz (1998) shows that, in recent years, many developing countries liberalised and deregulated their mining laws. Around 70 countries in Latin America, Africa, and the Asia-Pacific region are now fully liberalizing their mining laws and implementing deregulation in a wide range of areas, including land rights and mineral rights, taxation, environment protection, in order to attract foreign mining investors.

This liberalisation policy at national level is accompanied by the globalisation of mining operations. Mergers concentrate the power of mining TNCs even further, putting them in a better position to further expand their control over mineral lands. Mining TNCs are motivated to open up in the Third World because of the tightening environmental standards and increasing resistance from the indigenous peoples and environmentalists in their own countries and depletion of their mineral resources. To escape from environmental regulations requiring them to install expensive anti-pollution technologies and devices and other environmentally sound technologies, many companies transfer their operations to countries with no or low regulations.

A good illustration of the effects of the recent liberalisation of mining laws on sustainable development and people's livelihoods is provided in Khor (1997). In recent years, in the Philippines there has been a major policy shift, where land previously restricted to foreigners has now been opened up to foreign mining companies. Much of the untapped mineral lands are in regions populated by indigenous peoples, and also where small-scale local miners operate. The new Mining Act of 1995 allows foreign mining companies 100% control of their local subsidiaries (in contrast to previous requirement of 60% Filipino ownership). The law also provides for tax holidays and other exemptions, and gives other rights such as water rights and timber rights (or prior rights to the company in the use of water and forest resources) and "easement rights" (the right to evict people from the mineral areas). Mineral lands are also exempted from the issuance of ancestral land claims and ancestral domain claims.

According to Khor (1997), there are already hundreds of mining applications pending approval. Taking the lands applied for, and including existing and already approved mining operation areas, 45% of the entire 30 million-hectare land area of the country is affected by mining applications and operations. The indigenous people in particular have protested against the violation of their land rights and the dislocation the proposed mining activities would bring to large numbers of them.

The liberalisation of investment regimes will also likely have adverse ecological effects on forests and agriculture. Despite great public concern over the fate of the world's forests, logging activities are still undertaken, often by foreign companies. The increasing use of genetic engineering technology in agricultural crops has raised grave concerns by scientists and environmentalists that it will adversely affect biodiversity and also destabilise agricultural production. Some European countries have imposed a moratorium on the commercial use of genetically engineered crops. However, with the present investment liberalisation (even before the MAI) spreading to agricultural sector, some developing countries are already introducing such crops, even though they do not yet have the biosafety knowledge or capacity in place.

The MAI is likely to make it easier for foreign companies to operate with fewer regulations in many sectors in developing countries. This will correspondingly make it more difficult to implement environmentally sustainable development practices and policies.

Other Attempts at International Frameworks on Investment

Introduction: The initiatives on the MAI are of course not the first attempts at establishing an international framework on foreign investment. However, the approach taken by the MAI proponents is new in that it is an extreme and one-sided approach, which covers and greatly expands the rights of international investors, whilst not recognising and thus greatly reducing the authority and rights of host governments and countries. It also promotes investment liberalisation (through legally-binding rules) that would facilitate the international movement of capital and foreign corporations, with their great capacity to change the physical, economic and social environment of the host countries, whilst it contains little or no safeguards to oblige or ensure that the powerful international firms respect or promote sound environmental, social and development practices and principles. Moreover the proposal to have a very strong international enforcement mechanism either in the OECD's MAI framework, or in the WTO's dispute settlement system, means that the foreign investors' rights can be effectively enforced, and the host countries would be effectively disciplined to fulfil their obligations.

This one-sided approach on behalf of foreign investors' interests is in contrast to some earlier attempts within the UN system to set up an international framework on foreign investments, which attempted to balance the rights and obligations of foreign investors and host countries, as well as to balance the foreign investors' production activities with development, social, environmental goals.

UN Code of Conduct on Transnational Corporations

On a general level, the most well known has been the Draft UN Code of Conduct on Transnational Corporations, which underwent a decade of negotiations from 1982 to the early 1990s, under the UN Commission on Transnational Corporations, and serviced by the UN Centre on Transnational Corporations (UNCTC).

The draft text of the Code of Conduct on TNCs had two core content sections, one that dealt with the obligations of TNCs to host countries (Section on "Activities of TNCs"), and one with the obligations of host countries to TNCs (Section on "Treatment of TNCs"). A review of the February 1988 version of the text shows that the Code was an attempt at balancing the rights of host countries with the rights of foreign investors, and the obligations of TNCs with the obligations of host countries. The Code was also inclusive of many issues, including political dimensions (respect for national sovereignty, non-interference and human rights), development dimensions (transfer pricing, balance of payments, technology transfer) and social dimensions (sociocultural values, consumer and environmental protection).

The section on "Activities of TNCs" includes the following areas:

General aspects, including:

- Respect for national sovereignty and observance of national laws, regulations and administrative practices
- Adherence to economic goals and development objectives, policies and priorities of host countries
- Review and renegotiation of contracts and agreements
- Adherence to sociocultural objectives and values

- Respect for human rights and fundamental freedoms
- Non-collaboration by transnational corporations with racist minority regimes in southern Africa
- Non-interference in internal affairs of host countries
- Non-interference in intergovernmental relations
- Abstention from corrupt practices

Economic, Financial and Social Aspects, including:
- Ownership and control
- Balance of payments and financing
- Transfer Pricing
- Taxation
- Competition and restrictive business practices
- Transfer of technology
- Consumer protection
- Environmental protection

Disclosure of information

The section on "Treatment of Transnational Corporations" includes the following areas:

- General provisions relating to the treatment of TNCs;
- Nationalisation and compensation;
- Jurisdiction; and
- Dispute settlement.

A preamble setting out the overall aim states that a universally accepted Code of Conduct on Transnational Corporations is an essential element in strengthening international cooperation, in particular to "maximise the contributions of transnational corporations to economic development and growth and to minimise the negative effects of the activities of these corporations."

The Code was therefore placed in the context of international cooperation, recognised both the contributions and negative effects of TNCs, and sought to maximise the former and minimise the latter, towards the goal of development and growth. This is a more balanced approach than the MAI, which implicitly only makes claims for the benefits of liberalising and protecting foreign investments, and does not recognise or attempt to deal with the negative aspects.

The draft Code recognised both the rights of the host countries and the right of TNCs to fair and equitable treatment.

In the section on "Activities of TNCs", the Code contains many essential points obliging TNCs to recognise and respect the host government and country. In the section on "Treatment of TNCs", the Code lays out principles on the rights of TNCs (but with these rights balanced against the rights of host states). The following are among the key elements of both sections.

Section on Activities of TNCs

a. General

— TNCs shall respect the national sovereignty of host countries and the right of each States to exercise its permanent sovereignty over its natural wealth and resources.

— TNCs are subject to the laws and regulations of a country in which they operate, and shall also respect the right of each State to regulate and monitor the activities of their entities operating within its territory.

— Activities of TNCs should conform with the development policies, objectives and priorities of host governments and seriously work to contribute to achieve such goals. They should cooperate with host governments to contribute to the development process and respond to requests for consultation in this respect.

- TNCs should respect the social and cultural objectives, values and traditions of the countries in which they operate, and avoid practices, products or services which cause detrimental effects on cultural patterns and sociocultural objectives as determined by governments.
- TNCs shall respect human rights and fundamental freedoms in countries in which they operate. In their social and industrial relations, TNCs shall not discriminate on the basis of race, colour, sex, religion, language, ethnic origin or political or other opinion; and shall conform to government policies to extend equality of opportunity and treatment.
- TNCs shall not interfere in the internal affairs of host countries; shall not engage in activities of a political nature that are not permitted; and not interfere in intergovernmental relations.
- TNCS shall refrain from offering or giving payment to a public official as consideration to perform or not perform his duties; and shall maintain accurate records of any payment to any official.

b. Economic, financial and social

- TNCs should make every effort to allocate their decision-making powers among their entities to enable them to contribute to the development of host countries.
- TNCs should cooperate with governments and nationals of host countries to implement national objectives for local equity participation and for the effective exercise of control by local partners
- TNCs should carry out personnel policies in line with national policies of host countries which give priority to the employment and promotion of nationals in management to enhance effective participation of nationals in decision-making.
- TNCs should contribute to the managerial and technical training of nationals in host countries.
- Balance of payments: TNCs shall conform with host country policies on balance of payments (BOP) and financial transactions, and contribute to alleviating pressing problems of BOP and finance of host countries.
- TNCs should contribute to promotion and diversification of exports and to increased utilisation of goods, services and other resources locally available.
- TNCs should be responsive to requests by host governments to phase over a limited period the repatriation of capital in case of disinvestment or remittances of accumulated profits when the size and timing of such transfers would cause serious BOP difficulties.
- TNCs should not engage in short-term financial operations or transfers or defer or advance foreign exchange payments (including intra-corporate payments) in a manner which would increase currency instability and thereby cause serious BOP difficulties.
- TNCs should not impose restrictions on their entities on transfer of goods, services and funds that would cause serious BOP difficulties.
- Financing: When having recourse to money and capital markets of host countries, TNCs should not engage in activities which have adverse impact on the working of local markets, particularly by restricting availability of funds to other enterprises. When issuing shares or borrowing in the local market, they should consult with the government on the effects of such transactions on local markets.
- Transfer pricing: In intra-corporate transactions, TNCs should not use pricing policies that are not based on relevant market prices or the arm's length principle which adversely affect tax revenues and foreign exchange resources of countries in which they operate.
- Taxation: TNCs should not use their corporate structure and modes of operation, such as intra-corporate pricing, to modify the tax base on which their entities are assessed.

— Competition and Restrictive Business Practices: The provisions of the Set of Principles and Rules for Control of Restrictive Business Practices of December 1980 shall apply to this Code.

— Technology transfer: TNCs shall conform to technology transfer laws and regulations in host countries and cooperate to assess the impact of international technology transfers and consult with them on various technological options.

— TNCs should avoid practices that adversely affect the international flow of technology or otherwise hinder economic and technological development of countries.

— TNCs should help strengthen the scientific and technological capacities of developing countries and undertake substantial research and development activities in developing countries and make use of local resources and personnel in this process.

— Consumer protection: The operations of TNCs shall be carried out in accordance with laws and policies on consumer protection in host countries and shall follow international standards so they do not injure the health or threaten the safety of consumers or vary the quality of products in each market with detrimental effects on consumers.

— TNCs shall supply to any country they produce or market in information on their products and services concerning: characteristics that may injure health and safety of consumers; and prohibitions, restrictions, warnings and regulations imposed in other countries on health and safety grounds.

— TNCs shall disclose to the public information on contents and possible hazardous effects of their products through labelling and accurate advertising.

— Environmental protection: TNCs should operate in accordance with national laws and international standards on the environment. In their activities, they should protect the environment and if damaged rehabilitate it and apply adequate technologies for this purpose.

— TNCs should supply to the authorities information on: characteristics of these products, processes (including experimental uses) which may harm the environment and the measures and costs needed to avoid or mitigate the harmful effects; prohibitions, restrictions and regulations imposed in other countries on environmental grounds.

c. Disclosure of Information

— TNCs should disclose to the public in countries they operate in comprehensive information on structure, policies and activities of the TNC as a whole. The Code lists the kinds of financial and non-financial information needed.

— TNCs shall provide to trade unions in countries they operate in information in accordance with the International Labour Organization (ILO) Tripartite Declaration of Principles concerning Multinational Enterprises, including future prospects or plans having major economic and social effects on employees.

Treatment of TNCs

a. General Provisions on Treatment

— In matters relating to the Code, States shall fulfil their international obligations including international legal rules and principles.

— States have the right to regulate the entry and establishment of transnational corporations including determining the role that such corporations may play in economic and social development and prohibiting or limiting the extent of their presence in specific sectors.

— Subject to national requirements for public order and national security and consistent with national laws, and without prejudice to development objectives of developing countries, TNCs should be given treatment accorded to domestic enterprises in similar circumstances.

— Confidential business information furnished by TNCs to the authorities shall be accorded safeguards to protect its confidentiality.

— TNCs are entitled to transfer all payments legally due, subject to the host country's legislation, such as foreign exchange laws and restrictions emanating from exceptional BOP difficulties.

b. Nationalisation, Dispute Settlement

— It is acknowledged that States have the right to nationalise or expropriate the assets of a TNC operating in their territory, and that appropriate compensation is to be paid by the State in accordance with applicable legal rules and principles.

— An entity of a TNC is subject to the jurisdiction of the country in which it operates.

— Disputes between States and TNC entities shall be submitted to competent national courts or authorities. If they agree, such disputes may be referred to other mutually acceptable dispute settlement procedures.

c. Intergovernmental Cooperation

— States agree intergovernmental cooperation is essential to accomplish the Code's objectives and should be established and strengthened at bilateral, regional and interregional levels.

— States agree to consult on matters and application of the Code and with respect to developing international agreements and arrangements on issues related to the Code.

— States agree not to use TNCs as instruments to intervene in the internal or external affairs of other states and agree to take action to prevent TNCs from engaging in activities that interfere in internal affairs of or engage in political activities in host countries.

— Government action on behalf of a TNC operating in another country shall be subject to the principle of exhaustion of local remedies and procedures for dealing with international legal claims. Such action should not amount to the use of any type of coercive measures not consistent with the UN Charter.

d. Implementation

— At national level, States should implement the Code and report to the UNCTC on action to promote the Code.

— At international level, the UN Commission on TNCs shall be the institutional machinery to implement the Code, with the UNCTC as secretariat. The Commission's functions shall include: discussion at annual sessions matters related to the Code; periodically assess the Code's implementation; clarify the Code's provisions in the light of actual situations where the Code has been the subject of intergovernmental consultations; facilitate intergovernmental arrangements or agreements on specific aspects relating to TNCs upon request of governments.

— The UNCTC shall assist in the Code's implementation by collecting, analysing and disseminating information and conducting research and surveys.

— The Commission shall make recommendations to the General Assembly to review the Code, with the first review not later than six months after the Code's adoption.

The Code of Conduct Contrasted with the MAI

It is worthwhile to have another look at the provisions of this draft Code, as many of them deal with the same issues as the MAI but take a remarkably different or opposite position on many of them. The Code's main difference with the MAI is that the majority of its articles deal with the obligations of TNCs towards the host country, whilst the MAI is silent on this. In fact, the MAI has taken an opposite position, converting what were TNC obligations to observe the host country's rights, into the host

State's obligations to observe the foreign investors' rights not to be hampered by obligations or requirements by the host State.

For example, the Code requires (or encourages) TNCs to conform to the host country's policies on equity participation by nationals, on technology transfer, employment and training of nationals, use of local products and resources, and protection of balance of payments, whereas the MAI on these very same matters prohibits the governments of host countries from imposing these policies on foreign investors (and even on local investors). One of the most glaring of conflicting positions is in the treatment of the right of entry and establishment. Whereas the Code affirms the State's right to regulate the entry and establishment of transnational corporations, including determining the role that such corporations may play in economic and social development, and prohibiting or limiting the extent of their presence in specific sectors, the MAI specifically confers rights of establishment to foreign investors and denies States the right to regulate (except through country-specific exceptions).

The Code and the MAI are obviously the products of contrasting paradigms. The Code arose from the perception that the host developing countries, whilst having to accord some rights to TNCs, required an international understanding that 1) TNCs must comply with international guidelines recognising the countries' development needs and national objectives, and that 2) the hosts could by right allow the guest foreign investors to enter and operate on terms generally chosen by the hosts. The affirmation of the host countries' rights was seen to be important in light of the perceived growing economic power of TNCs and their potentially great economic, social, cultural and even political impacts on host developing countries. The Code also recognised the positive and negative effects of TNCs. As the UNCTC pointed out, the Code was meant to provide a stable, predictable framework to enhance the role of foreign investments in growth and at the same time minimise any negative effects associated with the activities of TNCs (UNCTC 1990, 20).

The MAI on the other hand has arisen from the perceived need by foreign investors to expand and protect their interests from the perceived interference by states that impose conditions on their operations. In this paradigm, the "borderless world" is the ideal construct, and any barriers to the free flow of investments and to the right to investment, property ownership and unhindered operations must be considered "distortions" and the denial of the investors' rights. The affirmation of these alleged investors' rights is seen as important to prevent states from constraining the expansionary reach and operations of foreign investors. Whilst the Code envisaged only a weak enforcement system, based on voluntary compliance and international cooperation, the MAI proponents suggested an extremely effective dispute settlement system to enforce the legally-binding rules. The MAI assumes that foreign investment brings only benefits to all countries, and does not recognise or attempt to deal with any negative effects.

A reading of the two texts gives the impression that the MAI was in some way a response to the Code, a substitution of one paradigm for another.

Negotiations on the Code started in 1976 and despite disagreements on many points through the years, agreement had been reached on about 80% of the text. "A draft text of the Code lies nearly complete, but blocked by continued disagreement over a few key issues," stated a UNCTC document in 1990 (UNCTC 1990, 1). The disagreements were never resolved. The attempt at a balanced approach through the Code failed, due mainly to the reluctance and hostility of some developed countries that did not favour the obligations placed by the Code on TNCs. In 1992, the Code process was abandoned. The UN Commission on Transnational Corporations itself was disbanded; the UN Centre on TNCs (which was secretariat for the process) was also closed down, and some of its staff were transferred to the Investment Division of the United Nations Conference on Trade and Development (UNCTAD), whose present functions are very different from those the Centre had performed.

Recent Clash of Frameworks on Foreign Investment

The aborted Code of Conduct on TNCs was the main set of international guidelines that were to have dealt generally with the relations between TNCs or foreign investors with states. However, there are a number of other codes and guidelines that the UN system has established or attempted to establish to cover more specific issues.

These include the UNCTAD-based Set of Multilaterally Agreed Equitable Principles and Rules for the Control of Restrictive Business Practices (adopted in 1980 by the UN General Assembly) and the Draft International Code of Conduct on the Transfer of Technology (which has not yet been adopted by the General Assembly); the ILO Tripartite Declaration of Principles Concerning Multinational Enterprises and Social Policy (1977); the World Health Organization's (WHO) International Code of Marketing of Breast-Milk Substitutes (1981); and the Guidelines for Consumer Protection (based on a UN General Assembly resolution in 1985). In the environmental field, there are also international legal agreements (such as the Basel Convention banning the export of hazardous wastes to developing countries) that have an influence on the behaviour of international companies.

These instruments have the intention of influencing the behaviour of foreign investors and TNCs so that they conform to development needs, or fulfil social and environmental obligations. Together they would also constitute elements of an alternative approach to an international policy or framework on foreign investment. Such a framework, encompassing the various existing instruments, could be further developed through additional instruments covering other areas by sector and issue.

However, such an approach would have to contend with the, at present, stronger international trend emphasising investors' rights to the exclusion of host country rights. At the same time as the Code of Conduct on TNCs was being downgraded and eliminated, and the UN Commission on Transnational Corporations was being eclipsed, negotiations were taking place on Trade Related Investment Measures (TRIMS) in the Uruguay Round of the General Agreement on Tariffs and Trade (GATT). The Uruguay Round approach to investment was to eventually supplant the more balanced approach of the Code of Conduct process.

The TRIMS proposal initially contained two components. The first involved foreign investment policy and rights per se (including the right of entry and establishment of foreign companies and granting of national treatment to them). The second dealt more narrowly with investment measures (such as local content policy) which have direct effect on trade.

Many developing countries initially objected strongly to TRIMS being brought into the General Agreement on Tariffs and Trade (GATT) system. They eventually succeeded in removing the first aspect (investment per se), on the grounds that governments had the sovereign right and the necessity on development grounds to regulate the entry and terms of operations of foreign investments, and that the GATT system was not the competent body to deal with the issue. The second aspect was developed in the Uruguay Round negotiations and established as the present TRIMS agreement in the WTO.

Some developed countries are now seeking to bring back the broader issues of investment policy per se into the WTO via a proposed MAI-type investment agreement.

The recent history of evolving an international framework for foreign investment shows that the proposed MAI (and models based on it) constitutes only one approach. It is an approach based on a paradigm that seeks to protect foreign investors' rights to the exclusion of their obligations and of host countries' rights. An alternative approach would take into account the rights and obligations of host countries and foreign investors, ensure that these are properly balanced, and be based on the primary objective of contributing to economic development and social and environmental objectives. It is however an issue for debate whether such an approach is possible in the present global environment, and also what would constitute an appropriate venue for discussions on the investment issue.

Proposals for Appropriate Management of Foreign Investment

Introduction: Previous sections have emphasised the following points:

(i) There are various categories of foreign investment, and it is important for governments to distinguish between the different types, understand the characteristics and effects of each type, and formulate policies to deal with each.

(ii) Even in the apparently most beneficial type, FDI, where there can be important contributions to development of host countries, it is academically recognised that there are also potential costs and risks, among the most important of which are financial instability and balance-of-payments difficulties.

(iii) Therefore a policy framework for managing FDI must take into account the need to attempt to maximise the benefits whilst reducing the costs and risks.

(iv) Thus, governments, especially of the developing countries, because of their greater vulnerability, need to be able to formulate policies that (a) distinguish between the types of FDI that are appropriate; (b) encourage the entry of FDI considered desirable whilst discouraging or disallowing FDI considered not so appropriate to the country; (c) impose certain conditions, if found necessary, on the operations of FDI; (d) subject FDI policy to the wider national objectives and development needs.

(v) The MAI approach is too one-sided in its objectives and functions of protecting and furthering foreign investors' interests whilst denying the interests of host states and countries. Moreover there is the assumption that there is no need to distinguish between different types of foreign investment, that all foreign investments bring only benefits but no costs, and the articles of the MAI are therefore drawn up under assumptions. Social, cultural, development, environmental and human rights concerns are also ignored in this approach.

(vi) There have been other attempts at creating international frameworks dealing with foreign investments or the behaviour of foreign enterprises. Some of these have been more accommodating to the rights and needs of host developing countries and to the imperatives of development. It would be useful to revisit some of these attempts and to examine the usefulness of reviving, improving or extending them, as well as to examine new approaches.

Given the above conclusions, this section attempts to provide suggestions for elements of an appropriate approach or framework for the management of foreign investment. Proposals will be confined mainly to foreign direct investment. The proposals are categorised as national-level and international-level approaches and actions.

National-Level Policies and Actions

1) Need for a Comprehensive Policy on Foreign Investments

Many developing countries may not have an adequate policy framework to deal with foreign investments as a whole. This is partly due to recent rapid global developments where the pace of changes in enterprise behaviour and development has exceeded the capacity of governments to adequately comprehend the trends or to formulate policy responses. Also, many developing countries that have come to depend on foreign loans or debt rescheduling often come under the influence of loan or aid conditionalities, which in recent years have included investment liberalisation. Thus, the ability or degree of freedom of governments to devise a comprehensive foreign investment policy is limited or constrained.

As a first step to remedy this situation, developing countries have to be given more space and freedom to make their own policies on foreign investment. This requires that the international financial and aid agencies and the bilateral aid agencies be more open to dialogue with and give more scope to the developing countries to own the policy process and search for the best policy options.

Given the nature of international capital flows, national governments need to have a comprehensive policy on the interface between domestic objectives and activities and foreign capital flows. Such a policy firstly requires a distinction to be made between different capital flows, such as FDI and its varieties, portfolio investment, foreign credit and loans, and highly speculative capital that takes advantage of money, currency and capital markets in developing countries. Each kind of capital has to be studied in terms of its behaviour, pattern and effects, and policies should be made to deal with each of these.

The need for countries to distinguish between different types of foreign capital is especially acute because the recent series of financial crises has shown up the dangers posed by some kinds of capital flows, but also because the MAI (which may become the prototype of investment agreements or frameworks since it is backed by the most powerful countries) has such a wide scope that covers all kinds of foreign investment and property rights.

It is beyond the scope of this paper to deal with the various forms of investment, so the suggestions here are confined to FDI.

2) Selective Policy on and Strategic Approach to FDI

In view of empirical evidence on the benefits and costs of FDI, developing countries should have a selective policy and strategic approach towards FDI. The right of entry and establishment should thus be conferred by a state on chosen foreign investors, and not be taken as inherent rights of the investors. Historically, many presently developed countries and the more advanced developing countries had such a selective policy. For example, Japan and South Korea had very little FDI: in 1984-94, FDI inflows to Japan were less than 0.1% of gross domestic capital formation, and South Korea and Taiwan had important restrictions on FDI entry and degree of foreign ownership. Yet these countries are among the fastest growing in the world. China and Malaysia have allowed much more FDI, but they also have a selective approach in terms of opening up of certain sectors where foreign firms can contribute to technological and export development, whilst discouraging FDI in other sectors where domestic companies are either weak (and need protection) or already possess technical capability (as in agriculture).

3) Need to Distinguish Between Differing Capacities and Needs of Local and Foreign Investors

An indiscriminate policy of opening up and of treating foreign firms on equal or better terms than local firms could lead to deindustrialisation in a country where the local enterprises are too weak to compete on equal terms with foreign firms. Thus, developing countries should be allowed to continue to protect certain sectors or industries where there is considerable local investment (or where the state is encouraging the attempting to build up local capacity).

In principle, state assistance to local enterprises should not be looked at as a "distortion", or necessarily wasteful or somehow unethical, but possibly as legitimate affirmative action to help the weak companies to eventually stand on their own. There are advantages to national development for local enterprise or farm development to occur, since institutions belonging to nationals are more likely to make use of local materials and talents, generate more domestic linkages, and to retain profits locally for reinvestment, all of which are positive for economic growth and development.

Thus a blanket "national treatment" policy towards foreign investment is inadvisable, as a "level playing field" for local and foreign investors is likely to result in more unequal results when the capacities are unequal, as foreign investors are larger and starting from a much stronger position.

4) Need to Ensure Acceptable Treatment of Investors

In order to obtain FDI that is considered beneficial for national development, developing countries have to establish conditions that are attractive to foreign firms. This may include guarantees for their unhindered operations, the exercise of expropriation only in extreme circumstances and even then with adequate compensation at rates that can in principle be worked out before (so that the investor knows what the terms are), and freedom to remit profits generated from FDI. Other, and perhaps more important, conditions include political and social stability, security, good infrastructure, a credible legal system with due process, a trained or trainable labour force, tax and other incentives, etc. Each country should however be given the space to determine the elements it chooses to adopt and act on.

5) Social and Environmental Screening and Obligations of Foreign Investors

Whilst developing countries may exert great efforts to attract the investors they desire, their right to request that foreign investors fulfil certain obligations and thus follow some conditions should be recognised. These may include the transfer of technology; the training and employment of local workers, professionals and executives; the development of linkages to the domestic sectors; and providing local participation or partnership in equity ownership.

In light of a country's social and environmental goals and the need to maintain or raise standards, governments should carefully screen foreign investment applications and discourage or reject those projects or enterprises that would be socially or culturally detrimental (for example, resulting in net loss of jobs, or endangering health and safety of workers or consumers, promoting unsustainable consumption patterns and lifestyles or adversely affect local cultural norms) or that would damage or pollute the environment (for example, through exploitation of natural resources that should be conserved; or use of harmful technology or introduction of products that endanger consumer safety).

As part of the processes of application, selection and approval, foreign investments should undergo an environmental impact assessment and a social impact assessment; only those that are positively assessed should be approved, and with conditions if necessary. Moreover, foreign investors may be asked not only to operate with respect for domestic laws, but also to positively contribute to social and environmental development.

6) Assessing the Effects on Local Sectors and Economy

In their FDI selection system, developing countries should include an assessment of the effects of the proposed investment on the local economy, especially the local enterprises, farms and informal sector. For example, selection criteria for projects under application could include that the projects do not compete with existing local enterprises or farms, that projects contribute new appropriate technologies, and that projects have significant linkages with the domestic economy. Factors militating against proposed investments could include significant displacement of existing local firms accompanied by loss of jobs, heavy dependence on imported inputs with little demand for local resources or locally produced inputs, and substitution of existing appropriate local products with inappropriate new products (e.g., expensive non-nutritious fast foods potentially replacing more nutritious local foods).

7) Protecting Financial Stability and the Balance of Payments

Most importantly, in formulating their FDI policies, governments of developing countries should take into account the need to protect their economies from the risks of financial instability and of getting into balance of payments or foreign exchange difficulties. Thus, foreign investors and their proposed projects should be carefully assessed as to the possible effects of their activities on the nation's financial stability, foreign exchange position and balance of payments. For example, it may be wise policy to discourage the entrance of firms or investors whose main operations are in highly speculative financial activities.

Conditions should be imposed that investors not indulge in activities such as transfer pricing and restrictive business practices, and efforts should be made by governments to develop more and more effective monitoring and implementation of national regulations prohibiting unethical practices.

Foreign investment proposals should also be made to undergo a "balance of payments assessment", with such indicators as impact on import payments and export earnings, profit level and the possible or predicted ratio between profit repatriation and retention for reinvestment. Investments that could lead to serious adverse effects on the BOP and on the state of foreign reserves could be discouraged; or else certain conditions or measures should be encouraged (such as local equity participation, use of more local materials and expertise within legal bounds keeping in view WTO rules, technology transfer) to help mitigate the adverse effects.

International-Level Policies and Actions

1) Need for a Fresh Look at the Nature and Effects of Foreign Investments

The nature and effects of cross-border foreign investments as a whole should be reviewed from the perspective of human-centred and socially and environmentally sustainable development. The dominant perspective, promoted by the secretariats of international financial and trade institutions amongst others, is that the free movements of capital have positive results for all countries and sections of society. Although there is now an increasing chorus of criticisms about the dangers of short-term speculative capital and calls for some regulatory mechanism, developing countries are likely to continue to face pressures for financial liberalisation. In the case of FDI, there is among the international financial and trade establishment an over-emphasis on the claimed benefits and a lack of appreciation of its potential negative effects on developing countries. Just as the claims about the unalloyed positive effects of short-term capital have been brought down to earth by the Asian financial crisis, it is possible that events will in future also show up that the positive aspects of FDI are also matched by some negative effects.

It is thus important that a comprehensive review be made of the nature and the positive and negative effects of all kinds of foreign investment, and of the conditions for the successful use and management of each. Such a comprehensive and balanced approach is especially needed now as the global financial crisis has left in its wake a desperate search for causes, solutions, and correct policies.

The United Nations could set up, or facilitate the establishment, of an independent commission or expert panel comprising academics, development practitioners, and agency experts to deepen and disseminate knowledge on this subject, taking a comprehensive and balanced approach, within the framework of promoting human sustainable development.

2) Reconsideration of an Appropriate International Approach to Foreign Investment and Investors' Rights

Given the inadequacies of theory and policies shown up by the financial and economic crises, it is timely for a reconsideration of international approaches to international investment. There should not be a continued "rush forward" with international policies and especially legally binding agreements that "lock" the vulnerable developing countries into a process of capital and investment liberalisation under a MAI or MAI-type model of international arrangements on investment.

The ongoing global financial and economic crisis, which is significantly related to cross-border capital flows, marks a new circumstance that calls for a deep study of and reassessment of recent trends in thinking on the nature of international capital movements. The international community should therefore devote the next few years to an educative process on a wide range of investment issues. Until such study process yields adequate insights to enable policy conclusions, there should not be initiatives to negotiate or promote a legally-binding international agreement furthering the rights of foreign investors in areas such as their movement and establishment, national treatment and compensation. In particular, there should not be any further initiatives for advancing international arrangements which constrict or deny the host states of their rights or capacity to determine the role of foreign investment in their economy and society, the entry and establishment (and conditions for these) of foreign investments, and to require that foreign investors fulfil obligations towards the national development, social and environmental goals of host countries.

The proposed study process should be carried out within the UN system, as it is the most representative of international fora, and it is a venue where the multidisciplinary dimensions of investment, economic and social development and environmental protection can be best integrated, in an atmosphere of objectivity (unlike trade or financial institutions where the atmosphere is less suitable for multidimensional, frank and free discussions and study).

3) Strengthening Existing International Arrangements and Promoting New Ones for Channelling Foreign Investments Towards Development, Social And Environmental Goals

International arrangements for facilitating or ensuring the implementation of the positive social, developmental and environmental roles of foreign investments and investors should be strengthened. For example:

- The implementation of the Set of Principles and Rules on Restrictive Business Practices (based in UNCTAD) should be strengthened, and the negotiations on the Draft International Code of Conduct on the Transfer of Technology could be revived.
- The WHO-based Code of Marketing of Breast-Milk Substitutes could serve as a model for similar guidelines relating to the marketing of other products.
- The UN General Assembly's Guidelines for Consumer Protection should be strengthened and subject to better monitoring and implementation.
- In the context of the implementation of Agenda 21, the Commission on Sustainable Development could establish a process of obliging enterprises, especially those engaged in cross-border investments, to respect international standards on environmental issues.
- An international effort can be initiated to facilitate a process or an arrangement whereby foreign investors are required to respect and contribute to the development, social and environmental objectives, policies and practices of host countries; this could incorporate some elements from the draft Code of Conduct on TNCs.
- The process of establishing new protocols and conventions to protect the environment should be accelerated whilst the existing agreements should be strengthened, in view of the increasing global environmental crisis. These agreements should specifically include provisions on criteria for good practices of and policies on foreign investments and the role and responsibilities of foreign investors. ■

References

Clarke, Tony and Maudhe Barlow (1997), MAI: The multilateral agreement on investment and the threat to Canadian sovereignty. (Stoddart, Toronto).

Corpuz, Victoria Tauli (1998), "The globalisation of mining and its impact and challenges for women", Third World Resurgence magazine, May.

European Economic Commission (1995), "A level playing field for direct investment worldwide". Unpublished paper.

Friends of the Earth US (1998), "How MAI would affect the South". Third World Resurgence magazine, February/March. (Penang).

Ghazali bin Atan (1996), The effects of DFI on trade, balance of payments and growth in developing countries, and appropriate policy approaches to DFI. (Third World Network, Penang).

Ghazali bin Atan (1990), "An empirical evaluation of the effects of foreign capital inflows on the economy of Malaysia (1961-1986)." PhD thesis, Faculty of Economics and Social Studies, International Development Centre.

Greer, Jed and Kenny Bruno (1996), Greenwash: the reality behind corporate environmentalism. (Third World Network, Penang).

Khor, Martin (1997), "Sustainable development and the limits to globalisation". Unpublished paper.

Kothari, Miloon and Peter Prove (1999), "A human rights response to globalisation". Third World Resurgence, December 98/January 99.

Kozul-Wright, Richard and Robert Rowthorn (1998), Transnational Corporations and the global economy. (Macmillan, London).

Kregal, J.A. (1996), "Some risks and implications of financial globalization for national autonomy." UNCTAD Review.

Nayyar, Deepak (1995), "Globalisation: the past in our present". Presidential address to annual conference of the Indian Economic Association.

OECD (1997a), Main Features of the MAI. 20 Feb, Paris.

OECD (1997b), Multilateral Agreement on Investment: Consolidated text and commentary. 1 Oct, Paris.

OECD (1998a), "Commentary to Consolidated Text" (DAFFE/MAI/NM(98)4). 6 March.

OECD (1998b), "The Multilateral Agreement on Investment: Consolidated Text". (DAFFE/MAI/NM(98)2/REV1), 23 April.

Phang Hooi Eng (1998), Foreign Direct Investment: a study of Malaysia's balance of payments position. (Pelanduk, Kuala Lumpur).

Preamble (1997), "Ethyl Corporation v. Government of Canada: Chemical firm uses trade pact to contest environmental law". Briefing paper, Preamble Center for Policy, Washington.

Public Citizen (1998a), "Another broken NAFTA Promise: Challenge by US Corporation leads Canada to repeal public health law". Press release, Public Citizen, Washington, August.

Public Citizen (1998b), "MAI provisions and proposals: an analysis of the April 1998 text." Briefing paper, Public Citizen, Washington.

South Centre (1997), Foreign Direct Investment, Development and the New Global Economic Order. Geneva.

UNCTC (1990), "The New Code Environment". UNCTC Current Studies, Series A, No. 16. (United Nations, New York).

UNCTAD (1996), International Investment Instruments: A Compendium. (United Nations, Geneva and New York).

SOCIAL IMPACTS OF THE ASIAN CRISIS: POLICY CHALLENGES AND LESSONS

*Jong-Wha Lee and Changyong Rhee**

Abstract

This paper documents the social impacts of the financial crisis in Asia. We provide a general overview of the causes and the evolution of the crisis and highlight the differences as well as the similarities among the affected Asian countries. In particular, the impacts of the crisis on unemployment, real wages, poverty, and income inequality are analyzed using a cross-country data set, which consists of all the countries that have received financial assistance from the International Monetary Fund (IMF) over the period from 1973 to 1994. The stylized pattern of employment growth in previous IMF program countries indicates that employment growth is more sluggish in the recovery process compared with other macroeconomic variables. Hence, unemployment rates can remain high for a long period even after the crisis in the Asian countries ends. We also find that the crisis aggravates poverty for marginal groups of the population over a significant period, although it does not exert a long-term effect on overall income distribution. Policy implications of our findings for building social safety nets in Asia are also discussed.

More than a year after its eruption in Thailand, the financial crisis in Asia has deepened and broadened more than anyone anticipated. The contagion has spread to Latin America and Russia and threatens to cause the global capitalist system to come apart at the seams. The financial crisis in Asia was followed by economic and social collapse. Asian countries are now struggling to escape from the miseries of declining income, rising unemployment, and increasing poverty.

While there has been much recent research on the causes and the economic impact of the Asian crisis, its social impacts have been relatively neglected. To remedy this discrepancy, this paper assesses the severity of the Asian crisis and its social consequences. For decades, Asian countries enjoyed high growth, low unemployment rates, relatively equal income distribution, and low crime rates. Therefore, compared with other crisis-hit countries, the social impacts of the crisis—such as rising unemployment and income inequality—have been felt more painfully in Asia. Indeed, the social consequences have been disastrous, as most Asian countries have not yet developed a meaningful social safety net. This paper documents the social impact of the crisis in the most affected Asian countries, notably Indonesia, Korea and Thailand, and attempts to draw policy implications.

The section on "Origins and Evolution of the Asian Crisis" begins with a general overview of the cause and extent of the Asian crisis and highlights the differences as well as similarities among countries in Asia. The key features of the Asian crisis are large inflows and sudden withdrawals of foreign capital. We review the extent of foreign capital inflows and outflows in these Asian countries and then analyze which factors caused the sudden change in foreign investors' confidence in these economies. The role of financial liberalization and globalization in the eruption of the crisis is closely examined. We also pay special attention to the role of International Monetary Fund (IMF) adjustment programs in handling the Asian crisis. In order to assess the economic and social impacts of the crisis and predict its future development, it is imperative to understand the conditionality that the IMF attached to its financial support for the Asian countries. The IMF adjustment program in Asia is being

* The authors are grateful to Hye Yoen Kim, Wonho Song, and Sam Ho Lee for their excellent research assistance. The authors email addresses are: jongwha@kuccnx.korea.ac.kr, and rhee5@plaza.snu.ac.kr, respectively.

severely criticized as the "same old belt-tightening" adjustment or "one-size-fits-all" approach. The frequent emergency IMF bailouts have also been blamed for contributing to moral hazard in international lending. To evaluate these criticisms, we review the general characteristics of IMF programs as well as the specific content of programs with Indonesia, Korea, and Thailand.

The next section, "Social Impacts of the Asian Crisis," analyzes the disastrous impacts of the financial crisis on societies in the region. We assess the current social impacts of the crisis in Indonesia, Korea and Thailand and then predict its long-term development. To make a long-term prediction, the social impacts of the financial crisis are analyzed from a broad historical and international perspective. We reviewed the records of all countries that have experienced a currency crisis and received conditional financial assistance from the IMF during the period of 1973 to 1994. From these cross-country data, we develop some stylized facts about the impacts of IMF programs on social variables such as unemployment, real wage, poverty, and inequality. Then we compare these stylized facts with the cases of the three most severely affected countries, namely Indonesia, Korea, and Thailand.

Our cross-country analysis shows some stylized patterns of the social impacts of the crisis. For example, we find that employment growth is more sluggish in the recovery process than other macroeconomic variables. This implies that unemployment rates can remain at a higher level for a long period after the crisis, even if output growth and inflation rates are restored to their pre-crisis level. We also find that the burden of the crisis is distributed unequally. It is marginal groups such as the poor, the less experienced, the less educated, women, and young workers who are most severely affected by the crisis. Consequently, although the crisis does not exert a long-term effect on overall income distribution, it definitely aggravates poverty for the victimized core group over a significant period. We think these findings have important policy implications, especially for building social safety nets in these Asian countries during the crisis. The third section, "Policy Implication and Lessons from the Asian Crisis," and the conclusion of the paper discuss and summarize the policy implications of our study.

Origins and evolution of the Asian crisis

Needless to say, the origins and the nature of the Asian crisis are multifaceted and the forms of evolution are significantly different among Asian countries. Nevertheless, they all share one common phenomenon: large-scale inflow of foreign capital and its sudden outflow. In evaluating various hypotheses for the origins of the Asian crisis, it is therefore important to understand what caused the sudden change of foreign investors' confidence in Asian countries. Under this opening section, we first review the pre-crisis macroeconomic conditions of Asian countries to see whether they had so deteriorated as to justify the sudden loss of foreign investors' confidence. In particular, macroeconomic policies such as fiscal, monetary, and exchange rate management before the crisis will be compared with those of Latin American cases in the 1980s. Then we examine in detail to what extent the globalization of international financial markets contributed to the changes in the amount and the structure of external liabilities of Asian countries. In this regard, we will try to highlight the differences as well as the commonality among Asian countries in the origins and the evolution of the crisis. After the crisis began, the highly affected countries—Thailand, Indonesia and Korea—requested IMF financial support and are currently under IMF adjustment programs. We also discuss the nature of IMF adjustment programs in general and the specific contents of the IMF policies for Indonesia, Korea, and Thailand.

Macroeconomic conditions and policies

Table 1 shows the macroeconomic performance of selected Asian countries from the mid 1970s until the onset of the crisis. The first three sub-tables are for the worst affected Asian countries; the other tables are for the less-affected countries. For comparison, the table includes Mexico and Argentina.

Growth, inflation, unemployment and macroeconomic policies

As can be seen in Table 1, Asian countries continued their solid growth performance throughout the 1990s. Except for Japan and Taiwan, their average rate of real growth of gross domestic product (GDP) from 1990 to 1995 was higher than or at least comparable to their historical averages. It is noteworthy that even the worst hit countries—Indonesia, Korea, and Thailand—all experienced average growth rates well above 7% during this period.

The performance was equally impressive in terms of price stability. Except for China and the Philippines, the inflation rates of Asian countries in the 1990s were modest at least by developing-country standards and remained at a single-digit level. Even the inflation rates of China and the Philippines were quite low compared with the hyperinflation Mexico and Argentina experienced before their debt crises in the 1980s. We can also see that China and the Philippines enjoyed virtually full employment prior to the crisis; unemployment rates were less than 3% in these economies.[1] Understandably, the experience of a long period of full employment is making the current crisis harder to swallow for the workers in this region.

Table 1: Macroeconomic Performance before the Crisis
Selected Economies in Asia and Latin America

ASIA

THAILAND	75-82	83-89	90-95	90	91	92	93	94	95	96	97
Growth	7.0	8.1	9.0	11.6	8.1	8.2	8.5	8.9	8.7	5.5	-0.4
Inflation	9.0	3.1	5.0	6.0	5.7	4.1	3.4	5.1	5.8	5.9	5.6
UE	-	3.2	-	2.2	2.7	1.4	1.5	-	-	-	-
CA/GDP	-5.6	-3.2	-6.7	-8.3	-7.7	-5.6	-5.0	-5.6	-7.9	-7.9	-2.2
Saving	19.6	25.4	34.4	32.6	35.2	34.3	34.9	34.9	34.3	33.7	32.9
Investment	23.6	27.7	40.4	40.2	41.6	39.2	39.4	39.9	41.8	41.7	35.0
Export	14.7	17.6	18.9	14.9	23.2	14.2	13.2	22.7	25.1	-1.3	-
Budget	-5.8	-3.0	3.0	4.4	4.2	2.6	2.1	2.0	2.6	1.6	-0.4
Money	19.3	18.8	18.4	26.7	19.8	15.6	18.4	12.9	17.0	12.6	16.4
RE(US$)	0.83	1.00	0.97	1	0.99	0.99	0.98	0.94	0.92	0.91	-
RE(Yen)	0.64	0.90	1.09	1	1.05	1.04	1.14	1.20	1.10	0.94	-
INDONESIA	75-82	83-89	90-95	90	91	92	93	94	95	96	97
Growth	6.2	5.5	8.0	9.0	8.9	7.2	7.3	7.5	8.2	8.0	5.0
Inflation	15.0	8.1	8.7	7.8	9.4	7.5	9.7	8.5	9.4	7.9	6.6
UE	-	2.6*	-	2.5	2.6	2.7	2.8	4.4	-	4.1	-
CA/GDP	-1.2	-3.5	-2.5	-2.8	-3.4	-2.2	-1.5	-1.7	-3.3	-3.3	-2.6
Saving	19.3	23.2	28.9	27.9	28.7	27.3	31.4	29.2	29.0	28.8	27.3
Investment	19.8	24.3	27.2	28.3	27.0	25.8	26.3	27.6	28.4	28.1	26.5
Export	16.0	0.8	12.7	15.9	13.5	16.6	8.4	8.8	13.4	9.7	-
Budget	-	-1.3	0.05	1.3	-	-1.2	-0.7	-	0.8	1.4	2.0
Money	29.3	27.0	24.9	44.6	17.5	19.8	20.2	20.0	27.2	27.2	-
RE(US$)	0.45	0.84	0.97	1	1.00	0.99	0.95	0.94	0.92	0.91	1.70
RE(Yen)	0.35	0.77	1.08	1	1.06	1.04	1.09	1.19	1.11	0.94	1.56

Table 1 cont'd

KOREA	75-82	83-89	90-95	90	91	92	93	94	95	96	97
Growth	7.0	9.6	7.8	9.5	9.1	5.1	5.8	8.6	8.9	7.1	5.5
Inflation	17.6	3.8	6.6	8.6	9.3	6.2	4.8	6.3	4.5	4.9	4.5
UE	-	3.4	2.4	2.4	2.3	2.4	2.8	2.4	2.0	2.0	2.7
CA/GDP	-4.6	2.5	-1.4	-0.9	-3.0	-1.5	0.1	-1.2	-2.0	-4.9	-2.0
Saving	25.7	32.7	35.3	36.1	35.9	35.1	35.2	34.6	35.1	33.3	32.9
Investment	29.4	29.4	36.7	37.1	38.4	36.6	36.0	35.7	36.6	36.8	36.6
Export	22.8	16.7	12.6	4.2	10.5	6.6	7.3	16.7	30.3	3.7	5.0
Budget*	-	-	-0.4	-0.9	-1.9	-0.7	0.3	0.5	0.4	0.3	0.03
Money	30.0	16.8	17.5	17.2	21.9	14.9	16.6	18.7	15.6	15.8	14.1
RE(US$)	1.02	1.16	0.99	1	1.01	1.02	1.03	0.97	0.93	1.00	1.97
RE(Yen)	0.79	1.03	1.11	1	1.08	1.07	1.19	1.23	1.12	1.03	1.80
CHINA	75-82	83-89	90-95	90	91	92	93	94	95	96	97
Growth	6.0	10.7	10.6	3.8	9.2	14.2	13.5	12.6	10.5	9.7	8.8
Inflation	2.1	9.0	9.9	2.1	2.7	5.4	13.0	21.7	14.8	6.1	1.5
UE	-	2.1	2.6	2.5	2.3	2.3	2.6	2.8	2.9	3.0	-
CA/GDP	0.7	-1.0	1.2	3.4	3.5	1.5	-2.7	1.4	0.2	0.9	2.4
Saving	39.3	35.2	39.7	38.1	38.3	37.7	40.6	42.6	41.0	42.9	40.8
Investment	21.3	29.5	32.0	25.5	27.5	31.2	37.5	36.0	34.7	35.6	35.8
Export	16.5	13.4	19.2	18.2	15.8	18.1	7.1	33.1	22.9	1.6	20.9
Budget	-1.0	-1.7	-2.0	-2.0	-2.2	-2.3	-2.0	-1.6	-1.7	-1.5	-1.5
Money	22.3	26.1	32.3	28.9	26.7	30.8	42.8	35.1	29.5	25.3	20.7
RE(US$)	-	-	1.05	1	1.05	1.07	0.97	1.17	1.01	0.96	0.95
RE(Yen)	-	-	1.18	1	1.11	1.13	1.12	1.49	1.21	0.99	0.87
HONG KONG	75-82	83-89	90-95	90	91	92	93	94	95	96	97
Growth	9.3	7.2	5.0	3.4	5.1	6.3	6.1	5.4	3.9	4.9	5.3
Inflation	8.6	6.7	9.3	9.7	11.6	9.3	8.5	8.1	8.7	6.0	5.7
UE	-	2.7	2.0	1.3	1.8	2.0	2.0	1.9	3.2	2.8	2.2
CA/GDP	1.9	8.3	4.5	8.9	7.1	5.7	7.4	1.6	-3.9	-1.3	-1.5
Saving	29.7	33.6	33.5	35.8	33.8	33.8	34.6	33.1	30.4	30.6	31.1
Investment	27.8	23.6	28	26.4	26.6	27.4	27.3	29.8	30.5	31.3	32.0
Export	18.0	20.1	15.6	12.3	20.0	21.2	13.2	11.9	14.8	4.0	4.0
Budget	1.5	1.6	1.6	0.7	3.2	2.5	2.3	1.1	-0.3	2.2	3.8
Money	-	-	-	-	-	8.5	14.5	11.7	10.6	12.5	8.8
RE(US$)	-	-	0.86	1	0.93	0.89	0.83	0.79	0.74	0.72	0.70
RE(Yen)	-	-	0.96	1	0.99	0.94	0.96	1.00	0.89	0.75	0.64

Table 1 cont'd

JAPAN	75-82	83-89	90-95	90	91	92	93	94	95	96	97
Growth	3.9	4.1	2.1	5.1	3.8	1.0	0.3	0.6	1.5	3.9	0.9
Inflation	6.6	1.4	1.7	3.1	3.3	1.7	1.2	0.7	-0.1	0.1	1.7
UE	-	2.6	2.5	2.1	2.1	2.2	2.5	2.9	3.2	3.3	3.4
CA/GDP	0.4	3.0	2.4	1.5	2.0	3.0	3.1	2.8	2.2	1.4	2.2
Saving	31.9	31.9	32.7	33.5	34.2	33.8	32.8	31.4	30.7	31.3	30.8
Investment	30.9	28.4	30.0	31.7	31.4	30.5	29.5	28.6	28.5	29.7	28.4
Export	10.4	10.4	8.4	5.0	9.5	8.0	6.6	9.6	11.6	-7.3	2.4
Budget	-4.0	-0.4	-0.05	2.9	2.9	1.5	-1.6	-2.3	-3.6	-4.3	-3.4
Money	10.7	9.2	3.1	8.2	2.5	-0.1	2.2	3.1	2.8	2.3	3.1
RE(US$)	1.31	1.18	0.89	1	0.94	0.95	0.87	0.79	0.83	0.97	1.09
RE(Yen)	1	1	1	1	1	1	1	1	1	1	1
MALAYSIA	75-82	83-89	90-95	90	91	92	93	94	95	96	97
Growth	7.1	5.4	8.8	9.6	8.6	7.8	8.3	9.2	9.5	8.6	7.8
Inflation	5.3	2.0	3.5	2.8	2.6	4.7	3.5	3.7	3.4	3.5	2.7
UE	-	7.3*	3.6	5.1	4.3	3.7	3.0	2.9	2.8	2.5	2.7
CA/GDP	-2.0	-0.7	-6.2	-2.1	-8.8	-3.8	-4.8	-7.8	-10.0	-4.9	-4.8
Saving	21.6	29.4	31.3	29.1	28.4	31.3	33.0	32.7	33.5	36.6	38.0
Investment	29.4	28.5	37.7	32.4	36.4	36.0	38.3	40.1	43.0	42.2	42.7
Export	15.0	12.0	19.9	17.4	16.8	18.5	15.7	24.7	26.0	5.1	-
Budget	-	-4.0	-0.3	-2.2	0.1	-3.5	-2.6	2.5	3.8	4.2	1.6
Money	20.2	9.2	19.3	10.6	16.9	29.2	26.6	12.7	20.0	25.3	17.5
RE(US$)	0.68	0.86	0.96	1	1.01	0.95	0.98	0.92	0.89	0.88	1.34
RE(Yen)	0.53	0.78	1.07	1	1.07	1.00	1.13	1.16	1.06	0.91	1.23
PHILIPPINES	75-82	83-89	90-95	90	91	92	93	94	95	96	97
Growth	5.6	1.1	2.3	3.0	-0.6	0.3	2.1	4.4	4.8	5.7	5.1
Inflation	11.0	15.4	10.8	12.7	18.7	8.9	7.6	9.0	8.1	8.4	5.1
UE	-	7.2	8.6	8.1	9.0	8.6	8.9	8.4	8.4	-	-
CA/GDP	-6.5	-0.3	-4.1	-6.1	-2.3	-1.6	-5.5	-4.6	-4.4	-4.7	-5.4
Saving	19.9	18.1	18.6	18.7	18.0	19.5	18.4	19.4	17.8	19.7	21.0
Investment	26.7	20.7	22.4	24.0	20.0	20.9	23.8	23.6	22.2	23.2	25.1
Export	11.9	7.2	14.9	4.0	8.7	11.2	13.7	20.0	31.6	16.7	22.9
Budget	-2.0	-2.8	-1.9	-3.5	-2.1	-1.2	-1.6	-1.6	-1.4	-0.4	-0.9
Money	20.5	21.4	21.5	22.5	17.3	13.6	27.1	24.4	24.2	23.2	26.1
RE(US$)	0.68	0.91	0.78	1	0.84	0.74	0.79	0.65	0.67	0.63	0.94
RE(Yen)	0.53	0.81	0.87	1	0.89	0.78	0.91	0.83	0.80	0.66	0.86

SINGAPORE	75-82	83-89	90-95	90	91	92	93	94	95	96	97
Growth	8.0	6.9	8.7	9.0	7.3	6.2	10.4	10.5	8.8	7.0	7.8
Inflation	4.2	1.0	2.7	3.5	3.4	2.3	2.3	3.1	1.7	1.4	2.0
UE	-	3.8	2.4	1.7	1.9	2.7	2.7	2.6	2.7	3.0	2.4
CA/GDP	-8.8	1.8	11.9	8.3	11.2	11.9	7.2	16.0	16.8	15.7	15.2
Saving	33.4	42.0	46.9	44.1	45.4	47.3	44.9	49.8	50.0	50.1	51.9
Investment	38.2	38.1	33.8	31.8	33.3	35.6	35.0	33.6	33.3	36.5	35.4
Export	16.4	12.4	17.9	18.1	11.9	7.6	16.6	30.8	22.1	5.7	0.0
Budget	0.6	4.8	12.2	11.4	10.3	11.3	14.3	13.7	12.0	9.1	10.3
Money	16.2	12.5	12.1	20.0	12.4	8.9	8.5	14.4	8.5	9.8	10.3
RE(US$)	0.93	1.07	0.92	1	0.94	0.96	0.94	0.85	0.83	0.84	1.01
RE(Yen)	0.72	0.96	1.03	1	1.00	1.01	1.09	1.08	1.00	0.87	0.92
TAIWAN	*75-82*	*83-89*	*90-95*	*90*	*91*	*92*	*93*	*94*	*95*	*96*	*97*
Growth	8.5	9.2	6.4	5.4	7.6	6.8	6.3	6.5	6.0	5.7	6.9
Inflation	8.6	1.2	3.8	4.1	3.6	4.5	2.9	4.1	3.7	3.1	1.1
UE	-	1.9	1.5	1.6	1.4	1.5	1.4	1.5	1.8	2.6	2.7
CA/GDP	1.6	12.9	4.3	6.8	6.9	4.0	3.2	2.7	2.1	4.0	2.3
Saving	30.2	35.0	28.2	29.3	29.5	27.8	27.7	27.1	28.0	28.0	27.9
Investment	27.8	20.4	22.8	22.4	22.2	23.2	23.7	22.9	22.9	21.0	21.0
Export	20.2	17.4	9.3	1.6	13.4	6.9	4.0	9.6	20.0	3.7	-
Budget	-	1.3	0.5	0.8	0.5	0.3	0.6	0.2	0.4	0.2	0.2
Money	22.3	24.4	15.0	10.5	19.7	19.6	15.5	15.2	9.6	4.7	-

Latin America

MEXICO	79-82	83-89	90-95	90	91	92	93	94	95	96	97
Growth	5.9	0.9	2.2	5.1	4.2	3.6	2.0	4.5	-6.2	5.2	7.0
Inflation	26.1	82.5	19.4	26.7	22.7	15.5	9.8	7.0	35.0	34.4	20.6
UE	-	-	-		2.2	-	2.4	-	4.7	3.7	-
CA/GDP	-5.1	1.00	-5.5	-3.2	-5.2	-7.4	-5.8	-11.1	-0.6	-0.6	-
Saving	34.4	24.3	19.6	21.7	20.3	18.9	17.0	17.1	22.7	23.4	-
Investment	23.7	18.6	18.7	18.4	19.2	20.5	18.6	19.3	16.1	17.2	-
Export	29.9	2.5	13.9	17.7	0.7	1.4	9.2	14.2	40.3	22.6	-
Budget	-4.5	-9.3	-0.4	-2.8	-0.2	1.5	0.3	-0.7	-0.6	-	-
Money	49.4	72.6	36.3	75.8	49.3	22.8	14.5	21.7	33.3	26.2	-
RE(US$)	2.76	1.46	1.00	1	0.88	0.80	0.75	1.23	1.34	1.06	0.93
RE(Yen)	0.72	1.34	1.14	1	0.94	0.85	0.87	1.57	1.61	1.10	0.86

Table 1 cont'd

ARGENTINA	*75-82*	*83-89*	*90-95*	*90*	*91*	*92*	*93*	*94*	*95*	*96*	*97*
Growth	0.2	0.0	4.9	-1.3	10.5	10.3	6.3	8.5	-4.6	4.2	8.4
Inflation	188.5	755.3	421.5	2314.	171.7	24.9	10.6	4.2	3.4	0.2	0.8
UE	-	5.3	10.5	9.2	5.8	6.7	10.1	12.1	18.8	18.4	-
CA/GDP	-1.0	-4.6	-1.1	3.7	-0.4	-2.4	-3.0	-3.6	-1.0	-1.3	-
Saving	32.8	21.9	17.2	19.8	16.3	15.1	16.4	17.4	18.1	17.4	-
Investment	26.1	18.5	17.0	14.0	14.6	16.7	18.4	20.0	18.0	17.6	-
Export	10.9	4.7	14.8	28.9	-3.0	2.1	7.2	19.4	33.9	13.6	-
Budget	-	-2.4	-0.4	-0.3	-0.5	-0.03	-0.6	-0.7	-0.5	-1.8	-
Money	-	-	230.0	1113	141.3	62.5	46.5	17.6	-2.8	18.7	-
RE(US$)	-	3.24	0.63	1	0.69	0.56	0.53	0.52	0.52	0.53	-
RE(Yen)	-	3.27	0.70	1	0.73	0.59	0.61	0.66	0.62	0.55	0.50

Note: 1. UE of 1983-1989 for Indonesia and Malaysia is calculated using only data for 1985-1989.
2. Budget data for Korea is a consolidated central government budget.
3. UE of 1983-1989 for Taiwan is calculated using data for 1980-1989.
4. In Mexico and Argentina, CA/GDP was calculated using data for 1977-1982.
5. In Mexico and Argentina, the saving rate was calculated using only private consumption data for 1977-1982.
6. In Argentina, investment was calculated using data only for 1978-1982.

Sources and Definition of Data:

Growth rate: real GDP growth rates, *World Economic Outlook* (IMF).
Inflation: CPI inflation rates, *World Economic Outlook*.
UE: Unemployment rates, *Yearbook of Labor Statistics* (ILO), *International Financial Statistics* (IMF).
CA/GDP: Ratio of Current Account Balance to GDP, *World Economic Outlook*.
Saving: Private saving rates, *World Economic Outlook*.
Invest Investment rates, *World Economic Outlook*.
Export: growth rates of export revenue in US dollar terms, *International Financial Statistics*.
Budget: Ratio of general government fiscal balance to GDP: *World Economic Outlook*.
Money: M2 growth rates (end of year), *World Economic Outlook, International Financial Statistics*.
RE: Real exchange rates based on CPI (end of year), *International Financial Statistics* (1990 = 100).
Data for Latin American countries are from *International Financial Statistics*.

Monetary and fiscal policies have been conservative, too. The growth rates of M2 during the 1990s were in line with their historical averages in the Asian countries, and incomparably lower than those of Mexico and Argentina. The absence of high inflation is indirect evidence of the discipline of monetary policies. Fiscal stance was, in general, prudent. Only China and the Philippines incurred persistent fiscal deficits during the 1990s, but the magnitude was very modest at less than 2% of GDP. Note that Thailand, where the Asian crisis first erupted in July 1997, maintained a fiscal surplus every year in the 1990s.[2] This is in sharp contrast with the Latin American debt crisis in the early 1980s. One of the key features of the Latin American debt crisis was the mismanagement of macroeconomic policies—large budget deficits and consequent monetary expansion.[3] To the contrary, the current Asian crisis was definitely not a result of profligate fiscal and monetary policies.

Current account and exchange rate management

In fact, a sign of disequilibrium is evident only from the behavior of current account balances. The three worst affected countries—Thailand, Indonesia, and Korea—along with Malaysia and the Philippines, incurred persistent current account deficits in 1990s. In Indonesia and Korea, the size of the current account deficits was modest, but in Thailand and Malaysia, they were well above 5% of GDP. In hindsight, it is hard to deny that the sizable current account deficits contributed to undermining foreign investors' confidence. However, there was good reason to underestimate their significance prior to the crisis. As presented in Table 1, these countries were maintaining very high private savings rates and even higher investment rates. The current account deficits during this period reflected shortfalls in savings relative to investment, instead of private or public dissaving.[4] High growth performance in the past decades had taught the Asian people to believe that investment is a virtue and that the current account deficits caused by the investment boom should not sound an alarm. Moreover, as will be explained later, the growing current account deficits in some countries in 1996 were mainly due to country-specific shocks, such as the drastic fall in international prices of export items, including semi-conductors, consumer electronics, and petrochemical products.[5] Since the sharp drop in export prices was regarded as temporary, the current account deficits were expected to quickly improve.

The sizable current account deficits in these Asian countries led many to suspect the possibility of mismanaged exchange rates. In fact Dornbush, Goldfajn, and Valdes (1995) argue that an overvalued peso played the most important role in the Mexican crisis in 1994. However, it is controversial whether the currencies in the Asian countries were significantly overvalued prior to the crisis. Most of the Asian countries effectively pegged their currencies to the US dollar. When the dollar weakened in 1990 and 1995, Asian currencies depreciated together with the dollar vis-à-vis the European currencies and the Japanese yen. Conversely, when the dollar appreciated markedly against the yen in mid-1995, they all appreciated sharply against the yen. This pattern can be confirmed from the behavior of real exchange rates (see Table 1). The table reports two real exchange rates—one against the US dollar and the other against the Japanese yen.[6] Between 1990 and 1996, in most Asian countries, real exchange rates against the US dollar did not change much. However, the real exchange rate against the yen depreciated slightly before 1995 and then sharply appreciated beginning in 1995.

In order to judge the extent of overvaluation, we have to look at real exchange rates in trade-weighted terms. Table 1 shows that the extent of overvaluation of each currency was not large against either the dollar or the yen during the 1990s.[7] For example, prior to its crisis in 1994, the Mexican peso was about 20% overvalued against the dollar and 13% overvalued against the yen. However, except for Hong Kong and the Philippines, no Asian currency shown in the table is comparably overvalued. Therefore, even without estimating trade-weighted real exchange rates, we can conjecture that the real exchange rates in the Asian countries were only mildly overvalued prior to the crisis.[8]

If their currencies were not seriously overvalued, why did export growth in the Asian countries (except the Philippines) begin to slow in the mid-1990s and then drop sharply in 1996? For example, Thailand's export revenue actually fell by 1% in 1996 after two years of growth in excess of 20%. In Korea, the growth rates of export revenue fell from 30% to 4% between 1995 and 1996. Several factors contributed to the loss of international competitiveness:

- the devaluation of the Chinese *yuan* in January 1994;
- added competitive pressure from Mexico after the establishment of the North American Free Trade Agreement (NAFTA) and the peso devaluation;
- a decrease in import demand coupled with economic downturn in Europe and Japan;
- the worldwide glut and sharp fall of the electronics market (particularly for Korea, Malaysia, and Singapore);
- slow growth in the Asian region itself—including China, Malaysia, and Thailand—after introducing policies to cool down overheating asset markets.

Nevertheless, it is important to remember that currency overvaluation was not a major factor in the loss of international competitiveness prior to the Asian crisis.

Policy mistakes in handling the crisis [9]

In this section, we argue that, unlike the Latin American countries in the early 1980s, Asian countries had not mismanaged macroeconomic policies prior to the crisis. Fiscal and monetary policies were conservative and currencies were not extremely overvalued. However, this does not imply that economic policymakers in these Asian countries were not responsible for the current crisis. In fact, by committing a series of policy mistakes in coping with the crisis in 1997, they unnecessarily aggravated the situation and completely lost reputations built on a history of prudent economic management. Among the policy mistakes, crucial ones include their mishandling of foreign reserves and domestic bankruptcy problems on the eve of the crisis; their unprofessional performance in negotiating with the IMF adjustment program; and inexperience in implementing economic policies within a global context. The following exemplify the mistakes.

1) On the eve of their respective crises, when their foreign currency reserves were quickly drying out, the Indonesian, Korean, and Thai governments did not recognize the seriousness of the problem and wasted a substantial part of foreign reserves in futile interventions in foreign exchange markets. Such intervention swiftly depleted the official reserves, which in turn started a vicious circle of impairing foreign investor confidence and accelerating capital outflows. It also contributed to the loss of policy credibility and transparency. For example, in early November 1997, Korea's central bank announced that its reserves were around $30 billion, but foreign investors estimated that actual usable reserves could be as low as $15 billion, the equivalent of only five weeks of imports and only a fifth of Korea's short-term debt. They correctly understood that the announced numbers did not include dollars borrowed in forward market intervention and recalled that Thailand had committed as much as two-thirds of its reserves in that way.
2) As the symptoms of the crisis developed in early 1997, foreign credit lines to these Asian countries started to decrease or terminate. To restore foreign investor confidence, the Thai and Korean governments pledged they would guarantee the foreign liabilities of domestic financial institutions and bail out troubled private banks. This was a crucial policy mistake, which, in its naivete, paved the way for a private banking crisis and then led to a sovereign crisis. This announcement made the previous distinction between sovereign and private problems less clear, and foreign investors began to seriously evaluate the potential fiscal cost in restructuring troubled private sectors.
3) After the crisis broke out, unwise and unnecessary discord with the IMF significantly undermined foreign investor confidence and aggravated the situation. Local news media described the IMF not as a counterpart for cooperation but as an invading army. In Korea, presidential candidates placed advertisements in newspapers vowing to renegotiate the IMF rescue pact if elected. In Indonesia, disagreement over the currency board proposal struck a further blow to deteriorating foreign investor confidence. The economic difficulty was compounded by political uncertainty, since the crisis happened during a politically unfortunate time. The three most affected countries—Indonesia, Korea, and Thailand—all faced general elections during this period, which delayed or made it impossible to implement necessary policy actions.[10]
4) One example showing the lack of global economic experience was the Korean government's decision to raise $US2 billion just one week after signing the $US55 billion IMF package. After signing the package, the government thought that the confidence problem was alleviated and tried to raise new capital through sales of Korea Development Bank bonds. The timing of the bond sales surprised foreign investors, who regarded it as a sign of desperation and speculated that the Korean situation was much worse than they had expected. As investors balked at the bond sales, and the yield spread increased by more than 200 basis points, the Korean government withdrew its sales plan. Nevertheless, it had already made the market more skeptical about the government's ability to handle the crisis.

In sum, considering the nature of the crisis, Asian policymakers may not have been able to prevent the crisis, but we think they are without doubt responsible for unnecessarily aggravating the situation through their policy mistakes in handling the crisis.

Globalization of Asian financial markets

Successful macroeconomic performance and prudent economic management in Asian countries contributed to rapid capital inflows into the region during the 1990s. However, we now see that this brought mixed blessings. Capital inflows boosted economic growth by stimulating investment. However, they simultaneously bred a lending boom and asset bubbles, and left financial markets more volatile and vulnerable to international capital flows.

Capital market liberalization and the subsequent huge capital inflows brought about more problematic consequences in Asia, where financial systems were not well developed. Most of Asia's emerging economies relied on government intervention rather than market forces in allocating financial resources. [11] In order to direct limited financial resources to strategic industries, private financial institutions were controlled and regulated as if they were public enterprises. Consequently, the liabilities of private financial intermediaries were perceived as having implicit government guarantees. Krugman (1998) points out that such perceptions contributed to the rapid formation of the financial market; however, it also fostered a serious moral hazard problem. Depositors flocked to financial institutions paying higher interest rates without giving much attention to their credit risks. Instead of making investment or loan decisions based on tradeoffs of risk and return, financial intermediaries and business enterprises alike ventured upon whatever projects paid higher returns in the event of success. Owners and managers believed that the government would bail them out should they be unlucky.

The problem of moral hazard intensified with economic growth, increased investment, and the opening of financial markets. As the economy grew, it became increasingly difficult for the government to monitor and supervise financial institutions. After capital markets opened, domestic enterprises recklessly expanded their investments in order to take advantage of low-cost foreign funds. Moreover, foreign investors provided funds to domestic financial institutions without due vigilance since they were perceived as having implicit government guarantees. In good times, this arrangement, despite its moral hazard, generated a virtuous circle of more investment and high growth. However, in bad times—such as from the mid-1990s, when financial intermediaries began to falter from a string of large-scale corporate bankruptcies—foreign investors could not help but start to take a fresh look at Asia. Consequently, as capital inflows abruptly slowed in late 1996 and early 1997, financial panic erupted and a much deeper crisis than anyone could have imagined began in Asia.

In this section, we review the extent of foreign capital inflows to the Asian countries and its relation to the globalization of the world capital markets. We then examine the amount and the structure of external liabilities in the Asian countries, and evaluate whether they became bad enough to justify the sudden reversal of foreign capital flows.

Globalization and capital flows to developing countries in an historic perspective

In terms of size and nature, capital inflows to emerging markets in the 1990s are often compared to those of the classical gold standard period (1870-1914). During the gold standard period, capital flowed from the United Kingdom, France and Germany to the then-emerging markets in Italy, Northern Europe and the new continents. Capital flows amounted to about 3.3% of GDP of the major capital-exporting and capital-importing countries.[12] Private flows, especially portfolio investments, played an important role during this period. After World War I, high capital mobility was sustained but the creditors and the debtors changed. The United States became the new capital exporter to Latin American and European borrowers.

International capital markets collapsed completely after witnessing the widespread and synchronized defaults during the Great Depression and World War II. Until the early 1970s, international capital flows had been minimal. Among them, official flows composed the major portion of the total flows, and foreign direct investment was the most important among private flows. Only after the first oil shock in 1973 did the international capital market begin to revive. From 1973 to 1981, oil revenues were recycled mostly to developing countries in Asia and Latin America through banks in developed countries. These bank loans were the major sources for non-oil-exporting countries of financing for their current account deficits, i.e., the gap between their investment and domestic saving. On the negative side, the ample supplies of financial resources made it possible for debtor countries to delay needed structural adjustment and maintain a loose fiscal and monetary stance. The consequent debt crisis in the early 1980s again stopped international capital flows.

After recovering from the debt crisis, capital flows to emerging markets soared again in the 1990s. Foreign direct investment and portfolio investments played a crucial role during this period while syndicated bank loans were the central factor from 1973 to 1981. In particular, bond financing accounted for a greater share of investment. Several factors contributed to this trend during the 1990s. The decrease in developed countries' real interest rates—notably in Japan and in Europe—and the improvement in the economic performance of developing countries increased these flows. The growth of institutional investors and securitization also promoted international portfolio investments. The revolution in information technologies and derivatives markets facilitated the flows. Competitive financial market liberalization to attract more foreign capital also accelerated the trend. Moreover, financial reforms in East Asia in the early 1990s that were intended to upgrade financial institutions tremendously expanded the banking sector and increased offshore bank borrowings.[13]

Capital flows in Asian financial markets in the 1990s

Tables 2 and 3 summarize capital flows in selected Asian countries during the 1990s. For comparison, we include the cases of several Latin American countries. Table 2 reports capital flows as a percentage of each country's GDP. Table 3 provides the same information in terms of millions of US dollars. Several features are apparent.

We can see that capital inflows to these countries (except Singapore) drastically increased in the 1990s compared with the 1980s. The increase was more dramatic than in Latin America, which had to export capital during the 1980s to repay external debt.[14] The magnitude of capital inflows was also remarkable. Between 1990 and 1996, financial capital inflows into the Asian countries averaged over 5% of GDP.[15] The most extreme cases were seen in Thailand and Malaysia. Capital inflows into these two countries averaged over 10% of GDP during the 1990s, reaching 13% and 17% of GDP in one year. Capital inflows abruptly reversed in 1997, and the magnitude was incomparably remarkable. In Thailand, for example, capital outflow reached 11% of GDP in 1997 alone. This means that between 1996 and 1997, Thailand experienced a sudden reversal of private capital inflows that amounted to about 20% of GDP. The other countries faced a similar fate. Net financial inflows to the five hardest hit Asian countries—Indonesia, Korea, Malaysia, the Philippines and Thailand—were $92.9 billion in 1996 and -$12.1 billion in 1997. The swing of $105 billion dollars in capital flows (from a $93 billion inflow to a $12 billion outflow) amounted to 11% of the pre-crisis dollar-denominated GDP of the five Asian countries.[16] It is no wonder that this large-scale shift in financial flows provoked deep economic contractions and financial embarrassment.

Before the sudden reversal, large inflows of capital had already had various economic impacts on the Asian countries concerned. First, these inflows contributed to appreciating real exchange rates. Despite enlarging current account deficits, the steady inflow of capital delayed currency devaluation in many countries and resulted in a loss of international competitiveness. Second, large capital inflows expanded domestic bank lending and increased the vulnerability of the financial system to reversals of capital inflows. A significant proportion of bank lending was used for purchasing real estate, property and equities, which consequently generated asset market bubbles. In good times, these bubbles accelerated bank lending by raising the value of the collateral. However, it simultaneously increased the vulnerability of financial institutions to the decline in domestic real estate and equity markets. The most notorious example is the Thai case. The credit crunch became a stark reality in Thailand after the crisis started because of the exposure of its financial institutions to the collapsing property market.

Table 2: Capital Flows in Selected Economies
(Units: % of GDP)

ASIA		83-89	90-95	90	91	92	93	94	95	96
KOREA	Financial flows	-0.8	3.0	1.1	2.3	2.3	1.0	2.8	3.8	5.0
	Direct investment	-0.1	-0.2	-0.1	-0.1	-0.2	-0.2	-0.5	-0.4	-0.4
	Portfolio investment	0.4	1.7	0.1	1.0	1.9	3.2	1.8	2.4	3.0
	Other investment	-1.1	1.5	1.1	1.4	0.6	-2.0	1.4	1.8	2.4
	Use of fund credit	-0.1	0.0	0.0	0.0	0.0	0.0	0.0	0.0	0.0
	Change in reserves	-1.1	-0.7	0.5	0.4	-1.2	-0.9	-1.2	-1.5	-0.3
INDONESIA	Financial flows	4.0	3.9	3.9	4.4	4.4	3.6	2.2	5.1	n.a.
	Direct investment	0.4	1.2	1.0	1.2	1.3	1.0	0.8	1.9	n.a.
	Portfolio investment	0.0	0.9	-0.1	0.0	-0.1	1.1	2.2	2.0	n.a.
	Other investment	3.5	1.9	3.1	3.3	3.2	1.4	-0.9	1.3	n.a.
	Use of fund credit	0.1	-0.1	-0.1	-0.2	-0.1	0.0	0.0	0.0	n.a.
	Change in reserves	-0.4	-1.0	-1.8	-0.9	-1.4	-0.4	-0.4	-0.8	n.a.
THAILAND	Financial flows	4.6	10.2	10.7	12.0	8.5	8.4	8.4	13.0	10.7
	Direct investment	1.1	1.5	2.7	1.9	1.8	1.3	0.6	0.7	0.8
	Portfolio investment	0.9	1.5	0.0	-0.1	0.8	4.4	1.7	2.4	2.0
	Other investment	2.6	7.1	8.0	10.2	5.9	2.8	6.1	9.9	8.0
	Use of fund credit	-0.1	-0.1	-0.3	0.0	0.0	0.0	0.0	0.0	0.0
	Change in reserves	-2.1	-3.5	-3.5	-4.7	-2.7	-3.1	-2.9	-4.3	-1.2
CHINA	Financial flows	1.3	3.0	0.8	2.0	-0.1	3.9	6.0	5.5	4.8
	Direct investment	0.4	2.9	0.7	0.9	1.5	3.8	5.9	4.9	4.6
	Portfolio investment	0.2	0.2	-0.1	0.1	0.0	0.5	0.7	0.1	0.2
	Other investment	0.7	-0.1	0.2	1.1	-1.5	-0.4	-0.5	0.6	0.0
	Use of fund credit	0.0	0.0	-0.1	-0.1	0.0	0.0	0.0	0.0	0.0
	Change in reserves	-0.3	-2.5	-3.0	-3.5	0.4	-0.3	-5.6	-3.2	-3.8
MALAYSIA	Financial flows	3.6	9.7	4.2	11.7	15.1	16.8	1.8	8.5	n.a.
	Direct investment	2.6	6.9	5.5	8.3	8.9	7.8	6.0	4.7	n.a.
	Portfolio investment	1.5	-1.0	-0.6	0.4	-1.9	-1.1	-2.3	-0.5	n.a.
	Other investment	-0.6	3.8	-0.7	3.0	8.1	10.1	-1.9	4.3	n.a.
	Use of fund credit	-0.1	0.0	0.0	0.0	0.0	0.0	0.0	0.0	n.a.
	Change in reserves	-2.1	-5.0	-4.6	-2.6	-11.4	-17.7	4.4	2.0	n.a.
PHILIPPINES	Financial flows	1.2	6.4	4.6	6.4	6.1	6.0	8.0	7.2	n.a.
	Direct investment	0.8	1.3	1.2	1.2	0.4	1.6	2.0	1.5	n.a.
	Portfolio investment	0.1	0.4	-0.1	0.2	0.1	-0.1	0.4	1.6	n.a.
	Other investment	0.3	4.7	3.6	5.0	5.5	4.5	5.6	4.1	n.a.
	Use of fund credit	0.4	-0.1	-0.8	0.4	0.1	0.2	-0.3	-0.5	n.a.
	Change in reserves	0.1	-2.0	0.9	-4.3	-3.3	-0.8	-3.3	-1.2	n.a.
SINGAPORE	Financial flows	4.9	-0.2	10.5	5.4	3.6	-1.9	-16.1	-2.9	0.6
	Direct investment	8.4	6.2	9.5	10.0	1.8	4.6	6.5	4.9	4.9
	Portfolio investment	-0.5	-5.5	-2.8	-2.1	5.0	-8.5	-15.3	-9.6	-7.6
	Other investment	-3.0	-0.9	3.9	-2.5	-3.2	2.1	-7.3	1.8	3.2
	Use of fund credit	0.0	0.0	0.0	0.0	0.0	0.0	0.0	0.0	0.0
	Change in reserves	-6.5	-11.0	-14.5	-9.6	-12.3	-13.0	-6.7	-10.1	-7.9

Table 2 cont'd

LATIN AMERICA		83-89	90-95	90	91	92	93	94	95	96
MEXICO	Financial flows	-0.8	4.8	3.4	8.7	8.1	8.4	3.7	-3.7	1.2
	Direct investment	1.2	1.8	1.0	1.6	1.3	1.1	2.6	3.3	2.3
	Portfolio investment	-0.4	2.2	-1.6	4.2	5.7	7.0	1.8	-3.6	4.4
	Other investment	-1.5	0.7	4.0	2.8	1.0	0.3	-0.6	-3.4	-5.4
	Use of fund credit	1.1	1.5	0.4	0.1	-0.2	-0.3	-0.3	9.1	-0.2
	Change in reserves	-0.5	-0.8	-1.3	-2.8	-0.4	-1.5	4.4	-3.4	-0.5
ARGENTINA	Financial flows	-1.5	1.1	-4.2	0.1	3.2	3.8	3.3	0.2	2.4
	Direct investment	0.6	1.4	1.3	1.3	1.8	1.3	1.1	1.7	1.6
	Portfolio investment	-0.4	2.3	-1.0	0.0	0.4	11.0	1.6	1.9	3.7
	Other investment	-1.7	-2.6	-4.5	-1.2	1.1	-8.4	0.6	-3.3	-2.9
	Use of fund credit	3.5	1.1	2.6	1.5	0.4	0.9	0.5	0.8	0.2
	Change in reserves	0.2	-1.1	-2.2	-1.1	-1.4	-1.7	-0.2	0.0	-1.3
BRAZIL	Financial flows	n.a.	n.a.	n.a.	-0.8	1.5	1.7	1.5	4.2	n.a.
	Direct investment	n.a.	n.a.	n.a.	0.0	0.5	0.2	0.4	0.5	n.a.
	Portfolio investment	n.a.	n.a.	n.a.	0.6	1.8	2.8	8.2	1.3	n.a.
	Other investment	n.a.	n.a.	n.a.	-1.5	-0.8	-1.3	-7.1	2.4	n.a.
	Use of fund credit	n.a.	n.a.	n.a.	0.8	1.0	0.4	0.1	0.0	n.a.
	Change in reserves	n.a.	n.a.	n.a.	0.1	-3.7	-2.0	-1.3	-1.8	n.a.
CHILE	Financial flows	-5.8	7.5	9.4	2.8	7.5	6.7	10.4	3.8	9.8
	Direct investment	6.8	2.2	2.2	2.0	1.3	1.3	3.3	3.4	5.1
	Portfolio investment	0.0	1.0	1.2	0.5	1.1	1.6	1.8	0.1	1.6
	Other investment	-8.1	3.5	6.1	0.2	5.1	3.7	5.3	0.4	3.1
	Use of fund credit	12.3	-0.6	-0.7	-0.6	-0.5	-0.6	-0.5	-0.6	-2.0
	Change in reserves	-1.1	-3.8	-7.0	-3.0	-5.6	-0.4	-5.7	-1.1	-1.6
COLOMBIA	Financial flows	2.8	2.3	0.0	-1.9	0.4	5.3	4.1	5.8	7.9
	Direct investment	1.4	1.7	1.2	1.0	1.5	1.4	2.2	2.5	3.8
	Portfolio investment	0.1	0.4	0.0	0.2	0.3	1.0	0.9	-0.2	1.9
	Other investment	1.2	0.3	-1.2	-3.1	-1.4	2.9	1.0	3.5	2.2
	Use of fund credit	0.0	0.0	0.0	0.0	0.0	0.0	0.0	0.0	0.0
	Change in reserves	-0.2	-1.7	-1.5	-4.3	-2.9	-0.9	-0.2	-0.4	-1.9
PERU	Financial flows	-3.4	1.1	-2.5	-2.1	1.1	-0.6	6.6	4.1	5.1
	Direct investment	0.0	2.0	0.1	0.0	0.3	1.6	6.1	3.5	5.9
	Portfolio investment	0.0	0.3	0.0	0.0	0.0	0.6	1.1	0.2	0.6
	Other investment	-3.4	-1.2	-2.6	-2.1	0.8	-2.8	-0.7	0.4	-1.3
	Use of fund credit	7.8	5.2	7.9	5.4	4.4	5.1	4.5	3.8	2.3
	Change in reserves	0.1	-2.2	-0.6	-2.1	-1.3	-1.6	-6.1	-1.6	-2.9

Note: Use of fund credit includes exceptional financing.
Source: IMF, *International Financial Statistics.*

Table 3: Capital Flows in Selected Economies (units: million US dollars)

ASIA		83-89	90-95	90	91	92	93	94	95	96
KOREA	Financial flows	-12850	68992	2866	6714	6969	3188	10610	17221	24025
	Direct investment	-151	-5310	-268	-320	-481	-773	-1715	-1753	-2099
	Portfolio investment	1780	37180	322	2934	5702	10530	6867	10825	14373
	Other investment	-14479	37122	2812	4100	1748	-6569	5458	8149	11751
	Use of fund credit	-1589	0	0	0	0	0	0	0	0
	Change in reserves	-13543	-16031	1208	1148	-3724	-3009	-4614	-7040	-1415
INDONESIA	Financial flows	24086	36178	4495	5697	6129	5632	3839	10386	n.a.
	Direct investment	2725	11245	1093	1482	1777	1648	1500	3745	n.a.
	Portfolio investment	232	9589	-93	-12	-88	1805	3877	4100	n.a.
	Other investment	21129	15344	3495	4227	4440	2179	-1538	2541	n.a.
	Use of fund credit	611	-643	-163	-319	-161	0	0	0	n.a.
	Change in reserves	-2294	-8158	-2088	-1210	-1909	-594	-784	-1573	n.a.
THAILAND	Financial flows	17442	74908	9100	11760	9474	10500	12166	21908	19486
	Direct investment	4163	9743	2304	1847	1966	1571	873	1182	1405
	Portfolio investment	3491	12822	-38	-81	924	5455	2481	4081	3544
	Other investment	9788	52343	6834	9994	6584	3474	8812	16645	14537
	Use of fund credit	-604	-274	-274	0	0	0	0	0	0
	Change in reserves	-8994	-25843	-2961	-4618	-3029	-3907	-4169	-7159	-2167
CHINA	Financial flows	30543	105829	3255	8032	-250	23474	32645	38673	39966
	Direct investment	10748	102017	2657	3453	7156	23115	31787	33849	38066
	Portfolio investment	4083	7318	-241	235	-57	3049	3543	789	1744
	Other investment	15712	-3506	839	4344	-7349	-2690	-2685	4035	156
	Use of fund credit	-44	-946	-492	-454	0	0	0	0	0
	Change in reserves	-6424	-78269	-11555	-14083	2060	-1769	-30453	-22469	-31705
MALAYSIA	Financial flows	7740	35669	1784	5621	8747	10805	1289	7423	n.a.
	Direct investment	6052	24993	2332	3998	5183	5006	4342	4132	n.a.
	Portfolio investment	3333	-4005	-255	170	-1122	-709	-1649	-440	n.a.
	Other investment	-1649	14681	-293	1453	4986	6508	-1404	3731	n.a.
	Use of fund credit	-263	0	0	0	0	0	0	0	n.a.
	Change in reserves	-4741	-16230	-1951	-1236	-6618	-11350	3160	1765	n.a.
PHILIPPINES	Financial flows	3109	21888	2057	2927	3208	3267	5120	5309	n.a.
	Direct investment	2059	4534	530	544	228	864	1289	1079	n.a.
	Portfolio investment	371	1507	-50	110	40	-52	269	1190	n.a.
	Other investment	679	15847	1577	2273	2940	2455	3562	3040	n.a.
	Use of fund credit	976	-574	-343	182	58	111	-220	-362	n.a.
	Change in reserves	82	-6722	388	-1937	-1746	-447	-2107	-873	n.a.
SINGAPORE	Financial flows	7015	-6869	3948	2345	1792	-1080	-11429	-2445	521
	Direct investment	12805	20299	3541	4361	887	2666	4622	4222	4635
	Portfolio investment	-682	-23502	-1037	-907	2489	-4966	-10872	-8209	-7102
	Other investment	-5108	-3666	1444	-1109	-1584	1220	-5179	1542	2988
	Use of fund credit	0	0	0	0	0	0	0	0	0
	Change in reserves	-9950	-36641	-5431	-4197	-6100	-7578	-4736	-8599	-7396

Table 3 cont'd

Latin America		83-89	90-95	90	91	92	93	94	95	96
MEXICO	Financial flows	-8624	99678	8441	25139	27039	33760	15786	-10487	4119
	Direct investment	13734	36572	2549	4742	4393	4389	10973	9526	7619
	Portfolio investment	-4598	52752	-3985	12138	19206	28355	7415	-10377	14698
	Other investment	-17760	10354	9877	8259	3440	1016	-2602	-9636	-18198
	Use of fund credit	12183	24238	1043	181	-572	-1175	-1199	25960	-788
	Change in reserves	-4460	-9895	-3261	-8154	-1173	-6057	18398	-9648	-1805
ARGENTINA	Financial flows	-8700	21352	-5884	182	7373	9827	9280	574	7033
	Direct investment	4100	19166	1836	2439	4019	3262	2982	4628	4885
	Portfolio investment	-2526	37544	-1346	-34	910	28304	4537	5173	10868
	Other investment	-10274	-35358	-6374	-2223	2444	-21739	1761	-9227	-8720
	Use of fund credit	24779	13424	3739	2846	990	2322	1394	2133	537
	Change in reserves	1033	-13271	-3121	-2040	-3106	-4512	-541	49	-3775
BRAZIL	Financial flows	-56519	40510	-5441	-4868	5889	7604	8020	29306	n.a.
	Direct investment	8804	8648	324	89	1924	801	2035	3475	n.a.
	Portfolio investment	-2592	77975	512	3808	7366	12322	44732	9235	n.a.
	Other investment	-62731	-46113	-6277	-8765	-3401	-5519	-38747	16596	n.a.
	Use of fund credit	74421	21473	10000	5055	4031	1819	617	-49	n.a.
	Change in reserves	-6166	-43619	-474	369	-14670	-8709	-7215	-12920	n.a.
CHILE	Financial flows	-7328	17732	2859	961	3131	2995	5296	2490	6780
	Direct investment	3771	6382	653	696	540	600	1673	2220	3561
	Portfolio investment	-14	2678	361	187	457	730	908	35	1098
	Other investment	-11085	8672	1845	78	2134	1665	2715	235	2121
	Use of fund credit	16439	-1501	-201	-208	-203	-258	-232	-399	-1397
	Change in reserves	-1742	-9341	-2122	-1049	-2344	-169	-2917	-740	-1107
COLOMBIA	Financial flows	7190	9550	-2	-776	182	2702	2782	4662	6784
	Direct investment	3732	5863	484	433	679	719	1515	2033	3254
	Portfolio investment	251	1120	-4	86	126	498	584	-170	1656
	Other investment	3207	2567	-482	-1295	-623	1485	683	2799	1874
	Use of fund credit	0	0	0	0	0	0	0	0	0
	Change in reserves	-255	-4615	-610	-1763	-1274	-464	-153	-351	-1598
PERU	Financial flows	-7562	4217	-831	-901	451	-259	3320	2437	3109
	Direct investment	89	6007	41	-7	136	670	3084	2083	3571
	Portfolio investment	0	945	0	0	0	228	572	145	341
	Other investment	-7651	-2735	-872	-894	315	-1157	-336	209	-803
	Use of fund credit	15774	13378	2668	2296	1852	2099	2241	2222	1386
	Change in reserves	731	-6315	-212	-899	-554	-667	-3068	-915	-1768

Note: Use of fund credit includes exceptional financing.
Source: IMF, *International Financial Statistics*

Structure of external liabilities

Not only the magnitude but also the structure of capital inflows is important in determining the scale of vulnerability and economic difficulty following a sudden shift in financial flows. The potential costs were much less associated with foreign direct investment and long-term capital flows than with short-term flows. Tables 4 and 5 examine the structure of external liabilities of the selected Asian and Latin American countries. Table 4 focuses on the amount and the maturity structure of external debt. Table 5 classifies the external debt by borrower type.[17]

Table 4: Structure of External Liabilities
(units: %)

ASIA		90	91	92	93	94	95	96	97
KOREA	Debt/GNP	12.5	13.3	13.9	13.2	14.9	17.2	21.6	27.3
	Short/Total	45.1	44.0	43.2	43.8	53.5	57.8	58.1	42.5
	Short/Reserves	95.9	124.5	107.4	94.3	118.0	138.5	183.1	251.5
	Total/Exports	48.8	54.5	55.9	53.3	59.2	62.7	80.7	88.7
	FDI+CA account/GNP	-0.8	-2.9	-1.4	0.1	-1.6	-2.2	-5.2	n.a
INDONESIA	Debt/GNP	64.0	64.9	66.2	58.7	63.3	64.6	59.7	64.2
	Short/Total	15.9	18.0	20.5	20.2	18.0	20.9	25.0	19.4
	Short/Reserves	128.6	138.2	157.9	143.8	146.4	174.3	165.7	160.2
	Total/Exports	234.1	237.4	230.2	212.6	231.8	234.1	221.4	n.a
	FDI+CA account/GNP	-1.7	-2.3	-0.8	-0.3	-0.8	-1.7	n.a	n.a
THAILAND	Debt/GNP	33.2	39.0	38.3	43.1	46.8	50.4	50.3	66.6
	Short/Total	29.6	33.1	35.2	43.0	44.5	49.4	41.4	31.2
	Short/Reserves	58.4	68.0	69.4	88.9	96.5	111.2	97.4	121.8
	Total/Exports	89.8	99.9	97.4	106.2	111.7	112.2	120.5	n.a
	FDI+CA account/GNP	-5.9	-5.9	-4.0	-3.9	-5.2	-7.5	-7.4	n.a
MALAYSIA	Debt/GNP	37.5	38.3	36.8	43.8	43.6	42.5	42.1	41.3
	Short/Total	12.4	12.1	18.2	26.6	21.1	21.2	27.8	31.8
	Short/Reserves	17.9	17.7	20.2	24.7	23.5	29.4	39.7	65.1
	Total/Exports	44.4	43.2	43.1	47.8	42.7	40.0	42.4	n.a
	FDI+CA account/GNP	3.6	-0.3	5.5	3.4	-0.3	-4.0	n.a	n.a
PHILIPPINES	Debt/GNP	68.6	70.5	60.7	64.9	60.8	51.8	47.3	70.6
	Short/Total	14.5	15.2	15.9	14.0	14.3	13.4	19.3	28.5
	Short/Reserves	217.4	111.4	98.6	84.8	80.2	68.1	68.0	204.1
	Total/Exports	230.1	219.4	187.1	187.3	163.4	118.5	97.6	n.a
	FDI+CA account/GNP	-4.9	-1.1	-1.4	-3.9	-2.5	-1.2	n.a	n.a
CHINA	Debt/GNP	15.6	16.0	16.3	19.9	18.6	17.2	16.0	17.1
	Short/Total	16.8	17.9	19.0	17.8	17.4	18.9	19.7	25.8
	Short/Reserves	27.0	22.4	55.4	55.9	30.3	27.8	22.7	29.2
	Total/Exports	91.4	86.3	85.6	94.1	80.2	77.3	71.3	n.a
	FDI+CA account/GNP	4.1	4.4	3.1	2.7	7.2	5.1	5.6	n.a
LATIN AMERICA		90	91	92	93	94	95	96	97
MEXICO	Debt/GNP	41.1	37.3	31.7	33.6	34.3	48.9	60.8	n.a
	Short/Total	15.4	19.2	21.9	27.6	28.1	19.1	22.5	n.a
	Short/Reserves	157.5	121.2	128.3	143.4	608.8	154.2	219.4	n.a
	Total/Exports	191.4	198.4	183.1	195.1	179.4	136.4	171.8	n.a
	FDI+CA account/GNP	-1.9	-3.3	-5.7	-4.9	-4.6	1.8	2.9	n.a
ARGENTINA	Debt/GNP	46.0	35.6	30.4	27.7	27.8	32.3	30.1	n.a
	Short/Total	16.8	20.7	23.7	12.3	9.3	13.0	12.2	n.a
	Short/Reserves	167.9	181.6	141.3	55.8	44.9	61.9	63.6	n.a
	Total/Exports	373.7	405.4	405.1	395.4	357.6	295.7	294.6	n.a
	FDI+CA account/GNP	4.7	1.0	-0.6	-1.7	-2.6	0.4	0.7	n.a
BRAZIL	Debt/GNP	28.1	32.2	34.9	33.9	27.7	24.5	23.6	n.a
	Short/Total	19.8	21.8	18.7	21.3	20.8	19.8	19.1	n.a
	Short/Reserves	257.8	300.9	103.6	96.5	81.5	59.4	59.2	n.a
	Total/Exports	325.3	327.7	301.4	312.5	285.1	293.2	270.7	n.a
	FDI+CA account/GNP	-0.8	-0.4	2.2	0.2	0.2	n.a	-2.2	n.a

Table 4 cont'd

CHILE	Debt/GNP	67.4	55.1	46.9	46.8	49.1	37.9	39.7	n.a
	Short/Total	17.6	12.3	16.9	20.0	26.0	25.5	27.2	n.a
	Short/Reserves	49.8	28.6	33.0	39.8	46.6	45.1	46.9	n.a
	Total/Exports	180.7	154.9	148.5	167.8	165.4	141.3	127.1	n.a
	FDI+CA account/GNP	0.6	1.8	-1.0	-4.4	0.2	-0.3	1.3	n.a
COLOMBIA	Debt/GNP	45.1	43.4	36.6	35.1	323	35.3	32.1	n.a
	Short/Total	8.4	10.2	14.8	19.3	20.5	20.4	22.1	n.a
	Short/Reserves	32.3	27.6	33.8	47.6	57.1	60.7	67.6	n.a
	Total/Exports	181.0	166.1	167.3	172.8	167.6	184.8	164.6	n.a
	FDI+CA account/GNP	2.7	7.0	3.4	-2.6	-2.4	-1.8	-2.7	n.a
PERU	Debt/GNP	63.0	75.9	49.9	59.2	54.7	49.1	54.1	n.a
	Short/Total	26.7	21.0	19.2	24.4	25.4	22.1	31.4	n.a
	Short/Reserves	282.9	140.9	112.8	146.5	90.8	58.7	111.9	n.a
	Total/Exports	452.2	446.1	411.2	487.1	415.8	352.4	400.2	n.a
	FDI+CA account/GNP	-4.2	-5.7	-4.9	-4.2	0.9	-0.1	-3.9	n.a

Note: FDI = foreign direct investment

Source: For the year 1990-96, World Bank, Global Development Finance; for the year 1997, JP Morgan "Emerging markets: Economic indicators" and "Asian Financial Markets"; all Korean data are from the Ministry of Finance in Korea.

Table 5: Structure of External Liabilities: Type of Borrowing (units: millions of US $)

			End 94	End 95	End 96	End 97
KOREA	Total Outstanding		56,599	77,528	99,953	94,180
	Obligations by sector (% of total)	Public	8.7	8.0	5.7	4.2
		Banks	65.4	64.4	65.9	59.4
		Non-bank Private	25.8	27.6	28.3	36.3
	Short term debt		40,143	54,275	67,506	59,444
	Short term/Reserves		1.57	1.66	1.98	2.82
INDONESIA	Total Outstanding		34,970	44,528	55,523	58,388
	Obligations by sector (% of total)	Public	19.9	15.1	12.5	11.8
		Banks	22.4	20.1	21.2	20.1
		Non-bank Private	57.7	64.7	66.2	68.1
	Short term debt		21,291	27,578	34,248	35,383
	Short term/Reserves		1.75	2.01	1.88	2.13
THAILAND	Total Outstanding		43,879	62,818	70,147	58,835
	Obligations by sector (% of total)	Public	6.3	3.6	3.2	3.0
		Banks	32.1	41.0	36.9	30.2
		Non-bank Private	61.5	55.2	59.6	66.6
	Short term debt		30,968	43,606	45,702	38,772
	Short term/Reserves		1.06	1.21	1.21	1.48
MALAYSIA	Total Outstanding		13,493	16,781	22,234	27,528
	Obligations by sector (% of total)	Public	18.1	12.4	9.0	6.3
		Banks	28.6	26.4	29.3	35.8
		Non-bank Private	53.2	60.4	61.8	57.8
	Short term debt		6,579	7,913	11,178	14,613
	Short term/Reserves		0.26	0.33	0.41	0.65

Table 5 cont'd

PHILIPPINES	Total Outstanding		6,830	8,327	13,289	19,732
	Obligations by sector (% of total)	Public	37.6	32.3	20.5	12.3
		Banks	25.1	27.0	39.5	45.3
		Non-bank Private	37.3	40.6	40.0	42.4
	Short term debt		3,171	4,067	7,737	11,924
	Short term/Reserves		0.53	0.64	0.77	1.64
CHINA	Total Outstanding		41,341	48,384	55,002	63,128
	Obligations by sector (% of total)	Public	29.4	19.9	15.4	11.3
		Banks	38.3	41.0	41.4	42.9
		Non-bank Private	32.3	39.1	43.1	45.8
	Short term debt		18,176	23,028	26,879	33,693
	Short term/Reserves		0.34	0.31	0.25	0.24
TAIWAN	Total Outstanding		21,068	22,534	22,363	26,173
	Obligations by sector (% of total)	Public	3.6	1.7	2.1	1.5
		Banks	64.9	63.7	57.8	55.4
		Non-bank Private	31.5	34.6	40.0	42.5
	Short term debt		19,048	19,650	18,869	21,402
	Short term/Reserves		0.30	0.32	0.31	0.34

Source: Bank for International Settlements (BIS) and IMF, *International Financial Statistics*

In Table 4, the total debt-to-GNP (gross national product) ratios were in general higher in Asian countries than those in Latin American countries, but there exist significant individual differences. The debt-to-GNP ratios were quite low in Korea and China until very recently. After the mid-1990s, the ratios increased sharply in Korea and Thailand. As explained before, the rapid growth of external debts was partly the result of financial reform that was aimed at building a regional financial center and upgrading domestic financial institutions. The higher debt-to-GNP ratios in the Asian countries do not necessarily imply the possibility of insolvency. On the contrary, this was made possible because of Asia's successful track record in economic development. Despite the larger amount of external debt, the debt-to-export ratios in Asian countries were lower than those in Latin American countries, which implies that they did not have difficulty in servicing their debt until recently.

Table 4 shows that the external debts in the Asian countries were highly concentrated in short-term debts. Thailand and Korea were the most extreme cases. Their short-term debt amounted to nearly 50% of total debt prior to the crisis.[18] The mismatch between the short-term debts and official foreign reserves was even more drastic. In the three worst affected countries—Indonesia, Korea, and Thailand—the ratio of short-term external debt to official foreign reserves exceeded 100% from the mid-1990s. This was in sharp contrast to China, Malaysia, and the Philippines. In China, short-term debt was a small fraction of total debt, as foreign direct investment dominated net private capital inflows. In Malaysia and the Philippines, total external debt was not small, but the proportion of short-term debt and its ratio with respect to foreign reserves were moderate. It is no wonder that the crisis erupted in Thailand and then propagated to Indonesia and Korea, leaving the other countries less affected.

Table 5 presents the debt structure by borrower type. In Thailand and Korea, external debts were predominantly borrowings by banks and financial institutions. On the other hand, in Indonesia, Malaysia, and the Philippines, the main borrowers were non-bank private corporations. Since financial institutions usually maintain steady long-term relationships with each other, it was believed that short-term inter-bank loans in Korea and Thailand would be rolled over without difficulty and were therefore equivalent to long-term debts. However, the current crisis taught us that the borrower type did not matter once the panic started. Even inter-bank loans played a role of "hot and speculative money" by not being rolled over.

In hindsight, it is ironic that the rapid buildup of short-term debts in these Asian countries was made possible because of Asia's successful track record of high growth. In fact, the shortening of the maturity of external debt could be interpreted as a sign of improvement in Asia's credit standing. Considering the term structure of interest rates in international financial markets, where long-term rates are typically higher than short-term rates, it would be natural for countries with higher credit ratings to rely more on short-term financing. Taiwan, which had a better credit rating than the other Asian countries, maintained a higher short-term to long-term debt ratio. Exchange rate management in Asia also contributed to the shortening of maturity. By pegging their currencies to the US dollar, with either very little variation or small predictable changes, the Asian governments virtually absorbed the exchange rate risks on behalf of investors. This strongly attracted foreign capital, particularly with short-term maturity.

IMF Adjustment Program for the Asian Crisis

After the crisis began, Thailand, Indonesia, and Korea requested IMF financial support and are currently under IMF adjustment programs attached to financial support. To analyze the economic and social impacts of the Asian crisis and to forecast its future development, it is imperative that we understand the IMF adjustment program. In this section, we first discuss how the IMF adjustment program has evolved over the last three decades. As the Asian crisis became deeper than initially expected, many cast doubts on the effectiveness of IMF policy and even questioned the *raison d'être* of the IMF itself. To address this issue, we describe the economic conditions before and after IMF intervention in these three countries and delineate IMF adjustment programs in each country.

The changing nature of the IMF Adjustment Program

The IMF provides financial support and economic advice to member countries facing severe macroeconomic imbalance. The conditionality attached to IMF resources—i.e., the policies that the IMF expects a recipient country to follow in order to avail itself of credit—is called an IMF financial or adjustment program. The theoretical framework and the nature of the IMF adjustment program has changed steadily as new economic theories develop and the world economic environment changes (Fischer 1998; IMF 1987; Polak 1991; Polak 1997; Schadler et al. 1995). The collapse of the fixed exchange rate system in the early 1970s and the rapid growth of international capital flows have increased the number of countries seeking financial assistance from the IMF, concurrently changing the nature of IMF adjustment programs. The changing nature of the IMF program since 1970 can best be understood by comparing the contents of its three large-scale arrangements. The first one was for the Latin American debt crisis in the 1980s, the second one for the Eastern European economic crisis in the early 1990s, and the third one for the recent crisis in Asia.

One of the main causes of the Latin American debt crisis in the 1980s was the mismanagement of macroeconomic policies. Profligate fiscal deficits resulted in excessive monetary expansion and consequent hyperinflation: overvalued exchange rates led to massive current account deficits. Accordingly, the IMF program focused on a policy of stringent management of aggregated demand to curb inflation and reduce current account deficits. By restoring macroeconomic stability and reducing external liabilities, the IMF tried to bring private foreign capital back to the region. When critics fault the IMF for applying the "same old belt-tightening" policy or "one-size-fits-all" approach to the Asian crisis, they are referring to this policy of restraining aggregate demand.

After the collapse of the Soviet Union in the early 1990s, many Eastern European countries including Russia joined the IMF. The economic crisis suffered by these countries during their transition to market economies created new demand for IMF financial resources. After the fall of communism, the disruption of trade within previously centrally planned economies caused a severe contraction of exports and a deep recession. The move to trade at world prices also inflicted a serious loss in their terms of trade and depleted their settlement currency. Unlike the Latin American case, which mainly focused on short-run demand management, the IMF program for Eastern Europe aimed at medium-term structural reforms to ensure their successful transition to a market economy. The "big bang approach" used in Eastern Europe consisted of three parts: liberalization, stabilization, and structural reform.[19] Through this program, the IMF tried to play a catalyst role in reviving international trade and inducing private capital inflows for economic development. Recurring crises in some Latin American countries that had previously received IMF support also contributed to the shift in emphasis from traditional demand management policy to supply-side policies, aimed at promoting the resumption of growth and building new institutions in the medium term.

The IMF program for the Asian crisis can be seen as a mixture of the two approaches described above, i.e., a mixture of aggregate demand management and structural reform. This choice reflects the IMF view of the origin of the Asian crisis (Fischer 1998). It places primary responsibility on the structural weakness of Asian capitalism, particularly its financial system. Inexperience and inefficiency among financial institutions in pricing and risk management, inadequate regulation and supervision of financial institutions, poor corporate governance—all had contributed to imprudent lending and inefficient investment spending, which in turn weakened the stability of the banking system. According to this view, the currency crisis in Asia was essentially a bank-run phenomenon where the creditors happened to be foreigners. Fearful about declining financial conditions in Asia, foreign creditors rushed to withdraw their capital, thereby intensifying exchange rate pressures.

For this reason, the design of the IMF program for the Asian crisis focused on fixing the structural weaknesses in the financial sector. But the IMF believed that the first order of business should be to restore confidence in the currency by implementing stringent demand management policy, because only after the exchange market is stabilized can these countries secure the necessary foreign funds for successful structural reform. In short, the best approach is to allow a sharp but temporary increase in interest rates to stem the outflow of capital, while making a decisive start on the medium-term tasks of economic restructuring. This IMF policy, which simultaneously pursues structural reform and stabilization of foreign exchange markets, poses a dilemma. In order to stabilize the foreign exchange market in the short run, contractionary fiscal and monetary policies are necessary. On the other hand, to alleviate pain from the credit crunch accompanying structural reform, expansionary policies are needed. Recent critiques of IMF policy argue that the program is too contractionary in the short run and that it reduces long-run growth potentials in the region, thereby hindering implementation of structural reform.[20]

The IMF financial program for Indonesia, Korea, and Thailand

So far, we have discussed the common features of the Asian crisis: weak financial systems; excessive, unhedged foreign borrowing (most of which is short-term borrowing by the domestic private sector); and a lack of transparency in accounting and business practices. Nonetheless, there exist significant differences among these countries regarding origins of the crisis and pre-crisis conditions. In Thailand, signs of deteriorating economic conditions and overheating pressures were more visible before the crisis than in Indonesia and Korea. Thailand had been running exceptionally large current account deficits (8% of GDP) since 1995, whereas those of Korea and Indonesia were at a more manageable level. It faced more difficulties in the property sector and a sharp fall in the stock market after the lending boom ended and asset bubbles burst. Inflexible management of exchange rates was more evident in Thailand.

In contrast, Korea's management of the economy was generally favorable before the crisis, but it suffered an unprecedented number of bankruptcies of highly leveraged conglomerates (*chaebols*) in early 1997. The bankruptcies rapidly increased the value of non-performing loans (in absolute terms and as a share of total bank assets) and exacerbated existing weakness in the banking system, eventually causing the loss of foreign investors' confidence. Compared with Thailand, corporate governance problems and the limitations of detailed government intervention at the micro level were more visible in Korea.

Indonesia's economic performance also was quite sound until mid-1997, but its own structural weakness left Indonesia unable to escape contagion from Thailand and Korea in the latter half of 1997. Besides its weak financial system, import monopolies and domestic trade regulations impeded economic efficiency and competitiveness. Political uncertainty arising from the general elections of 1997 and the presidential election in March 1998 compounded economic problems. Meanwhile, the cyclical weather pattern known as El Niño brought extended drought, which in turn ignited forest fires, all occurring at a most unfortunate juncture for the country. The drought and fires caused serious damage to the forestry and agriculture sectors of the economy, reducing exports and raising food prices.

The design of the IMF programs in these countries reflected these similarities and differences. Table 6, Table 7, and Table 8 briefly summarize the major contents of the initial IMF programs and their revised agreements. All three programs called for an initial, substantial rise in interest rates to prevent a downward spiral of currency depreciation. In fact, in Indonesia, the decline in the exchange rate was so precipitous that monetary and interest rate policies were subordinated to the exchange rate target. Instead of aggregate money supply, interest rates were controlled because the deterioration of the financial markets was so rapid and extreme. All three programs focused on up-front action to put the financial system on a sounder footing as quickly as possible. In addition, they called for a fiscal tightening that would cover the carrying costs of financial sector restructuring.[21] Despite these similarities, however, there still exist differences among countries. Improving corporate governance was emphasized in Korea; deregulation, privatization, and trade liberalization had more weight in the Indonesia program; and the Thailand program focused relatively more on correctly macroeconomic imbalance and coping with the burst of the real estate bubble.

Table 6: IMF Programs for Korea

KOREA	Dec 97	First review (8 Jan 98)	Second review (17 Feb 98)	Third review (29 Apr 98)
Gross official reserve	$ 35.4 bil		$ 39.1 bil	$ 43.0 bil
Reserve money growth	9%		1st Qtr; 15.2% 2nd Qtr; 15.7%	2nd Qtr; 13.5%
Fiscal balance	Balanced or a little surplus	Deficit permitted	-0.8%	-1.7%
Growth rate	3%	1–2%	1%	-1%
Inflation	Less than 5%	About 9%	9–10%	9–10%
Current account balance	$ 4.3 bil	$ 3 bil	$ 8 bil	$ 22 bil
Unemployment rate	3.9%	4.7%	5.0–6.0%	6.4%

Table 6 cont'd

Financial sector restructuring	1. Passing of the financial sector reform bill 2. Restructuring and recapitalization of troubled financial institutions 3. Disposal of non-performing loans 4. Timetable for all banks to meet Basel standards 5. Replacement of present blanket guarantees by a limited deposit insurance scheme 6. Action program to strengthen financial supervision and regulation 7. Improvement of accounting standards and disclosure rules 8. Bringing Bank of Korea's international reserves management standards in line with international best practices		1. Assessment of rehabilitation plans of merchant banks and following actions including suspension and closure 2. Appointment of outside experts and selection of lead managers for privatization of Korea First Bank and Seoul Bank 3. Establishment of a unit for bank restructuring and ordering submission of recapitalization plans from commercial banks whose capital adequacy ratios fall below the Bank for International Settlements (BIS) standard 4. Strengthening of prudential supervision and regulations 5. Additional financial legislation 6. Keeping all public support for financial restructuring on a transparent basis	
KOREA	Dec 97	First review (8 Jan 98)	Second review (17 Feb 98)	Third review (29 Apr 98)
Other	1. Trade liberalization (elimination of trade-related subsidies, restrictive import licensing and the import diversification program) 2. Capital account liberalization (increase of the ceiling of individual foreign ownership of equity, opening of corporate bond markets, etc.) 3. Improvement of corporate governance and structure (generally accepted accounting standards, plan for the restructuring of corporate finance, etc.) 4. Labor market reform to improve labor market flexibility 5. Improvement of dissemination of key economic data		1. Widening capital account liberalization (full liberalization of money market instruments, lifting of restrictions on corporate borrowing, providing transparent guidelines for foreign investment in financial institutions, prudential controls on short-term external borrowing, eliminating aggregate ceiling on equity investment)	

Source: *IMF Stand-By Arrangement for Korea*, available at the IMF Internet site.

Table 7: IMF Programs for Indonesia

INDONESIA	05 Nov 97	First review (15 Jan 98)	Second review (10 Apr 98)
Gross official reserves	5 months of import		
Fiscal balance	0.5–1%	-1%	-3.8%
Growth rate	3%		-5%
Inflation	9%	Less than 20%	45%
Current account balance	-2%		2.7%

Table 7 cont'd

Financial Sector Restructuring	1.Closure of non-viable banks and implementation of rehabilitation plans for weak institutions 2. Establishment of enforcement mechanisms and clear exit policy	1. Establish and implement rules for resolving liquidity and solvency problems of private banks 2. Program for efficiency improvement and privatization of state banks 3. Amendment of the Banking Law 4. Enforcement of prudential regulation (capital adequacy rules, upgrading of the reporting and monitoring procedures for foreign exchange exposure of the banks, strengthening of the central bank's capacity for risk-based supervision) 5. Strengthening of the policy and institutional infrastructure for banking (revising the legal framework for banking operations, improving transparency and disclosure in banking, leveling the playing field for foreign investors in banking, eliminating all restrictions on bank lending)	1. Government guarantees for all depositors and creditors of locally incorporated banks 2. Establishment of the Indonesian Bank Restructuring Agency (IBRA) 3. Additional prudential regulation on new credits and payment of dividends 4. Establishment of an Asset Management Company (AMC) for the debt recovery of troubled assets 5. Minimum capital requirement for locally incorporated banks
INDONESIA	05 Nov 97	First review (15 Jan 98)	Second review (10 Apr 98)
Other		1. Liberalization of foreign trade and investment (elimination of import monopolies, tariff reduction program, abolition of import and export restriction, removal of foreign investment restriction, etc.) 2. Deregulation and privatization (dissolution of restrictive marketing arrangement, deregulation of agricultural product trade, abolition of inter-provincial and inter-district trade tax, establishment of framework for the management and privatization of government assets, etc.) 3. Social safety net (introduction of community-based work programs, increased social spending)	1. Support for small- and medium-scale enterprises 2. Corporate debt restructuring 3. Bankruptcy and judicial reforms (update of the bankruptcy law, creation of Special Commercial Court, etc.)

Source: IMF Stand-by Arrangement for Indonesia, available at the IMF Internet site.

Table 8: IMF Programs for Thailand

THAILAND	20 Aug 97	First review (25 Nov 97)	Second review (24 Feb 98)
Gross official reserve	4.4 months of import	$ 24.8 bil	$ 23-25 bil
Reserve money growth		1%	6.6%
Fiscal balance	1%	1%	-2%
Growth rate	3.5%	0–1%	-3 to -3.5%
Inflation	5%	10%	11.6%

Table 8 cont'd

Current account balance	-3%	-1.8%	3.9%
Financial Sector Restructuring	1. Up-front separation, suspension, and restructuring of non-viable institutions 2. Immediate steps to instill confidence in the rest of the financial system 3. Strict conditionality on the extension of FIDF resources 4. Phased implementation of broader structural reforms to restore a healthy financial sector	1. Restructuring of the 58 suspended finance companies (establishment of institutional framework, determination by the Financial Restructuring Agency (FRA) which finance companies would be suspended, disposal of assets of closed finance companies) 2. Recapitalization and strengthening of the remaining financial system (the early tightening of loan classification rules, timetables for the recapitalization of all undercapitalized financial institutions, streamlining of bankruptcy procedures, reaffirmation of disclosure and auditing requirements)	1. Asset disposal of the 56 closed finance companies 2. Strengthening of the core financial system through a combination of more realistic loan provisioning and private sector-led recapitalization 3. Establishment of sound legal, regulatory, and institutional frameworks for the supervision of financial institutions
Other		1. Privatization (legislation to facilitate the privatization of the state enterprises) 2. Social sector support program 3. Bringing the legal and regulatory framework in line with international standards	1. Drawing up a strengthened social safety net program 2. Amendment of the bankruptcy and foreclosure laws to facilitate corporate restructuring

Source: IMF Stand-by Arrangement for Thailand, available from the IMF Internet site.

It is too early to tell whether the IMF adjustment programs in these countries will be effective. Between July 1997 and January 1998, the Indonesian rupiah depreciated by 432%, falling from 2,430 to 12,950 rupiah to the US dollar. The Indonesian stock price index declined by 54%. Between January and December 1997, the Korean won depreciated by 121% and the composite stock price index declined by 50%. The value of the Thai baht and composite stock price index declined by 139% and 52%, respectively, during a similar period. For reference, we plot the behavior of the exchange rates in each country and describe major economic events in Figures 1 to 3.

As the Asian crisis deepened, many critics cast doubt on the effectiveness of the IMF programs, or even blamed them for worsening the situation. We think, however, that this verdict is premature. The further deterioration following IMF intervention does not necessarily imply the failure of IMF policy. Without IMF support, the situation might have deteriorated even more than it actually did. Moreover, as we argued in the discussion of macroeconomic conditions and policies, the governments in these countries must take the primary responsibility. They aggravated the situation unnecessarily by committing a series of policy mistakes after IMF intervention. The disagreement over the currency board proposal between the Indonesian government and the IMF is a representative example.

Social impacts of the Asian crisis and the IMF program

In this section, we analyze the social impacts of financial crises and IMF adjustment programs in East Asia. Over the past 20 years, East Asian countries were remarkably successful in reducing poverty and achieving high employment growth. The present crisis, however, has jeopardized this hard-won reputation for economic performance that has provided better living standards for millions of Asians and offered millions more people in other regions the hope of lifting themselves out of poverty. The financial meltdown in Asia, currently translating into rising social and political unrest, has resulted in more people being thrown out of employment and joining the ranks of the poor.

As we write, the Asian crisis is still unraveling, and only limited information is available for assessing its social impact. Given this difficulty, this paper will focus only on its impact on employment, real wages, income distribution, and poverty. To examine how the financial crisis affects these social variables, we consult the records of countries that experienced past currency crises and received conditional financial assistance from the IMF. In order to accurately measure the impact of both the financial crisis and the IMF adjustment program, we have to evaluate the performance of program countries in comparison with the performance that would have prevailed in the absence of the crisis and adjustment program. In other words, we have to evaluate whether the IMF programs were associated with better or worse social outcomes *than would otherwise have occurred.* It is very difficult both conceptually and practically to identify the hypothetical reference point and to disentangle the effects of IMF programs from those of other factors. In this section, we first briefly discuss several methodologies for evaluating the effects of IMF programs. We then analyze the social impact of IMF programs in past program countries from 1973 to 1994. Based on these empirical results and specific East Asian characteristics, we attempt to assess the social impact of the recent financial crisis and IMF programs in East Asia.

Methodology to evaluate the programs in a cross-country framework

A number of previous studies have tried to assess the effects of IMF programs based on cross-sectional country data. The methodology for evaluating IMF programs can be classified into three categories: the "before-after" approach; the "control group" approach; and the "modified control group" approach.[22] The first and most popular method is the "before-after" approach, which compares performance during a program with that prior to the program. It uses non-parametric statistical methods to evaluate whether there is a significant change in some essential variables over time. Therefore, while easy to employ and seemingly objective, this approach often gives biased results due to the assumption that had it not been for the program, the performance indicators would have taken their pre-crisis-period values.

The "control group" methodology attempts to overcome some of the limitations of the "before-after" approach. Here, the behavior of key variables in the program countries was compared to their behavior in non-program countries (a control group). Thus, it implicitly assumes that only the imposition of the IMF program itself distinguishes the group of program countries from the control group. The external environment is assumed to affect program and non-program countries equally.

The third methodology is the "modified control group" approach, which consists of regressions that control for differences in initial conditions and policies undertaken in program and non-program countries. That is, this approach identifies the differences between program and non-program countries in the pre-program period, and then controls these differences statistically in order to find out the isolated impacts of the programs in the post-reform performance.

A substantial body of research has adopted these approaches to assess the impact of IMF programs. In particular, since the primary purpose of the IMF program is to assist the member country in restoring a sustainable balance of payments, reducing inflation, and creating the conditions for sustainable income growth, most of the studies focused on evaluating how successfully these primary macroeconomic goals have been achieved (see Goldstein and Montiel 1986, Khan 1990, and Conway 1994). However, little investigation has been conducted on the analysis of the social impact of IMF programs. A notable exception is a study by Garuda (1998), which conducts an extensive cross-country investigation into the distributional effects of IMF programs in 39 countries from 1975 to 1991.

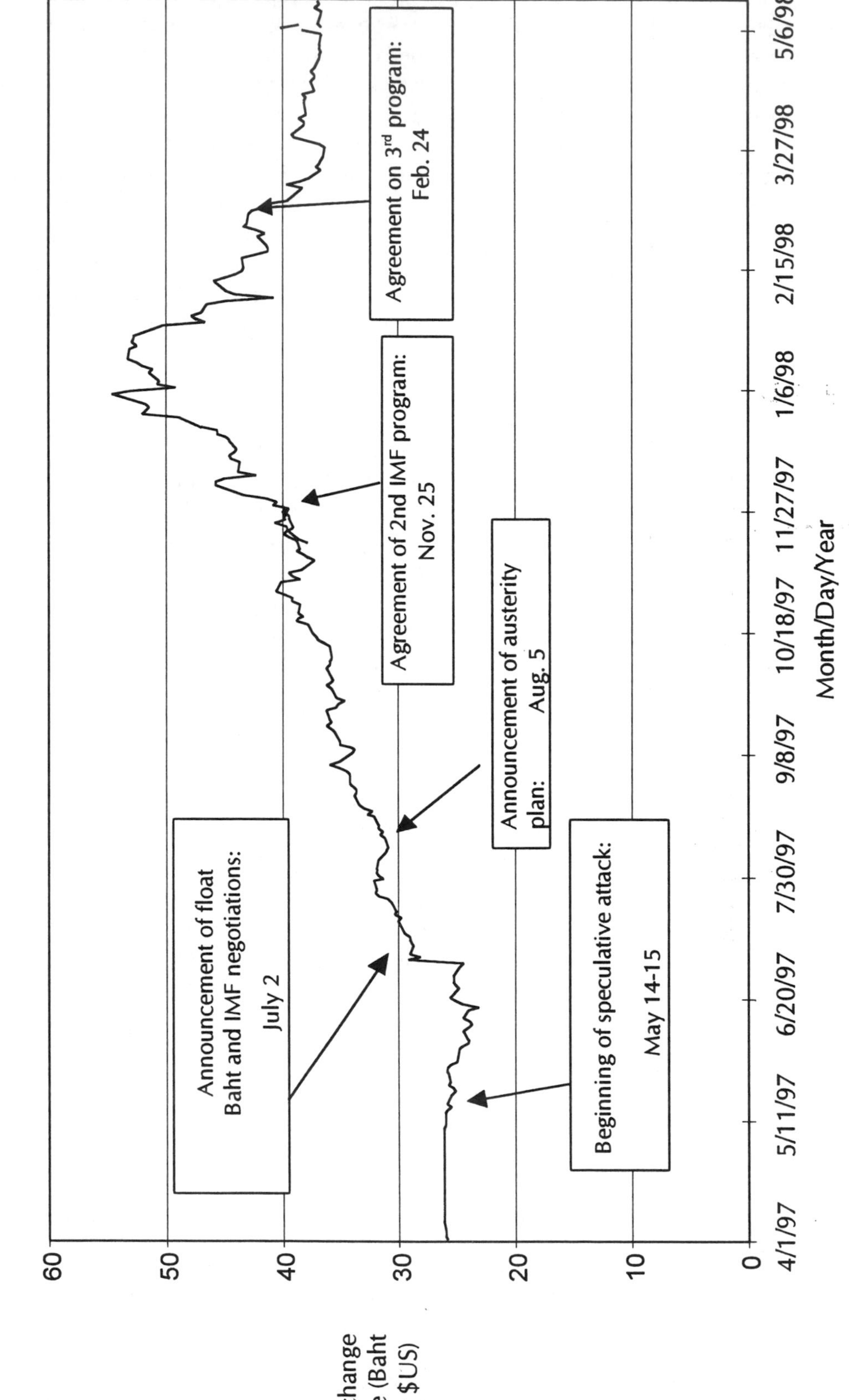

Figure 1: Exchange Rate in Thailand
Exchange rate (Baht per $US)
60
50
40
30
20
10
0
4/1/97
5/11/97
6/20/97
7/30/97
9/8/97
10/18/97
11/27/97
1/6/98
2/15/98
3/27/98
5/6/98
Month/Day/Year
Announcement of float Baht and IMF negotiations: July 2
Beginning of speculative attack: May 14-15
Announcement of austerity plan: Aug. 5
Agreement of 2nd IMF program: Nov. 25
Agreement on 3rd program: Feb. 24

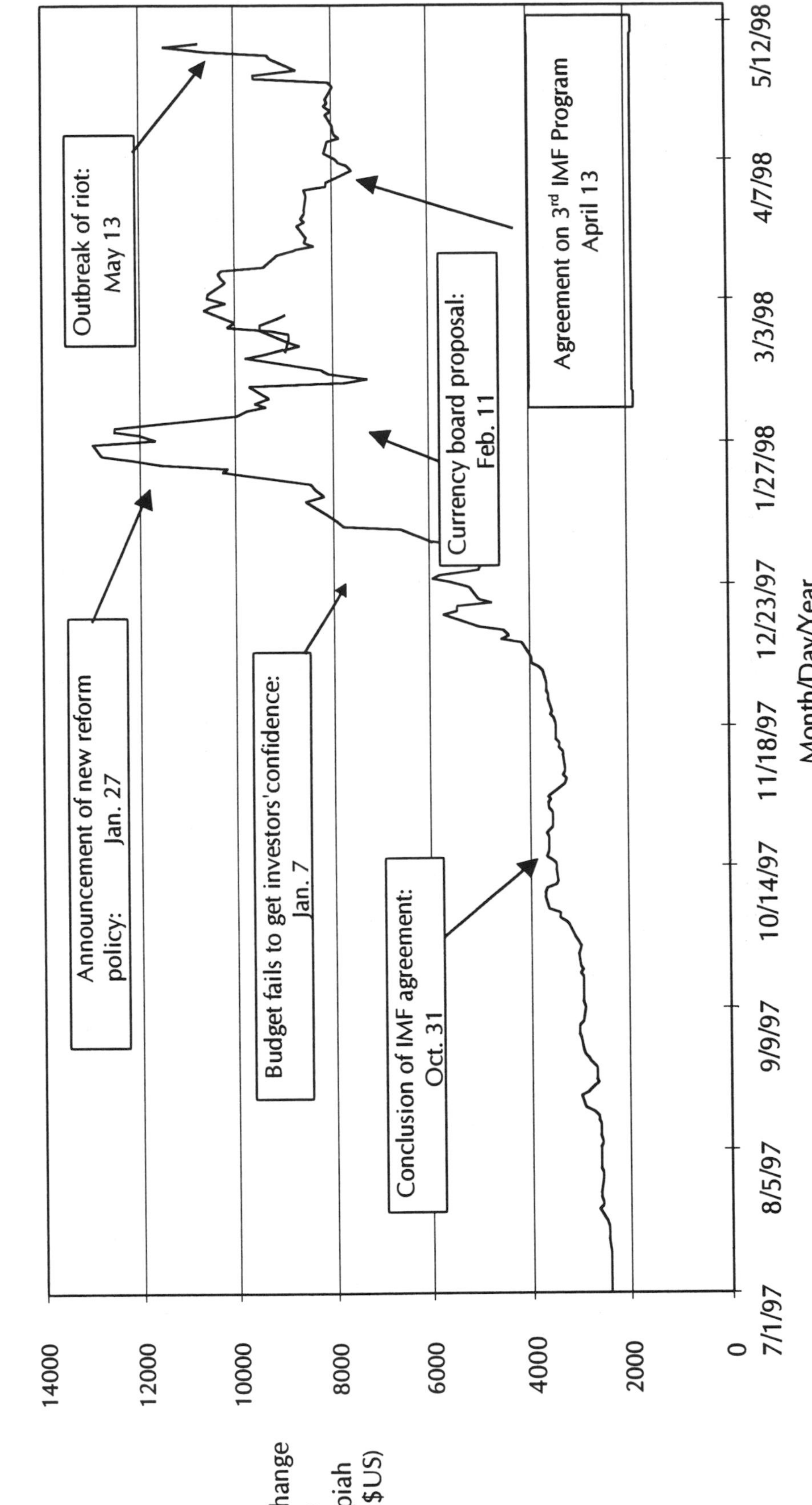

Figure 2: Exchange Rate in Indonesia

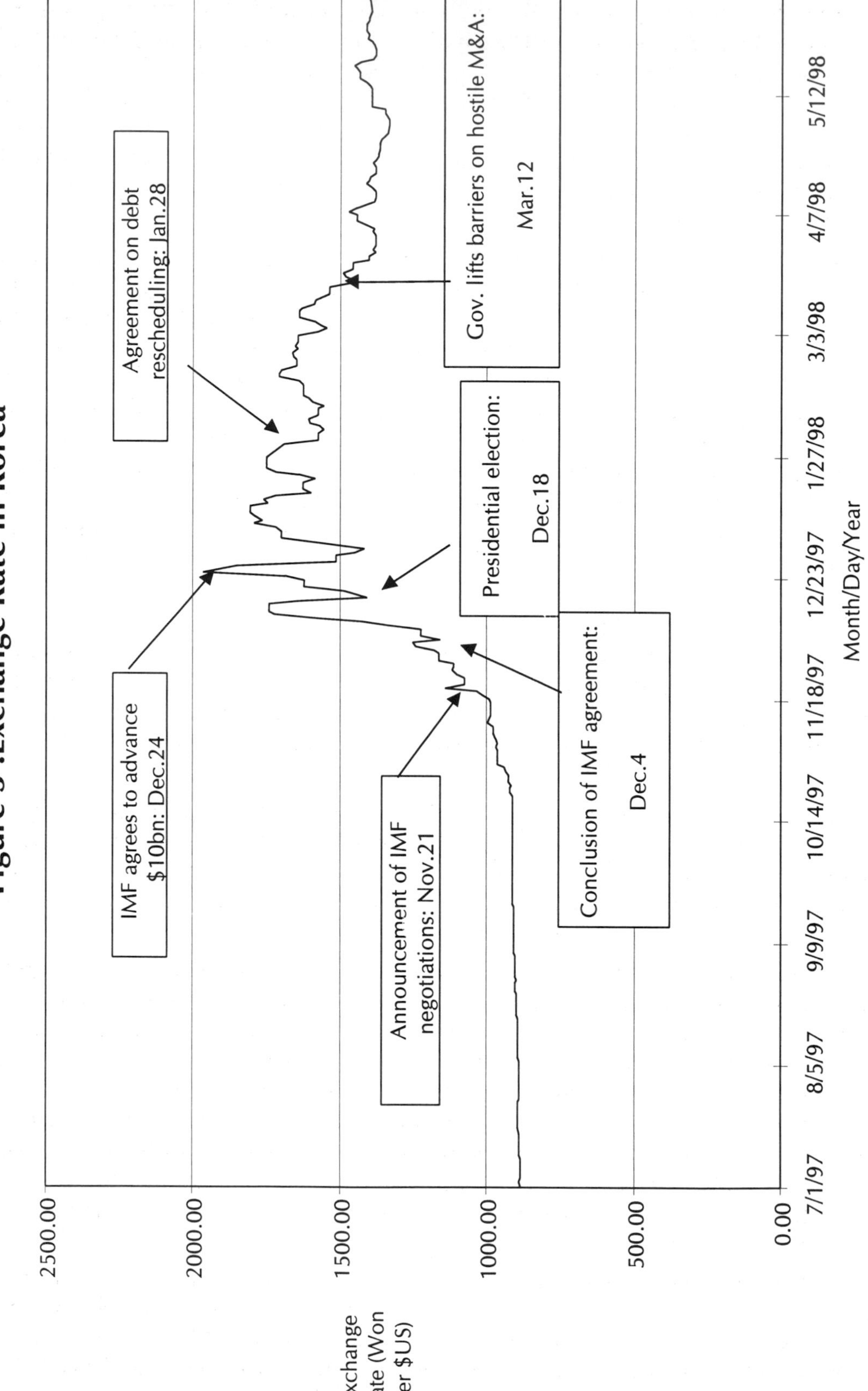

Figure 3 :Exchange Rate in Korea

Evaluation of the social impact of the IMF Programs, 1973-1994

We examine the social impact of IMF programs, using data of all developing countries that received stand-by and extended arrangements from mid-1973 to mid-1994. During this period, 88 non-OECD (Organization for Economic Cooperation and Development) countries received financial support from the IMF at least once; the total number of programs was 455.[23] In order to avoid "double counting" of economic crises or IMF programs, we pay special attention to programs that were continued from the previous year. That is, in our sample, a consecutive approval of a program or programs of more than one year in length is counted as only one program and is identified by the first year of the program. This procedure yields a total of 313 programs.

For each program in our sample, we estimate the social outcomes following the "before-after" approach, and then compare them to the average outcomes of non-program countries following the "control group" approach. We focus on two key social outcomes: employment and real wages on the one hand, and poverty and income distribution on the other hand. The changes in these social variables are measured over the period of three years preceding, and one to five years following, the approval of an IMF program. We also construct a control group of "tranquil" observations. If a country had not been subject to any IMF program within a window of plus or minus five years surrounding a specific year, it is counted as a non-program country in that specific year. We use all these observations as our control group of non-program "tranquil" observations. We have not tried to control statistically for the differences between program and non-program countries as in the "modified control group" approach.

Changes in employment and real wages

To analyze the effects of IMF programs on employment and real wages, we use data on manufacturing employment and wage growth rates available from the World Bank's *World Tables*. The data were compiled for the period of 1968 to 1994 to examine the lagging effects of IMF programs. The data cover 1,306 observations for employment and 1,157 for the real wage, of which 138 and 126 observations, respectively, correspond to IMF program years.[24]

Figure 4 shows the changes in rates of employment and real wage growth before and after the initiation of IMF programs. In panel (a) of Figure 4, we plot the behavior of the average employment growth rate at the onset of the IMF programs, over the three preceding years, and in each of the following five years. For comparison, we include a straight line in the panel, which indicates the average employment growth rate of the control group of "tranquil" observations.

We can clearly see that employment growth rates in program periods were significantly lower than those in non-program periods. It is not hard to understand why: the lower level of employment growth indicates deteriorating economic conditions in the program countries prior to the onset of the crisis. What is surprising is the fact that the employment growth rate did not recover its pre-crisis level even five years after the onset of the crisis. The average employment growth rate was 3.2% in the initial program year, which was essentially identical to the average of the three years before the program. As programs proceeded, the employment growth rate fell to 2.5% in the year following program initiation, fluctuated for the next three years, and stood at 2.4% in the fifth year. We discuss the causes for the slow recovery of employment growth rates following an examination of the behavior of real wage growth rates.

Panel (b) of Figure 4 portrays the change in real wage growth rates. The growth rates dropped a little in the year of program initiation, and then declined further in the year following the crisis. Wage growth recovered in the second year after the program. Since most IMF programs contained measures to restrain wage bills by such measures as wage freezes, reduced work hours, and cuts in fringe benefits, the initial drop in wage growth seemed inevitable (Sisson 1986). The real wage growth in subsequent years is also consistent with the changes in output and inflation over the period of IMF involvement. Schadler et al. (1995) show that output growth rates declined in the program year and then subsequently recovered.

Figure 4: Changes in Employment and Real Wages Before and After IMF Programs

(a): Employment growth

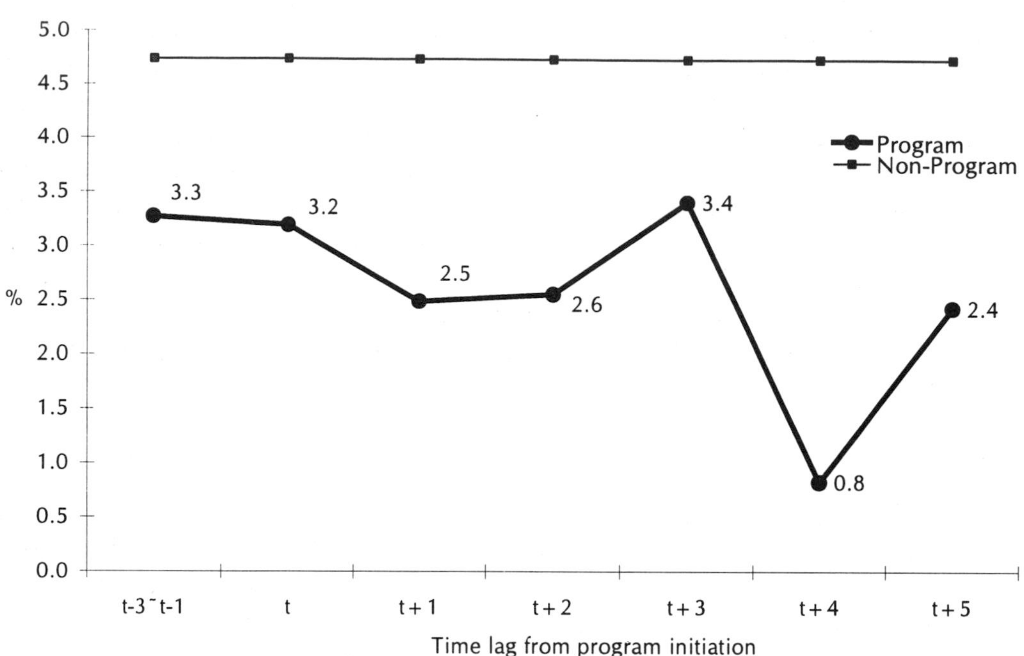

(b): Real Wage Growth

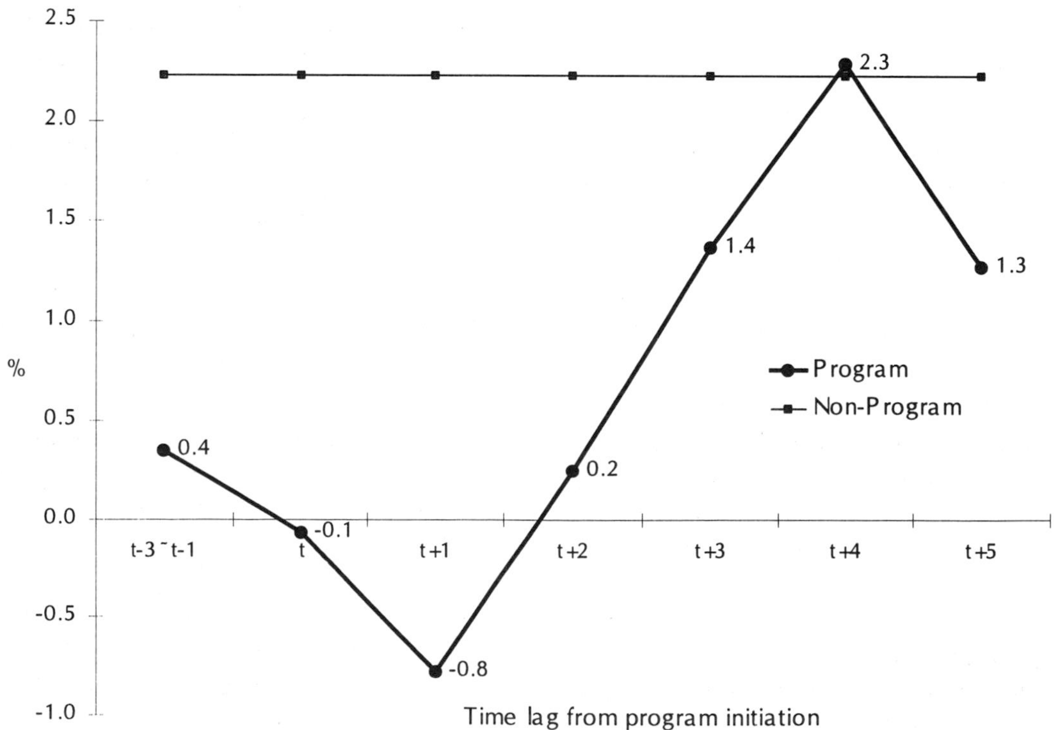

The initiation of the programs was in general accompanied by lower inflation rates.[25] Higher output growth and lower inflation certainly contributed to higher real wage growth following IMF involvement.

Considering the strong surge of real wage and output growth, the relatively weak performance of employment growth after IMF programs is surprising. It implies that even after output growth rates, exchange rates, and interest rates recover their pre-crisis levels, one cannot expect the same recovery for employment. This fact, ironically, may be the result of labor productivity increases due to the adjustment program. After the crisis, program countries implement various structural reforms to enhance economic efficiency. Among them, increasing labor productivity by cutting over-employment is usually a primary objective. In other words, the reform has the same *short-run* effect as a laborsaving technology progress. Therefore, even after output demand returns to its pre-crisis level, labor demand is not fully recovered in the *short run*. Only after the beneficial effects of enhanced labor productivity have worked their way through the economy can employment growth rates be significantly increased. In any case, the weak performance of employment growth indicates that unemployment rates can remain at a higher level for a long period after economic crises and IMF programs. This has a very important policy implication that we will discuss in the section on "Social Policy Options for the Affected Economies".

Changes in income distribution and poverty

When we analyze the distributional effects of IMF programs, the quality of cross-country data on income distribution raises a serious concern regarding the reliability of estimated results. A database recently constructed by Deininger and Squire (1996) considerably mitigates the data constraint faced in previous works. Deininger and Squire reviewed major studies on income distribution that had been conducted during the last 40 years and then constructed a fairly accurate and comparable data set across countries and time.

From their "high quality" database, we focus on two indicators of income distribution: Gini coefficients and the income share of the lowest quintiles. Our data set covers the period from 1968 to 1994 and consists of 322 observations of Gini coefficients and 274 observations of the lowest quintile's income share for the sample of developing countries. Of these observations, 29 and observations for the Gini and 25 for the quintile income shares correspond to the IMF program years.

Figure 5 plots the behavior of Gini coefficients and the lowest quintile's income share. Panel (a) of Figure 5 shows that countries initiating IMF programs experienced gradual deterioration of income distribution over the period of the initial program year and the following two years after the programs. The average Gini coefficients increased to 42.8 in the first year following program initiation from 42.4 over the preceding three years; it then further increased to 43.7 in the second year after program initiation. However, over the longer run, income distribution showed substantial improvement. Gini coefficients dropped to 41.5 three years out and to 39.9 in the fifth year following program initiation. Hence, on average, income distribution during the program period improved substantially relative to the pre-program years, and approached the level of the non-program control group.

The lowest quintile's income share shows a similar pattern. Panel (b) of Figure 5 shows short-term deterioration and long-term improvement of income distribution in terms of the lowest quintile's income share. However, there exists an important difference. The immediate adverse effects of IMF programs on income distribution are more visible in the quintile indicator. The lowest quintile's share of income dropped on average from 6.16% over the three years preceding the crisis to 5.72% at program initiation. It then fluctuated for the next two years, eventually increasing to 6.12% in the fifth year following program initiation. Note that, five years after the onset of crisis, income distribution as measured by Gini coefficients improved significantly relative to the pre-program years, while the income share of the poorest 20% had not even fully recovered to its former level.

Figure 5: Changes in Gini Coefficient and Income Share of the Lowest Quintile, Before and After IMF Programs

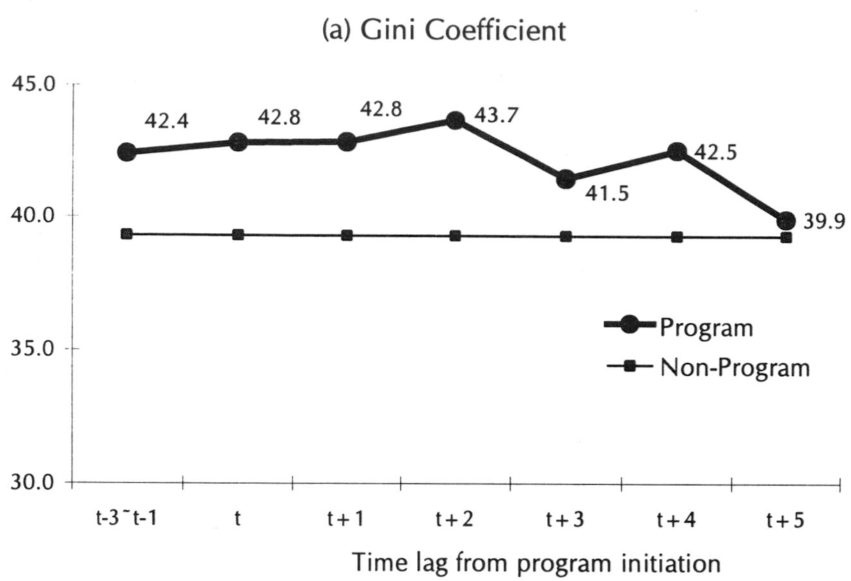

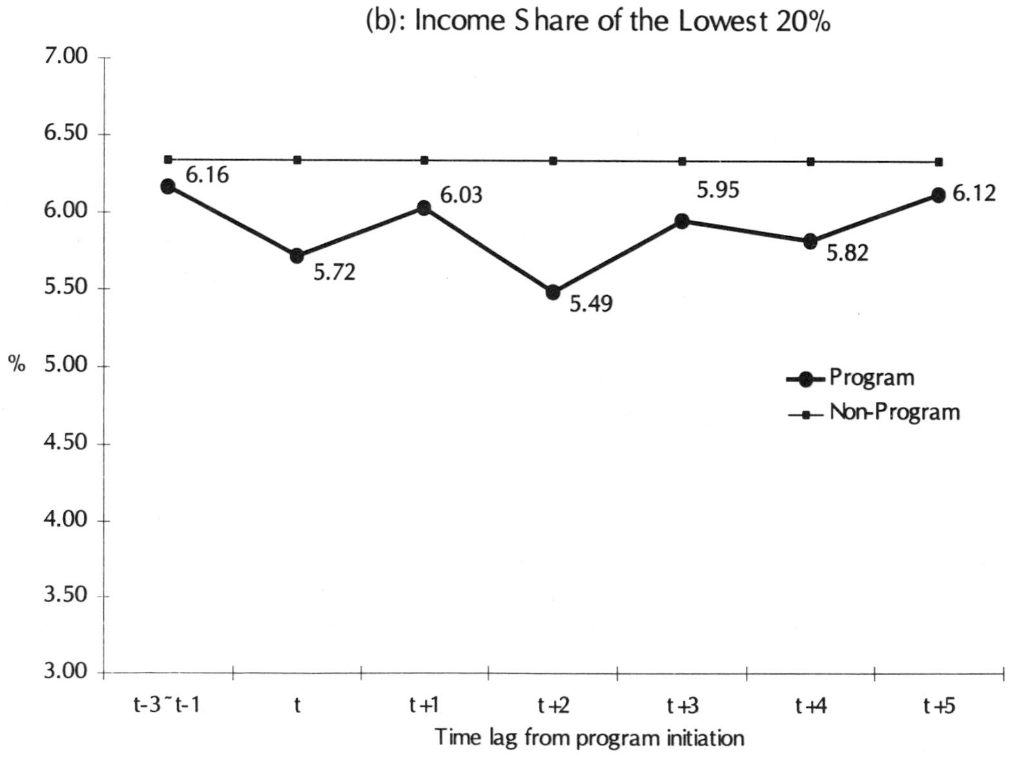

Although the estimated magnitude of the distributional impact of the IMF program may vary depending on sample countries, we think the pattern of short-term deterioration and long-term improvement of income distribution is quite a robust phenomenon.[26] The initial deterioration of income distribution can be attributed to government policy changes. The stabilization programs in general consist of contractionary monetary and fiscal policies and real exchange rate devaluation. Since these policy changes immediately lead to increases in bankruptcies, unemployment and the slow growth of real wages, there is likely to be a severe deterioration of income distribution. Poverty is aggravated as prices of items such as food, public transportation, and energy, which account for a large share of the consumption of low-income households, rise. In the long run, however, distribution started to improve when successful programs led to increases in foreign capital inflows, investment, and output growth.

There are other channels through which the IMF stabilization programs can affect income distribution. First, fiscal constraints have significant effects on income distribution and poverty through changes in both revenue and expenditure. IMF programs typically require the government to increase its revenues and/or decrease its outlays to reduce its overall deficit. Increased taxes on income or imported luxury goods would influence income equality more favorably. The distributional effects of reduction in government expenditure depend on where the specific reductions are made. Workers in the public sectors as a whole tend to experience a decline in real wage or salary earnings with the downsizing of the public sector. Reduction of social expenditures—particularly subsidies to the poor, such as food subsidies—results in perverse distributional effects (Sisson 1986).

Monetary and credit policy also affects income distribution in various ways. A credit crunch and tight monetary policy hurt small and medium-sized firms more severely than large firms, which negatively impacts income equality (Johnson and Salop 1980). Increasing real interest rates have an additional effect by redistributing income from borrowers to lenders, which is likely to render relative gain for households in the richest quintile, considering their interest-bearing asset holdings. Real depreciation of exchange rates causes a relative increase in the price of traded goods, leading to increases in the incomes of producers in the export and import-competing sectors.

Impact of the Asian Crisis on unemployment and real wage

For the last two decades, Asian countries enjoyed virtually full employment prior to the crisis. As shown in Table 1, the unemployment rates in Indonesia, Thailand, and Korea were remarkably low, at less than 3-4% during the 1990s.[27] However, their performance has drastically deteriorated since the crisis began. Bankruptcies due to credit crunches, contractionary fiscal and monetary policy, and the lift of legal restrictions on layoffs have contributed to a rapid increase in unemployment. Unemployment rates have been rising faster in these countries than in Mexico in 1994. According to the estimates reported in ILO (1998), the unemployment rate in Indonesia was expected to reach 8-10%, compared with about 5% in 1996. In Thailand, it was expected to increase from 1.54% in 1996 to 5.6% in 1998. In Korea, the unemployment rate had already risen drastically from 2.0% in October 1997 to 6.7% in April 1998. Given that Korea had not fully completed economic restructuring, the unemployment rate was expected to increase further, to 7.5% by the end of 1998. Since the Asian crisis was so unexpectedly drastic, there exists a pessimistic view that the recovery may not be as rapid as that of Mexico and Argentina following the "tequila crisis" in 1994. Moreover, the stylized pattern of employment changes discussed earlier showed that unemployment rates are likely to remain high for a long time, and may even rise further still.

One important thing to note is that the crisis had diverse impact on unemployment across different groups. In Thailand and Indonesia, the wave of layoffs affected urban white-collar workers the most (Tambunlertchai 1998; Azis 1998). In general, however, the crisis hit hardest on marginal workers such as women, young workers, the less educated, recent school dropouts, and first-time job seekers (Kim 1998). Tables 9 and 10 clearly exhibit this pattern in Korea. Table 9 shows the changes in employment by gender, age, and schooling. Between April 1997 and April 1998, employment declined by 3.8% among men, but by 7.1% among women. Young workers aged between 15 to 29 accounted for the lion's share of job loss, especially young female workers. Employment of those with no high school diploma fell by 11.1%, whereas the employment of college graduates increased by 7.2%. The increase is not surprising, because it reflects the deterioration of the job market. Displaced college graduates are settling for jobs that used to be taken by high school graduates. We also see that employment of older workers— particularly older women who were more likely to be forced to accept early retirement—declined more than employment of primary workers. This pattern is consistent with the internal labor market hypothesis that marginal workers—young, female, less-experienced, less-educated workers—are likely to bear more of the burden of adjustment to external shocks than primary workers. The policy implications of this phenomenon will be discussed in the latter part of this paper.

Table 9: Employment by Gender, Age, and Schooling in Korea
units: thousands; (%)

Age	*April 1996*	*April 1997*	*April 1998*	*Δ96/97 (%)*	*Δ97/98 (%)*
Total					
All	20,743	21,219	20,127	476 (2.3)	-1,092 (-5.1)
15/19	394	398	335	4 (1.0)	-63 (-15.8)
20/29	4,775	4,811	4,162	36 (0.8)	-649 (-13.5)
30/39	6,100	6,007	5,915	-93 (-1.5)	-92 (-1.5)
40/49	4,621	4,825	4,802	204 (4.4)	-23 (-0.5)
50/59	3,000	3,161	2,973	161 (5.4)	-188 (-5.9)
60+	1,852	2,017	1,939	165 (8.9)	-78 (-3.9)
Men					
All	12,349	12,446	11,976	97 (0.8)	-470 (-3.8)
15/19	151	150	137	-1 (-0.7)	-13 (-8.7)
20/29	2,528	2,513	2,178	-15 (-0.6)	-335 (-13.3)
30/39	3,969	3,867	3,841	-102 (-2.6)	-26 (-0.7)
40/49	2,836	2,893	2,912	57 (2.0)	19 (0.7)
50/59	1,819	1,910	1,805	91 (5.0)	-105 (-5.5)
60+	1,045	1,112	1,103	67 (6.4)	-9 (-0.8)
Women					
All	8,395	8,773	8,151	378 (4.5)	-622 (-7.1)
15/19	243	248	198	5 (2.1)	-50 (-20.2)
20/29	2,248	2,299	1,985	51 (2.3)	-314 (-13.7)
30/39	2,131	2,139	2,074	8 (0.4)	-65 (-3.0)
40/49	1,784	1,933	1,890	149 (8.4)	-43 (-2.2)
50/59	1,181	1,251	1,169	70 (5.9)	-82 (-6.6)
60+	807	904	836	97 (12.0)	-68 (-7.5)

Table 9 cont'd

Schooling					
No HS Diploma	7,637	7,715	6,870*	78 (1.2)	-845 (-11.1)
HS Diploma	9,009	9,163	8,582*	154 (1.6)	-581 (-6.2)
College Diploma	4,098	4,341	4,675*	243 (6.4)	334 (7.2)

Note: * = projected number.
Source: National Statistical Office, Korea, *The Economically Active Population Survey*, cited in Kim (1998).

Table 10: Change in Employment in Korea by Industry, Occupation, and Worker Classification units: thousands; (%)

Industry	*April 1997/ April1998 (% Change)*
Agriculture/Fishery	216 (8.8)
Manufacturing	-619 (-13.7)
Construction	-392 (-19.3)
Utility/Transportation/Finance, Insurance, Real Estate	11 (0.6)
Retail/Wholesale	-234 (-4.0)
Services	-66 (-1.5)
Occupation	
Professional/Administration	15 (0.0)
Clerical	-117 (-4.5)
Sales/Service	-103 (-2.1)
Operatives/Laborer	-1,072 (-13.9)
Farmers/Fishermen	186 (7.9)
Worker Classification	
Wage/Salary Workers	-1,041 (-7.8)
Regular Workers	-727 (-10.0)
Non-Wage Workers	-50 (-0.6)
Unpaid Family Workers	201 (10.5)
1 to 17 hours per week	47 (14.0)
18 to 35 hours per week	96 (9.0)
36 hours or more	-1,256 (-6.4)

Source: National Statistical Office, Korea, *The Economically Active Population Survey*.

Table 10 examines the changes in employment by industry, occupation, and work hours. It shows there have been substantial retrenchments, especially in manufacturing and construction industries. To a lesser degree, employment in retail and service sectors decreased, while the agricultural and fishery industries gained in employment. This implies that displaced workers and unsuccessful job seekers in the primary sector are involuntarily settling for inferior employment in the rural or the urban informal sector. No doubt, this trend will increase underemployment. Underemployment will also rise because unpaid family workers and part-time workers gained employment whereas regular workers lost it. The influx of displaced workers into the rural or the urban informal sectors and the decline of regular jobs will reduce even more the already low average income in those sectors, and is likely to increase the number of people below the poverty level.

Table 11: Participation Rate in the Korean Workforce, by Gender and Age (units: %)

Gender	Age	April 1996	April 1997	April 1998	Δ96/97	Δ97/98
All	All	62.2	63.0	61.3	0.8	-1.7
	15/19	11.2	11.2	10.7	0	-0.5
	20/29	66.8	68.0	65.2	1.2	-2.8
	30/39	76.3	77.6	75.6	1.3	-2.0
	40/49	80.5	81.1	79.7	0.6	-1.4
	50/59	71.9	73.3	71.0	1.4	-2.3
	60+	40.1	41.7	39.3	1.6	-2.4
Men	All	76.5	76.3	75.8	-0.2	-0.5
	15/19	8.6	8.6	9.0	0	0.4
	20/29	76.6	76.3	75.4	-0.3	-0.9
	30/39	97.2	97.3	96.6	0.1	-0.7
	40/49	96.4	95.9	95.2	-0.5	-0.7
	50/59	88.7	89.4	87.7	0.7	-1.7
	60+	55.3	56.2	54.1	0.9	-2.1
Women	All	48.7	50.5	47.4	1.8	-2.8
	15/19	13.8	14.0	12.5	0.2	-1.5
	20/29	58.4	60.7	56.5	2.3	-4.2
	30/39	54.3	56.7	53.6	2.4	-3.1
	40/49	63.7	66.0	63.3	2.3	-2.7
	50/59	55.6	57.3	54.3	1.7	-3.0
	60+	29.5	31.6	28.8	2.1	-2.8

Source: National Statistical Office, Korea, *The Economically Active Population Survey.*

Table 12: Distribution of Unemployment in Korea, by Age and Schooling units: thousands; (%)

	Number of Unemployed Workers (Share in Total Unemployment)		Unemployment Rate	
	April 1997	*April 1998*	*April 1997*	*April 1998*
All	603	1,434	2.8	6.7
Age				
15/19	41 (6.8)	75 (5.2)	9.3	18.3
20/29	277 (45.9)	527 (36.8)	5.4	11.2
30/39	141 (23.4)	359 (25.0)	2.3	5.7
40/49	84 (13.9)	272 (19.0)	1.7	5.4
50/59	46 (7.6)	156 (10.9)	1.4	5.0
60+	15 (2.5)	45 (3.1)	0.7	2.3
Schooling				
No HS Diploma	141 (23.3)	391 (27.3)	1.8	5.4
HS Diploma	308 (51.1)	731 (51.0)	3.3	7.8
College Diploma	155 (25.7)	311 (21.7)	3.5	6.2

Source: National Statistical Office, Korea, *The Economically Active Population Survey.*

Table 11 shows the changes in participation rates by gender and age. Between 1997 and 1998, participation rates declined by 0.5% among men but by 2.8% among women. Age differences do not seem to exist, although the decline is slightly more visible among older workers. Considering the extent of gender discrimination in the Korean labor market, it is no wonder that participation rates among female workers, who were more likely to be second-income earners in a family, dropped significantly more than those of male workers. Table 12 reports the distribution of unemployment and unemployment rates. We can see that the unemployment rates of young workers (15-29 years old) are the highest and that they accounted for 42% of total unemployment in April 1998. Nevertheless, it is important to note that primary workers, not just marginally attached workers, are also losing jobs on a large scale, indicating the severity of the crisis. In terms of the rate of change in employment, unemployment increased faster for primary workers. For example, unemployment of workers aged between 40 to 49 tripled within one year, rising from 1.7% to 5.4%.

Table 13: Changes in Real Wages in Korea

	1997					1998		
	1st Quarter	2nd Quarter	3rd Quarter	4th Quarter	Annual	1st Quarter	April	May
Nominal Wage (all industries)	11.6	9.7	6.8	0.9	7.0	0.0	-	-
Inflation (CPI)	4.7	4.0	4.0	5.1	4.5	8.9	8.8	8.2
Real Wage Growth	6.9	5.7	2.8	-4.2	2.5	-8.9	-	-

Note: Percentage change compared with the same period in the previous year.
CPI – Consumer Price Index.
Source: Korea Development Institute, *Monthly Economic Outlook.*

Table 13 reports changes in the real wage in Korea. It is noteworthy that the growth rate of the nominal wage, which used to be about 10% per year, dropped sharply after the crisis. In the first quarter of 1998, the nominal wage did not increase at all. On the other hand, the inflation rate increased significantly following substantial currency devaluation. As a result, the real wage decreased by 8.9% in the first quarter of 1998. In the section, "Evaluation of the Social Impact of the IMF Programs, 1973-1994," we saw that the growth rate of real wages should recover soon after the sharp initial fall. At this moment, it is premature to judge whether real wages in Korea will follow this general trend. The freeze in nominal wages in Korea in the first quarter of 1998 was not due solely to the decline in labor demand after the crisis. It was mainly a temporary phenomenon negotiated in the Tripartite Committee, which consists of representatives from the government, workers' and employers' organizations. Whether the Tripartite Committee can fully accomplish its mission of creating social consensus on economic restructuring is very uncertain. As restructuring proceeds and mass layoffs begin, it is likely that labor unions will protest against their unfair suffering. Then labor strikes and nominal wage hikes will follow.

Impact of the Asian Crisis on income distribution and poverty

The rapid economic growth in East Asia significantly reduced the number of people living under the absolute poverty line. However, even before the crisis began, there had been widespread concern that the accelerating trend toward globalization in the 1990s could exacerbate the prevailing income distribution. This concern is now being reinforced. The current crisis may reverse the trend toward increasingly equitable distribution of income in the region. In this section, we provide a summary of trends in income distribution in the three worst-affected Asian countries and then discuss the impact of the present crisis on their income distribution.

Trends in inequality and poverty

To see the changes in income inequality since the crisis began, we look at the data on Gini coefficients and the quintile shares of total national income. Although methods of collection, degree of coverage, and specific definitions of personal income may vary among countries, Table 14 and 15 depict a general trend of increasing income inequality in Indonesia, Korea and Thailand.

Table 14 shows that Indonesia has made steady progress in reducing income inequality during the past two decades. Gini coefficients increased a little in the 1970s, reaching a peak in 1978. From then on, they declined consistently until 1993, the year up to which data are available. In the Republic of Korea, Gini coefficients showed an increasing trend from 29.8 in 1969 to 39.1 in 1976, and then continued to drop to 29.5 in 1996. Hence, according to the data, Indonesia and Korea have at least succeeded in preventing serious deterioration in income distribution over the last three decades. In contrast to the good performance of Indonesia and Korea, Thailand experienced a persistent deterioration in income distribution despite high income growth. Gini coefficients steadily increased from 41.7 in 1975 to 51.5 in 1992. The share of income of the lowest quintile decreased from 0.049 to 0.037 during the same period. According to the UN (1998), the deterioration of income distribution can be attributed to a widening income differential between the urban and rural poor.

Table 15 presents cross-country comparisons of income distribution. In general, countries in Asia appear to be more egalitarian than those in Latin America. The relationship between growth and equity is not clear. Countries such as Taiwan and Korea have successfully combined the reduction of inequality with high income growth. The superior performance of these countries is in contrast to that of countries such as Hong Kong, Mexico and Malaysia, all of which had high economic growth rates but failed to reduce income inequality.

Table 14: Gini Coefficient and Quintile Income Shares for Three Asian Countries

Country	Year	Gini	Income (Expenditure) Share				Data Characteristics		
			Bottom 20%	Bottom 40%	Top 20%	Top 20%/ Bottom 20%	Inc[1]	Pers[2]	Gross[3]
Indonesia	1964	33.3					E	P	
	1967	32.7					E	P	
	1970	30.7					E	P	
	1976	34.6	0.080	0.196	0.425	5.3	E	P	N
	1978	38.6	0.080	0.181	0.453	5.7	E	P	N
	1980	35.6	0.073	0.196	0.423	5.8	E	P	N
	1981	33.7	0.077	0.204	0.421	5.5	E	P	N
	1984	32.4	0.083	0.208	0.420	5.9	E	P	N
	1987	32.0	0.080	0.209	0.417	5.2	E	P	N
	1990	33.1	0.092	0.213	0.420	4.6	E	P	N
	1993	31.7	0.087	0.210	0.407	4.7	E	P	
Korea, R.	1965	34.3	0.058	0.193	0.418	7.2	I	H	G
	1966	34.2	0.065	0.184	0.406	6.3	I	H	G
	1968	30.5	0.086	0.214	0.392	4.6	I	H	G
	1969	29.8	0.084	0.214	0.382	4.6	I	H	G
	1970	33.3	0.073	0.196	0.416	5.7	I	H	G
	1971	36.0	0.072	0.187	0.434	6.0	I	H	G
	1976	39.1	0.057	0.169	0.453	8.0	I	H	G
	1980	38.6	0.051	0.161	0.454	8.9	I	H	G
	1982	35.7	0.070	0.188	0.430	6.2	I	H	G
	1985	34.5	0.068	0.205	0.419	6.2	I	H	G
	1988	33.6	0.074	0.197	0.422	5.7	I	H	G
	1993	31.0	0.074	0.204	0.392	5.3	I	H	G
	1996	29.5	0.076	0.212	0.374	4.9	I	H	G
Thailand	1962	41.3	0.080	0.166	0.498	6.2	I	H	G
	1969	42.6	0.051	0.152	0.501	9.8	I	H	G
	1975	41.7	0.049	0.150	0.484	9.8	I	H	G
	1981	43.1	0.043	0.137	0.511	11.9	I	H	G
	1986	47.4	0.042	0.129	0.531	12.6	I	H	G
	1988	47.4	0.041	0.126	0.542	13.2	I	H	G
	1990	48.8	0.040	0.123	0.552	13.8	I	H	G
	1992	51.5	0.037	0.113	0.585	15.8	I	H	G

Note: 1) Inc = Indicates whether the Gini coefficient is calculated based on income (I) or expenditure (E).
2) Pers = Indicates whether the recipient unit is the person (P) or the household (H).
3) Gross = Indicates whether the income reported is gross (G) or net of taxes (N).

Source: Deininger and Squire (1996); for Korean data for 1993 and 1996, National Statistical Office, *Social Indicators of Korea 1997*.

Table 15: Gini Coefficients and Quintile Shares for Latest Available Year in Selected Economies

Country	Year	Gini	Income (Expenditure) Share			Data Characteristics		
			Bottom 20%	Top 20%	Top20%/ Bottom20%	Inc	Pers	Gross
Bolivia	1990	42	0.056	0.482	8.6	E	P	N
Botswana	1986	54.2	0.036	0.589	16.4	E	H	N
Brazil	1989	59.6	0.025	0.652	26.3	I	P	G
Chile	1994	56.5	0.035	0.609	17.3	I	P	
China	1992	37.8	0.06	0.416	6.9	I	P	G
Colombia	1991	51.3	0.036	0.544	15.1	I	P	G
Gabon	1977	63.2	0.029	0.663	22.9	I	H	N
Hong Kong	1991	45	0.049	0.494	10.1	I	H	G
India	1992	32	0.088	0.411	4.7	E	P	N
Indonesia	1993	31.7	0.087	0.407	4.7	E	P	
Japan	1982	34.8	0.059	0.418	7.1	I	H	G
Korea, R.	1988	33.6	0.074	0.422	5.7	I	H	G
Malaysia	1989	48.3	0.046	0.537	11.7	I	P	G
Mexico	1992	50.3	0.041	0.553	13.4	E	P	
Nigeria	1993	37.5	0.04	0.493	12.4	E	P	
Philippines	1988	45.7	0.052	0.525	10.1	I	P	G
Taiwan	1993	30.8	0.071	0.387	5.4	I	P	N
Thailand	1992	51.5	0.037	0.585	15.8	I	H	G
USA	1991	37.9	0.045	0.441	9.8	I	H	G
Zimbabwe	1990	56.8	0.04	0.623	15.7	E	P	N

Note: See notes for Table 14.
Source: Deininger and Squire (1996).

Table 16: Trends in Poverty in Indonesia, Thailand, and Korea units: poor people as % of total population; (millions of poor people)

Indonesia	1976	1981	1987	1993	1996
Total:	40.1	26.9	17.4	13.7	11.3
	(54.3)	(40.6)	(30.3)	(25.9)	(22.5)
Urban	38.8	28.1	20.1	13.4	9.7
	(10.0)	(9.3)	(9.7)	(8.7)	(7.2)
Rural	40.3	26.4	16.1	13.8	12.3
	(44.2)	(31.3)	(20.8)	(17.2)	(15.3)
Thailand	1975	1981	1988	1992	1996
Total	30	23	22	13	-
	(12.4)	(11.0)	(11.9)	(7.5)	
Korea	1975	1980	1985	1990	1995
Urban	20.0	14.4	14.2	10.5	7.4

Note: Poverty estimates are based on country-specific poverty lines.
Source: Data for Indonesia are from *Statistical Yearbook of Indonesia*; for Korea, Chanyong Park and Meesook Kim, *Current Poverty Issues and Counter Policies*, Korean Institute for Health and Social Affairs, cited in ILO (1998); for Thailand, UN (1998).

In addition to income distribution and relative poverty, another important issue focuses on the extent and magnitude of absolute poverty. Until the recent crisis, all three countries enjoyed improving living standards, as the population living in poverty fell substantially. Table 16 demonstrates that all three Asian countries reduced poverty as a result of remarkable growth rates. In Korea for instance, the level of absolute poverty decreased from 21.5% in 1975 to 8.5% in 1995.[28] However, despite these impressive successes, a substantial proportion of the population still lives below the poverty line, particularly in the rural areas of Indonesia and Thailand. Some 22 million Indonesians were still living below the official poverty line in 1996. The poor in Indonesia are predominantly located in the rural and agricultural sectors. Similarly, in Thailand, though the absolute population living below the poverty line continued to decline, poverty is much higher in the rural areas, particularly among less-educated households, agricultural workers, and large families.

<u>*Distributional impact of the Asian crisis*</u>

Although we do not a this stage have precise statistics or information on the evolution of poverty and income distribution, the current economic crisis is considered to have already had significant adverse effects on equitable growth in this region.

The immediate impacts of economic crises and IMF programs on income distribution were increases in unemployment and inflation. The increases in unemployment and underemployment directly aggravated poverty. The total number of unemployed has increased in unprecedented numbers in this region and will continue to mount. The newly unemployed are obviously suffering a drastic drop in income and living standards. Loss of jobs or relegation to low-wage occupations has led to a sizeable increase in the number of people living below the poverty line. Hence, the decline in job opportunities has definitely contributed to increased poverty.

Price increases lowered the real wages of those still employed, exacerbating poverty even more. Average annual inflation rates reached 44% in Indonesia in May 1998, and around 11% in Korea and Thailand. Because nominal wages did not adjust to offset the effect of price increases, and compensation from social safety nets was minimal, real income of a typical household declined by almost the full extent of the price increases. The price increases of specific commodities also had a great impact on household consumption. They had a differentiated impact on households, depending on the shares of food and necessary items in a household's consumption basket. Because the price increases concentrated on the items that account for a large share of the consumption of low-income households, they further adversely affected income distribution. For example, food constitutes 70% of the total expenditure of the households in the lowest income decile in Indonesia and 55% in Thailand. The corresponding expenditure shares for the top decile households are 35% and 21%, respectively (Gupta et al., 1998). Thus, price increases in these countries have more significant adverse impacts on the consumption of the poor.

In addition to the severe adverse effects of rising unemployment and inflation, poverty could be further aggravated by "social income poverty" (Ranis and Stewart 1998). During a crisis, higher prices and fewer employment opportunities deprive people of primary (or private) income. Moreover, a crisis reduces secondary (or social) income from the state via public works or income transfers (e.g., unemployment benefits). Although it is not clear whether total government expenditure itself was reduced after the crisis, social expenditure for education, public health, and social services was negatively affected. In Thailand, for example, the government budget in 1997 was reduced by 32%, 15%, and 11% for the social services, public health, and education sectors, respectively, after the crisis (Siamwalla and Sobchokchai 1998). The cuts in social expenditure have had an immediate, adverse effect on social incomes of the poor, and will also have long-run consequences on the private incomes of all economic agents. Since it is expenditure for education and health care that has a significant effect on human capital formation, the cuts in these social sectors can hurt long-run growth potential and prolong considerably the adverse poverty situation.

The combined effects of higher prices, job losses, and reduced social expenditures indicate that the crisis will have a deep adverse effect on (absolute and relative) poverty in these Asian economies. However, its impact on overall income inequality is rather ambiguous. The impact of job losses on income inequality is hard to predict; it depends on the composition of job losses. If the crisis hurts urban middle class workers more severely than those in the upper and bottom quintiles, how the Gini coefficients will change is not clear.

Moreover, not all population groups lose from the crisis. Some households will gain from exchange rate depreciation. Incomes of those engaging in export and tourism sectors can improve. The sharp increase in interest rates can benefit those holding a larger stock of interest-bearing assets. Diverse impacts of the crisis on income distribution imply that the increase of Gini coefficients during the crisis will be marginal. The cross-country evidence in the section on "Evaluation of the Social Impact of the IMF Programs, 1973-1994," confirms this prediction. It shows that income inequality tended to increase immediately after the IMF programs but that the degree of deterioration was not substantial. Individual country experience also supports the prediction that the crisis aggravates poverty significantly, but that the change in overall income distribution is relatively small. For instance, according to Hernandez and Mayer (1998), the Gini coefficient in Chile worsened only marginally during the 1982-83 economic crisis (from about 52 in 1980-81 to about 55 in 1982-83) even though poverty indices deteriorated significantly. The share of population below the poverty line increased from 33% in 1981 to about 58% in 1983. This finding has an important policy implication for building a social safety net during a crisis. In view of the significant deterioration of poverty and the minimal rise in overall income inequality, welfare policy should be targeted to the core group of the poorest and hardest-hit victims, instead of trying to maximize the number of beneficiaries.

In sum, although the short-term deterioration of poverty and income distribution is inevitable, the longer-run impact of the crisis on income distribution is less clear. It clearly depends on the nature and implementation of government policy in handling the crisis. The cross-country evidence shows the possibility of income distribution improving with the recovery of economic growth in the long run. However, without adequate government policies, we cannot expect the level of income equality to soon recover to what it was before the crisis in Asia.

Policy implications and lessons from the Asian crisis

In this section, we draw policy lessons and implications from our early analysis. We will first discuss the implications of globalization for financial markets. As discussed in the opening section, large capital inflows and sudden withdrawal of foreign capital were key features of the crisis, and the management of erratic and volatile movement of short-term capital has become an important policy issue. Then, we review the current social policies and programs in the worst-affected Asian countries and discuss the problems in establishing social safety nets in those countries.

Policy challenges and lessons from the globalization of the Asian financial markets

The current Asian crisis clearly shows the benefits and risks of financial market globalization. Capital inflows to emerging markets boost growth by igniting investment. They also increase the opportunity for risk diversification and consumption smoothing, and help to improve the efficiency of the financial sector by increasing international competition. However, they simultaneously breed a lending boom and asset bubbles, and make financial markets more volatile and vulnerable to international capital flows. International financial flows can be abruptly reversed not only by rational causes, but also by irrational causes such as the herd behavior of foreign investors. A sudden outflow of foreign capital entails a strong negative impact on the debtor country's investment, growth, and economic welfare.

Globalization can also have significant effects on social welfare in the debtor countries. For the last three decades, Asian economies have demonstrated that there are enormous economic gains in opening international trade and financial markets. The fast and sustained growth of the East and Southeast Asian countries was spurred by increased integration into world markets (Radelet, Sachs, and Lee 1997). Despite overall economic benefits, however, international integration produces winners and losers within a country and thus possibly increases inequality.[29] International trade, for instance, requires a continuous change of industrial structure and shifts of workers from low- to high-productivity sectors to maintain international competitiveness. The rising demand for skilled labor and the commensurate decline in demand for unskilled labor could lead to rising inequality among workers.[30] A study of seven countries in East Asia and Latin America shows that wage inequality increased after trade liberalization (Robbins 1996). Increased capital mobility can also put pressure on either wages or working conditions. Concerns remain that multinational firms will exploit workers in developing countries who are desperate to find jobs. Although financial globalization *per se* promotes higher employment and real wage growth, it might also increase volatility of employment and wage growth in response to external shocks.

Financial market globalization, therefore, provokes various policy issues. Sound macroeconomic management becomes more essential in containing the negative effects of globalization. Policymakers should find effective tools to contain the negative effect of capital inflows. An early warning system for the crisis should be developed. Monetary and fiscal policies consistent with the choice of an exchange rate system become more important. It is well known that free capital mobility has important implications for the effectiveness of macroeconomic policies. As capital mobility increases, fiscal policy becomes more effective while independent monetary policy becomes less feasible. Loose fiscal policy together with real overvaluation of exchange rates is known usually to be very detrimental.

More than anything else, strengthening the domestic financial system should be the most important policy agenda. The current Asian crisis demonstrates that the downside costs of globalization become magnified when the debtor country's financial system shows structural weakness. Lack of prudent regulation and supervision of the financial sector can lead to large-scale capital inflows, imprudent lending, consumption booms, and asset bubbles, which result in the real appreciation of currencies and the loss of international competitiveness. Consequently, it makes the economy extremely vulnerable to adverse developments. Many policy prescriptions have been suggested for strengthening the financial system. Establishing transparent accounting standards and practices and increasing the public disclosure of information are important for improving financial infrastructure. Strengthening banks' profitability and capitalization, restricting connected lending, and tightening asset classification and loan loss provisions are essential elements in the regulatory and supervisory framework. Providing the right incentive structure, such as abolishing implicit government guarantees, is an essential precondition.

In view of the recent Asian crisis, it is natural that the call for restricting international capital flows, especially short-term capital flows, is getting more attention and sympathy. Many think that the most important lesson to be learned from the Asian crisis is that a developing country should be more cautious in opening its capital market. In particular, various measures aimed at regulating the magnitude and composition of international capital flows are proposed. They include the Tobin tax and a compulsory deposit on exchange transactions as introduced in Chile. Considering the pains that the crisis-hit countries are suffering, it is hard to deny that some regulation on short-term capital mobility is necessary for stability.

However, we do not think that raising a barrier to international capital flows or delaying the opening of capital markets is the lesson to take away from the Asian crisis. We believe that those policy goals cannot be achieved by an individual country's efforts alone. The current experience in Korea is an important example. In the past, the Korean government favored a gradual opening of its financial market to avoid the speculative movement of hot money. Instead of opening capital markets directly to foreign investors, the government chose to do it indirectly. In other words, it allowed domestic financial institutions to borrow from abroad and to distribute the obtained funds in domestic markets. That policy was aimed at securing low-cost financing while preventing speculative capital flows. It was presumed that domestic financial institutions were easier to supervise than foreign hedge funds. However, considering non-performing loans, reckless offshore investment, and imprudent foreign exchange risk management of domestic financial intermediaries, we cannot help but doubt the validity of this presumption *ex post facto*.

In addition, the government did not understand the down side of this indirect approach. Since the domestic bond market was not open to foreign investors, the high interest rates since the inception of the crisis could not deter massive outflows of foreign capital. The adjustment burden thus fell entirely on the foreign exchange market. Only after fully opening domestic financial markets at the request of the IMF did domestic interest rates start to work as a policy instrument for controlling capital flows.

In sum, it is true that financial liberalization exposes domestic financial markets to the possibility of speculative attacks. However, the Korean experience shows that a currency crisis can occur even in countries whose domestic financial markets are partially and indirectly open to foreign investors. The Korean experience shows that, once a financial market is developed above a certain threshold level, to believe that a small country can control the speed of capital market opening is pure fantasy. If one country tries unilaterally to restrict short-term capital mobility through the Tobin Tax or a compulsory deposit, foreign capital will switch to other countries without regulation. Therefore, to effectively regulate short-term capital mobility, international policy coordination is essential. Until we have a worldwide system for restricting short-term capital flows, the correct lesson to draw from the Asian crisis is the importance of improving domestic financial infrastructure rather than trying to control capital inflows to prevent a crisis.

Social policy options for the affected economies

The sharp increase in unemployment, substantial decrease in real earnings, and widening income inequality have led to disastrous social unrest in crisis-hit Asian countries. Since they have for decades enjoyed high growth, low jobless rates, relatively equal income distribution, and low crime rates, this sudden social distress has been felt keenly and impatiently. To make matters worse, most Asian countries have not yet developed meaningful social safety nets. In this section, we review existing social policy programs in the Asian economies and discuss how to contain the social costs of the crisis effectively.

Reviewing the existing social protection system

As the crisis unfolded, it became clear that the existing social welfare systems in the crisis-hit Asian countries were completely incapable of meeting the needs of the sufferers. As Table 17 shows, existing social policies and programs in Indonesia, Korea, and Thailand provide protection for formal sector workers only to a very limited extent. In Indonesia, old age and disability benefits are limited to firms with more than 10 employees. In Thailand, the pension system covers only 10% of the labor force.

Table 17: Existing Social Programs in Korea, Indonesia, and Thailand (as of 1997)

Korea	Indonesia	Thailand
A. Old age, Disability		
Coverage: Social insurance system covering the employed in firms with 5 or more workers and agricultural workers aged 18-59. Voluntary coverage for those employed in firms with less than 5 workers and self-employed. Separate systems for public employees, military, and private school teachers. Funding: 6% of payroll paid by employer and 3% of wage earnings paid by employees. Voluntarily insured persons contribute 9% of wage earnings. Eligibility: Old-age pension: 60 years of age, insured 20 years or more. Disability: insured at least 1 year, no longer working and disability occurred during the insured period. Benefits: Old-age: Non-taxable. Adjusted for price changes. 2.4 times the sum of average of monthly earnings of all insured in the proceeding year and the average monthly earnings of the retiree over the entire contribution period. Total disability: the same as old-age.	Coverage: Provident fund system paying lump-sum benefits only, covering firms with 10 or more employees or a payroll above 1 million rupiah per month Funding: Employers pay 3.7 % of payroll, plus 0.3 % of payroll for death benefit. Insured persons pay 2% of earnings. Government provides no additional funding. Eligibility: Old-age pensions: 55 years of age, 66 months more of contributions. Disability benefit: total incapacity for work and age under 55. Benefits: Old-age, disability and survivor benefits: Lump-sum equal to total employer contributions paid in, plus accrued interest.	Coverage: Limited social insurance system covering firms with 10 or more employees. From September 2, 1998, voluntary coverage for self-employed will become available. Separate systems for civil servants and private school teachers. Funding: Employer pays 1.5% of payroll and insured person pays 1.5% of wages. Government provides annual grant equal to 1.5% of covered wages. Eligibility: New system. To be payable starting in 1998. Benefits: Disability: same as sickness benefits. A person must have received the sickness benefit for one year. Permanent disability: 50% of prior wage for life.
B. Sickness and Maternity		
The system covers all permanent residents, except government and private school employees and those under Medical Aid program. Separate systems for public employees and private school teachers. Funding: employer pays 1-4% (average 1.52%) of standard monthly wage; employees pay also 1-4% (average 1.52%) of standard monthly wage. Government pays a part of the benefits and all administrative costs.	Social insurance system (medical benefits). Coverage being gradually extended to various industries. Employees with more comprehensive benefits exempt from coverage. Employer pays 6% of payroll for married employees and 3% for single employees. Insured persons and government bear no cost.	Limited insurance system with coverage and funding as for old-age pensions. Cash sickness eligibility: 90 days of contribution in 15 months before date of treatment.

Table 17 cont'd

C. Work Injury		
Mandatory public insurance, covering all industrial firms with 5 or more employees. Separate systems for public employees. Employer pays 0.6% to 29% of the payroll, depending on the "industry risk." Employees pay no contribution. Government pays the cost of administration. Temporary disability benefits pay 70% of average earnings. For total disability, annual pension between 138 and 329 days average earnings or lump sum (55–1,474 days' earnings) according to degree of disability.	Social insurance system covering firms with 10 or more employees. Voluntary coverage available. Special system for public employees. Employer bears the whole cost, 0.24-1.74% of the payroll according to "industry risk." Permanent disability benefit varies with the degree of disability with maximum 70% of previous monthly earnings times 60.	Compulsory public insurance covering firms with 10 or more employees, but excluding workers in agriculture, fishing, and a number of other sectors. Funding: employer pays 0.2-2% of payroll according to "industry risk." Temporary disability: 60% of wages, payable up to 52 weeks.
D. Unemployment Insurance		
Coverage and eligibility: In January 1998, it will cover firms with at least 10 workers. To qualify, employees must be employed for at least 12 months during 18 months before involuntary unemployment occurred. Benefit, financed by 0.6% payroll tax shared between workers and employers, is equal to ½ of the average worker's daily salary during the preceding 12 months.	No programs	No programs
E. Social Assistance		
Korea's social assistance system consists of two components: (i) public assistance (livelihood protection, medical aid, veteran relief, disaster relief): and (ii) social welfare services (for the disabled, elderly, children, women and the mentally handicapped). Public assistance provides services and financial assistance to needy people with low incomes. Social welfare services focussed on maintaining family welfare of the disadvantaged groups.	No programs	No programs

Source: US Department of Health, Education, and Welfare, *Social Security Programs throughout the World 1997,* August 1997, and Gupta et al. (1998).

Indonesia and Thailand do not have unemployment insurance systems, while Korea introduced it only recently. Korea implemented an unemployment benefit scheme in 1995 under the terms of the Employment Insurance Act of 1993, but its coverage and benefits are very limited.[31] The limited level of social protection in these Asian countries is partly a reflection of policy choices. High economic growth prior to the crisis reinforced the belief that economic growth would effectively alleviate poverty and income distribution problems. Together with a reliance on traditional private support systems through the family, this belief resulted in only limited priority being given to the development of social protection systems.

Table 17 also shows that Korea, compared with Indonesia and Thailand, has more developed social safety protections. Korea has public assistance programs such as livelihood protection, medical aid, veteran relief, and disaster relief. Yet even Korea's social assistance scheme is still quite rudimentary compared with those of developed countries. The majority of employees have not yet had the opportunity to build up any unemployment benefit entitlements. Moreover, the lifetime-job tradition in Korea has meant that workers have relied on welfare programs provided by the firm, rather than relying on a social safety net supported by the government. In normal times, this company-funded welfare system as well as the traditional family-based system can be more efficient than the public social safety net. However, the problem is that they cease to function when the private sector is deeply affected by the crisis, and therefore, public support is the most needed.

Social policies for adjustment to the crisis

Since the existing social programs were not able to cope adequately with the social consequences of the crisis, it is necessary for governments to implement various programs to prevent social unrest. In the short term, the two most damaging problems arising from the crisis are increases in unemployment and inflation rates. Sudden increases in prices, especially of items mainly consumed by low-income households, hit the poor the hardest. To soften this adverse effect, it might become inevitable to subsidize some essential items such as food, energy, and public transportation.

In dealing with unemployment, there are several alternative approaches. First, some policy measures aim to minimize the extent of unemployment. For instance, workers and employers can negotiate alternatives to layoffs and cooperate to stabilize employment through redeployment within the enterprise or wage reduction. However, these measures are effective only when the firms face a temporary liquidity crisis rather than permanent insolvency; therefore, the scope of their application is very limited.

The second approach is to create new employment. This job creation policy includes public work programs and schemes promoting self-employment. In Indonesia and Korea, governments have already started public work programs to create temporary job opportunities. (See ILO 1998 for details.) They also set up financial programs to provide credit targeted at encouraging self-employment. However, growing unemployment and expected large-scale layoffs in these countries cannot be sufficiently dealt with by worker-employer voluntary negotiations or public job creation programs.

The third approach is to provide unemployment benefits and other income-support programs for the unemployed. In Indonesia and Thailand, where no formal unemployment scheme exists, the government must first introduce minimum social safety nets.

Our findings in the section "Impact of the Asian Crisis on Unemployment and Real Wage" have an important implication for building social safety nets. We demonstrated that it is marginal workers—young, female, less experienced, and less educated—who are most severely affected by the crisis. They are more likely to be the long-term unemployed and the people living under the poverty level. Given the reality that only limited resources are available in building up the social safety net, benefits should be directed to this small number of core groups instead of the unemployed in general. In other words, maximizing the number of people covered under the social safety net should not be the primary concern in designing a new system. Asian countries should learn from Europe's mistakes. Overly generous coverage of unemployment benefits can discourage displaced workers from seeking or accepting inferior jobs. Safeguarding existing jobs for regular workers can inhibit the creation of new jobs.

However, even if it is socially just and economically efficient, targeting the core unemployed group is politically difficult. In building up the social safety net, the core group does not have a political channel to represent itself. They are usually non-union members not represented by workers' representatives at the negotiation table. Often, policies adopted under the name of social consensus place an unfair burden on them.[32] That is why we have to emphasize the government's parental role in targeting the worst-affected core group when designing social safety nets. Several techniques can be undertaken in selecting or targeting the beneficiary groups (see UN 1998, p.141). One technique is means testing, which uses an income cut-off point to limit the eligibility of the benefits to persons whose incomes are below a certain level. Geographical targeting is another technique in which programs are implemented in areas where the poor are concentrated. A third technique, known as categorical targeting, uses various characteristics of poverty, such as small landowners, joblessness, and number of dependents to identify the poor. The fourth technique, self-targeting, has no direct screening of the beneficiaries but designs programs in such a way that the non-poor have no incentive to join them. For example, public work programs that make payments to the beneficiaries at a rate below the minimum wage discourage persons who might have better opportunities for employment. Thus, self-targeting seems the most efficient way to concentrate the benefit of the programs on the poor group.

In addition, the new social safety net should be comprehensive rather than focusing only on unemployment. It should also pay attention to improving the health, nutrition, and educational status of the poorest populations. Social security and pension reform, health care policies that provide wider access to low-income groups, and education policies that provide improved labor skills will strengthen social protection. In particular, educational factors—higher levels of educational attainment and more equal distribution of education among the population—can make significant contributions to the equality of income distribution (see De Gregorio and Lee 1998). Furthermore, these social programs should give special attention to vulnerable groups such as children and women.

Another consideration in introducing new social programs is how to finance the necessary expenses. Because these programs entail additional government funds, extra revenue or the reallocation of expenditures is required. However, it is desirable that the expenses for the programs are not fully covered by the government budget. Programs that distribute benefits free of charge to the poor can lead to a moral hazard on the part of the beneficiaries, and they often fail. The programs could be more cost-effective and more sustainable if participants are at least partially charged for the benefits they receive.

So far IMF assistance in these Asian countries has focused on restoring macroeconomic stability and reforming financial markets and has paid relatively little attention to social issues, such as human and social protection systems development. However, they are important tasks in maintaining social cohesion in the short run and growth potential in the long run. In this regard, cooperation and partnership between a country and international institutions such as the World Bank, the Asian Development Bank (ADB), and the United Nations Development Programme (UNDP) seems highly desirable. The expertise in these institutions can play a vital role as advisers and technical supporters in dealing with social issues during the crisis.

Concluding remarks

The unexpected financial collapse in Asia has been followed by massive economic and social collapse. Millions of people have lost their jobs, and the problems of poverty and income inequality have rapidly worsened. A substantial part of the gains in living standards that have accumulated in the last decades have evaporated in one year. The lack of adequate social safety nets in the midst of the crisis has led to disastrous social consequences in these countries.

The stylized pattern of employment growth in the previous IMF program countries indicates that employment growth takes more time to adjust than other macroeconomic variables. It implies that unemployment is unlikely to be alleviated in the near future in the Asian countries. In addition, the paper finds that the crisis exacerbates poverty for a significant period, although it does not have a long-run effect on overall income distribution. This pattern arises because the burden of the crisis tends to be distributed unequally. The poor, less-educated, less-experienced, young and female workers are most severely affected. They are more likely to become the long-term unemployed and to remain below the poverty level even after the economy recovers from the crisis.

This fact has important implications for policies to build social safety nets in Asian countries. In view of the significant rise in poverty, but only minimal increase in overall income inequality, welfare policy should be targeted to the core group of the poor and the hardest-hit victims, instead of trying to maximize the number of beneficiaries. In particular, this core group is not represented by unions and has little political power. One has to be aware that, oftentimes, policies adopted under the name of social consensus place an unfair burden on them.

The key features of the Asian crisis are large inflows and sudden withdrawals of foreign capital. It is therefore understandable that the call for restricting international capital flows, especially short-term capital flows, is gaining more support and sympathy. However, this paper argues that unilaterally raising a barrier to international capital flows is not the policy lesson to be learned from the Asian crisis. There is no doubt that managing erratic and volatile movements of short-term capital flows is an important policy challenge, and that this goal cannot be achieved by one country's unilateral effort. The Korean case is a good example: It is fantasy to think a small country can effectively control the extent and the speed of globalization once it opens its financial markets partially or indirectly. If a country tries to restrict capital mobility unilaterally, either it pays a higher cost for financing or foreign capital will leave that country and flow into another country. Effective regulation of short-term capital flows is possible only through international policy coordination. Until a global financial governance system is developed, improving the domestic financial infrastructure rather than trying to control capital flows seems to be the more practical policy option.

The Asian crisis presents extraordinary policy challenges not only to the affected countries but also to their trade partners and the international community. International partnership among the affected Asian countries, advanced countries, and international institutions is essential in overcoming the current economic and social disaster, in preventing it from spreading to the rest of the world, and in ensuring stability in the global capitalist system.■

Notes

[1] It is widely recognized that unemployment statistics in these countries are considerably underestimated. Discouraged workers and the underemployed in informal sectors still account for a large portion of the population. In fact, employment growth rates in these countries were less impressive compared with their unemployment rates.

[2] In the cases of Korea and Malaysia, extrabudgetary and quasi-fiscal operations account for a large proportion of public finance, so that true fiscal positions were not as tight as the official statistics suggest. For example, in Korea, Cho and Rhee (1995) find that the estimated fiscal deficits were on average twice as large as the announced figures when extrabudgetary special funds and public enterprise operations were included in measuring fiscal balances.

[3] Unlike their earlier experience, the fiscal conditions in Mexico and Argentina were healthy during the 1990s.

[4] This fact is in sharp contrast with the Mexican crisis that erupted in late 1994. In Mexico, the large current account deficit before the crisis was largely the result of sustained increases in private consumption. See IMF (1997b, pp.10-11).

[5] For example, Korea's export price index fell by 13% in 1996 alone.

[6] The estimated real exchange rates are based on consumer price indices. The rates are normalized so that the 1990 value is equal to 1. A decrease in the index indicates real appreciation of the currency concerned.

[7] We are implicitly assuming that the 1990 rate is an equilibrium value, as in Radelet and Sachs (1998b).

[8] In fact, the trade-weighted real exchange rates in IMF (1998, p.8) confirm the conclusion. Radelet and Sachs (1998b) estimate that the real exchange rates appreciated about 25% between 1990 and early 1997 in the crisis-hit Southeast Asian countries. But they conclude that the real appreciations in Asia were relatively modest compared with Brazil and Argentina, which have seen real appreciations of more than 40% since 1990.

[9] For more detailed information, refer to Park and Rhee (1998).

[10] Thailand held a general election in November 1996. Korea and Indonesia held presidential elections in December 1997 and March 1998, respectively.

[11] Borensztein and Lee (1998) show evidence that, in Korea, government intervention in the financial sector resulted in inefficient allocation of bank credit.

[12] The number for the 1990s is 2.6%. It is measured by the ratio of current account deficits relative to GDP for major capital-exporting and capital-importing countries. See IMF (1997a).

[13] The notorious cases are Thailand's establishment of the Bangkok International Banking Facility (BIBF) and financial market reforms in Korea in the mid-1990s. BIBF was established in 1992 to compete with Singapore and Hong Kong as a regional financial center. BIBF and the Korean reform greatly expanded the number of financial institutions that could access short-term international loans. See Park (1998).

[14] Colombia is an exception. Korea was also a capital exporting country during the late 1980s, when it enjoyed a large current account surplus due to an export boom.

[15] The financial capital flows in Table 2 and 2.3 are not totally private. They include portfolio investment and direct investment by the governments.

[16] Cited from IIF (1998).

[17] The data for Table 4 and 5 come from the World Data and BIS, respectively. Note that the coverage and the classification of external debt differ one from the other. Since the data from the Bank for International Settlements (BIS) are based on reports of lending international banks at reporting area, they are different from those officially released by each country. The classification of short-term debt is also different: the world data are based on the maturity on the date of issuance, whereas the BIS data are based on the remaining maturity.

[18] Even these figures turned out to underestimate the true short-term liabilities since offshore borrowings were not accounted for.

[19] For a detailed policy description, refer to Polak (1997).

[20] See Bandow and Vasquez (1994), Danaher (1994), Feldstein (1998), and Radelet and Sachs (1998a, 1998b) for critical views of IMF policies.

[21] Whether the fiscal policy in the IMF program is stringent is a subtle issue. For example, the consolidated budget balance in Korea does not include the quasi-fiscal and extra-budgetary activities in Korea. The newly issued public bonds to finance banking sector reform and social safety nets in the IMF program are not included in the consolidated budget balance, since they were issued by special funds. For example, in 1998, the government issued bonds worth about 35 trillion Korean through two special funds—the Korea Asset Management Fund and the Employment Stabilization Fund—to buy non-performing loans from the financial industry and to pay unemployment benefits. The total value of the bonds issued was equal to almost 50% of the regular budget. However, these bonds were not included in measuring the official "consolidated budget deficits" (unlike in other advanced countries) since they were classified in the accounts as "public bonds" instead of "government bonds." Needless to say, the government is held wholly responsible for servicing these "public bonds." In this regard, the argument that the IMF is demanding the same belt-tightening policy is not convincing, at least as far as fiscal policy in Korea is concerned.

[22] For discussions on the methodology of evaluating the effects of the IMF programs, see Khan (1990); Killick (1995); Killick and Malik (1993); Killick, Malik, and Manuel (1993); and Corbo and Fisher (1995).

[23] The 455 programs approved during the sample period consist of 345 stand-by arrangements, 42 extended fund facility (EFF) arrangements, and 44 arrangements under structural adjustment facility (SAF) or enhanced structural adjustment facility (ESAF). The remaining 21 cases were combined programs of two or more arrangements.

[24] We have excluded some extreme observations such that annual growth rate of employment or real wage is higher than 50% or lower than -50%. The results are essentially identical when these observations are included.

[25] The stabilization effects of IMF programs appear dependent on the exchange rate regime: in countries with nominal exchange anchors, which could add substantial credibility to the stabilization package, inflation rates fell dramatically from the first program year. See Schadeler et al. (1995, part I) for more details.

[26] Garuda (1998) claims that distributional effects of IMF programs may depend on a country's pre-program economic situation. He finds evidence of a significant relative improvement in income distribution in the program countries, in which external imbalance prior to the program initiation was not severe, while countries with the most severe pre-program external problems showed deterioration in income distribution relative to non-program countries with equally severe conditions. We have not tried the same experiment because the sample size becomes too small with the further classification of data.

[27] On the labor market front, the performance of Indonesia during the pre-crisis period had been least impressive of the three countries. However, it is widely noted that the underemployment problem is most severe in Thailand and therefore, its unemployment rate is significantly underestimated.

[28] See Whang and Lee (1997) for detailed analysis of changes in income distribution and poverty in Korea.

[29] There is growing literature that focuses on the distributional effects of globalization both on industrialized and developing countries. See ILO (1996), Rodrik (1997,1998), World Bank (1995), Slaughter and Swagel (1997), Wood (1995), Robbins (1996), and Williamson (1998).

[30] Globalization can contribute to rising wage dispersion by widening "within industries" wage differentials among workers with different levels of skill and education, as well as by widening the "inter-industry" dispersion of wage. ILO (1996) shows that intersectoral wage dispersion has increased within manufacturing sectors in Indonesia and Thailand since the 1970s, though it has decreased in Korea.

[31] According to current estimation, it covered only 22% of job losers in Korea as of April 1998.

[32] In fact, the findings in the section on "Impact of the Asian Crisis on Income Distribution and Poverty" might reflect this reality.

References

Aziz, Iwan J., 1998. "The Transition From Financial Crisis to Social Crisis," Paper presented at the International Conference on Social Implications of the Asian Financial Crisis, Organized by the KDI and UNDP, Seoul, Korea, July 29-31, 1998.

Bandow, Doug and Ian Vasquez, eds., 1994. *Perpetuating Poverty: the World Bank, IMF, and the Developing World,* Cato Institute: Washington D.C.

Borensztein, Eduardo and Jong-Wha Lee, 1998. "Financial Distortions and Crisis in Korea," mimeo., International Monetary Fund.

Cho, Yoon Je and Changyong Rhee, 1995. "A Study on the Budget Deficit Policy and Measurement in Korea," Policy Research Report 95-06, Korea Tax Institute, December.

Conway, Patrick, 1994. "IMF Lending Programs: Participation and Impact," *Journal of Development Economics* 45: 365-391.

Corbo, Vittorio and Stanley Fischer, 1995. "Structural Adjustment, Stabilization and Policy Reform: Domestic and International Finance," in *Handbook of Development Economics,* ed. J. Behrman and T.N. Srinivasan, Elsevier Science B.V.

Danaher, Kevin, ed., 1994. *50 Years is Enough: the Case against the World Bank and the IMF*, South End Press: Boston.

De Gregorio, Jose and Jong-Wha Lee, 1998. "Education and Income Distribution: New Evidence from Cross-Country Data," a working paper, Korea University, February.

Deininger, K. and L. Squire, 1996. "A New Data Set Measuring Income Inequality," *World Bank Economic Review* 10: 565-91.

Dornbush, R., Goldfajn I. and R. Valdes, 1995. "Currency Crises and Collapses," Brookings Papers on Economic Activity 2:219-294.

Feldstein, Martin, 1998. "Refocusing the IMF," *Foreign Affairs* 77, March/April.

Fischer, S., 1998. "The Asian Crisis: A View from the IMF," Address at the Midwinter Conference of the Bankers' Association for Foreign Trade.

Garuda, Gopal, 1998. "The Distributional Effects of IMF Programs: A Cross-Country Analysis," Seminar thesis, Harvard University.

Goldstein, Morris and Peter Montiel, 1986. "Evaluating Fund Stabilization Programs with Multicountry Data," *IMF Staff Papers* 33, June.

Gupta S., C. McDonald, C. Schiller, M. Verhoven, Z. Bogetic, and G. Schwartz, 1998. "Mitigating the Social Costs of the Economic Crisis and the Reform Programs in Asia," IMF Paper on Policy Analysis and Assessment 98/7, June.

Hernandez, Leonardo and Ricardo Mayer, 1998. "On the Social Impact of the Chilean Financial Crisis of 1982," Paper presented at the International Conference on Social Implications of the Asian Financial Crisis, Organized by the KDI and UNDP, Seoul, Korea, July 29-31.

Institute of International Finance, 1998. *Capital Flows to Emerging Market Economies.*

International Labour Office, 1996. *World Employment 1996/97: National Policies in a Global Context.*

International Labour Office, 1998. "Social Impact of the Financial Crisis in East and South-East Asia," Working paper prepared for ILO's High-Level Tripartite Meeting, April.

International Monetary Fund, 1987. *Theoretical Aspects of the Design of Fund-Supported Adjustment Programs,* IMF Occasional Paper No. 55.

International Monetary Fund, 1997a. *International Capital Markets: Developments, Prospects, and Key Policy Issues.*

International Monetary Fund, 1997b. *World Economic Outlook: Interim Assessment*, IMF: Washington D.C.

International Monetary Fund, 1998. *World Economic Outlook*, IMF: Washington D.C.

Johnson, Omotunde and Joanne Salop, 1980. "Distributional Aspects of Stabilization Programs in Developing Countries," *IMF Staff Papers* 27:1-23.

Khan, Mohsin S., 1990. "The Macroeconomic Effects of Fund-Supported Adjustment Programs," *IMF Staff Papers* 37 (2): 195-231.

Killick, Tony and Moazzam Malik, 1993. "Country Experiences with IMF Programmes in the 1980s," *World Economy*16, June.

Killick, Tony, 1995. "Can the IMF Help Low-Income Countries? Experiences with its Structural Adjustment Facilities," *World Economy* 18, June.

Killick, Tony, Moazzam Malik, and Marcus Manuel, 1993. "What Can We Know About the Effects of IMF Programmes?" *World Economy*16, June.

Kim, Dae Il, 1998. "The Social Impact of the Crisis in Korea," Paper Presented at the International Conference on Social Implications of the Asian Financial Crisis, Organized by the KDI and UNDP, Seoul, Korea, July 29-31.

Krugman, Paul, 1998. "What Happened to Asia?" mimeo, MIT, January.

Park, Yung Chul, 1998. "Financial Crisis and Macroeconomic Adjustments in Korea, 1997-98," unpublished draft, Korea University.

Park, Daekeun and Changyong Rhee, 1998. "Currency Crisis in Korea: Could It Have Been Avoided?" Working paper at Seoul National University.

Polak, Jacques J., 1991. "The Changing Nature of IMF Conditionality," *Essays in International Finance* No. 184, Princeton University: Princeton, New Jersey.

Polak, Jacques J., 1997. "The IMF Monetary Model at Forty," IMF Working Paper 97-49.

Radelet Steven and Jeffrey Sachs, 1998a. "The Onset of the East Asian Financial Crisis," a working paper, Harvard Institute for International Development (HIID), February.

Radelet Steven and Jeffrey Sachs, 1998b. "The East Asian Financial Crisis: Diagnosis, Remedies, Prospects," Working paper prepared for the Brookings Panel, HIID, March.

Radelet, Steve, Jeffrey Sachs, and Jong-Wha Lee, 1997. "Economic Growth in Asia," Development Discussion Paper No.609, HIID, November.

Ranis, Gustav and Frances Stewart, 1998. "A Pro-Human Development Adjustment Framework for the Countries of East And South East Asia," Paper Prepared for the UNDP Regional Bureau for Asia and the Pacific.

Robbins, Donald, 1996. "Trade, Trade Liberalization, and Inequality in Latin America and East Asia: Synthesis of Seven Countries," Discussion Paper, HIID.

Rodrik, Dani, 1997. *Has Globalization Gone Too Far?* Institute of International Economics: Washington D.C.

Rodrik, Dani, 1998. "Globalization, Social Conflict and Economic Growth," *World Economy*, January.

Schadler, Susan, Adam Bennett, Maria Carkovic, Louis Dicks-Mireaux, Mauro Mecagni, James H.J. Morsink, and Miguel A. Savastano, 1995. *IMF Conditionality: Experience Under Stand-By and Extended Arrangements, Part I and Part II*, IMF: Washington D.C.

Siamwalla, Anmar and Orapin Sobchokchai, 1998. "Responding to the Economic Crisis and Impact on Human Development in Thailand," Paper presented at the International Conference on Social Implications of the Asian Financial Crisis, Organized by the KDI and UNDP, Seoul, Korea, July 29-31.

Sisson, Charles A., 1986. "Fund-Supported Programs and Income Distribution in LDCs," *Finance and Development*, March, 33-36.

Slaughter, Matthew J. and Philip Swagel, 1997. "The Effects of Globalization on Wages in the Advanced Economies," *IMF Working Papers* 97/43, April.

Tambunlertchai, Somsak, 1998. "The Social Impact of the Financial Crisis in Thailand and Policy Responses," Paper Presented at the International Conference on Social Implications of the Asian Financial Crisis, Organized by the KDI and UNDP, Seoul, Korea, July 29-31.

United Nations, 1998. *Economic and Social Survey of Asia and The Pacific 1998,* United Nations: NY.

Whang, Seong-Hyeon and Joung-Woo Lee, 1997. "The Problems of Income Distribution and Related Policy Issues in Korea," Working paper, Korea Development Institute, May.

Williamson, Jeffrey G., 1997. "Globalization and Inequality, Past and Present," *The World Bank Research Observer*12: 117-135.

Wood, Adrian, 1995. "How Trade Hurt Unskilled Workers," *Journal of Economic Perspectives* 9: 57-80.

World Bank, 1996. *Involving Workers in East Asia's Growth*, World Bank: Washington D.C.

World Bank, 1997. *Private Capital Flows to Developing Countries*, World Bank: Washington D.C.

World Bank, 1998. *Global Development Finance*, World Bank: Washington D.C.

Globalization, Employment And Gender

Süle Özler

There is by now a large body of work in the academic literature on linkages between globalization and labor markets. In particular, focusing mostly on the US experience, researchers have analyzed the impact of globalization on the wage gap between skilled and unskilled workers.[1] Some view the source of increased wage inequality in the US as the shift towards industries that use skilled labor relatively more intensely because of increased import competition from low-wage countries (Leamer 1993; Leamer 1994; Borjas and Ramey 1995; Wood 1994). In sharp contrast, others argue that technological change has caused firms to adopt production techniques that are biased in favor of skilled workers (Lawrence and Slaughter 1993; Berman, Bound and Griliches 1994; Krugman 1995). There are fewer studies in this literature focusing on developing countries. Among these, Feenstra and Hanson (1997) attribute the increased wage gap in Mexico to foreign direct investment, and Hanson and Harrison (1995) attribute the increased wage gap in Mexico to the reduction of tariff protection, which primarily affected low-skilled industries.[2]

Gender differences have been outside the realm of analysis of most of this literature, which is surprising, given an entire field in labor economics on gender gap.[3] It is mostly in the field of women and development, among feminist economists, and in international institutions such as the United Nations Development Programme (UNDP) and the World Bank, that gender has been included as a category of analysis.[4] In this literature, recent efforts have been directed toward analyzing gender aspects of international trade at the conceptual and empirical levels (for recent overviews, see Fontana, Joekes and Masika 1998).

One area where there is considerable empirical evidence on linkages between globalization and gender is paid employment in the manufacturing sector, in particular in developing countries. Evidence suggests that export promotion and trade liberalization policies have led to the feminization of labor force.[5] In fact, over the last two decades there has been a significant increase in women's share of industrial employment as export-oriented industrialization has spread from its initial bases in Mexico and the four Asian tigers (Hong Kong, South Korea, Taiwan and Singapore) (Pearson 1998). This expansion, however, has not been universal. In South Asia, for example, export-led industrialization has taken off only in Bangladesh; in East Asia, the only countries where the expansion has taken place other than the initial four tigers are Malaysia, Indonesia, Thailand, and the Philippines. In Latin America, the expansion has been primarily limited to Mexico. The expansion has also taken place in various small economies of Central America and the Caribbean. In sub-Saharan Africa and the Middle East, in sharp contrast to other regions, various economic and political factors have precluded the emergence of export-oriented manufacturing (except in Mauritius). Despite this regional patchwork, industrialization of developing countries in the post-war period has been described as being as much female-led as export-led (Joekes 1987).

Despite the evidence on linkages between export-led growth and feminization of the labor force, there is some evidence suggesting that the association of increased intensity of female employment with export-oriented industrialization might be reversed. This reversal has been observed in South Korea (Joekes 1985) and in the *maquiladora* industry along the US-Mexico border (Beneria 1995). Where it is observed, the reversal is attributed to the introduction of new technologies, skill upgrading of export producers, and reorganization of production, especially multitasking of flexible labor engaged in high-performance production. Women who remain in the labor force in the face of such technological and organizational change emerge as multi-skilled workers crucial to the new flexible and just-in-time production cultures (for example, in electronics and garment-making in Mexico) (Pearson 1998).

It is also important to note that the declining share of women workers in manufacturing factories fails to capture the relocation of industrial processes and production from factories to home-production or the informal sector. Since the early 1980s, along with deregulation of labor markets, new, unconventional forms of work arrangements have emerged. Among a variety of unconventional work arrangements, home-working and informal sector work have been the most important (World Survey 1999).

Most evidence on feminization of the labor force resulting from export promotion and trade liberalization policies has been based on case studies. Though a large collection of case studies offers insights on overall patterns, it is still difficult to make generalizations based on case studies. In order to complement the existing evidence, some recent efforts have been directed towards using cross-country data. To shed light on the sources of aggregate changes and uncover the nature of relevant linkages, efforts have also been directed at using plant-level data. In recent papers, we have undertaken some of this task in an attempt to fill the existing gap. The primary purpose of this essay is to provide a review of the findings in these studies, a task that we undertake in the first section below. In the concluding remarks, we provide an assessment of gender-differentiated work effects of trade liberalization and export promotion.

Globalization and Labor Markets: An Overview of Statistical Evidence

Two demand-side explanations are suggested for feminization of the labor force in export-oriented enterprises in developing countries. One reason is that developing countries have comparative advantage in sectors that tend to use labor-intensive production techniques and unskilled labor, and traditionally employ women.[6] Thus, feminization of the labor force in the face of export promotion and trade liberalization is a consequence of the shift of production to export-oriented industries.

A second demand-side explanation for feminization of the labor force in the process of globalization is based on the notion that women constitute a "cheaper" source of labor. In this literature, "...'cheap' labor is deconstructed beyond wage levels to include employee protection, employer's contribution to social wage, taxation, investment and working conditions in combination with non militancy, docility and manual dexterity and conscientious application to often monotonous production process..." (Pearson 1998, 5). Standing (1989) argues that labor deregulation and reorganization of production along lines of labor flexibility has rapidly altered the nature of jobs, leading to a substitution of women's "cheap labor" for that of men. Elson (1996), on the other hand, points out that the growth of women's share of industrial employment is a consequence of the decline of jobs that were previously done by men, rather than the substitution of "cheaper" women in men's jobs.

Women's availability for paid employment in the manufacturing sector is attributed in some cases to "push factors". The structural adjustment program of the 1980s in Mexico, for example, has been associated with declining real wages and rising poverty, especially in urban areas. In such households, women have been "pushed" into paid employment to compensate for husbands' loss of job, or declining real wages, representing "distress sale of labor" (see, for example, Beneria 1992). In some situations, young women are also pressured to work in factories to support their natal families (Salaff 1990). Women's entry into the manufacturing sector, however, does not always represent "distress sale of labor," as is evident among garment factory workers in Bangladesh (Kabeer 1995). It is noted that women in these factories come from a variety of economic categories, and their entry into the workforce is likewise in response to a variety of needs and incentives, not only in response to the "necessity" to support family income. Daughters' choice of factory employment in the face of opposition from parents, for example, is interpreted as their route to personal liberation (Wolf 1992).

> <u>Stylized Fact:</u>
> *Export promotion and trade liberalization policies have led to feminization of the labor force in developing countries, although feminization might be reversed through technological change and reorganization of production.*
>
> <u>Factors that explain feminization of the labor force</u>:
> ***Demand side**: 1) Developing countries have comparative advantage in sectors that traditionally employ women. 2) Employers substitute women who constitute a "cheaper"* source of labor, either because of creation of new forms of jobs more suitable for "cheap" sources of labor, or increased labor market availability of women in the process of globalization.*
>
> ***Supply side:** In some cases, it is the worsening of real incomes and increased poverty in urban areas during trade reform periods that lead women to seek paid employment to support family incomes. In others, it is the new economic opportunities and incentives that lead women to seek paid employment.*
>
> ** "Cheap" refers not only to wage levels, but all other conditions, practices, and requirements of a job.*

A. Export Share of Output and Female Share of Employment

A.1. Cross-Country Evidence

In Cagatay and Özler (1995), we ask whether female share of employment has increased in countries where trade openness has increased. The investigation is undertaken for a set of 165 countries and for the years 1985 and 1990, to assess whether findings from case studies could be generalized. The main finding is that increased openness has led to an increase in the female share of employment.

In earlier cross-country empirical studies it has been noted that female share of the labor force exhibits a U-shaped pattern as a function of the level of development (Goldin 1984). In these studies, gross national product (GNP) per capita has been used as a proxy for the level of development. The primary empirical result, supporting the presence of feminization, "U," is that the female share of the labor force is a quadratic function of GNP per capita. The conceptual underpinning of this inquiry dates back to Boserup (1970), who argued that women were "marginalized" during economic development. She points out that men's privileged access to new technologies and education leads to growing productivity differences between men and women, and hence a decline in women's share of the labor force. It is noted, however, that with industrialization, more education for women, "commodification" of domestic labor, and declining fertility rates women's labor force participation increases, giving rise to the U-shaped pattern.

We investigate whether structural adjustment programs, through their impact on increased openness, and their impact on income share of workers in manufacturing industries, have led to feminization of the labor force once feminization "U" (FEMU) is taken into account. The model estimated is described by the following equation:

FEMINIZATION = f (FEMU, DEMOGRAPHIC, ECONOMIC, ADJUSTMENT)

The explained variable, FEMINIZATION, is the female share of the labor force. Turning to the explanatory variables, FEMU is the feminization "U," which is measured by log of GNP per capita, and its square. DEMOGRAPHIC characteristics have long been known to be relevant for feminization.

The most important of such characteristics, including fertility levels, levels of urbanization, and levels of female education are used as control variables. ECONOMIC variables are included to capture economic characteristics other than GNP variables that might be relevant for feminization. These include the degree of expansion of the economy (as measured by investment-to-GNP ratio) and trade openness, as well as changes in income distribution (measured as labor's share in manufacturing value added). ADJUSTMENT is a measure of structural adjustment, constructed in two alternative ways. The first is a dummy variable indicating the countries that have undertaken adjustment programs (which might be weighted by the number of adjustment programs undertaken). Alternatively, the economic impact of adjustment programs is measured. The three economic categories incorporated under ECONOMIC are also those that are known to have been impacted by adjustment programs in a number of countries. Hence, in Cagatay and Özler (1995), we construct measures of the degree of change in these three categories stemming from adjustment programs. Employing the changes of the variables in these categories for adjusters along with the long-term averages of the same variables allows us to separate the impact of the two.

The impact of ADJUSTMENT on feminization is the primary result of interest for this overview. We report that female share of employment is significantly higher in countries that have undertaken structural adjustment programs (controlling for other determinants of the female share of employment). This result is found to be robust to alternative measures of adjustment. Furthermore, in our attempt to identify the channels through which adjustment programs lead to feminization of the labor force, we find that, in intensively adjusting countries that have experienced an improved performance of exports share of GNP, there has been a feminization of the labor force. Another channel, which leads to feminization, is worsening income distribution.

Feminization "U" refers to the U-shaped relationship between women's share of the labor force and GNP per capita. Evidence based on cross-country data for 165 countries pooled for 1985 and 1990 indicates that structural adjustment policies have led to an increase in feminization of the labor force after controlling for the feminization "U." Increased feminization has been via worsening income distribution, and increased openness of adjusting countries.

A.2. Plant-Level Evidence

In Özler (1999a), we investigate the impact of increased export share of output on intensity of female employment. For this purpose, we use plant-level data for manufacturing plants located in the larger metropolitan area of Istanbul, Turkey during the 1983-85 period. The significance of the period is that the Turkish economy was set onto an export-oriented industrialization path in 1980. The sample contains observations for 1,345 plants, which have at least 10 employees. The results are obtained from estimations that use averages of plant data over the three years in the sample.[7]

The equation estimated is described as follows:

FEMALE = g (SIZE, AWAGES, SKILL, POWER,V-ADDED, INV-MACHIN, EXP/OUT)

FEMALE represents intensity of female employment.[8] SIZE is total number of employees, including administrative and production workers. AWAGES represent alternative wages for production workers and non-production workers separately. Alternative wages are computed using average wages of plants that are in the same industry as the one being considered. SKILL is measured by summing over high-level technical personnel, medium-level personnel, and foreman categories, and scaling the sum by the number of unskilled workers. POWER is the total power used by engines working with electrical energy, generators and other equipment, scaled by total employment. V-ADDED stands for real value added per worker. To compute INV-MACHIN, we sum new investment in machinery including new purchases, upgrades, own production and upgrade, secondhand purchases, and research expenditures for machinery less depreciation. The sum is then scaled by total employment. EXP/OUT is exports scaled by output. All variables used in the estimation of the above equation are at plant level, except for the export output ratio, which is at the three-digit level of the Standard Industrial Classification (SIC).

The primary result in this study is that as the ratio of exports to total output within a given sector increases, the female intensity of employment at the plant level also increases. It is difficult to attribute this finding to the fact that most women work in "unskilled" jobs, and that the exporting sectors in developing countries tend to use unskilled workers, since the estimates that are reported are obtained after controlling for skill composition of workers at plant level.

Two closely related studies are Berik and Cagatay (1990) and Kasnakoglu and Dikbayir (1997), both of which use Turkish data. In the former, the authors use data at the three-digit SIC level for the period of 1966-1982. In the latter, the authors use four-digit SIC data for 1990-1992. In both studies, a high share of output in exports is found to lead to a high share of female employment.

Studies on the Turkish economy indicate that industries with a high share of output in exports employ a larger fraction of women. These findings are observed not only at the sectoral level but also at a plant level. Controlling for the ratio of skilled workers at the plant level, an increase in the ratio of exports to total output of the sector leads to an increase in plants' female intensity of employment.

B. Export Status, Job Creation and Job Persistence

In Özler (1999b), we focus on the gender gap in jobs and ask whether the gap is different for exporting plants than for non-exporting plants. The issues we consider regarding the gender gap are job growth rates, job reallocation rates, and persistence of jobs created. For this purpose, we use plant-level information from Colombia for the period of 1983 to 1991. The data contain information on a balanced panel of 1,151 plants, each employing more than 10 people, in the following eight industries: food products, other agricultural products, textiles, clothing and apparel, leather products, paper, industrial chemicals, and other chemicals. The Colombian data are particularly well suited to this study because they contain a breakdown along gender lines of the number of employees in different occupational categories. Using this breakdown, we create a measure of skilled females (males) by adding females (males) who are managers, skilled workers, and technicians. The unskilled females (males) category includes only unskilled female (male) workers. Furthermore, the data include information on a plant's export activity for each year. In our analysis, we separate plants into two groups: plants that are exporting in a given year, and plants that are not.

Overall, the results indicate that during the period of rapid export growth in Colombia, unskilled workers in general lost jobs. However, unskilled women workers in exporting plants gained jobs. Skilled workers in general gained, with the gain of skilled women exceeding that of skilled men. Women experience a higher rate of job turnover than men do, but more of the jobs created for women persist at least two years. These results suggest that the rise of exporting industry has led to employment gains for women. [9]

Let us now turn to a more detailed description of our findings. First, we investigate whether there are gender differences in job growth rates. We find gender differences in employment growth rates among non-exporters but not among exporters. In particular, among non-exporters, the growth rate of jobs for unskilled males is significantly higher than unskilled females, while the growth rate of jobs for skilled males is lower than the growth rate of skilled jobs for females.[10]

Next, we measure gender differences in job reallocation rates.[11] Since jobs are simultaneously created and destroyed, only by considering both can we measure total job reallocation. For this purpose, we create two new measures. NEG is the size-weighted average of shrinking firms' employment growth rate. NEG is calculated separately for exporters and non-exporters. Hence, the weights are the ratio of a firm's average employment to the average employment of all plants in that export group. An analogous measure is calculated by a weighted sum of expanding firms' growth rates, and is denoted POS. Using these measures, we can calculate net reallocation rates as the difference between POS and NEG. The upper bound of gross reallocation rate is calculated as the sum of NEG and POS.

Among non-exporters, there is a net destruction of jobs for unskilled females as well as males, though the rate of destruction is higher for males. Among exporters, there is a net creation of unskilled female jobs, while unskilled male jobs are destroyed. A comparison of skilled males and females also yields interesting results. Among non-exporters, there is a net creation of skilled female jobs, while there is a net destruction of male jobs. Among exporters, on the other hand, net creation of jobs for skilled females is slightly greater than creation of jobs for skilled males. Gross job reallocation rates also indicate gender differences. For both types of workers, and in both export categories, gross job reallocation is higher for females, though the difference is smaller among exporters.

We investigate gender differences in persistence of jobs that are created and destroyed. By persistence, we mean the fraction of new jobs that still exist after two years. We observe that jobs created for females—both unskilled and skilled—have a higher percentage of persistence than those of their male counterparts. This result holds for both exporters and non-exporters, though the gap is larger among exporters. Persistence of job destruction is greater for skilled males than skilled females, and the gender gap does not change with export status. The gender gap in persistence rates of job destruction shows different patterns for unskilled males versus females when exporters are compared with non-exporters. Among exporters, the persistence of job destruction is greater for unskilled males, whereas among non-exporters, it is greater for unskilled females.

From 1983 to 1991, a period of rapid export growth in Colombia:

a) The net job creation rate *for skilled (unskilled) females is higher than it is for skilled (unskilled) males; the gender gap in net job creation is smaller among exporters than non-exporters.*

b) The gross job reallocation rate *for skilled (unskilled) females is higher than their male counterparts; the gender gap is smaller among exporters than non-exporters.*

c) The persistence rate of jobs created *for skilled (unskilled) females is higher than their male counterparts; the gender gap is higher among exporters than non-exporters.*

d) The persistence rate of jobs destroyed *is lower for skilled females than it is for skilled males; export status does not have an impact on the gender gap. Persistence rate of unskilled female jobs that are destroyed is higher than it is for males among non-exporters, but lower than it is for males among exporters.*

C. Worker Composition and Firms' Export Decision

In Orbay and Özler (1999), we ask a related, but different question. In particular, we ask whether a given worker composition, such as the ratio of unskilled workers, or the ratio of female workers, influences the decision of a firm to participate in export activity. Conceptually, this effect might arise two possible ways. The first is what might be referred to as the indirect effect, through plant efficiency. Since plants that are more efficient are more likely to participate in export markets[12], if a certain worker composition has a bearing on plant efficiency, we would expect to see the effect on export participation as well. Second, worker composition might have a direct impact on the export participation decision. This can be rationalized by assuming that the worker composition bears in some manner on the benefits from exporting, and that it is costly to adjust worker composition. As an example, suppose it is true that females increase the value of exported goods due to an unobservable characteristic associated with being a woman (e.g., nimble fingers for embroidery, docility in the work environment). Consequently, firms entering export markets will hire and train more females to increase output value; this can be thought of as a fixed cost of exporting. Meanwhile, a firm that already has a stock of female workers for this activity will not have to pay the training and other costs associated with hiring new workers, and hence will be more likely to participate in export activity.

We undertake an empirical investigation, simultaneously using a census of manufacturing data for Colombia for the period of 1983 to 1991, a period of rapid export growth. The data used are from plants from four major industries: clothing and apparel, textiles, industrial chemicals, and other chemicals. We estimate simultaneously the decision to participate in export activity, and the average variable cost of the firm.[13] Both the participation decision equation and the average cost equation include two measures of worker composition—namely, the unskilled worker ratio and the ratio of female workers. Hence the estimated equations are:

EXPORT = f (Z, REXCHR, FEML, UNSL)

AVC= g (Z, FEM, UNS)

where **Z = (AGE, AGESQ, REALCAPL, BTYPE, AVCL1, AVCL2, EXPORTL).**

The presence of "L" at the end of any variable name indicates that the value of the variable is lagged (by one or two years). EXPORT is a dummy variable equal to one if the firm is exporting in a given year and zero otherwise. AGE and AGESQ measure a plant's age and the square of its age, respectively. REALCAPL is real capital, lagged by one year. BTYPE indicates whether a firm is a corporation or not. AVC stands for average variable cost. REXCHR is the dollar-based real exchange rate. Finally FEM is the ratio of females to total employees, and UNS is the ratio of unskilled workers to all workers. With this specification of the participation decision, i.e., EXPORT equation, we attempt to capture variables that help predict future marginal costs and demand as well as those that effect current profitability and fixed costs of exporting.

The results of the econometric analysis indicate the following with regard to gender composition effects. First, an increase in the ratio of female workers is associated with an increase in export activity in textiles and industrial chemicals. Note that, in these two industries, the unskilled ratio does not have a statistically significant effect. (The correlation between the two ratios is .12 in textiles and -.40 in industrial chemicals.) Second, an increase in the ratio of female workers increases costs in other chemicals, but does not affect costs in the other industries. One striking aspect of all these results is that the female worker ratio does not appear to be a mere proxy for the unskilled worker ratio, measured with standard classifications of skilled/unskilled workers.

Furthermore, the positive significant impact of the female ratio on participation in exports does not appear to be based on cost considerations, since the female ratio is not found to have an impact on costs in industries where it increases the likelihood of participation in export activity. For the textiles industry, there might be several possible interpretations of this finding. Unfortunately, these are not easily testable with available quantitative data.

One interpretation is that women are more "skilled" in certain jobs (such as embroidery), which is not captured with the typical definition of "skilled" jobs. Another interpretation might be "docility." Women workers might be "better suited" for subservient positions in highly demanding and competitive work environments, or for jobs that require more "flexibility." In industrial chemicals, on the other hand, the ratio of skilled to unskilled females is nearly ten, which is in sharp contrast to the other industries. It appears that females are working as technicians or doing the service jobs in large plants where men do the unskilled work.

The significance of the findings in this study is that they highlight the importance of gender differences in deriving trade. Most studies on trade and labor markets ask how trade policy, or changes in trade performance, influence labor markets. This study indicates that a plant's worker composition is an important determinant of its export participation decision.[14]

From 1983 to 1991, textiles and industrial chemicals plants in Colombia that employed a high share of females (controlling for the skill composition of the plant) were more likely to become exporters.

Concluding Remarks

The issues we have raised so far suggest important linkages between globalization and women's work in developing countries. Evidence suggests that globalization does not have gender-neutral effects on employment. Women appear to gain jobs. The evidence indicates not only that women and men are impacted differently in the process of globalization, but also that they have potentially different influences on the process of globalization. Women's attributes not captured with typical measures of skill appear to be increasing the likelihood of firms' participation in exporting. An evaluation of these findings from women's point of view is not an easy task, and the studies reviewed here do not have direct implications for policy. However, we raise some important issues that ought to be considered in such discussions.

An increase in women's paid employment has positive dimensions in the light of evidence linking access to paid employment to women's power. Women's degree of empowerment in family and community decisions is enhanced as a consequence of having paid work. Evidence indicates that women's say in areas of fertility, economic decisions such as purchases and sales, and domestic decisions such as mobility, appear to increase.

Additional evidence suggests that there are significant differences in expenditure of income controlled by women versus income controlled by men. Women spend a higher fraction of their incomes on family nutrition, health and education, which are important factors in human resource development and enhancement of human capabilities. This suggests that women's increased access to paid employment is not only beneficial for women because it increases women's power, but also has potential economic benefits for society as a whole.

A source of debate concerns the working conditions of jobs that women have access to, as discussed in the *1999 World Survey*. One view is that, since in general the jobs women have access to are lower-paying jobs with inferior work conditions, integration of women into paid employment should not be interpreted positively. Alternatively, women's conditions in factory jobs, both in terms of pay and working conditions, fare better than alternative low-skilled female occupations, such as domestic work and small-scale local industry activities. The empirical evidence on the relationship between globalization and the gender gap in wages, however, is scarce, unreliable, and difficult to interpret.

Similar sources of concern apply when women's increased employment in informal sector jobs and home-working is considered. Typically, jobs in the informal sector have precarious working conditions and very low wages, with no social benefits attached. Although conditions of work may be better in home-working than other informal-sector jobs, home-working can still be undesirable, as it perpetuates women's position in traditional roles.

Yet another issue is what happens to women's overall burden of work. Evidence from structural adjustment episodes indicates that, in families and communities that are adversely affected by such an episode, women's unpaid work increases and intensifies. Daughters' burden of domestic work is also found to increase significantly in such families, resulting in increased bias against girls' education. A number of case studies suggest that such consequences for women's overall burden of work have important implications for human resource depletion, as they erode the quality and quantity of the current and future labor force.■

Notes

[1]Since Katz and Murphy (1992) convincingly showed that relative supply shifts could not explain the dramatic change in the labor market, attention has turned to demand-side explanations.

[2] Others have investigated the impact of trade reforms on manufacturing sector wages and employment. Currie and Harrison (1997) estimate a reduced form industry wage and employment equations in the spirit of Grossman (1987) and find that employment in the average firm was unaffected by the tariff reductions and quota elimination, but employment was significantly reduced in exporting firms in Morocco. Revenga (1995) finds that in Mexico, trade reforms have led to a reduction in wages and employment. Feliciano (1993) finds that increase in returns to education explains the rise in wages to skilled labor in Mexico. Similar results are also documented for Chile (Robbins (1994)).

[3] Levinsohn (1999), Özler (1999b), Orbay and Özler (1999) are among the few exceptions.

[4] See Cagatay, Elson and Grown (1995) for an overview of approaches to gendered macroeconomic analysis.

[5] See, for example, Standing (1989), Wood (1991), Joekes and Weston (1994), Joekes (1995), and Cagatay (1995).

[6] The concentration of women workers in export-oriented industries or export processing zones with especially labor-intensive production techniques has been widely documented in case studies (see Berik and Cagatay (1990) for an overview).

[7] A number of features of the data impinge on the choice of estimation technique. Without dwelling on the technical details, let us note that we chose this approach because not every plant has observations in every year in the sample, and this unbalanced nature of the panel data is not random. This approach also diminishes potentials for measurement error over the years.

[8] FEMALE is measured in log-odd form. In other words, let FSH stand for female share of total employment, then FEMALE = Log (fsh/1-fsh).

[9] The inferences we can draw about the conditions of this employment are limited and contaminated with potential measurement error. However, our analysis indicates that the gender wage gap is larger in exporting plants than in non-exporting plants. This finding is based on imputations, since the data we use contain wage information only at the plant level. However, using information on ratios of workers, we imputed male and female wages. These imputations suggest that, within non-exporting plants, male wages are more than twice that of females. Among exporting plants, men earn three times as much.

[10] To determine statistical significance, we performed the Wilcoxon rank-sum test.

[11] The method is the same as in Davis and Haltiwanger (1992).

[12] See Clerides, Lach, and Tybout (1999).

[13] The reason for the simultaneous equations estimation is to address the issue of whether more efficient firms (measured with low average variable costs) *self-select* into export activity or, alternatively, firms become more efficient as a *consequence* of entering into export activity.

[14] Berge and Wood (1997) ask whether manufacturing exports depend more on education of women than of men. Their cross-country regressions give weak support to this view. This finding is contrary to evidence based on case studies, which argue that education of females is an important determinant of manufacturing export performance.

References

Beneria, L., 1992, "The Mexican Debt Crisis: Restructuring the Economy and the Household," Pp. 83-104 in *Unequal Burden: Economic Crises, Persistent Poverty, and Women's Work*, ed. L. Beneria and S. Feldman. Oxford: Westwood Press.

_______, 1995, "Toward a Greater Integration of Gender in Economics," *World Development* 23 (11).

Berge, K. and A. Wood, 1994, " Does Educating Girls Improve Export Opportunities?" *IDS Working Paper* Number 5, Institute of Development Studies, University of Sussex.

Berik, G. and N. Cagatay, 1990, "Transition to Export-Led Growth in Turkey: Is There a Feminization of Employment?" *Review of Radical Political Economics* 22:115-134.

Berman, E., J. Bound and Z. Griliches, 1994, "Changes in the Demand for Skilled Labor within U. S. Manufacturing: Evidence from the Annual Survey of Manufacturers," *Quarterly Journal of Economics* 109:367-398.

Borjas, G. J. and V. A. Ramey, 1995, "Foreign Competition, Market Power, and Wage Inequality: Theory and Evidence," *Quarterly Journal of Economics* 110:1075-111.

Boserup, E., 1970, *Women's Role in Economic Development.* New York: St. Martin's Press.

Cagatay, N. and S. Ozler, 1995, "Feminization of the Labor Force: The Effects of Long-term Development and Structural Adjustment," *World Development* 23:1883-1894.

Cagatay, N., D. Elson, and C. Grown, 1995, "Introduction" in *World Development* vol. 23, number 11. Special Issue on Gender, Adjustment and Macroeconomics, ed. N. Cagatay, D. Elson, and C. Grown.

Clerides, S.K., S. Lach, and J.R. Tybout, 1999, "Is Learning by Exporting Important? Micro-Dynamic Evidence from Colombia, Mexico and Morocco," *Quarterly Journal of Economics.*

Currie, J. and A. Harrison, 1997, "Sharing the Costs: The Impact of Trade Reform on Capital and Labor in Morocco," *Journal of Labor Economics* 15(3): 44-72.

Davis, S.J., and J. Haltiwanger, 1992, "Gross Job Creation, Job Destruction and Employment Reallocation," *Quarterly Journal of Economics* 107(3): 819-863.

Elson, D., 1996, "Appraising Recent Developments in the World Market for Nimble Fingers", in *Confronting State, Capital and Patriarchy: Women Organizing in the Process of Industrialization*, ed. A. Chhachhi and R. Pittin. Basingstoke, England: Macmillan.

Feenstra, R. C. and G. H. Hanson, 1997, "Foreign Direct Investment and Relative Wages: Evidence from Mexico's Maquiladoras," Journal of International Economics 42:371-393.

Feliciano, Z., 1993, "Workers, and Trade Liberalization: The Impact of Trade Reforms in Mexico on Wages and Employment," mimeo, Harvard University.

Fontana, M., S. Joekes, and R. Masika, 1998, "Global Trade Expansion and Liberalization: Gender Issues and Impacts," Department for International Development, U.K.

Goldin, C., 1994, " The U-shaped Female Labor Force Function in Economic Development and Economic History," NBER Working Paper Series, Number 4707, Cambridge: National Bureau of Economic Research.

Grossman, G. M., 1987, "The Employment and Wage Effects of Import Competition in the U.S.," *Journal of International Economic Integration*, Vol.2.

Hanson G. H. and A. Harrison, 1995, "Trade Technology and Wage Inequality," NBER Working Paper Number 5110.

Joekes, S., 1987, *Women in the World Economy.* Oxford: Oxford University Press.

_______, 1995, "Trade-Related Employment for Women in Industry and Services in Developing Countries," Occasional Paper Number 5. Geneva: UNRISD.

Joekes, S. and Weston, A., 1994, *Women and the New Trade Agenda*. New York: UNIFEM.

Kabeer, N., 1995, " Necessary, Sufficient or Irrelevant? Women, Wages and Intra-household Power Relations in Bangladesh," IDS Working Paper Number 25, Institute of Development Studies, University of Sussex.

Kasnakoglu, Z., and G. Dikbayir, 1997, "Determinants of Women's Employment in Selected Sub-sectors of Turkish Manufacturing Industry," Middle East Technical University Working Paper, Ankara.

Katz, I. and K.M. Murphy, 1992, "Changes in Relative Wages, 1963-1987: Supply and Demand Factors," *Quarterly Journal of Economics* 107:35-78.

Krugman, P.R., 1995, "Technology, Trade, and Factor Prices," NBER Working Paper Number 5355.

Lawrence, R. Z. and M. J. Slaughter, 1993, "Trade and U.S. Wages: Great Sucking Sound or Small Hiccup?" *Brookings Papers an Economic Activity* 2:161-227.

Leamer, E. 1993, "Wage Effects of a U.S.- Mexico Free Trade Agreement," Pp. 57-128 in *The Mexico-U.S. Free Trade Agreement*, ed. P.M. Garber. Cambridge: MIT Press.

________, 1994, "Trade and Wages, and Revolving Door Ideas," NBER Working Paper Number 4716.

Levinsohn, J., 1996, "Firm Heterogeneity, Jobs and International Trade: Evidence from Chile," NBER Working Paper Number 5808.

Orbay, H. and S. Ozler, 1999, "Worker Composition and Export Decision: Evidence from Colombia," mimeo, Koc University, Turkey.

Ozler S., 1999a, "Exporting and Female Share of Employment: Evidence from Turkey," mimeo, Koc University.

Ozler, S., 1999b, "Jobs and Exporting," mimeo, Koc University.

Pearson, R., 1998, " Nimble Fingers Revisited: Reflections on Women and Third World Industrialisation in the late Twentieth Century" in *Feminist Visions of Development: Research, Analysis and Policy*, ed. C. Jackson and R. Pearson. London: Routledge.

Revenga, A., 1995, "Employment and Wage Effects of Trade Liberalization: The Case of Mexican Manufacturing," World Bank Policy Research Working Paper Number 1524.

Robbins, D., 1994, "Relative Wage Structure in Chile: The Effects of Liberalization," mimeo, Harvard Institute for International Development.

Salaff, J., 1990, " Women, the Family and the State: Hong Kong, Taiwan and Singapore - Newly Industrialised Countries in Asia" Pp. 98-136 in *Women, Employment and the Family in the International Division of Labor*, ed. Stichter and Parpart, Philadelphia: Temple University.

Standing, G., 1989, "Global Feminization Through Flexible Labor," *World Development* 17: 1077-1095.

Wolf, D., 1992, *Factory Daughters: Gender, Household Dynamics and Rural Industrialisation in Java*. Los Angeles: University of California and Oxford University Presses.

Wood, A., 1991, "North-South Trade and Female Labor in Manufacturing: An Asymmetry," *Journal of Development Studies*, vol. 27.

________, 1994, *North-South Trade, Employment and Inequality*. Oxford: Clarendon Press.

World Survey, 1999, "The Role of Women in Development," United Nations.

GLOBALIZATION AND ENVIRONMENT

Theodore Panayotou

Globalization has been the defining trend in the closing decade of the 20th century. The dawn of new millenium heralds a new era of interaction among nations, economies and people. Globalization is an ongoing process of global integration that encompasses (i) economic integration through trade, investment and capital flows; (ii) political interaction; (iii) information and information technology and (iv) culture. While all dimensions of globalization affect the natural environment and through it human development, for the purposes of tracing the main lines between globalization and environment, we will focus on the economic dimensions of trade, investment and capital flows. An unprecedented flow of capital, technology, goods and services crosses national borders daily. Nearly US$20 billion in capital flows around the world each day.

Economic globalization impacts the environment and sustainable development in a variety of ways and through a multitude of channels. Globalization contributes to economic growth and thereby affects the environment in many of the same ways that economic growth does: adversely in some stages of development, favorably at others. Globalization accelerates structural change, thereby altering the industrial structure of countries and hence resource use and pollution levels. Globalization diffuses capital and technology: depending on their environmental characteristics relative to existing capital and technology, the environment may improve or deteriorate. Globalization transmits and magnifies market failures and policy distortions that may spread and exacerbate environmental damage; it may also generate pressures for reform, as policies heretofore thought of as purely domestic attract international interest. While it improves the prospects for economic growth worldwide and increases overall global output, globalization could conceivably reduce economic prospects in individual countries, sectors and industries; such marginalization of economies and people may result in poverty-induced resource depletion and environmental degradation.

Globalization diffuses world product standards and, to the extent that environmental standards are higher in the dominant consumer markets, it *may* create a trend toward rising standards globally. On the other hand, concerns over the possible loss of competitiveness due to "unfair practices" or lax standards may lead to a "race to the bottom." Economic globalization changes the government-market interface: it constrains governments and enhances the role of the market in economic, social and environmental outcomes. On the other hand, it creates new imperatives for states to co-operate both in managing the global commons and in coordinating domestic environmental policies.

The purpose of this paper is to (a) identify the key links between globalization and environment; (b) identify major issues included in multilateral economic agreements in trade, finance, investments and intellectual property rights that affect environmental sustainability; and (c) review priority policy issues affecting multilateral economic agreements and environment, to analyze incentives implicit in trade and investment policy measures that affect environmental sustainability.

Since this is a vast area to cover, we have divided it into the main dimensions of economic globalization: trade liberalization, investment and finance, and technology diffusion and intellectual property rights. In the case of the trade-environment interface, we consider both the impact of trade on the environment and of the environment on trade. An integrative section on the effects of globalization on the environmental policy and performance leads to domestic and international priority policy issues and recommendations.

Trade and Environment

Trade liberalization and its outcome, freer trade, are both drivers and manifestations of globalization. They are also major channels through which globalization impacts the natural environment and affects environmental quality. World trade has grown faster than world output indicating a growing trade-intensity of the global economy. While global output grew at an average annual rate of 4% during 1950-94, the world merchandise trade grew at an average annual rate of over 6% during the same period. As a result, over the 45-year period, world merchandise trade grew by 14 times compared to only 5.5 times for the world merchandise output. The trade intensity of the global economy increased further during 1990-1995 (WTO 1995).

Trade theory has demonstrated that free trade maximizes the efficiency of resource allocation by channeling economic activities to least-cost producers; it thus produces a given level of output at the least cost. If natural and environmental resources are efficiently priced (i.e., all relevant social costs are accounted for), the global output resulting from free trade is also produced at the least environmental cost. Free trade maximizes social welfare. For example, countries with high levels of agricultural protection use more than ten times as much chemical fertilizers and pesticides per hectare as countries with low-level protection (see Figure 1 below).

Figure 1: Relationship between agricultural producer subsidy equivalent (PSE) for 1979-89 and the use of chemical fertilizers and pesticides per hectare of cropland*

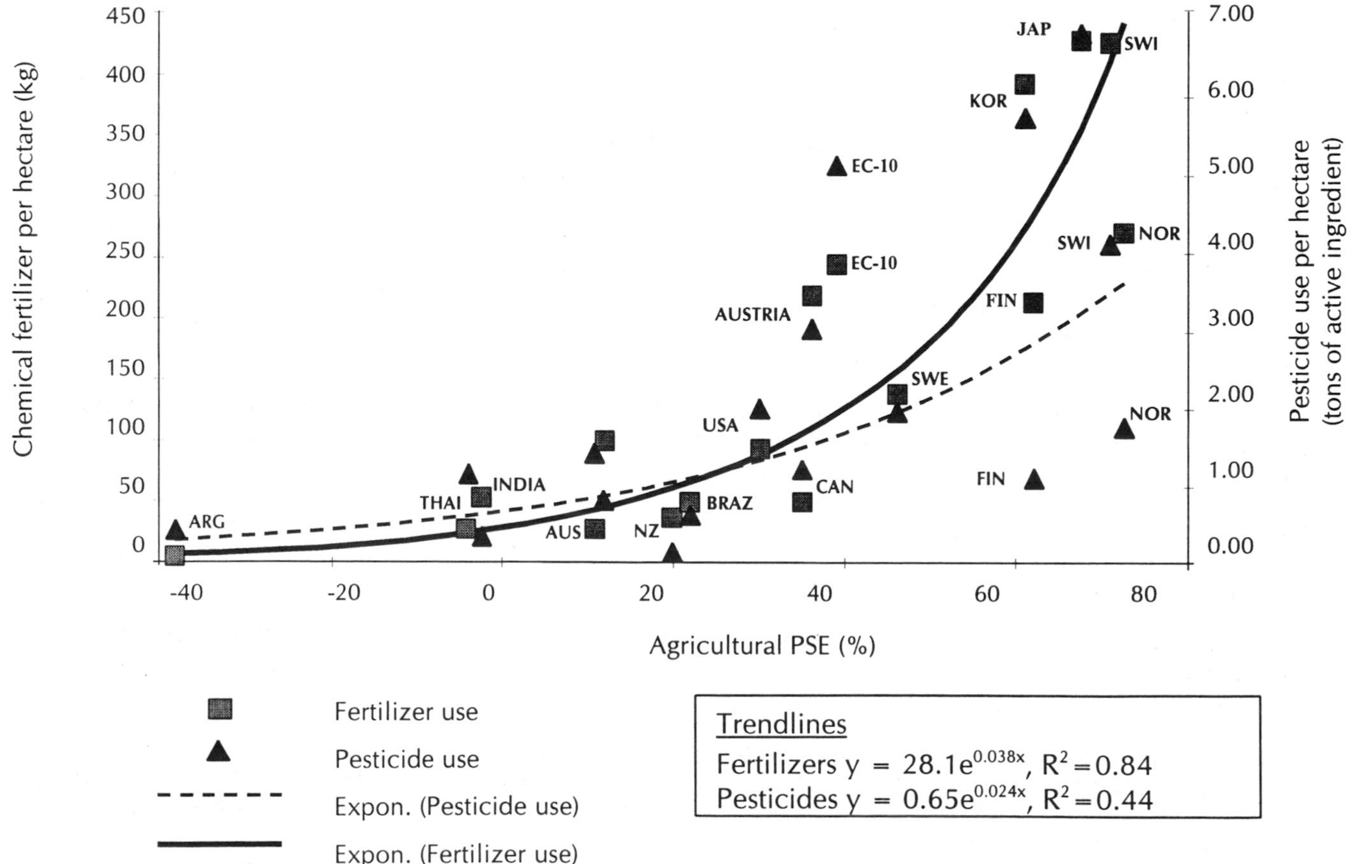

Source: Anderson (1992, Figure 1) and World Resources Institute (1990, Table 18.2), in Anderson and Strutt (1994).

In this case, trade liberalization would significantly reduce the use of agrochemicals—and hence environmental degradation—in protectionist countries and increase it marginally in low protection countries resulting in overall gains in environmental protection and sustainability. If, however, there are market failures (such as unpriced or underpriced resources or unaccounted for externalities), or policy failures (such as environmentally harmful subsidies) that are not removed, resources are misallocated to start with and removal of barriers to trade may exacerbate this misallocation. Under such conditions, freer trade would not maximize social welfare. There would still be efficiency gains (positive effects) but there would also be welfare losses, as wasteful resource depletion and environmental degradation are exacerbated (negative effects). The net effect on social welfare would depend on the relative magnitude of the positive and negative effects.

There are few studies attempting to estimate and compare the efficiency gains from trade liberalization with the costs of increased environmental degradation or needed additional environmental protection measures. Repetto (1993) attempted such a comparison and concluded that there is no *a priori* case for giving trade policy a priority over environmental policy. Efficiency gains from trade liberalization were estimated to range from 1-2% of GDP to 3-4% for economies with severe economic distortions. Environmental control costs and residual environmental damage costs, on the other hand, range from 1-2% of GDP to 3-5% of GDP in countries with lax environmental policies.

To better understand how globalization-induced free trade impacts the environment, it is necessary to examine the channels through which such impacts are transmitted. There are six such channels: (a) scale of economic activity; (b) income growth; (c) changes in structure of economic activity; (d) product composition; (e) technology diffusion; and (f) trade-induced regulations. (See Box 1 below for a summary of these effects.)

Box 1. Trade-related Environmental Effects

Scale effects — either negative effects, when increased trade leads to more pollution without compensating product, technology or policy developments, or positive effects, when increased trade induces better environmental protection through economic growth and policy development that stimulates product composition and technology shifts that cause less pollution per unit of output.

Structural effects — changes in the patterns of economic activity or microeconomic production, consumption, investment, or geographic effects from increased trade that either exert positive environmental effects (e.g., reducing production of crops that rely on chemical intensive methods, in favor of more extensive agriculture), or cause negative consequences (e.g., encouraging the drainage of wetlands to satisfy new trade demands).

Income effects — positive effects, including increased willingness to pay with increased personal incomes brought about by growth-induced trade; also increased budgetary resources allocated to environmental protection both in absolute and relative terms.

Product effects — either positive effects, from increased trade in goods that are environmentally-beneficial, e.g., biodegradable containers, or negative effects, from more trade in environmentally-damaging products, e.g., hazardous wastes.

Technology effects — either positive effects from reducing pollution per unit of product, e.g., precision farming that reduces excess fertilizer use, or negative effects from the spread of "dirty" technologies, e.g., highly toxic and persistent pesticides, through trade channels.

Regulatory effects — either through improved environmental policies, in response to economic growth from enhanced trade or through measures included in the trade agreement, or the relaxation of existing environmental policies, because of specific trade pressures or restrictions on environmental policy by trade agreements.

Source: OECD (1994) for 1 - 2 and 4 - 6; author for 3.

Scale effects

To the extent that trade liberalization stimulates economic growth, both the scale of economic activity and incomes increase. A larger volume of economic activity would certainly raise the aggregate level of natural resource use and environmental pollution, unless improved resource efficiency and structural change reduce resource use and pollution intensity per unit of output more than proportionally. For a given structure and level of resource-use efficiency, the scale effects on the environment of trade liberalization are unambiguously negative. Negative scale effects are more pronounced where there are market failures such as ill-defined property rights, unpriced ecosystems, uninternalized externalities and underprovided public goods. Policy failures such as energy subsidies or forced industrialization further exacerbate the scale effects of trade liberalization.

Income effects

The gains from trade and trade-induced economic growth result in substantial income increases, which impact the environment in a variety of ways. First, higher incomes result in both higher levels of consumption and associated environmental externalities, and in higher willingness to pay for environmental improvement, and associated increases in both private and public environmental expenditures. There is considerable empirical evidence that environmental quality is income-elastic, in the sense that increases in income result in more than proportionate increases in environmental expenditures. Second, economic growth makes more resources available for environmental protection, and raises environmental quality in a country's list of priorities, prompting governments to increase environmental expenditures both in absolute terms and as a percentage of GDP. This is true of virtually all the newly industrializing countries (from China and South Korea to Mexico and Brazil). The reverse is also true, when income growth slows down (as after the recent Asian financial crisis), environmental expenditures tend to fall more than proportionally.

Third, to the extent that trade and growth benefits are widely distributed, trade liberalization may help reduce the pressures placed by poverty on the environment through the encroachment of natural resources. If, on the other hand, poor people (either rural or urban) are further marginalized by global competition without access to technology, capital and other means to compete, encroachment and degradation of natural resources (forest, pastures, fisheries, public lands) are likely to intensify. Trade liberalization may actually reinforce the vicious circle between poverty and environmental degradation, especially when open access resources, heretofore poor people's last resort source of livelihood, are now being exploited for exports. Ironically, economic collapse may not reduce the pressure on natural resources, if impoverished urban dwellers return to the rural areas reclaiming their traditional sources of livelihood as indeed happened in Thailand and Indonesia following the recent financial crisis. Finally, economic growth may result in reform of environmental policies and enactment of new laws and regulations and new institutions to enforce them.

Studies of the relationship between income levels and environmental degradation, not controlling for scale and structural change effects, found an inverted U-shape relationship, especially for localized effects. (Grossman and Krueger 1995; Panayotou 1997a). At low income levels (early stages of development), income growth is associated with higher levels of environmental degradation until a turning point is reached (between US$5,000-10,000), beyond which further income increases result in environmental improvement. This finding, which came to be known as the Environmental Kuznets Curve, tends to suggest that environmental degradation is a "growing up" problem to be overcome through rapid economic growth rather than through targeted environmental policies. To the extent that free trade speeds up economic growth and raises per capita incomes, any restrictions on trade or diversions of resources away from export-led growth slow down the transition to a positive income-environment relationship.

This is clearly a misinterpretation of an empirical relationship that is devoid of policy significance in its reduced form. First, it ignores the role of market and policy failures in determining the level of environmental damage cost per additional unit of GDP, and the scope for policy reform to reduce it. Second, it ignores threshold effects and the risk of irreversible environmental damages were environmental degradation to cross such thresholds before reaching the turning point. Third, current income levels of developing countries are nowhere close to the turning point, hence environment-intensive production would continue for a long time, resulting in significant and possibly irreversible environmental damage.

Policy formulation calls for a more analytical and disaggregated approach to the income-environment relationship. One such attempt (Panayotou 1997a) decomposed the income-environment relationship into 1) a scale effect, which was found to be unambiguously negative; 2) a pure income effect, which was found to be unambiguously positive; and 3) a composition or structural change effect, which was found to be negative at earlier stages of development (shift from agriculture into industry) and positive at later stages of development (shift from industry to services). The speed of income growth was also found to matter, resulting in somewhat higher levels of environmental degradation per unit of GDP. However, it was also found that effective policy intervention is a potent means to reducing the environmental cost of growth at all stages of economic development. Thus, while some deterioration of environmental quality is inevitable along a country's development path up to the turning point, policy interventions to remove distortions and mitigate market failures can reduce the environmental cost of growth, and hence of trade, and keep it at reversible levels below critical ecological thresholds.

Structural or Composition Effects

Globalization in general and freer trade in particular result in a shift in industrial structure more in line with a country's comparative advantage. In the absence of market and policy failures, the composition of output under free trade would be better suited to a country's environmental resource endowment than under austerity. Controlling for scale effects and for stage of development, trade liberalization tends to make the structure of the economy less pollution-intensive. It speeds up the transition from resource extraction and processing to light manufacturing and eventually, services. Since most developing countries are more richly endowed in low-cost labor than any other factor of production, trade liberalization tends to shift labor-intensive activities to developing countries. Indeed, Lucas, Wheeler and Hettige (1992) found that toxic intensity increased more rapidly in inward-looking developing countries, while outward-oriented, high-growth developing countries had a slowly increasing or declining toxic intensity of manufacturing. They found that highly protected economies had experienced rapid growth in capital-intensive smokestack sectors, while more open economies had experienced high growth in less pollution-intensive, more labor-intensive activities.

Developing countries may also have significant national resource endowments and income-constrained demand for environmental quality. The extent to which trade liberalization would contribute to sustainable development, under these conditions, depends critically on whether environmental assets are properly valued, and whether these values have somehow been taken into account by world markets. Otherwise, trade liberalization may result in structural shifts towards increased specialization in unsustainable activities. A recent study by Strutt and Anderson (1998), however, found that, even under a business-as-usual scenario (i.e., no change in resource pricing or environmental regulation), implementation of the Uruguay Round trade reforms would have a positive impact on natural resource conservation in developing countries and most other regimes of the world, except for Western Europe where resource policies are well developed and can cope with any increase in resource exploitation (see Table 1).

Product and Technology Effects

Liberalized trade facilitates the diffusion of products, technologies and processes across borders. The environmental impacts of this diffusion depend on the characteristics of the products and technologies that are being diffused. The trade in products that are patently harmful to the environment—such as toxic chemicals, hazardous waste, endangered species and disease-bearing pests—is strictly regulated or prohibited by international conventions. A very important channel through which globalization impacts the environment is the trade in environmentally preferred "producer" and "consumer" goods. The global market for environmental goods and services is around $300 billion annually and is expected to grow rapidly (OECD 1996). Trade liberalization expands the potential market for both more efficient capital equipment and "cleaner" production technologies on the production side, and "greener" products, such as organic foods, low-emission vehicles and recyclables, on the consumption side.

While other dimensions of globalization— such as investment, intellectual property rights and economic integration—have technology implications impacting the environment, three-quarters of all technology transfers arise from trade flows (OECD 1995), especially the trade in machinery and equipment, which amounts to almost 40% of total global trade (UN 1996). These trade flows result in diffusion of more efficient (and, one hopes, cleaner) technologies: almost 80% of the global trade in machinery and equipment comes from developed countries, and about a third is imported by developing countries (UN 1996). Technology diffusion also takes place through the trade in services such as engineering and consulting services and technology licensing.

Table 1. Percentage changes in resource-sector output levels in various regions of the world following Uruguay Round trade reform (including China), 2010

	Indonesia	Other APEC developing economies	Other developing & transition economies	APEC high-income economies	Other high-income economies (W. Europe)	Total World
Paddy rice	-0.3	2.9	-1.3	-1.0	-3.1	0.48
Non-grain crops	-4.6	4.3	-0.4	2.0	-2.9	0.59
Livestock	0.1	-1.4	-1.6	0.9	1.2	-0.06
Forestry	-1.1	-0.7	-0.1	-0.0	1.9	-0.03
Fisheries	-0.7	-7.4	0.1	-0.4	5.1	-0.21
Coal	-7.1	-0.6	0.2	-0.3	1.0	-0.03
Oil	-3.3	-2.9	0.2	0.1	0.4	-0.04
Gas	-3.4	-1.4	0.1	0.5	0.1	0.06
Other minerals	-5.2	-5.0	-1.4	-1.4	1.9	-0.39

Source: Strutt and Anderson (1998).

Liberalized trade contributes not only to technology diffusion and transfer but also to technological progress through economies of scale, enhanced incentives to innovate, and less duplication of research and development efforts due to fewer protectionist barriers (Grossman and Helpman 1995).

Does the trade-induced generation and diffusion of technology benefit or harm the environment? The technology-environment relationship is a complex one, consisting of both demand and supply factors and policy effects. On the demand side, pressures by regulators, customers, shareholders and the community drive firms to demand technology with environmental characteristics, such as "cleaner" production technology and pollution-abatement equipment. While regulatory and community pressures usually aim at process characteristics, customer pressure is directed towards product characteristics. Studies of firm behavior in developed countries tend to find regulatory pressure as the most potent driver of environmentally preferred technologies (e.g., Henriques and Sadorsky 1996) while studies of firm behavior in developing countries tend to find community pressures as the most important determinant of firms' environmental behavior (Pargal and Wheeler 1995; Panayotou *et. al.* 1997). On the supply side, environment-related technological change is driven by abatement costs and the ability of innovating firms to benefit from environmental damage mitigation (which in turn depends on the regulatory regime) and to appropriate the benefits from innovation with wider applications (which in turn depends on the intellectual property right regime). According to Johnstone (1997), in addition to these factors the level of industrial research and development is likely to be an important factor in the supply of environment-relevant technological innovations. Indeed, Nentjes and Wiersma (1987) found that the most active industries in environment-related research and development (R&D) were the chemicals, petroleum, and machinery and vehicles industries.

Finally, environmental policy plays a key role in technological innovation. Clarity, predictability and stability of environmental policy are critical for the necessary investments to take place. Equally important is the flexibility of policy instruments to allow firms to seek the least-cost methods of compliance, to take advantage of cost differentials in pollution abatement, and to benefit from continuous innovation. In this regard, market-based instruments such as pollution taxes and tradable permits have significant advantage over command and control regulations. The case has also been made (Johnstone 1997) for a mixed system of pollution taxes (to internalize the negative environmental externality of pollution) *and* technological innovation subsidies (to encourage the positive technological innovation externality).

Regulatory effects

The regulatory effects of trade liberalization on the environment arise from (a) improved environmental policies, standards and enforcement in response to economic growth from enhanced trade; (b) environmental measures included in trade agreements; and (c) relaxation of existing environmental policies due to specific trade pressures or restrictions on environmental policies by trade agreements.

With regard to the first effect above, World Bank research based on data from 145 countries has found a positive association between economic growth and environmental regulation and security of property rights. With regard to the second effect, the North American Free Trade Agreement (NAFTA) demonstrates how trade liberalization can serve as a catalyst for improvements in both the level and the enforcement of environmental regulations. Trade agreements in general may promote harmonization of environmental standards and influence policies towards environmental subsidies and environment-related fiscal and trade measures. While the multilateral trading system encourages the use of international standards, and allows for higher levels of environmental protection, there is a widespread fear that trade liberalization and the resulting drive for competitiveness would "drag down" environmental standards in a race towards the bottom. There is no evidence that this has happened thus far.

Empirical evidence

There are many analytical studies of the effects of trade liberalization on the environment (e.g., Bhagwati and Srinivasan 1997) but few empirical studies. A recent study (Sprenger 1997) of the countries of the Organization for Economic Cooperation and Development (OECD) has simply indicated the likely direction of the various impacts. The scale of economic activity has, as one would expect, unambiguously detrimental effects on the environment, while technology and income have beneficial effects (see Table 2). Since these effects are in opposite directions and the remaining impacts (structural and product effects) are ambiguous, it is not possible to determine the net effect of trade on the environment in the absence of quantitative assessment of these impacts.

One attempt to quantify the effects of trade liberalization on the environment is a recent study by Strutt and Anderson (1998) on Indonesia. Using a modified version of the global general equilibrium model (GGE) known as GTAP, they project the world economy to 2010 and 2020 with and without trade reforms. The effects of trade liberalization on the Indonesian environment (air and water pollution) are traced through a special environmental module attached to the Indonesian part of the GTAP. They then identify the effects on key air and water quality indicators of changes in the level and consumption of output and in production technology arising from (a) full global implementation of Uruguay Round commitments by 2010 and (b) an additional move to a free trade zone among APEC countries by 2020. Without the trade reforms, the aggregate activity (scale) effects of economic growth on pollution are, as expected, positive and the technology effect negative; the intersectoral composition (or structural effects) are mixed but mostly positive (see Table 3). The scale effects dominate. The implementation of the Uruguay Round trade reforms results in intersectoral composition (structural change) effects that dominate the scale effect. These structural effects further result in reduction of pollution levels except for suspended solids (see Table 4). The authors conclude that, for Indonesia, trade policy reforms slated for the next two decades in many cases would improve the environment (at least with respect to air and water pollution) and reduce the depletion of natural resources, and in the worst cases add only slightly to environmental degradation and resource depletion even without toughening the enforcement of environmental regulations or adding new ones. The economic gains from the trade reforms and the scope for adopting well-targeted environmental and resource policies to reduce any serious damage are such that social welfare almost certainly is going to be improved substantially by these liberalizations. (Strutt and Anderson 1998, 13-14)

Table 2. "Most likely" impacts of trade liberalization on employment and environment in OECD (home) countries

Globalization-related activity	*Anticipated economic effects*	*Anticipated employment effects*	*Anticipated pollution/resource use effects . . .*	
			... at home	*. . . on transboundary transport*
International Trade				
• Scale effects	Change in the volume of exports and imports; increase in cross-border transport	(+,-)	(+)	(+)
• Structural effects	Change in the composition of exports and imports; increase in cross-border transport	(+,-)	(+,-)	(+,-)
• Product effects	Change in the composition of exports and imports; increase in cross-border transport	(+,-)	(+,-)	(+,-)
• Technology effects	Change in the composition of exports and imports; increase in cross-border transport	(+,-)	(-)	(-)

Source: Sprenger (1997).

Table 3. Decomposition of Changes in pollution as a consequence of economic growth and structural changes, Indonesia, 1992-2010 and 2010-2020

(a) 1992-2010	Total pollution change[a]		Aggregate activity effect	Intersectoral composition effect	Technology effect
Carbon (kt)	65,346	[134]	104,607	10,149	-49,409
Sulphur (kt)	799	[132]	1,302	214	-716
Nitrogen (kt)	7,427	[162]	1,897	392	-862
Water in (bm^3)[b]	-12	[-4]	685	-388	-309
Water out (bm^3)[b]	0.8	[126]	1.3	0.7	-1
BOD (kt)	81	[52]	337	176	-433
COD (kt)	341	[64]	1,149	726	-1,534
DS (kt)	-17	[-46]	79	-47	-48
SS (kt)	105	[23]	1,002	638	-1,532
(b) 2010-2020	Total pollution change[b]		Aggregate activity	Intersectoral composition	Technology effect
Carbon (kt)	63,982	[56]	107,244	16,904	-60,166
Sulphur (kt)	707	[50]	1,323	276	-893
Nitrogen (kt)	1,495	[65]	2,165	366	-1,035
Water in (bm^3)[b]	-109	[-36]	296	-167	-236
Water out (bm^3)[b]	0.4	[29]	1.3	1.0	-2
BOD (kt)	-13	[-5]	223	146	-382
COD (kt)	2	[-0]	822	587	-1,412
DS (kt)	-13	[-65]	19	-12	-19.5
SS (kt)	-211	[-37]	545	474	-1,231

[a] *Percentage changes from base case are shown in square parentheses.*
[b] *This does not include the change in household water use.*
Note: kt = kilotons; bm^3 = billions of cubic meters; BOD = biological oxygen demand; COD = chemical oxygen demand; DS = dissolved solids; SS = suspended solids

Source: Strutt and Anderson (1998).

Table 4. Decomposition of pollution effects from Uruguay Round trade reform (including in China), Indonesia, 2010

	Total change	Aggregate activity	Intersectoral composition
Carbon (kt)	-733 (-0.6) [-1.1]	1,585 (1.4) [2.4]	-2,318 (-2.0) [-3.5]
Sulphur (kt)	-8 (-0.6) [-1.0]	20 (1.4) [2.4]	-27 (-1.9) [-3.4]
Nitrogen (kt)	-22 (-1.0) [1.5]	32 (1.4) [2.2]	-54 (-2.3) [3.8]
Water in (bm^3)[b]	-0.8 (-0.3) [-7]	4 (1.4) [35]	5- (1.6) [-42]
Water out (bm^3)[b]	0.01 (0.6) [1.1]	0.02 (1.4) [2.4]	-0.01 (-0.8) [-1.3]
BOD (kt)	-2.0 (-0.9) [-2.5]	3 (1.4) [4.1]	-5 (-2.3) [-6.6]
COD (kt)	-6.5 (-0.7) [-1.9]	12 (1.4) [3.6]	-19 (-2.1) [-5.5]
DS (kt)	-0.5 (-0.3) [-0.3]	0.3 (1.4) [1.6]	-0.3 (-1.7) [-2.0]
SS (kt)	5.3 (0.9) [5.0]	8 (1.4) [7.6]	-3 (-0.5) [-2.5]

Note: % change from 2010 baseline level shown in parentheses (); % of the 1992-2010 absolute change shown in brackets [ ].

Source: Strutt and Anderson (1998).

The approach used by Strutt and Anderson—i.e., using a side environmental module rather than a fully integrated emissions-damage-abatement feedback system—has been criticized by Smith and Espinosa (1996). Using a new GGE model for the European Union (EU) incorporating local and transboundary externalities, they illustrate how environmental and trade policies become intertwined. The model is extended to include three air pollutants (particulate matter (PM), nitrogen oxides (NO_x), and sulfur oxides (SOx)) and their health effects on influences on household preferences. They then evaluate the welfare implications of a 50% reciprocal reduction of non-tariff barriers for durables traded between UK and each of its EU trading partners, combined with a 25% increase in emission rates reflecting the entry of marginal plants in response to trade liberalization. When the effects of emissions on morbidity, and of morbidity on labor endowments and threshold demand for services, are ignored, the balance of trade to GDP ratio is positive. When the income and substitution effects of health damages from pollution are considered (including mortality), the welfare implication of the 50% reduction in non-tariff barriers (as measured by the ratio of balance of trade to GDP) turns negative (see Table 5). Ignoring the air-pollution-induced effects on mortality results in a 12 % overstatement of the gains relative to GDP. Thus, when the gains from trade are considered, trade liberalization enhances social welfare. If the accompanying increase in air pollution and its health effects are considered, there may be net welfare loss, depending on the magnitude of increase, the sector affected, and the nature of environmental impacts.

Allowing for the environmental impacts of emissions and their feedback to the economy via revaluation of endowments or changes in rents and substitutions for other marketed goods (i.e., allowing for the full general equilibrium effects to play themselves out), one obtains a larger increase in emissions than otherwise. As shown in section B of Table 5, a 50% reduction in trade barriers results in a more than 30 times greater increase in emission of particulates and an increase rather than a reduction in NOx and SOx. It is also of interest that Germany, a UK trading partner, enjoys smaller welfare gains from trade when the impact of the increased output on emissions and the transboundary effects of emissions from the UK on Germany are considered (see Table 5).

Is there a Case for Trade Measures to Protect the Environment?[1]

As the General Agreement on Tariffs and Trade (GATT) has gone beyond tariffs, quotas and other border instruments to address internal policies and measures such as standards, production subsidies, and intellectual property rights, environmental concerns and policies began to be projected beyond national borders, even when no transboundary or global impacts are involved. Whether the underlying motivation is to counter "unfair trade" practices, to disguise protectionism or to advance a genuine environmental concern, trade contraction, rather than trade expansion has come to be viewed as the way to go. For example, Subramanian (1992, 135) reports that "of the 48 bills on environmental matters introduced in the 101st Congress in the United States, 33 included provisions affecting international trade of which 31 took the form of restrictive trade measures."

Trade measures may take the form of either direct trade interventions or supporting trade provisions. Direct trade interventions usually aim at the environmental externality, e.g., bilateral measures such as the US import ban on dolphin-unsafe Mexican Tuna, and multilateral agreements such as the trade ban on endangered species under the Convention on the International Trade in Endangered Species (CITES) or trade restrictions on the transport of hazardous wastes under the Basel Convention.

Direct trade interventions may also aim at compensating for environment-related loss of competitiveness. One such example is proposed legislation in the United States (the proposed Pollution Deterrence Act of 1991, introduced by Senator Boren and thus known as the "Boren Proposal") for automatic levying of countervailing duties on imports from countries with low environmental standards. Also, GATT's border tax adjustment rules allow the use of trade measures to

---

[1] This section draws heavily on Subramanian (1992).

offset taxes imposed on environmental grounds. Supporting trade provisions are trade measures aiming to assist the enforcement of a related action or provision. For example, Denmark banned the imports of soft drinks bottled in non-reusable containers to enforce a domestic consumption ban. The Montreal Protocol restricts trade of CFC-related products with non-signatories to enforce the production and consumption obligations on the signatories.

Table 5. Welfare implications and environmental effects of trade liberalization (50 % reduction in non-tariff barriers for durables)

	Market effects only (no environmental effects)	Non-market environmental effects and feedbacks added
I. United Kingdom		
A. Welfare change		
1. Balance of Trade/GDP (%) (excluding mortality)	0.198	0.177
2. Balance of Trade/GDP (%) (including mortality)	0.198	-0.166
B. Environmental effects		
% Emission Particulates	0.161	6.693
NOx	-0.111	2.064
SOx	-0.098	2.406
% Health effects		
Morbidity	–	1.647
Mortality	–	6.693
II. Germany		
A. Welfare change		
1. Balance of Trade/GDP (%) (excluding mortality)	0.013	0.012
2. Balance of Trade/GDP (%) (including mortality)	0.013	0.007

Source: Smith and Espinosa 1996.

Trade measures may also be used as rewards and punishments for inducing a change in environmental behavior, participation in an international environmental agreements, or compliance with its provisions. They may take the form of sanctions as in the case of the Pelly Amendment, which authorizes trade measures against unrelated products for failing to observe US tuna fishing methods. Sanctions have also been threatened against countries to force them to raise or lower their standards. For example, the US has threatened the EU with withdrawal of trade concessions to force it to lower its hormone standards on beef products. Finally, trade inducements may take the form of incentives, as in the case of NAFTA, whereby Mexico is provided with increased market access in exchange for raising its environmental standards in general and for reducing transborder pollution in particular.

Are all the above uses of environment-related trade measures (summarized in Table 6) justified or are they inefficient at best and disguised protectionism at worst? Subramanian (1992, 151) analyzed the use of environment-related trade measures and reached the following conclusions. First, with regard to domestic environmental problems, the use of trade measures aims to negate a source of comparative advantage that is legitimately "conferred by differences in environmental endowments, pollution assimilation capacities, or social preferences regarding environmental outcomes." Therefore, the intent of trade measures in relation to domestic environmental problems is largely protectionist.

Second, with regard to transboundary environmental problems, trade measures are inefficient and often inequitable instruments for correcting market failures. Assignment of property rights, creation of markets, and production or consumption interventions are superior to trade interventions. Trade restrictions imply unilateral allocation of property rights, which may be unfair to poor countries and counterproductive for environmental outcomes, if income and environmental quality are positively related.

Third, trade measures nonetheless have a useful role to play in securing participation in and compliance with multilateral environmental agreements. The threatened use of trade sanctions may be sufficient to alter the behavior of would-be free riders. In general, the use of restrictive trade measures for environmental purposes is generally more legitimate when it is multilateral and aims at enlisting participation and compliance for addressing global environmental problems. Appendix Table A.1 lists selected multilateral trade agreements with possible trade effects and trade measures aiming to protect the environment (e.g. CITES) or to secure compliance (e.g. Montreal Protocol).

Environment and Trade

Do environmental regulations act as barriers to trade? Do multilateral trade rules permit restrictions on trade for environmental purposes?

Globalization in general and trade liberalization in particular have accorded international importance to policies previously considered to be purely domestic. Included among such policies are competition policy, intellectual property rights and environmental policy. Furthermore, the reduction of tariff barriers has heightened the relative importance of non-tariff barriers as potential constraints on trade. At the same time, protectionist forces, having lost the use of tariff barriers, are inclined to focus their attention on non-tariff barriers. Environmental concerns, because of their emotive nature, are a prime candidate. This in turn has raised concerns that some environmental measures might be protectionism in disguise. Sorting out legitimate environmental policy from disguised protectionism is not easy. For example, some environmental regulations such a tax on imported large cars or a subsidy for pollution abatement, afford protection to domestic producers and reduce imports.

Multilateral trade rules make a fundamental distinction between (a) products standards and (b) process and production methods (PPMs). The two are treated very differently: national requirements on product standards and product-related PPMs are allowed, but non-product related PPMs are not. We examine these in turn.

Product Standards

Multilateral trade rules permit national requirements for products to meet certain environmental, safety and health standards provided that they are transparent and non-discriminatory between domestic and foreign sources. Taxes and charges for environmental or other resources may be imposed on important products and to exempt exports as an application of the principle of national sovereignty.

Table 6. Interactions Between Trade and Environment

Type of measure	Features	Transborder Examples	Domestic Examples
1. Direct Trade Interventions			
(a) Unilateral	Aimed at directly affecting the substantive problem, either a loss in competitiveness or an environmental externality. Restrictive measure will have penalizing effects (incidental or otherwise) on actions creating the pollution.	(a) US import ban on Mexican tuna. EC's threatened ban on imports of tropical timber and of fur products produced from animals caught in leghold traps.	(a) Countervailing duty against products produced under allegedly "low standards" (e.g., Boren Initiative). Export subsidies for pollution equipment.
(b) Multilateral		(b) Trade ban on ivory and on several other endangered species under CITES. Trade restrictions in Basel Convention on Hazardous Wastes.	(b) Proposals in the Uruguay Round to exempt from countervailing action certain kinds of production subsidies for pollution abatement. Multilaterally sanctioned use of trade measures to offset production taxes imposed on environmental grounds, such as the Superfund Panel Case.
2. Supporting Trade Provisions			
(a) Unilateral	Intended to enforce *other* actions or interventions addressing the substantive problem or externality. By its nature, measure will be in the related area and could have incidental penalizing effects.	(a) Circle of Poison Act, intended to stop exports of harmful pesticides on the grounds that they may be reimported on imported produce. Import ban to enforce domestic consumption ban or domestic standards (e.g., Danish beer bottles case).	

Table 6. Interactions Between Trade and Environment, cont'd

Type of measure	Features	Transborder Examples	Domestic Examples
(b) Multilateral		(b) Trade restrictions against non-signatories of Montreal Protocol. National actions that are sanctioned multilaterally.	
Trade Inducements			
3A. Sanctions:			
(a) Unilateral	Measures intended to change environmental behavior and taken in *unrelated* areas, hence substitutable in principle by equivalent actions, e.g., financial sanctions for trade sanctions and technology transfer for trade incentives. Often sanctions will only be threatened and, if credible and effective, need not be taken.	(a) Pelly Amendment and Packward-Magnuson Amendment to the US Fisherman's Protective Act of 1967, under which imports of fish products in general can be restricted or prohibited. (e.g., recent US action against Japan for policies endangering the sea turtle.)	(a) Use of trade restrictions to *raise* pollution standards abroad. Use of trade restrictions to *lower* standards, e.g., threatened US actions in beef hormone case.
(b) Multilateral		(b) None so far.	
3B. Incentives			
(a) Unilateral			
(b) Multilateral		(b) US-Mexican negotiations under NAFTA for market access in return for reduced transborder pollution.	(b) US-Mexico negotiations under NAFTA for provision of market access in return for higher standards

Source: Subramanian (1992).

Border adjustments are permitted: the consumption of a product that can cause environmental damage may be taxed, provided that the tax is applied in a transparent and non-discriminatory manner. Packaging and recycling requirements are more controversial, as they are part of a domestically focused waste reduction policy that can impose higher costs on importers; as such, these measures act as a non-trade barrier to trade. The trade effects of this policy can be mitigated by giving advanced notice to allow foreign suppliers to adjust.

Given their direct impacts on trade, product standards are prime candidates for harmonization. Two agreements of the WTO system—the Agreement on Technical Barriers to Trade and the Agreement on Application of Sanitary and Phytosanitary Measures—encourage harmonization of product standards and where possible, adherence to international standards.

Process and production methods[2]

How natural resources are extracted and products are produced can have significant environmental impacts, which countries attempt to control through harvesting restrictions, emission controls and specified production techniques. Extending such production-methods- based standards (or taxes and charges) to imported products raises trade issues and conflicts with the principle of national sovereignty: standards adopted by one country attempt to enforce a particular production method (that does not affect the final product) on another country.

If the method of production affects the characteristics of the imported product, then border tax adjustments are allowed under WTO rules, i.e., product-related PPMs are treated in the same way as product standards. Charges or standards on non-product-related PPMs (i.e., on production methods that do not affect the product characteristics) violate the principle that "like products" must be accorded "like treatment," and are prohibited by WTO rules. Border tax adjustments or countervailing duties for non-product-related PPMs are not allowed, i.e., the prices of imported products cannot be adjusted for the extra cost incurred by the domestic industry operating under such requirements.

Thus, differences in domestic environmental policies are seen as part of the many variations that constitute a country's comparative advantage, and do not justify compensating levies or export rebates to offset price differences. Where transboundary and global environmental issues are concerned, harmonization of non-product PPM requirements may be necessary, at least on a consensual basis, as in the context of regional or multilateral agreement. An interesting issue currently under consideration is the potential for using border tax adjustments in combination with domestic process taxes to reduce greenhouse gases (Adams 1997).

In conclusion, unlike "product standards," "methods standards" are not candidates for harmonization; it would be both more difficult to do so and less beneficial. While some convergence is to be expected over time, production methods and solutions to local environmental problems are best tailored to local conditions. Yet the globalization of environmental concerns such as tropical deforestation and biodiversity loss pits the emerging product life-cycle perspective, whereby consumers want to know the overall environmental characteristics of the products they buy, against conventional notions of national sovereignty and of products as their physical characteristics (Adams 1997).

Does environmental policy influence the pattern of trade?

Since differences in environmental policies and standards and their enforcement are translated into production cost differences, it is a legitimate concern that such differences may alter the pattern of trade. There is substantial evidence, however, that differences in environmental standards and environmental control costs have had very limited effect on trade patterns. The main reason is that

---

[2] This section is based on Adams (1997).

environmental control costs are a very small fraction of production costs. Any comparative advantage created by lax environmental standards is overwhelmed by other sources of comparative advantage such as differences in resource endowments, technologies, human and physical capital, infrastructure and the macroeconomic policy environment. For example, Walter (1973) found that environmental control costs (ECC) amounted, on average, to 1.75% of the total value of US exports and 1.52% of US imports. Robison (1988) estimated the average ECC as a share of total exports as 0.37% in 1973 and 0.72% in 1982 and found that a doubling in ECC has negligible impacts on output and trade: the trade balance is reduced by only 0.67%. Low (1992) has found that the traditionally lenient environmental standards in Mexico did not result in specialization in dirty industries. Grossman and Krueger (1993) found that pollution abatement costs in the US have not affected US imports from Mexico. If this is the case with Mexico and the US, which share a long common border, have a large volume of trade, and have substantially different environmental standards, it is unlikely that environmental regulations have a significant impact on net exports in other cases.

Another test of the relationship between environmental regulations and competitiveness is whether an increasing share of trade in pollution-intensive products comes from developing countries, which on the whole have less stringent environmental laws (or more lax enforcement). While the share in world trade of pollution-intensive products from North America fell from 21% to 14%, and that of Southeast Asia rose from 3% to 8%, between 1965 and 1988 (Low and Yeats 1992), these trends are more indicative of increased demand for pollution-intensive products in newly industrializing countries than of any shift of pollution-intensive production to developing countries.

Capital flows, foreign investment and environment

Capital flows in general, and direct foreign investment in particular, are major channels through which globalization impacts the environment. Foreign investment is a major vehicle of economic integration, technology diffusion and trade expansion. Globally, capital flows are larger than trade flows. Nearly US$20 billion per day or US$7 billion per year cross national borders. Private capital flows to developing countries in 1996 were six times the value of official development assistance (ODA), accounting for 86% of the total capital flows to these countries (World Bank 1997). Unlike ODA, which has been steadily falling, private capital flows have been rising steadily right up to the recent financial crisis. Private capital flows are driven by the opportunity to earn a commercial return. These opportunities have increased considerably in the past decade, as an increasing number of countries have assumed a greater market orientation, begun to privatize state enterprises and welcomed foreign investment.

However, private capital flows, which are motivated by market opportunities rather than capital needs or development priorities, tend to be concentrated in a dozen or so emerging economies. Poor countries with high risk, undeveloped institutions and poor infrastructure are seldom the recipients of large amounts of private capital. Moreover, private capital flows are not usually guided by sustainability considerations, and indeed are very volatile and sensitive to changing market conditions. There is little information available about their environmental and social impacts.

Of the nearly US$280 billion of private capital flows to developing countries, 45% were accounted for by foreign direct investment, 33% by debt finance and 19% by portfolio equity investments. Foreign direct investment (FDI) goes mostly into manufacturing plants, mining development, power stations, telecommunications, port development, airport and road construction, water supply, and sanitation, all of which have environmental and natural resource use implications. As such, FDI has the most direct and pronounced links to and effects on the environment and sustainable development. It is also a primary vehicle of technology transfer. Portfolio equity investments have only indirect links to the environment through their effect on the value of companies that they are directed to. If they build up the value of companies with high environmental performance, they have positive impacts; if instead, they increase pressure for short-term profitability, they create disincentives for environmental performance. Debt financing or commercial lending to private companies gives the lender a stake in the borrower's financial performance, which may be affected by environmental risks. This is not usually the case with investors in government bonds since the governments' solvency is usually unrelated to its environmental performance (Gentry et. al. 1996).

Private capital flows are highly concentrated (see Table 7). Developing countries received only about a quarter of global FDI and portfolio flows. Within the developing world, 12 countries in Asia, Latin America and Eastern Europe received 80% of the total flows to developing countries; sub-Saharan Africa, arguably the region with the greatest need for capital infusion, received only 2% of these flows. At the other extreme, China receives more than half of all FDI directed to Asia, and a third of total global capital flows to developing countries.

Table 7. Leading host economies for FDI, 1985-1995 (based on cumulative inflows)

Rank	Country	FDI billion $
1	United States	477.5
2	United Kingdom	199.6
3	France	138.0
4	China	130.2
5	Spain	90.9
6	Belgium-Luxembourg	72.4
7	Netherlands	68.1
8	Australia	62.6
9	Canada	60.9
10	Mexico	44.1
11	Singapore	40.8
12	Sweden	37.7
13	Italy	36.3
14	Malaysia	30.7
15	Germany	25.9
16	Switzerland	25.2
17	Argentina	23.5
18	Brazil	20.3
19	Hong Kong	17.9
20	Denmark	15.7

Source: As cited in WTO (1996).

What does the rapid growth of private flows mean for sustainable development? First, private capital flows are not a substitute for ODA, since poor countries that need them most attract the least. Moreover, private investment is not automatically channeled to sustainable development activities. To the contrary, the social and environmental areas traditionally have been among the activities least attractive to foreign investors, partly because of government regulations that limited foreign (and even domestic) private sector involvement. Moreover, without enforcement of environmental regulations and freedom to charge user fees or raise tariffs to cover costs (including an acceptable reform to capital), these sectors are not attractive to private capital.

However, during the past five to seven years, a number of positive changes, such as deregulation, privatization, and financial innovation, have increased the availability and attractiveness of these sectors to both domestic and foreign private capital. The development of innovative financing strategies, such as build-own-transfer (BOT), build-own-operate (BOO), and build-own-lease (BOL), have made it possible for the private sector to enter into infrastructure development. The increased use of competitive bidding, coupled with environmental performance bonds or bank guarantees, has improved the efficiency and environmental performance of FDI, and hence its contributions to sustainable development. The past five years have witnessed a strong trend toward privatization of state-owned enterprises and public utilities and concessions to private developers of infrastructure inducing power generation, transportation, water supply and sanitation, and waste treatment, among others. The privatization of electric utilities in Argentina and concessions to private developers for public transport and waste management in Thailand and for water and sanitation in the Philippines are cases in point. Indeed, there is a clear trend in the 1990s of FDI shifting from resource extractive industries to environmental services, which are generally more environmentally benign.

The net effect of FDI and portfolio investment on the environment and sustainable development is difficult to determine in the absence of data and quantitative models. On the one hand, FDI provides risk capital, which contributes to economic growth, employment (see Table 9) and poverty alleviation. It also creates positive externalities in terms of increased competition, improved management skills, and access to greener markets and cleaner technologies.

On the other hand, fears have been expressed that foreign direct investment gravitates toward countries with lower environmental standards or lax enforcement (the "pollution haven" hypothesis). Alternatively, capital mobility results in lower environmental standards as governments compete with each other to attract scarce investment by lowering environmental standards below efficient levels (the "race to the bottom" hypothesis).

On theoretical grounds, Bhagwati and Srinivasan (1997) argued that capital mobility does not lead to a "race for the bottom" if the economy is competitive and distortion-free and there are no constraints on the use of tax instruments. Capital mobility does not enter a government's benefit-cost analysis calculus in choosing environmental standards if the first-best instrument of a tax or user fee is available and can be set equal to the cost that a firm's operations impose on the country. This cost includes the cost of providing public goods and services to the firm as well as the use of the environment for waste disposal (environmental cost). Weaker environmental standards may attract additional (foreign) investment but this will neither benefit nor harm the country since firms subject to an optimal (Pigovian) tax fully and efficiently compensate the country for any environmental cost associated with their investment (Bhagwati and Srinivasan 1997). But of course, economies are neither fully competitive nor undistorted. The authors show that even monopoly power in capital and product markets does not destroy this benchmark efficiency: as long as the government can use tax instruments to exploit its market power, it is free to set its environmental policy efficiently. It is only when governments fail to tax capital efficiently that environmental policy becomes distorted; if governments overtax capital, they may have an incentive to lower environmental standards to attract capital.

Is there evidence that lax environmental standards actually attract more foreign investment? Repeated tests of the "pollution haven" hypothesis failed to find evidence of a systematic tendency of manufacturing plants to be located in countries with lax environmental standards. In choosing how much to invest and where, firms take into account many factors in addition to environmental regulations, such as size of the local market, the quality of the labor force, the available infrastructure, ability to repatriate profits, political stability, and the risk of expropriation. In this context, evidence indicates that the stringency or laxity of environmental regulations is insignificant as a determinant of location decisions. Indeed, Wheeler and Mody (1992) found that multinational firms base their investment decisions primarily on labor costs and market access, while corporate tax rates and, by extension, environmental control costs play little or no role. In a 1997 World Economic Forum survey, 3,000 business executives from 53 countries were asked to rank environmental regulations and 26 non-environmental factors —ranging from government tax and investment policies to the quality of the workforce and infrastructure—according to their role in their investment location decisions. The stringency of environmental regulations ranked 22nd. Figure 2 slows the importance attached to environmental regulations compared to 11 of the non-environmental factions. (A complete list of factors affecting industrial locations is given in Figure 3.) Thus executives who actually make investment location decisions report that environmental regulations do not figure significantly in those decisions. Similar results have been obtained by many surveys of the importance of environmental regulation in plant location decisions in the United States (see Table 8).

Table 8: Surveys of the Importance of Environmental Regulations to Plant Location in the United States

Survey	Sample	Result
Epping (1986)	Survey of manufacturers (late 1970s) that located facilities 1958-1977	"Favorable pollution laws" ranked 43rd to 47th, out of 54 location factors presented.
Fortune (1977)	*Fortune*'s 1977 survey of 1,000 largest U.S. corporations	11% ranked state or local environmental regulations among top 5 factors
Schmenner (1982)	Sample of Dun & Backstreet data for new *Fortune* 500 branch plants opening 1972-1978	Environmental concerns not among the top 6 items mentioned
Wintner (1982)	Conference Board survey of 68 urban manufacturing firms	29 (43%) mentioned environmental and pollution control regulations as a factor in location choice
Stafford (1985)	Interviews and questionnaire responses of 162 branch plants built in the late 1970s and early 1980s	"Environmental regulations are not a major factor," but more important than in 1970. When only self-described "less clean" plants were examined, environmental regulations were "of mid-level importance."
Alexander Grant (various years)	Surveys of industry associations	Environmental compliance costs given an average weight of below 4%, though growing slightly over time.
Lyne (1990)	*Site Selection* magazine's 1990 survey of corporate real estate executives	Asked to pick 3 of 12 factors affecting location choice, 42% of executives selected "state clean air legislation."

Source: Levinson (1997).

The results of these surveys are corroborated by *ex post* analysis of foreign direct investment in pollution-intensive industry. If environmental regulations affect FDI location decisions, we would expect foreign direct investment in pollution-intensive sectors to account for a larger share of foreign direct investment *from* countries with stringent environmental regulations today than it did in the 1960s or 1970s. Repetto (1995) showed that the reverse is true. He concluded that, to the extent that "greener" countries seem to be exporting their "dirty" industries, they are predominantly sending them to each other, not to developing countries with weaker regulations. In 1995, only 5% of US direct investment in developing countries was in pollution-intensive sectors, compared to 24% in developed countries with equally stringent (compared to the US) environmental regulations.

Figure 2: Comparative Impact on Industrial Location Decisions

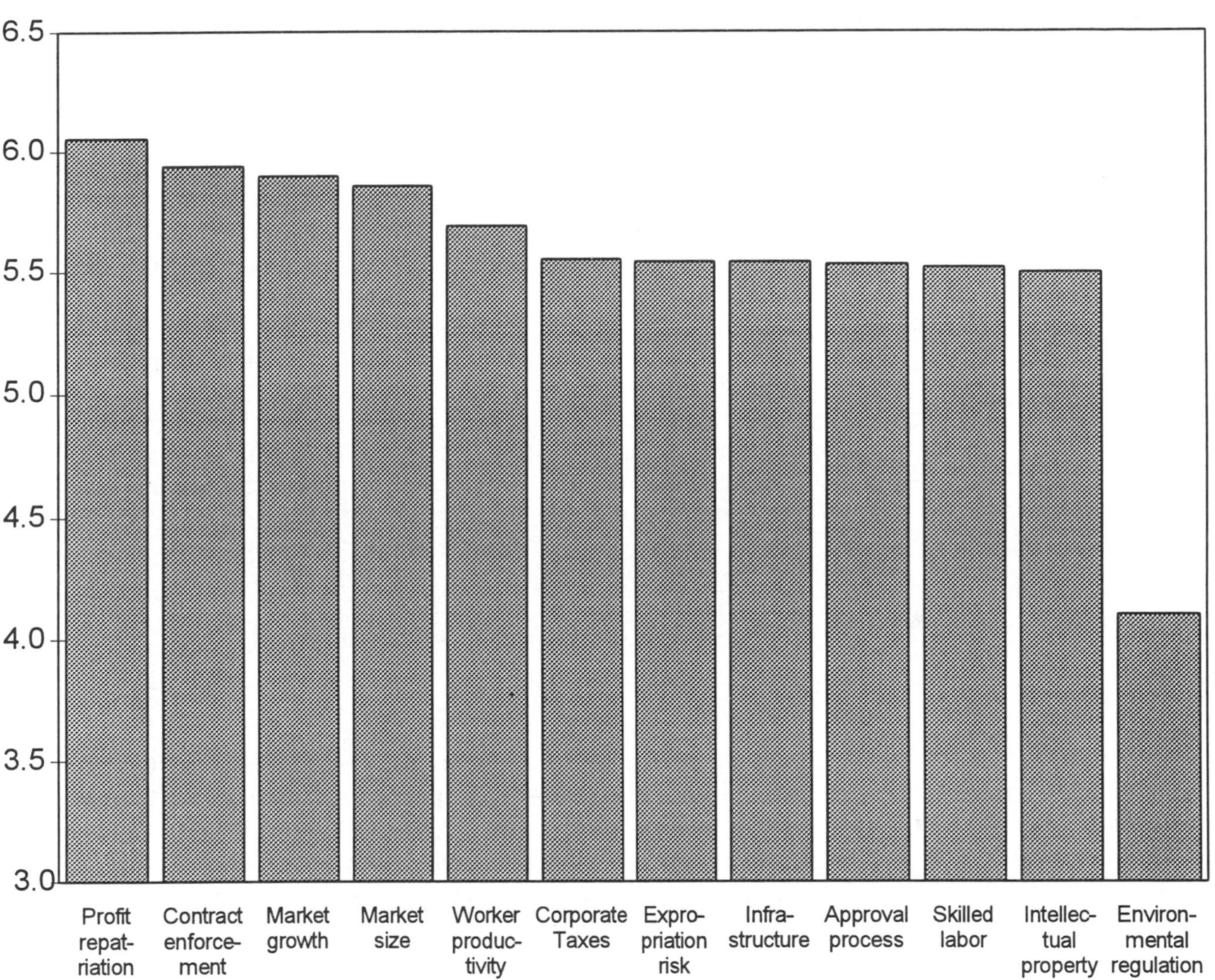

Note: Y-axis is "Rating in Terms of Significance" (1 = unimportant to 7 = very important.)

Source: Executive Survey, World Economic Forum (1997) in Panayotou and Vincent (1997).

Figure 3: Industrial Location Factors
Decision factors for industrial location

Market-related factors	Production-and-cost-related factors	"Soft" location factors
• Proximity to market • Preservation and/or expansion of market share • Import restrictions and other trade barriers • Developing of new market • Avoiding foreign exchange risk	• Securing stable supply of raw materials and natural resources • Social security contributions • Skills of foreign labor force • Business-related infrastructure • Corporate taxes • Energy costs • Transport costs • State Aids • Obtaining technological know-how • Environmental stringency	• Political stability • General social conditions • Unionization • Risk of strikes • Public acceptance of new technologies • Quality of living conditions • Environmental quality • Infrastructure for leisure activities

Source: Sprenger (1997).

To the contrary, there is a growing evidence that foreign-owned firms or joint ventures tend to be cleaner than local firms (in general and state-owned enterprises in particular) for at least five reasons:

(a) the usually higher environmental standards of the developed countries are embedded in the technology of the overseas subsidiary (it is too costly to design different production processes for each location and regulatory regime);
(b) they export to environmentally sensitive markets;
(c) a degree of control is exercised by parent firms that do not want their image to be tarnished by environmentally irresponsible overseas operations;
(d) in case of environmental accidents, they may still be subject to liability claims; and
(e) pollution-intensive industries happened to be among the least footloose industries.

Furthermore, foreign investors exhibit a strong preference for a stable and predictable policy environment, which requires clear, transparent and consistently enforced environmental regulations approaching international standards. Having invested in the cleaner technology of the advanced countries, multinational firms have an incentive to lobby for higher environmental standards to raise the costs of their domestic rivals. Thus, the cleaner technology of the multinational firms constitutes another argument for the liberalization of capital controls and encouragement of capital flow.

Despite the likely positive influence of FDI on a country's environmental policy, the environmental performance of FDI cannot be taken for granted; it should be continuously monitored, as should that of domestic firms. FDI that is made in the absence of effective environmental policy, like any other type of investment, can result in environmental degradation, especially if the FDI flows are so large as to overwhelm the regulatory capacity of usually weak environmental authorities. As seen in Table 9, FDI inflows are "most likely" to add to pollution and resource use even as they increase employment (and hence curtail resource encroachment) and reduce pollution arising from transboundary transport.

In conclusion, the overall net effects of a foreign direct investment on the environment and sustainability of host countries could be positive or negative. On the one hand, FDI generates employment, growth and wealth that makes larger investments in environmental protection possible, and it may even reduce pollution per unit of output through cleaner technology. On the other hand, it leads to increased industrial production and hence increased aggregate pollution levels (scale effect) as well as increased consumption of pollution goods such as electricity, fossil fuels for automobiles, etc.

Table 9. "Most Likely" Impacts of Foreign Direct Investment on Employment and Environment in OECD (home) countries

Globalization-related activity	**Anticipated economic effects**	**Anticipated *employment* effects**	**Anticipated pollution/ resource use effects . . .**	
			. . . at hom e	**. . . on transboundary transport**
FDI outflows				
• Plant closure/relocation	Reduction in local output; increase in imports of final products; increase in cross-border transport	(-)	(-)	(+)
• Export substitution	Reduction or change in the composition of output for export	(-)	(-)	(+)
• Re-imports	Reduction in output; increase in imports of final products; increase in cross-border transport	(-)	(-)	(+)
• Complementary exports	Increase in output of intermediate goods or capital goods; increase in cross-border transport	(+)	(+)	(+)
• Increased competitiveness	Increase/no change in output; increase in cross-border transport	(+,-)	(+,-)	(+,-)
FDI inflows				
• Mergers or acquisitions	Shift in output; reduction in imports and cross-border transport	(+,-)	(+,-)	(-)
• Greenfield investment	Increase in output; reductions in imports and cross-border transport	(+)	(+)	(-)
• Import substitution	Increase in output; reductions in imports and cross-border transport	(+)	(+)	(-)
• Substitution of domestic production	Shift in output	(0)	(+,-)	(+,-)
• Change in competitiveness	Increase/no change in output for export; increase/no change in cross-border transport	(+,0)	(+,0)	(+,0)

Source: Sprenger (1997).

Since developing countries need both more investment and more improvements of their environmental performance, it behooves them to design a clear, transparent, stable and consistently applied environmental regulatory system. Such a system can serve as an attraction for foreign investors, who want to be able to predict their costs and returns and to be assured that these costs are stable and common to all competitors.

In recognition of the growing importance of foreign direct investment, OECD has attempted to negotiate a multilateral agreement on investment (MAI) among its members and non-members willing and able to meet is obligations. (Argentina, Brazil, Chile, Hong Kong, and Slovak Republic joined the negotiations as observers.) The MAI attempts to establish rules of investment and create an inclusive investment climate, analogous to what has been negotiated and agreed upon for trade and services through GATT and GATS (General Agreement on Trade in Services). The main objectives of a multilateral agreement on investment are to meet the foreign investors' need for (a) long-term stability of rules and procedures, (b) open markets and equal competitive opportunities with domestic investors, (c) protection of existing investments and (d) an international mechanism for settling disputes with national governments. OECD took the initiative of drafting MAI in recognition of (1) its major stake in investment rules, as it accounts for 85% of FDI outflows and 60% of inflows; (2) the common view of the benefits from free investment flows; and (3) its need for more comprehensive and effective rules. MAI was intended to include direct investments, portfolio investment, real estate investments and rights under contract. The main provisions of MAI were:

- Non-discrimination: foreign investors must be treated no less favorably than domestic investors (*National Treatment*) and all investors should be accorded *Most-Favored- Nation Treatment.*
- Transparency of laws, regulations and procedures
- Free transfer of funds to and from the host country
- Expropriation only for public purpose and with full compensation
- Dispute resolution through binding arbitration.

General exceptions were allowed for national security, and integrity and stability of the financial system; temporary safeguards in response to balance of payments crisis; and country specific exceptions and regulations as negotiated among the parties. Exceptions for culture were also considered.

With regard to the environment, MAI allowed freedom to governments to implement policies to protect the environment as long as these policies are not more stringent for foreign investors than for domestic ones, and MAI parties do not lower their environmental standards to attract foreign investment. The NAFTA provisions against environmental measures that constitute disguised restrictions on trade and investment were in effect expanded to include all OECD countries under MAI.

MAI has been heavily criticized on a variety of fronts, from national sovereignty and cultural protection to public health and the environment. The environmental criticism included among others: (1) concerns that corporate challenges to environmental regulations will accelerate; (2) the intellectual property rights provisions giving patents full protection may conflict with provisions of the biodiversity convention; (3) while logging concessions are protected by MAI, acquiring land for preservation is not protected; and (4) governments are unduly constrained by provisions on rights from concessions, licenses, and permits in regulating corporations developing natural resources in their jurisdictions (Clarke 1998).

In the end, MAI did not receive the necessary support from key parties to come into effect. However, new efforts to negotiate a multinational agreement on investment are anticipated in coming years.

Globalization, technology and environment[3]

Economic globalization affects both the nature and the rate of technological innovation and diffusion through a variety of channels: (a) more liberalized international trade, (b) more liberalized capital flows and a more favorable investment climate, (c) improved institutional and communication links, and (d) increased protection of intellectual property rights.

As we have already seen, 75% of international technology transfer arises from trade flows and 18% from investment flows (OECD 1995). Technology transfer arises from the trade of both goods and services including licensing of particular technologies through arms-length transaction with foreign firms. Expanded trade also advances the rate of technological innovations by (a) enlarging the size of the market and generating economies of scale, (b) by realizing more monopoly profits from successful innovation and (c) by reducing dislocation of R&D efforts as protectionist barriers are removed. Capital flows, especially FDI, contribute to technological innovations and diffusion by (a) generating greater finance from capital-exporting countries for financing investments in equipment, embodying more advanced technologies than are available in the host country, (b) by investing in R&D overseas, and (c) by generating technological spillover to national firms, through imitation, employment turnover, and by supplying multinationals demanding higher quality standards.

For at least two reasons, the technology transfer by multinationals tends to be more advanced than what already exists in the host country. First, 80 % of FDI originates in countries that are primary sources of technological innovations such as the US, UK, Germany and Japan. Second, in order to overcome institutional, regulatory, cultural, and other hurdles in the host country, multinationals tend to apply advanced technology which, along with management, tend to be their most important competitive advantages (Grossman and Helpman 1995). It is estimated that 75% of industrial R&D is done by multinationals. Finally, the flow of technical expertise between countries encouraged by globalization results in international exchange of information, which reduces the costs of developing new technologies. Archibugi and Michie (1995) report that 75% of patent applications in OECD countries come from outside OECD. However, again it is the middle-income and newly industrializing economies that have benefited most from the international flow of technology and knowledge. This creates a new source of inequality among developing countries, as some converge technologically while others are left further behind.

Having established the link between globalization and technological innovation and transfer, we turn to the link between technological change on the one hand and environmental quality and resource use on the other. What has been the environmental intensity of technological change? Table 10 indicates that the material intensity of output in all regions of the world fell during the period 1970-1988. This includes most basic material inputs such as wood, metals, minerals, steel and raw agricultural materials. While world GDP during 1970-1991 increased by 38% (Young and Sachs 1995), carbon dioxide emissions per unit of GDP declined (WRI 1996). This decline, of course, is in part due to structural change as well as technological change. Furthermore, aggregate resource use and pollution levels continue to rise as the scale effect of global output growth outweighs the effects of structural and technological change.

[3] This section draws heavily on Johnstone (1997).

Table 10. Technological Innovation with Significant Environmental Impact

Innovation	Form of Change	Primary Investment	Secondary environmental effect	Primary motivation
Coal scrubbers	End-of-pipe	Reduced SO_2 emissions	Increased energy use (-)	Environmental
Electric arc furnace	Process	Reduced energy consumption	Increased use of scrap (+/-)	Economic
HCFCs	Input substitution	Reduced ozone depletion		Environmental
Biodegradable packaging	Product change	Reduced waste accumulation	Reduced waste from plastics manufacturing (+)	Environmental
Thermomechanical pulping	Process	Reduced waste water discharges	Increased energy use (-)	Economic
Low-solvent paint	Product change	Reduced smog		Environmental
Reverse osmosis purification	End-of-pipe	Reduced waste water discharges	Increased solid waste (-)	Environmental
Counter-current rinsing	Process	Reduced heavy metal waste	Reduced metal inputs (+)	Environmental/ Economic

Source: Johnstone (1997).

Is there a trend for technological innovations to be less environment-intensive or cleaner? Environmental intensity changes when there is a change in the product or the production process, when one input is substituted for another, and when the technology is used more efficiently. There is no comprehensive analysis of recent technologies as to their environmental intensity. Table 11 presents a list of selected technological innovations with significant (positive) environmental impacts, which have been widely adopted in recent years and are spreading throughout the developing world. (For a discussion of the determinants of the environment-intensity of technology, see section on technology effects of trade liberalization.)

Table 11. Average annual rate of change in material-intensity of output, by region

	1970-1973	1974-1983	1984-1988
OECD (except USA)			
Raw Agricultural Materials	-3.39	-3.88	0.42
Wood	-1.9	-1.4	-0.17
Metals & Minerals	-0.38	-2.22	-1.66
Steel	-3.87	-2.09	-3.6
NADCs			
Raw Agricultural Materials	-1.99	-2.01	2.58
Wood	-3.37	-0.96	-2.28
Metals & Minerals	12.48	2.82	1.14
Steel	-5.29	-3.39	-3.86
USA			
Raw Agricultural Materials	1.73	-3.86	4.08
Wood	-2.73	0.24	-1.07
Metals & Minerals	10.03	2.36	2.87
Steel	-5.12	-3.12	-2.63
Asia			
Raw Agricultural Materials	-3.26	-1.29	1.47
Wood	-3.79	-1.52	-3.18
Metals & Minerals	11.19	3.67	0.02
Steel	-5.45	-3.52	-4.79

NADCs = Non-Asian Developing Countries
Source: Hoffman and Zivkovic (1992).

In conclusion, globalization could, in principle, improve the environmental characteristics of technology through (a) increased exposure to foreign markets from which cleaner technologies and more effective pollution abatement equipment than those available at home can be imported; (b) increased access to export markets that may be more environmentally demanding than local markets; (c) foreign investment that brings with it the technologies and practices of the home country with more stringent environmental standards than the host country; (d) increased diffusion of the fast-growing export-oriented environmental goods and services industry. However, empirical evidence on the quantitative effect of globalization-driven technological innovation and diffusion, especially on developing countries, is extremely limited.

Intellectual property rights

One result of the Uruguay Round that liberalized trade and created the WTO was the Agreement on Trade-Related Aspects of Intellectual Property Rights, Including Trade in Counterfeit Goods, known as the TRIPS Agreement. TRIPs came into force with the WTO on January 1, 1995. The TRIPS Agreement sets up the rules that WTO members must follow in establishing a system to protect intellectual property rights within their borders. Unlike other WTO rules describing what countries may not do, TRIPS prescribes what countries must do. For example, it requires that any intellectual property rights granted to domestic innovators must also be granted to foreign innovators (*national treatment*) and no party should be favored over others (*non-discrimination*). Contravening the TRIPS Agreement may bring "cross-retaliation" through goods covered by other agreements. Developing country members and economies in transition have five years and less-developed countries ten years to set up the required laws and meet the standards set up in the TRIPS agreement. This is a challenge for countries that have no related legislation in place or have developed entire sectors based on imitations of innovations developed elsewhere (e.g., India's pharmaceutical industry).

It is certain that complying with TRIPS will impose significant social and financial costs on countries through higher prices (due to payment of royalties and industry concentration). For example, small-scale seed and pharmaceutical companies in India and other developing countries are likely to go out of business and prices will rise beyond the reach of many poor people.

TRIPS also is likely to have significant but not easily predictable effects on the environment. For example, concentration of the seed market in the hands of a few major producers who specialize in a few strains may result in loss of biodiversity and impoverishment of the genetic pool. Loss of thousands of land races that began with the Green Revolution would accelerate. A narrow genetic base and extensive monocultures will be more vulnerable to epidemics of pests and blight.

A related effect arises from the different treatment of formal and informal innovation. While TRIPs protects varieties resulting from formal innovation (i.e., scientific research by firms or individuals), no protection is afforded to varieties produced informally by farmers selecting the desired characteristics through traditional knowledge. This pits breeders' rights against farmers' rights and is criticized as unfair, especially since breeders and other formal innovators search for new crop traits and medicines by studying the products in use by traditional societies. As traditional medicines and land races developed over many generations do not fit the standard model of innovation, they are not protected by TRIPS, with the consequence that a steady flow of information from South to North worth billions of dollars goes uncompensated (Runnalls 1998).

Another concern relates not just to cultivated crops but to biodiversity in general. The release of new life forms, such as genetically modified plants, animals and microorganisms, protected by TRIPS, raises concerns relating to the ability of such "new life forms' to multiply, mutate and migrate. Genetically modified organisms (GMOs), once they have been released into the environment, may multiply and spread widely, affecting existing species. Even harmless GMOs without side effects may eventually mutate and assume unintended qualities or migrate to other organisms through pollination or sexual reproduction. Because of these concerns, the TRIPS Agreement allows for exceptions to patenting animals and plants, but the fact that countries can choose to patent life forms is considered contrary to the Precautionary Principle, which is fundamental to sustainable development. These threats to biodiversity are expected to be addressed in the Biodiversity Protocol to the Convention on Biological Diversity now under negotiation.

Globalization and environmental policy and performance

Economic globalization changes the "balance of power" between markets, national governments and international collective action. It enhances the influence of markets on economic, social, and environmental outcomes and reduces the degree of freedom and unilateral management capabilities of national governments. It creates the necessity for states to cooperate both in the management of the global commons and the coordination of domestic policies (Zarsky 1997). Globalization creates market driven political pressures to gain or maintain competitiveness and this forces premature and not necessarily appropriate convergence of environmental policy. In the presence of diversity of environmental endowments, assimilative capacities and preferences, efficient environmental management requires sensitivity to local ecological and social conditions. Diversity of conditions calls for a diversity of policies. Yet, in the absence of collective action, globalization leads to uniformity and inertia in environmental policy.

The main channel through which globalization influences environmental policy is through the cost of production. To the extent that environmental policy raises or is perceived to raise the cost of production, globalization-inspired concerns about gaining or maintaining competitiveness mitigate against any change of policy that might change the cost parameters, unless competitors are subject to the same policy. This creates inertia, pressures toward uniformity, and a shift of power from national governments to market and global governance.

Zarsky (1997) advanced the hypothesis that globalization creates forces that: (a) lead to domestic environmental "policy paralysis" and (b) puts the market in the driver's seat with regard to environmental policy and performance. On the one hand, diverse or weaker environmental policies raise concerns among competitors that the country is somehow trying to subsidize exports to attract foreign investors at their expense. On the other hand, any attempt to raise environmental standards raise concerns among domestic producers about higher costs of production and loss of competitiveness, and hence loss of market share and foreign investment to competitors. Between the concerns of domestic producers and those of foreign competitors, environmental policy makers have very little room to maneuver. This room has narrowed further as profit margins became smaller and smaller under the competitive pressures of globalization. Even if the increase in production costs is negligible and temporary, the fear or threat of being priced out of the market or losing a hard-won export market or foreign investment leads to "policy paralysis" and a strong bias towards the status quo. But the status quo does not favor the environment, since as Zarsky (1997, 32) notes

> relative market prices and patterns of competitive advantage usually grow out of an institutional context in which environment is left out of the equation. The pressures of globalization mean that improvements in environmental performance will be slow. Given the large new demands on global ecosystems posed by rapid economic growth in developing countries, slow progress—even if steady—points toward a pessimistic assessment of the prospects for global sustainability.

The pressures to maintain the status quo or make only small gradual changes in step with competitors is not a temporary phenomenon but one that gathers momentum over time: as the share of income derived from trade and foreign investment rises, the political pressures and lobbying not to disturb competitiveness intensify.

This "Zarsky hypothesis" leads to a number of testable predictions. First globalization-generated pressures to maintain competitiveness keep governments and enterprises from taking any initiatives to improve their environmental performance, if such measures entail significant costs on domestic producers. Second, developing-country product standards will be slowly pulled up towards those of large markets and PPMs towards those of main competitors. Third, the benchmark-setting developed-country standards will improve only slowly and gradually out of fear of loss of competitiveness to slowly converging developing countries.

There has been no direct test of the Zarsky hypothesis and its predictions. Zarsky presents some indirect evidence that tends to support the hypothesis, at least in part:

- The 1993 proposed BTU tax in the US was defeated on account of its perceived threat to US industry's international competitiveness, despite the fact that (a) US energy prices are about one-half of those of the rest of OECD; (b) the estimated impact on even the energy-intensive industries (aluminum, chemicals, fertilizers) was negligible (1-2% of the value of shipments); and (c) the economic and environmental benefits were assessed to be substantial in terms of deficit reduction, improved energy efficiency, decreased pollution and reduced dependence on foreign oil.
- The proposed EU-wide carbon/energy tax in the early 1990s was postponed indefinitely on the grounds that Japan, the US and other EU trading partners were not prepared to adopt similar measures. A similar greenhouse levy of only $3 per ton of carbon was defeated in Australia in 1994 despite the exemption for transport fees and fossil fuel exports, and the estimated negligible impact on the other energy-intensive industries such as aluminum. Industry's contention—that the perceived effects, however small, could drive investment away towards low-energy-cost countries—carried the day.

- China, India, and many other developing and transitional economies, which continue to subsidize fossil fuels and electricity to the order of 30-50% of the world price, are reluctant to remove these subsidies due to fear of loss of competitiveness. Meanwhile, the original rationale for these subsidies—the promotion of state-owned internally oriented industrial growth—is no longer relevant.

The implication of the Zarsky hypothesis is that nation-states face a prisoner's dilemma with regard to environmental policy: pressures to compete for market and investments in a global economy compel them to pursue individual policies that result in lower payoff than if they acted collectively. Cooperation and coordination of policy in internalizing environmental costs, while recognizing the need for diversity, would result in greater welfare for all countries. The absence of effective global governance or enforceable coordination condemns countries to a suboptimal policy of premature and inefficient convergence to slowly improving environmental standards.

Yet there are counter-threads that tend to improve environmental performance even as environmental policy is caught in classic prisoner's dilemma. Growing public environmental awareness and rapidly spreading information about industry's environmental performance, both spearheaded by the revolution in information technology, give rise to a global environmental ethic. Under pressure from communities, customers, shareholders and employees, industry self-regulation is advancing ahead of formal regulations. The rigors of competition compel firms to intensify their search for more efficient, resource-saving, waste-reducing technologies. Moreover, the cross-border flows of capital, commodities, people and ideas promote technological and managerial change: resources are better allocated, cleaner and more efficient technologies are disseminated and the environmental standards of worst performers are gradually pulled up. These trends are fully consistent with the Zarsky hypothesis that globalization makes markets, the drivers of environmental performance, at the same time as it tends to "paralyze" official environmental policy.

Managing the process of globalization to protect the environment and enhance sustainability

Countries and people have the potential to derive significant benefits from the globalization process but there is still the problem of realizing this potential. Too much attention has been paid to the economic benefits of globalization and not enough to the social and environmental implications. As a result, the promise and potential of globalization as a force of sustainable human development may not be achieved. Furthermore, even as globalization improves the prospects for economic growth worldwide, it may reduce the economic prospects in individual countries, sectors and communities. A variety of factors contribute to wide disparities within and between nations:

- Lack of access to more efficient technologies
- Lack of access to capital
- Inadequate flexibility to respond to changes in market demand
- Inability to manage structural change
- Weak institutions and absence of effective safety nets.

To the extent that globalization marginalizes economies, sectors, and people, it results in poverty-induced resource depletion and environmental degradation, which lead to further human deprivation, disparity and disempowerment.

Globalization is likely to place significant stresses on the environment if perverse subsidies and other distortions are not removed and environmental costs fully internalized, or if "social adjustment" policies are not in place to cushion economic dislocation and avert marginalization of the poor. Globalization, by driving a wedge between what is produced and what is consumed in any given location, alters the distribution of environmental impacts and the costs of avoiding them within the current generation and between current and future generations.

The environmental consequences of globalization differ from the economic effects both in time and space: (1) environmental impacts are more long-term, dynamic, cumulative and beset with uncertainty; and (2) environmental impacts involve both physical and non-physical spillovers that may or may not be transmitted through markets, such as cross-border pollution, aesthetics, ethical or moral concerns of parties not involved in the transaction. Globalization generates international interest in what traditionally were considered purely domestic policies, since economic integration implies that trade and investment are now being affected by such policies. Globalization increasingly brings into conflict notions of national sovereignty over production processes with globally oriented lifecycle perspectives, where consumers want to know the overall environmental impact of what they buy and consume.

In conclusion globalization brings with it potentially large benefits as well as risks. The challenge is to manage the process of globalization in such a way that it promotes environmental sustainability and equitable human development. The ability of nation-states to manage risks, inequalities and change is severely restricted by taxation constraints and the need to remain competitive. Hence, the traditional instruments of trade barriers and command and control regulations would not work because they would have unacceptably high costs in a globalized world and at the same time be less effective. To manage globalization in the interest of both people and the environment, it would be necessary to implement more efficient and innovative policies domestically and more effective global governance internationally.

National policies

1. Accelerate democratization and institutional development to keep in pace with globalization.
2. Increase accountability and transparency throughout the economy, and especially in the formulation and implementation of public policy.
3. Channel more public investment to human capability formation.
4. Preserve as much as possible of the autonomy of the state to exercise fiscal and monetary policies to achieve both macroeconomic stability and growth.
5. Reform domestic policies that both distort trade and have negative environmental impacts (e.g., energy subsidies).
6. Correct existing market failures through efficient incentive systems (economic instruments) that internalize environmental costs, to avert their magnification by trade liberalization and economic integration.
7. Improve the effectiveness of environmental policy (benefit per dollar spent) through the involvement of businesses and local communities in monitoring and enforcement rather than relying on the state's limited budget and weak regulatory enforcement capacity. Instruments of empowerment include information disclosure in environmental performance of firms, and provision of training and other capacity building services to communities.
8. Institute social adjustment policies to cushion economic dislocation and avert the marginalization of the poor.

It must be recognized, however, that the autonomy of the state to act deliberately to protect the environment or to cushion the impact on the poor of structural or other changes brought about by globalization is limited by the need to compete in the global economy for capital, jobs and markets, on the one hand, and by the interest that competitors and trade partners take in a country's domestic environmental and social policies, on the other. Countries facing financial crisis are further constrained by limitations imposed on their fiscal and monetary policy by creditors, the International Monetary Fund, and the crisis itself.

International policies

As we have seen, globalization constrains the state's unilateral management capacities and creates new imperatives for states to coordinate their domestic environmental policies as well as to cooperate in the management of the global commons. Without effective global governance (or effective multilateralism, as Zarsky calls it) nation-states, subject to the pressures of globalization, drift towards a low-level environmental policy convergence that is insensitive to local ecological conditions and does not respect the diversity of preferences and priorities across and within nations. The challenge is to mobilize collective action among governments, firms and civil societies to overcome the gravity towards the sterile uniformity and inertia created by narrow competitiveness concerns and create a broader environmental policy framework, which will (a) recognize and allow for the diversity of environmental endowments and preferences; (b) raise the terms of environmental policy convergence; and (c) allow for continuous improvement in environmental performance. In such a framework, policy coordination, harmonization and convergence would not be understood as homogenization or standardization of the objectives and instruments of environmental policy regardless of local circumstances, but a collective move towards sustainable development at different speeds depending on stage of development, environmental endowments, etc.

Unfortunately, the one international "body" entrusted with the responsibility of building a bridge between environmental and trade policy, WTO's Committee on Trade and Environment (CTE), did not focus on finding "a synergy between environment and trade as two equal policy objectives. Rather they have explored how to fit environmental concerns within the framework of existing trade regimes" (Ewing and Taresofsky, 1996). CTE saw its role as one of limiting unilateral state actions in the name of environmental protection in order to protect the trading system, rather than one of a paradigm shift from a negative to a positive trade-environment relationship and a "collective responsibility to promote sustainable trade, investment and growth" (Zarsky 1991). Rather than focusing on how trade rules can promote sustainable development CTE focussed narrowly on (a) whether there should be a "safe harbor" within WTO for trade-restricting measures included in multilateral environmental agreements (MEAs); and (b) on whether ecolabelling schemes constitute non-tariff trade barriers. These issues are important as guidelines are urgently needed for both ecolabelling schemes and MEA negotiators, but they cannot be resolved in isolation from other important issues in the interface of trade and environment, and without an overarching framework of sustainable development in which both environment and trade are critically important and synergistic. As Zarsky (1997, 41) put it, "First, the Organization [WTO] as a whole needs to affirm its commitment to a development agenda...Among other things, this would entail abandoning the idea that the primary goal of trade-environment diplomacy is to enhance the capacities of developed countries to restrict market access on environmental grounds."

Besides MEAs and ecolabelling, other unresolved issues, central to the trade-environment relationship are: (1) non-product-related process and production methods (PPMs) for which WTO rules have come increasingly in conflict with globally-oriented product life-cycle perspectives; and (2) the gradual removal of domestic policies such as energy, chemical and water subsidies, which distort trade and damage the environment; and (3) internalization of environmental costs.

The latter two issues, while domestic in nature and unilaterally beneficial are politically unpalatable because of concerns about loss of competitiveness, not unlike the concerns that limited unilateral trade liberalization and necessitated several rounds of trade negotiations and coordinated action, culminating with the Uruguay Round. What is needed is a "Green Round" to coordinate joint action on the elimination of environmentally damaging subsidies and internationalization of environmental costs (with due recognition of diversity among countries). The question is whether WTO is up to the task of convening such a "Green Round" and coordinating the implementation of multilateral agreements on resource subsidies and internalization of environmental costs. WTO has thus far provided no evidence that is either prepared to view the trade-environment relationship in a broader development context, or willing to address it in a more holistic manner.

A "Global Environment Organization" as called for by Esty (1994) may be necessary to fill the gap, which in its absence is now partially filled by regional groupings such as NAFTA, APEC, OECD and others attempting policy coordination among their members. That such regional initiatives are not a substitute for effective global governance and multilateralism can be seen from the now defunct efforts of OECD to negotiate a Multilateral Agreement on Investment (MAI) among is members. First, the main motivation behind the MAI was to promote foreign investor interests by reducing political risk and ensuring "national treatment" rather than to encourage investment for good environmental management and sustainable development. Second, MAI was met with suspicion by developing countries, which viewed it as a run around WTO to conclude an agreement (without their participation) that, in letter, would bind only OECD members, but in effect would apply to them as well. This gave rise to calls for exceptions to MAI provisions to protect the environment, and ultimately for a much broader sustainable development investment agreement. Belated offers by OECD negotiators to include a "pollution haven" clause and to append environmental guidelines for multinationals did not constitute substitutes for effective policy coordination.

Clearly, private capital flows into developing countries, especially emerging markets, will continue to grow rapidly into the foreseeable future. The challenge is to attract more foreign investment into the poorer countries and to direct it to sustainable development activities. In this regard, official development assistance (ODA) has a critical role to play in leveraging private capital flows, both directly and through encouragement of better policies (including prudent macroeconomic policies and outward-oriented trade policies) in the recipient countries. Governments can ensure through regulations, incentives, and voluntary agreements that new investment is directed towards sustainable goals or, at a minimum, that it does not jeopardize environmental, social and long-term development goals.

At the multilateral level, there has been a clear trend since the early 1990s to take into account more consistently the environmental and social effects of projects. This is true of both the Multilateral Investment Guarantee Agency (MIGA), which guarantees funds to governments and the private sector to reduce risks, and the International Finance Corporation (IFC), which provides loans, equity and other financial instruments to private-sector development. In cooperation with national governments, international organizations should support monitoring and the development of a database for tracking the environmental impacts of foreign capital flows on environmental quality and sustainability.

With regard to technology, globalization can play a key role in generating and diffusing resource-saving and cleaner production technologies to developing countries. For this to happen, however, several policy concerns must be resolved. First, the fact that developed countries dominate the generation of technological innovations means that some of these technologies and their environmental features are ill suited to the factor endowments and economic and environmental circumstances of developing countries. Second, developing countries may lack the capacity to successfully absorb technological innovations, including those aimed at mitigating negative environmental impacts. It is therefore important that developing countries themselves develop their own institutional frameworks and capacity for adoption and adaptation of foreign technologies as well as for domestic generation of innovations (Johnstone 1997). Since domestic and foreign technological capacities tend to be complementary rather than substitutable, domestic capacity building should be coupled with removal of domestic barriers to diffusion of foreign technology, such as import tariffs on capital equipment, local content requirements, or foreign exchange restrictions. Lack of protection of intellectual property rights is another barrier to diffusion, since foreign firms may be concerned that transferring or licensing a technology may result in their losing market advantage. Developing countries should undertake to increase their own capacity to assimilate transferred technology by fostering research and development and improving their skills in negotiation and management, with the aim of strengthening their intellectual property rights.

International policies also have an important bearing on technology transfer. While MEAs such as the Montreal Protocol and the Basel Convention provide for transfer of best available, environmentally safe technologies to developing countries, care must be taken so that the transferred technology reflects the economic and environmental conditions of the recipient country rather than those of the donor (Johnstone 1997). For this to happen, it is necessary to develop cooperation between donors and recipients in R & D related to environmental technologies. Tropical environments and materials differ fundamentally from temperate ones in ways that impact the effectiveness and efficiency of environmental technologies designed for temperate environments.

Finally, there is scope for governments to ease the terms of access to some cleaner production technologies for developing countries as a form of development assistance. Technologies, such as newly developed vaccines or clean coal technologies that benefit diversity, the environment and human health, could be made freely available to developing countries. Developed countries can soften the impacts of trade-related aspects of intellectual property rights (TRIPs) on developing countries by specifying very liberal terms of protection for environmental and clean production innovations involving public financing.

There is a need for an Amendment or Understanding among WTO members that the rights of informal innovators are protected, and for a broader interpretation of TRIPs to include patents for land races and other products of traditional knowledge, in exchange for a commitment by the developing countries to preserve these varieties. There are many innovative ideas including granting of special status, such as free or concessional access or royalty sharing, to source communities for commercial products "derived" from traditional knowledge or products in traditional use. The Convention on Biological Diversity already provides that the benefits from commercial use of genetic resources should be shared with the country of origin in a "fair and equitable way."

Finally, with regard to the risks posed to the biodiversity of flora and fauna, any patent protection afforded to the genetically modified organisms under TRIPs must incorporate the highest standards of protection according to the "precautionary principle," which is fundamental to sustainable development.

In conclusion, the more integrated environmental and trade policies are, the more sustainable economic growth will be and the more globalization can be harnessed for the benefit of the environment. At a rather modest level, this integration may take the form of institutionalization of environmental issues in future bilateral, multilateral and regional trade agreements. At a more ambitious level, new institutions of more effective and equitable global governance can be created to bring together governments, the private sector and civil society in a dialogue to achieve consensus for action in dealing with globalization-induced volatility, inequality and threats to environmental sustainability.■

Appendix

Table A.1: Selected Multilateral Environmental Agreements with Possible Trade Impacts

Major Global Environmental Agreements with Significant Trade Impacts

Convention on the Prevention of Marine Pollution by Dumping of Wastes and Other Matter, 29 December 1972

Convention on International Trade in Endangered Species, 3 March 1973

Vienna Convention for the Protection of the Ozone Layer, 22 March 1985

Montreal Protocol on Substances that Deplete the Ozone Layer, 16 September 1987

Basel Convention on the Control of Transboundary Movements of Hazardous Wastes and Their Disposal, 22 March 1989

United Nations Framework Convention on Climate Change, 9 May 1992

Convention on Biological Diversity, 5 June 1992

Global Commodity/ Environmental Agreements with Trade Impacts

Treaty for the Preservation and Protection of Fur Seals, 7 July 1911

ILO Convention (#13) concerning the Use of White Lead in Painting, 25 October 1921

FAO Agreement for the Establishment of the Indo-Pacific Fisheries Commission, 26 February 1948 (amended and superseded 20 January 1961)

Washington International Convention for the North-West Atlantic Fisheries, 8 February 1949

Washington Convention for the Establishment of an Inter-American Tropical Tuna Commission, 31 May 1949

Paris International Convention for the Protection of Birds, 18 October 1950

FAO International Plant Protection Convention, 6 December 1951

Tokyo International Convention for the High Seas Fisheries of the North Pacific Ocean, 9 May 1952

Washington International Convention for the Regulation of Whaling and 1956 Protocol, 10 November 1948; Protocol, 4 May 1959

Convention on Fishing and Conservation of the Living Resources of the High Seas, 29 April 1958

London North-East Atlantic Fisheries Convention, 24 January 1959

Varna Convention concerning Fishing in the Black Sea (as amended 30 June 1965), 7 July 1959

Paris International Convention on the Protection of New Varieties of Plants, 2 December 1961

Rio de Janeiro International Convention for the Conservation of Atlantic Tunas, 14 May 1966

Phyto-sanitary Convention for Africa South of the Sahara, 13 September 1968

FAO Convention on the Conservation of the Living Resources of the South-East Atlantic, 23 October 1969

Canberra Convention on the Conservation of Antarctic Marine Living Resources, 20 May 1980

International Tropical Timber Agreement, 18 November 1983

Reykjavik Convention for the Conservation of Salmon in the North Atlantic Ocean

Pacific Islands Regional Fisheries Treaty, 2 April 1987

Convention for the Establishment of a Latin American Tuna Organization, 1989

Wellington Convention on the Prohibition of Driftnet Fishing in the South Pacific, 24 November 1989

Table A.1: Selected Multilateral Environmental Agreements with Possible Trade Impacts (cont'd)

Other Global Environmental Agreements Paris International Convention for the Protection of Birds, 18 October 1950 International Convention for the Prevention of Pollution of the Sea by Oil, 12 May 1954 Brussels International Convention relating to Intervention on the High Seas in Cases of Oil Pollution Casualties, 29 November 1969 Brussels International Convention on Civil Liability for Oil Pollution Damage, 29 November 1969 Ramsar Convention on Wetlands of International Importance, Especially as Waterfowl Habitat, 2 February 1971 World Heritage Bonn Convention on the Conservation of Migratory Species of Wild Animals, 23 June 1979 Convention on Desertification ***Other Multilateral Environmental Agreements with Trade Impacts*** European Convention for the Protection of Animals During International Transport, 13 December 1968 Convention on the Prevention of Marine Pollution by Dumping of Wastes and Other Matter, 29 December 1972 Convention on International Trade in Endangered Species, 3 March 1973 London International Convention for the Prevention of Pollution from Ships (MARPOL), 2 November 1973	European Convention for the Protection of Animals kept for Farming Purposes, 10 March 1976 Bonn Convention for the Protection of the Rhine River against Pollution by Chlorides, 3 December 1976 European Convention for the Protection of Animals for Slaughter, 10 May 1979 European Convention for the Protection of Animals Used for Experimental and Other Scientific Purposes, 18 March 1986 European Convention for the Protection of Pet Animals, 13 November 1987 Bamako Convention on the Ban of Import into Africa and the Control of Transboundary Movement and Management of Hazardous Wastes within Africa, 30 January 1991 Other Multilateral Environmental Agreements London Convention for the Protection of Wild Animals, Birds and Fish in Africa, 19 May 1900 Washington Convention on Nature Protection and Wildlife Preservation in the Western Hemisphere, 12 October 1940	Bern Convention on the International Commission for the Protection of the Rhine against Pollution, 29 April 1963 Convention for the Prevention of Marine Pollution by Dumping from Ships and Aircraft (Oslo Convention), 15 February 1972 Helsinki Convention for the Protection of the Marine Environment of the Baltic Sea Area, 22 March 1974 Paris Convention for the Prevention of Marine Pollution from Land-Based Sources, 4 June 1974 Barcelona Convention for the Protection of the Mediterranean Sea against Pollution, 16 February 1976 Apia Convention on the Conservation of Nature in the South Pacific, 12 June 1976 Kuwait Regional Convention for Co-operation on the Protection of the Marine Environment from Pollution, 24 April 1978 ECE Convention on Long Range Transboundary Air Pollution, 13 November 1979 Abidjan Convention for Co-operation in the Protection and Development of the Marine and Coastal Environment of the West and Central African Region, 23 March 1981

Table A.1: Selected Multilateral Environmental Agreements with Possible Trade Impacts (cont'd)

Other Global Environmental Agreements (cont'd) Lima Convention for the Protection of the Marine Environment and Coastal Area of the South-East Pacific, 12 November 1981 Jeddah Regional Convention for the Conservation of the Red Sea and Gulf of Aden Environment, 14 February 1982	Cartagena Convention for the Protection and Development of the Marine Environment of the Wider Caribbean Region, 24 March 1983 Nairobi Convention for the Protection, Management and Development of the Marine and Coastal Environment of the Eastern African Region, 21 June 1985	Noumea Convention for the Protection of the Natural Resources and Environment of the South Pacific Region, 25 November 1986 ***Voluntary International Environmental Agreements with Trade Impacts*** ISO 9000 ISO 14,000

Source: von Moltke (1996).

References

Adams, J. (1997). "Globalisation, trade, and environment." *Globalization and Environment.* OECD Proceedings. Paris: OECD.

Alexander Grant and Company. Various years. *Annual Study of General Manufacturing Climates of the Forty-Eight Contiguous States of America.* Chicago: Alexander Grant and Company.

Anderson, K. (1992). "Agricultural trade liberalization and the environment: A global perspective." *The World Economy* 15(1): 153-71.

Anderson, K. and A. Strutt (1994). "On measuring the environmental impacts of agricultural trade liberalization." Center for International Economic Studies, Seminar paper 94-06. Adelaide: University of Adelaide.

Archibugi, D. and J. Michie (1995). "The globalisation of technology: A new taxonomy." *Cambridge Journal of Economics* 19:121-140.

Bhagwati, J. and T.N. Srinivasan (1997). "Trade and the environment: Does environmental diversity detract from the case for free trade?" in *Fair Trade and Harmonization: Prerequisites for Free Trade? Vol. 1: Economic Analysis* ed. J. Bhagwati, and R. Hudec. Cambridge, MA: MIT Press.

Clarke, T. (1998). "MAI-Day! The Corporate Rule Treaty: The Multilateral Agreement on Investments (MAI) seeks to consolidate global corporate rule." http://www.nassist.com/mai/mai(2)x.html.

Epping, M. (1986). "Tradition in transition: The emergence of new categories in plant location." *Arkansas Business and Economic Review* 19(3):16-25.

Esty, D.C. (1994). *Greening the GATT, Trade, Environment, and the Future.* Washington, DC: Institute for International Economics.

Ewing, K.P. and R.G. Taresofsky (1996). *The "Trade and Environment" Agenda: Survey of Major Issues and Proposals form Marakesh to Singapore.* Environmental Law Centre, World Conservation Union (IUCN). Bonn: IUCN.

Gentry, B.S. et. al. (1996). *Private Capital Flows and the Environment: Lessons from Latin America.* Center for Environmental Law and Policy, Yale University (draft report).

Grossman, G.M. and E. Helpman (1995). "Technology and trade." *Centre for Economic and Policy Research (CEPR) Discussion Paper* 1134. London: CEPR.

Grossman, G.M. and A.B. Krueger (1993). "Environmental impacts of a North American Free Trade Agreement." Pp. 13-56 in *The US-Mexico Free Trade Agreement*, ed. P. Garber. Cambridge, MA: MIT Press.

Grossman, G.M. and A. Krueger (1995). "Economic growth and the environment." *Quarterly Journal of Economics* 110(2): 353-77.

Henriques, I. and P. Sadorsky (1996). "The determinants of an environmentally responsive firm: An empirical approach." *Journal of Environmental Economics and Management* 30: 381-95.

Hoffman, U. and D. Zivkovic (1992). "Demand growth for industrial raw materials and its determinants: An analysis for the period 1965-1988." *UNCTAD Discussion Paper* No. 5. Geneva: UNCTAD.

Johnstone, N. (1997) "Globalization, technology, and environment." *Globalization and Environment.* OECD Proceedings. Paris: OECD.

Levinson, A. (1997). "Environmental regulations and industry location: International and domestic evidence." in *Fair Trade and Harmonization: Prerequisites for Free Trade? Vol. 1: Economic Analysis*, ed. J. Bhagwati and R. Hudec. Cambridge, MA: MIT Press.

Low, P., ed. (1992). "Trade and the environment: A survey of the literature." in *International Trade and the Environment*, ed. P. Low. World Bank Discussion Paper 159. Washington, DC: The World Bank.

Low, P. and A. Yeats (1992). "Do 'dirty' industries migrate?" in *International Trade and the Environment*, ed. P. Low. World Bank Discussion Paper 159. Washington, DC: The World Bank.

Lucas, R., P. Wheeler and H. Hettige (1992). "Economic development, environmental regulation and international migration of toxic pollution 1960-1988." in *International Trade and the Environment*, ed. P. Low. World Bank Discussion paper 159. Washington, DC: The World Bank.

Lyne, J. (1990). "Service taxes, international site selection and the 'green' movement dominate executives' political focus." *Site Selection*, October.

Nentjes, A. and D. Wiersma (1987). "Innovation and pollution control." *International Journal of Social Economics* 17(4): 247-65.

OECD (1994). *The Environmental Effects of Trade*. Paris: OECD.

OECD (1995). *Foreign Direct Investment, Trade and Employment*. Paris: OECD.

OECD (1996). *Globalization of Industry: Overview and Sector Reports*. Paris: OECD.

OECD (1997). *Globalization and Environment*. OECD Proceedings. Paris: OECD.

Panayotou, T. (1997a). "Demystifying the Environmental Kuznets Curve: Turning a Black Box into a Policy Tool." *Environmental and Development Economics* 2(4): 465-484.

Panayotou, T. (1997b). "Taking stock of trends in sustainable development since Rio." Pp. 35-72 in *Finance for Sustainable Development: The Road Ahead*. Proceedings of the Fourth Group Meeting on Financial Issues of Agenda 21, Santiago, Chile. New York: United Nations.

Panayotou, T. and J.R. Vincent. (1997). "Environmental regulation and competitiveness." *Global Competitiveness Report*. Geneva: World Economic Forum.

Panayotou, T., T. Schatzki and Q. Limvorapitak. (1997). "Differential Industry Response to Formal and Informal Environmental Regulations in Newly Industrializing Economies: The Case of Thailand." A Case Study for the HIID Asia Environmental Economics Policy Seminar.

Pargal, S. and D. Wheeler (1995). "Informal regulation of industrial pollution in developing countries." *World Bank Policy Research Working Paper* 1416. Washington, DC: The World Bank.

Repetto, R. (1993). *Trade and Environment Policies: Achieving Complementarities and Avoiding Conflicts*. Washington, DC: World Resources Institute.

Repetto, R. (1995). *Jobs, Competitiveness, and Environmental Regulation: What are the Real Issues?* Washington, DC: World Research Institute.

Robison, H.D. (1988). "Industrial pollution abatement: The impact on the balance of trade." *Canadian Journal of Economics* 21(1).

Runnalls, (1998). "Shall we dance?" Trade and Sustainable Development Research Guide, International Institute for Sustainable Development (IISD). http://iisd1.iisd.ca/trade/dance.htm

Schmenner, R. (1982). *Making Business Location Decisions*. Englewood Cliffs, NJ: Prentice-Hall.

Smith, K. and J.A. Espinosa (1996). "Environmental and trade policies: Some methodological lessons." *Environment and Development Economics*: 19-40.

Sprenger, R.U. (1992). *Umweltschutz als Standortfaktor*. Bonn: Friedrich Ebert Stiftung.

Sprenger, R.U. (1997). "Globalization, employment and environment." *Globalization and Environment*, OECD Proceedings. Paris: OECD.

Stafford, H.A. (1985). "Environmental protection and industrial location." *Annals of the Association of American Geographers* 75(2):227-240.

Strutt, A. and K. Anderson (1998). "Will trade liberalization harm the environment? The case of Indonesia to 2020." Seminar Paper 98-04. Center for International Economic Studies, University of Adelaide.

Subramanian, A. (1992). "Trade measures for environment: A nearly empty box?" *The World Economy*15(1).

United Nations (1996). *World Economic and Social Survey*. New York: UN.

Von Moltke, K. (1996). "International environmental management, trade regimes and sustainability." Paper prepared for the International Institute for Sustainable Development, Winnipeg, Manitoba, Canada, January.

Walter, I. (1973). "The pollution content of American trade." *Western Economic Journal* 11:61-70.

Wheeler, D. and A. Mody (1992). "International investment location decisions: The case of US firms." *Journal of International Economics* 33: 57-76.

Wintner L. (1982). *Urban Plant Siting.* New York: Conference Board.

World Bank (1997). *Can the environment wait? Priorities for East Asia.* Washington, DC: The World Bank.

World Resources Institute (1990). *World Resources 1990-91.* New York: Oxford University Press.

World Resources Institute (1996). *World Resources: A Guide to the Global Environment.* Washington, DC: World Resources Institute.

World Trade Organization (1995). *International Trade Trends and Statistics.* Geneva: WTO.

World Trade Organization (1996). *Trade and Foreign Direct Investment.* Geneva: WTO.

Young, J.E. and A. Sachs (1995). "Creating a sustainable materials economy." in *State of the World 1995,* ed. L. Brown et. al. London: Earthscan.

Zarsky, L. (1991). *Trade-Environment Linkages and Ecologically Sustainable Development.* Report to Department of Arts, Sports, Environment, Tourism and Territories, Environmental Strategy Branch, Australia, October.

Zarsky, L. (1997). "Stuck in the mud? Nation-states, globalization, and environment." *Globalization and Environment,* OECD Proceedings. Paris: OECD.

The Impact Of Globalization On National Film Industries

Alejandro Ramírez Magaña

The economic output of the United States, measured in tons, is barely any heavier today than it was 100 years ago, even though the real value of the gross domestic product (GDP) increased twenty-fold during this period. This points to the fact that the world is entering a new era, characterized by the expansion of the knowledge-based economy, where production will increasingly be in the form of intangibles, such as information services, advertising and entertainment, rather than material goods.

A recent report by the Organization for Economic Cooperation and Development (OECD) estimates that more than half of total GDP in the rich economies is now knowledge-based, including industries such as telecommunications, computers, software, education, television and filmmaking. As production has shifted from steel and heavy copper wire to microprocessors and fine fiber-optic cables, and as services have increased their share of the total, output has become lighter and less visible, a phenomenon sometimes referred to as the weightless economy.

In fact, the largest single export industry of the US is not aircraft, computers or automobiles, but entertainment—movies and television programs. In 1997, Hollywood films grossed over $30 billion worldwide, and in 1998, a single movie, *Titanic*, grossed over $1.8 billion internationally in its theatrical release (that is, in movie theaters, not counting video, satellite, cable and free TV).[1] Furthermore, the US movie industry has created more jobs since 1990 than carmakers, pharmaceutical firms and hotels combined.

The film industry was the first media industry to globalize, long before the birth of television. During the 1930s, Hollywood films were being shown in Europe and European films in America. Not all national film industries, however, have become global industries. In fact, there is a case to be made that the only film industry that has become truly global is the American film industry. The United States dominates world cinema today. It may not make the most feature films—India leads the world in terms of numbers of films produced each year, and Hong Kong produces most per capita. But American films are the only ones that reach every market in the world.

The United States claimed 70% of the film market in the European Union in 1996, up from 56% in 1987. In Latin America, US films took 83% of the box office in 1996. Even in Japan, American films now account for more than half the film market.

Hollywood's domination of the international film market has grown steadily in the past two decades. Hollywood now gets 51% of its revenues from overseas, up from just 30% in 1980.[2] At the same time, few foreign films make it big in the United States, where they account for 2.5% of the market. In 1996, Europe's trade deficit with the United States in films and television stood at $5.65 billion, up from $4.8 billion the previous year.[3]

The rise of American films in virtually every major market around the world has prompted national governments everywhere to devise mechanisms to protect and support their national film industries. All across the European Union, there are complex systems of support for European films. Argentina and Brazil have recently passed laws securing financial support for their film industries. The legislatures of Mexico, Poland and Hungary are currently analyzing proposals to protect and support national film production.

In fact, some countries that have embraced free trade policies have tried to exclude films and other cultural industries from free trade pacts. In 1993, France threatened to sabotage the Uruguay Round of the General Agreement on Tariffs and Trade (GATT) in order to exempt audio-visual material from free trade agreements. Last June, Canada organized a meeting in Ottawa with nineteen other countries with the purpose of finding ways of exempting cultural goods from treaties lowering trade barriers, on the basis that free trade threatened national cultures. In 1997, 96% of films shown on Canadian screens were foreign, primarily American.

With the exception of India, China and Hong Kong (where the indigenous films' share of the domestic market is 95%, 67% and 58%, respectively), all other major markets are dominated by American films. This domination, however, has not been a historical constant. In fact, most European and Latin American film industries dominated their domestic markets in the 1940s, 1950s, and 1960s. The 1970s and 1980s saw a sharp decline in movie attendance all over Europe and Latin America, which hurt national film industries. In the 1990s there has been a significant increase in movie attendance, with a parallel revival of filmmaking in some European and Latin American countries.

The first part of this paper analyzes the decline of various national film industries around the world and the rise of American films to their current position of leadership in world film markets. The second part looks at the support schemes that governments around the world have implemented to assist their film industries and analyzes the outcomes of such programs. A third section looks at consumer preferences in films and analyzes the evolution and the globalization of the exhibition industry (i.e., movie theaters) and its impact on film production. The fourth part presents some conclusions.

The rise and fall of national film industries

Virtually everywhere in Europe, Latin America and East Asia, domestic film industries have enjoyed a golden age of abundant production and massive movie attendance, followed by a period of stagnation and decline. The expansion of television in the 1960s marked the beginning of the decline. Television had a tremendously negative impact on movie attendance in practically all countries. The United Kingdom, for example, had over 500 million admissions in 1960; by 1970 the figure had dropped to 193 million. Similarly, movie admissions in Germany fell from 604 million in 1960 to 160 million in 1970; in France from 354 million in 1960 to 184 million in 1970; and in Italy from 744 million in 1960 to 241 million in 1980.[4] As a consequence of this drastic decline in movie attendance, many national film industries, such as the British and the German, almost disappeared. Table 1 shows the trend in European movie admissions during the past three decades, and the dramatic plunge that occurred after 1960.

The decline that began during the 1960s in virtually every major European market continued until 1990. The significant fall registered between 1980 and 1990 is partly attributable to the rise of home video.

In 1960, admissions in most European countries stood at about ten per person per year. Italians, for example, visited a movie theater, on average, 14.7 times a year, Spaniards 12.5, and Germans 11.4. By 1990, movie admissions per person had dropped to 2.2 in Italy, 2.0 in Spain, and 1.6 in Germany. Figure 1 illustrates this significant fall in admissions per head.

Table 1: Movie Admissions in Europe 1960-1997 (in millions)

Country	1960	1970	1980	1990	1995	1996	1997
U.K	500.8	193.0	101.0	91.0	108.0	124.0	139.5
Germany	604.8	160.1	143.8	102.5	124.5	132.9	143.1
France	354.6	184.4	175.4	121.9	130.2	136.6	148.8
Italy	744.7	525.0	241.8	123.1	91.4	95.8	101.0
Spain	370.0	330.9	176.0	78.5	89.9	104.2	101.4
Belgium	79.5	30.3	20.6	17.8	19.2	21.2	22.1
Netherlands	55.4	24.1	25.5	14.6	17.2	16.8	18.9
Luxembourg	4.5	1.3	0.8	0.5	0.7	0.7	1.1
Ireland	41.0	20.0	9.5	8.08	9.8	11.4	11.0
Austria	106.5	32.8	17.5	10.1	11.9	12.3	13.7
Denmark	43.9	23.8	15.9	9.6	8.8	9.8	10.8
Norway	35.0	18.5	17.4	11.3	10.9	11.4	10.9
Sweden	55.0	28.2	24.0	15.3	14.8	15.4	15.2
Finland	24.6	11.7	9.9	6.1	5.3	5.5	5.9
Iceland	Na	na	3.06	1.45	1.40	1.44	1.48
Switzerland	40.0	33.0	20.9	14.3	14.9	15.1	15.55
Greece	61.2	128.6	42.9	12.0	7.0	7.7	9.0
Portugal	26.5	27.9	30.7	9.5	10.0	11.5	12.5
Czech Rep.	Na	na	na	51	9.2	8.8	9.8
Hungary	Na	na	na	31.5	14.3	12.1	15.5
Poland	Na	na	na	na	22.2	21.3	22.4
Bulgaria*	Na	na	na	19.5	11.0	12.2	11.4
Romania*	Na	na	na	41.0	31.9	25.6	17.3
Slovakia**	Na	na	na	9.0	6.5	5.6	4.9
Slovenia**	Na	na	na	2.3	2.8	2.8	3.0
Russia**	Na	na	na	489.0	389.7	75.4	na
Belarus**	Na	na	na	29.5	na	na	na
Croatia**	Na	na	na	3.7	4.6	3.7	na
Yugoslavia**	Na	Na	na	1.8	1.4	2.2	na
Ukraine**	Na	Na	na	126.6	na	na	Na

* Figures correspond to the period 1992-1995. ** Figures correspond to the period 1993-1996.

Sources: Central Statistical Office, Hauptverband Deutscher Fillmtheater, Centre National de la Cinematographie, Associazione Nazionale Esercenti Cinema, Ministerio de Educación y Cultura, Federation des Cinemas en Belgique, Nederlands Federatie voor Cinematografie, Centre National de l'Audiovisuel, Fachverband der Lichtspieltheater, Danmarks Statistik, Suomen Elokuvateatteriliitto, Hagstofa Islands, Kommunale Kinematografers, Svenska Filminstitutet, Magyar Filmunio, MEDIA Salles, Screen Digest, Procinema, Dodona Research.

Figure 1: Admissions per capita in Europe, 1960-1997

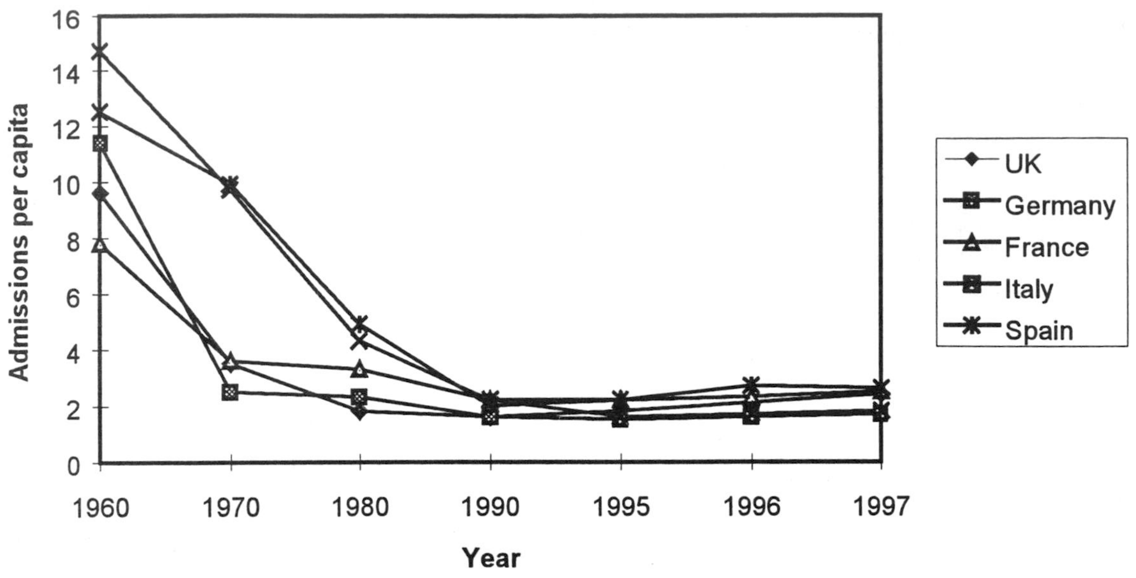

Source: Central Statistical Office, Hauptverband Deutscher Fillmtheater, Centre National de la Cinematographie, Associazione Nazionale Esercenti Cinema, Ministerio de Educación y Cultura.

In 1990, the declining trend in admissions ended in most Western European markets. In absolute terms, admissions began rising in Germany, the United Kingdom, France, Spain, Belgium, the Netherlands, Ireland, Austria, Luxembourg, Switzerland and Portugal. More importantly, admissions per person also began to rise. Admissions per person increased between 1990 and 1997 from 1.6 to 2.4 in the United Kingdom, from 2.0 to 2.6 in Spain, and from 2.2 to 2.5 in France.

The reversal of this trend was brought about by the construction of modern multiplexes—movie theater complexes of numerous screens (usually more than five) and equipped with the most advanced sound and projection technologies. With admissions falling since the 1960s, European exhibition companies had not invested much in modernizing their movie theaters and, with a few exceptions, had not introduced the multiplex concept to Europe before the 1990s. Aging and decrepit facilities were a key factor—in addition to competition from TV and videos—driving out crowds from cinemas.

Table 2 shows the number of movie screens in Europe between 1960 and 1997. The close positive correlation that exists between number of screens and the absolute number of admissions is evident. The plunge in movie admissions between 1960 and 1990 is mirrored in the massive closure of movie screens during the same period. Similarly, the opening of new multiplexes since 1990 is igniting the recovery of movie admissions throughout the continent.

Unlike most Western European countries, Hungary and the Czech Republic have only begun recovering lost audiences in the last year, thanks to the entrance into the market of multinational exhibition companies, which opened new multiplexes in Prague and Budapest. Bulgaria, Romania, Slovakia and the Russian Federation are still clearly on a downward spiral of fewer audiences and fewer screens.

Table 2: Number of Movie Screens in Europe, 1960-1997

Country	1960	1970	1980	1990	1995	1996	1997
U.K	3034	1529	1562	1715	2005	2222	2349
Germany	6950	3673	3422	3269	3901	4070	4284
France	5821	4381	4540	4518	4378	4519	4640
Italy	10393	9439	8453	3293	3816	4004	4200
Spain	6922	6911	4096	1773	2090	2354	2530
Belgium	1506	714	508	440	447	442	447
Netherlands	559	434	523	423	435	440	444
Luxembourg	52	31	20	17	17	17	27
Ireland	272	237	163	172	197	215	243
Austria	1291	917	499	399	382	421	433
Denmark	462	374	475	347	313	322	320
Norway	670	463	444	399	394	399	396
Sweden	2403	1357	1239	1144	1168	1165	1165
Finland	610	330	352	340	330	325	327
Iceland	60	40	48	37	49	51	50
Switzerland	626	595	483	402	488	489	521
Greece	560	1034	1103	500	260	260	280
Portugal	437	485	423	276	282	323	333
Czech Rep.	n.a.	n.a.	n.a.	n.a.	947	848	600
Hungary	4558	3879	3624	1726	597	580	590
Poland	n.a.	n.a.	n.a.	n.a.	788	829	830
Bulgaria*	n.a.	n.a.	n.a.	319	134	156	160
Romania*	n.a.	n.a.	n.a.	420	408	402	436
Slovakia**	n.a.	n.a.	n.a.	433	430	326	234
Slovenia**	n.a.	n.a.	n.a.	94	98	98	113

* Figures correspond to the years 1992-1995.
** Figures correspond to the years 1993-1996.
Source: Compiled from various sources, including government statistical agencies and national film organizations (see listing at Table 1).

But even for Hungary and the Czech Republic, recovering pre-1990 levels of admissions seems quite difficult. Between 1990 and 1995, when most of Western Europe was already in a recovery phase, Hungary lost over half of its audience, and the Czech Republic lost four-fifths of it. Simultaneously, Hungary closed down 60% of its screens, and the Czech Republic a similar proportion. Although both countries have recently succeeded in stopping the trend of falling admissions, the Czech Republic's recovery is limited by competition from a new commercial TV network, by a crumbling exhibition sector, and by continued controls on ticket prices in the remaining state-owned cinemas, which the government is reluctant to privatize.

The dramatic fall of movie admissions throughout Europe had a devastating effect on film production. For a film to be profitable, it has to attract audiences first and foremost in its home market. But with audiences shrinking rapidly and steadily from 1960 onwards, many European film industries were almost completely wiped out. The British and the German film industries, which produced above one hundred feature films a year during the 1950s, saw the number of productions drop to less than twenty in the mid 1970s. Italy and Spain also saw a significant contraction in the number of films they produced a year. The only Western European country that was able to maintain an active film industry despite the admissions crisis was France, due to a complex system of government support, which had been implemented by Malraux during the De Gaulle administration (and which will be described in Section 3 of this paper).

Admissions, the number of screens, and the number of films produced in a country are intimately related. The higher the admissions in a country, the more screens it will have and thus, the greater the potential for the recovery of domestic production. On the contrary, the lower the admissions, the fewer screens there will be and thus, the smaller the potential of recovery for domestic films.

These negative trends—sharply falling admissions, massive closure of cinemas and the subsequent contraction of national film production—were not unique to Europe. Latin America and Asia also experienced this tendency.

Mexico, for example, produced over a hundred feature films a year during the 1940s and 1950s. Not only was the quantity of films produced each year significant, their quality was, too. During that period, Mexican films constituted the second largest export industry in the country and provided employment to over 30,000 Mexican workers.

The stagnation and decline of the Mexican film industry was caused by an overly protectionist law introduced in 1952, which required 1) that half of the screen time in all movie theaters was devoted to domestic films, 2) forbade the dubbing of foreign films into Spanish (so that the illiterate population would have no option but to watch Mexican films), and 3) established a ceiling price for movie tickets. The fact that Mexican films had, by law, 50% of the screen time in all movie theaters regardless of quality, and the fact that with the dubbing restriction they had a captive market of moviegoers, took away any incentive to produce good quality films. In addition, the Mexican government created the *Banco cinematográfico*, a financial institution that gave out subsidies to movie producers. This financing basically removed the last element of risk from the film industry: money to produce was readily available, screen time guaranteed and a market niche secured. The lack of any risk in the production of films acted as a disincentive to quality productions.

During the same period, the government nationalized the largest cinema chains, becoming the largest exhibitor in the country with the movie theater chain, *Compañía Operadora de Teatros* (COTSA). Because the government could operate its movie theaters at a loss, it strictly enforced the ticket price ceiling in all cinemas throughout the country, causing Mexico to have an excessively low admission price (around $0.3). This, in addition to the requirement to reserve half of the screen time to Mexican films, regardless of quality or commercial potential, drastically reduced the profitability of most independent (i.e., non- government) cinema chains. The result was that during the period of high inflation in the 1980s, over half of Mexican cinemas went bankrupt. In 1980, Mexico had more than 2,800 movie screens. By 1993 it had about 1,400, less than half the 1980 level.

Movie attendance dropped in parallel with the massive closure of cinemas. In 1980, 385 million movie admissions were registered in Mexico. By 1995 that number had dropped to 63 million. Evidently, this had a negative impact on the profitability of Mexican productions. In 1985, the highest grossing Mexican film had 1.9 million admissions in Mexico City. By 1995, the most successful Mexican film only received about 270,000 admissions.

The number of films Mexico was able to produce a year was also negatively affected by the crisis in exhibition and movie attendance. In 1980 Mexico was still producing around 100 films a year. By 1995 that figure had dropped to 39 productions, and by 1997 to only 16.

In 1992, a new motion picture law eliminated the screen quota for Mexican films, removed ticket price controls and reduced municipal taxes on cinemas. As a result of the new legislation, new exhibition companies began building multiplexes all over Mexico, reversing the negative trend of the past decade and a half. Between 1993 and 1998, there was steady growth in movie theaters (see Figure 2), and since 1995 there has also been significant growth in movie attendance.

Figure 2: Movie Screens in Mexico, 1980-1998

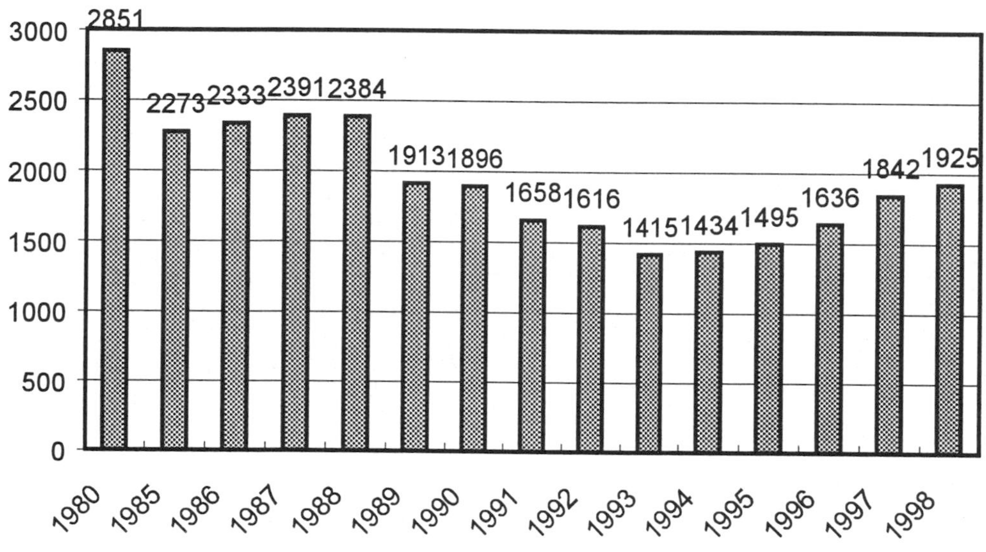

Source: Cámara Nacional de la Industria Cinematográfica de México

The negative trend has not yet been reversed for film production; in 1998, only eight Mexican films were produced. But the recovery of the exhibition sector has a strong potential for helping to revive film production, as it has already done in other countries such as Italy. What is clear is that excessive government intervention in every stage of the life of a film—production, distribution and exhibition—is what destroyed the competitiveness of the Mexican film industry and eventually plunged it into a deep crisis.

The predominance of US films in global markets

Hollywood's share of most major film markets around the world has increased significantly during the past twenty years, particularly during the past decade. American films generally take more than 70% of most European markets and over 90% of most Latin American markets. Hollywood's penetration of Asian markets has also been growing during the past five years, but is, on average, significantly smaller than the dominance it enjoys in Europe and Latin America. Indian, Japanese, Chinese and Hong Kong films regularly take a significant share of Asian markets.

Table 3 shows the market share of American films in several countries, the number of American films in the top ten (in terms of box office receipts) in each market in the latest year for which data were available (usually 1995, 1996 or 1997), and the market share and number of domestic releases.

Table 3: US films' penetration of world markets

Country	Number of American films in the top 10	Market share of American films	Number and market share of domestic productions
Belgium	8	na	20 / 2.1%
France	5	na	150 / 34%
Netherlands	8	82%	18 / 5.4%
Italy	4	51%	69 / 29%
Spain	9	68%	78 / 13%
Portugal	9	88%	10 / na
Greece	na	na	17 / 4%
Ireland	8	90%	18 / na
United Kingdom	8	90%	49 / 11%
Austria	7	na	11 / na
Germany	4	75%	47 / 17%
Switzerland	6	69%	41 / 4.3%
Denmark	4	73%	17 / 19%
Finland	7	70%	10 / 7%
Norway	8	60%	10 / 6%
Sweden	7	68%	24 / 20%
Iceland	7	na	2 / 6.3%
Czech Republic	5	na	na / 35%
Hungary	6	85%	9 / 1.1%
Poland	6	na	15 / 20%
Romania	9	na	9 / 17%
Slovakia	10	na	na
Argentina	8	78%	50 / na
Brazil	na	88%	40 / na
Chile	na	95%	na
Colombia	9	95%	10 / na
Mexico	10	90%	8 / 3%
Venezuela	na	93%	9 / na
South Africa	8	na	na
Japan	6	53%	na / 37%
Hong Kong	na	na	90 / 58%
China	na	na	150 / 67%
India	na	1.5%	750 / 95%
Indonesia	na	10.5%	12 / na
Philippines	10	na	150 / 61%
Singapore	10	na	na
South Korea	8	na	na
Taiwan	6	55%	na
Australia	9	na	13 / 4%
Canada	9	96%	na
United States	10	97%	290 / 97%

Source: Compiled from various sources, including government statistical agencies and national film organizations (see listing at Table 1).

As Table 3 reveals, US films dominate in most markets around the world. In most countries, the majority of the top ten grossing films in 1997 were American. In Europe, the market share of American films is above 50% in all countries, and around 70% on average. In Latin America, it is above 75% in all markets, and 83% on average. In Asia, US penetration is not as strong as in Europe and Latin America. Taiwan is the country where US penetration is the highest, and US films account for 55% of the market.

It is interesting to see, however, that even with the undeniable dominance of Hollywood productions, many countries continue to produce successful films, even when financial resources for film production are limited. The next section explores which countries have the most successful film industries, and how they have managed to survive in the face of competition from Hollywood.

Successful film industries and support schemes

One reason for the US domination of the European film market is the large number of American films produced and, more importantly, released in European country markets. Taken individually, European countries produce a fraction of the number of films produced in the United States. European films also find more difficulty in export markets, including those of other European countries. They rarely find strong distributors and, in foreign markets, lose the advantage of speaking directly to a national audience. In their domestic markets, however, European films are often enormously successful.

Table 4 shows how many domestic films reached the top ten, measured by box office, in their European national markets in 1997. Four of the top ten places were occupied by domestic films in the Czech Republic, France and Italy, and three in Germany, Poland and Denmark. In Hungary and the United Kingdom, two local films made it into the top ten, and in Belgium and Sweden, one. Given the scale and cost of film production in Europe, this suggests a comparatively successful industry. It also emphasizes the degree to which the high share of US films in European markets is due not only to successful films but also the large volumes of unsuccessful ones which find theatrical release dates. It is not only the highly successful motion pictures that sustain America's large market share, but also the pictures of indifferent quality that play week in and week out on the secondary screens of theaters.

Table 4: Domestic Films in Top Ten, 1997

Country	Number
Czech Republic	4
France	4
Italy	4
Germany	3
Poland	3
Denmark	3
Hungary	2
United Kingdom	2
Belgium	1
Sweden	1
Austria	0
Netherlands	0
Ireland	0
Iceland	0
Finland	0

Source: Dodona Research, Cinema Going Europe 1998.

Table 5 lists all the films that reached positions one, two or three in national movie charts in 1997 in the same sixteen European countries as above. *Men in Black* was the most popular film in these countries, reaching the number-one position in four and one of the top three places in twelve. The second most popular was a European picture, *Bean*, top in three countries and in the top three in ten. The third film that attained consistently high popularity across the continent was *The Lost World: Jurassic Park*. Nine of the other thirteen films to occupy first, second or third position in these markets were European, most attaining a top spot in only one country. This degree of isolated popularity was also true of the remaining American films. Only *101 Dalmatians*, balanced by Britain's *The Full Monty*, made the top three in more than one country.

Table 5: Top Performing Films in European Country Markets, 1997

Film Title (Country)	#1	#2	#3
Men in Black (US)	4	6	2
Bean (UK)	3	3	4
The Lost World: Jurassic Park (US)	3	2	5
The Full Monty (UK)	2	-	-
101 Dalmatians (US)	-	1	2
Klier (Poland)	1	-	-
The Fifth Element (France)	1	-	-
Adam and Eva (Sweden)	1	-	-
Fuochi D'Artificio (Italy)	1	-	-
Space Jam (US)	-	1	-
Smilla's Sense of Snow (Denmark)	-	1	-
Liar, Liar (US)	-	1	-
Il Ciclone (Italy)	-	1	-
La Verite Si Je Mens! (France)	-	-	1
The English Patient (US)	-	-	1
Barbara (Denmark) (US)	-	-	1

Source: Dodona Research. Cinema Going Europe 1998.

Virtually every government in Europe has devised a scheme to support film production. Of all European film industries, the French is consistently the strongest in its home market. This situation is the result of strong government action to support the industry, not only at the level of production, or even distribution. Almost alone among Europeans, the French understand that a strong movie industry requires a matching exhibition sector, not tied to Hollywood studios by links of ownership, habit or otherwise. Part of the tax levied on cinema tickets (11% of gross box office) is therefore returned to exhibitors investing in cinemas. (The largest proportion of the tax on admission tickets is devoted to film production through subsidies and soft loans.) The amount collected through this cinema tax is significant, reaching FF564 million.

Around 150 French features and co-productions are released each year and take about a third of the market. French television, especially Canal+, is a major source of production finance, funding about 37% of the budgets of the 125 French films made in 1997.

Unlike some protectionist policies promoted by France concerning television programming (e.g., the European Union decree that 40% of TV programs should be domestic), the only protectionist regulation France has put in place for the film industry is that it does not allow films to be shown on commercial television on popular moviegoing evenings (Friday and Saturday evenings).

European films also fare relatively well in Spain, due to a system of screen quotas and dubbing licenses. These mean, effectively, that 25% of screen space must be devoted to showing European Union films, while distributors must distribute one European picture to obtain a license to dub three non-European (usually US) films. Spain also has a government fund that supports the financing of Spanish productions.

In the United Kingdom, a recent run of successes is creating hopes that a long-term renaissance of the industry may be taking place. A variety of factors have contributed to the industry's recent good run. The highest profile development has undoubtedly been the provision of significant new public funding for the business through the National Lottery.

In Germany, a tax of about 12% of box office receipts is levied on behalf of the national film fund. In the past, this has been criticized for supporting films that had few prospects at the box office. Subsidies from federal and state film boards continue to make up a significant proportion of film budgets with, in recent years, larger amounts becoming available. There is, however, a new focus on the commercial prospects of projects, as the purpose of funding shifts from cultural goals to employment creation.

A further potential source of film finance in Germany comes from the generous tax write-offs available to investors in firms. The ability of German taxpayers to write off 100% of such investments immediately against taxable income has led to the establishment of a number of investor funds, notably Global Entertainment Productions, an off-balance-sheet funding vehicle for Sony Pictures Entertainment. Sony has also announced its plans to spend at least DM100 million in Berlin, notably on post-production at Babelserg studios. Details of the deal aside, it is a concrete manifestation of Sony's strategy of spreading its production activities worldwide.

Other European countries that have special cinema taxes to support their film industries are Austria, with a tax of 1.4%, Belgium, with a tax that varies between 0 and 18.7%, the Netherlands, with a tax of 5.7%, Sweden, with a 10% tax, and Greece with a tax of 12%.

In Latin America, Argentina and Brazil recently passed new motion picture laws, which are helping to revive their moribund film industries. In Argentina, the law requires that 10% of gross box office go to a fund to finance Argentine productions. Ten percent of video rentals and sales, as well as 25% of the taxes received by the Federal Committee on Radio Transmission, also go to the film production fund.

The Argentine law went into effect in 1994. In 1995, 23 feature films were produced. In 1996, 37, and in 1997, 51. In 1997, the Film Production Fund (known as INCAA) received $53 million. Before 1994 the annual budget for film production was $8 million. Half of the resources are devoted directly to financing films. The other half finances the institute that manages the fund, to organize the *Festival de Mar del Plata*, and to give soft credits for production and other industry-related activities.

Three of the four highest takes in the Argentinean market in 1997 were achieved by local offerings, and within the top eight films, the local industry and Hollywood placed four each. At the box office, the home team had the edge, with a cumulative of $25.9 million versus $23.3 million of imports.

In Brazil, film subsidies were drastically reduced by the Collor de Mello administration, but in 1993 it passed a new Law of Support to the Audiovisual Industry. The new law provides attractive corporate tax shelters for investors in the film industry. For example, the remittance tax that the

Hollywood studios have to pay the government for repatriating their profits can instead be invested in domestic filmmaking. In 1997, the shelter provided $60 million to film production. In 1998, it was estimated that the tax shelter stream could rise to $100 million. The law stipulated that the shelter would last for ten years, with the idea that, after a decade of incentives to produce films locally, domestic filmmaking could become self-supporting.

The law has had impressive effects. In 1994 only three feature films were released. In 1995 this number went up to six, and in 1995 to 18. But in 1997, 41 Brazilian films were released. Their box office success, however, has not been comparable to the case of Argentina. In 1997, no Brazilian film hit the top 20.

Three other countries with very successful film industries are India, China and Hong Kong. In the case of India and China, the film industries have flourished within a very protective framework. In India, film imports dubbed into an Indian language were first permitted only as recently as 1992. The success of foreign films has been quite low, because domestic product is quite entrenched and so radically different in style.

American films accounted for only 1.5% of the Indian box office in 1995. The Indian movie industry produced around 750 films in 21 languages in 1995. Indian admissions totaled 5.2 billion in 1996, averaging 5.5 admissions per person. Indian passion for movies continued unabated, as the average ticket price rose from $0.04 in 1990, to $0.10 in 1995.

In the past five years, television has made rapid advances in the Indian market. The rapid increase in TV households was directly responsible for the closure of over a thousand cinemas in the past two years. Indian films are mainly produced for the huge domestic markets, but a few are exported to some Arab and East African countries, and to other neighboring Asian countries with Indian populations.

China's admissions have dropped drastically in the past seven years, from 14.3 billion admissions in 1991, to 2.4 billion in 1996. Two factors partially explain this massive decline in movie attendance: the poor quality of Chinese cinemas, and the advance of TV and video. But another important factor is the ironclad censorship of movie production. New censorship regulations include prohibitions on "long kisses that arouse strong feeling of excitement" and anything that "romanticized crime." Full frontal nudity is not allowed, nor is homosexuality. The new regulations even banned "low-quality background music".

China's state studios produced more than 100 features in 1996. But in Shanghai, the largest film market, nine of the top ten films at the box office in 1996 were from Hollywood. China requires by law that two-thirds of all screen time be devoted to domestic films.

Finally, Hong Kong was the fourth largest producer of films in 1994, and stood behind only the US in terms of exports. At its height, the Hong Kong movie industry produced about 150 titles per year, though fewer than 90 were produced last year. These productions cater for the international market, especially Asian countries such as Malaysia, Indonesia, Philippines, Taiwan, South Korea, Thailand, Japan and, as of late, China.

Conclusions

The United States dominates world cinema today. Several countries, however, continue to produce important domestic box office successes. It is evident that, when given the choice, audiences still prefer homegrown films to imported ones. People want to see their own stories, reflecting their tastes and realities. In Mexico, a recent survey revealed that 91% of the population would like to see more Mexican films.[5]

Even with limited resources, it is possible to compete with Hollywood, as demonstrated by the many small productions that have outperformed substantially more expensive Hollywood films. In 1997, for example, an Italian, an Argentinean and a Czech film, each costing less than $2 million (*Il Ciclone, Comodines* and *Kolya*, respectively) outperformed in domestic box office the biggest Hollywood blockbusters of the year (*The Lost World: Jurassic Park* and *Men in Black*, each costing over $100 million).

Many support schemes for national film industries are working well, such as the ones implemented in France, Germany, the United Kingdom, Spain, Argentina and Brazil. Protectionist policies like screen quotas and dubbing restrictions, however, hurt quality and do not produce internationally competitive industries in the long run, as the Mexican case attests. Furthermore, protectionist policies are becoming rapidly outdated, as new technologies offer, in different formats, the film diversity that quotas are intended to prevent. With satellite TV, video and cable, there is always a foreign film to be watched even if there is a screen quota for domestic productions in cinemas and commercial TV. Furthermore, with new formats to see a film at home, like the Digital Video Disk (DVD), it is possible to get around other protectionist policies, like the dubbing restriction implemented in Mexico, since different languages are already registered in the DVD. Moreover, movie trailers can already be seen through the Internet. It will not be long before full feature-length films will be available through this medium. Finally, quotas have the perverse effect of encouraging "quota quickies"—banal local productions designed only to satisfy official mandates and to capture the subsidies that often come with them.

Filmmaking, however, does need to be supported. First, because film is a cultural manifestation, it would be a great loss if national film industries around the world disappeared in favor of Hollywood. Cultural homogenization would undoubtedly be a negative effect of the global dominance of American films. Second, film is an extremely risky industry. The economists De Vany and Walls have shown that the film industry is, mathematically speaking, chaotic, or borderline chaotic, in the sense that the commercial success of a film is basically impossible to predict.[6] They describe the film industry as a "complex adaptive system poised between order and chaos." Using chaos theory, they try to explain the instability of the industry. Chaos theory seeks to demonstrate how a few simple variables can interact to generate results that are so complicated and unpredictable that they appear to be completely random (i.e., the evolution of the weather or the flow of a river). According to De Vany and Walls, the chaos of the film industry has to do with the way millions of filmgoers and potential filmgoers exchange information. Since people don't know whether they will like a movie until they see it, they have to rely on what others tell them. If they hear good things—from friends, critics or whomever—they will probably go and see the film; if they hear bad things, they probably won't. This process, known as an information cascade, is impossible to forecast.

To demonstrate this mathematically, De Vany and Walls turned to a statistical distribution specified by Albert Einstein and Satyendra Nath Bose to describe the way gas molecules bouncing around a room tend to gather in balls. The position of the balls cannot be predicted, but they always turn up somewhere. After examining the box-office records of three hundred movies released between 1985 and 1986, De Vany and Walls concluded that film viewers were behaving like the gas molecules described by Einstein and Bose.

The evidence showed that audiences were repeatedly attracted to a small number of films. Four releases accounted for a fifth of total box-office revenues over the sample period, and twenty percent of the films accounted for eighty percent of the total. Moreover, it was impossible to say why audiences were attracted to certain films and not to others. The only reliable predictor of a film's box-office take was its performance the previous week. Nothing else seemed to matter—neither the genre of the film, nor its cast, nor its budget. "The strong evidence supporting the Bose-Einstein distribution points to the stark uncertainty facing the motion picture industry," De Vany and Walls concluded. "Neither genre nor stars can guarantee success, and a disaster can bankrupt a studio."

Given the uncertainty of filmmaking, it is important that governments around the world develop support schemes to help their national film industries manage the risks inherent in this activity. In most countries, the risks intrinsic to filmmaking are magnified by competition from Hollywood. In particular, the large marketing budgets American films have can substantially alter box office results.

Moreover, because one-fifth of the movies garners four-fifths of the revenues, eighty percent of films are destined to lose money. This indicates that the volume of production is important for the long-term success of a studio. Again, support schemes are essential for a country to achieve the volume of films necessary to assure a few successes. Temporary subsidies, tax shelters and credit schemes for film production have worked well in several countries, such as Brazil and Spain.

Subsidies, however, should not eliminate the risks of filmmaking altogether, because it could lead to the production of films with no commercial potential, as happened in France in the 1970s and in Mexico in the 1980s. At present, there is a proposal being discussed in the Mexican legislature that attempts to eliminate much of the risk associated with filmmaking: the proposed law would reserve 30% of screen time in movie theaters for Mexican films; it would create a new tax of 5% of box office grosses to subsidize the production of Mexican films; and it would maintain the prohibition on dubbing foreign films into Spanish. In other words, if the new cinema law gets approved, Mexican filmmakers would have a permanent subsidy for the production of Mexican films; they would not have to compete with foreign films for screen time; and they would have a guaranteed market niche with the functionally illiterate population (because, with the dubbing restriction, they would have no other option but to watch Mexican movies). This type of protectionist policy will never lead to the creation of an internationally competitive Mexican film industry. Thus, support mechanisms for film production are necessary, but they should never eliminate competition as the driving force of the industry. If a national film industry is shielded from international competition, it will never become self-sustaining.

The United States will continue to have great influence in world cinema for many years. It has the advantage of a huge domestic market, a language that is rapidly becoming the international language, and very good marketing techniques. Despite the dominance of American films in world markets, however, there are hopeful signals for a sustained revival of national film industries.

First, the evolution of the exhibition sector, from one-screen theaters to multiplexes of up to thirty screens in one site, provides enough windows of exhibition for national films. In the past, when cinemas consisted mainly of one, two or three screens, only the biggest blockbusters could be exhibited, and these were usually American films. Even when national films found their way to the movie theaters, the exhibition time was usually short because there were always films waiting for a screen. With the new multiplexes that are sprouting in many countries, there are enough screens for national productions to be shown, and the time they remain in exhibition has increased substantially, which obviously raises the potential for recovering the investment.

The past three years have seen a boom in the international exhibition sector. National and multinational exhibition companies are building multiplexes all over Western and Eastern Europe, Latin America and East Asia. Dodona Research, a British firm specializing in research on the European film industry,[7] estimates a 30% increase in movie attendance in Europe in the next five years, and attributes it to 4,000 new multiplex screens that will be built in the 1997-2002 period throughout the continent. Similarly, American and Australian exhibition companies have opened new multiplexes in Argentina, Chile, Brazil, Uruguay, Ecuador, Peru, Panama, Costa Rica, El Salvador, Mexico, Malaysia, Thailand, South Korea, Japan, Indonesia and Taiwan.

Second, the evidence shows that audiences around the world still prefer domestic films if given the choice. The fact that so many low-budget domestic films have outperformed much more expensive Hollywood films is a very important signal of the potential of national film industries. Third, countries are finding mechanisms (like the ones described in Section 3 of this paper) to successfully support national film production.

With more movie screens and more financial incentives to produce films domestically, national film industries around the world will be able to endure the fierce competition from Hollywood. As long as people around the globe seek in their films a reflection of their culture, aspirations and dreams, national film industries will have a reason to exist and the potential to compete.

Notes

[1] Data from the Motion Picture Association of America in AC Nielsen, *Box Office Statistics* and also published in *Weekly Variety*, 12-18 October, 1998.

[2] Ibid.

[3] The Economist Intelligence Unit, *World Trade Figures 1997*.

[4] Dodona Research, *Cinema Going Europe*, 1998.

[5] Cámara Nacional de la Industria Cinematográfica, *Encuesta sobre Preferencias del Público,* Covarrubias y Asociados, Octubre, 1998.

[6] Arthur De Vany and David Walls, "Bose-Einstein Dynamics and Adaptive Contracting in the Motion Picture Industry," *The Economic Journal*, November 1996.

[7] Dodona Research is one of the most reliable sources of statistics for the European film industry, including production, distribution and exhibition. It is now expanding to cover the US and Latin American film industries.

References

Baskerville Communications Corporation, 1996, *Global Film Exhibition & Distribution*.
——, 1998, *Global Film Exhibition & Distribution*, Second Edition.

Instituto de la Cinematografía y de las Artes Audiovisuales de España, 1997, Boletín Informativo: Películas, Recaudaciones, Espectadores.

Boudier C., 1997, *El modelo francés de apoyo a la industria cinematográfica*, Ministère de Culture, France.

Brazilian Ministry of Finance, 1993, *Brazilian Law* 8.685, "Audiovisual activities," 20 July.

Brazilian Official Gazette, 1996, 20 August.

Cámara Nacional de la Industria Cinematográfica y del Videograma de México, 1997, *Análisis comparativo internacional de legislaciones de cinematografía casos: Francia, España, Brasil, Argentina y México*.

De Vany A and Eckert R.D., 1991, "Motion Picture antitrust: the paramount cases revisited," *Research in Law and Economics*, Volume 14.

De Vany A. and Walls W.D., 1996, "Bose-Einstein dynamics and adaptive contracting in the motion picture industry," *The Economic Journal*.
——, 1997, "The market for motion pictures: rank, revenue, and survival," *Economic Inquiry*.

Dodona Research, 1998, *Cinema Going Europe: France & Benelux, Germany & Eastern Europe, Southern Europe, United Kingdom & Ireland, Scandinavia & Finland, Summary*.

Giornale dello Spettacolo, Informazioni professionali, 1994, "La nuova legge cinema."

Hong Kong Regulations on Administration of the Films Industry, 1996.

Ley Argentina sobre el Fomento y Regulación de la Actividad Cinematográfica, 1994.

Media Research & Consultancy Spain, 1997.

Ministerio de Información y Difusión del gobierno de la India, 1998, *India 1998*.

Organization for Economic Cooperation and Development, 1998, *Human Capital Investment*.
——, 1998, *Information Technology and the Future of Post-Secondary Education*.

Ovaciones, 1997, "Cierre masivo de cines en la India", 27 Junio.

Ovaciones, 1997, "El embate de Hollywood es el mayor desafío para lograr colocarse en salas," 22 Septiembre.

Rajadhyaksha A. and Willemen P., 1995, *Encyclopaedia of Indian Cinema*.

Reforma, 1998, "Albania: muchas películas, ningún cine," 23 Julio.

Sangham A. K, 1995, *Indian performing arts in the last 25 years*. Vol. II.

TDC News & Messages, 1998:
"Filmart aims at helping film and TV firms to open up new markets," 5 June.
"Over 600 buyers from around the world visited Filmart '98," 5 July. "TDC Hosts Filmart '98 to promote Local Film Industry," 17 May.

The Economist, 1998, "Moreover: Culture wars," 12 September.

Variety Deal Memo, 1997:
"China shifts position as audiences drop," 9 June.
"Former Czechoslovakia teeters on verge of multiplex boom as admissions drop," 7 July.
"Italy tempts fate with longer movie season," 7 July.
"New Hungary film law declares war on Hollywood," 29 September.
"New investment, competition looks to stop film decline and break cartel control," 9 June.

Variety Deal Memo, 1998:
"Byzantine maze of taxes confounds Euro cinema biz," 25 May.
"Cinema protectionism rears with push from filmmakers," 8 June.
"Forecast: Euro admissions to increase 30% in five years," 8 June.

Weekly Variety, 1998:
"Argentine pix heat up at home," 23-29 March.
"Brit pic policy goosed by report's proposals," 30 March-5 April.
"Filmmakers rise from ashes of Yugoslav war," 27 April-3 May.
"Global kudos shine on Brazil pix," 23-29 March.
"Italo prod'n edges toward renaissance," 15-21 June.
"South African gov't grant boosts local filmmakers," 29 June-12 July.
"Spanish pix in cash crunch," 23-29 March.
"Venezuela looks to make a little coin go a long way," 23-29 March.

OPENNESS, POVERTY AND INEQUALITY

J. Mohan Rao

Over the past decade and a half, economic reforms in much of the developing world were necessitated, in the first instance, by a rapid accumulation of internal and external imbalances. This is evident most of all among the countries that underwent severe payments and debt rescheduling problems in the aftermath of the Reagan-Volcker recession and the consequent Mexican debt crisis of the early 1980s. But even in a country such as India, which has undergone reforms only since 1991, the immediate provocation was a similar problem with external indebtedness. More recently, the rapid growth of short-term debt in South Korea is held mainly accountable for the International Monetary Fund (IMF) bailout package and attendant changes in the policy regime.

Although short-term crisis, particularly external imbalance, has been the proximate trigger of reforms, the substantive content of reforms has been largely shaped by diagnoses of long-term structural problems in these economies. It is a remarkable fact that most such diagnoses converged on insufficient external integration of these economies as a primary structural constraint. Consequently, trade reforms and externally oriented financial liberalization have been the cornerstones of structural adjustment. Such *policy* convergence in favor of external integration or what may be termed "openness" has been a major vehicle of globalization in our time. But globalization has also been speeded up by other factors such as internationally coordinated policy changes—including the last round of the General Agreement on Tariffs and Trade (GATT) creating the World Trade Organization (WTO)—improvements in communications technologies and the changing opportunities for new divisions of labor across nations (brought about by both technical change and changing production conditions).

The prevailing opinion in economics favors external openness as a way to promote economic growth. In turn, economic growth is expected to reduce poverty and promote human development more or less automatically. This is not to say that economists neglect the sometimes large redistributions of income or straight misery that a changing global economy may inflict upon an externally integrated country. On the contrary, trade-driven effects on factor prices, wage dispersion and the distribution of income continue to excite much interest within the profession. But it remains the case that economists are loath to encourage trade and macroeconomic interventions aimed at income redistribution or alleviating poverty. The other remarkable aspect of the prevailing opinion is that it harbors no exceptions. It is meant to apply with equal, perhaps even greater, force to the poorer nations of the world where most of the world's poor and much egregious inequality are concentrated.

This paper presents the results of an exercise in stocktaking following two decades of externally oriented reforms in the developing world. It puts together available evidence on indicators of globalization, poverty and inequality for a wide cross-section of nations taking as much care as feasible to choose indicators that are comparable across countries. The aim of this exploration of the empirical record is to provide inputs toward *Human Development Report 1999* whose theme will be globalization and human development. The immediate object of establishing this database is to gauge the degree to which nations have progressed on the path to openness and globalization and whether there are discernible and correlated trends in the extent of absolute poverty and relative inequality. The exercise is also intended to inform us of the extent of continuing diversity across nations with respect to globalization. This allows us to classify country experiences and provide the basis for selecting a sample of countries for intensive study, with a view to identifying the channels through which globalization and openness affect the prospects for poverty alleviation and human development.

The paper is organized as follows. The first section on "Indicators of globalization" summarizes available evidence on a variety of both "input" and "output" (or policy and outcome) indicators of globalization. The evidence is presented for aggregates of countries by income level and region and broad conclusions drawn for those aggregates. We also provide a brief review of the literature concerned with measuring openness and the limitations of commonly used indicators (which arise from the paucity of data and/or from problems of interpretation). The evidence shows large average differences in globalization (in terms of trade, export and trade-taxation ratios, for example) among low-income, middle-income and high-income nations. In the section "From globalization to openness," we construct a trade-based index of openness to take into account structural differences in globalization across nations, differences that are related to economic size (proxied by population size) and, as just noted, the level of development (proxied by per capita income). The "Trade Index" and "Export Index" that we construct are derived respectively from the ratio of trade to gross domestic product (GDP) and the export/GDP ratio for 1970-79, 1980-87 and 1988-95. Countries are then ranked in terms of the Trade Index and changes in rank across the three periods to give an indication of the speed of opening up.

The section on "The evidence on inequality and poverty" examines the available evidence on poverty and inequality in developing nations. Unlike the data on nations' global transactions, this evidence is neither abundant in quantity nor even nearly uniform in quality. In addition, particular difficulties of international comparability arise and these are duly noted. Comparability and quality problems are especially salient when we try to gauge levels of poverty and inequality in different countries or at different points of time. Some of these difficulties are alleviated if we focus on trends rather than levels. Accordingly, our effort is concentrated in this direction, even though the time-series are scarce and too much should not be read into "trends" calculated from pairs of annual observation (except as one may surmise that poverty and inequality are apt to change relatively smoothly over time).

The final section brings together the indicators of openness, poverty and inequality in both level and especially trend forms. Our purpose here is twofold. The first is to look for broad associations, if any, between (trends in) openness on the one hand and poverty and inequality on the other; our intent is not to explore causality in any rigorous sense but simply to establish a rough classification of the diversity of experience. Our second purpose is to search for "outliers" in the charts—countries that may have been leaders or laggards in opening up and whose poverty and inequality trends are similarly removed from the crowded middle.

Indicators of globalization

Many years of structural adjustment, much of which has been oriented toward trade liberalization and external integration, have created the strong expectation that observable indices must show significant increases in the degree of globalization. This section and the next investigate whether and to what extent this expectation is borne out in cross-country evidence for the period 1970-95. While there is a fairly large body of cross-country data from which indicators of globalization may be constructed, researchers have not been able to agree universally on any particular indicator.

First, a definition of key terms is appropriate. By *globalization* we mean a process by which an economy becomes increasingly integrated with the world economy. The term is sometimes used interchangeably to refer to both a country's position at a point in time and changes over time. Increased integration is itself indicated by rising cross-border transactions normalized relative to income or other appropriate denominator[1]. The items transacted include goods, services, technologies, financial flows, direct investments, labor migrations, information and cultural flows, so there can be at least as many indicators of globalization. The term *openness* will refer to a country's receptivity to cross-border flows. Thus, indicators of openness ought to implicitly capture policy actions that either resist or promote globalization. This is why it is easy to deploy observable data to measure globalization as compared to measuring openness. Even so, a single indicator of globalization cannot capture important dimensions of the nature of external integration. For example, two countries may have identical trade and export ratios but these would miss an important aspect if the composition of exports (as between primary and manufactured goods) and imports (say, between capital goods and consumer goods) were not considered[2].

Evidence on a number of globalization indicators is presented in aggregative form in Tables 1 and 2[3]. Table 1 groups countries, by their level of income, into low-, middle- and high-income categories[4]. The periodization is designed roughly to capture different points in "world time": 1970-79 partly overlaps the so-called Golden Age of high growth (which in the case of the less developed countries was stretched beyond the crisis years of 1973-75 by the recycling of petrodollars by international banks); 1980-87 includes the bulk of the years of the lost decade of growth; and 1988-95 witnessed a new era of liberalization and convergence in policy regimes.

TABLE 1: Structural variation in some measures of globalization

	GDP pc (US$1987)	Trade (% of GDP)	Exports (% of GDP)	Trad.Taxes (% of Trade)	Net FDI (% of GDP)	Net PCF (% of GDP)	Prm.Exprts. (% of GDP)	BToT (1987=100)
LOW-INCOME COUNTRIES								
1970-79	426	52.4	22.8	14.0	0.7	1.8	72.2	..
	(197)	(20.1)	(9.4)	(16.5)	(0.2)	(0.6)	(62.6)	..
1980-87	412	54.0	21.7	13.3	0.4	1.5	69.4	114.2
	(252)	(25.7)	(11.4)	(20.8)	(0.3)	(1.1)	(61.5)	(118.4)
1988-95	393	56.5	23.3	12.6	0.9	1.0	54.2	96.6
	(355)	(33.3)	(15.8)	(19.5)	(1.9)	(3.1)	(30.1)	(102.4)
MIDDLE-INCOME COUNTRIES								
1970-79	1740	67.7	30.8	9.0	1.2	3.2	64.3	..
	(1251)	(35.1)	(16.5)	(7.1)	(0.7)	(3.4)	(63.1)	..
1980-87	1975	72.8	33.3	6.4	1.2	2.8	57.4	115.5
	(1449)	(40.3)	(20.3)	(6.1)	(0.7)	(2.3)	(56.0)	(122.0)
1988-95	2106	75.4	35.3	5.5	1.5	2.3	47.9	103.5
	(1537)	(44.3)	(21.0)	(4.7)	(1.3)	(2.7)	(41.2)	(101.1)
HIGH-INCOME COUNTRIES								
1970-79	10700	76.1	36.9	2.8	..	..	28.7	..
	(12081)	(33.2)	(16.5)	(2.0)	..	..	(23.6)	..
1980-87	12838	88.1	43.7	0.8	..	..	30.7	98.0
	(14266)	(36.1)	(17.8)	(1.3)	..	..	(23.3)	(95.3)
1988-95	15277	84.1	42.7	0.7	..	..	25.9	100.7
	(17023)	(37.7)	(19.0)	(0.8)	..	..	(15.6)	(101.6)
ALL COUNTRIES								
1970-79	3415	64.2	29.4	8.4	1.0	2.6	56.9	..
	(2884)	(32.5)	(16.0)	(3.5)	..	..	(29.6)	..
1980-87	3849	69.3	31.3	7.5	0.8	2.1	53.1	111.1
	(3099)	(36.0)	(17.8)	(3.7)	..	..	(29.3)	(100.3)
1988-95	4432	70.5	32.7	6.3	1.2	1.7	41.5	100.2
	(3435)	(38.1)	(19.0)	(2.7)	..	..	(18.8)	(101.5)

Notes: Figures in parentheses are weighted means
GDP pc = GDP per capita
Trad. Taxes = Export and import tax revenues
FDI = Foreign Direct Investment;
PCF = Private Capital Flows
Prm. Exprts = Primary Exports
BtoT = Barter Terms of Trade

TABLE 2: Regional variation in some measures of gobalization

	pc GDP (US$1987)	Trade (% of GDP)	Exports (% of GDP)	Trad.Taxes (% of Trade)	Net FDI (% of GDP)	Net PCF (% of GDP)	Prm.Exprts. (% of GDP)	BToT (1987=100)
SUB-SAHARAN AFRICA								
1970-79	700	66.1	27.8	13.0	1.0	2.3	73.7	..
	(650)	(49.4)	(24.2)	(5.2)	(0.6)	(2.1)	(63.4)	..
1980-87	723	70.1	28.3	10.9	0.9	2.0	73.4	114.6
	(557)	(48.8)	(23.9)	(5.1)	(0.4)	(1.5)	(62.5)	(123.6)
1988-95	732	69.5	29.1	10.8	1.0	1.2	61.9	99.9
	(514)	(54.0)	(25.7)	(5.1)	(0.7)	(1.5)	(47.7)	(103.8)
SOUTH ASIA								
1970-79	208	27.8	11.5	15.1	0.1	0.1	41.3	..
	(235)	(15.8)	(6.9)	(18.0)	(0.1)	(0.1)	(41.4)	..
1980-87	256	35.2	12.9	15.7	0.2	0.9	48.6	104.1
	(280)	(19.4)	(7.5)	(22.8)	(0.1)	(0.9)	(39.0)	(99.4)
1988-95	314	39.8	16.4	13.8	0.4	0.7	23.7	96.9
	(359)	(25.0)	(11.0)	(21.4)	(0.2)	(1.2)	(21.6)	(105.9)
EAST ASIA								
1970-79	2661	79.7	38.8	8.9	1.0	2.9	51.5	..
	(1417)	(28.7)	(14.5)	(8.8)	(0.3)	(1.1)	(22.9)	..
1980-87	3731	94.5	46.4	6.3	1.5	4.1	40.2	107.2
	(1798)	(34.6)	(18.1)	(5.7)	(0.6)	(1.9)	(20.7)	(94.4)
1988-95	5236	101.8	51.2	5.0	3.0	4.4	26.0	100.7
	(2326)	(32.9)	(17.2)	(4.4)	(3.0)	(5.0)	(10.8)	(104.7)
MIDDLE EAST & NORTH AFRICA								
1970-79	2236	65.2	30.0	15.4	0.7	3.4	67.7	..
	(1179)	(64.0)	(26.8)	(16.9)	(0.8)	(4.9)	(75.4)	..
1980-87	2744	68.3	30.4	16.7	1.1	3.0	60.9	130.0
	(1529)	(60.1)	(27.1)	(18.5)	(0.9)	(2.5)	(69.9)	(136.2)
1988-95	2941	74.7	33.7	11.7	1.7	2.0	38.4	100.5
	(1591)	(63.6)	(28.8)	(12.6)	(1.2)	(3.1)	(35.9)	(103.4)
LATIN AMERICA & CARIBBEAN								
1970-79	1785	59.4	28.1	9.0	1.1	3.2	66.2	..
	(1718)	(27.2)	(12.8)	(5.9)	(0.7)	(3.6)	(61.9)	..
1980-87	1906	58.7	28.1	6.5	0.6	1.9	63.5	118.2
	(1884)	(29.9)	(15.8)	(6.1)	(0.7)	(2.4)	(59.8)	(126.8)
1988-95	1946	61.0	28.8	5.5	1.0	1.6	60.7	100.9
	(1888)	(28.9)	(13.9)	(4.5)	(1.1)	(2.5)	(49.0)	(99.1)

Note: See Table 1.

Table 1 shows that trade and export ratios rose over the whole period for both middle-income and low-income countries[5]. But the rise was both significantly higher and more sustained for the middle- than for the low-income countries. The high-income countries witnessed the sharpest trade and export increases of all three groups between the first two periods, but there has been an actual decline in trade and export ratios between the second and third periods[6]. Thus, according to observable trade indicators, the world has become more globalized over the last quarter century. But the relative weight of low-income countries in world trade has declined and international differences in the extent of globalization continue to be strongly related to the level of development. The last point shows up clearly in Figures 1 and 2.

FIGURE 1: Trade ratios by income level and over time

FIGURE 2: Export ratios by income level and over time

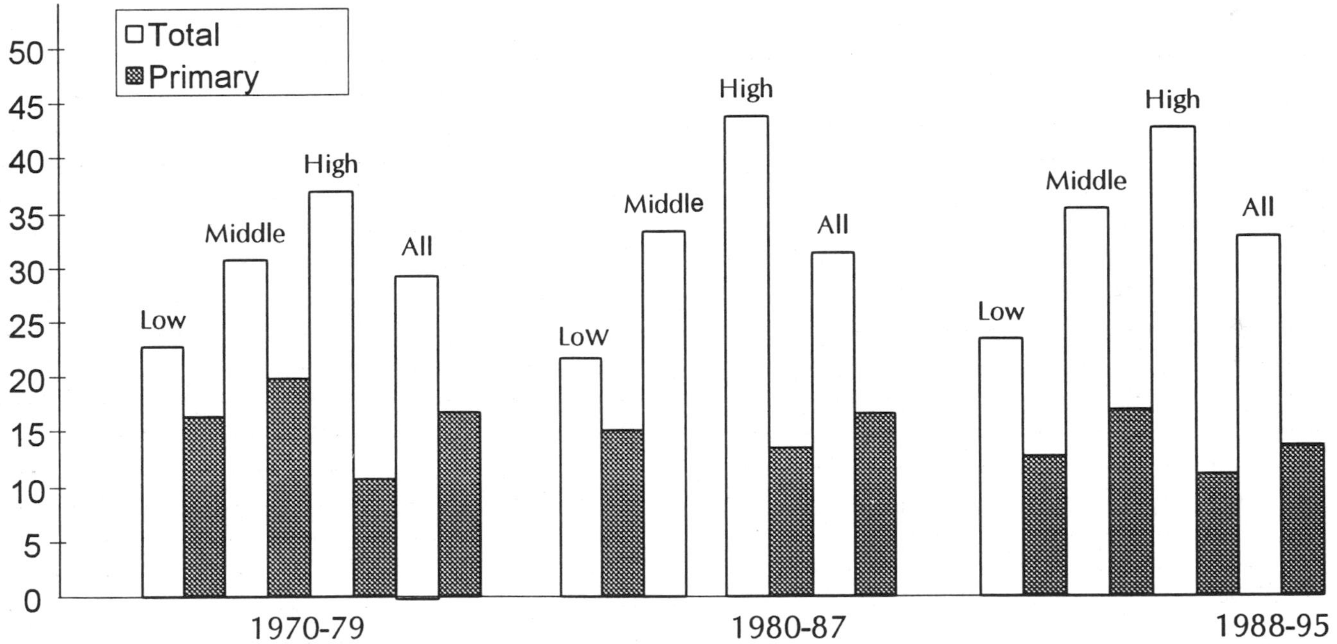

Import tariffs and export taxes are primary instruments by which a country may pursue trade-restrictive policies. Column 3 in Table 1 (and also Figure 3) shows the differences in trade taxation relative to trade across income groupings and over time[7]. Though undoubtedly related to the instruments of policy, the trade taxation ratio is an ambiguous indicator at best of policy openness. This is because it has both a trade policy and a fiscal policy dimension. For now, it is sufficient to note the very large differences across the income groups. Thus, low-income countries seem to be heavily reliant upon trade taxation and/or heavily restrictive of international trade compared to the middle- and high-income nations.

Two further indicators connected with international trade are shown in the last two columns of Table 1. The first of these shows that there has been some change in the character of global trade as measured by the share of primary exports (which include food, minerals and other non-food items). The share of manufactured exports has risen while the primary share has fallen in all three groups. But the greater dependence on primary exports among the low- and middle-income countries as compared to the high-income group shows that these economies are not, in a qualitative sense, symmetrically integrated into the world economy.

FIGURE 3: Trade taxes (% of trade) by income level and over time

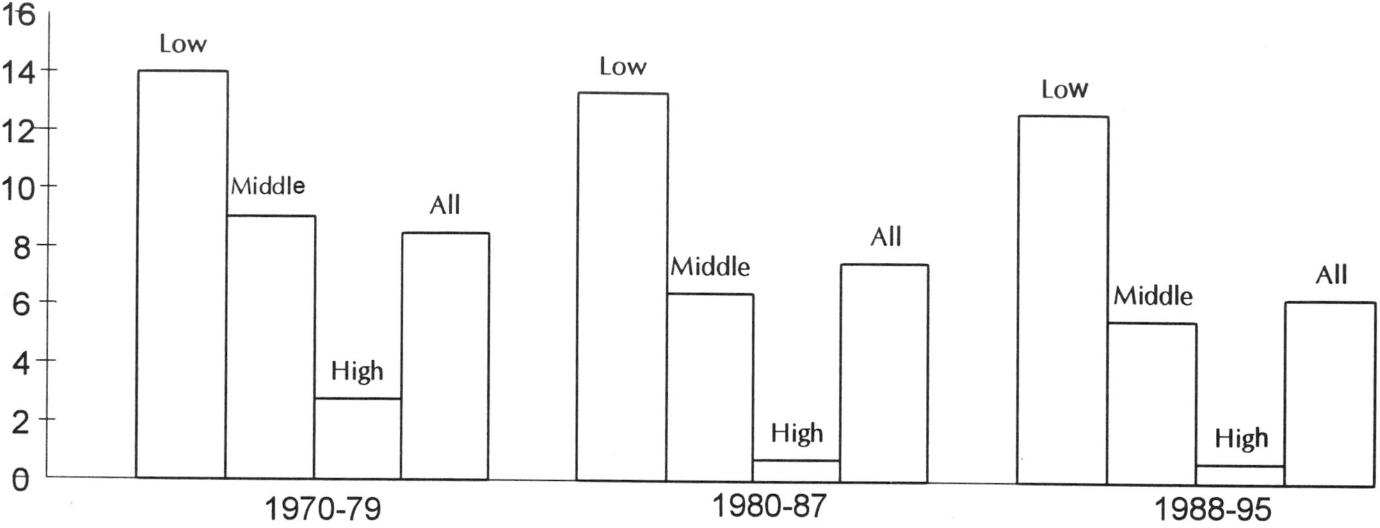

A higher share of primary exports often means that the country is vulnerable to large terms-of-trade shocks and associated instability in import capacity and the growth process. The last column shows the net barter terms of trade with base 1987. It is clear that both low- and middle-income countries suffered large reductions in their terms of trade between the first and second pairs of time periods. In conjunction with the stability of the terms of trade in the rich countries, and the fact that the bulk of the trade from the less developed countries is with the rich countries, this shows that there has been a deterioration in the terms of trade of the poorer vis-à-vis the richer nations. These observations underline the fact that trade is a source of both potential gains and, especially for poor countries, potential losses so increased external integration per se is not a virtue.

The remaining two columns of Table 1 relate to financial globalization measured by net flows of foreign direct investment (FDI) and net private capital flows (PCF). The data in this respect are much less complete both across nations and over time than are the trade data. The key point here is that net FDI flows and PCF still remain relatively small proportions of GDP for most countries. In net terms, there has been a shift in favor of FDI reflecting the continuing high debt-service ratios that many in the developing world face. According to World Bank data, our source here, total capital flows amounted to $273 billion in 1995. But this was a mere 1% of world GDP in that year and only 4.3% of gross investment worldwide. And even this flow is heavily concentrated among a handful of nations. Just eighteen countries, each receiving at least 1% of the world total, account for 91.4% of the total flow. Low-income countries received a mere $20 per capita, middle-income countries got $44 per capita and the high-income nations received $185 per person (see Rao 1997).

That these flows can, in some countries, finance a sizable portion of gross domestic investment is of course true. Leaving the high-income countries aside, we find that a half dozen countries (Hungary, Nigeria, Namibia, Poland, Nicaragua and Mauritius) financed at least a fifth of their domestic investment from foreign sources. But these exceptions confirm the general rule that finance—in the sense of sources of net funds to finance domestic investment—tends to be strongly national rather than international. Even among the rich nations of the West, saving and investment rates are strongly correlated. Note from Table 1 that capital flows (whether direct investments or portfolio flows) follow development rather than lead it: middle-income countries on average receive more net foreign finance than do low-income countries. If we suppose that in a properly functioning (or "integrated") market, capital would flow from capital-abundant to capital-scarce regions, then, we must conclude that the global capital markets are profoundly fragmented and localized.

Table 1 suggests another broad conclusion of some significance for the interpretation of globalization indicators. We have shown weighted means for all indicators—with weights being the appropriate natural denominator[8]—by the figures in parentheses. Roughly speaking, the weighted means reflect the influence of the economic size of nations while the simple means give equal weight to each nation. The influence of size may be quickly summarized. Larger countries are decisively less "globalized" than the average country in that they have much lower trade and export shares in GDP. For the low-income group alone (but not for the other two groups), the weight of trade taxes is greater among the larger countries, reflecting either greater fiscal dependence on such taxes or a greater proclivity to restrict imports and exports.

Table 2 summarizes the aforementioned indicators for various geographical groupings (excluding the developed countries). East Asia unsurprisingly has the highest trade and export ratios among all regions and (barring only South Asia which had the lowest export ratios to start with) has also witnessed the highest rate of increase in the export ratio (see also Figures 4 and 5). Perhaps somewhat surprising is the observation that sub-Saharan Africa (SSA), which is mostly low-income, has trade and export ratios that are equal to or surpass those of Latin America and the Caribbean (LAC) and Middle East and North Africa (MENA), regions which are predominantly middle-income. While some of this may be explained as the apparent influence of size (this seems the case for the LAC-SSA comparison), no such inference seems sustainable for the MENA-SSA comparison. In regard to net financial flows, once again SSA and LAC have broadly similar levels and trends (a steady decline between periods). The gains in this respect are of course heavily concentrated in East Asia. Finally, dependence on primary exports is greatest in the LAC and SSA groups and least in East Asia. The former two have also experienced the lowest declines over time in such dependence (see Figure 5).

Broadly similar conclusions are developed by the World Bank (1996). Most measures of integration point to wide disparities across less developed countries in both the level and the speed of integration, whether as outcomes or as policies. They also show a heavy concentration of gains, with the high-income countries continuing to make the biggest gains in terms of their international integration. The Bank document notes that in 1995, 54 of 126 countries (with a D rating) were essentially shut out from access to private lending. A further 33 nations had a C rating, which required them to pay 500 or more basis points over benchmark US rates of interest. The A-rated countries are exclusively in the high-income group and, prior to the recent Asian crisis, the B-rated countries included only Korea, Malaysia and Thailand.

From globalization to openness

A country's policy stance towards external integration of its economy (which we have termed openness) is not easily measured. To begin with, this section considers some reasons why this is so and why a consensus on this matter has eluded researchers. Following this, we focus on the construction of a trade-based index of openness. We believe this index captures the *degree of policy openness* (accounting for both direct and indirect, and external and internal policy influences on a country's capacity to participate in the international economy) as distinct from either *trade policy* in the narrow sense (tariffs and quotas and other direct restrictions) or *trade integration* as an outcome variable (which we considered in the preceding section).

FIGURE 4: Regional differences in trade ratios

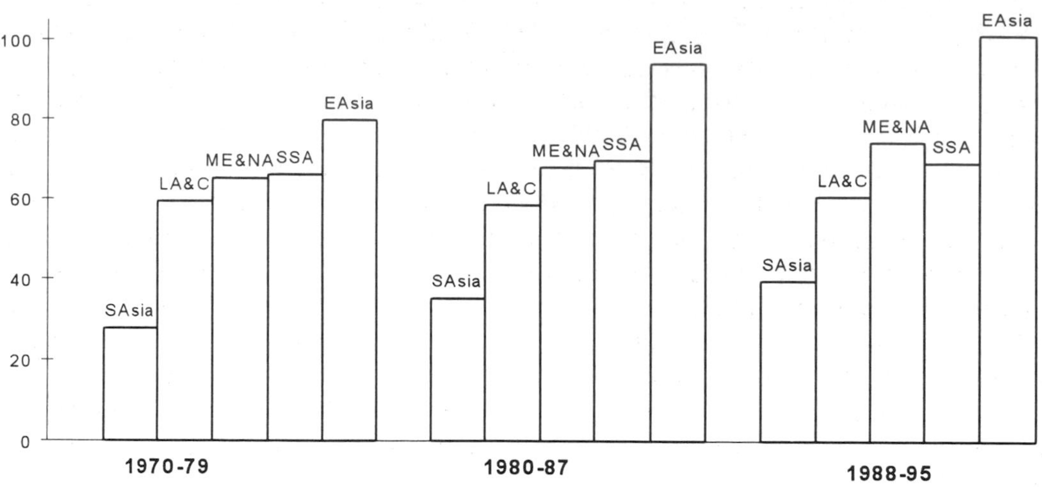

FIGURE 5: Regional differences in export ratios

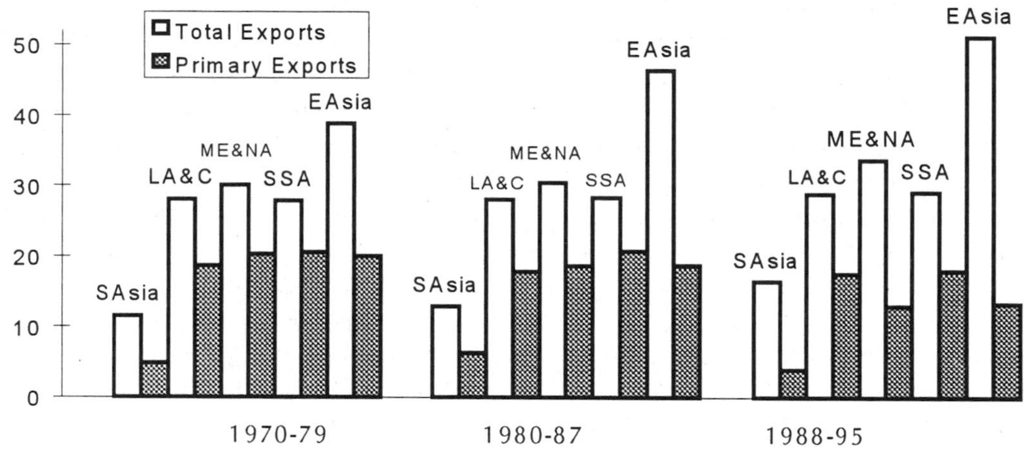

FIGURE 6: Regional Differences in Trade Taxation

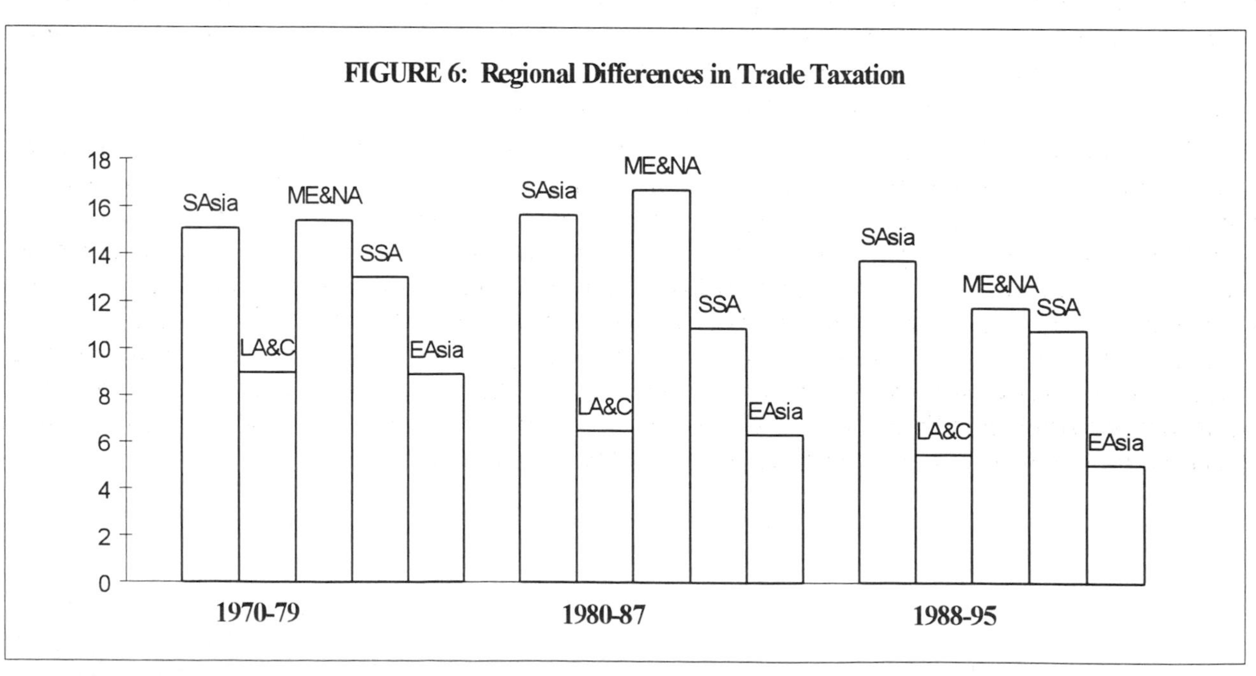

Increased policy openness would, in some respects, be manifest in the policy regime itself. Thus, the growth of openness could be gauged by reduced average tariffs, lifting of quotas, greater freedom of mobility of capital and the like. Such "administrative" measures of openness or barriers have been employed in the literature but confront a number of important difficulties. Tariff rates and quotas applied to various goods must be aggregated to arrive at an economy-wide index of tariffs or quota coverage, but the aggregation entails various arbitrary assumptions[9]. A second difficulty is that average tariff rates are available for a broad sample of countries only for the mid-to-late 1980s so that no trends could be built on their basis. Even if these narrowly technical and data problems could be overcome, there remains a more basic problem. This has to do with the fact that external integration is affected not merely by avowedly "trade" policies such as tariffs or quotas but also by financial policies, macroeconomic policies, labor policies, etc. For example, increased trade may result from increased investments in human capital, which may in turn flow from policies designed to reduce income inequality. It is even possible that a liberal "trade" policy turns out not to be. Consider tariffs or other trade taxes. While such taxes can, in general, be expected to restrict trade directly, they may well increase a country's trade capacity indirectly if the revenues are critical to, say, public investment in infrastructure or other factors complementary to trade[10].

Sachs and Warner (1995) have approached the problem of measuring openness by combining several instruments of external policy in a single index. But it is noteworthy that they take a country's trade regime to be a proxy for the soundness of its whole policy package and that is why they choose to focus on trade policy. As they state the matter, "Trade reform is almost always accompanied by a much broader range of reforms, including macroeconomic stabilization, internal liberalization, legal reforms.... Our results [relating economic growth causally to the trade regime] cannot, therefore, distinguish between the effects of trade policy per se and the effects of other parts of the policy package" (p. 57). Following this rationale, Sachs and Warner define an economy to be "closed" if any of the following criteria applies: average tariffs in excess of 40%, coverage of non-tariff barriers in excess of 40%, exchange rate black-market premium exceeding 20%, socialist economy and state export monopoly. An economy is taken to be "open" if none of these criteria holds. One problem with this approach is that its binary treatment does not accord with commonly held notions of openness. A second difficulty is that, as the authors themselves note, "In many instances, the black market premium was the decisive variable in categorizing economies as closed or open" (p. 106). This has been questioned on the grounds that the premium (a) is endogenous; (b) reflects the thinness of the market; and (c) is affected by penalties, the prevalent interest rates, etc. (Srinivasan 1995).

Since it has proved difficult to measure openness by its instrumentalities, many researchers have resorted to measuring it by its presumed consequences such as the observed trade share in GDP. In other words, openness has often been proxied by globalization[11]. But if policy openness may not be unambiguously indicated by measures of policy, such as average tariffs, that are manifestly oriented toward external transactions, measures of those transactions themselves (the various outcome indices of globalization we have considered) suffer from being hybrid effects of a country's *capacity* to trade and its *willingness* to trade. It is the latter that we mean to measure through an index of openness.

Our analysis of globalization in the earlier section has indicated two variables—country size and per capita income—that seem to strongly condition average levels of external integration. Our approach here is to take these variables as proxies for a range of determinants of globalization that are essentially beyond the control of policy. On average, population size is positively related to an economy's resource base and perhaps also to transport costs. Hence, internal diversification is easier for large than for small countries. Per capita income may be similarly related to external trading possibilities though the influences here are more complex. At low levels of development, the share of industry in GDP is low so that exports are generally limited to the extractive sectors. With low per capita incomes, there is also less scope for intra-industry trade due to limited product differentiation. Low incomes can also be a proxy for high transport costs, poor infrastructure, low levels of human capital, etc., all of which limit trade[12].

Given the premise that population and income are "structural" determinants of a country's capacity to trade, we have statistically isolated their effects on observed trading shares and constructed an openness index from the latter after purging them of the structural effects. That is, we take the average cross-country effects of size and income to be structural factors. And by implication, deviations of trade ratios (whether positive or negative) from the structural relationship are taken to be the influence of policies towards openness. We employed both the trade/GDP ratio and the export/GDP ratio as the dependent variable in the regressions (see Table 3) since many developing countries run persistent balance-of-trade deficits. The independent variables are population size and per capita GDP (at 1987 national prices in US$) both taken in log form. The regressions show that large size makes for lower trade and export ratios whilst high income raises trade and export ratios, with both effects being statistically significant[13].

We have constructed a Trade Index and an Export Index from the residuals of the corresponding regression equations using a scale of 0 to 100. Although the two indices differ substantially in a few cases, they are very similar for the vast majority of nations. Table 4 reports mean values of the Trade Index for each country for the three periods of the study and ranks them in ascending order. Changes in rank between periods are shown in the last two columns and may be taken to be indicative of the relative speed of opening up. Figure 7 plots the computed Trade Index (in ascending order) against the observed trade ratio. The results show that Austria, Belgium, Denmark and New Zealand are among the high-income countries with Trade Index values that are less than two-third their respective trade ratios. The corresponding list of low- and medium-income nations includes Botswana, the Congo, Lesotho, Mauritius, Namibia, Costa Rica, Trinidad and Tobago and Malaysia. These are of course all small countries. On the other side of the distribution, Japan and the US are the high-income countries with Trade Index values that were greater than one and one-half times their trade ratios. In the less developed world, countries with a similarly understated level of openness include China, India, Bangladesh, Argentina, Brazil, Peru, Sudan and Ethiopia.

TABLE 3: Effects of Population Size and Income on the GDP Share of Trade (Annual data, 1970-95)

Independent Variable	Dependent variable	
	Trade/GDP	Exports/GDP
Constant	237.5***	95.5***
	(5.03)	(2.91)
LG(POP)	-12.4***	-6.0***
	(0.28)	(0.16)
LG(pcGDP)	3.1***	4.0***
	(0.32)	(0.18)
Adj. R-Sq.	0.44	0.42
Mean dependent variable	62.3	29.1
Standard Error	24.2	14.2
Sample size	2739	2818

Notes:
LG(POP) = logarithm of population size
LG(pcGDP) = log of GDP per capita in 1987 US$.
*** Indicates coefficient is significant at the 1% level.

TABLE 4: A Trade-Based Openness Index

Country	Trade-Index of Openness			Country Rankings			Rise In Rank (+)	
	(1970-79)	(1980-87)	(1988-95)	(1970-79)	(1980-87)	(1988-95)	(1980-87)	(1988-95)
Low-Income	43.9	45.6	48.6	65.1	64.1	61.2	1.0	3.0
Guyana	68.5	57.6	71.7	2	22	7	-20	15
Mozambique	.	46.9	67.8	56	56	9	0	47
Gambia, The	43.4	57.9	65.2	60	21	13	39	8
Nigeria	48.2	52.2	64.7	42	36	15	6	21
China	53.9	59.5	62.5	24	18	18	6	0
Tanzania	.	39.9	61.8	91	91	21	0	70
Congo	54.9	63.1	60.9	20	10	3	10	-13
Sri Lanka	52	57.2	60.5	30	23	24	7	-1
Mauritania	56.4	70.6	59.2	19	6	27	13	-21
India	51.5	54.5	56.6	33	30	29	3	1
Dem. Rep. Congo	38.8	47.6	56.4	88	51	30	37	21
Togo	58.8	62.9	55.8	11	11	31	0	-20
Kenya	53.2	50.7	54.4	27	42	34	-15	8
Angola	.	43.4	54.2	73	73	35	0	38
Zimbabwe	43.3	44.6	53.2	61	70	36	-9	34
Pakistan	46.2	51.1	53.2	48	39	37	9	2
Myanmar	.	.	50.7	41	41	41	0	0
Malawi	49.4	45.2	50.4	39	67	43	-28	24
Nicaragua	40.7	32.2	50.2	69	107	45	-38	62
Zambia	57.3	53.9	49.7	14	31	48	-17	-17
Senegal	51.2	52.2	48.6	34	37	55	-3	-18
Somalia	43.6	56	48.5	59	27	56	32	-29
Honduras	45.1	41.7	48.5	51	82	57	-31	25
Bangladesh	42.4	47.2	47.7	67	53	61	14	-8
Liberia	62	55.3	47.1	9	28	65	-19	-37
Nepal	31.5	38.8	46.9	109	94	67	15	27
Ghana	34.4	30.3	46	102	112	70	-10	42
Chad	44.2	45.5	44.9	58	64	76	-6	-12
Ethiopia	.	42.7	43.8	77	77	82	0	-5
Madagascar	35.7	35.5	43.8	100	103	83	-3	20
Sudan	35.8	35.5	43.5	99	102	84	-3	18
Benin	40.6	47.6	42.6	71	52	86	19	-34
Guinea	.	45.5	42.5	63	63	88	0	-25
Mali	35.5	45.8	40.9	101	61	92	40	-31
Sierra Leone	42.8	32.1	40.4	64	108	93	-44	15
Niger	36	42	38.5	95	80	97	15	-17
Burkina Faso	33.7	39.1	37.4	105	93	102	12	-9
Cameroon	40.7	45.5	37.2	70	65	104	5	-39
Rwanda	29.3	31.8	36.6	111	110	105	1	5
Uganda	.	33.9	36.3	104	104	106	0	-2
Guinea-Bissau	22.1	30	36	118	113	107	5	6
Burundi	27.4	31.6	35.8	113	111	109	2	2

Table 4 (Low income) cont'd

Country	Trade-Index of Openness			Country Rankings			Rise In Rank (+)	
	(1970-79)	(1980-87)	(1988-95)	(1970-79)	(1980-87)	(1988-95)	(1980-87)	(1988-95)
Haiti	33.1	38.2	33.6	106	98	112	8	-14
Cent. Afr. Rep.	40	40.2	33.4	80	89	113	-9	-24
Comoros	.	29.6	28.2	115	115	116	0	-1
Middle-Income	46.3	49.4	51.2	53.3	56.3	55.5	-3.1	0.8
Malaysia	62.1	75.4	81.1	7	4	1	3	3
Swaziland	66.8	74.2	77.5	4	5	3	-1	2
Lesotho	62.4	84.9	77.1	6	2	4	4	-2
Puerto Rico	68.3	77.7	72.9	3	3	5	0	-2
Jordan	.	61.7	72.2	13	13	6	0	7
Thailand	48.3	53.9	70.5	40	33	8	7	25
Jamaica	45	60	67.1	53	17	10	36	7
Mauritius	54.5	56.9	65.2	22	25	14	-3	11
Philippines	50.4	53.9	63.3	37	32	17	5	15
Botswana	53.3	64.7	62.5	26	9	19	17	-10
Namibia	.	68.6	62.3	8	8	20	0	-12
Tunisia	44.8	54.7	61.5	55	29	22	26	7
Indonesia	56.6	60.9	60.1	18	15	25	3	-10
Papua N. Guin.	51.9	59.1	59.5	31	19	26	12	-7
Egypt	52.4	58.6	58.2	28	20	28	8	-8
Fiji	47.3	45.9	55.5	45	60	32	-15	28
Syrian Arab Rep.	40.5	37.9	52.9	75	99	38	-24	61
Morocco	45.4	49.4	51.7	49	45	39	4	6
Paraguay	25.8	32.1	50.5	114	109	42	5	67
South Africa	49.6	51	50.3	38	40	44	-2	-4
Seychelles	60.2	48.3	50	10	50	47	-40	3
Poland	.	45.2	49.4	68	68	50	0	18
Hungary	57.2	57	49.3	15	24	51	-9	-27
Romania	.	48.7	49.3	46	46	52	0	-6
Oman	54.8	48.5	49.1	21	48	53	-27	-5
Costa Rica	40.4	44.5	48.3	76	71	58	5	13
Venezuela	40.6	40.7	47.2	72	85	63	-13	22
Mexico	35.8	42.5	47.1	98	78	64	20	14
Panama	.	43.2	47	74	74	66	0	8
Chile	36	42.7	46.8	96	76	68	20	8
Turkey	31.9	41	45.8	108	84	71	24	13
Ecuador	39.7	39.7	45.6	84	92	74	-8	18
Dominican Rep.	37.7	40.6	45.3	90	86	75	4	11
Trinidad & Tob.	45	38.3	44.9	52	97	77	-45	20
Gabon	51.1	48.5	44	35	47	81	-12	-34
Greece	33.7	40.6	43	103	88	85	15	3
Algeria	50.7	45.4	41.5	36	66	89	-30	-23
Colombia	38.1	37.9	41.4	89	100	90	-11	10
Brazil	39.8	41.8	40.3	82	81	94	1	-13
Barbados	56.9	56.1	39.4	17	26	95	-9	-69
Guatemala	36.2	32.5	39.3	94	106	96	-12	10

Table 4 (Middle Income) cont'd

Country	Trade-Index of Openness			Country Rankings			Rise In Rank (+)	
	(1970-79)	(1980-87)	(1988-95)	(1970-79)	(1980-87)	(1988-95)	(1980-87)	(1988-95)
Peru	37.1	38.7	38.1	93	95	99	-2	-4
El Salvador	44.9	40.2	37.9	54	90	100	-36	-10
Bolivia	39.7	29.6	35.9	83	114	108	-31	6
Cape Verde	46.6	53.8	35.5	47	34	110	13	-76
Uruguay	24.6	29.1	29.4	117	116	114	1	2
Argentina	27.5	29	29.4	112	117	115	-5	2
Suriname	58.5	46.2	24.4	12	58	118	-46	-60
High-Income	44.2	48.5	47.9	61.4	57.2	64.1	4.2	-6.9
Belgium	69.5	86.9	79	1	1	2	0	-1
Ireland	53.6	62.5	66.7	25	12	11	13	1
Netherlands	62.5	70.5	65.4	5	7	12	-2	-5
Reunion	.	.	63.3	16	16	16	0	0
Korea, Rep. Of	53.9	61.6	55	23	14	33	9	-19
United King.	51.7	51.7	50.9	32	38	40	-6	-2
Portugal	40.2	48.4	50	78	49	46	29	3
Switzerland	42.9	47.1	49.4	62	54	49	8	5
Cyprus	52.4	53.2	48.9	29	35	54	-6	-19
Sweden	39.1	44.6	47.9	85	69	59	16	10
Austria	44.4	49.9	47.8	57	44	60	13	-16
Canada	42.4	45.8	47.6	66	62	62	4	0
Spain	37.5	42.8	46.2	92	75	69	17	6
Italy	45.2	46.9	45.8	50	55	72	-5	-17
France	42.6	46.6	45.6	65	57	73	8	-16
Israel	47.6	50.1	44.5	44	43	78	1	-35
United States	40	42.4	44.2	79	79	79	0	0
Norway	47.9	45.9	44.2	43	59	80	-16	-21
Germany	.	.	42.6	87	87	87	0	0
Denmark	39	43.6	40.9	86	72	91	14	-19
Japan	39.8	41.1	38.2	81	83	98	-2	-15
New Zealand	32.9	37.3	37.7	107	101	101	6	0
Finland	36	38.4	37.3	97	96	103	1	-7
Australia	30.6	32.9	34.3	110	105	111	5	-6
Iceland	25.4	25.4	24.8	116	118	117	-2	1

Note: Indices based on residuals from regression reported in Table 3.

FIGURE 7: Two Indices of Openness: The Trade Ratio Vs. the Trade Index (Country-wise Means for 1988-95)

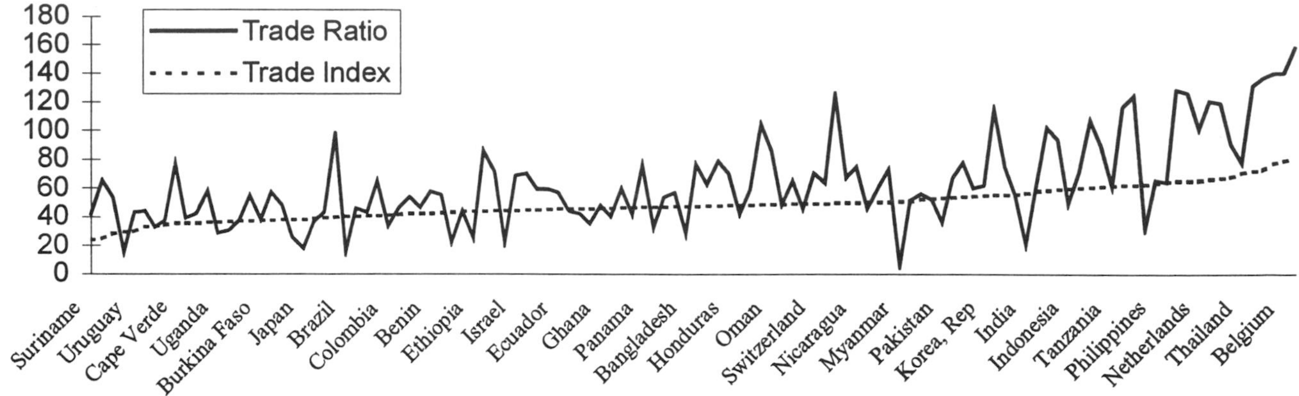

Note: Not all country names are shown on the x-axis.

FIGURE 8: Trade Ratio Vs. the Trade Index (Income-Group-Wise Means)

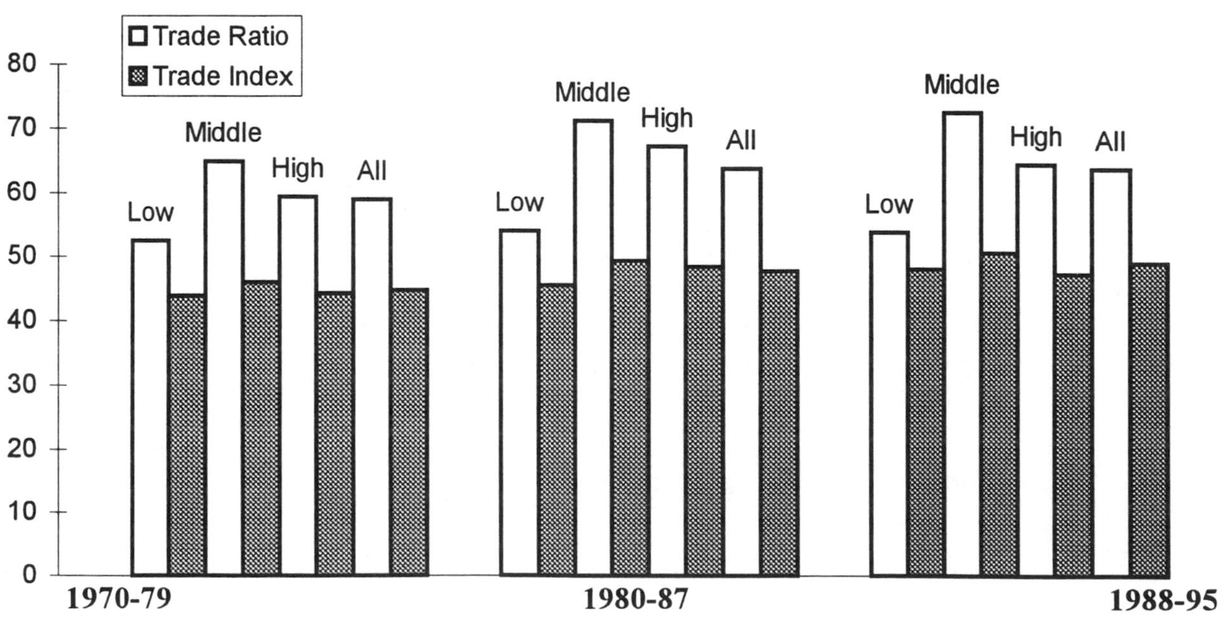

FIGURE 9: Country-wise Changes in the Trade-Index Plotted Against Initial Values

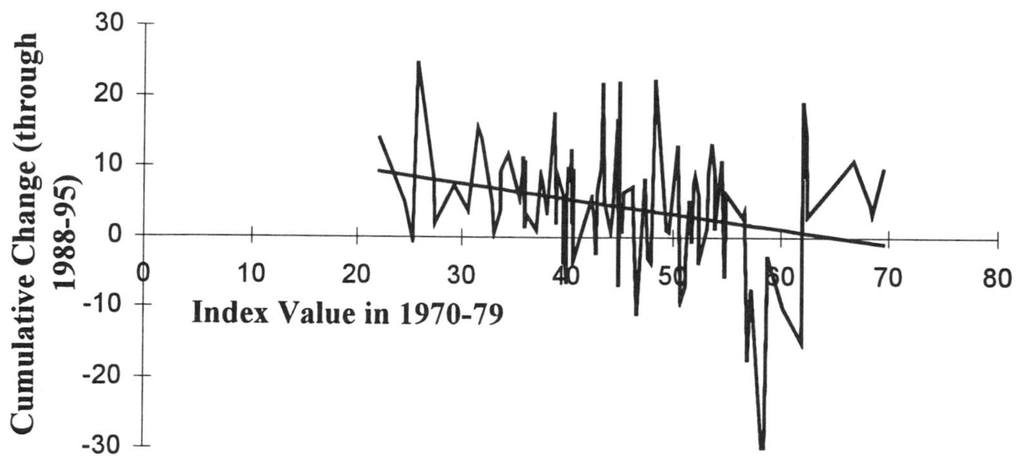

TABLE 5: Correlation Among Policy and Outcome Indices of Openness
(based on annual values for 1970-95)

	LG(pcGDP) (US$1987)	Trad.Taxes (% of Trade)	Avg Tariff (% of Imports)	Trade Indx (% of GDP)	Exprt Indx (% of GDP)	Trade (% of GDP)	Exports (% of GDP)
LG(pcGDP)	1	-0.63***	-0.57***	0.00	0.00	0.24***	0.35***
		(784)	(80)	(2735)	(2818)	(2849)	(2854)
Trade Taxes		1	0.66***	0.10***	0.12***	-0.32***	-0.35***
			(33)	(765)	(784)	(786)	(786)
Avg Tariff			1	0.08	0.19	-0.28**	-0.28**
				(76)	(76)	(80)	(80)
Trade Indx				1	0.81***	0.70***	0.63***
					(2731)	(2735)	(2734)
Export Indx					1	0.66***	0.76***
						(2812)	(2818)
Trade						1	0.95***
							(2906)
Exports							1

Notes: *** and ** denote correlation significant at the 1% and 5% levels (2-tailed) respectively

Figures in parentheses denote the number of (paired) observations.

The evidence on inequality and poverty

In this section, we briefly review the available evidence on measures of absolute deprivation and relative inequality before turning, in the following section, to a classification of country experience in terms of trends in openness, inequality and poverty. The most general indicators of absolute deprivation are various measures of poverty. From a human development standpoint, the most pertinent of these is the Human Poverty Index (HPI) proposed in the *Human Development Report 1997* (UNDP 1997). Like the Human Development Index (HDI) from which it derives, the HPI incorporates not only income but also other elements of human capability such as education and life expectancy. As such, it is a more inclusive index than income-based measures. Whereas the HDI is built up from *average* measures of key elements of human capability, the HPI takes account of the *distribution* of the same elements in a given population. This it does by stipulating minimum levels of income, longevity and education. The proportion of the population that falls below those levels defines the HPI.

Table 6 shows countries for which the HPI can be put together for 1990 and a year around 1970, thus permitting trend calculation. Country coverage is clearly very limited and most of the countries in Table 6 belong to the middle-income group. Though distinctly preferable to more conventional measures of poverty, the HPI is of limited use for present purposes because it has not been applied widely enough to generate sufficient time-series information from which trends could be discerned. Other more specific indicators such as numbers of underweight children, the population with access to health services, safe water and sanitation, etc. may also be considered. Like the HPI and unlike conventional measures of poverty, these have the advantage of greater comparability and also perhaps of being more immediately sensitive to various sorts of public action and policy change. But they are also rather partial indices, overly so in our judgment, to be used in establishing associations with openness and globalization[14].

Conventional measures of the incidence of poverty are usually reckoned with respect to a poverty line, which is the amount of private income or expenditure required to buy the bare necessities[15]. Typically, the cost of the minimum food requirement is estimated normatively, while the allowance for other needs such as shelter and clothing is based on empirically observed expenditure levels that would seem to be the irreducible minimum required. But such measures of income poverty, even for the same country and time period, vary widely depending on the poverty line employed. International comparisons are that much more complicated as a quick perusal of the most detailed available compendium of international poverty statistics (Tabatabai 1997) will show.

For example, in Latin America the non-food component varies between 50% and 60% of the poverty line whereas in India the share of non-food in the basic basket is as low as 20%. No attempt is made to include public services such as health and education that may be available free (Streeten 1994).

The World Bank has published head-count indices of poverty for a number of countries based on a poverty line of one US dollar per day per person. The latter is preferable to the conventional poverty lines because it is internationally comparable as a measure of absolute deprivation. Unfortunately, the $1-a-day poverty incidence data are available only for single years (during the late 1980s or early 1990s) and only for 49 countries.

The dilemma therefore is that, whereas poverty data based on a uniform income standard across countries will not permit trends in poverty to be determined, those based on diverse and essentially non-comparable poverty lines are available for more than one year for a fairly large number of countries. For purposes of country classification, we have chosen to provide information on both indicators (see Table 7), with the $1-a-day index obviously in level form and the national poverty-line-based data in trend form. The level indicator is shown in column 2. "Absolute" poverty trends, based on diverse standards and for diverse periods of time, can be calculated for 40 countries and are shown in column 6 together with the periods (in column 5) for which the trends have been determined[16]. The critical assumption underlying this compromise is that the available trend indicators of poverty are at least roughly comparable across nations[17].

Table 6: Trends in the Human Poverty Index

Country	*HPI,1970*	*HPI,1990*	*Trend**
Trinidad	8.9	4.1	-3.8
Chile	13.2	5.4	-4.4
Costa Rica	15.0	6.6	-4.0
Argentina	16.7	..	..
Panama	17.4	11.1	-2.2
Mauritius	19.4	12.5	-2.2
Peru	28.0	22.8	-1.0
Mexico	29.5	10.9	-4.9
Kuwait	32.0	..	..
Thailand	34.3	11.7	-5.2
Sri Lanka	35.3	20.7	-2.6

Source: Human Development Report Office, United Nations Development Program.

* *Annual compound rate of growth.*

Relative poverty or inequality indices may as before be determined for a broad index such as the HDI or confined to private income or expenditure (or more narrowly defined elements of consumption or capability). Hicks (1997) has constructed an inequality-adjusted Human Development Index for 20 developing countries. But his sample is composed mostly of middle-income countries and lacks time-series—limitations that are critical from the present standpoint. Data on income or expenditure inequality (summed up, say, by the Gini coefficient) are available for a number of countries (see Deininger and Squire 1996 and Tabatabai 1997). Virtually all of our inequality numbers are from the high-quality set in the Deininger-Squire database.

Like their national poverty counterparts, the time-series on inequality are very sparse and, when available, for very unevenly separated years. We could determine inequality trends for 39 countries, virtually the same number (40) as for poverty trends[18]. But the two sets of countries together yielded only 22 countries for which *both* poverty and inequality trends could be computed—Uganda, Bangladesh, China, India, Pakistan, Indonesia, Malaysia, Philippines, Thailand, Brazil, Chile, Colombia, Costa Rica, Guatemala, Jamaica, Mexico, Venezuela, Egypt, Hungary, Jordan, Morocco and Poland. Even within this subset, the poverty and inequality trends in some cases are for rather varied periods.

In closing this section, we should like to note further limitations of the data we have assembled. First, our time rates of change in poverty and inequality are not based on continuous time-series and therefore too much should not be read into "trends" calculated from pairs of annual observation, except as one may surmise that poverty and inequality are apt to change relatively smoothly over time. Second, in comparing poverty and inequality across time and space, one ought to be mindful of relative price differences if these are known, systematic and significant. Lacking the means to determine if they are, we have chosen to ignore them. Third, our inequality data include both expenditure and income Ginis and some doubt may be entertained whether differences in their trends can be neglected. For these and earlier noted reasons, our poverty and inequality data must be regarded with a modicum of skepticism.

TABLE 7: Levels and Trends in Poverty, Inequality, Income and Openness

Country	Poverty Headcount	Inequality Gini	Trade-to-GDP	Poverty Period	Poverty Headcount	Inequality Period	Inequality Gini	GDP pc (1987US$)	Exports-to-GDP	Trade Index	Barter Terms of Trade
	(Mean Level over 1988-95)						(Trend over Relevant* Period)				
	(% <$/day)	(%)	(%)		(% pa)		(% pa)	(% pa)	(% pa)	(% pa)	(% pa)
Low Income Sub-Saharan Africa											
Burundi	..	..	39.1	1978-91	-0.73		..	0.83	-4.10	0.91	-5.94
Cameroon	..	..	37.2	1978-91	-3.26		..	0.39	-1.61	-1.28	-5.28
Chad	..	..	58.9	1978-91	-3.28		..	-0.06	-1.18	0.33	1.63
Ghana	..	35.1	47.9		..	1988-92	-1.42	1.31	-4.06	-0.31	-8.46
Kenya	50.2	54.4	60.1	1978-91	-1.73		..	0.89	-1.85	-0.40	-3.86
Malawi	..	62.0	60.7	1977-91	-0.21		..	-0.05	-1.71	-0.28	0.95
Mali	..	54.0	43.1	1975-91	-1.36		..	0.81	1.55	-0.08	1.52
Nigeria	28.9	39.3	64.5		..	1986-93	0.17	1.48	10.09	4.88	-8.35
Tanzania	16.4	38.1	61.3	1978-91	-2.61		..	0.60	-0.80	4.46	-3.77
Tanzania	16.4	38.1	61.3		..	1977-93	-0.90	0.36	2.42	5.00	-4.12
Uganda	50.0	36.9	28.7	1990-92	36.01	**1989-92**	7.31	1.85	3.65	3.63	-20.10
Zambia	84.6	49.1	63.6		..	1976-91	-1.05	-2.47	-0.40	-1.75	-1.19
Zambia	84.6	49.1	63.6		..	1991-95	4.76	-3.39	-3.40	1.99	-10.00
Low Income Asia											
Bangladesh	..	28.6	28.4	1984-92	-0.64	**1983-92**	-2.65	1.74	4.72	0.22	-1.23
China	29.4	35.9	31.7	1981-90	-8.85	**1982-90**	2.32	7.73	7.07	-4.53	-1.38
India	52.5	31.2	20.7	**1971-78**	-0.82	1972-77	0.18	1.30	7.14	1.05	
India	52.5	31.2	20.7	1978-92	-1.94	**1977-92**	-0.02	2.48	2.28	0.65	0.00
Nepal	53.1	..	41.9	1977-89	-0.06		..	1.18	0.22	1.23	-2.79
Pakistan	11.6	31.3	36.1	1979-85	-3.69	**1979-85**	0.06	3.58	2.71	1.25	-1.62
Pakistan	11.6	31.3	36.1		..	1985-91	-0.67	2.73	4.86	0.41	-1.63
Sri Lanka	4.0	30.1	71.9	1981-86	-6.11			3.72	-5.10	-4.10	-1.43
Sri Lanka	4.0	30.1	71.9		..	1979-87	1.02	3.33	-3.58	-1.31	-0.96

Table 7 cont'd

Country	Poverty Headcount	Inequality Gini	Trade-to-GDP	Poverty Period	Poverty Headcount	Inequality Period	Inequality Gini	GDP pc (1987US$)	Exports-to-GDP	Trade Index	Barter Terms of Trade
	(Mean Level over 1988-95)						(Trend over Relevant Period)				
	(% <$/day)	(%)	(%)		(% pa)		(% pa)	(% pa)	(% pa)	(% pa)	(% pa)
Low Income Latin America & Caribbean											
Honduras	46.5	52.9	70.5			1986-93	-0.25	0.74	2.81	3.16	-5.37
Middle Income Sub-Saharan Africa											
Botswana	..	..	125.0	1976-86	2.26		..	7.08	4.78	0.97	0.84
Lesotho	..	..	140.6	1979-91	-3.01		..	0.77	-2.53	3.39	
Lesotho	..	..	140.6		..	1987-93	0.29	3.83	3.11	-0.56	
Mauritius	..	36.7	128.6		..	1980-91	-1.98	3.41	3.23	2.40	2.95
Middle Income Asia											
Indonesia	14.5	32.4	49.3	1978-90	-6.38	**1978-90**	-1.27	4.64	0.39	-1.81	-4.01
Malaysia	5.6	48.4	159.2	1970-87	-6.80	**1970-89**	-0.18	4.03	2.92	2.38	-4.05
Philippines	27.5	45.4	65.7	1985-91	-3.11	**1985-91**	-0.39	-0.20	2.90	1.95	0.41
Thailand	0.1	49.2	77.6	1981-89	0.38	**1981-90**	1.39	5.87	3.44	4.55	-1.23
Middle Income Latin America & Caribbean											
Argentina	..	..	15.6	1986-94	0.00		..	2.11	-6.05	-0.22	-0.35
Brazil	28.7	59.6	15.5	**1981-90**	-1.37	1981-89	0.91	-0.49	-2.34	-2.15	-1.88
Chile	15.0	57.2	59.8	1968-87	0.98	**1971-89**	1.28	1.57	4.60	2.75	0.00
Chile	15.0	57.2	59.8	1987-94	-6.70	1989-94	-0.48	5.12	-0.39	0.03	0.99
Colombia	7.4	51.3	33.8	**1978-93**	-1.65	1978-91	-0.46	2.00	-0.12	0.66	-4.92
Costa Rica	18.9	46.1	79.0	1980-85	6.52	**1979-86**	-0.98	-1.37	1.33	0.15	-1.32
Costa Rica	18.9	46.1	79.0	**1985-91**	-5.13	1986-89	1.03	1.01	1.56	1.96	-3.84
Domin. Rep.	19.9	49.7	59.1		..	1984-92	1.56	0.52	5.73	3.92	0.52
Guatemala	53.3	59.1	43.0	1980-86	0.55	**1979-87**	2.00	-2.12	-3.38	-1.07	-5.01
Jamaica	4.7	41.0	119.4	1988-90	-45.93	**1988-90**	-1.60	4.18	1.07	-8.43	2.28
Jamaica	4.7	41.0	119.4		..	1990-93	-3.19	3.06	3.66	2.90	-2.52

Table 7 cont'd

Country	Poverty Headcount	Inequality Gini	Trade-to-GDP	Poverty Period	Poverty Headcount	Inequality Period	Inequality Gini	GDP pc (1987US$)	Exports-to-GDP	Trade Index	Barter Terms of Trade
	(Mean Level over 1988-95)						(Trend over Relevant Period)				
	(% <$/day)	(%)	(%)		(% pa)		(% pa)	(% pa)	(% pa)	(% pa)	(% pa)
Mexico	14.9	52.6	32.9	1984-94	0.57	**1984-89**	1.68	-0.76	-3.04	1.03	-7.16
Panama	25.6	56.5	75.9	1986-91	1.21		..	-3.51	1.22	8.16	-2.87
Panama	25.6	56.5	75.9		..	1979-89	1.48	-0.23	1.75	-0.98	-3.46
Peru	49.4	44.9	25.9	1979-86	1.79		..	-0.20	-4.96	-1.57	-6.32
Peru					..	1986-94	0.60	-0.63	-7.77	-1.59	-3.59
Puerto Rico	..	50.9	137.3		..	1979-89	0.14	2.49	1.57	0.54	
Suriname	..	..	41.8	1969-83	1.31		..	0.72	-2.44	-0.96	-1.13
Trinid & Tob.	..	..	69.8		..	1971-81	2.03	4.73	0.21	-0.59	6.70
Trinid & Tob.	..	..	..	1970-90	-3.80		..	0.83	0.11	4.04	-3.35
Uruguay	..	..	42.8	1981-89	4.44		..	-0.78	5.85	2.05	0.83
Venezuela	11.8	49.0	53.8	1981-91	6.88	1981-90	2.58	-1.01	0.77	1.05	-4.98
Other Middle Income Countries											
Egypt	7.6	32.0	64.2	1982-91	1.28	**1975-91**	-1.07	4.17	2.63	0.99	-2.75
Greece	..	35.2	55.2		..	1981-88	0.80	0.69	1.61	1.18	0.09
Hungary	0.7	27.8	65.2	1978-87	-1.21	**1978-87**	1.15	2.50	-0.88	-1.08	-1.65
Hungary	0.7	27.8	65.2		..	1987-93	2.46	-0.78	-5.80	-2.84	-0.56
Jordan	2.5	40.7	132.1	1987-88	13.90	**1987-91**	3.02	-9.54	15.13	9.75	0.95
Morocco	1.1	39.2	56.4	1985-91	-20.44	**1984-91**	0.00	2.62	1.46	0.47	2.26
Poland	6.8	27.7	45.9	1980-90	10.99	**1980-90**	0.54	-0.76	0.17	0.56	0.60
Poland					..	1990-93	8.00	-3.42	4.61	3.37	-2.54
Romania	17.7	25.8	48.6		..	1989-94	4.16	-4.43	-0.44	2.15	2.31
Tunisia	3.9	40.2	89.5	1985-90	-8.81		..	0.89	4.64	2.92	-2.78
Tunisia	3.9	40.2	89.5		..	1980-90	-0.66	1.38	1.01	1.23	-2.12
Turkey	..	..	35.4		..	1973-87	-1.03	2.10	6.71	2.14	1.89

* The relevant period for trend calculation is the same as that for the poverty or inequality trends; where both are available, the period chosen for trend calculation is shown in bold.

Recent trends in openness, poverty and inequality

Our purpose here is twofold. The first is to look for broad associations if any between trends in openness on the one hand and poverty and inequality on the other; our intent is not to explore causality in any rigorous sense but simply to establish a rough classification of the diversity of experience. Our second purpose is to search for "outliers" in the charts—countries that may have been leaders or laggards in opening up and whose poverty and inequality trends are similarly removed from the crowded middle. The reader is referred to the Appendix, which describes the results of regression analyses of the relationship among levels of openness and globalization, on the one hand, and levels of absolute poverty, inequality and growth rates on the other.

Table 7 provides the database for making the above determinations. The first three columns provide, for each country, level indicators of its headcount below one-dollar-a-day, the income inequality Gini coefficient and the trade/GDP ratio for the period 1988-95. The next four columns indicate the *trends* in poverty and inequality together with the time periods over which the trends apply. The final four columns indicate average annual trends in GDP per capita, the export/GDP ratio, the Trade Index and the net barter terms of trade. These latter trends are calculated for the corresponding period for which the poverty trend or inequality trend is available[19].

Consider first the relationship between changes in openness and poverty. Figure 10 shows a scatter-plot of the trends in openness (as indicated by both the export/GDP ratio and the Trade Index) against the trend in poverty. The majority of countries became more open (as indicated by the Trade Index as well as the export ratio) and so lies in the upper quadrants. There are a number of countries in which poverty increased though there were more in which poverty decreased. But the sample as a whole shows a positive (and statistically significant) relationship between changes in the Trade Index measure of openness and changes in poverty with an adjusted R^2 of 0.29. There is, however, no statistically significant link between poverty changes and trends in the export/GDP measure of openness. In other words, poverty increases are positively related to our measure of policy openness but bear no relationship to an export measure of globalization. Countries with declining poverty had on average an openness trend of 0.1% per annum whilst those with rising poverty had an average openness trend of 2.1% (the corresponding figures for the export/GDP index of globalization were 0.7% and 2.0% per annum).

Figure 11 constructs the similar link between changes in openness and inequality. Few observations in this scatter-plot fall in the southwest quadrant, i.e., there were few countries that witnessed a decline in both openness and inequality. Observations showing a rise in inequality are rather evenly divided among those with rising openness and falling openness. Countries opening up similarly show roughly equal proclivity to become less unequal as more unequal. Although there is a positive relationship between the trend in openness (Trade Index) and the trend in inequality, the regression coefficient is not statistically significant at any conventional level. In the case of the export measure of globalization, the regression explained little of the variation in inequality. In terms of sample means, countries with declining inequality had an openness trend of 0.6% per annum while those with rising inequality opened up at 1.1% per annum (the corresponding figures for trends in globalization are 2.0% and 1.6% per annum).

Finally, Figure 12 classifies countries by trends in both poverty and inequality. Growth in openness, the third dimension in the Figure, is indicated as high (if the trend change exceeded 1% per annum), medium (if the trend change lies between 1% and -1% per annum) and as low (when the trend change fell below -1% per annum). Unsurprisingly, trends in poverty and inequality show a statistically significant correlation of 0.64.

Figures 13 and 14 provide a three-way classification of the countries in Table 7 using a four-quadrant graph. The vertical and horizontal axes refer to trends in inequality and poverty respectively. Countries for which both inequality and poverty trends have been determined above fall inside one of the four quadrants. Countries for which only one of these trends is known are placed on the corresponding axis. Figure 13 classifies countries further according to the trend in openness (measured by the Trade Index) while Figure 14 does so according to the trend in globalization (measured by the exports/GDP ratio). The openness and globalization categorization is as indicated previously, i.e., H if the trend change exceeds 1% per annum, M if the trend change lies between 1% and -1% per annum and L when the trend change fell below -1% per annum.

FIGURE 10: Trends in Openness and Poverty

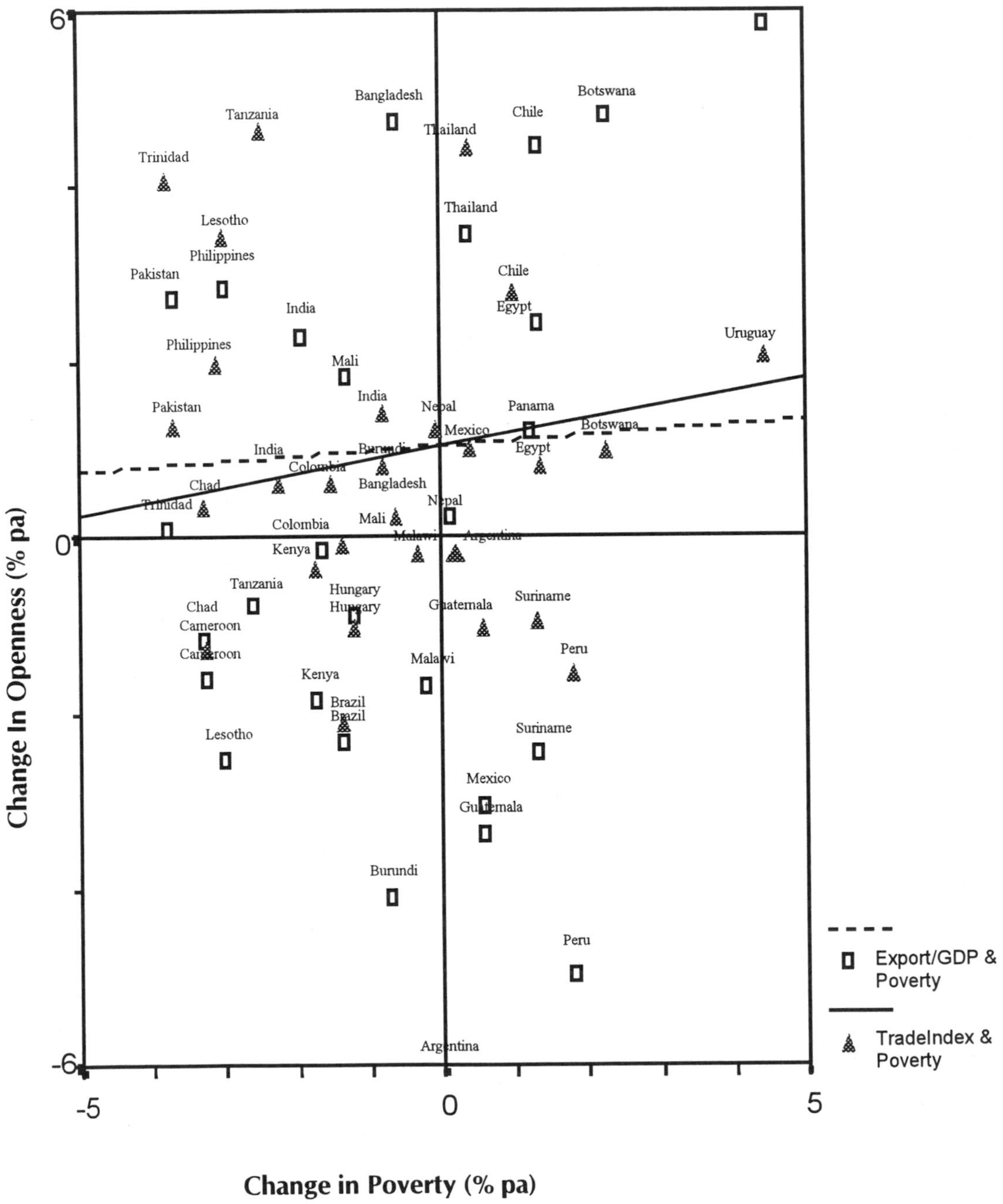

Change In Openness (% pa)

Change in Poverty (% pa)

Export/GDP & Poverty

TradeIndex & Poverty

FIGURE 11: Trends in Openness and Inequality

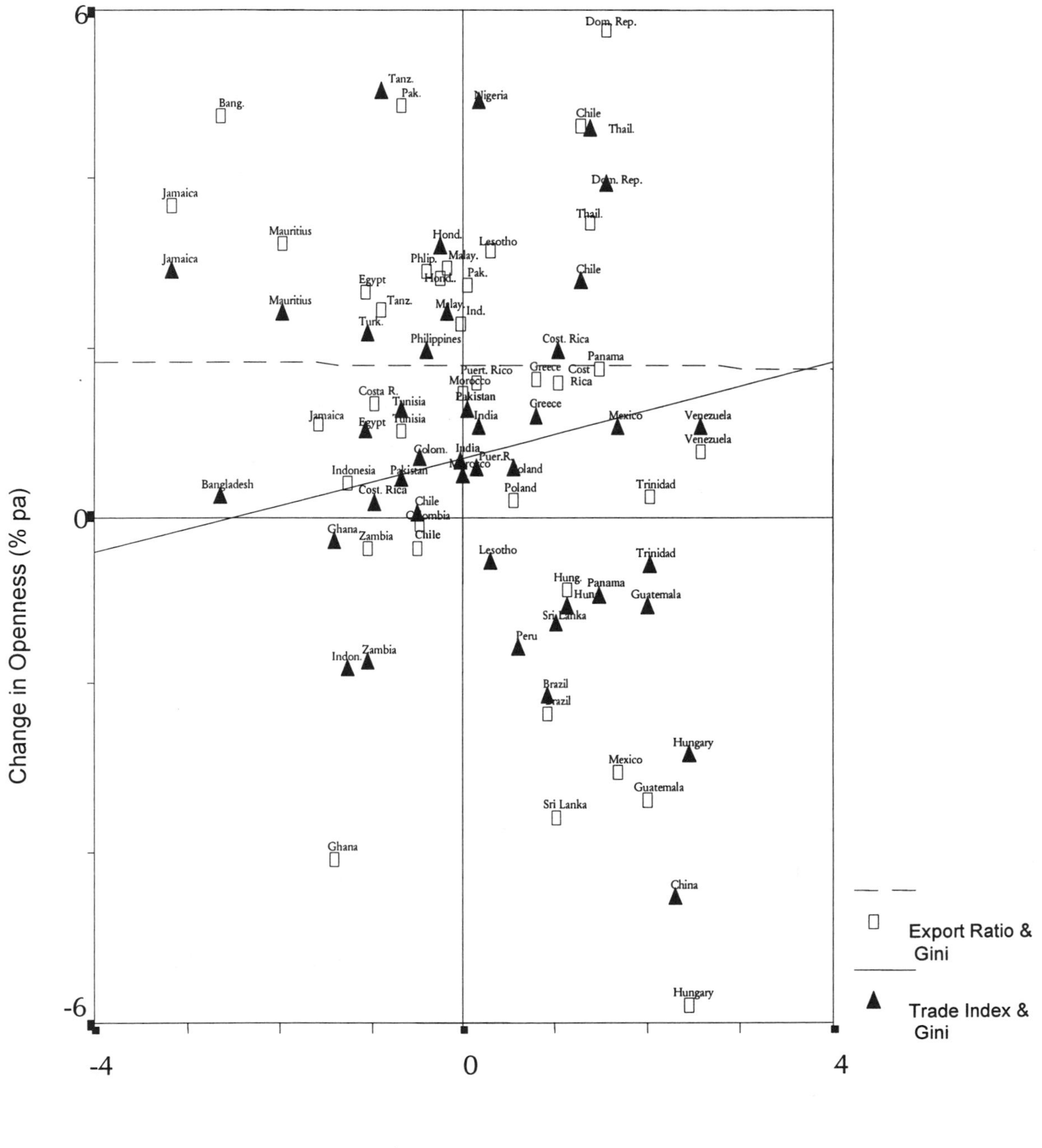

Change in Openness (% pa)

6

0

-6

-4 0 4

Change in Inequality (% pa)

Export Ratio & Gini

Trade Index & Gini

FIGURE 12: Trends in Openness, Poverty and Inequality

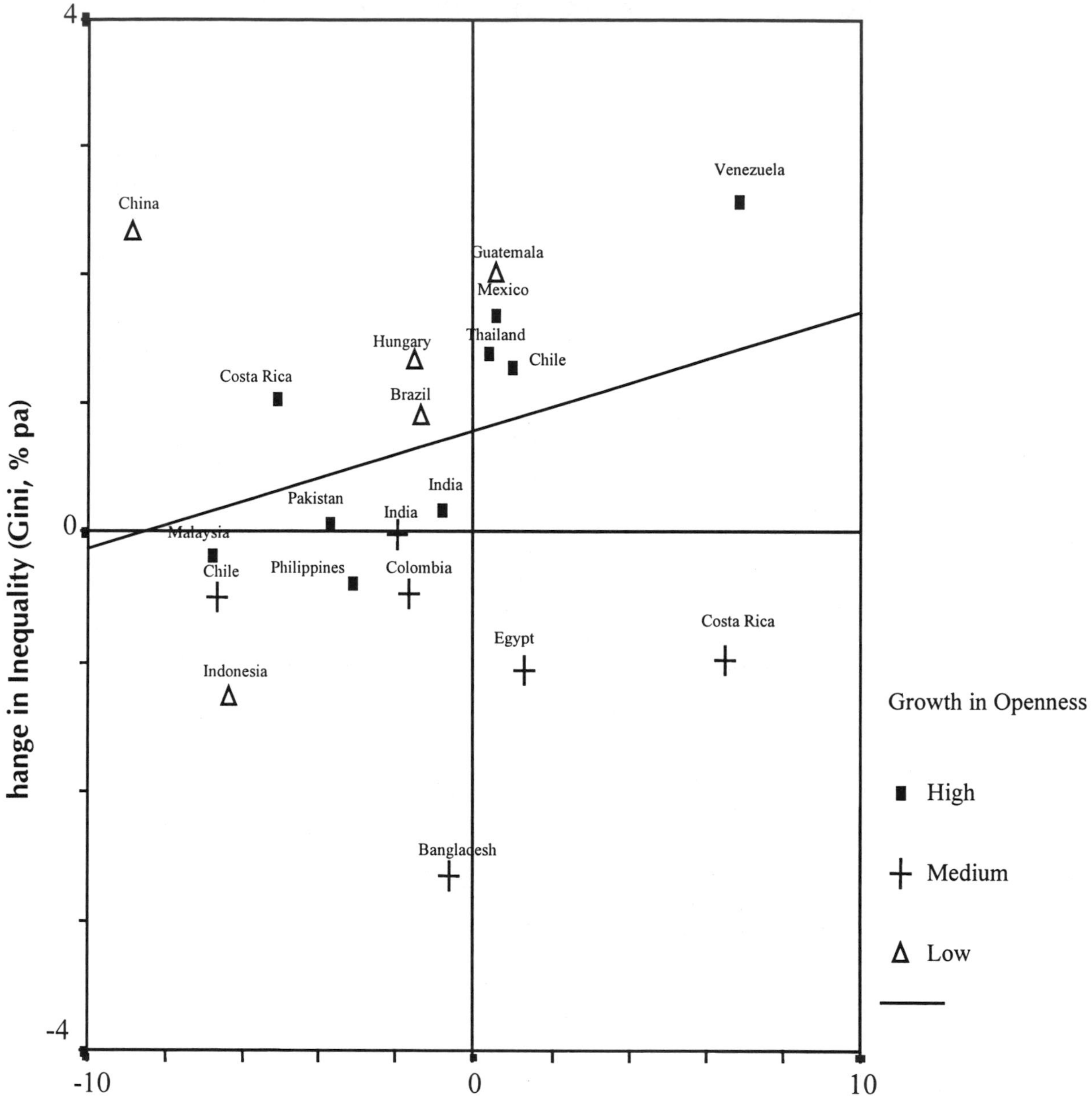

FIGURE 13: Country Classification with the Trade Index

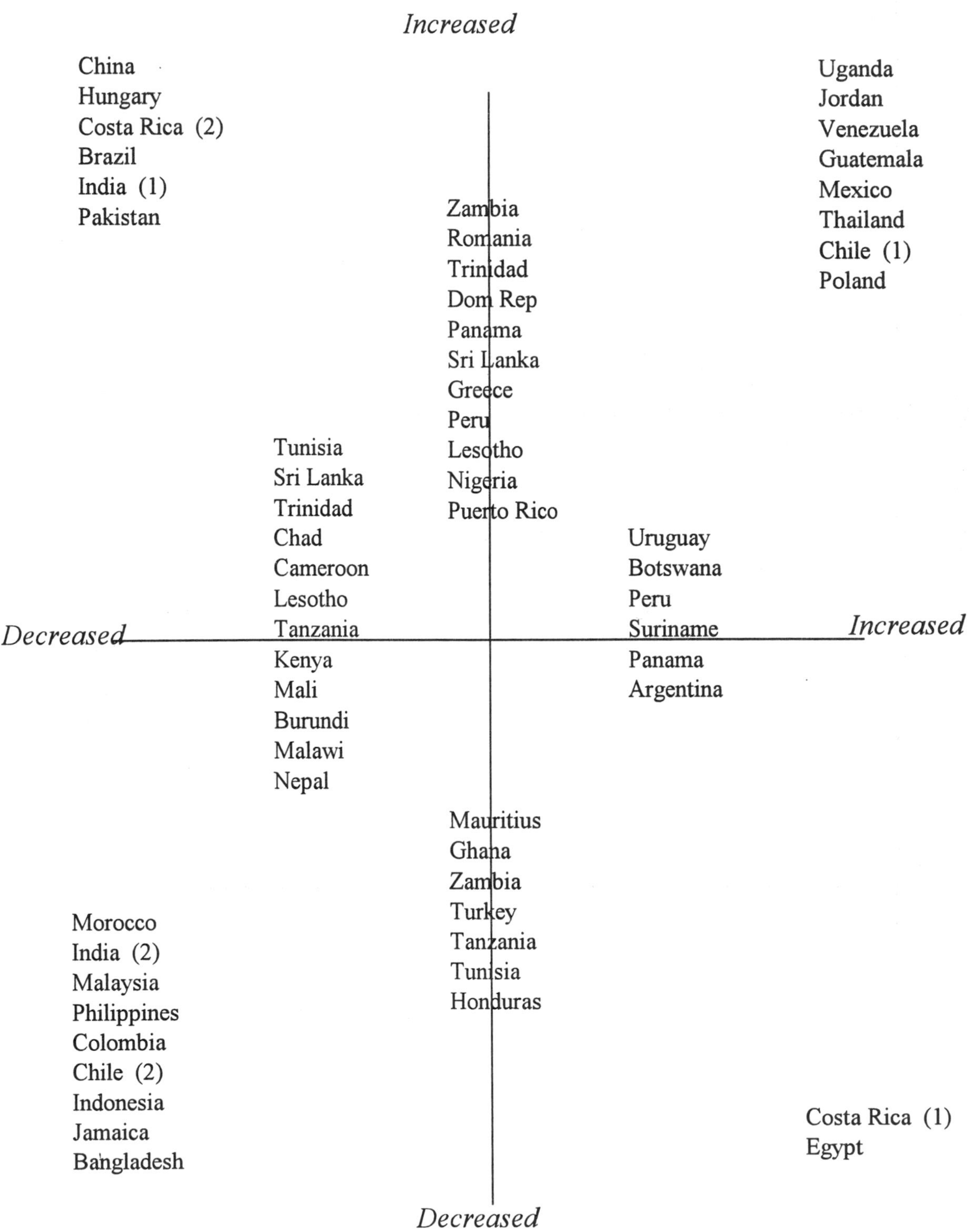

FIGURE 14: Country Classification with the Export/GDP Ratio

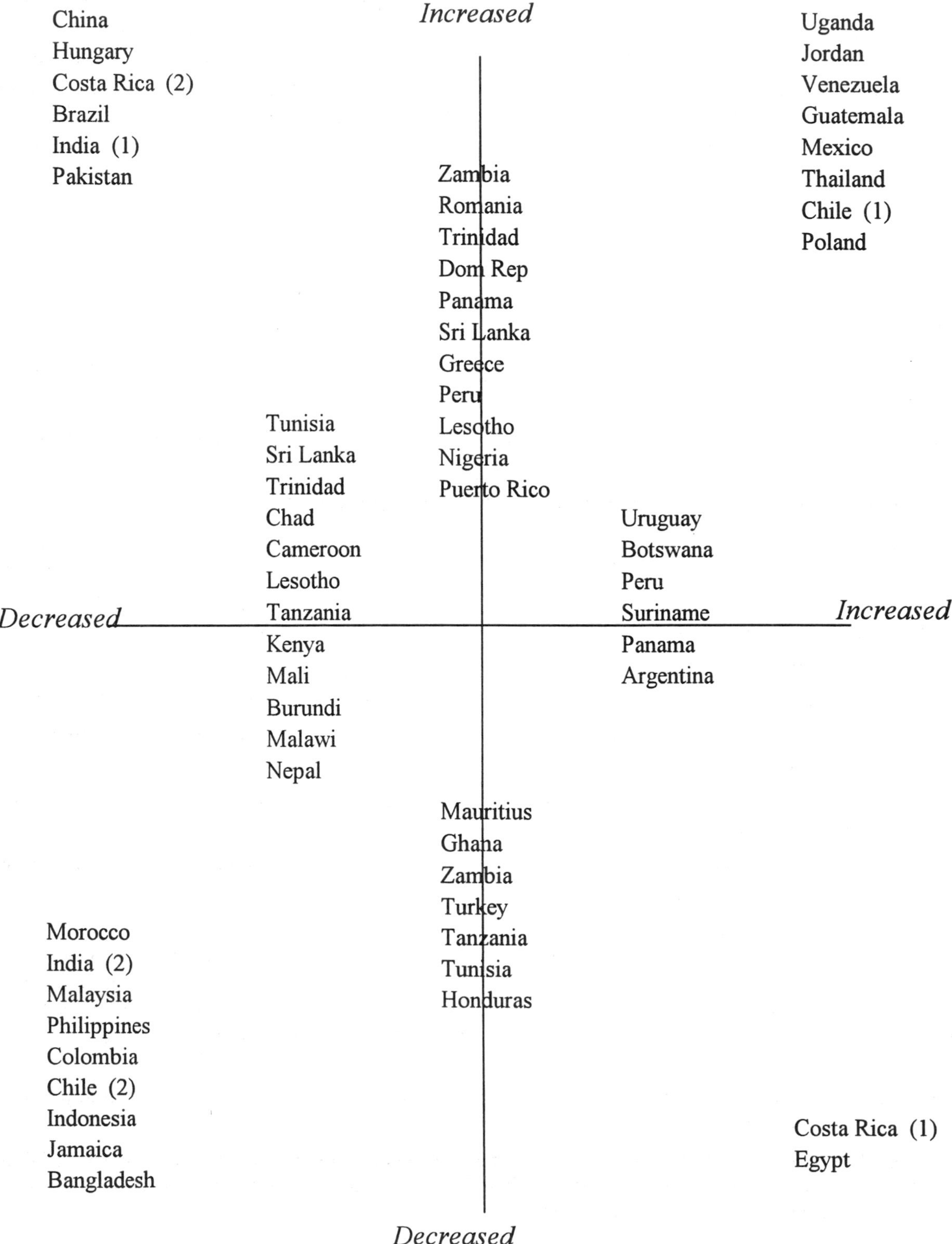

The above results relating trends in openness, poverty and inequality, when taken together with the results (described in the Appendix) relating *levels* of openness, poverty and inequality, present a paradox. On the one hand, increasing openness is positively associated with increasing poverty and increasing inequality. On the other, the level of openness is itself negatively related to levels of poverty and of inequality. In general, these results are stronger for our measure of openness than for the measure of globalization. Two conclusions are therefore warranted. First, a policy regime of openness may be expected to have poverty-alleviating, inequality-reducing and growth-enhancing effects. However, "openness" here is to be construed broadly as the whole policy regime, including appropriate domestic policies, that conduces to increased trade rather than narrowly as border policies of "liberalized" trade. In particular, liberalized trade may well have adverse impacts on poverty, inequality and growth if it undermines the conditions for pursuing optimal domestic policies. Second, from the viewpoint of pursuing equitable growth, our evidence indicates that developing countries, on average and over the past two decades, may have pushed liberal trade policies too far. These conclusions call for further exploration of the channels through which domestic and border policies complement or conflict with each other, and thereby influence poverty, inequality and growth.■

Notes

[1] Ideally, international market integration is indicated by the extent of price integration (based on comparisons of domestic prices, wages and interest rates with those prevalent in international markets). But price data are difficult to come by and we have in practice to rely on quantity indices such as ratios of trade or foreign direct investment to GDP.

[2] A related observation is that we should be wary of imputing normative significance to any given measure of globalization without situating it within a considered causal analysis.

[3] The source of the basic data here is the World Bank's *World Indicators 1997*.

[4] The categorization is as follows: "low-income" economies are those with a GNP per capita of $765 or less in 1995; "middle-income" economies have a GNP per capita of more than $765 but less than $9386; "high-income" economies have a GNP per capita of $9386 or more. See World Bank (1997).

[5] All numbers in the Table are pooled country means for the period concerned.

[6] This last anomaly may well be due to some combination of a saturation process on the one hand and, on the other, the continued growth of services (which are much less tradable than goods) in the GDP of rich countries.

[7] The trade tax ratios are obtained by aggregating revenues from import taxes and export taxes, which are available separately, and dividing the result through by the value of trade.

[8] For example, trade ratios are weighted by GDP shares, trade taxes are weighted by trade shares, and per capita incomes by population shares.

[9] For example, the quota coverage ratio tells us how widespread quotas are but does not tell us whether they are binding or how much trade is affected by them.

[10] From this standpoint, the trade-tax ratio that we considered in the previous Section also cannot serve as a measure of openness since it is a composite of both the administrative measures in place and of the consequent market responses. Note also that, although globalization as external market integration is ideally defined by price comparisons, we must still decide whether imperfect integration is due to policy impediments or due to market imperfections—failures of "the law of one price" to hold cannot be taken to automatically indicate policy impediments.

[11] See Harrison (1996) for a review of studies in which this and similar measures have been employed to examine the link between openness and growth.

[12] These determinants must be set against the fact that high-income countries have a high share of GDP in services, which are generally less tradable. The evidence from Section 2 may be taken to imply that this factor is outweighed by the other determinants referred to in the text.

[13] There is a large literature devoted to examining the effect of "openness" on income *growth*. It is pertinent to note that the regressions here are rather of trade ratios on income *level* and population size. The measures of openness constructed here can of course be employed in growth regressions.

[14] They must obviously have an important place in any detailed investigation of diverse indicators of deprivation and their inter-relations.

[15] See Lipton (1997) for an extended discussion of the concepts of poverty.

[16] All trend calculations reported here refer to annual average rates of change (%). Note also that we have an additional trend observation for India, Chile and Costa Rica.

[17] Data on the national poverty head-count ratios were obtained from an International Labor Organization (ILO) compendium (see Tabatabai 1997) except that for data on Argentina, Chile, Colombia and Mexico, we have relied on Altimir's (1997) detailed study of absolute poverty trends.

[18] For eight of these countries—Zambia, India, Pakistan, Chile, Costa Rica, Jamaica, Hungary and Poland—we could determine two trend observations involving varied pairs of years.

[19] Where both trends are available, the period chosen for the income and globalization or openness trends is generally the longer and more recent period available.

APPENDIX: Some determinants of poverty and inequality

Figure A1 plots the Trade Index, absolute poverty incidence ($-a-day poverty line) and inequality, based on annual data. With countries arranged in ascending order of the Trade Index, the Figure suggests a broadly inverse relationship between openness on the one hand, and poverty and inequality on the other. This relationship is explored further in Tables A1 and A2.

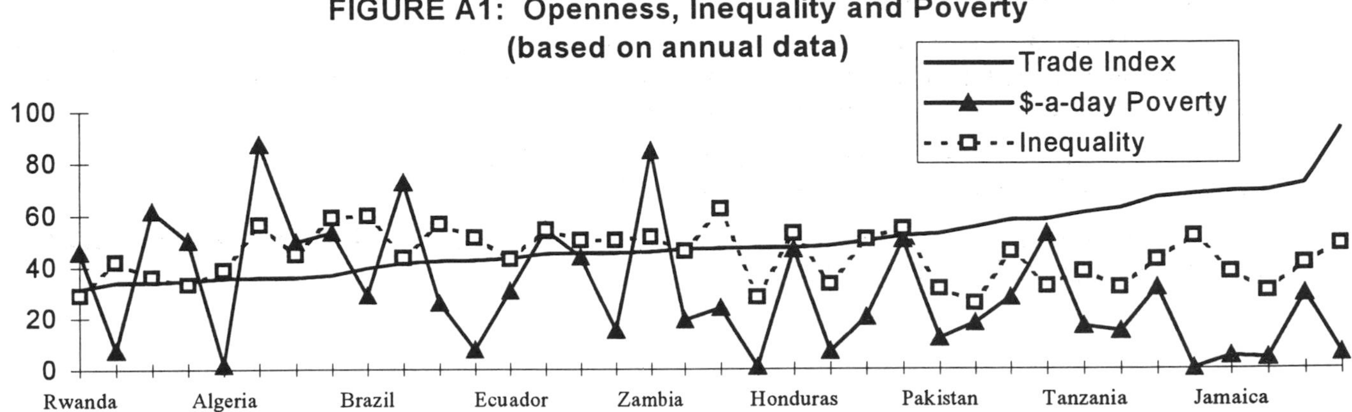

Note: Both expenditure and income inequality measures are included.

Table A1 reports the results of regressions with absolute poverty as the dependent variable. Regressions (1) and (2) have respectively the trade/GDP ratio (or globalization) and the Trade Index (or openness) on the right hand side. Both regressions control for the influence of the level of development (log of GDP per capita) and the index of the net barter terms of trade. Unsurprisingly, the incidence of poverty is inversely related to the level of development, with the coefficient being identical and statistically significant in both equations. The terms-of-trade index also has a negative though statistically insignificant influence on the incidence of poverty. But it is with regard to the influence of openness and globalization that the regressions bring out an interesting contrast. Whereas regression (1) shows that the trade/GDP ratio has a negative but statistically insignificant effect on poverty, regression (2) indicates that the Trade Index of openness has a considerably larger negative and statistically significant effect. A one percentage point rise in the Trade Index reduces absolute poverty incidence by more than half a percentage point. But recall that the Trade Index is not simply an indicator of border policies—such as tariffs and quotas—in relation to trade. Indeed, Table 5 shows a statistically significant and *positive* correlation between, on the one hand, the trade taxation ratio and, on the other, the trade index and the export index. While excluding the structural effects of income levels and economic size on trade, the Trade Index is a broad index of "openness", which captures the effects of both trade policies proper and of domestic policies that may influence globalization. It is in this broad sense that the negative effect of openness on poverty must be construed.

Table A2 reports a parallel set of results for the relationship between trade measures and inequality using available annual data within our sample of countries. Three measures of trade are employed: the trade/GDP ratio, the ratio of trade taxes to trade and the Trade Index. All three regressions in the table control for the "Kuznets Hypothesis", the expectation that there is a non-linear relationship between inequality and the level of development (per capita GDP). The Kuznets Hypothesis emerges intact and statistically significant in all three equations, showing an inverted U-shaped relationship between inequality and per capita income. Whereas the trade taxation ratio is positively related to inequality but is statistically insignificant (regression (2)), the trade/GDP ratio and Trade Index bear a negative and significant relationship with inequality. Note however that our index of trade openness has a coefficient almost six times as large as our indicator of globalization (-0.17 versus -0.03). Once again, the evidently beneficial effect of openness on inequality must be understood in the light of an interpretation recognizing that both external and domestic policy stances are captured in the Trade Index measure of openness.

Finally, Table A3 tests the relationship between openness or globalization and the rate of growth of per capita income. As before, the two equations are distinguished by the fact that the first has the trade ratio while the second has the Trade Index on the right hand side. Both equations in the Table show a positive effect of initial per capita GDP on growth (or "divergence") but the coefficient in regression (2) is both statistically significant and considerably larger as compared to regression (1). Growth is also positively affected by changes in the barter terms of trade. While both the trade/GDP ratio and the Trade Index have a positive effect on growth rates, the positive coefficient on openness is over five times as large as the coefficient on globalization (0.073 versus 0.014).

TABLE A1: Levels of Development, Openness and Absolute Poverty (Annual Data)

Independent Variable	Dependent variable: % Population Below PPP$1/day (1)	(2)
Constant	158.7***	177.4***
	(30.1)	(28.4)
LG(pcGDP)	-16.5***	-16.5***
	(3.8)	(3.4)
Net Barter Terms of Trade (1987=100)	-0.15	-0.11
	(0.22)	(0.20)
Trade/GDP (%)	-0.11	
	(0.10)	
Trade Index (%)		-0.56***
		(0.20)
Adj. R-Sq.	0.36	0.45
Mean dependent variable	27.3	27.3
Standard Error	18.6	17.2
Sample size	42	42

****, ** and * indicate coefficient is significant at the 1% , 5% and 10% level respectively.*

TABLE A2: Levels of Development, Openness and Inequality (Annual Data)

Independent Variable	Dependent variable: Gini Coefficient of Income Inequality (1)	(2)	(3)
Constant	-41.7***	-98.5***	-27.8*
	(14.8)	(21.5)	(14.6)
LG(pcGDP)	25.1***	41.1***	23.4***
	(3.9)	(5.3)	(3.8)
Sq(LG(pcGDP))	-1.8***	-2.9***	-1.7***
	(0.25)	(0.33)	(0.24)
Trade/GDP (%)	-0.03*		
	(0.02)		
Trade Taxes (% Trade)		0.17	
		(0.20)	
Trade Index (%)			-0.17***
			(0.04)
Adj. R-Sq.	0.29	0.63	0.32
Mean dependent variable	37.9	38.8	37.9
Standard Error	8.4	6.0	8.2
Sample size	330	116	330

****, ** and * indicate coefficient is significant at the 1% , 5% and 10% level respectively.*

TABLE A3: Openness, Growth and Divergence (Annual Data)

Independent Variable	Dependent variable: Growth Rate of Income (1)	(2)
Constant	-0.56	-3.90***
	(0.71)	(0.91)
LG(Initial pcGDP)	0.076	0.179*
	(0.095)	(0.094)
Change in Barter Terms of Trade	0.035***	0.033***
	(0.012)	(0.012)
Trade/GDP (%)	0.014***	
	(0.004)	
Trade Index (%)		0.073***
		(0.011)
Adj. R-Sq.	0.01	0.04
Mean dependent variable	0.76	0.76
Standard Error	4.84	4.78
Sample size	1295	1295

***, ** and * indicate coefficient is significant at the 1% , 5% and 10% level respectively.

References

Altimir, Oscar. 1997. Trends of Absolute Poverty in Latin American Countries. Paper prepared for the United Nations Development Programme (UNDP), New York.

Deininger, Klaus and Lyn Squire. 1996. A New Data Set Measuring Income Inequality. *The World Bank Economic Review* (September): 565-91.

Harrison, Ann. 1996. Openness and Growth: A Time-Series, Cross-Country Analysis for Developing Countries. *Journal of Development Economics* 48:419-47.

Hicks, Douglas. 1997. The Inequality-Adjusted Human Development Index: A Constructive Proposal. *World Development* 25:1283-98.

Lipton, Michael. 1997. Defining and Measuring Poverty: Conceptual Issues. *Poverty and Human Development: Human Development Papers 1997*. New York: United Nations Development Programme.

Rao, J. Mohan. 1996. Globalization: A View from the South. Paper prepared for the International Labour Organization (ILO), Geneva.

Rao, J. Mohan. 1998. Development in the Time of Globalization. Paper prepared for UNDP, New York.

Sachs, Jeffrey and Andrew Warner. 1995. Economic Reform and the Process of Global Integration. *Brookings Papers in Economic Activity*. 1-118.

Srinivasan, T. N. 1995. Comment on Sachs and Warner, Economic Reform and the Process of Global Integration. *Brookings Papers in Economic Activity*. 1-118.

Streeten, Paul. 1994. Poverty Concepts and Measurement. In *Poverty Monitoring: An International Concern*, ed. Rolph van der Hoeven and Richard Anker. New York: St. Martin's Press.

Tabatabai, Hamid. 1997. *Statistics on Poverty and Income Distribution: An ILO Compendium of Data*. Geneva: International Labour Organization.

United Nations Development Programme. 1997. *Human Development Report 1997*. New York: Oxford University Press.

World Bank. 1996. *Global Economic Prospects and the Developing Countries*. Washington, DC: The World Bank.

World Bank. 1997. *World Indicators*. Washington, DC: The World Bank.

GLOBALIZATION AND THE FISCAL AUTONOMY OF THE STATE

*J. Mohan Rao**

Public finance in less developed countries is the focal point—both as source and destination—of many of the dilemmas and conflicts posed by development. Revenue mobilization for the allocative, distributive and stabilization functions of the state is severely constrained by the narrowness and instability of the tax base. The latter, in turn, is the result of political constraints rooted in socioeconomic inequalities, economic constraints arising from the structures of production and trade, and administrative constraints reflecting a weakly developed state apparatus. As a consequence, public infrastructure and human development expenditures, which are among the most effective vehicles available for reaching the poor and promoting growth at the same time, persistently fall short of socially desired levels. While fiscal constraints do not always reflect the need to finance current and capital outlays for development, public investment is often the first victim of fiscal troubles. Moreover, states must typically resort to modes of taxation and budget financing that violate accepted canons of economic efficiency and "good" macroeconomic policy. For much the same reasons—political, economic and administrative—social transfers through the budget must also rely on inefficient and leaky buckets. Hence, from both the expenditure and revenue sides, public squalor exacerbates private squalor.

Overcoming fiscal constraints is both cause and consequence of a cumulative process of *internal integration*. The intra-national division of labor, as Adam Smith observed, is limited by the extent of the market: specialization is a public good producing external benefits that are jointly consumed. In addition, public infrastructure investment (in transport and communications, education, research, extending the land frontier, etc.) raises productivity both directly and by extending the home market while, the development of state institutions (enactment and enforcement of laws, tax-collecting machinery, maintaining order, etc.) serves to expand the state's revenues. As the market expands, the costs of running the state and delivering infrastructure services fall and state revenues increase at the same time. These make possible an increased supply of public goods and services, which further extends the home market. Hence, the expansion of the home market and modern state formation feed on each other in cumulative fashion and add to national competitiveness and productivity. Similarly, while an initially significant productivity lag seems almost inevitable in agriculture relative to industry, and in informal activities relative to the formal, a successful process of internal integration must dissolve these lags progressively over time. Such internal convergence and integration is both the hallmark and the principal mechanism of development. It is also the basis for raising national competitiveness and achieving international convergence.

Consistent with this formulation, states have played a pivotal role in capitalist transformations throughout the world. The development of the market system has required the simultaneous development of institutions, including the state itself, to support it. Late developers have found it necessary to fashion state institutions and policies that are more actively engaged, both qualitatively and quantitatively, in the development process. Nurturing local development against competing global forces has become a progressively more delicate affair. Strategic direction of the economy, macroeconomic management to secure internal and external balance, and selective engagement in global markets to exploit its opportunities and thwart its constraints have been added to the more traditional tasks of establishing new forms of property relations and associated legal and enforcement systems, ensuring order, supplying infrastructural and educational services and, above all, resolving the fundamental political conflicts arising in the process of constructing a market system.

But internal integration is not a mechanistic process that is guaranteed to succeed. It requires coordinated structural change and investments, and hence a major role for public policy and public finance. This is the reason for ensuring that the conditions in which national economies are integrated with global markets do not jeopardize national autonomy. Globalization or *external integration* of weakly integrated national economies forces unpleasant tradeoffs between the requirements of internal integration and those of external integration. In a globalizing world, the problem for developing countries is not so much that external integration threatens internal disintegration. Rather, external integration may abort a healthy process of internal integration that is practically a defining element in successful development. At the very least, management of these tradeoffs requires a modicum of national autonomy, which can only be sustained with a measure of fiscal autonomy from the pressures of globalization.

At the same time, a half century of experience shows that it does not follow, merely from demonstrating the developmental value of national autonomy, that the state will exercise its autonomy successfully. Modern state formation has been no less problematic than the process of economic modernization or development, as the history of Western Europe reveals. Constraints originate both from conflicts in civil society and from failures within the state. In many parts of the developing world, the four or five decades following the retreat of colonialism have seen intense state-building activity and attempted modernization. The complementarity between these processes noted above does not imply that they will be successfully implemented. The failures and reversals (as also the successes) in this effort cannot be understood except in *political* terms, i.e., in terms of the conflicts generated by the social "embeddedness" of both state and economy.

Yet, economic and ideological compulsions arising from the very lack of economic success has strengthened a rather optimistic vision of development through globalization. Liberalized markets, in this view, are the optimal route to both internal *and* external integration. This view is based on both economic and political arguments. On the economic side, this is illustrated by the gains from international trade. The main instruments include trade policy reform (dismantling quantitative restrictions, reducing tariff rates and ensuring currency convertibility), openness to capital and technology flows, unhindered flow of domestic investment and labor across sectors (flexibility and free exit), financial reform to permit market determination of investment and saving, and public sector disinvestment. On the political side, it is argued that the global market provides the ideal antidote to political cupidity and stupidity since states, when not bound to a minimalist agenda by the global market system, are liable to be captured by sheltered special interests or fall victim to erroneous ideas. Hence, globalization is not merely useful for *extending the gains* from trade; it is in fact the most effective means available to achieve the minimalist state, thus also *avoiding the much larger losses* from "rent-seeking". Clearly, the most important implication of this policy agenda is that internal and external integration are strictly complementary.

In keeping with this orthodox formulation, the fiscal effects of liberalization have received far less attention in the literature than their "real" effects on exports, resource allocation across sectors, and on the trade or external balance. By contrast, this paper focuses on the fiscal impact of globalization on the theory that government budgets have been a principal site at which the tradeoffs between internal and external integration make themselves felt. Using cross-country evidence for the period 1970-96, the paper explores the revenue and expenditure implications of trade and financial liberalization. Such liberalization has been effected, particularly in the 1980s and 1990s, not only through the structural adjustment packages and conditionalities of international lending institutions, but also by reform efforts undertaken by countries fearful of losing access to global markets and capital flows.

The plan of the paper is as follows. The first section provides an overview of trends in economic openness and in fiscal aggregates. It also suggests a theoretical basis for understanding the emergence of fiscal constraints in less developed countries (LDCs) from the viewpoint of both economic growth and human development. The second section analyzes trends in the tax structure of LDCs during the period of liberalizing reforms. Apart from a comparison in tax structures across levels of development, the main object of the analysis is the decline in government revenues from trade following tariff and export tax-rate reductions. Decomposition of revenue effects shows that trade failed to rise sufficiently to compensate for the rate reductions in most countries. The third section looks at the fiscal effects of rising national debts and financial liberalization particularly in low-income countries. A crude aggregate index of the fiscal impact flowing from liberalization—in the form of trade revenue losses and rising public debt-servicing burdens—suggests that globalization has indeed produced a fiscal squeeze for LDC governments. The fourth part looks at the effects of the fiscal squeeze on government investments in public capital and human capital. International experience in this respect seems varied, reflecting perhaps the diverse policy responses to the fiscal squeeze and the initial conditions faced. Nevertheless, the cross-national evidence shows that the fiscal squeeze has dampened overall (physical and human capital) investment in developing countries. The section ends with a consideration of the redistributive effects of globalization and their implications for maintaining or strengthening feasible social safety nets. Then the paper presents its conclusion.

The fiscal constraint under economic liberalization

For any given configuration of political and social forces, policy maneuverability in LDCs is severely restricted by the feasible instruments of policy. Hence, policy tradeoffs are sharper and policy-makers must worry not only about the "direct" effects of policy changes on social groups, but also the gap between the resource demands needed to engineer compromises and the fiscal resources available. Put differently, fiscal actions or policies must seek not merely to close social-political gaps but also ensure that fiscal gaps are not widened in the process. When countries are more or less chronically confronted with a fiscal gap, policy change has to be particularly sensitive in this regard. In particular, changes that promise overall social gain may nonetheless provide no room for fiscally-mediated compensation policies or may even reduce the room available. Such countries may properly be said to lack fiscal autonomy.

In standard neoclassical economics, the allocation of resources between the public and private sectors (hence the choice of both tax and expenditure policies) is seen to derive from an optimizing calculus. Such a calculus is unproblematic if it is assumed that there exists a well-defined social welfare function and that needed resource transfers between the public and private sectors (or within the private economy) can be arranged through non-distortionary lump-sum transfers. These assumptions ensure that a social contract is costlessly defined and costlessly implemented. Fiscal autonomy here is absolute and the budget is a first-best outcome.

A dose of realism may be added to this formulation with the recognition that real-world taxes to finance the budget are bound to distort resource allocation and that there will also be costs in reaching a social contract. In other words, resource allocation between the public and private sectors entails tradeoffs that go beyond the purely technologically defined opportunity costs. These additional tradeoffs arise essentially from incentive effects, the transactions costs of political bargaining, and the costs of administration to effect needed taxes and transfers. If it is assumed that these added tradeoffs in the budget are essentially calculable, even if only through a social-political bargaining process, then the budget will be a second-best outcome.

From such a viewpoint, therefore, the fiscal autonomy of the state, even allowing for economic feedbacks, can never be compromised. At worst, fiscal autonomy may be monopolized by a narrow interest group or by a runaway state not answerable to civil society, a particular outcome of the "social contract" rather than the absence of a contract. There can be no room, in this conception, for economic forces to directly constrain fiscal maneuverability. Even openness to liberalized markets and globalization that narrowly limit state options is seen as a policy *choice*.

In practice, LDC governments confront financing constraints of greater or less severity in pursuing otherwise feasible growth-enhancing or human development-enhancing policies. While these may be formally seen, as above, to flow from the prevailing political-economic equilibrium, the very existence of fiscal constraints suggests that there are multiple equilibria. The economy may get stuck in a bad equilibrium when political and economic factors reinforce each other. Suppose, for example, that equilibrium A produces a more equitable, human development-enhancing outcome compared to equilibrium B. Assume also that A requires a larger budget than B but that political-economic factors, by constraining the budget, make B the prevailing, self-enforcing equilibrium. If new economic policy choices serve to relax the fiscal constraint, the economy may then be able to move to equilibrium A[1].

A fiscal constraint arises in developing countries chiefly from the facts that the tax base is usually narrow and there are strict limits to how far tax rates can be raised on that narrow base when adjustment involves the whole economy. LDCs tend to have a relatively large share of economic activity in low-taxed sectors such as agriculture, informal industry and services; in addition, a significant part of the potential revenue at legislated rates fails to be realized on account of collection problems, corruption and evasion.

The problem also has a dynamic dimension. As an economy grows, its fiscal requirements are also expected to grow. This association has causal factors going both ways. A larger economy is easier to tax but a larger economy also requires larger fiscal outlays. This does not necessarily mean that economic growth and government budget outlays can grow in a smooth and balanced fashion. There are important lags in the redesigning of the fiscal structure since political and administrative obstacles must be overcome.

Conversely, there may also be important leads from fiscal effort to economic growth, i.e., growth itself may depend on a rise in fiscal outlays. Such dynamic fiscal lags and leads can conspire to hold back growth itself.

Apart from limits on taxation, other ways of financing government deficits also quickly run into diminishing political and economic returns. Foreign financing, which mostly takes the form of grants and loans to governments, cannot be directly controlled by the borrowing government. They also come with conditionalities that may narrow policy choices and fiscal autonomy. Similarly, domestic finance is limited by the underdeveloped state of domestic financial markets on the one hand and the inflationary potential of bank financing on the other.

Following the worldwide slowdown in growth and rise in interest rates, many developing countries emerged from the 1980s with the need to make massive external transfers due to accumulated debt. At the same time, a large internal transfer had to be effected, since much of this debt was incurred on public account whilst the export earnings that would pay for it were mostly private. Apart from the narrow fiscal choices available to effect this internal transfer, the adjustment process itself tended to be contractionary with attendant losses rather than gains in public revenue. As a consequence, fiscal retrenchment became the order of the day in most countries undergoing adjustment. Reductions in the non-interest part of expenditure tended to hurt public capital expenditure with further growth-reducing effects.

Conditionalities accompanying accommodation of creditors included a general program of market liberalization. Thus, many developing economies have engaged in external liberalization while faced with balance-of-payments and fiscal constraints. In particular, trade liberalization—which has almost invariably reduced public revenues—has had to be undertaken alongside public expenditure reductions and/or non-trade-based tax increases. Moreover, devaluations undertaken as part of the reform package have raised government debt-service obligations. Trade and exchange reforms thus added a further important fiscal burden leading to cuts in domestic capital accumulation. It is in this sense that adjustment to debt and adjustment to liberalization have had major fiscal, growth and redistributive effects. As persistent fiscal deficits added to the public debt, financial liberalization and increased reliance on foreign financing of public deficits did not help, since interest rates on market borrowing by states rose to add to the burden.

The quality of fiscal adjustment is a matter of sustaining, indeed raising, the levels of public capital investment on the one hand and of widening the tax net on the other. Liberalization tends to militate against both objectives in the short to medium term. When this is coupled with the argument above that the policy regime reinforces politics and vice versa, liberalization aimed at globalization may also produce adverse longer-term impacts. While it might be supposed that once the transition is weathered, growth cannot decline and possibly will rise, the fiscal constraint has remained at the center of the dilemma of how to effect the transition without hurting growth prospects.

For these reasons, the following analysis of fiscal trends must be placed in the context of growing globalization. Table 1 summarizes the broad picture of economic globalization in terms of exports plus imports relative to gross domestic product (GDP); the taxation of trade whether for protective or fiscal purposes; and the flow of net foreign direct investment (FDI).

TABLE 1: Trends in Economic Openness

	Trade (% of GDP)	Net FDI (% of GDI)	Avg Tariff (% of Trade)	Trade Index (%)	Trade Taxes (% Trade)
LOW-INCOME COUNTRIES					
1970-75	51.4	3.5	..	42.6	11.1
1976-80	59.7	3.3	..	47.5	10.6
1981-85	57.5	3.3	..	46.4	10.2
1986-90	54.8	1.7	..	46.7	9.9
1991-96	61.3	7.1	26.9	50.2	9.4
LOWER MIDDLE-INCOME COUNTRIES					
1970-75	57.4	4.4	..	43.5	8.6
1976-80	72.3	3.7	..	49.3	8.3
1981-85	67.3	3.9	..	48.9	6.6
1986-90	67.8	3.6	..	48.7	5.8
1991-96	75.8	7.5	17.5	51.2	5.1
UPPER MIDDLE-INCOME COUNTRIES					
1970-75	71.2	6.1	..	46.0	5.7
1976-80	82.8	6.3	..	49.1	4.7
1981-85	79.7	5.6	..	50.4	4.8
1986-90	79.4	6.8	..	49.4	5.2
1991-96	80.2	10.3	11.8	48.0	3.6
HIGH-INCOME COUNTRIES					
1970-75	73.2	4.7	..	44.1	2.7
1976-80	83.6	3.6	..	46.4	2.0
1981-85	89.9	3.9	..	49.4	1.6
1986-90	88.1	6.8	..	48.0	1.3
1991-96	87.7	7.9	6.6	47.5	0.9
ALL COUNTRIES					
1970-96	69.3	4.8	17.4	47.5	6.3

Note: GDI = Gross Domestic Investment

Trade openness may be measured directly in terms of the trade share in GDP and also in terms of a *Trade Index* which is constructed from the trade share after controlling for the facts that richer countries are more open and so are smaller countries (Rao 1998). Trade taxation is indicated both *ex ante*, i.e., based on weighted-average published tariff rates *circa* 1992, and as *ex post* realized tax rates, i.e., total trade tax revenues divided by total trade (hereafter the "trade tax ratio"). The trade ratio and the Trade Index are highly correlated, and so are the *ex ante* import tariff and *ex post* trade tax ratio[2]. The correlation between the trade/GDP and the FDI/GDP ratios is also statistically significant though less pronounced. Nevertheless, openness and globalization are not the same thing. The latter refers to outcomes in terms of cross-border transactions; the former to policy inputs, whether at the border or not, that may affect globalization.

The main conclusions from Table 1 may be summarized as follows. (1) Low-income countries, as well as other groups, have shared in the global growth of trade relative to national incomes of the past quarter century, even though this period has seen a continuing divergence in economic growth performance. However, trade growth has not been uniform across all groups reflecting the uneven spread of the benefits of globalization and, not any less, its costs. (2) Taxes on trade have declined everywhere but the relative decline is itself inversely related to income levels (i.e., trade taxes have fallen most in the high-income and least in low-income countries); in consequence, the worldwide dispersal of trade taxation has increased substantially[3]. (3) Countries that had higher trade ratios and Trade Indices also tended to have higher net FDI inflows; trade openness and investment openness and/or attractiveness seem to go together. Notably also, whereas low-income countries were at the low end in terms of FDI inflows during the 1980s, the 1990s have witnessed a correction[4].

Table 2 reveals trends in the main fiscal aggregates. Tax revenues as a proportion of GDP clearly rise with per capita income. In the high-income countries, this proportion is, on average, more than double that in low-income countries. Non-tax revenues are also substantially higher (5.4%) in the upper middle-income countries than in the low-income countries (2.6%). Low-income countries have clearly lost tax revenue relative to GDP during the 1980s and 1990s (the fall represents 14% of the tax/GDP ratio, i.e., from 15.3% in 1981-85 to 13.1% in 1991-96). Upper middle-income countries also lost revenue to the tune of 11% in the tax/GDP ratio. By contrast, lower middle-income countries lost but little between the two halves of the 1980s, and then more than made up the loss to end with a higher average tax/GDP ratio during the 1990s. The high-income group never saw any decline in their tax/GDP ratio throughout the quarter century, until 1996. Even between the 1980s and 1990s, their tax effort rose by 5%.

What accounts for these trends in the tax/GDP ratio? The following regression estimates the relationship between the tax/GDP ratio and per capita income after controlling for size, trade taxation and the trade ratio.

$$\underset{}{TAXREV/Y} = \underset{\substack{(7.77)\\(0.00)}}{-23.62} + \underset{\substack{(0.49)\\(0.00)}}{3.28\mathrm{Ln}(pcY)} + \underset{\substack{(0.35)\\(0.13)}}{0.54\mathrm{Ln}(Pop.)} + \underset{\substack{(0.10)\\(0.00)}}{0.32(TradTax/Tr.)} + \underset{\substack{(0.02)\\(0.00)}}{0.12(Trade/Y)} \qquad (1)$$

(with $R^2=0.42$ and $N=217$)[5].

Per capita income raises the tax/GDP ratio from both supply and demand sides. On the supply side, income growth and the accompanying structural change increases the taxable part of national income.

On the demand side, income growth requires greater public investment in physical and financial infrastructure and/or increases the demand for government social services (especially social transfer programs)[6].

TABLE 2: Trends in Fiscal Aggregates

	Nontax Rev	Tax Rev	Cur Rev	Tot Exp	Fis Bal	For Fin
	(% of Gross Domestic Product)				(% of GDP)	(% of Fis Bal)
LOW-INCOME COUNTRIES						
1970-75	2.0	13.6	15.6	18.9	-3.5	56.1
1976-80	2.2	14.1	16.3	22.0	-5.5	47.5
1981-85	2.3	15.3	17.7	24.5	-6.6	45.0
1986-90	2.6	13.9	16.6	24.7	-6.3	42.5
1991-96	2.6	13.1	15.7	22.5	-5.2	53.9
LOWER MIDDLE-INCOME COUNTRIES						
1970-75	3.8	14.8	18.7	20.9	-2.4	80.1
1976-80	4.9	16.2	21.2	26.0	-4.4	54.3
1981-85	5.0	17.1	22.1	26.0	-3.9	50.8
1986-90	5.3	16.6	22.0	23.6	-1.3	38.1
1991-96	4.5	17.8	22.3	23.6	-0.7	55.1
UPPER MIDDLE-INCOME COUNTRIES						
1970-75	6.7	19.4	26.1	29.5	-4.7	48.0
1976-80	6.7	21.0	27.7	29.5	-2.3	34.4
1981-85	6.7	22.7	29.3	32.6	-4.9	36.5
1986-90	6.3	22.5	28.7	33.7	-5.1	23.3
1991-96	5.4	20.2	25.5	29.7	-3.3	26.4
HIGH-INCOME COUNTRIES						
1970-75	2.5	24.0	26.7	27.4	-2.4	22.9
1976-80	3.0	26.5	29.5	32.6	-4.4	27.4
1981-85	3.9	28.4	32.3	36.8	-5.3	24.6
1986-90	3.9	28.4	32.3	36.8	-5.3	24.6
1991-96	3.7	29.8	33.5	37.1	-3.2	40.5

If the above structural relationship indeed holds, then it stands to reason that attempting to change the *structure* of taxation in the direction of developed country norms—the thrust of trade liberalization—particularly in a period of stagnant or falling per capita incomes cannot be achieved easily. Alternatively, such a movement may well be accompanied by increased fiscal deficits, higher foreign financing and/or reduced expenditures. For the low-income group, equation (1) predicts a drop of 0.2 percentage point in the tax/GDP ratio from the first half of the 1980s to the 1990s on account of the 8% fall in real GDP per capita, and another 0.25 percentage point on account of the drop in the trade taxes ratio relative to trade. This drop is matched, however, by the predicted rise in the tax ratio on account of the rise in the trade ratio during this period. Yet, the overall tax ratio has fallen as noted above. This suggests that revenue losses have occurred on account of significant policy and/or structural shifts that accompanied the reforms package implemented in these economies.

Total government expenditure fell steeply in all the three LDC groups between the early 1980s and the 1990s but it rose somewhat in the high-income group of countries. For the low-income group, total expenditure relative to GDP fell 2 percentage points, the same as the fall in current (tax and non-tax) revenues. Total expenditure fell in the lower middle-income countries by 2.3 percentage points, despite the stability of government revenues, while the fall in expenditure in the upper middle-income group equalled two-thirds of the fall in government revenues. Thus, fiscal adjustment to the decline in revenues has involved varying degrees of reduction in government expenditure.

Table 2 shows that the average fiscal deficit was highest (5.2%) in the low-income countries during the 1990s. Deficits averaged 3.3% and 3.2%, respectively, in the upper middle-income and high-income countries. The lower middle-income countries had the lowest average fiscal deficit ratio of all the groups, at just 0.7%. These comparisons should be viewed against the fact that aggregate fiscal expenditure and the overall fiscal take are considerably higher in the higher-income groups than in low-income countries.

All country groupings witnessed significant fiscal adjustment between the 1980s and 1990s in the form of falling average deficit ratios, but the low-income countries seem to have had the most difficulty in making the adjustment. The relative reduction in the fiscal deficit between the first half of the 1980s and the 1990s averaged as much as 82% for the lower middle-income countries, 33 % for the upper middle-income group, 40% for the high-income group and only 21% for the low-income nations. Many developing countries were under the International Monetary Fund (IMF) lending programs during the late 1980s and 1990s. Domestic financing of fiscal deficits has fallen while foreign financing has risen in low-income and lower middle-income countries during the 1990s.

Equation (1) suggests that the partial effect of greater globalization or openness (as measured by the trade ratio) is to raise the tax/GDP ratio. But the causal mechanisms involved cannot be presumed to be the same in developed and less developed countries. In less developed countries, with relatively high rates of trade taxation in place, a higher trade ratio increases the ability of the government to garner revenues from trade. This effect is reinforced by the fact that revenues from domestic indirect taxation are also more easily collected from trade than from many domestic sectors. Clearly, therefore, while trade increases tax revenues in LDCs, trade taxation is a requirement for this favorable linkage, even though trade taxes themselves hurt trade[7]. The policy implication is equally clear. While fostering trade is one route to raising revenues, reducing trade taxation typically fails to accomplish this (see the next section), and a policy of free trade—implying zero taxation of trade—certainly will not. On the other hand, domestic policies and investments designed to raise the trade ratio without lowering trade taxation will help the fisc.

In developed countries, with rates of trade taxation close to zero, if a trade-fisc association holds, it cannot be due to a revenue-side effect. It has been argued that the worldwide link between openness and the size of government reflects the greater expenditure-side *demand* for public services, especially social safety nets and transfers (Rodrik 1998). The argument above suggests, instead, a possible contrast across the world: trade and trade taxation augment the budget from the *revenue* side in LDCs whereas trade may increase the budget from the *expenditure* side in developed countries.

To examine whether this contrast holds, separate regressions were run for the developed and developing countries in the sample, with government current expenditure as the dependent variable and with per capita income, population, the trade/GDP ratio and the trade-tax ratio as the independent variables. The regression for the developed country sample is:

$$CUREXP/Y = 102.8 - 1.4Ln(pcY) - 3.0Ln(Pop.) - .006(Trade/Y) - 3.1(TradTax/Tr.) \quad (2)$$

(33.5)	(2.46)	(0.96)	(0.03)	(0.85)
(0.00)	(0.57)	(0.00)	(0.02)	(0.00)

(with $R^2=0.31$ and $N=73$)

while for the LDC sample, the regression is

$$CUREXP/Y = -18.2 + 3.53Ln(pcY) + 0.35Ln(Pop.) + 0.11(Trade/Y) + .24(TradTax/Tr.) \quad (3)$$

(10.5) (0.67) (0.48) (0.02) (0.14)

(0.09) (0.00) (0.47) (0.00) (0.09)

(with $R^2 = 0.28$ and $N = 205$).

These results are broadly consistent with the contrast drawn above. Equation (3) shows that government expenditure in LDCs rises with the trade ratio as well as with trade taxation. By contrast, equation (2) shows that globalization and trade taxation both have negative effects on the size of public expenditure though the size of the effects is notably small. The fact that current expenditure levels in developed countries actually fall with openness throws into question the notion that openness raises the demand for social transfers. On the other hand, the positive link between globalization and public expenditure in LDCs may be understood as flowing from the supply- or revenue-side effect of trade taxation which serves to relieve the fiscal constraint that was described at the beginning of this section.

Apart from the structural constraints on revenue mobilization, tax revenues are also substantially more unstable in LDCs than in industrialized economies. This difference reflects the greater reliance on trade taxes, which are affected by the boom-bust cycles in commodity prices and realized export revenues. Instabilities in the tax/GDP ratio are markedly greater in Africa than in any other region of the world (Zee 1996). Moreover, in terms of instability, the largest (unfavorable) difference between LDCs and the industrialized countries of the Organization for Economic Cooperation and Development (OECD) pertains to trade tax revenues (relative to GDP) (Zee 1996, 1663). Fluctuations in export revenues affect aggregate income and import demand, both from the demand side and from foreign exchange constraints. In turn, revenues from import taxation also suffer fluctuations (Chu 1990). Chu finds that the impact of a revenue shock in LDCs was partly met by a change in government expenditure in the same direction whereas, by contrast, revenue shocks in industrial countries lead to deficit increases that are larger than the revenue shortfalls. The difference is clearly traceable to the lack of "diverse policy instruments" (p 124, Chu) that underlies the ubiquitous public financing constraint in developing economies. The large variability in revenues means that even if a government is willing to extend its planning horizon to the medium and long terms, its ability to sustain plans is strongly limited by this form of the fiscal constraint.

Tax structure, globalization and revenue effects

Structural adjustment and policy changes oriented towards increased external integration of developing economies have entailed a significant transformation of the tax structure. This transformation arises not only because fiscal policies are among the main instruments for such reorientation, but also because the resultant change in economic structure reacts upon the structure of public revenues. In the normal course of economic development, the fiscal structure undergoes a patterned transition reflecting the transformation in the economic structure that accompanies development. This section begins with evidence on these structural differences across countries at different stages of development. It then considers the results of globalizing policy changes of the past decade and half before focussing on changes brought on by trade liberalization in particular.

Table 3 brings out the salient differences across countries and over time in the structure of taxation. Most obviously, the weight of direct taxation rises with per capita income levels. This becomes clearer still when we include social security taxes under the "direct taxes" rubric[8]: the share of direct taxes rises from just 26.7% in the low-income countries to 39.80% in the lower middle-income, 47.2% in the upper middle-income and 60.5% in the high-income countries. But it is also noteworthy that the share of direct taxes fell in both low-income and high-income countries by about 10%. It rose somewhat in the lower middle-income and significantly in the upper middle-income countries. Barring this last group, the overall trend augurs poorly for redistributive policies aimed at advancing human development. All three developing country groups also witnessed declines in social security tax collections, a similarly unpleasant development.

Less developed countries are more reliant on corporate than personal income taxes as compared to developed countries. The ratio between these two elements was around 1:3 for the OECD countries while for non-OECD countries, the ratio was about 2:3 (Zee 1996). At first glance, this seems very surprising since corporate organization and corporate profits are undoubtedly a much smaller share of national income in LDCs than in developed countries. The observed inversion of shares may be attributed directly to the problems of tax administration. Thus, the very difficulty of collecting the personal tax levy in less developed countries raises their reliance on corporate taxation.

The other major development of course relates to collection of trade tax revenue. Trade taxation remains far more important to the developing, especially low-income, countries than the high-income nations. Although its share has fallen everywhere—by a fifth in the low-income group and by two-thirds in the high-income group—the change in fiscal structure this represents is far more significant in the lower two income groupings. The weight of this point is especially evident when we note that the last two decades have been a period of falling or stagnant per capita incomes in many of these developing countries. Hence, the move is not just the manifestation of a structural pattern characteristic of "normal" development. Rather, it is principally a reflection of the powerful tendency toward trade liberalization and other forms of policy liberalization.

In developing countries generally, much of the slack created by the decline in trade taxes has been taken up (in relative, not absolute, terms) by rising domestic indirect taxation. This is particularly the case for the low-income countries for which Table 3 suggests a law of invariance: the sum of domestic taxes and trade taxes on commodities has remained at 70% throughout the 26-year period. In many of these countries, the transition within the structure of indirect taxation—from trade toward domestic taxes—is also more apparent than real. Even value added taxes (VAT) are collected disproportionately from tradables (particularly importables), primarily because of the "law" of fiscal structure, i.e., "tax policy is tax administration". This follows from the observation that fiscal structures follow definite patterns correlated to income levels, which in turn is not easily explained, except by recourse to administrative impediments and aids in conjunction with the structure of the economy[9]. Hence, too much should not be made of the relative movements in the incidence of indirect taxation at the border versus within borders, which is shown in the last two columns of Table 3. While domestic indirect taxes as a proportion of the non-service GDP have moved up worldwide, this represents a real increase in developing country rates, whereas, for the high-income countries, it is the falling share of industry in GDP (and growing tax coverage of the rising services sector) that, in all likelihood, is captured in this movement.

TABLE 3: The Structure of Taxation

	Dir Taxes	Soc Secur.	Dom Indir.	Trade	Imports	Exports	Trade	Dom Indir.
	(% of Total Tax Revenue)				(% of Imports)	(% of Exports)	(% of Trade)	(% of NS VA)
LOW-INCOME COUNTRIES								
1970-75	26.1	2.0	29.3	40.8	18.1	6.3	11.1	5.84
1976-80	25.2	2.5	28.3	39.3	17.3	7.5	10.6	7.86
1981-85	25.5	2.4	32.0	37.0	17.7	6.3	10.2	6.78
1986-90	27.0	1.6	33.5	35.1	18.9	5.1	9.9	7.72
1991-96	25.4	1.3	37.8	32.2	18.9	2.4	9.4	8.30

Table 3 cont'd

	Dir Taxes	Soc Secur.	Dom Indir.	Trade	Imports	Exports	Trade	Dom Indir.
	(% of Total Tax Revenue)				(% of Imports)	(% of Exports)	(% of Trade)	(% of NS VA)
LOWER MIDDLE-INCOME COUNTRIES								
1970-75	29.9	4.8	26.7	31.9	15.9	3.9	8.6	4.90
1976-80	30.4	7.6	24.0	30.0	14.0	4.6	8.3	5.15
1981-85	32.8	8.1	25.0	25.5	13.0	2.8	6.6	5.14
1986-90	32.0	8.4	28.6	23.3	13.9	2.1	5.8	5.65
1991-96	32.7	7.1	33.9	20.3	12.7	0.7	5.1	6.88
UPPER MIDDLE-INCOME COUNTRIES								
1970-75	36.7	13.7	24.5	20.8	10.0	3.6	5.7	4.05
1976-80	42.4	11.5	24.8	17.0	10.7	3.7	4.7	5.24
1981-85	36.5	14.1	30.3	15.7	11.4	2.8	4.8	7.01
1986-90	29.5	16.8	31.1	18.2	13.3	1.8	5.2	7.88
1991-96	32.4	14.8	33.8	15.9	12.0	0.6	3.6	6.95
HIGH-INCOME COUNTRIES								
1970-75	37.7	17.9	30.8	7.5	6.0	**0.4**	2.7	5.53
1976-80	37.4	21.4	29.7	6.3	4.9	0.3	2.0	7.87
1981-85	37.7	22.1	30.3	4.9	3.9	0.2	1.6	8.48
1986-90	37.9	21.0	31.6	3.8	3.5	0.1	1.3	8.31
1991-96	36.1	24.4	31.4	2.3	2.4	0.0	0.8	8.00

Note: NS VA = Non-service value added

It is noteworthy also that high-income countries—whose dependence on trade taxation has remained minuscule and falling throughout the whole period—also experienced a rise in their overall tax/GDP ratios, in contrast to many developing (particularly low-income) countries which suffered a decline. In other words, changes in the fiscal structure in the LDCs documented here may be considered to be "premature", inasmuch as they have entailed revenue losses exacerbating the fiscal constraint, rather than a "normal" transition.

A final point of some policy significance emerging from Table 3 is the observation that export taxation has fallen rather more steeply on average than import taxation. Indeed, for the low-income group, import taxes relative to imports have actually risen or remained stable between the last three quinquennia covered. For the other two LDC groups, however, as steep as the decline in export taxation has been, import taxation has also fallen especially over the 1990s.

The major shift in the weight of trade taxes noted above calls for closer scrutiny. Although most economists view trade taxes only in terms of their effects on resource allocation across various production activities—particularly protection for import-competing sectors—their fiscal function cannot be overemphasized. As noted earlier, the positive argument for a reliance on trade taxes arises from administrative or structural imperatives in revenue mobilization. To the extent that this holds, the protective effects of trade taxation may be incidental rather than fundamental to policy choice.

But even if the protective function is the primary motive of policy, fiscal feasibility may constrain the choice of policy instruments. The point may be illustrated in relation to protection of infant industries against import competition. The orthodox argument against protective tariffs has always been that they are inefficient instruments for nurturing infant industries: since the need for intervention must arise from some market failure, the proper response is to correct or compensate for that failure rather than to impose tariffs. Thus, if the failure is in the capital market, a capital subsidy should be extended. The fact that most LDCs have instead pursued import protection at least suggests the rationale that the subsidy option is fiscally costly whilst the tariff option adds to state coffers. Fiscal factors are among the most important reasons why LDC governments violate the canons of standard efficiency arguments.

As against the fiscal arguments, the principal advantages claimed for trade liberalization in LDCs include increased efficiency in resource allocation and faster productivity gains through knowledge spillovers from trade. But the size of these effects remains an object of intense controversy, especially when allowance is made for the fact that a budding industrial sector, under protection, generates gains from increased division of labor and knowledge spillovers of its own. Moreover, *free trade* is hardly necessary for garnering the benefits promised by trade. It may, on the contrary, even be harmful, by destroying an industrial base without which the benefits of trade-based knowledge and learning spillovers would be irrelevant.

Even if it be understood that trade liberalization at the margin is socially beneficial, endemic fiscal constraints subject actual policy choices in developing countries to the economics of the second-best. Accounting for the costs of opportunities forgone due to fiscal constriction, liberalization may not confer net benefits. Nonetheless, there is a further question raised by these arguments. If governments are dependent on trade taxes, it would seem natural to suppose that government would want to *encourage trade* purely for revenue reasons, quite apart from any direct benefits to the economy or indirect gains to the treasury that trade expansion may bring. But it is not obvious what the means for doing so are. European states in the age of absolutism and mercantilism were inclined to "promote" trade through the creation of trade monopolies and colonial conquests, which fed their bullion store. Lacking such options, modern governments might consider fostering trade by lowering trade taxes. But this has obvious limits since the so-called Laffer curve has a positive slope below some level of tax rate: further reductions in rates will call forth revenue declines rather than gains[10]. Indeed, it can be argued that although trade taxation reduces trade volumes *directly* and therefore confronts unpleasant Lafferian tradeoffs from a revenue standpoint, it may well be an instrument for promoting trade *indirectly,* if the revenues obtained are used to augment infrastructure and human capital and thereby increase international competitiveness of the economy.

The revenue effect of trade liberalization is not easily predicted. Apart from uncertain Laffer effects, trade liberalization is in practice part of a package of policy moves, including the relaxation and/or tariffication of quantitative trade restrictions, and real devaluation of the exchange rate. Consider the quota regime first. Unlike tariffs, quotas are not only unambiguously protective; they also do not—at least directly—contribute to the fisc. Why governments that are fiscally strapped take recourse to quotas is therefore an interesting question. One reason may be that quota rents generated in the protected sectors are more easily taxed or, where they are publicly owned, accrue to the public sector. Another has to do with their effectiveness in protection. While under certainty, tariffs and quotas have equal trade incentive effects, uncertain changes in foreign prices will alter the degree of protection afforded the local industry under a tariff, whereas under a quota this is unchanged. So quotas need not be inconsistent with a fiscal constraint[11]. Quota liberalization, similarly, is certain whilst tariff liberalization may be neutralized by exchange rate devaluation. At any rate, the tariffication of quotas (a common element in recent liberalizations) is indeed revenue-enhancing. But once quotas have been tariffized, further liberalization must involve uncertain revenue effects.

Exchange rate policy before and after trade liberalization can make both the protective and fiscal effects of a particular liberalization package ambiguous. While a devaluation raises import values and hence import tax collections, the import tax base also erodes as import prices rise[12]. Prior to reforms, the protective effect of prevalent tariffs and quotas may be at least partly nullified by overvaluation of the exchange rate, which reduces the relative price of tradables. The revenue effect of the overvaluation will be ambiguous. Conversely, a real devaluation accompanying trade "liberalization" can exceed tariff reductions, in which case there will be an increase in the rate of protection. Again, revenue effects are ambiguous.

When adjustments are occurring concurrently in competing countries, trade liberalization and devaluation may also produce terms-of-trade losses. Declining terms of trade limit the tax take of governments since they reduce the tax base of readily taxed sectors. Moreover, falling commodity prices create a dilemma for governments that have price stabilization and marketing boards. They must choose between 1) letting the fall pass through to producers, which might erode the tax base and 2) stabilizing producer prices, which would reduce the tax or raise the subsidy implicit in such arrangements.

Table 4 and Table 4A report the results of an exercise to decompose changes in trade tax *revenues* (relative to GDP) into changes in the realized *rate* of trade taxation (trade taxes relative to trade) and changes in the *tax base* (trade relative to GDP). The analysis is based on mean values of the variables for developing countries for three periods, viz., 1970-79, 1980-87 and 1988-96 (periods 1, 2 and 3, respectively). Changes in the mean values were converted into annualized average rates. The individual country results appear in Table 4A while Table 4 shows the averages of the country results for four country groupings, viz., low-income sub-Saharan Africa (SSA), other low-income, lower middle-income and upper middle-income. The decompositions naturally incorporate the net effects of all policy changes that countries may have undergone, including changes in published tax rates, changes in quota regimes and exchange rate changes. They also include terms of trade and other exogenous changes. Note also that both export and import taxes are included in the results.

The decomposition is employed here to see whether and how far trade growth compensates for reduced protection accompanying globalization and increased economic openness. Between periods 1 and 2, 31 of the 50 countries represented in the sample had declining average trade tax rates while between periods 2 and 3, 41 of 58 countries saw a decline, and the average rate of decline in trade taxes was 1.8% and 2.6% per year, respectively. In terms both of the proportion of countries and the rate of change in trade taxation, therefore, there was a clear and cumulatively large trend of effective trade liberalization.

Table 4 shows that all developing country groups experienced revenue declines in period 3 (which includes the 1990s). While low-income SSA and non-SSA countries saw their trade tax revenues rise in period 2 (i.e., from period 1 to period 2), the trade tax rate was virtually unchanged in the case of the former while it rose significantly in the case of the latter. Thus, no country group in either period experienced a favorable "Laffer effect", i.e., rising revenues from falling trade taxes (with the possible exception of low-income SSA in period 2). These results underline the complementary rather than competitive nature of imports and exports relative to domestic production in developing economies.

Table 4A shows that five of the 50 countries in period 2, and 15 of the 58 in period 3, experienced favorable Laffer effects (whether from raising or reducing trade taxation). The revenue gainers in period 3 that also reduced tax rates were Ghana, India, Nicaragua, Fiji, Thailand, Jordan, Paraguay, Poland, Chile and Mexico. In the case of low-income sub-Saharan Africa, while Ghana, Zambia and Zimbabwe were the only countries that saw rising trade tax revenues in period 3; Ghana was alone in realizing this gain from *reduced* trade tax rates. In period 2, trade tax revenues increased in Kenya, Lesotho, Malawi, Niger, Zambia and Zimbabwe, and *all* of them saw *increased* realized trade tax rates. Hence, low-income countries in general, and SSA in particular, have been especially hard-hit by the adverse fiscal impact of trade liberalization. Most of these economies have operated on the rising part of the realized Laffer curve, and therefore confront a tradeoff between reduced protection and reduced revenues from liberalizing reforms.

TABLE 4: Decomposition of Changes in Trade Tax Revenues Relative to GDP

Country Group	Period	Trade-to-GDP (%)	Avg. Tax Rate (%)	Revenues-to-GDP	Avg. Tax Rate	Trade-to-GDP	"Laffer" Effect
				(Avg. Annual Rate of Change, %)			
Low-Income SSA	2	60.4	9.5	0.4	-0.1	0.5	Yes
	3	60.1	8.1	-1.6	-1.6	0.0	x
Other Low-Income	2	41.8	14.0	1.6	1.5	0.1	x
	3	50.5	10.9	-1.0	-3.4	2.4	x
Lower Middle-Income	2	53.6	6.8	-1.7	-2.4	0.7	x
	3	59.8	5.6	-1.5	-2.9	1.4	x
Upper Middle-Income	2	79.8	4.4	-2.3	-3.8	1.5	x
	3	87.7	3.4	-4.4	-5.5	1.1	x

Note: Average annual rates of change were computed from period means, where Periods 1, 2 and 3 stand for 1970-79, 1980-87 and 1988-1996 respectively.

In addition to the factors already noted, changes in the structure of the economy following trade liberalization also underlie the overall fiscal impact. That is, the fiscal impact of trade liberalization is not confined to trade taxation alone but may also be felt in domestic tax collections. Two such structural changes are the expected shift in resources from import-competing to export sectors and, from capital-intensive to labor-intensive sectors. If the latter of these pairs are low-taxed sectors, then liberalization will impose additional revenue losses. There are two reasons to expect this to be the case. First, sectors such as agriculture and small-scale export production typically escape the domestic tax net because they are legally exempt or effectively untaxed. Second, large-scale enterprises that are more easily taxed tend to be concentrated in the capital-intensive and import-competing sectors. In addition, cost pressures following trade liberalization prompt larger enterprises to sub-contract production to the small-scale and informal sectors. While these shifts may provide employment gains, there may also be revenue losses. These secondary revenue losses are likely to outweigh any revenue gains from increased allocative efficiency that orthodox theory claims for trade liberalization.

Import tariff reductions do not usually provide any concomitant reduction in government outlays. The chief reason is that government expenditures tend to be heavily concentrated on non-tradable goods and especially services. A secondary reason is that governments, as consumers, often do not pay import tariffs (defense is an example). On the other hand, transfer expenditures can be expected to rise in the wake of trade liberalization. Transition subsidies may have to be raised in sectors hit by import competition; retrenchment and retraining of workers organized enough to make their demands felt will add to the fiscal burden; rising food and other relative prices may have to be cushioned through compensatory wage increases for government employees, and through food and other subsidies to politically sensitive consumer groups.

Clearly, both the argument and the evidence underscore the fiscal squeeze, from revenue *and* expenditure sides, that accompanies trade liberalization[13]. One response might be that trade taxation should be resorted to at best for protection and not for revenue reasons. Such an argument might be made on second-best grounds on the trade side and on first-best grounds on the fiscal side. Apart from the presumed optimality of the resulting policy regime, its feasibility may be secured by switching from a reliance on trade taxes to trade-neutral excise taxation or value-added taxes. Although this proposal may seem attractive, its feasibility is largely a function of a country's level of development. A number of countries have introduced value added taxes (VATs) within the past decade or modified their VATs in seeking alternative revenue sources. However, the revenue results have often been mixed. Countries that had the lowest initial levels of tax revenue relative to GDP also fared the worst in terms of successfully introducing the VAT or other reforms in fiscal structure as well as in generating additional revenues. This holds the important lesson that "programs designed to raise revenue over time in low-income countries should take account of administrative constraints" (Abed et al. 1998, 4). Efficient and effective revenue mobilization may be more important in these countries than aiming fiscal reforms toward a textbook ideal of minimizing allocative inefficiency. In many countries, moreover, even the VAT is not "trade-neutral" in the sense that a greater part of the tradable sectors is subject to the VAT than is the case for domestic non-tradables, so that the efficiency rationale for the shift is blunted.

Another policy argument is that the fiscal squeeze is only a short-run or transitional problem that will remedy itself once the economy settles into a new steady state with liberalized trade. However, the promise of income gains in the long run must be viewed with caution if major distortions remain in the rest of the economy[14]. With widespread infrastructure and human capital constraints typical of poor countries—which are closely related to the fiscal constraint—the long-run gains (if they do exist) may prove unrealizable since the transition entails a worsening fisc, and this could lock the economy into a bad but politically self-sustaining equilibrium. In the presence of such distortions, liberalization may even end up reducing income and welfare.

Under the circumstances, the success of trade "liberalization" is to be judged not by how close to free trade a country gets but rather by how well it mediates between the fiscal and foreign exchange constraints endemic to developing countries. At the margin, a relaxation of the exchange constraint would give a potentially strong boost to investment, provided that the means by which the relaxation is effected do not worsen government finances. The qualification is necessary because a relaxation of the fiscal constraint also would provide an investment spur. Trade liberalization can be useful in this sense but, for the reasons and evidence given above, only within fairly narrow limits. Beyond this, no persistent net growth contribution should be expected; such a potential remains in the realm of speculation.

TABLE 4A: Decomposition of Changes in Trade Tax Revenues Relative to GDP

Country	Period	Trade-to-GDP (%)	Avg. Tax Rate (%)	Revenues-to-GDP	Avg. Tax Rate	Trade-to-GDP	"Laffer" Effect
				(Avg. Annual Rate of Change, %)			
Low-Income SSA	2	60.4	9.5	0.4	-0.1	0.5	
	3	60.1	8.1	-1.6	-1.6	0.0	
Burkina Faso	2	42.5	9.7	-2.0	-3.4	1.4	x
Burundi	3	32.7	11.6	-1.8	-2.1	0.4	x
Cameroon	2	54.4	8.6	-3.8	-4.6	0.8	x
Cameroon	3	37.0	7.1	-6.8	-2.3	-4.5	x
Chad	3	60.6	3.3	-1.3	0.6	-1.9	Yes
Congo, Dem. Rep.	2	40.8	7.9	-3.3	-7.3	3.9	x
Congo, Dem. Rep.	3	47.1	5.6	-2.4	-4.1	1.7	x
Ethiopia	3	21.2	12.8	-4.4	-1.8	-2.7	x
Gambia, The	3	148.7	6.3	-3.3	-6.1	2.8	x
Ghana	2	20.2	16.9	-4.3	0.1	-4.4	Yes
Ghana	3	44.9	10.6	4.0	-5.4	9.4	Yes
Kenya	2	53.9	8.2	1.5	3.2	-1.7	x
Kenya	3	58.4	5.5	-3.8	-4.8	0.9	x
Lesotho	2	153.6	17.0	6.2	2.3	3.9	x
Lesotho	3	149.4	16.5	-0.7	-0.4	-0.3	x

Table 4A cont'd

Country	Period	Trade-to-GDP (%)	Avg. Tax Rate (%)	Revenues-to-GDP	Avg. Tax Rate	Trade-to-GDP	"Laffer" Effect
				(Avg. Annual Rate of Change, %)			
Malawi	2	53.8	7.6	3.5	5.6	-2.1	x
Malawi	3	57.1	6.0	-2.1	-2.8	0.7	x
Mali	2	51.2	5.7	-1.1	-4.3	3.2	x
Mali	3	50.7	4.6	-2.7	-2.6	-0.1	x
Niger	2	62.9	8.4	3.1	1.6	1.5	x
Nigeria	2	34.1	5.1	-4.5	-3.3	-1.2	x
Rwanda	2	40.8	13.3	-0.9	-3.1	2.3	x
Rwanda	3	23.6	14.2	-5.6	0.8	-6.4	Yes
Senegal	2	79.6	9.2	0.0	-0.9	0.9	Yes
Sierra Leone	2	65.0	5.7	-7.5	-7.6	0.1	x
Sierra Leone	3	47.6	6.8	-1.6	2.1	-3.7	Yes
Sudan	2	34.8	17.0	-1.9	-3.7	1.8	x
Togo	2	101.1	8.7	-1.4	0.3	-1.7	Yes
Zambia	2	74.9	5.1	7.1	8.4	-1.3	x
Zambia	3	73.7	5.5	0.6	0.8	-0.2	x
Zimbabwe	2	55.6	6.8	15.1	14.8	0.3	x
Zimbabwe	3	71.3	7.3	3.8	0.8	2.9	x
Other Low-Income	2	41.8	14.0	1.6	1.5	0.1	
	3	50.5	10.9	-1.0	-3.4	2.4	
India	2	15.3	21.2	4.7	3.3	1.4	x
India	3	20.6	16.7	0.7	-2.8	3.5	Yes
Pakistan	2	34.9	15.2	0.9	-0.3	1.3	Yes
Pakistan	3	36.0	14.2	-0.4	-0.8	0.4	x
Sri Lanka	2	68.9	10.4	-2.0	-3.1	1.1	x
Sri Lanka	3	70.6	6.9	-4.6	-4.9	0.3	x
Nicaragua	2	48.0	9.0	2.9	6.4	-3.5	x
Nicaragua	3	74.8	5.9	0.2	-5.0	5.2	Yes
Lower Middle-Income	2	53.6	6.8	-1.7	-2.4	0.7	
	3	59.8	5.6	-1.5	-2.9	1.4	
Botswana	2	103.7	9.9	-1.1	-3.3	2.1	x
Botswana	3	95.7	8.5	-2.8	-1.8	-0.9	x
Namibia	3	113.5	8.7	0.8	1.4	-0.6	x
Swaziland	3	165.8	7.1	-4.7	-5.9	1.2	x
Fiji	3	115.9	5.6	0.3	-2.5	2.9	Yes
Indonesia	2	48.6	2.2	-7.5	-8.8	1.3	x
Indonesia	3	49.8	1.8	-2.0	-2.2	0.3	x
Papua New Guinea	2	94.3	5.0	4.5	3.7	0.8	x
Papua New Guinea	3	92.2	6.3	2.4	2.7	-0.3	x
Philippines	2	49.6	6.1	-2.6	-3.4	0.8	x
Philippines	3	68.1	6.6	4.7	1.0	3.7	x
Thailand	2	50.8	6.4	-0.9	-2.7	1.8	x
Thailand	3	77.2	4.4	0.5	-4.4	4.9	Yes
Egypt, Arab Rep.	2	57.1	11.9	-4.2	-3.6	-0.6	x
Egypt, Arab Rep.	3	54.9	6.5	-7.6	-7.2	-0.5	x
Jordan	3	132.2	6.1	1.1	-0.7	1.8	Yes

Table 4A cont'd

Country	Period	Trade-to-GDP (%)	Avg. Tax Rate (%)	Revenues-to-GDP	Avg. Tax Rate	Trade-to-GDP	"Laffer" Effect
				(Avg. Annual Rate of Change, %)			
Morocco	2	52.7	8.0	1.5	0.3	1.2	x
Morocco	3	54.9	8.3	0.9	0.4	0.5	x
Tunisia	2	77.1	11.5	3.2	1.2	2.0	x
Tunisia	3	89.0	9.4	-0.7	-2.4	1.7	x
Bolivia	3	42.2	2.7	-6.2	-8.6	2.4	x
Colombia	2	27.8	7.2	-2.1	-1.3	-0.8	x
Colombia	3	33.4	5.5	-0.9	-3.1	2.1	x
Costa Rica	2	71.1	6.6	2.9	2.5	0.5	x
Costa Rica	3	77.5	6.8	1.3	0.3	1.0	x
Dominican Rep.	2	47.9	7.9	-6.6	-6.3	-0.4	x
Dominican Rep.	3	65.9	9.2	5.5	1.8	3.8	x
Ecuador	2	57.7	3.7	-6.1	-4.6	-1.5	x
El Salvador	2	54.0	7.2	-2.9	-0.6	-2.3	x
El Salvador	3	47.9	3.9	-8.5	-7.1	-1.4	x
Guatemala	2	34.5	5.7	-5.2	-1.9	-3.3	x
Guatemala	3	41.9	4.4	-0.6	-2.9	2.3	x
Jamaica	2	97.9	2.0	1.6	-1.1	2.7	Yes
Panamà	3	175.9	1.4	-1.0	-3.5	2.4	x
Paraguay	2	39.2	3.9	-7.4	-9.0	1.6	x
Paraguay	3	53.6	3.7	3.2	-0.5	3.7	Yes
Peru	2	35.2	9.0	1.2	1.3	0.0	x
Peru	3	25.5	5.4	-9.9	-6.1	-3.8	x
Venezuela	2	40.7	7.6	8.8	10.4	-1.6	x
Venezuela	3	53.9	3.2	-7.0	-10.3	3.3	x
Poland	3	47.4	6.1	0.4	-2.9	3.3	Yes
Turkey	2	26.8	3.9	-8.8	-17.0	8.2	x
Turkey	3	35.1	2.1	-4.3	-7.5	3.2	x
Upper Middle-Income	2	79.8	4.4	-2.3	-3.8	1.5	
	3	87.7	3.4	-4.4	-5.5	1.1	
Mauritius	2	106.0	10.0	3.7	3.4	0.3	x
Mauritius	3	129.0	7.3	-1.4	-3.7	2.3	x
Seychelles	3	118.9	20.2	3.8	3.8	0.0	x
South Africa	2	54.0	1.6	-3.6	-3.2	-0.4	x
South Africa	3	47.2	2.3	2.6	4.2	-1.6	x
Malaysia	2	109.3	5.7	-0.9	-3.4	2.5	x
Malaysia	3	156.9	2.6	-5.1	-9.4	4.3	x
Oman	3	85.4	1.1	1.6	1.9	-0.3	x
Argentina	3	16.1	7.5	-1.3	-2.0	0.8	x
Barbados	2	124.7	3.6	-3.7	-3.8	0.1	x
Barbados	3	98.7	3.8	-2.0	0.8	-2.8	Yes
Brazil	3	15.3	3.3	-5.4	-2.9	-2.5	x
Chile	2	50.2	4.2	-2.2	-6.0	3.9	x
Chile	3	59.2	3.6	0.1	-1.8	2.0	Yes
Mexico	2	26.6	3.1	-5.1	-9.9	4.8	x
Mexico	3	37.8	2.4	1.1	-3.1	4.1	Yes

Table 4A cont'd

Country	Period	Trade-to-GDP (%)	Avg. Tax Rate (%)	Revenues-to-GDP	Avg. Tax Rate	Trade-to-GDP	"Laffer" Effect
				(Avg. Annual Rate of Change, %)			
Trinidad	2	84.1	3.3	-0.6	-0.2	-0.4	x
Trinidad	3	85.4	2.4	-3.6	-3.8	0.2	x
Uruguay	2	40.9	6.9	3.3	1.4	1.9	x
Uruguay	3	42.6	4.4	-4.8	-5.3	0.5	x
Greece	2	39.6	1.1	-12.4	-14.4	2.0	x
Greece	3	44.0	0.1	-32.7	-33.9	1.2	x
Hungary	3	66.0	4.5	-1.9	0.2	-2.1	Yes
Malta	2	162.9	4.5	-2.0	-1.8	-0.2	x
Malta	3	175.9	4.9	1.8	0.9	0.9	x

Note: Average annual rates of change were computed from period means, where Periods 1, 2 and 3 stand for 1970-79, 1980-87 and 1988-1996 respectively.

Financial liberalization and the fiscal squeeze

Apart from trade liberalization, liberalization of the external account and of the domestic financial system has been at the core of attempts at globalization. The liberal presumption has been that 1) barriers to financial mobility across borders are essentially policy-induced, and that 2) these are costly. A relatively closed financial system has or entails controls on interest rates, exchange rates and the capital account, and the regulation of credit allocation—in short, financial "repression" that produces inefficiencies in both portfolio holdings and investment allocation. Internal liberalization stimulates domestic saving and improves its allocation via financial markets. External integration permits global market forces to determine interest rates, bond and equity prices and the foreign exchange rate.

Although global financial flows have increased sharply in the 1990s, both foreign direct investment and portfolio flows seem to follow development rather than lead it. Long-term global financing of investment still remains a small share of total investment, as revealed by the persistent and high correlation between national saving and investment rates. International interest rate differentials also remain stubbornly high (Avramovic 1993). And much of that long-term flow is heavily concentrated in a dozen or so countries. Yet, the potential returns not merely to physical capital investments but also to human capital and infrastructure investments in LDCs are undoubtedly high. It is evident therefore that global financial markets and flows are deeply fragmented rather than integrated.

While it might be argued that this anomaly arises from the pursuit of improper macroeconomic policies and government control of the financial system, such an assessment ignores, on the one hand, the underlying structural constraints and market failures and, on the other, the limited scope for liberal policy choices without imposing potentially costly tradeoffs including exacerbation of fiscal constraints. Indeed, fragmentation characterizes even the *domestic* financial markets in LDCs. Finance flows but unevenly among the modern industrial sector (where much of the learning process must concentrate), the informal and agricultural sectors (which are the prime sources of employment and livelihoods), and the public sector (which must play the leading role in creating physical infrastructure and human capital). Uneven access to finance and wide differences in interest rates arise essentially from financial market failures owing to significant externalities and information asymmetries, and from the finance-fisc nexus (see below). In other words, intra-national fragmentation of finance is not unlike the global fragmentation noted above. Moreover, different parts of indigenous financial markets, even when not closed by policy, are highly unevenly connected with global markets.

The fiscal constraint and the uneven development of finance interact strongly to limit policy choices. The fiscal constraint, particularly the dynamic lag in relation to growth, implies that the public-sector financing requirement runs well ahead of government revenues and borrowing capacities. Governments have resorted to forced finance: by monetizing the deficit and forcing saving via inflation, or by requiring domestic banks, through reserve and portfolio requirements, to accommodate government finance. Forced saving and financial repression both have their economic and political limits, but so does revenue mobilization. Prudential regulation apart, a major reason for controls over banking in LDCs arises from the fiscal constraint. But note also that such controls cannot be sustained without a captive supply, which, in turn, is a prime motive for external capital controls. Thus, financial repression together with capital controls may be understood as stemming, in major part, from financial market fragmentation and the infeasibility of first-best policies for public financing.

Hence, it is to be expected that attempts at liberalizing and opening up the financial system are liable to impose fiscal costs. One source of this cost is the relaxation of financial repression: it has been estimated that the implicit fiscal gain from repression amounted to 2% of GDP (Giovannini and de Melo 1993). Similarly, reduced monetization of the fiscal deficit that is compelled by financial liberalization results in the loss of seignorage revenues; as inflation declines, the inflation tax also falls, as governments cannot reduce their debt obligations through a declining real value of money. Thus, in LDCs with large fiscal deficits, while the loss in real value of government liabilities held by the private sector averaged 2.7% of GDP in 1983-89, it fell to 1.7% of GDP in 1990-95. The corresponding figures for countries with moderate fiscal deficits were 3.5% and 2.8% respectively (IMF 1996).

Exchange rate changes matter not only for the external balance but also for the fiscal balance. Devaluations directly raise debt service burdens that rest disproportionately on the budget while benefiting the private export sectors, which may not be easily taxed. It should also be kept in mind that there are secondary fiscal impacts flowing from losses in trade tax and other sources of revenue, as noted in the previous sections. Revenue losses induce a rise in the domestic and/or foreign debt, which may force up the interest rate and thus the interest burden on the budget.

Table 5 draws attention to contrasting trends across country groups in public debt and the burden of servicing that debt. Between the early 1980s and the 1990s, the debt/GDP ratio remained essentially stable in the high-income and lower middle-income groups (at about 50%), but doubled from about 50% in the low-income group. The upper middle-income group has stabilized its debt/GDP ratio over the last decade, after an initial rise. The trend in the public interest burden follows these trends rather closely. In particular, interest expenditure relative to GDP in low-income countries has risen sharply—from 1.5% to 3.6%—in the space of a decade. While the interest burden in low-income countries is not much above that in the lower middle-income group (and is in fact lower than in the other two groups) when measured relative to GDP, it represents a much greater and growing fiscal constriction given their much lower tax/GDP ratio, which has also been falling in this period. Thus, as a share of total current expenditure, the interest burden has risen from 6.1% in the early 1980s to 15.5% in the 1990s.

The period of adjustment represented in Table 5 has not seen any rise, but rather some decline, in the ratio of gross domestic investment to GDP. There has been a noticeable trend toward privatization in investment (witness the rise in the private sector proportion of gross domestic fixed investment) everywhere, especially in the middle-income groups. At least in terms of raising the realized domestic investment ratio, the trend toward privatization and greater reliance on foreign investment has not helped.

A revealing if crude index capturing the fiscal impact of trade and financial liberalization is provided by changes in government interest expenditure and trade tax revenues (both relative to GDP). First, define a fiscal index by the difference between trade taxes and interest expenditures:

$$\text{F-INDX} = (\text{TradTax}/Y) - (\text{IntExp}/Y) \quad (4)$$

Between-period reductions in this index may be taken to represent the degree of fiscal "squeeze" related to trade and financial liberalization. Thus,

$$\text{F-SQZ} = \Delta\,(\text{TradTax/Y}) \quad -\Delta\,(\text{IntExp/Y}) \qquad (5)$$

TABLE 5: Public Debt, Interest and Investment

	Pub Debt (% of GDP)	Interest (% of GDP)	Interest (% of CurExp)	Int. Rate on Pub Debt	Gr. Dom. Inv (% of GDP)	Priv. GDFI (% of GDFI)	Net FDI (% of GDI)
LOW-INCOME COUNTRIES							
1970-75	34.6	1.1	5.1	3.6	17.7	**65.4**	3.5
1976-80	63.3	2.5	9.8	5.1	19.5	46.4	2.8
1981-85	50.9	1.5	6.1	3.9	20.8	50.4	3.2
1986-90	87.3	2.8	11.6	5.2	19.3	50.5	2.4
1991-96	98.4	3.6	15.5	3.9	20.7	55.0	7.3
LOWER MIDDLE-INCOME COUNTRIES							
1970-75	21.4	0.8	3.8	3.7	23.8	64.0	4.4
1976-80	23.9	1.3	5.2	4.3	27.5	59.0	4.1
1981-85	45.2	2.2	8.8	5.1	24.2	56.3	3.9
1986-90	48.6	2.5	11.4	7.2	22.7	63.1	3.7
1991-96	46.3	2.7	12.0	6.6	23.6	66.4	8.3
UPPER MIDDLE-INCOME COUNTRIES							
1970-75	24.6	1.2	4.8	4.5	25.7	**62.7**	6.2
1976-80	28.0	1.5	5.6	5.5	27.2	62.7	6.3
1981-85	35.4	2.9	10.8	12.6	23.3	65.4	5.6
1986-90	45.8	5.2	16.9	10.0	21.4	73.0	6.8
1991-96	45.7	4.3	14.5	7.8	21.1	76.2	10.7
HIGH-INCOME COUNTRIES							
1970-75	27.8	1.4	4.7	10.8	26.8	81.6	5.5
1976-80	37.5	2.2	6.5	6.5	26.0	**78.1**	3.9
1981-85	52.0	4.1	10.4	8.1	23.7	**75.2**	3.9
1986-90	51.4	4.6	12.2	8.6	23.3	**79.3**	6.8
1991-96	50.8	4.1	10.6	7.2	22.3	**80.7**	8.4

Tables 6 and 6A show the results for a cross-section of LDCs. As before, the time periods for which the fiscal squeeze index and its components are calculated are 1970-79, 1980-87 and 1988-1996 (periods 1, 2 and 3, respectively). Based on underlying level variables that are averages for the respective periods, between-period changes are computed as changes in those averages between successive periods. Accordingly, change indicators pertain to periods 2 and 3.

The first three columns of Table 6 summarize the fiscal squeeze variables for the four LDC country groups (low-income SSA, other low-income, lower middle-income and upper middle-income) while the corresponding columns in Table 6A show individual country results. A negative value for the fiscal squeeze variable indicates an adverse fiscal impact. For virtually all country groups and both time periods, Table 6 shows both revenue losses on the trade account and expenditure rises on the interest account.

The rise in interest expenditure was the dominant contributory factor except for low-income SSA and lower-middle-income countries in period 3 when losses from trade taxation constituted a sizable share of the fiscal squeeze. The fiscal squeeze ranged between 1% and 2% of GDP in both periods. Between the two periods, the index rose in both the low-income groups, fell in the lower middle-income group and was unchanged in the upper middle-income group. Table 6A shows that 46 of 58 countries in period 2, and 45 of 61 countries in period 3, experienced a fiscal squeeze.

While the fiscal squeeze index is only an accounting device, the following regression, after controlling for changes in the trade/GDP ratio, shows that it is closely related to both trade liberalization and the financial consequences of opening up[15].

$$-\text{FISSQZ} = \underset{(0.05)}{\underset{(0.23)}{0.46}} - \underset{(0.00)}{\underset{(0.02)}{0.07}}\,\Delta\,(\text{TradTax/Tr.}) + \underset{(0.00)}{\underset{(0.03)}{0.17}}\,\Delta\,(\text{IntExp/CurExp}) - \underset{(0.03)}{\underset{(0.07)}{0.17}}\,\Delta\,(\text{Trad/Y}) \qquad (6)$$

(with $R^2 = 0.26$ and $N = 163$).

Trade liberalization is here indexed by changes in the ratio of trade tax revenues to the value of trade, whilst financial policy changes are captured by changes in the ratio of government interest expenditure to total current expenditure. Both variables have the expected signs and are statistically significant. The regression also shows that countries that improved their trade shares of GDP reduced the fiscal squeeze.

TABLE 6: Liberalization, Fiscal Impact and Accumulation in Developing Countries

Country Group	Period	Trade-Tax Rev.	Interest Expend.	Fiscal Squeeze	Gov. Educ. Expend.	Gov. Cap. Expend.	Gr. Dom. Invest.	P.C Income Avg. Ann. Growth (%)
		(Change between periods, % of GDP)						
Low-Income SSA	2	0.4	1.4	-1.1	.	0.9	-1.4	-0.6
	3	-0.7	0.9	-1.6	-0.1	-1.1	1.7	2.7
Other Low-Income	2	0.3	1.4	-1.2	.	3.1	4.3	0.5
	3	-0.6	1.2	-1.7	0.0	-2.8	0.7	3.1
Lower Middle-Income	2	-0.4	1.5	-1.9	.	-1.2	-1.0	1.6
	3	-0.4	0.6	-1.0	0.2	-1.2	-0.8	5.6
Upper Middle-Income	2	-0.1	1.6	-1.7	.	-0.7	-1.8	3.9
	3	0.1	1.8	-1.7	0.2	-1.5	-1.5	3.9

Note: Change between periods was computed from period means, where Periods 1, 2 and 3 stand for 1970-79, 1980-87 and 1988-1996, respectively.

TABLE 6A: Liberalization, Fiscal Impact and Accumulation in Developing Countries

Country Group	Period	Trade-Tax Rev.	Interest Expend.	Fiscal Squeeze	Gov. Educ. Expend.	Gov. Cap. Expend.	Gr. Dom. Invest.	PC Income Avg. Ann. Growth (%)
		(Change between periods, % of GDP)						
Low-Income SSA	2	0.4	1.4	-1.1	.	0.9	-1.4	-0.6
	3	-0.7	0.9	-1.6	-0.1	-1.1	1.7	2.7
Burkina Faso	2	-0.8	0.2	-1.0	.	0.0	-1.9	-0.9
Burundi	3	-0.6	1.0	-1.7	1.1	-0.1	-3.9	1.2
Cameroon	2	-1.9	0.0	-1.9	.	2.7	3.6	-0.3
Cameroon	3	-2.1	1.6	-3.7	0.1	-4.4	-8.5	4.1
Chad	3	-0.2	0.1	-0.3	.	-1.9	6.4	4.7
Congo, Dem. Rep.	2	-1.1	0.6	-1.8	.	-0.3	-5.3	-1.6
Congo, Dem. Rep.	3	-0.6	-0.3	-0.2	.	-1.1	-2.9	-0.6
Ethiopia	3	-1.2	0.4	-1.6	.	-0.5	2.0	0.5
Gambia, The	2	1.5	0.8	0.8	.	3.8	7.6	.
Gambia, The	3	-3.1	3.0	-6.1	0.2	-5.0	-1.0	12.4
Ghana	2	-1.6	-0.2	-1.4	.	-2.4	-3.1	-0.2
Ghana	3	1.4	0.3	1.1	0.2	1.3	8.0	4.9
Kenya	2	0.6	2.1	-1.6	.	-0.4	0.4	0.4
Kenya	3	-1.2	2.9	-4.1	-0.6	0.1	-2.4	2.9
Lesotho	2	11.2	3.6	7.5	.	19.0	22.0	0.3
Lesotho	3	-1.6	1.1	-2.6	-0.1	-7.4	34.6	0.7
Liberia	2	-0.2	2.9	-3.1	.	-2.3	-11.5	.
Liberia	3	0.4	-0.5	0.9	.	-3.2	.	0.3
Malawi	2	1.1	3.4	-2.3	.	1.6	-9.0	-0.6
Malawi	3	-0.7	-0.4	-0.3	0.0	-2.3	-0.9	3.8
Mali	2	-0.3	0.5	-0.8	.	-0.1	0.4	-0.7
Mali	3	-0.6	0.3	-0.9	-1.6	-0.4	6.6	2.4
Niger	2	1.3	0.2	1.1	.	3.5	0.7	-1.0
Nigeria	2	-0.9	5.5	-6.4	.	0.3	-6.8	-0.8
Rwanda	2	-0.4	0.1	-0.5	.	1.4	4.0	-0.7
Rwanda	3	-2.1	1.1	-3.2	0.8	1.5	-3.5	-1.9
Senegal	2	0.0	1.5	-1.5	.	2.0	-5.3	-0.7
Sierra Leone	2	-3.6	0.3	-3.8	.	-0.1	-2.0	-1.3
Sierra Leone	3	-0.5	1.6	-2.1	-1.7	-0.6	-4.1	1.8
Sudan	2	-1.1	0.1	-1.2	.	-1.1	-0.6	-0.9
Togo	2	-1.2	3.4	-4.6	.	-11.7	-7.8	-0.5
Zambia	2	1.8	0.3	1.5	.	0.2	-12.8	-0.4
Zambia	3	0.2	0.0	0.2	-1.4	4.8	-4.1	2.3
Zimbabwe	2	2.8	2.1	0.8	.	0.4	1.0	0.2
Zimbabwe	3	1.4	1.9	-0.5	1.5	1.3	-0.8	3.8

Table 6A cont'd

Country Group	Period	Trade-Tax Rev.	Interest Expend.	Fiscal Squeeze	Gov. Educ. Expend.	Gov. Cap. Expend.	Gr. Dom. Invest.	PC Income Avg. Ann. Growth (%)
		(Change between periods, % of GDP)						
Other Low-Income	2	0.3	1.4	-1.2	.	3.1	4.3	0.5
	3	-0.6	1.2	-1.7	0.0	-2.8	0.7	3.1
India	2	1.1	1.0	0.2	.	0.5	2.7	0.0
India	3	0.2	1.7	-1.5	0.7	-0.1	1.9	4.1
Pakistan	2	0.4	1.0	-0.6	.	-0.6	2.7	0.3
Pakistan	3	-0.2	2.6	-2.8	0.4	1.0	0.4	3.9
Sri Lanka	2	-1.4	2.0	-3.4	.	6.2	9.5	2.5
Sri Lanka	3	-2.3	1.3	-3.6	0.4	-6.9	-2.9	3.7
Nicaragua	2	1.0	1.8	-0.8	.	6.3	2.1	-0.8
Nicaragua	3	0.1	-0.9	1.0	-1.7	-5.2	3.2	0.7
Lower Middle-Income	2	-0.4	1.5	-1.9	-0.3	-1.2	-1.0	1.6
	3	-0.4	0.6	-1.0	0.2	-1.2	-0.8	5.6
Botswana	2	-1.1	0.2	-1.3	-0.4	-2.3	-10.7	2.3
Botswana	3	-2.1	-0.2	-2.0	2.0	-1.5	-1.5	6.4
Namibia	3	0.7	-1.7	2.4	7.0	-1.9	3.0	4.3
Swaziland	2	2.0	0.9	1.2	.	-1.0	1.3	.
Swaziland	3	-5.7	0.0	-5.8	0.0	-4.0	-6.1	0.7
Fiji	2	-0.5	1.4	-1.9	.	-0.9	0.1	.
Fiji	3	0.2	0.5	-0.3	-0.9	-0.7	-8.6	2.8
Indonesia	2	-1.0	1.0	-2.0	.	2.6	4.8	1.3
Indonesia	3	-0.2	0.4	-0.6	-0.2	-2.4	3.3	7.2
Papua New Guinea	2	1.6	1.2	0.3	.	-1.9	0.0	-0.4
Papua New Guinea	3	1.1	0.2	0.9	.	-0.2	-1.8	5.8
Philippines	2	-0.8	1.6	-2.4	.	0.5	-3.9	1.0
Philippines	3	1.5	3.0	-1.5	1.1	0.3	-0.8	4.0
Thailand	2	-0.3	1.2	-1.5	.	0.1	2.5	3.5
Thailand	3	0.2	-1.1	1.3	0.2	0.0	11.2	9.6
Egypt, Arab Rep.	2	-3.1	1.1	-4.2	.	-2.6	4.4	0.4
Egypt, Arab Rep.	3	-3.3	2.4	-5.7	-0.8	-0.6	-5.1	7.0
Jordan	2	-1.5	1.1	-2.6	.	-4.8	-4.7	0.8
Jordan	3	0.7	2.5	-1.8	-1.8	-3.4	0.4	8.3
Morocco	2	0.5	2.6	-2.1	.	-1.9	2.2	0.8
Morocco	3	0.3	1.3	-0.9	-0.4	-1.4	-2.7	2.6
Tunisia	2	2.2	1.2	1.0	.	1.9	4.2	1.8
Tunisia	3	-0.5	1.1	-1.7	0.5	-3.5	-5.0	7.2
Bolivia	3	-0.8	0.6	-1.4	0.4	3.0	2.9	6.1
Colombia	2	-0.4	0.3	-0.7	.	-1.2	0.7	3.5
Colombia	3	-0.2	0.5	-0.7	0.8	-0.5	0.3	7.4

Table 6A cont'd

Country Group	Period	Trade-Tax Rev.	Interest Expend.	Fiscal Squeeze	Gov. Educ. Expend.	Gov. Cap. Expend.	Gr. Dom. Invest.	PC Income Avg. Ann. Growth (%)
		(Change between periods, % of GDP)						
Costa Rica	3	0.5	1.6	-1.0	-1.3	-0.8	0.5	6.9
Dominican Republic	2	-3.1	0.4	-3.5	.	-2.7	0.2	1.2
Dominican Republic	3	2.3	0.1	2.2	-0.3	3.1	2.1	6.5
Ecuador	3	-0.8	2.1	-2.9	-1.8	-0.8	-1.5	7.1
El Salvador	2	-1.2	1.1	-2.3	.	-0.1	-6.7	0.8
El Salvador	3	-2.0	0.1	-2.1	-1.7	-0.5	4.1	3.8
Guatemala	2	-1.2	0.3	-1.5	-0.1	0.2	-3.8	0.2
Guatemala	3	-0.1	0.3	-0.4	-0.3	-1.3	1.7	4.0
Jamaica	2	0.3	8.6	-8.3	.	-2.7	-2.8	2.2
Panama	2	-0.5	2.9	-3.5	.	-3.5	.	1.5
Panama	3	-0.2	-3.8	3.6	0.5	-1.9	-0.4	11.0
Paraguay	2	-1.4	0.2	-1.6	.	-0.6	4.3	0.9
Paraguay	3	0.5	0.4	0.0	0.9	-0.1	-3.4	3.6
Peru	2	0.3	1.8	-1.5	.	-0.1	5.2	0.2
Peru	3	-1.8	-0.3	-1.5	.	-1.1	-4.6	6.5
Suriname	2	-1.0	2.2	-3.2	.	-4.8	-10.1	.
Venezuela	2	1.7	1.7	0.0	.	-1.2	-12.9	2.0
Venezuela	3	-1.4	1.4	-2.8	-0.3	-1.8	-4.0	5.2
Poland	3	0.1	3.1	-3.0	0.6	-1.2	-3.8	4.7
Romania	3	0.8	0.0	0.7	0.5	-6.9	-6.7	2.9
Turkey	2	-1.3	1.1	-2.3	.	-0.4	2.2	3.1
Turkey	3	-0.3	1.6	-1.9	0.1	-2.1	5.9	3.4
Upper Middle-Income	2	-0.1	1.6	-1.7	0.7	-0.7	-1.8	3.9
	3	0.1	1.8	-1.7	0.2	-1.5	-1.5	3.9
Mauritius	2	3.0	3.4	-0.4	.	-1.1	-2.1	5.7
Mauritius	3	-1.1	-2.1	0.9	-0.7	0.3	7.7	5.0
Seychelles	3	6.6	3.7	2.9	-0.3	-3.0	-2.2	6.8
South Africa	2	-0.3	1.4	-1.8	.	-0.2	-2.6	1.6
South Africa	3	0.2	2.0	-1.8	1.0	-0.4	-7.5	1.1
Malaysia	2	-0.5	2.9	-3.4	.	3.1	5.9	3.9
Malaysia	3	-2.2	-0.4	-1.8	-0.9	-2.4	3.6	4.8
Oman	2	0.2	0.1	0.1	.	-6.1	-2.7	.
Oman	3	0.1	1.1	-0.9	0.8	-4.2	-9.5	5.1
Argentina	2	1.3	1.7	-0.3	.	1.4	-5.4	2.3
Argentina	3	-0.1	-0.6	0.5	0.7	-0.6	-3.5	7.3
Barbados	2	-1.7	1.0	-2.7	.	-0.5	-3.5	6.6
Barbados	3	-0.7	0.6	-1.3	1.1	-0.1	-4.3	-1.9
Brazil	3	-0.3	11.5	-11.8	-0.5	-0.6	1.1	5.7
Chile	2	-0.5	-0.3	-0.1	.	-3.4	-0.7	5.7
Chile	3	0.0	0.2	-0.2	-1.5	0.2	9.2	5.5

Table 6A cont'd

Country Group	Period	Trade-Tax Rev.	Interest Expend.	Fiscal Squeeze	Gov. Educ. Expend.	Gov. Cap. Expend.	Gr. Dom. Invest.	PC Income Avg. Ann. Growth (%)
		(Change between periods, % of GDP)						
Mexico	2	-0.5	7.2	-7.6	.	0.6	0.7	2.1
Mexico	3	0.1	-2.4	2.5	0.8	-1.9	0.1	6.1
Trinidad and Tobago	2	-0.2	0.1	-0.3	.	-0.7	-2.8	3.9
Trinidad and Tobago	3	-0.7	4.5	-5.3	-1.1	-9.4	-10.1	1.7
Uruguay	2	0.7	0.9	-0.2	.	-0.3	-4.9	3.4
Uruguay	3	-0.9	0.4	-1.4	0.4	0.2	-2.8	2.4
Greece	2	-0.9	2.0	-2.9	0.7	-0.5	-5.7	4.7
Greece	3	-0.4	6.6	-7.0	0.2	-0.5	-2.4	5.9
Hungary	3	-0.5	1.5	-2.0	1.4	-2.5	-4.5	-4.6
Malta	2	-1.4	-0.8	-0.6	.	-0.7	1.7	3.0
Malta	3	1.2	0.6	0.6	1.2	1.9	2.1	7.8

Note: Change between periods was computed from period means, where
Periods 1, 2 and 3 stand for 1970-79, 1980-87 and 1988-1996 respectively.

Infrastructure and Human Development Impacts

The adverse fiscal effects of liberalization and globalization have implications for both economic development and income distribution. These flow directly from the fiscal squeeze that can reduce both infrastructure and human development expenditures on the public account. There are also important indirect effects to be considered. One such effect arises from the greater amplitude of fluctuations in incomes and relative prices—not to mention financial crises of the sort seen recently in Asia, Russia and elsewhere—that globalization brings in its train. These are apt to hurt especially the poor and vulnerable segments of the population. Another indirect effect flows from income redistribution due to reductions in real wages, increased informalization, and increased skilled/unskilled wage differentials. Real reductions in the incomes of the poor may also be induced by increased relative prices of food, cuts in food and other wage goods subsidies, higher user charges for health and educational services, etc.

Low-income countries with low levels of human development seem to be in particular danger of marginalization due to globalization. One reason is that these countries are especially hard hit by the fiscal impact discussed in the preceding sections. Second, with low levels of human development, they lack the capabilities to benefit from globalization. Human development and good infrastructure are key to both industrialization and raising international competitiveness. Third, lacking established safety nets, they are liable to experience the backwash effects of globalization, such as de-industrialization, terms-of-trade losses, and trade-induced instability.

Raising the level of human development is principally a matter of raising investment, especially public investment, and of reaching large sections of the population bypassed by the market. Both factors originate from pronounced externalities in such areas as health, education, and training, and market failures in insurance, credit, and infrastructure creation. On the face of it, the required investments and provision of opportunity should have nothing to do with a policy of globalization, i.e., they have to be undertaken as part of any program of economic development, quite independently of policies with respect to external integration. But this is simply not so. While low levels of human development and infrastructure make poor countries more vulnerable to the costs of globalization without being able to benefit from it, globalization also makes it more difficult for them to raise their levels of human development and infrastructure. This suggests a cumulative process that can hold back development. Clearly, the government budget is a crucial link in this process.

Tables 6 and 6A provide cross-country evidence on changes in government expenditure on the capital account and on education as well as changes in gross domestic investment (all relative to GDP). As the tables show, time-series data on government education expenditures are less abundant than for capital expenditure. Although ideally health expenditures and other human development expenditures should also be considered, adequate cross-country time-series data were unavailable. The group-wise averages in Table 6 show that government capital expenditure fell in all four groups in period 3 (which includes the 1990s). Note also that low-income SSA suffered a decline in education expenditures in the latest period.

On the other hand, gross domestic investment recovered in low-income SSA after a decade of decline (accompanied by decreasing per capita incomes) but this recovery was marginal at best, a bit above neutralizing the earlier decline. The other low-income group experienced rising investment, but investment growth slowed down substantially between the two periods. By contrast, middle-income countries witnessed a continuation of falling investment ratios, with only a small drop in the rate of decline.

The declines in government capital expenditure and gross domestic investment are related to each other, but, more importantly, these declines took place in a period when the fiscal squeeze from globalization was also taking effect. As we argue below, the trend in public educational expenditures is also related to the fiscal squeeze, though this may not be immediately apparent. The following regression reveals the link between the fiscal index (defined in equation 4) and public capital expenditure, controlling for income, size and the trade ratio.

$$PUBINV/Y = 5.46 - 0.58Ln(pcY) + 0.06Ln(Pop.) + 0.04(Trade/Y) + 0.25(F\text{-}INDX) \quad (7)$$

(5.07)	(0.32)	(0.24)	(0.01)	(.08)
(0.28)	(0.07)	(0.81)	(0.00)	(0.00)

(with $R^2 = 0.26$ and $N = 196$).

This result supports several interesting conclusions. First, public investment is inversely related to per capita income levels. This shows that infrastructure and related capital expenditure requirements are larger in countries at the beginning stages of modern economic growth and/or that a greater part of such capital expenditures tend to be publicly organized and financed in such countries. Either way, this indicates the greater importance of the public finance constraint in countries at low levels of development. Second, this last conclusion is directly confirmed by the positive and statistically significant coefficient for the fiscal index. Countries that were fiscally squeezed by lowered trade tax revenues and/or increased interest expenditures tended to have a lower rate of public capital expenditure. Capital expenditure falls by one quarter of any drop in the fiscal index. Finally, the positive coefficient on trade shows that, all else being the same, enlarged trade increases public capital expenditure. Since the tax-base effect of trade on public revenues is already captured by F-INDX, this coefficient probably reflects a foreign exchange constraint: higher trade volumes indicate a relaxation of that constraint, which serves to push up public investment.

The above specification was repeated using the total of public capital and public education expenditures as the dependent variable and the following result obtained:

$$EDU/Y + PUBINV/Y = \underset{\substack{(6.94)\\(0.34)}}{6.65} - \underset{\substack{(0.43)\\(0.29)}}{0.46Ln(pcY)} + \underset{\substack{(0.32)\\(0.71)}}{0.12Ln(Pop.)} + \underset{\substack{(0.01)\\(0.00)}}{0.05(Trade/Y)} + \underset{\substack{(0.10)\\(0.00)}}{0.37(F\text{-}INDX)} \quad (8)$$

(with $R^2=0.387$ and $N=127$).

Note that the income coefficient is not statistically significant although it remains negative as in equation (7). The smaller size of the sample than that for equation (7) may be a factor here. At any rate, equation (8) reveals a large and significant coefficient for the fiscal constraint as indexed here. With a $1 decline in trade-tax revenues or rise in government interest expenditure, public expenditure on capital formation and human capital falls by $0.37. This result is consistent with the one obtained in equation (7) for public capital formation alone.

It is of considerable interest to see how gross domestic investment, as the key determinant of economic growth, reacts to the fiscal index. Apart from income per capita and size, the specification below controls for the trade ratio, public capital expenditure and educational expenditure.

$$GDI/Y = \underset{\substack{(9.29)\\(0.00)}}{-61.74} + \underset{\substack{(0.59)\\(0.00)}}{2.75Ln(pcY)} + \underset{\substack{(0.42)\\(0.00)}}{3.24Ln(Pop.)} + \underset{\substack{(0.02)\\(0.00)}}{0.08(Trade/Y)} + \underset{\substack{(0.14)\\(0.00)}}{0.69(F\text{-}INDX)} \quad (9)$$

$$+ \underset{\substack{(0.14)\\(0.00)}}{0.67(CapExp/Y)} + \underset{\substack{(0.30)\\(0.02)}}{0.72(EducExp/Y)}$$

(with $R^2=0.49$ and $N=132$).

All variables bear the correct sign and are statistically significant. The investment ratio is an increasing function of both per capita income and population size. Following the previous interpretation, the positive coefficient on the trade ratio indicates a foreign exchange constraint on accumulation. As for the fiscal constraint, a $1 loss of revenue from trade or increase in the interest burden leads to a decline of $0.69 in gross domestic investment. Again, this result provides further confirmation of the fiscal fetter on accumulation. Two further conclusions may be noted. Educational expenditure has a large and positive impact on domestic capital formation. Thus, public investment in education and total investment in physical capital are strong complements. Finally, the coefficient on public capital expenditure, though positive, is less than unity. While this seems to indicate a crowding-out of private investment, this result should be seen together with the large positive coefficient on F-INDX. Thus, enhanced fiscal capacity would seem to have a strong direct effect of crowding in private investment as well.

The above results regarding the determinants of public investment expenditure, public educational expenditure, and domestic capital formation, underline the centrality of the fiscal constraint for economic growth and human development. Together with the results in preceding sections showing significant adverse fiscal effects from globalization, this refutes the notion that human development need have nothing to do with a policy of globalization. Rather, it indicates an important tradeoff between external integration and internal integration, with the government budget providing the fulcrum of that tradeoff. Liberalization shifts resources from the public to the private sectors, thus exacerbating the budget constraint. This not only lowers public investment but, in the end, also serves to lower economy-wide accumulation.

While externally oriented liberalization has been promoted mainly with a view to the efficiency gains that it is promised to deliver, its distributional effects may in fact be more important, in both political and economic terms. One such effect is the redistribution from government to the private economy, which we have just considered. The other of course pertains to redistributions within the private sector. Such redistributions arise from relative price changes and the consequent resource reallocations and factor price changes. Attempts at liberalizing domestic economies and integrating with world markets impose costs on some groups while benefiting others; hence they pose political problems which may show up in the budget.

Yet, these budget demands produced by globalization come in the wake of reduced revenues and increased debt obligations. The paradox of globalization is that it places the strongest demands on the weakest states after weakening them further. This is related to two considerations. On the one hand, the fiscal losses from globalization are largest for the poor countries. On the other, it is the poor countries that have small and fiscally weak states to begin with; the developed economies have large governments whose capabilities have been built up in the course of development. As Tanzi (1998) has pointed out, "The reason is not that the [advanced industrial countries] need more government than the [poor countries] but because *they can collect more taxes*" (emphasis added). Yet, it is the poorer countries that need fiscally stronger states to cope with widespread market failures and complex distributional changes.

Relative price shifts accompanying globalization may also weaken the fisc. Liberalizing agricultural prices, for example, can produce large real transfers from poor consumers (for whom food is the overwhelming part of private expenditure) to agricultural rentiers and traders[16]. When developing countries as a group face pressures to get their agricultural-exportable prices "right", i.e., alignment with world price levels, this will also produce a net transfer of resources to the consuming countries via terms-of-trade losses. These effects are additional to the permanent increase in the variability of producer prices and export earnings that openness entails, and to the transitory costs of de-industrialization and unemployment that adjustment requires.

The real income loss of poor food consumers due to liberalized food and agricultural prices will be reinforced if food or fertilizer subsidies are cut at the same time. In such cases, the redistribution does not implicate the fisc directly. But note that indirect effects on the budget are likely, e.g., if government employees demand and secure compensatory nominal wage increases, government current expenditure will rise or, if private non-agricultural employees are similarly compensated, government tax revenues decline along with non-agricultural profits. But political compulsion might force the government also to extend or at least maintain food subsidies. The rise in food prices, however, entails a larger fiscal outlay for such subsidies to achieve the same real subsidy level. As in the present example, the budget rarely goes unscathed from major price realignments.

In standard trade theory, when trade arises from factor endowment differences rather than intra-industry competition, trade liberalization will reduce the income of the scarce factor while benefiting the abundant factor of production. A great deal of trade between rich countries and developing countries is probably largely complementary in this sense (with specialization predicted by comparative advantage). The usual presumption in a two-factor world is that abundant labor will gain at the expense of scarce capital in LDCs. There are a number of qualifications however. First, with large reservoirs of underemployed or surplus labor, the relative price shifts from trade opening will produce employment rather than wage increases. Second, trade opening can be expected to reduce employment and wages in import-competing sectors, and as firms seek to reduce costs, lower workplace standards and weaken trade unions, minimum wage enforcement, etc. Third, with a third factor present in the form of skilled labor, a rise in unskilled wages is no longer assured. If skilled and unskilled labor are easily substituted, then, the skilled-unskilled wage differential may widen and wage-based inequality may rise. This last effect may be reinforced if technical change favoring substitution of skilled-labor and capital for unskilled labor accompanies liberalization. Similarly, with agricultural land as the third factor, a real wage increase from liberalization is not assured.

For developing countries, evidence on changes in absolute poverty and relative inequality (both in terms of the personal distribution of income) are rather more available than evidence on the functional distribution of income to which the foregoing arguments relate. Of course, the two distributions are closely related in general. Accordingly, cross-country evidence over the period 1970-95 has been examined to see if there are broad associations between trends in openness on the one hand and poverty and inequality on the other (Rao 1998). Openness is measured by the export/GDP ratio and the Trade Index (which is the trade/GDP ratio after eliminating the effects of per capita income level and population size). The majority of countries in the sample witnessed a rise in their openness. There were a number of countries in which poverty, as measured by the head-count ratio below US $1 per day, increased though the numerical edge was on the side of those where poverty decreased. The sample as a whole shows a *positive* (and statistically significant) relationship between *changes* in the Trade Index measure of openness and *changes* in poverty with an adjusted R^2 of 0.29[17]. Countries with declining poverty had on average an openness trend of 0.1% per annum whilst those with rising poverty had an average openness trend of 2.1% (the corresponding figures for the export/GDP index of globalization were 0.7% and 2.0% per annum).

Turning to the link between changes in openness and inequality, few countries in the sample witnessed a decline in both openness and inequality. Rises in inequality were rather evenly divided among those associated with rising openness and those associated with falling openness. Countries opening up similarly showed roughly equal proclivity to become less unequal as more unequal. Although there was a positive relationship between the trend in openness (Trade Index) and the trend in inequality, the regression coefficient was not statistically significant at any conventional level[18]. In terms of sample means, countries with declining inequality had an openness trend of 0.6% per annum while those with rising inequality opened up at 1.1% per annum (the corresponding figures for trends in the export ratio or globalization are 2.0% and 1.6% per annum).

From a policy standpoint, dealing with the poverty, dislocation, volatility and distributive effects of globalization may be considered in terms of tax and expenditure policies. Consider the tax policy potential. Ideally, taxes must be designed so as to strengthen the fisc and promote human development—objectives that would seem best served by a progressive structure of taxes. As already seen, this need not have a net disincentive effect on domestic investment; on the contrary, such a structure would be complementary to economic growth.

But administrative (and political) constraints related mainly to low levels of development remain formidable barriers. Tangible wealth and property, which constitute the real base of taxable incomes, have been particularly difficult to tax in poor countries, whereas human capital, which constitutes the larger taxable element in rich countries, is more easily taxed in the rich countries. Though much is made of the influence of tax rates on tax compliance, lax enforcement allows ample scope for evasion of both direct and indirect taxes whatever the rates. Most taxable incomes in the informal sectors simply escape the tax net, agricultural incomes and wealth are typically exempt from taxes, and corporations and the well-to-do in the formal sector get away with legal concessions and artful subterfuge. Official corruption imposes its own tax on the state's rightful take. Similarly, public services though formally offered free are often subject to informal charges. A major problem arising from the heterogeneity of enterprise structures in developing countries is that of horizontal inequity: the unequal treatment of equals. Thus, small entrepreneurs escape taxes, which the salaried classes with similar incomes must cough up. In turn, of course, this inequity affects the economic structure and enlarges the range and scope of activities where tax evasion is less costly. Yet, global integration tends to shift the tax structure further in a regressive direction. Thus, regressive shifts from corporate and personal income taxes—and trade taxes—towards consumption-based taxes like VAT are increasingly accepted as inevitable or, result from competitive concessions. One of the ironies of globalizing liberalization is that administratively insecure tax bases are increased at the expense of secure tax bases.

TABLE 7: Trends in Social Investment

Public Expenditure on:

	Education	Health	Capital	Educ + Health	Educ, Health & Cap
	(% of Gross Domestic Product)			(relative to Interest Expenditure)	
LOW-INCOME COUNTRIES					
1970-75	..	..	4.3		
	..	..	(21.8)		
1976-80	3.7	..	5.8		
	(16.2)	..	(25.6)		
1981-85	3.4	..	5.9		
	(15.4)	..	(23.1)		
1986-90	3.5	1.8	6.5	2.0	**4.2**
	(16.5)	**(7.1)**	(26.7)		
1991-96	3.9	1.6	6.1	1.8	**3.4**
	(17.0)	(7.2)	(24.9)		
LOWER MIDDLE-INCOME COUNTRIES					
1970-75	..	..	5.8		
	..	..	(27.1)		
1976-80	**4.2**	..	7.7		
	(17.2)	..	(29.5)		
1981-85	**4.1**	..	5.9		
	(16.1)	..	**(23.0)**		
1986-90	**4.0**	**2.4**	4.7	4.2	6.3
	(17.1)	**(11.7)**	(19.3)		
1991-96	4.1	2.7	4.4	4.1	7.3
	(16.5)	(9.9)	(20.2)		
UPPER MIDDLE-INCOME COUNTRIES					
1970-75	..	..	5.8		
	..	..	(18.8)		
1976-80	**3.9**	..	5.9		
	(14.5)	..	(19.9)		
1981-85	**4.4**	..	5.6		
	(12.9)	..	(16.3)		
1986-90	**4.5**	**3.5**	4.4	2.8	3.6
	(13.6)	**(13.8)**	(12.9)		
1991-96	4.4	3.3	4.0	3.3	**4.3**
	(16.9)	**(12.4)**	(13.4)		
HIGH-INCOME COUNTRIES					
1970-75	..	..	2.9	..	..
	..	..	(11.6)		
1976-80	**5.6**	..	3.0	..	..
	(18.2)	..	(9.9)		
1981-85	**5.3**	..	3.0	..	..
	(15.8)	..	(8.8)		
1986-90	**5.2**	**5.2**	2.9	3.5	**4.4**
	(15.8)	**(15.8)**	(8.5)		
1991-96	5.5	5.8	2.5	6.7	9.1
	(15.7)	(16.7)	(7.4)		

Notes Figures in parentheses are relative to public current expenditure. Bold-faced figures indicate less than 30 observations.

Expenditures on social safety nets take diverse forms across countries, but in developing countries, as a rule, the chief free forms are access to health and education, subsidies for items consumed by the poor, especially food, and temporary measures for those in distress. Pensions, health insurance and unemployment benefits, programs characteristic of advanced economies, are virtually non-existent[19]. Table 7 puts together readily available data on public expenditures on health and education, and also public capital expenditures. Data of adequate quality are sparse both in country and time-period coverage. It is notable that government capital expenditure (as a share of GDP) is considerably higher in low-income countries than in rich countries (6.1% in 1991-96, compared to 2.5%). This gap is higher still when capital expenditure is reckoned relative to current expenditure (27.1% for low-income countries in the 1990s, compared to only 6.7% for high-income countries). After falling in the 1980s, education expenditures relative to GDP in low-income countries have recovered lost ground in the 1990s. On the other hand, health expenditures have fallen (from 1.8% of GDP in the late 1980s to 1.6% in the 1990s). Both health and education public expenditures have stagnated or fallen in the middle-income groups.

Combating poverty, whether endemic or transitional, with pure cash tax-and-transfer programs is not administratively practicable and subject to even greater leakage to unintended beneficiaries than the conventional in-kind transfers. Yet, there are strong advocates of cost recovery even from the slender safety nets provided by in-kind transfers in poor countries. User charges, not to mention private alternatives, are advocated even in the areas of urban hospitals, clinics, universities, and transport. The assumption is that secondary and tertiary education, as well as most curative care, are private goods, which will find private alternatives if government did not commit to footing the bill. The implication is that greater social security can be achieved at lower costs by relying on communities and households to take up the slack. The principle that user charges be confined to curative care and for tertiary education while primary care and education is supplied free seems sensible enough. But there are overwhelming administrative problems in maintaining user charges, policing informal charges, and confining subsidies to the deserving poor[20].

Infrastructure expenditures fulfill a vital allocative function of governments in LDCs primarily because of the presence of large market failures and externalities. They are also arguably the most important—or at least most accessible—instruments by which the benefits of development can be diffused across the population. But unless these expenditures are financed mainly through taxation, the resulting fiscal deficits are likely to work against equitable outcomes.

Conclusion

This paper has been concerned primarily with the fiscal consequences of various measures of policy liberalization designed to increase the global integration of developing countries. Its principal conclusions are that globalization has further accentuated the fiscal constraints facing states, and that there is a cumulative process of causation between liberal policies and the fiscal constraint. These conclusions imply that the fiscal basis of constructive state action to promote human development and resolve distributive conflict is now more limited than before.

But globalization is not just an autonomous development, resulting from technological imperatives; it is also driven by policy choices. Liberalization has been the principal policy instrument of globalization in trade and finance. Thus, not only international financial institutions, but also states as policymakers, have played an essential determining role in this process of external integration. Hence, it appears as something of a paradox that states are seen as helpless in the face of the forces of globalization. The paradox dissolves once it is recognized that the global arena of policy has both powerful and weak players, countries able to take advantage of the global marketplace and those vulnerable to its compulsions, individual countries and various collectivities of nations, active agents of change and passive onlookers. The fiscal autonomy of states has been trimmed, in part, by states acting autonomously and powerfully.

Even if there are significant long-run benefits to globalization (this remains a controversial claim), the transition to greater global integration in developing countries requires strong public action and a stable fiscal base. The push to globalization can and has been premature from this viewpoint. Globalization and human development are not orthogonal to each other. There are significant tradeoffs between them mediated especially through the fisc. Developing country governments are especially constrained by the paucity of tax and expenditure instruments that do not conflict with accepted canons of economic efficiency and "good" macroeconomic policy, which globalization is supposed to enforce. States must retain the autonomy from global market forces necessary to pursue nationally and politically determined tradeoffs.■

Notes

[1] To be sure, moving out of the fiscally constrained initial equilibrium cannot be a matter only of the right policy choice being technically feasible. But an "outside" observer or policy analyst ought to take into account how, in economic terms, policy recommendations relax or reinforce the constraint, and how, in political terms, they enlarge or constrict the room for left-out groups in society to participate in the process that determines budgets and to make their valuations relevant.

[2] The correlation coefficients are respectively 0.69 ad 0.73 over the sample of 123 countries for 1970-96.

[3] This is subject to the qualification that the influence of non-tariff barriers is not captured by trade tax measures nor even entirely by measured trade outcomes. The trade tax ratio is obviously a more accurate measure of the fiscal aspect of trade taxation than of the protective aspect of trade policies.

[4] This is not to say that capital necessarily flows from the best-endowed regions nor that it flows to the worst endowed, much less that the flows are in (inverse) proportion to existing endowments.

[5] Observations are means of annual values for the following three periods 1970-79, 1980-87 and 1988-96. Here as elsewhere in this paper, the first row of figures in parentheses are standard errors and those in the second row in parentheses indicate the level of significance.

[6] It is noteworthy, however, that the proportion of non-tax revenues relative to total revenue is a *decreasing* function of per capita income. This may be accounted for by the greater involvement of LDC governments in production activities, services provision (from which some user charges are collected), monopoly trading, and the like.

[7] For the cross-country sample here, the simple correlation between the trade/GDP ratio and the trade tax ratio was 0.21 and statistically significant.

[8] This is justified because social security contributions are based on employment incomes and (business) profits.

[9] This conclusion is also supported through cluster and principal components analyses of a wide range of countries and tax structure variables (Hitiris 1990).

[10] Lacking precise knowledge of the trade Laffer curve, states are therefore likely to develop a schizophrenic attitude toward trade taxes.

[11] Quotas may also be a route to bestowing unearned rents on politically favored or politically powerful groups.

[12] An IMF study of the SAF/ESAF (Structural Adjustment Facility/Extended Structural Adjustment Facility) countries found that "a currency devaluation usually has a greater impact on raising current and capital expenditure in local currency than on raising revenue in local currency terms, which leads to a large increase in the fiscal deficit/GDP ratio." (Nashashibi et al. 1991, 3ff)

[13] The fiscal impact of trade liberalization documented in this paper illustrates the "double jeopardy" to public finance that globalization threatens (Grunberg 1998).

[14] Following the theorem of the second-best, given major distortions elsewhere in the economy, liberalization may end up reducing income and welfare.

[15] The fiscal squeeze index is entered with a negative sign in the regression.

[16] Higher agricultural prices will also lower the real wage of labor to the extent that agricultural (food and raw material) goods figure heavily in labor's consumption bundle even though agriculture is labor-intensive. "Peasants", on the other hand, gain as owners of land but may lose as food consumers or labor suppliers.

[17] There was, however, no statistically significant link between poverty changes and trends in the export/GDP measure of openness.

[18] Similarly, the export measure of globalization explained little of the variation in inequality.

[19] While many relatively high-income East Asian economies have relatively low tax-GDP ratios (Zee 1996), this seems due, considering their levels of income, in major part to their lack of significant government-mandated safety nets. In the past, this seemed defensible given labor-market institutions and norms that limited the unemployment-generating impact of business fluctuations. But this is now changing as the norms are tested by the deep financial crises of the recent past.

[20] Improved targeting of subsidies to maximize budgetary savings ignores ground realities. For example, generalized commodity subsidies, it is believed, should be replaced with subsidies or cash transfers that are narrowly targeted to the "truly needy" (see Chu and Gupta 1998, p. 91). In many cases, just the opposite recommendation seems to be called for from the viewpoint of meeting both administrative constraints and fiscal sustainability.

References

Abed, George T. et al. 1998. *Fiscal Reforms in Low-Income Countries*. Washington DC: International Monetary Fund.

Avramovic, Dragoslav. 1992. Developing Countries in the International Economic System: Their Problem and Prospects in the Markets for Finance, Commodities, Manufactures and Services. *Human Development Report* Occasional Papers No. 3. New York: United Nations Development Program.

Chu, Ke-young. 1990. "Commodity Exports and Public Finances in Developing Countries." in *Fiscal Policy in Open Developing Economies*, ed. V. Tanzi. Washington, DC: International Monetary Fund.

Chu, Ke-young and Gupta, Sanjeev. 1998. *Social Safety Nets: Issues and Recent Experiences*. Washington DC: International Monetary Fund.

Giovannini, A. and de Melo, M. 1993. "Government Revenue from Fiscal Repression." *American Economic Review* 83:953-963.

Grunberg, Isabelle. 1998. "Double Jeopardy: Globalization, Liberalization and the Fiscal Squeeze." *World Development* 26:591-606.

Hitiris, Theo. 1990. "Tax Structure, Trade Taxes, and Economic Development: An Empirical Investigation." in *Fiscal Policy in Open Developing Economies*, ed. V. Tanzi. Washington, DC: International Monetary Fund.

International Monetary Fund. 1996. *World Economic Outlook*. Washington DC: International Monetary Fund.

Nashashibi, K., Gupta, S., Liuksila, C., Lorie, H. and Mahler, W. 1991. *The Fiscal Dimensions of Adjustment in Low-Income Countries*. Washington, DC: International Monetary Fund.

Rao, J. Mohan. 1998. "Openness, Poverty and Inequality." In *Human Development Papers 1999*. New York: UNDP.

Rodrik, Dani. 1998. *Has International Integration Gone Too Far*? Princeton: Princeton University Press.

Tanzi, Vito. 1998. "Fundamental Determinants of Inequality and the Role of Government." Washington, DC: International Monetary Fund.

Zee, Howell. 1996. "Cross-country Tax Revenue Comparisons." *World Development* 10:1659-71

INCOME INEQUALITY WITHIN AND BETWEEN COUNTRIES: MAIN ISSUES IN THE LITERATURE

Pablo Rodas-Martini *

Atkinson, in "Bringing income distribution in from the cold" (1997), has highlighted the fact that the issue of income distribution is again receiving attention, after years of marginalization. Krugman (1994) is more skeptical. He certainly says that, by the 1990s, the distribution of income in the United States was as unequal as it was in the 1920s; a "Great Compression" had taken place since 1973. Krugman, however, does not necessarily see a comeback for the issue of income distribution, since there is no clear understanding of why it is rising, nor the political will to reverse the trend. Baumol et al. (1994) see a revival of interest in the subject of convergence—the evolution of increasingly similar economic modes between countries—because of its profound implications for the welfare of nations and for the design of policy.

This paper surveys current thinking on the distribution of income, with a strong emphasis on empirical studies that depict (Section 1) and explain its trends. The causes of income inequality are considered for both developing and industrial countries (Sections 2 and 3), as the forces tend to be quite dissimilar. It also surveys, though to a lesser degree, the relationship between poverty and inequality (Section 4) and the study of historical and current convergence of economic growth (Sections 5 and 6). Closing remarks explore the uses for this type of study (Section 7).[1]

1. Trends on income inequality within countries

Income distribution varies widely across countries (see Figures 1.1-1.6).[2] In industrial countries, Gini coefficients cluster from the mid-20s to the upper 30s. During the early 1990s, income distribution worsened relative to the 1980s in most countries. Smeeding (1997) found the lowest levels of inequality in Scandinavian countries (Finland, Sweden, and Norway) and in Northern Europe (Belgium, Denmark, and Luxembourg). Central and Southern Europe are next (Italy, Germany, Austria, Switzerland, and France), followed by other industrial countries (New Zealand, Canada, Japan, Spain, and Israel). Australia, the United Kingdom and the United States have the most unequal income distribution.

Awad and Israeli (1997) agree strongly with Smeeding's opinion. They say that, during the 1980s, the industrial countries were divisible into three groups: those with highest degree of inequality (the US, Israel, Italy, and Australia); a second layer with better distribution (the UK, France, Canada, the Netherlands, and Germany); and a third with the highest equality levels (Belgium, Norway, and Sweden). During the 1990s, however, the classification changed somewhat. The UK and France moved to the most unequal group, Italy improved and moved to the second, and the third group remained constant. Bradshaw and Chen (1996) stress that the UK and the US have the most unequal income distribution, and point out that the UK and Germany experienced the largest increases in inequality during the 1980s. A good summary of these trends can be found in Table 1.1.

Eastern and Central European countries enjoyed a better income distribution than the industrial region until the 1990s, but have recently seen a clear trend toward rising inequality as their economies restructure. Milanovic (1998) argues that inequality has increased overall, with the exception of the

* I gratefully acknowledge comments from Juan Alberto Fuentes, John Whalley, colleagues at the HDRO, and participants at a workshop organized by the HDRO. I am also very grateful to Marixie Mercado and Giovanni Reyes, who helped in editing the manuscript.

Figure 1.1 Changes in income inequality in OECD countries

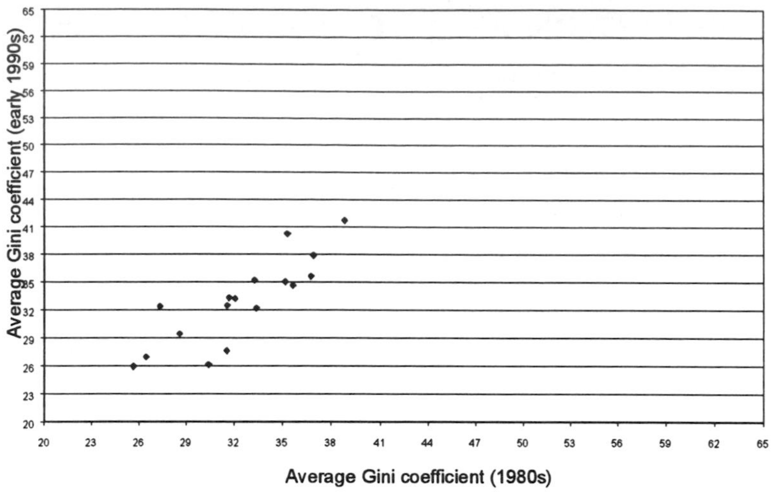

Average Gini coefficient (early 1990s)

65 62 59 56 53 50 47 44 41 38 35 32 29 26 23 20

20 23 26 29 32 35 38 41 44 47 50 53 56 59 62 65

Average Gini coefficient (1980s)

Figure 1.2 Changes in income distribution in transition countries

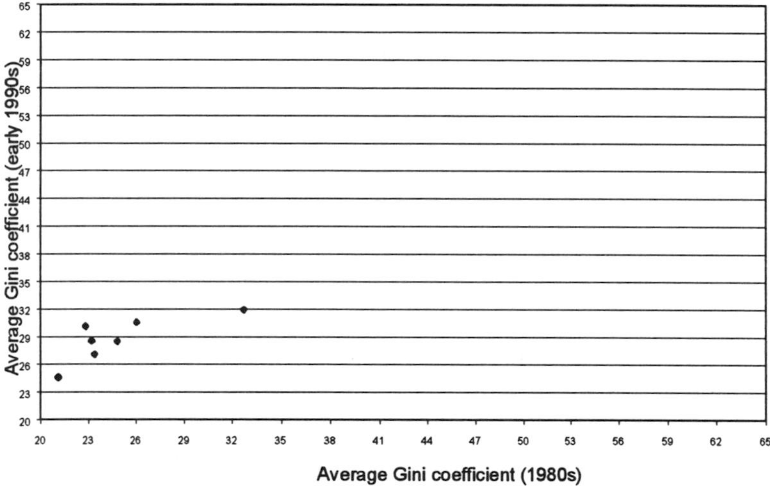

Figure 1.3 Changes in income distribution in Latin America and the Caribbean

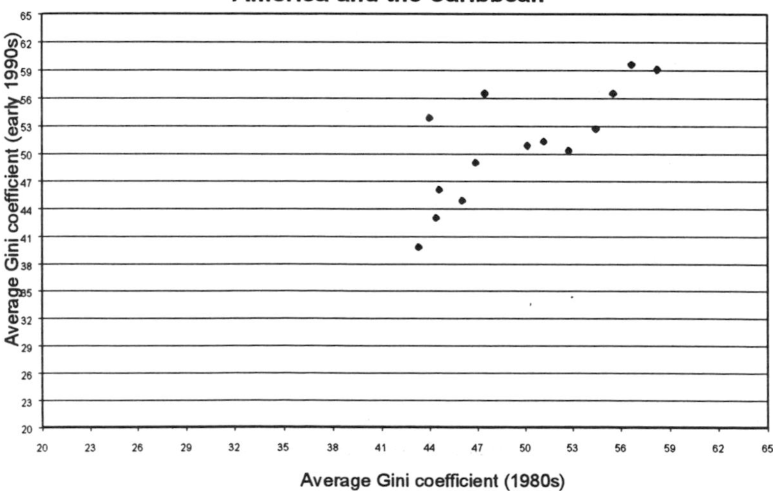

Figure 1.4 Changes in income distribution in East and South Asia

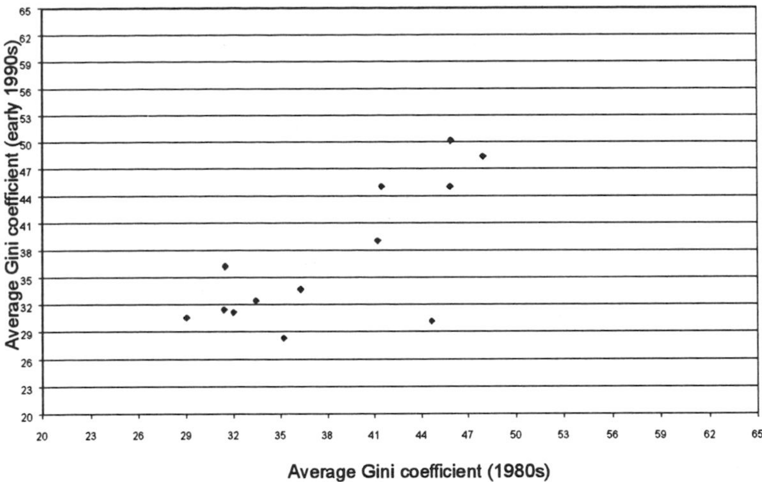

Figure 1.5 Changes in income distribution in the Middle East and North Africa

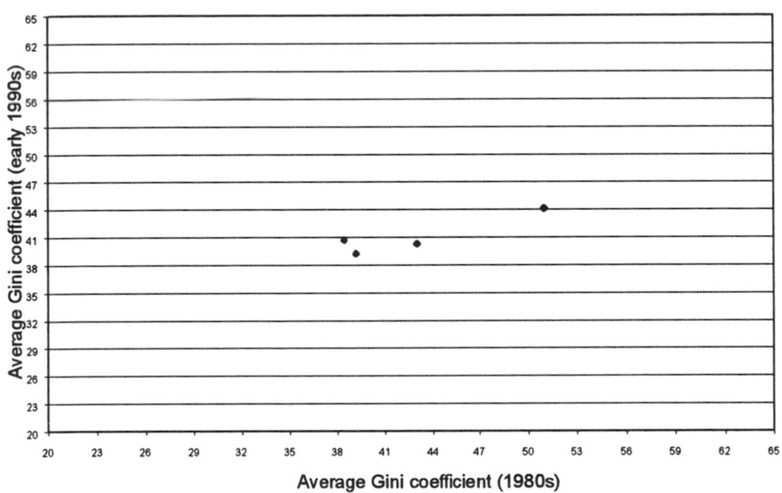

Figure 1.6 Changes in income distribution in sub-Saharan Africa

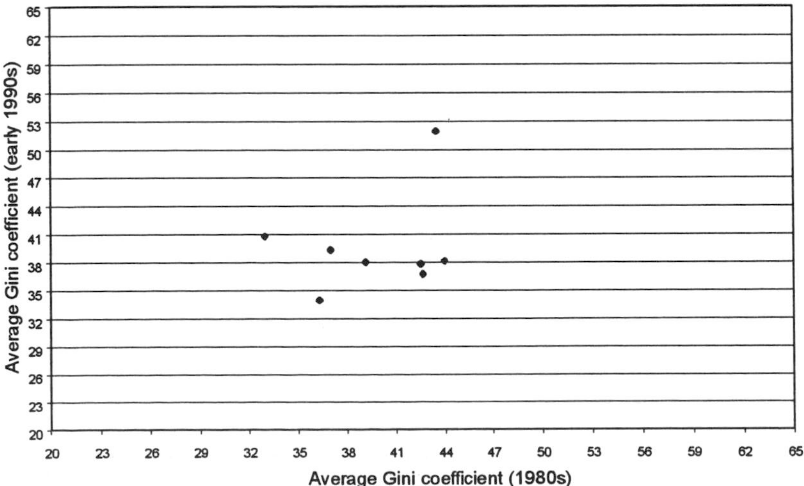

Source for Figures 1.1-1.6: Based on data from Deininger and Squire (1992) and updated information from the World Bank.

Slovak Republic. The increase in the Gini coefficients has been sharp: nearly nine points, an average of 1.5 points per year. This is almost three times as fast as the rise recorded in those industrial countries where inequality has increased in recent years. Moreover, the relative homogenization among former socialist countries is disappearing with increasing dispersion.

Latin America has one of the most unequal income distributions in the world: no country in that region has an average Gini coefficient of less than 40. The 1980s saw an increase in inequality in Latin America. Morley (1995a), however, argues it was not universal; in four countries—Colombia, Costa Rica, Uruguay and Paraguay—inequality decreased. Londoño and Székely (1997b) do not see any substantial improvement in inequality in the 1990s. The Inter-American Development Bank (1998) points out that one of the most striking features of the poor income distribution in Latin America is the huge gap between the families in the highest income decile and everyone else.

Asia's performance lies between industrial and transition countries on one side, and Latin America, on the other. Within that region, however, very different patterns of inequality occur. The scarcity of data on Arab states and sub-Saharan Africa makes it difficult to formulate reliable judgments on those regions. Ahuja et al. (1997) note that East Asia is more egalitarian than sub-Saharan Africa or Latin America, but that it is far from being one of the world's most egalitarian regions. They point out that, in the 1990s, income disparities have increased.

Bruno et al. (1998) detected greater variation across countries (around 87%) than within them (about 6%) over time. This trend suggests that the inequality rankings of countries are highly stable over the long run. In fact, the rank correlation between the average Gini coefficients from the 1960s and 1980s is 0.85.

Comparisons of Gini coefficients, however, need to be taken with some degree of skepticism.

- Deininger and Squire (1996) found that the share of income received by specific quintiles is not always congruent with the Gini coefficient. On the contrary, intersecting Lorenz curves are present in most cases (55% of the countries), implying that income shares could change substantially within countries, despite the apparent stability of the Gini coefficient.
- Some Gini coefficients are based on expenditure data—generally considered as tending to understate inequality—and others on income data.
- Osberg and Xu (1997) tested the sensitivity of income distribution indicators to sampling variability,[3] finding in some cases substantial variations (see Figure 1.7).
- A Gini coefficient for an entire country does not necessarily capture important trends like geographical inequality within countries. Ahuja et al. (1997) show the growing spatial disparity within China, mainly between rural and urban areas and across provinces (see Figure 1.8).
- Market forces, acting through wages, certainly have the most important effect on income distribution. The state, however, also plays an important role: it can partially offset the impact of those market forces, or fail to do so if social and fiscal policies are inadequate. Bradshaw and Chen (1996) show that the reduction in Gini coefficients due to social benefits and taxes can be substantial (see Figure 1.9). Smeeding (1997) confirms the importance of social transfers on income distribution (see Figure 1.10).
- Even the inclusion of social transfers and direct taxes may not be enough, particularly in the case of industrial countries. Steckmest (1996) claims that not only cash benefits, but also non-cash benefits, must be taken into account, since these in-kind benefits increase the income that families can allocate to other consumption. Governments in fact treat cash and non-cash benefits as complementary rather than substitutable for meeting redistributive goals. Steckmest (1996) takes government final consumption less defense spending as a proxy for non-cash benefits (see Figure 1.11); the impact should be to clearly improve income distribution. She acknowledges, however, that recipients may value non-cash benefits differently from cash ones.

In summary, Gini coefficients give a picture of income distribution, but only a very blurred one.

Figure 1.7 Cross country Gini comparisons, circa 1990

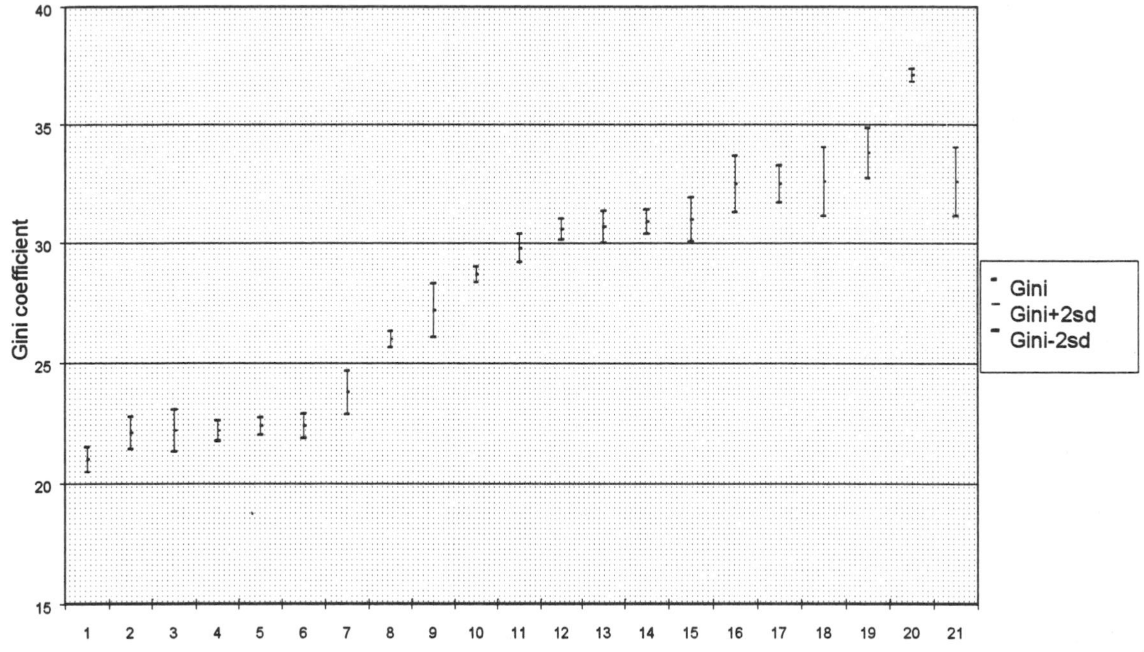

Source: Osberg and Xu (1997)

Figure 1.8 Components of China's rising inequality, 1985 and 1995

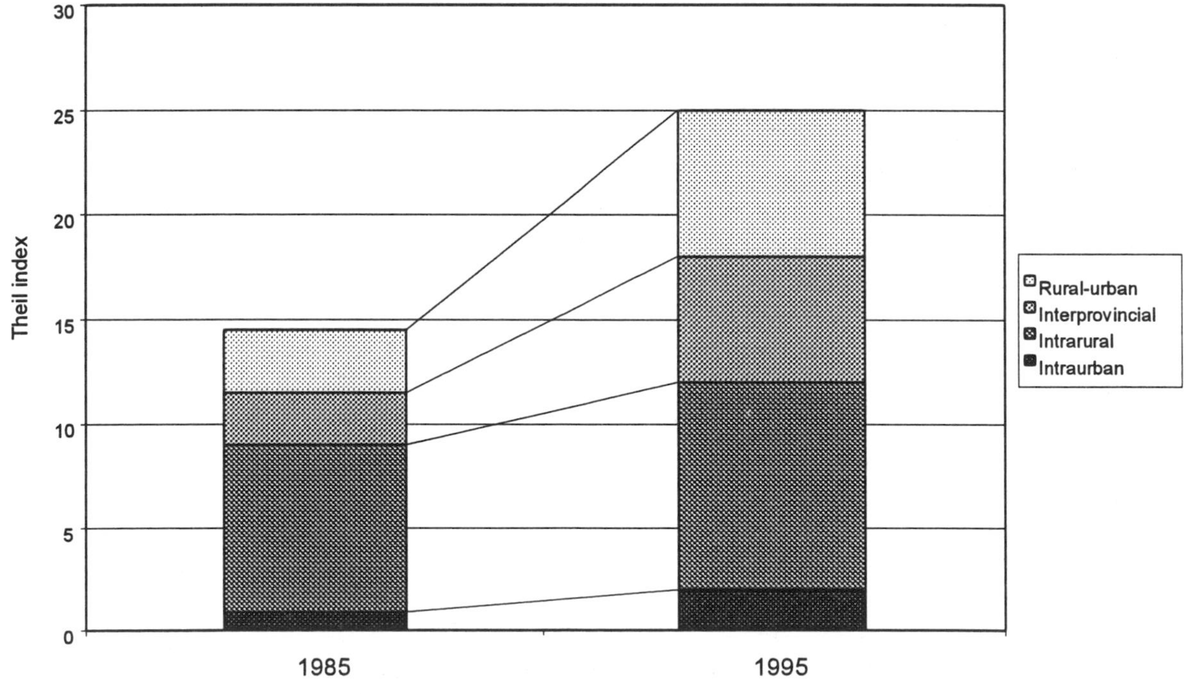

Source: Ahuja et al. (1997)

Figure 1.9 Impact of social security benefits and direct taxes on Gini coefficients, circa 1990

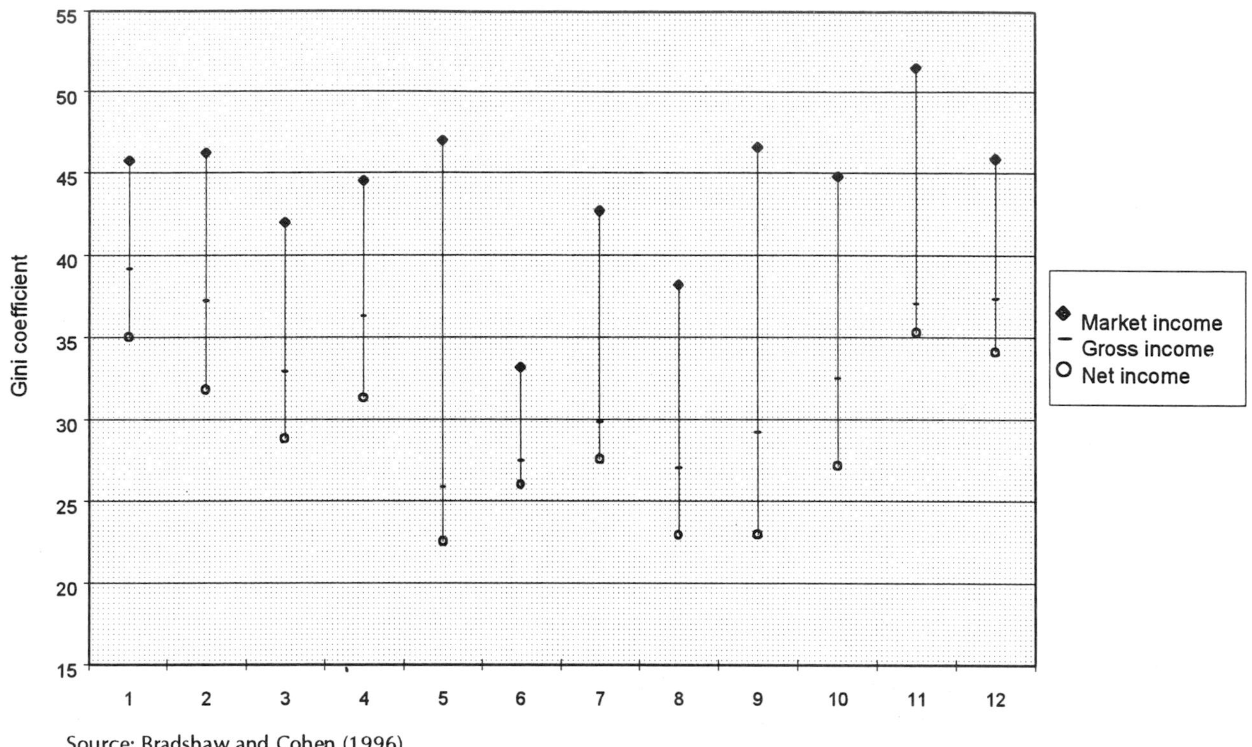

Source: Bradshaw and Cohen (1996)

Figure 1.10 Relationship between income inequality and social transfers in developed countries

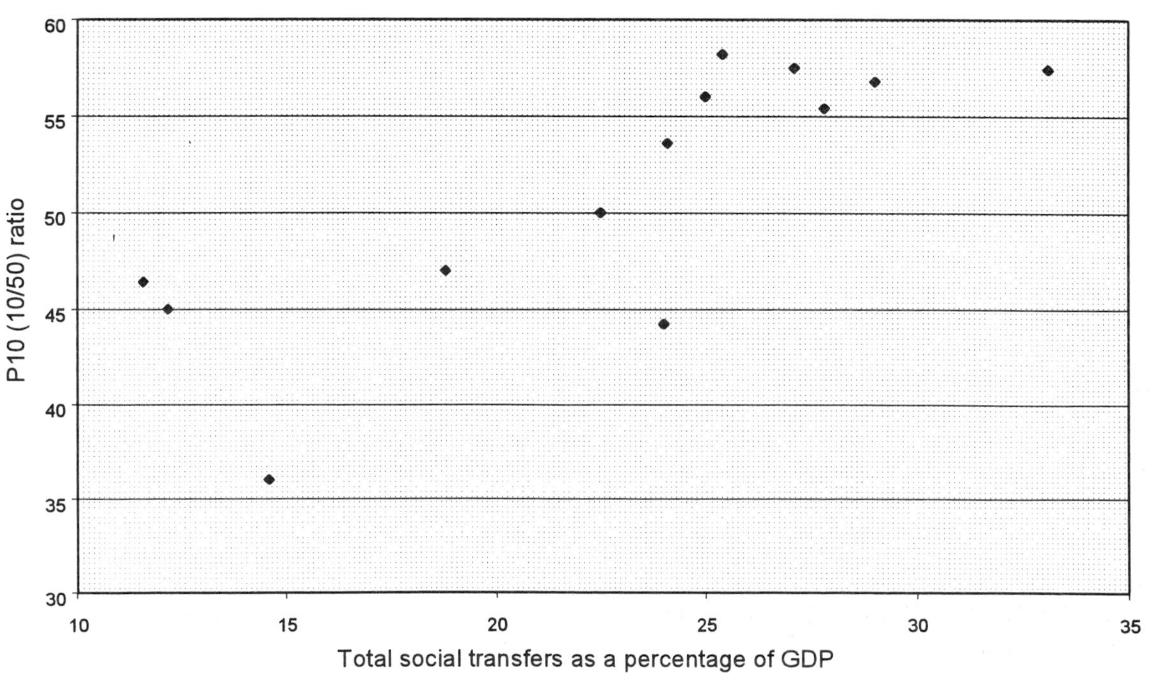

Source: Smeeding (1997)

Figure 1.11 Cash and non-cash benefits as a percentage of GDP 1986

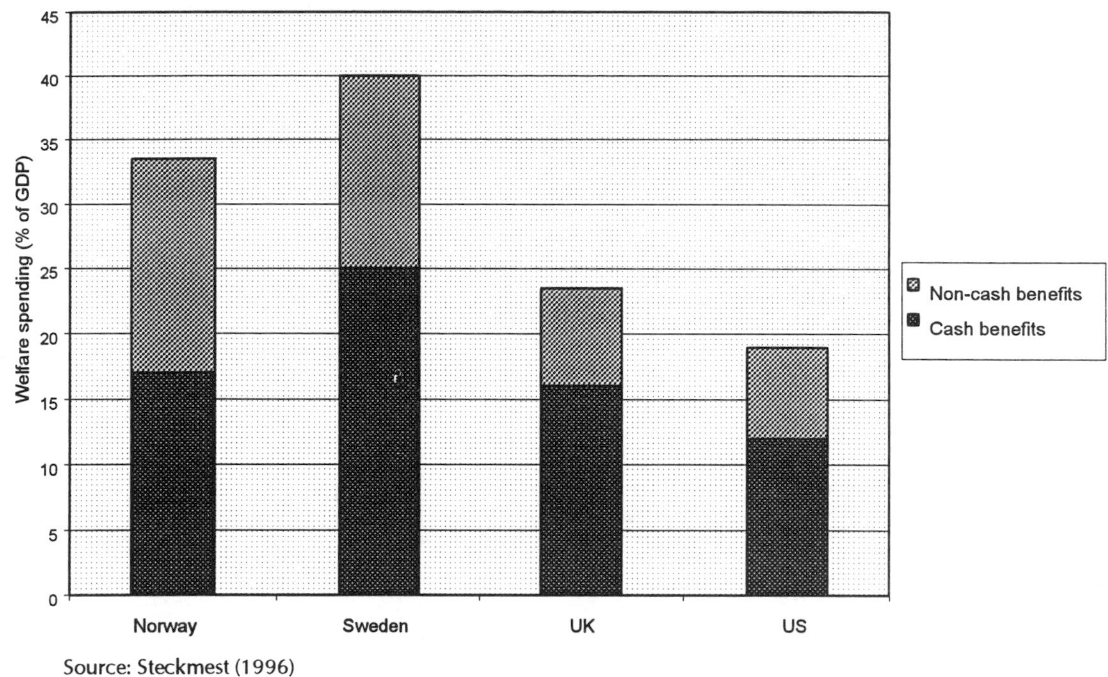

Source: Steckmest (1996)

2. Main determinants of inequality within developing countries

Income inequality is not rooted in a single cause. In the case of developing countries, the recent literature identifies some factors affecting inequality: economic crises, stabilization and structural adjustment, economic growth, and distribution of assets. These factors of course do not affect all countries at all times in the same way.

2.1 Impact of economic crises in the absence of social safety nets

Economic crises worsen income distribution in developing countries. Indicators such as the Gini coefficient may not register the impact immediately, but forces increasing inequality eventually spread. Bulir (1998), for instance, determines that inflation has a non-linear effect on income distribution: hyperinflation, at times of crises, clearly increases inequality, but once a low inflation rate has been achieved, further reductions in its level do not improve income distribution. Inflation is regressive because it affects fixed-income earners most: the rich and the upper middle classes are generally better shielded from inflation (Alesina 1998).

Hyperinflation, however, is just one of the many channels through which economic crises impact income distribution. There are many others: currency exchange depreciation, job loss, bankruptcy, and so on. Economic crises can have a devastating effect on income distribution in developing countries that—unlike industrial countries—rarely have social safety nets to cushion negative shocks. Workers have only three options in a crisis: to accept wage reduction, move to the informal sector, or become unemployed (Morley 1995b). In each case, income distribution is affected. The ones who suffer most are those most marginalized—the unemployed, the elderly, the poor.

Morley (1995b) clearly illustrates the negative impact of economic crises on income distribution in Latin America: during recessions, income distribution worsened (see Table 2.1).[4] This phenomenon does not seem to be confined to a particular region (e.g., Latin America) or to a particular crisis (e.g., the debt crisis). Lee and Rhee (1999) claim that the recent Asian financial crisis will also increase inequality in these countries.[5,6]

Table 2.1 Income inequality and the business cycle in selected Latin American countries, selected periods, 1979-90

Income distribution	Recession	Recovery
More equal or same	Argentina 1981-82 (+)a Argentina 1982-85 (+) Brazil 1979-83	Brazil 1983-86 (-) Chile 1983-87 (-), 1987-90 (+) Colombia 1980-89 (+) Costa Rica 1983-86 (+), 1981-89 (+) Uruguay 1981-89 (-) Venezuela 1989-90 (+)
Less equal	Argentina 1980-89 (-) Bolivia 1986-90 (+) Brazil 1986-89 (-), 1979-89 (-) Chile 1980-83 (-) Costa Rica 1980-82 (-) Guatemala 1981-86 (-) Mexico 1984-89 (-) Panama 1979-89 Peru 1981-84 (-), 1984-89 (-) Venezuela 1981-85 (+), 1981-89 (-)	Chile 1979-87 (-) Guatemala 1986-89 (-)

Source: Morley (1995).
a -The signs that follow each entry reflect the direction of change in the real minimum wage in each period. No sign means no change.

The transition from socialist economies toward free markets has brought a new kind of economic crisis to many countries.[7] Unemployment, almost non-existent before, has started to spread. Social transfers such as health and education, once free and taken for granted, were abruptly curtailed; relative prices experienced major changes, and so on (Cornelius and Weder 1996). The crises there have been deep and long; Milanovic (1998) says that gross domestic product (GDP) fell in all transition countries since 1990 for at least three years in a row. In Romania and Estonia, the recession has lasted five years; in Hungary, Slovenia and Belarus, six; and in Moldavia, Russia and Ukraine, seven. For these transition countries, the recession of the 1990s has definitely been much worse than the Great Depression from 1929 to 1933. Milanovic (1998) and Cornelius and Weder (1996) agree that transition has negatively affected income distribution in those countries, and that the longer the recession, the greater the impact on income distribution.

2.2 Short- and long-term effects of adjustment on income distribution

After an economic crisis erupts, stabilization and structural adjustment usually follow to curb capital flight, lower hyperinflation, and reduce the trade and fiscal deficits. A standard conclusion among economists is that inequality rises during the first stages of the stabilization and adjustment process, but tends to fall in the medium and long term (Bruno et al. 1998). Inequality thus follows an inverted J-curve, a dynamic tradeoff between the short, medium and long terms. Lee and Rhee (1998) found empirical support for this thesis. They assessed the impact of International Monetary Fund (IMF) programs on income distribution for 313 programs from 1968 to 1994 (see Figure 2.1) and showed that the Gini coefficient effectively worsens in the first stages of the adjustment process, but improves later on.[8]

Figure 2.1 Changes in income distribution before and after IMF programs

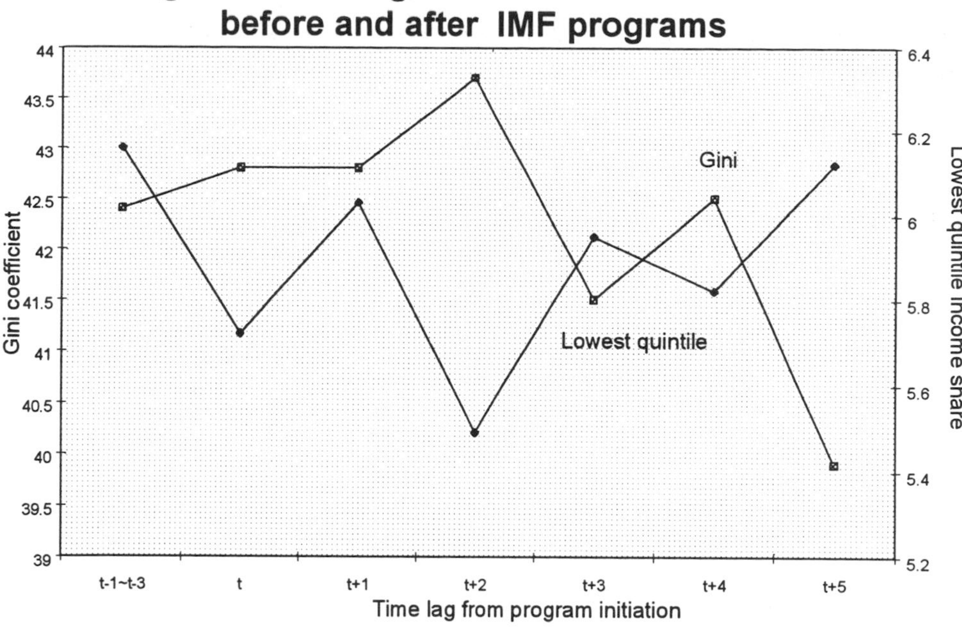

Source: Lee and Rhee (1998).

Stabilization and structural adjustment tend to harm income distribution because monetary and fiscal policies become contractionary, implying that somebody's consumption must fall (Bruno et al. 1998). Meanwhile, depreciation of the exchange rate depresses real wages. On the one hand, the middle and the working class suffer wage freezes, limits on employment, and cuts in fringe benefits; on the other, they also face price increases for goods and service produced by the public sector (such as electricity, water and transportation) due to reduced subsidies, and for staple goods (such as food). Increases in income inequality are a natural outcome.[9]

Regarding transition economies, Milanovic (1998) shows that movements in the Gini coefficient relate to the kind of adjustment that takes place (see Table 2.2). He defines as "populists" those countries that tried to cushion the living standard of their people from GDP declines; "compensators" are those with some kind of social transfers, and "non-compensators" are those that did not try to offset the costs of transition in any way. The "populist" adjustment results in minor changes in income distribution; in the case of the other two adjustments, the relationship is weaker, but "non-compensators" still tend to have a wider income inequality (in particular Russia and Ukraine) than "compensators." Another issue that has been pointed out by Altimir (1998) for Latin America, but that may also be at stake in transition countries, is "capitalist shock"—i.e., massive privatizations. Privatization has transferred asset value into a few private hands, and hence contributed to income inequality.

One may question what would have happened without the adjustment. Morrison (1992), among many others, emphasizes that the usual complaint against adjustment does not recognize that, without it, economic crises would have been even deeper and income inequality would have risen even higher. In the case of Latin America, Morley (1995) claims that part of the income distribution improvement before the debt crises was in fact borrowed from the future.

Some deny that income distribution follows an inverted J-curve. Alesina (1998), for instance, argues that a reduction in government expenditure during the adjustment process does not affect the poorest in society, since many of them are reached barely or not at all by government programs. On the contrary, he adds, the pattern of expenditure mainly benefits the upper and the middle classes,[10] and often results in patronage and corruption.[11] He defends, in summary, the feasibility of adjustment without worsening income distribution.

Table 2.2 Relationship between type of adjustment and increase in Gini coefficient

Country	Increase in Gini
Non-Compensators	
Russia	24
Ukraine	24
Estonia	12
Moldova	12
Czech Republic	8
Romania	6
Slovakia	-1
Compensators	
Lithuania	14
Bulgaria	11
Latvia	8
Belarus	5
Populists	
Slovenia	3
Poland	2
Hungary	2

Source: Milanovic (1998).

2.3 Dismissal of the Kuznets hypothesis

Once macroeconomic equilibrium has been achieved, growth usually follows. Kuznets suggested in 1955 that income distribution and growth would behave in a particular way: income inequality follows an inverted U-curve, i.e., inequality increases in the early stages of a country's economic development, but falls in later stages (see Figure 2.2). Kuznets' hypothesis is based on the observed long-term transition in developing countries from mainly rurally based economies toward urban-based ones: when industrialization starts and the first workers migrate to the cities, inequality increases. Once most workers are in the urban sector, any additional migration decreases inequality rather than increasing it. In other words, in Kuznets' hypothesis, income inequality is a byproduct of growth and structural change.[12]

Deininger and Squire (1996) did not find support for the Kuznets hypothesis in 90% of the countries they studied. They say that earlier studies were mistaken in drawing inferences about longitudinal relationships from cross-sectional studies. As a whole, they did not find a systematic relationship between growth and income inequality,[13] in part because changes in Gini coefficients tend to be small with respect to much larger changes in income per capita.[14] Bruno et al. (1998) also claim that Kuznets' hypothesis has not withstood the test of time. They say that previous tests finding support for the hypothesis were not technically sound: they did not take country effects into account, and consequently gave biased results. Bruno et al. (1998) conclude that economic growth—with some exceptions—is not immiserizing since it benefits all layers of a society more or less in proportion to their initial level of living.

The East Asian experience, a virtuous circle of growth and improvements in income distribution, is usually portrayed as an historical demonstration of the failure of the Kuznets hypothesis (see also Figure 2.2). Ranis and Stewart (1998) argue that the East Asian success was due to growth based on labor-intensive exports, in contrast to the Latin American vicious circle of unequally distributed growth based on investment in capital-intensive industries. In the same sense, Morley (1995) stresses that growth is important, but that the kind of growth also matters.

Figure 2.2 Relationship between economic growth and income

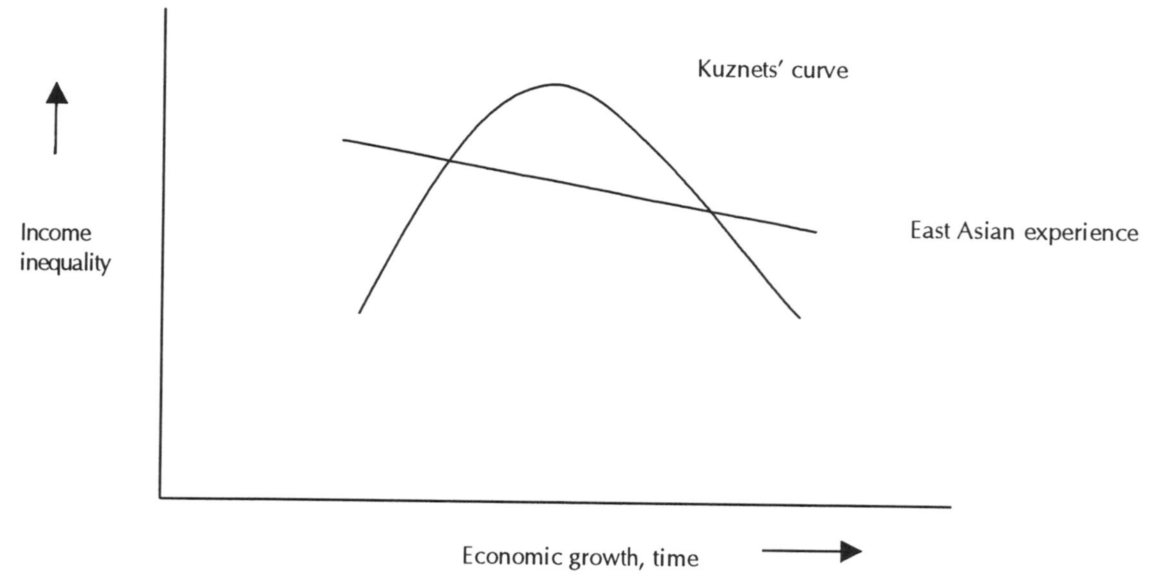

While Kuznets' hypothesis relates to growth in a long-term sense, there is also the short-term issue of recovery as part of the business cycle. Morley (1995) shows the countries in which income distribution became more equal or stayed the same during times of economic expansion (see Table 2.1, northeast quadrant). He claims that there is symmetry between recessions and expansions, and that consequently income inequality is counter-cyclical (i.e., increases during recessions, and decreases during expansions). Altimir (1998) disagrees; he says that recovery does not necessarily bring distributive improvements, so symmetry is not necessarily warranted.

In tests of Kuznets' hypothesis, usually the Gini coefficient (or an alternative measure of income distribution) is the dependent variable and growth is one of the explanatory variables, i.e., the causality runs from the latter to the former. However, some have suggested that the causality is reversed, i.e., growth is the dependent variable and the income distribution is the explanatory variable (Bruno et al. 1998). Two main theses have been suggested for this alternative.[15] First, inequality causes social discontent, unrest, threat to private property, policy volatility, government fragility—in sum, political instability that affects growth. Second, inequality increases grievances of median voters, creating pressure for a redistributive agenda through higher taxes that also affect growth. Thus, both theses suggest that the higher the inequality, the lower the growth, which is contrary to the more traditional argument (i.e., that the higher savings elasticities of the rich are the engines of growth).

2.4 Education levels as a determinant of income distribution

Income distribution depends on how people are endowed with factors of production, e.g., physical and human capital, and land. Income is the *flow* produced by a *stock* of assets; thus, low inequality reflects an egalitarian society in which assets are more or less evenly distributed.

In the past, when developing countries were mainly agrarian, land tenure was the most important determinant of income distribution. In many developing countries today, land is no longer the crucial factor of production. Londoño (1996) estimated that, even in Latin America, with one of the highest levels of inequality, land contributes scarcely 10% of GNP and provides employment to little more than 20% of the population, on average. Of course, in the poorest countries, land still remains the main determinant of inequality, and that is reflected in the concentration of rents from mineral and agricultural exports in a few hands (Bruno et al. 1998). In most developing countries, with increasing urbanization, manufacturing, and services production, the main culprit of inequality must be found elsewhere.

Urban and financial assets have become increasingly prominent in recent decades. Regrettably, there are no major studies on the impact of the former on income inequality (Londoño 1996). Regarding the latter, there is disagreement. Londoño (1996) dismisses the importance of financial assets, arguing that despite their increased share in the total portfolio assets of investors, financial deregulation has made that market more competitive. Morley (1995a), however, claims that structural adjustment in regions such as Latin America has required a rise in interest rates of government bonds (for fiscal and monetary reasons), resulting in increased inequality since bondholders are few.

Londoño (1996) also dismisses monopolistic and oligopolistic forces as agents of increasing inequality. Since the opening of economies and concomitant lowering of trade and non-trade barriers, increased competition and made it more difficult for companies to take advantage of market power.

By far, human capital—as represented by education—now seems to be the most important factor of production. The Latin American experience illustrates this fact. Fiszbein and Psacharopoulos (1995) show how inequality of education produces the largest marginal contribution to income inequality in that region (see Figure 2.3). Londoño and Székely (1997b) illustrate how education inequality aggravated the income inequality caused by macroeconomic policy in Latin America during the debt crisis of the 1980s, and how education inequality has offset the positive impact of changes in macroeconomic policy during the recovery process that has taken place in recent years (see Figure 2.4).

Spilimbergo et al. (1997) provide an intuitive reason for the importance of education in a more egalitarian society. In the case of other factors of production (e.g., land, physical capital), there are no limits to the amount that can be possessed by one person; with education, there is a natural limit to how much knowledge one person can have. As a consequence, a society richly endowed with education tends to be more egalitarian. Bruno et al. (1998) say that there is, in fact, a positive correlation between higher ratios of primary and secondary enrollment and improvements in income distribution in developing countries.

A final point is Londoño's (1996) contention that there is a nonlinear relationship between education and inequality (see Figure 2.5). The higher the level of development, the greater the rise in income attributable to higher educational attainment. Londoño says that the maximum inequality results when average education levels reach around 6.3 years.

These are not the only causes of inequality within developing countries; there are many more. Gupta et al. (1998), for instance, say that the returns to corruption accrue to the better connected in society, contributing to the perpetuation of inequality.[16] These studies focus on long-term development trends (e.g., economic growth and distribution of assets) or on macroeconomic fluctuations (e.g., economic crises, stabilization, and structural adjustment). In the case of developing countries, there are not yet many regional or cross-country studies related to current trends such as globalization.[17] In some cases, however, technological change is seen as affecting inequality (Ahuja et al. 1997).

3. Main determinants of income inequality within industrial countries

Industrial countries have suffered from a clear increase in inequality in the last decades. The wage premium, defined as the difference in the average wages of college graduate workers and high-school graduate workers,[18] has increased for most of the industrialized countries of the Organization for Economic Cooperation and Development (OECD). Economists agree that the demand for unskilled workers has shifted down while demand for skilled workers has shifted up, though they are still discussing the causes of the movement.

Figure 2.3 Marginal contributions of individual variables to inequality, seven-country averages

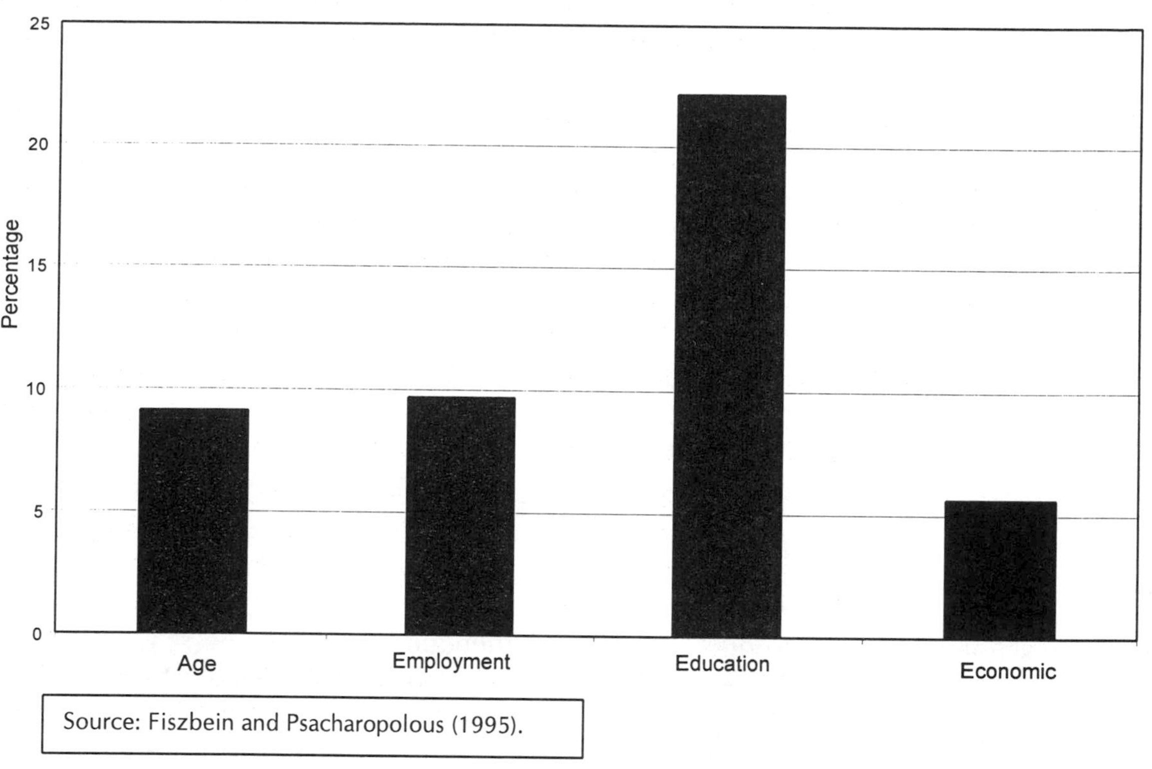

Source: Fiszbein and Psacharopolous (1995).

Figure 2.4 Inequality factors in Latin America

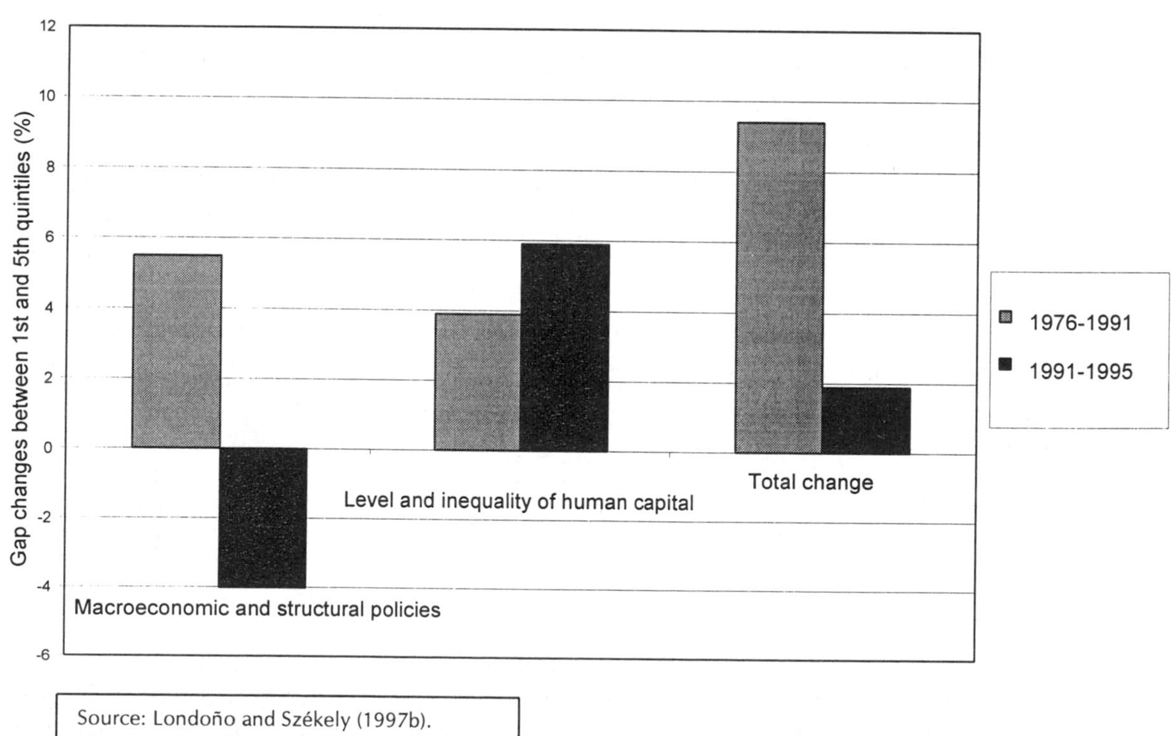

Source: Londoño and Székely (1997b).

Figure 2.5 International perspective on educational insufficiency

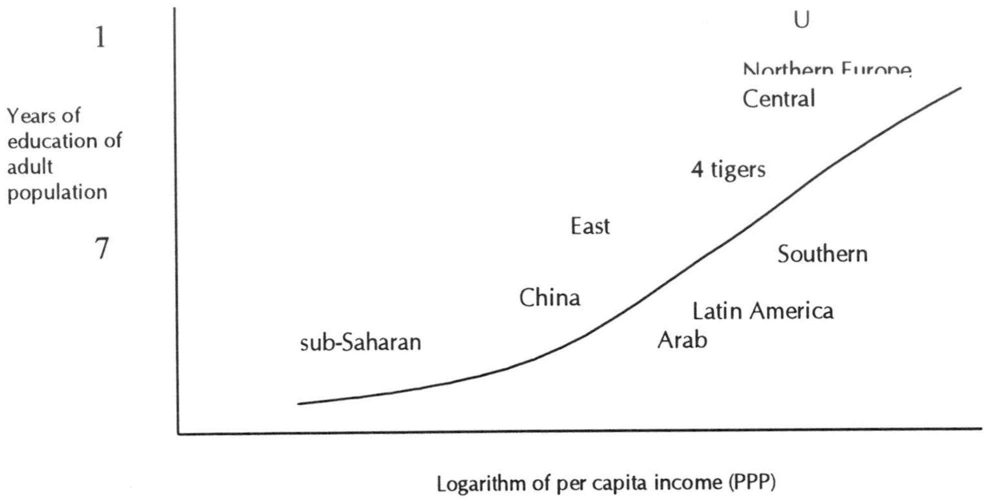

1

Years of education of adult population

7

U

Northern Europe

Central

4 tigers

East

Southern

China

Latin America

sub-Saharan

Arab

Logarithm of per capita income (PPP)

Source: Londoño (1996).

3.1 Impact of trade with the South on income distribution

Standard trade theory claims that North-South relations would be characterized by flows of skilled-labor products from the former in exchange for unskilled-labor products from the latter.[19] Although factors of production may not be totally mobile—particularly labor, which faces migrant restrictions—trade itself becomes a substitute, since traded commodities are really bundles of factors of production (Leamer 1995). In other words, trade changes the "real endowments" of factors of production: imports of unskilled-labor products from the developing countries lower the demand curve for those workers in the developed ones. The same standard theory predicts that North-South trade will widen the wage gap between skilled and unskilled labor in industrial countries since imports from the South—composed of mainly unskilled-labor products—would lower the relative wages of workers producing similar items in the North.[20] Most economists, even those such as Krugman, who have proposed new trade theories of increasing returns and imperfect competition as an explanation of North-North trade, agree that these forces are behind North-South trade. The disagreement arises about the magnitude of their impact on industrial countries. Some think that that impact is almost nil, while others give it more weight.

The main argument made by those who dismiss imports from the South as a major determinant of increasing inequality in the North is that those imports represent just 2% of GDP in the OECD—a low share despite recent increases. Krugman (1995) says that such low figures cannot, for instance, explain the roughly 30% increase in the US wage premium that took place during the 1980s. A second argument is that, according to standard trade theory, the fall in the relative wages of unskilled labor would have implied a similar fall in the relative prices of the goods they produce; there is no empirical evidence that this has taken place (Rowthorn and Ramaswamy 1997). Finally, the critics also claim that non-tradable services such as education, government, finance, insurance, real estate, and wholesale and retail trade represent a large share of output in industrial countries (Slaughter and Swagel 1997).

Other economists, however, assign a more important role to trade with the South. Rodrik (1997a) points out that trade has not just shifted down the demand curve for unskilled workers in industrial countries, but it has also flattened it (see Figure 3.1), increasing its elasticity. This additional movement reflects the fact that unskilled labor can be more easily substituted for by similar workers in other countries via either trade or foreign direct investment. He adds that trade has increased the elasticity of demand for goods—a fact revealed by reductions in price-cost margins—and that such demand is directly related to the demand for labor. Thus, he claims that openness should not be

Figure 3.1 Effect of openness on labor markets reaccion to shocks

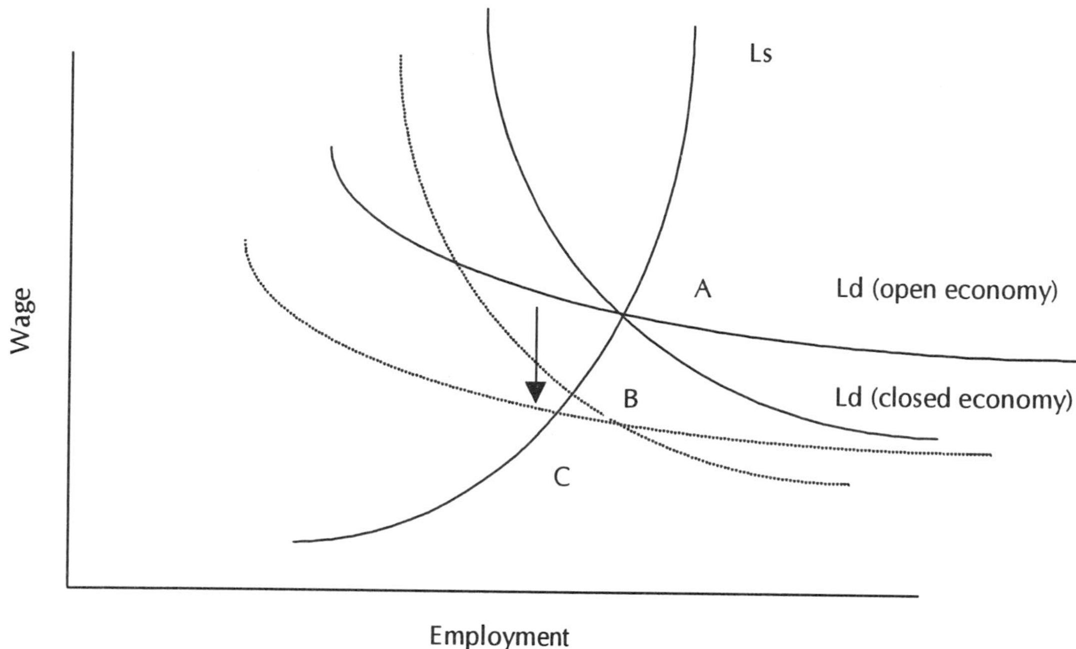

Source: Rodrik (1997a).

measured by traditional proxies such as the percentage of imports on GDP—as Krugman (1995) does—but by the ease in carrying out international transactions. Finally, Rodrik (1997a) claims the dismissal of the impact of trade on wages in industrial countries sits uncomfortably with the usual claim that the world has had substantial gains from trade. Wood (1994) and Leamer (1994) had already picked up the main argument behind this explanation; they say that even a small import share can have a large effect on wages, provided that trade changes the competitive structure of an economy, and that prices—determined on the margin—matter more than quantities.

Rodrik (1997a) suggests that another consequence of the flattening of the demand curve for unskilled labor would be greater instability in labor markets in both earnings and hours worked compared to more stable labor markets in closed economies. In Figure 3.1, for instance, a negative shock to an open economy depresses wages more than a similar shock to a closed economy. Hence, openness, by making product and factor prices more volatile, has magnified the impact of any shock, whether in a positive or in a negative direction.

Despite the importance placed on trade,[21] Rodrik (1997b) does not accept the thesis that wages are the driving forces behind trade. He absolutely dismisses the usual complaint against low wages, since countries such as Bangladesh or some African countries would be formidable exporters. He brings out the standard argument that wages relate closely to labor productivity.[22]

Borjas and Ramey (1994) give a twist to the trade argument, claiming that the wage premium in industrial countries is positively correlated with net imports of durable goods. They found that import competition has recently affected industries that historically made—and shared—high profits with workers.[23]

3.2 Technological change and bias against unskilled labor

While economists strongly disagree on the trade argument, the idea that skill-biased technological change (SBTC) plays a major role in the increase of inequality enjoys a greater consensus of opinion.[24] Murphy et al. (1998) say that technological change need not be biased in one direction or the other, but that everything indicates current technology has been biased against unskilled labor and toward skilled labor, mainly due to automation and information technology processes. The trend seems to have begun in the 1970s, and its continuation during the 1980s and 1990s is closely related to the use of computers. In the 1950s and 1960s, technological change was more neutral and most levels of skill qualifications benefited from it.

SBTC explains why, despite increases in the supply of skilled labor, and despite the worldwide increases in education, there has not been a fall in the relative price of skilled labor. On the contrary, the wage premium has increased and the demand for unskilled labor has fallen. SBTC, a phenomenon that has permeated almost every industry, has counteracted the increase in the supply of skilled labor.[25,26] SBTC may explain the finding by Sullivan and Smeeding (1997) that industrial countries with higher levels of educational attainment do not necessarily have lower levels of income inequality—a different pattern from the one usually stressed for developing countries.[27]

3.3 Erosion of trade union power and its impact on inequality

The increase in income inequality in industrial countries can also be partially explained by the gradual and irreversible fall in the power and political influence of trade unions. Globalization in general, and imports from developing countries in particular, exert downward pressure on wages and employment in many unionized industries. Jacoby (1995) argues that the global economy has eroded one of the major roles that trade unions had in the past: they cannot take wages out of competition any longer, meaning wages cannot standardize across borders as they generally had within particular countries.

Workers' worries, however, are not confined to wages: they also involve job losses. Companies may threaten to relocate if trade unions' claims are too high, e.g., outsourcing of production in developing countries. This happens mainly in labor-intensive industries.[28] Rodrik (1997a) points out that globalization creates a new kind of arbitrage; in addition to traditional arbitrage of prices across markets, arbitrage in national norms and social institutions is now possible, with arbitrage in labor markets particularly important. He adds that that labor-market arbitrage introduces asymmetry of bargaining power between employer and employee, a situation that sixty years of US labor legislation has sought to prevent. This asymmetry is clearly seen in the fact that employers can move abroad if they do not like the social norms of one country, but employees cannot (Rodrik, 1997b).

Erosion of trade union power, however, is not uniform across countries. Jacoby (1995) shows large differences in unionization across the OECD countries (see Table 3.1)[29] and tries to encapsulate the main features of industrial relations according to two main criteria: whether wage bargaining is centralized or decentralized, and whether government plays a large or a small role in the economy, with particular emphasis in industrial relations (see Figure 3.2). This classification yields three types of systems: "macrocorporatism," "statist microcorporatism," and "voluntarism." A fourth type, "regionalism," combines elements of the other three.[30]

Figure 3.2 Industrial relations systems

		Government role	
		Large	**Moderate**
	Centralized	Macrocorporatism (Scandinavia, Germany)	
Wage bargaining		Regionalism (France, Italy)	
	Decentralized	State Microcorporatism (Japan)	Voluntarism (UK, US)

Source: Jacoby (1995).

Table 3.1 Union density trends, 1950-1987

	1950	1970	1987
High density			
Belgium	37	66	n.a.
Denmark	53	66	95
Finland	33	56	85
Sweden	68	79	96
Moderate density			
Australia	56	52	56
Austria	62	64	61
Canada	33	32	36
Germany	36	37	43
Ireland	39	44	51
Italy	44	39	45
Netherlands	36	39	35
Norway	46	59	61
United Kingdom	44	51	50
Low density			
France	31	22	15
Japan	46	35	28
United States	28	31	17

Source: Jacoby (1995).

Most empirical evidence indicates that different systems of industrial relations impact variously on income distribution. European countries, and especially those in which the wage bargaining process is centralized, tend to have lower inequality than more decentralized countries such as the US. This does not, however, imply that unionization, centralized wage bargaining, or a large government role will provide a shield against the forces of globalization. Gottschalk and Joyce (1995) point out that the presence of such labor market institutions do not necessarily imply that constraints are binding, since market forces can instead play out via changes in unemployment rates. In other words, outcomes impact either wages or unemployment, depending on which industrial relation system a country has in place (Slaughter and Swagel 1997).[31]

3.4 Impact of deindustrialization on inequality

Deindustrialization is a long-term trend affecting the processes of development. Rowthorn and Ramaswamy (1997, 1998) show that deindustrialization involves a reduction in manufacturing employment, but not in manufacturing output (see Figure 3.3). Figure 3.4 shows that as employment in manufacturing industries decreases, employment in the service sector tends to increase, potentially absorbing displaced workers.

Rowthorn and Ramaswamy (1998) defend deindustrialization as a sign of a successful economy.[32] Deindustrialization is explained by the fact that manufacturing is technically progressive, i.e., processes can be readily standardized and prepared for mass production, while services tend to be technically stagnant (the exceptions are impersonal services such as telecommunications, whose production functions resemble those of manufacturing). Therefore, the shrinking of manufacturing employment reflects successful industrial development, since it implies that fewer workers are needed to produce the same output.[33,34]

Deindustrialization, however, impacts income inequality; while manufacturing wages tend to be rather uniform, in the service sector, highly paid jobs coexist with poorly paid ones (Gustafsson and

Johansson 1997). Moreover, unionization rates tend to be higher in manufacturing than in services (Jacoby 1995) because, once again, standardization of manufacturing facilitates organization of

Figure 3.3 Evolution of the manufacturing share

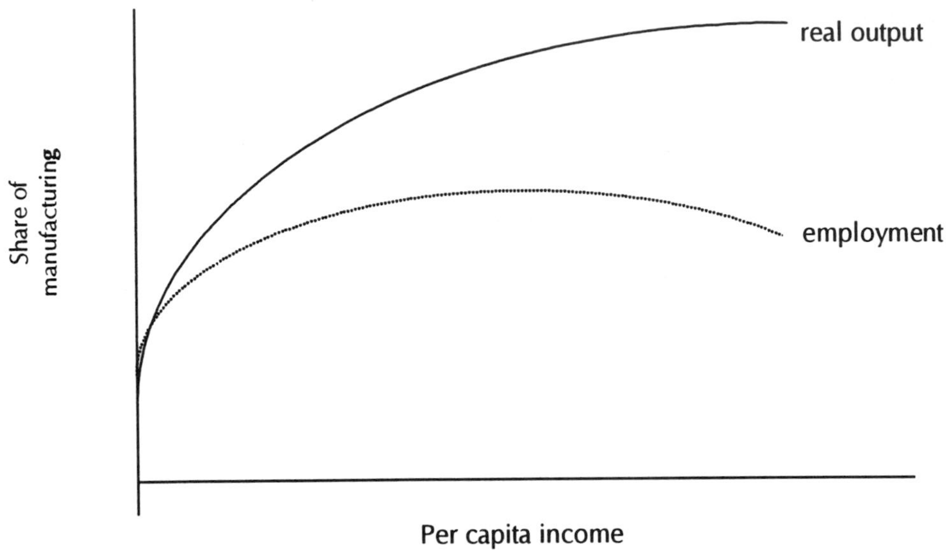

Source: Rowthorn and Ramaswamy (1998).

Figure 3.4 The changing structure of employment

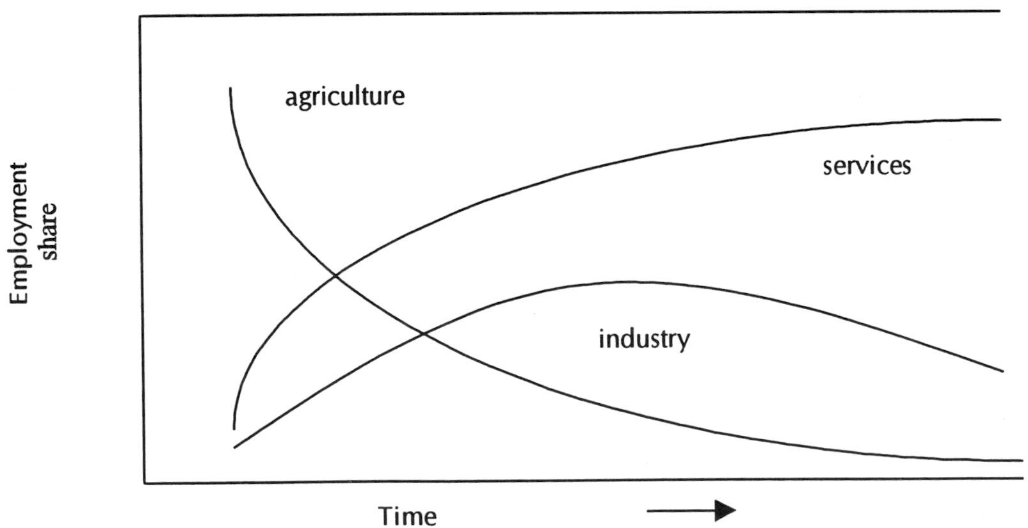

Source: Rowthorn and Ramaswamy (1997).

workers, while wide differences in services make organization more difficult. In sum, these factors make services more prone to wage inequality than manufacturing.

3.5 Inequality under varying types of social welfare systems

Korpi and Palme (1998) use three criteria—bases of entitlement, benefit levels, and forms of governance of social insurance programs—to distinguish the types of welfare systems currently in place in industrial countries.[35] Based on these criteria, they define four types of welfare systems (see Figure 3.5):[36] 1) "targeted" systems, which are directed mainly at those defined as needy; 2) "corporatist" systems, with compulsory membership for the economically active population, but which produce separate social programs according to the occupation or branch of industry; 3) "basic security" systems, based either on contribution or on citizenship; and 4) "encompassing" systems, based on contributions and citizenship.[37] The authors acknowledge that, in practice, one finds crossbreeds, not purebred welfare systems.

Figure 3.5 Typical models of social insurance institutions

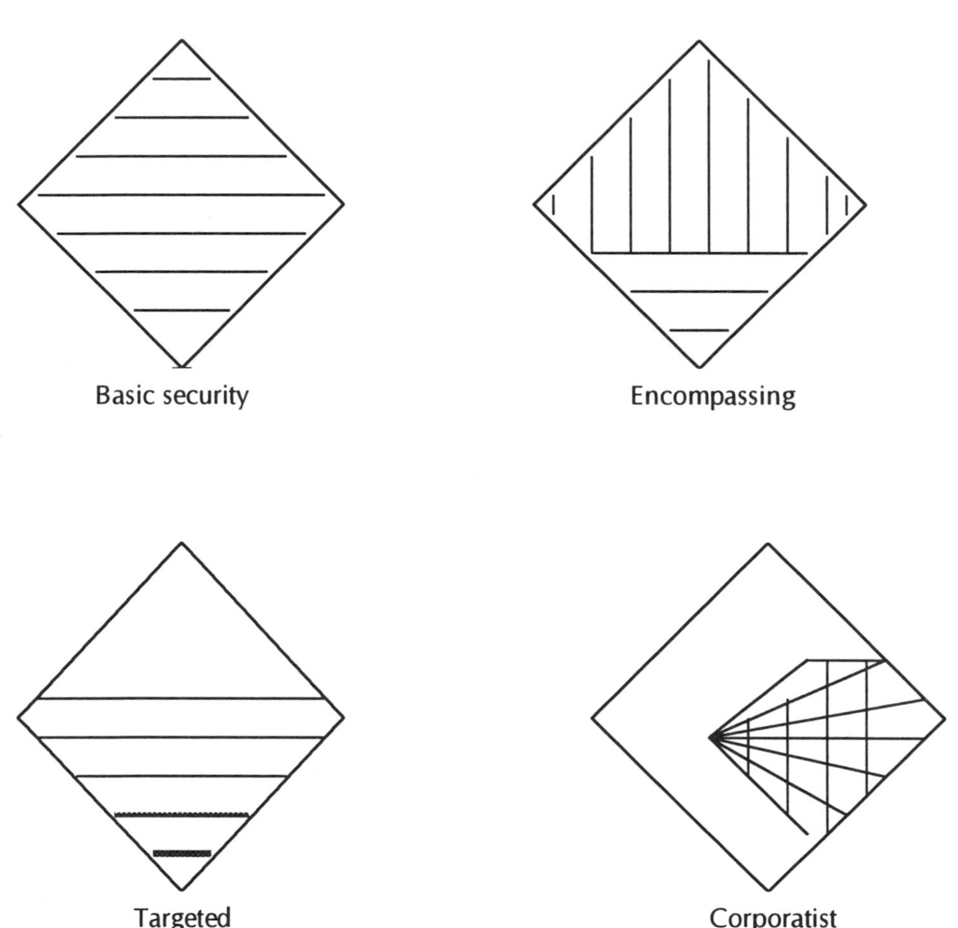

Source: Korpi and Palme (1998).

Table 3.2 summarizes the findings of Korpi and Palme (1998) on differences in inequality across welfare systems. More even distribution of income is found in the three countries with "encompassing" systems—Finland, Norway and Sweden. Greatest inequality is found in the "basic security" and "targeted" models, especially in the US, Switzerland, Australia and the UK. The two countries with "corporatist" systems, France and Germany, have intermediate levels of inequality. Korpi and Palme call this result the paradox of redistribution, since the more governments target benefits at the poor (the "Robin Hood" strategy of taking from the rich to give to the poor), the more inequality results, and the less likely that poverty falls. On the contrary, the "encompassing" model, with its Matthew principle of giving more to the rich than the poor, produces in industrial countries less inequality and poverty. The "basic security" system with its egalitarian strategy produces intermediate results.[38]

Once again, as in the case of developing countries, the factors described here are not the only ones that attempt to explain the growing inequality in industrial countries. Many others exist, but their importance may be minor.

Table 3.2 Gini coefficient by type of social insurance institutions

Type of social insurance institutions	Gini coefficient
"Encompassing"	
Finland	23.1
Norway	23.2
Sweden	21.5
"Corporatist"	
France	29.2
Germany	24.3
"Basic security"	
Canada	27.9
Netherlands	25.2
Switzerland	32.0
United Kingdom	29.3
United States	33.3
"Targeted"	
Australia	31.0

Source: Korpi and Palme (1998).

4. Relationship between income inequality and poverty

Krugman (1994) argues that most people would prefer to live in a society where low levels of income inequality prevail rather than in one where the gaps are wide. High income inequality, however, is bad not only in itself, but also in its strong relation to poverty. Londoño and Székely (1997b) and Osberg and Xu (1997) show a clear positive correlation between poverty levels and the Gini coefficients: the higher the former, the higher the latter (see Figures 4.1-4.2).

Ravaillon (1997) explains the correlation. First, higher income inequality may reduce growth rates (see the arguments in Section 2.3), and hence make it more difficult to reduce poverty (he calls this the "induced-growth argument"). Second, even assuming that growth benefits all levels of income in similar proportions, higher income inequality would affect poverty reduction, since the poor will receive a smaller share of income, making the reduction of poverty slower (the "growth-elasticity argument").

Figure 4.1 Poverty and inequality in Latin America, mid-1990s

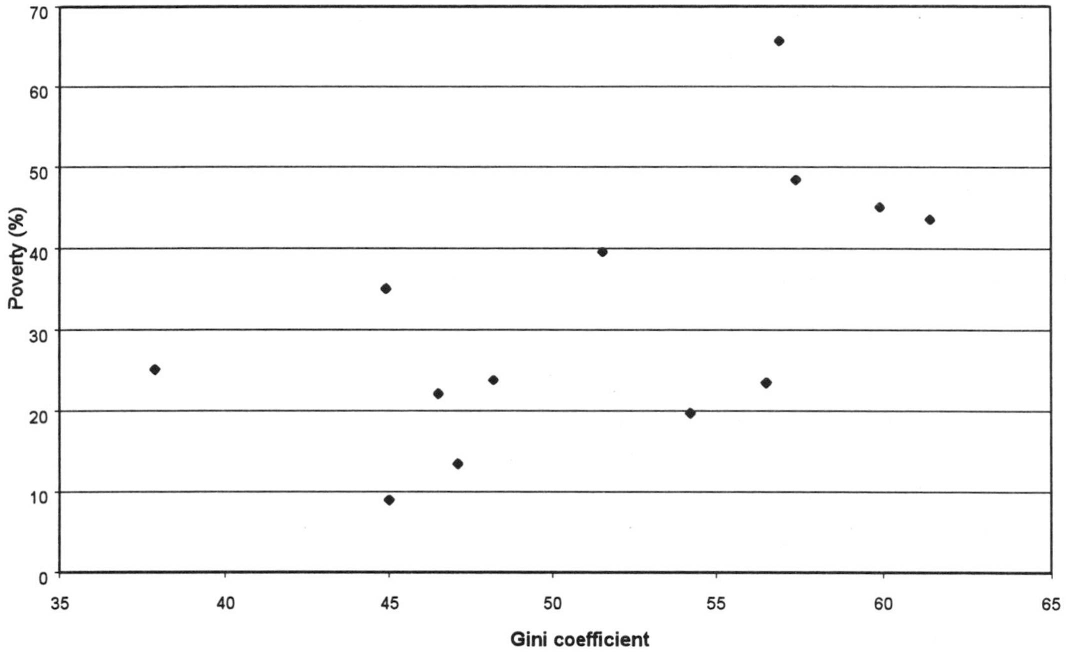

Source: Londoño and Szèkely (1997B).

Figure 4.2 Relationship between poverty and inequality in developed countries

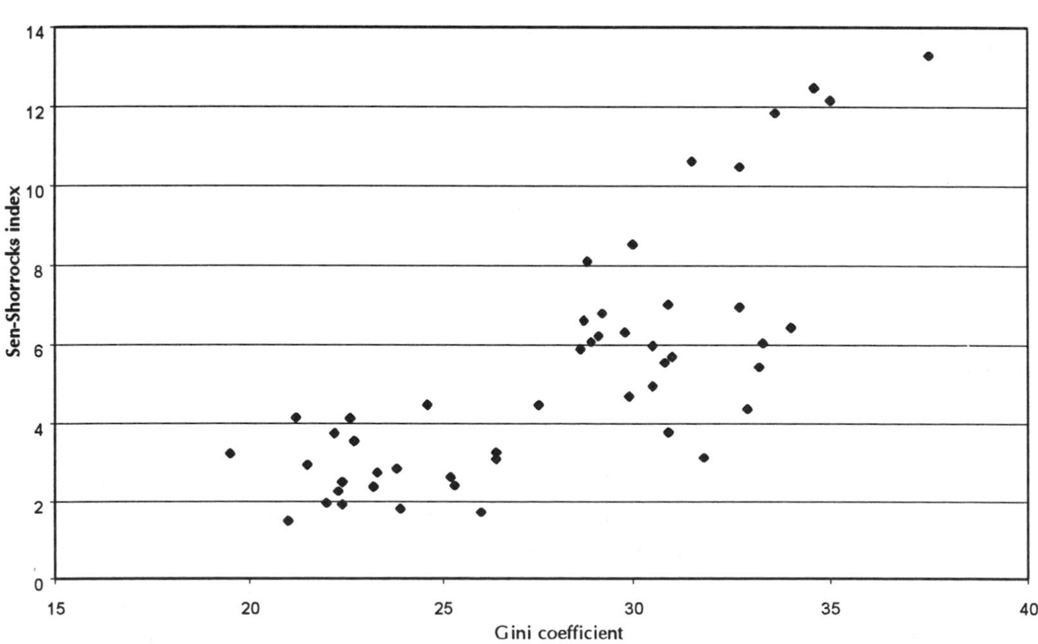

Source: Osberg and Xu (1997).

In practice, the two effects are so difficult to disentangle that they must be analyzed together. Chatterjee (1995) points out that growth definitely impacts positively on poverty reduction, and there is no doubt that sustained growth will eliminate poverty in the very long run. However, that does not mean that growth alone will suppress poverty in the short and medium term: the kind of growth also matters (see again Section 2.3). Chatterjee (1995) notes that there are two kinds of poverty: one is between the ambit of economic forces, the other not. The first may be reduced by growth alone, while the other requires social measures.[39] Bruno et al. (1998) say that growth is very important, but only one of the many factors that impact poverty; they add that poverty is countercyclical, increasing during recessions and declining during expansions.

Londoño and Székely (1997b), however, found that the recent recovery in Latin America did not show benefits for the poorest of the poor. They suggest that this may be due to high income inequality, which would make poverty a distributive problem rather than a growth one. They also found empirical support for the elasticity argument: the growth elasticity of poverty declines as the distribution worsens. Milanovic (1998) found that, in East European countries, poverty has risen substantially since the transition to market economies for two main reasons: growth has fallen, and income inequality has worsened. Figure 4.3 shows a hypothetical level of poverty if the recession in Eastern Europe had not affected income distribution, as well as the actual level of poverty, in which the two effects (recession and worsening income distribution) are combined.[40] However, he claims that poverty in transition countries is different from the poverty in regions like Latin America. In the latter the poor tend to be an "underclass," which is not the case in former socialist countries, where the poor are more educated and poverty is shallower. Finally, Osberg and Xu (1997) claim that some countries, such as Switzerland, perform better in preventing poverty than in reducing income inequality.

Figure 4.3 Change in poverty and income at times of economic crisis

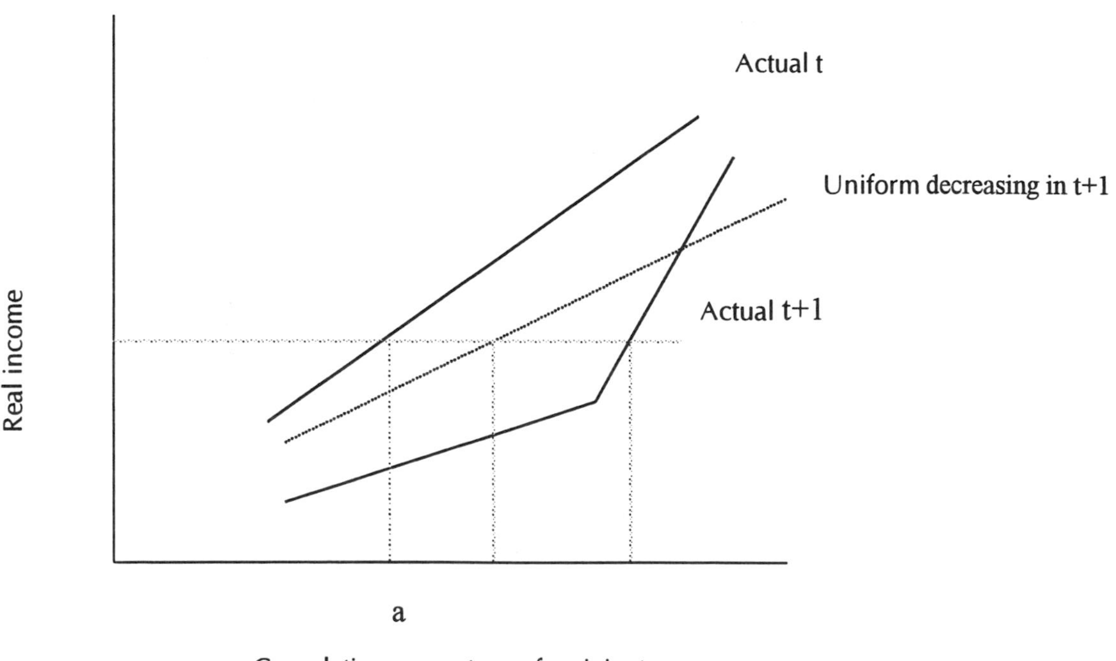

Source: Milanovic (1998).

5. Trends in growth convergence across countries

So far, this paper has surveyed income inequality studies *within* countries. Income inequality *between* countries is another aspect of the issue, which may be equally important.

Previous studies on the phenomenon of growth convergence focused on already industrialized countries. As such, growth convergence became almost tautological since industrialized economies were by definition economies that had already achieved convergence (Pritchett 1997). Empirical studies of growth, however, have been revived in recent years due to the availability of data.

Maddison (1994, 1995) extracted the following major conclusions from his analysis. First, economic growth progressed quickly from 1820 to 1992: per capita product increased eight-fold in that period (population rose five-fold, and world GDP forty-fold).[41] Second, countries have differed widely in their growth rates, resulting in major divergence (see Figure 5.1). In 1820, the gap between the lead country and the worst performer was about 3:1, in 1870 7:1, in 1913 11:1, in 1950 35:1, in 1973 44:1, and 72:1 in 1992.[42] Third, except for Asia, regional performance has had some degree of homogeneity. Fourth, growth has not been constant over the entire period. The period of highest growth was between 1950 and 1973, followed by the period 1870-1913, and by 1973-92. One important caveat from Maddison (1995) is that even if the global picture is one of divergence, history also shows some experiences of successful convergence. Income inequality between Western Europe, on the one hand, and Southern Europe, Eastern Asia and oil-exporting countries, on the other, has declined. It is possible for regions to "catch up."

Bairoch and Kozul-Wright (1996) agree that most available evidence indicates divergence between countries, and that only a small group of countries exhibited convergence. Alonso-Gamo et al. (1997) argue that countries have become more polarized into high- and low-income clusters. Barbone and Zalduendo (1997) are skeptical about cases of convergence; they stress that even the Southern European countries (Greece, Portugal and Spain) have reduced their initial income differentials with the European Union average by only one-half during the last 34 years.

Figure 5.1 GDP per capita in all 43 countries

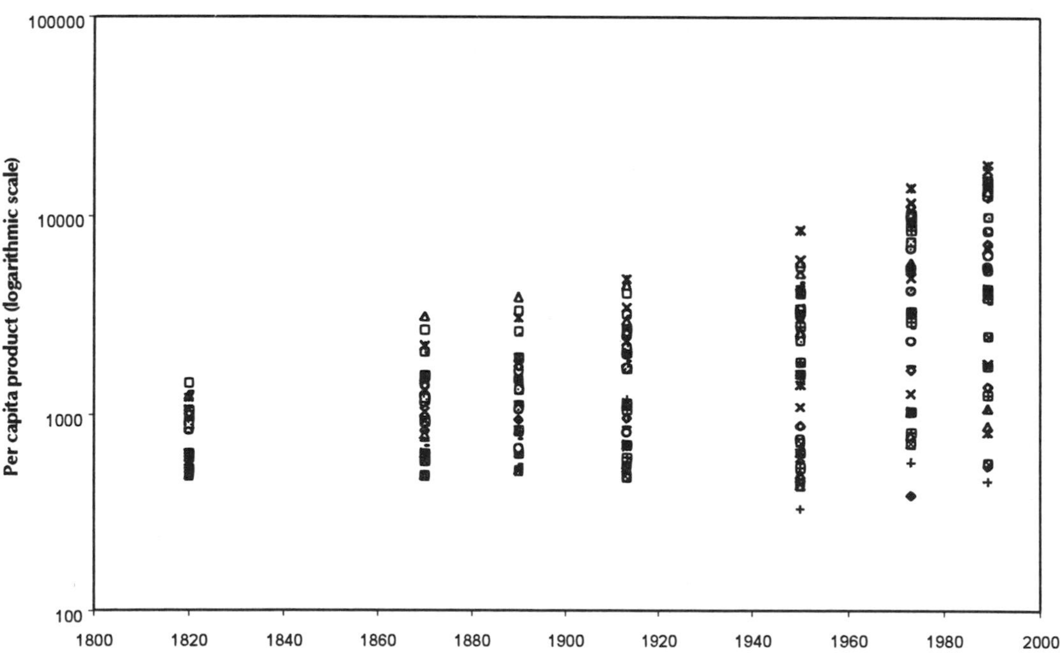

Source: Madison (1995).

Pritchett (1997) took a different approach than most traditional growth convergence studies. Based on household surveys, extreme poverty lines, and nutritional intakes, he asked: what is the lowest GDP per capita that any country could have had in 1870? He then compared that hypothetical amount to the highest GDP per capita at that time (that of the US), to see if there had been convergence or divergence. He found (see Figure 5.2) that the lowest GDP per capita any country could have had in 1870 was US$250 (in 1985 purchasing power equivalents) since that amount is well below any current poverty line (no one has ever seen a lower poverty line) and with less than that amount the population could not have survived.

Using this approach, Pritchett (1997) also reached the conclusion that divergence has been the predominant trend. He says that the ratio of per capita income in the richest country to per capita income in the poorest country increased from about 9:1 in 1870 to about 39:1 in 1960 and 45:1 in 1990. Moreover, there has not been an acceleration of growth in most poor countries; consequently, there have been no major reversals of the trend toward divergence in recent years. The growth rates between developing countries varied significantly: from –2.7% to 6.1% during the period 1960-1990.

Pritchett (1997) points out that the divergence could be greater still if one looks over a longer time frame, as some claim that the income gaps between countries were even smaller prior to 1870.[43] Finally, he agrees with Maddison that some countries stagnate while others show a rapid convergence.

Those very long-term perspectives, however, have a "small" problem, as Maddison (1994) acknowledges: those exercises compare the present situation with that of dead ancestors who did not experience air and motor transport, radio, television, cinema, or most household electrical appliances. Even contemporary cross-sectional studies compare incomes across countries whose lifestyles are vastly different.

Figure 5.2 Simulation of divergence of per capita GDP, 1870-1985, showing only selected countries

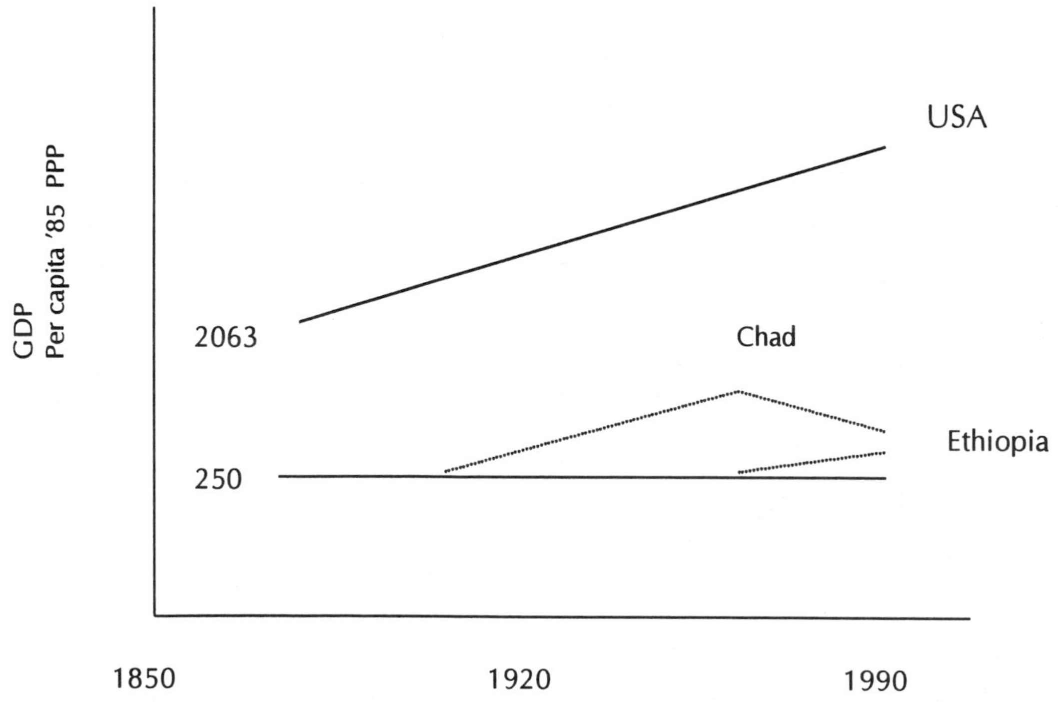

Source: Pritchett (1997).

6. Determinants of inequality between countries

In recent years, growth economists have been testing so-called conditional convergence theories[44] to find the engines of growth. They call it conditional convergence because a simple absolute convergence (i.e., rich countries grow more slowly than poor ones because of diminishing return to capital), does not account for factors and conditions other than the impact of that capital stock. Barro (1997) gives a simple example: a rich country may grow faster than a poor one if its saving rate is higher.

Growth theory, however, is not explicit about what variables matter, and even if the theory were clear in pointing out specific variables, the problem of which proxy should be used is always present (Sala-i-Martin 1997). He identifies around 60 explanatory variables that have been found statistically significant in at least one econometric study of conditional convergence (see Table 6.1). The expected sign of the variables is shown in parentheses; this may or may not be the sign actually found by statistical regression.

Table 6.1 Names of tested variables, conditional convergence effect
Impact on level of income: (+) or (-)
Human development variables: life expectancy (+), primary school enrolment (+), secondary school enrolment (+), average years of secondary school (+), higher education enrollment (+), average years of higher school (+)
Demographic variables: Average age of the population (?), growth rate of population (-), urbanization rate (+)
Labor market: Size of labor force (?), ratio of workers to population (?)
Macroeconomic and financial variables: Average inflation rate (-), standard deviation of inflation rate (-), average interest rate (-), ratio of liquid liabilities to GDP (+), standard deviation domestic credit (?), growth of domestic credit (?), terms of trade growth (+)
Government: Defense spending share (-), public consumption share (-), public investment share (?), government education spending share (+)
Geographic and regional variables: Area (?), Sub-Saharan Africa (-), Latin America (-), East Asia (+), absolute value of latitude (far away from the equator) (+)
Political variables: Rule of law (+), political rights (+), civil liberties (+), number of revolutions or military coups (-), war dummy variable (-), political assassinations (-), index of democracy (+), political instability (-)
Religious variables: Confucius (+), Buddhist (+), Muslim (+), Protestant (-),Catholic (-)
Market distortions and market performance: Real exchange rate distortions (-), standard deviation of black market premium (-)
Types of investment: Equipment investment (+), non-equipment investment (+)
Primary sector production: Fraction of primary products in total exports (-), fraction of GDP in mining (+)
Openness: Number of years an economy has been open (+), outward orientation (+), tariff restrictions (-), free trade openness (+)
Type of economic organization: Degree of capitalism (+)
History and language: Former Spanish colony (-), former French colony (?), former British colony (?), fraction of population that speaks English (+), fraction of people speaking a foreign language (+), fraction of population that is Jewish (+), fraction of population that is Hindu (?), ethnolinguistic fractionalization (-)

Source: Sala-i-Martin (1997).

7. Concluding remarks[45]

Beyond a review of the main issues in the literature, what else can be gleaned from this survey? What practical and policy implications may be drawn? Will inequality within and between countries always be analyzed as two separate branches with almost no interconnection?

First, conditional convergence studies can be used to forecast growth scenarios. Once the key explanatory variables have been identified, the coefficients obtained from the regressions may be used to predict future growth rates. It is also feasible to explore different growth paths by changing certain assumptions, as, for example, a government official analyzing alternative policies. The results for two studies of this sort are shown in Tables 7.1-7.2. Barbone and Zalduendo (1997), in particular, tested different policies in order to estimate the degree of convergence for some transition countries, using the average GDP per capita of the European Union. For some countries, convergence never occurs.

Table 7.1 Convergence: a long road ahead

Countries	Per capita growth rate (%)[a]	GDP per capita (% of OECD)	Number of years to reach 50% of GDP per capita in OECD	
	1970-95	1995	Scenario 1[b]	Scenario 2[c]
Algeria	7.8	29.0	16	10
Djibouti	2.1	5.0	never	43
Egypt	7.2	20.7	32	17
Jordan	7.2	25.2	25	13
Lebanon	-1.0	16.8	never	20
Libya	2.4	44.1	never	2
Mauritania	5.0	8.5	270	33
Morocco	7.3	17.7	37	19
Somalia	3.1	4.7	never	44
Sudan	4.9	7.7	329	35
Syria	8.0	29.7	15	10
Tunisia	8.5	28.0	15	11
Yemen	8.5	9.3	42	32

Source: Alonso-Gamo et al. (1997).

[a] Annual average.

[b] Scenario 1 is based on the per capita growth rate in the Arab countries over the last 25 years and the average growth rate of per capita GDP in the industrial economies over the period 1990-2000.

[c] Scenario 2 is based on a uniform 10% average growth rate for the Arab countries and the average growth rate of per capita GDP in the industrial economies for the period 1990-2000.

Table 7.2 Years of convergence

	GNP capita	GNP (PPP estimates)	Number of years to reach 75% of GNP per capita in EU	
	1994	1994	Scenario 1[a]	Scenario 2[b]
Czech	17	53	15	10
Republic	20	36	41	18
Hungary	13	33	never	20
Poland	13	38	41	17
Slovakia	37	37	91	18
Slovenia				

Source: Barbone and Zalduendo (1996).

[a] Scenario 1 assumes each Easter European country maintains the same growth determinant values that it currently has.

[b] Scenario 2 assumes Eastern European countries follow the best possible policies (e.g., a policy framework similar to Hong Kong, no labor force growth, level of human capital equal to the highest in the European Union, and a high investment level of 30% of GDP).

Second, the interaction between income distribution, poverty, and growth can be used to forecast important goals like poverty reductions rates, as Londoño (1996) does for Latin America (see Figure 7.1). What is interesting about this exercise is that it accounts for direct and indirect (through income distribution) effects of growth on poverty (see Section 4). This may become the logical extension of growth convergence studies, since different growth scenarios can be combined with country estimates of inequality and poverty to predict further results.

Londoño's (1996) exercise, however, should not be taken as a demonstration that the two branches—inequality within countries and inequality between countries—have been integrated. For the most part, they remain on separate tracks: one takes a microeconomic perspective using microeconomic data, while the other does the opposite by focusing on macroeconomic variables. Taking Figure 7.2 as a reference, most studies run along each of the horizontal lines with almost no research following the vertical line. The exceptions are few: Londoño and Székely (1997a) build a Lorenz curve for Latin America that ranks each quintile (not each individual, since that information is not available) for each country according to their position in the Latin American population (in Figure 7.3, the references are for the average citizen). One of the main difficulties confronted in these kind of exercises is that, despite the homogenization of household surveys by institutions such as the World Bank and the Luxembourg Income Study Group, many differences still remain in the way those surveys are realized across countries. They are not strictly comparable, unlike macroeconomic indicators such as GDP per capita.

Figure 7.1 Poverty projections for Latin America scenarios of economic growth (alternative and income distribution)

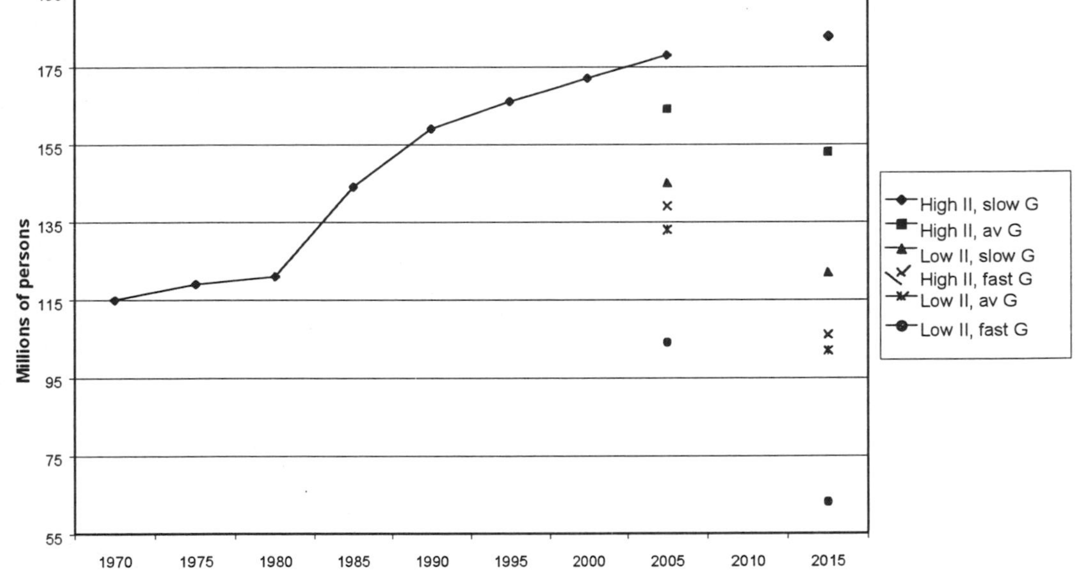

Source: Londoño (1996). Note: II = income inequality; G = growth

Figure 7.2

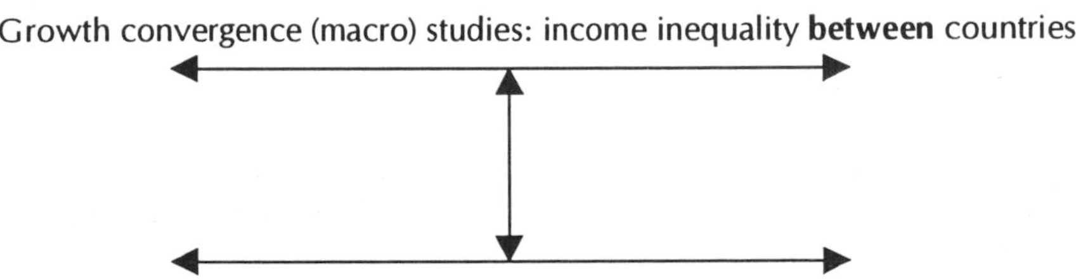

Notes

[1] The first draft also included suggestions on inequality for the *Human Development Report 1999.*

[2] Figures 1.1-1.6 are based on Gini coefficient data made available by Deininger and Squire (1996), in particular the latest update available at the World Bank's Internet site (www.worldbank.org). Deininger and Squire claim that their 682 observations have national coverage and came from trusted sources. They indicate that it is the largest available set of Gini coefficients. I included only the "accepted" or "high-quality" data identified by the authors. An alternative source of inequality indicators is the Luxembourg Income Study (LIS), until recently confined to industrial countries, but which has started to include information from East Asian countries.

[3] They simply dropped the top five income observations from the household surveys.

[4] Morley (1995) and Altimir (1998) disagree about symmetry at times of recovery; see Section 2.3 below.

[5] Ranis and Stewart (1998) add that financial crisis mainly reduces primary income (i.e., income derived from the economic system), but also affects secondary income (i.e., derived from the state via social production of free—or subsidized—goods and services and income transfers). This latter fall is as not as strong as the former because government expenditure may have its own momentum and rarely reverses quickly.

[6] Economic crises also affect human development indicators such as infant mortality and life expectancy, but in a different way: those indicators tend to increase even during a recession, but they may grow at a slower rate (Lustig 1995).

[7] In some cases, of course, there were also non-economic factors (e.g., civil wars) aggravating the negative impact of the transition.

[8] Lee and Rhee (1998) find that income distribution worsens in the year of the program's initiation and for the next two years, but subsequently improves.

[9] Bruno et al. (1998) mention another issue: most countries were not capable of monitoring the welfare impact of adjustment in the 1980s since they did not have high-quality household surveys.

[10] It is mostly evident with subsidies to higher education.

[11] Alesina (1998) also claims that expenditure reduction affects social expenditure less than public investment and infrastructure. He says that the former has an index of vulnerability of about 0.4 (i.e., social spending decreases by 0.4 percentage point for each percentage point that public expenditure is cut), while the index of vulnerability of the latter is about 1.7. The latter, he adds, affects future growth.

[12] Birdsall et al. (1996) remind us of an alternative to the Kuznets hypothesis. Galenson and Leibenstein in 1955 and Kaldor in 1978 argue for a reverse causation: income inequality prompts growth, since the rich have a higher marginal propensity to save than do the poor.

[13] However, they say that even in those cases in which both growth and inequality rise, incomes for the members of the lowest quintile increase in more than 85% of the cases.

[14] Deininger and Squire (1996) found that the annual rate of change of the Gini coefficient was only 0.28%, while for per capita income it was about 2.16%.

[15] See, among others, Alesina (1998), Birdsall et al. (1996), Bruno et al. (1998), and Lustig (1995).

[16] Gupta et al. (1998) argue that corruption creates incentives for higher investment in capital-intensive projects and lower investment in labor-intensive projects, while the latter would be of greater benefit to the poor.

[17] Rao (1998) say that openness and globalization must affect poverty, income inequality, and human development, through a rather wide range of intermediate variables such as employment, wages, public investment and the like.

[18] Another proxy usually utilized is high-school drop-outs workers

[19] This is the Heckscher-Ohlin theorem, i.e., a country exports (imports) commodities that use intensively abundant (scarce) factors of production in that country.

[20] This is the Stolper-Samuelson theorem, i.e., an increase in the relative price of one commodity raises (lower) the real returns to the factor used intensively (scarcely) in producing that commodity.

[21] He says that Cline's (1997) conclusion—that trade may explain 20% of the wage premium in the US—is reasonable. Cline also found that trade has mainly raised skilled wages, due to new export opportunities, rather than reduced unskilled wages.

[22] Most economists also agree that trade may cause short-term adjustment costs in industrial countries (Slaughter and Swagel 1997), and that some firms (even in traditional sectors such as textile, footwear, and apparel) have been able to upgrade their product mix.

[23] The industries are motor vehicles and parts, primary metals, and nonelectrical machinery.

[24] See Atkinson (1997), Rodrik (1997b), and Slaughter and Swagel (1997), among many others.

[25] Moreover, Rodrik (1997a) claims that unskilled laborers suffer more from changes because their skills are more job-specific, while the skills of the college educated are more transferable across firms or industries.

[26] In manufacturing, the industries that have experienced the greatest upgrading of workers' skills are those associated with the spread of microprocessor technology (electrical, machinery—including computers—and printing and publishing). However, retail and financial services have also changed their pattern of production since the introduction of microprocessors and information technologies.

[27] See above, Section 2.4.

[28] Jacoby (1995) says that the US and the UK are among the industrial countries prone to have those pockets of low-technology manufacturing. In other countries, such as Sweden or Switzerland, such pockets are rarely found.

[29] Jacoby (1995) says that disparities in rates of unionization have existed between industrial countries since the beginning of the century.

[30] See Jacoby (1995) for a full discussion.

[31] Rowthorn and Ramaswamy (1998) add that, because of globalization, centralized unions also have difficulty in making the decisions that the fast-changing environment requires.

[32] Deindustrialization is taking place not only in industrial countries, but also in the newly industrializing countries of East Asia.

[33] Rowthorn and Ramaswamy (1998) say that the increase in demand created by falling manufacturing prices has not been able to offset the reduction in employment, since productivity growth has been even stronger.

[34] Rowthorn and Ramaswamy (1998) say that Clark in 1957 had suggested an alternative hypothesis for deindustrialization, one not based on supply-side considerations but on demand-side ones. He thought that manufacturing would suffer a fate under Engel's Law similar to that of agricultural products, i.e., the income propensity to consume would be less than one, and hence countries would demand less manufacturing as they developed.

[35] They say that other typologies are possible. An alternative is the one by Esping-Andersen (1990), who defines three major types according to main ideological currents: conservative, liberal, and social democratic.

[36] The diamond-shaped figure symbolizes the socioeconomic stratification system, with high-income earners at the top and low-income earners as well as the poor at the bottom. The horizontal lines represent minimum benefits, and the vertical lines, income-related benefits.

[37] In fact, Korpi and Palme (1998) identify five types: the fifth is the "voluntary state-subsidized" system, an older form of social welfare system. Its main characteristic was that tax money helped mutual societies and voluntary organizations to protect their members against loss of earnings.

[38] In developing countries, the International Monetary Fund, the World Bank and even the European Union have favored "targeted" programs.

[39] He adds that poverty reduction has more to do with primary sector growth—especially food production—than growth in general.

[40] Milanovic (1998) found that a decline in income of 10% increased the poverty headcount from 5% to 6%.

[41] World trade grew much faster: 540-fold.

[42] The British living in 1820 had an income about six times higher than Ethiopians living in 1992.

[43] Bairoch (1993) argues that, as late as 1800, there were almost no income gaps between the now developed and developing countries.

[44] Growth convergence is different from factor price equalization; see Slaughter (1997) for a discussion of this issue.

[45] The first draft also included suggestions on inequality for the *Human Development Report 1999*.

Social Stratification Under Tension in a Globalized Era

Víctor E. Tokman and Emilio Klein[*†]

The objective of this paper is to explore the effect of globalization on the labor market and social stratification. There is general acceptance that globalization will bring about progress for nations and people. This, however, is far from clear, since almost two decades of experience are shedding increasing doubts on the potential net gains but, particularly, on the distribution of such gains. Clearly, there are winners and losers both among countries and people.

We will concentrate on the effects on people within countries and only refer to one region: Latin America. Our search is to identify winners and losers in the process of globalization and, particularly, the impact on social stratification. Is globalization leading toward greater social integration within nations, or is social disintegration the result (because only some groups are being integrated, while a majority is progressively excluded)?

To analyze this issue, the paper is structured in four parts. The first treats globalization as an integral part of a policy compact, as it is necessary to refer to the impact of the whole package rather than trying to isolate partial effects. The second concentrates on the effects on employment, incomes and equity. The third explores changes in the social structure associated with some of the main processes accompanying globalization. Finally, we draw some conclusions about the social structure of Latin America during the reform period.

Globalization as part of a policy compact

Globalization in a restricted sense refers to major changes in trade, finance and information that have taken place in the international economy. This process has not happened in isolation, but as an integral part of a policy package combining internal adjustment measures with changes in the relationship of countries to the international economy. Three main processes characterize the emerging scenario: *globalization, privatization and deregulation* (Tokman 1997). In fact, the policy compact followed by most countries, at least in Latin America, became to be known after 1989 as the "Washington Consensus" (Williamson 1990).

Globalization means that national economies are today more integrated with the international economy and that goods, capital and communications and people are closer than ever before in the past. This has been the result of the opening up of economies as well as rapid technological change. Trade and financial liberalization have been the result of the reduction of tariff and non-tariff barriers by 1) multilateral agreements in the General Agreement on Tariffs and Trade (GATT) and the creation of its successor, the World Trade Organization (WTO); 2) new or reactivated integration schemes, such as the North American Free Trade Agreement (NAFTA) and the South American free trade association

[*] V.E. Tokman is Assistant Director General and Regional Director for the Americas, ILO- Lima. E. Klein is Director, Multidisciplinary Team, ILO-Santiago de Chile. This paper was written at the request of UNDP as a contribution to the *Human Development Report 1999*.

known as Mercosur; 3) an explosion of bilateral trade agreements during recent years; and most important, by 4) a unilateral tariff reduction as a key component of the adjustment policy package. Latin American tariffs decreased from an average of 35-100% (for minimum and maximum levels) in 1985, to 14-22% in the early 1990s. Diversification of the tariff structure also was greatly reduced, and is now limited in most countries to three tariff categories or fewer.

Globalization opens new opportunities for growth and job creation, but at the same time affects the determinants of employment and wages and requires regulation to avoid unfair international competition. On one hand, given the differences in factor endowments, it is expected that trade from developing to developed countries will be concentrated in goods that are intensive in the use of unskilled labor. This could increase the demand for these types of jobs and decrease the gap between the wages of skilled and unskilled labor.

This expected result could also be combined with the prevailing differences of remuneration and labor regulations between countries that could generate a trade expansion based on unfair labor practices or increased exploitation of workers. This has sparked an international discussion about how to avoid this outcome and whether there is need for additional regulation. While there was no general agreement on how to proceed, it is clear that nobody postulates the equalization of wages between countries since this would affect the competitive position of developing countries, nor is it accepted that trade expansion should be based on labor exploitation. Trade sanctions for those who do not comply with minimum international standards have also been discussed, but so far the danger of misuse as an instrument for trade protection has prevented its acceptance. There is, however, a more general agreement about the need for international and national monitoring of whether economic progress is accompanied by social progress and, particularly, by compliance with basic labor standards by all trading partners. This has been incorporated in the International Labor Organization (ILO) Declaration on Fundamental Principles and Rights at Work and its Follow-up, adopted by the International Labor Conference on 18 June, 1998.

Globalization also affects the determinants of job creation and wages, because in open economies the capacity to compete becomes a major factor and introduces constraints to wage adjustments. Unlike in the previous economic environment, there is a need for a closer link between wages and productivity. In closed economies, wage increases in excess of productivity growth can be transferred to prices, resulting in inflation; in open economies, the outcome is a reduced capacity to compete. In addition, demand fluctuations require a faster capacity to adapt and more flexibility in production and labor processes.

Privatization is the second feature of the new scenario. Privatization decreases the size and functions of government and increases the importance of the private sector and markets in the management and allocation of resources. Public employment falls and public enterprises are transferred to national or international capitalists. Both are mainly the result of the need to reduce fiscal deficits during adjustment. In addition, the responsibility for investment is increasingly transferred to the private sector, limiting public investment to basic infrastructure and social sectors, and with increasing participation of the private sector in the execution and management of these sectors.

Deregulation is the third process introduced in the new scenario. This has meant reducing protection and government intervention in trade, finance and labor markets. As mentioned above, trade and financial liberalization are leading to increased globalization, while reduced protection in product and labor markets is introduced to increase economic efficiency and to allow for a greater role of markets in the allocation of resources. The process of deregulation has in part been led by substantial legal reforms, but there has also been an important *de facto* increase in flexibility caused by the unfettered operation of markets.

The triple processes of *globalization, privatization and deregulation* are occurring in an international environment, characterized by a "universalization" of economic and social problems, and by increased ideological homogeneity. Today, the problems of employment and social exclusion are no longer present exclusively in developing countries, but constitute a major challenge even in the more developed economies of the world. Unemployment in some of the industrialized countries of the Organization for Economic Cooperation and Development (OECD) is stubbornly high; more than 30 million people are officially classified as unemployed, while an additional 10 million are no longer actively searching for jobs (OECD 1994; ILO 1996). The average rate of unemployment exceeds 10%, and for some vulnerable groups, like youth, one of five is unemployed in many countries. The end of the Cold War broke ideological barriers, and present conflicts are caused less by ideological divergence and more by local interests or as a natural reaction against the social cost of adjustment.

The three processes are interrelated on both analytical and *de facto* grounds. On the analytical side, globalization could not have advanced if it were not accompanied by the other components of adjustment that reduce trade protection as well as by financial liberalization and privatization to open opportunities for increased trade, capitals flows and direct foreign investment. All these policies contributed to achieving macroeconomic balance, but they were also necessary conditions for integration in the world economy. These sets of policies were fully incorporated in the Washington Consensus with the addition of those instruments geared to obtaining fiscal discipline. The latter were included with the main objective of ensuring price stability, but they also play an important role to create incentives for capital inflows in a more stabilized framework. Indeed, the one thing that has not been liberalized is the movement of unskilled workers. Only *ex post facto* policies of regularization of illegal migration were introduced, but the policy continues to be one of closed borders or at least, of tied regulation of flows.

De facto, the recent economic history of Latin American countries shows that globalization has been accompanied by privatization and deregulation. The timing and policy mix varied according to countries and it is perhaps early to evaluate the results. Only five countries—Brazil, Chile, Colombia, Costa Rica and Uruguay—have reached a per capita income level higher than in the pre-crisis period. Even fewer were able to achieve a high and sustained rate of growth; Chile and Colombia were the only countries able to grow at more than 5% per year for four consecutive years. Rates of growth have been erratic and stop-and-go cycles prevailed. In addition, three other features influence performance. Initial conditions were different in each country: some started the reform process early, while others only at the end of the 1980s or at the beginning of the 1990s. The policy mix in each stage was also different.

In spite of the differences, after a decade and a half of adjustment, it can be concluded that all Latin American countries were involved in the process of globalization and adjustment, and that privatization and deregulation were an integral part of the policy compact. The results are still unclear and the policy instruments are continuously evolving, but it is clear that the region is today more open and integrated in the world economy, more privatized and less regulated than pre-1980. All these things happened simultaneously; hence, any analysis of results should incorporate the context. This is what we will do in the rest of this paper.

Employment, incomes and equity under globalization

1. Expected effect

Globalization is expected to generate two main effects on labor and incomes. First, productivity gains, particularly in tradable sectors, should result in increased employment and price reductions in those sectors. The latter would also result in an expansion of real income and welfare for the population. Second, increased wages in export sectors, assumed to be more unskilled-labor-intensive, should result in decreased wage differentials by skills and, hence, in increased equity.

The reduction or elimination of tariffs and non-tariff barriers should generate a decrease in the relative prices of tradable goods. This would result, on the production side, in a reallocation of factors toward the export sectors, and on the consumption side, in a reallocation of expenditure toward imported goods and services. Consequently, export increases should generate a positive effect on employment, while the relative reduction in the price of importable goods should generate an increase in real incomes. Trade liberalization, hence, should result in increased welfare.

However, in the short run, the expansion of employment derived from increased exports could be offset by a decrease in employment in import-competing sectors. Increased competition in these sectors forces enterprises to increase productivity, generally at the cost of employment. The net employment effect of economic opening will depend on the behavior of the demand for labor in both tradable and non-tradable sectors, and on the labor supply dynamics. This will, in turn, affect average wages in each sector.

Another expected result of trade liberalization is that it should produce an increase in the relative price of unskilled labor-intensive goods in developing countries. This would induce an increase in the demand for unskilled labor and an expansion of their relative wages. As a consequence, wage dispersion would diminish.

2. Observed Performance

a) <u>Productivity gains and international competitiveness</u>

The first expected outcome recorded in most countries is the expansion of productivity in tradable sectors, particularly in manufacturing industry. As will be seen below, this outcome is associated with a reduction in the employment level of the sector. During the 1990s, productivity per employee expanded at annual rates of 5-7% in Argentina, Brazil, Mexico and Peru, while the rate was around 3% in Chile.

International competitiveness is variously affected, depending on the country studied and the indicators used to measure labor costs. It is usually argued that overpriced labor can affect access to international markets. Indeed, in a more competitive environment, costs matter. Overpriced labor can be the result of higher wages or high non-wage labor costs or both. The situation in most Latin American countries does not seem to justify the priority allocated to this issue (except for some required adjustments).

Wages in most Latin American countries, in spite of the recent tenuous recuperation, are still lower than in 1980. Minimum wages on average were 30% lower in 1997 than in 1980, and wages in manufacturing industry are down 2.9% in the same period. Non-wage labor costs vary from country to country, ranging from 38-64% of wages. In the case of Chile and Argentina, non-wage labor costs are higher than in Korea, similar to those of the United States, and much lower than those prevailing in European OECD countries. Labor costs per hour in Latin American manufacturing industry range from US$2.10 to US$6.50; this is between one-third and one-eighth of the US level and even less than in the Southeast Asian countries. Labor cost differences per unit of output are smaller due to higher productivity in competing countries (see Table 1). This denotes the importance of productivity improvements rather than only cost reductions as a major priority to gain competitiveness (Martínez and Tokman 1997).

The fact that relative labor costs are not high does not exclude the introduction of some adjustments in the labor cost structure to reduce them further and, particularly, diminish the cost of unskilled labor. Labor taxes on unskilled labor tend to reduce employment, while some of the existing taxes on the wage bill would be more efficient if transferred to other sources of revenue, particularly those that finance housing or other investments.

The evolution of labor costs in the 1990s also denotes additional policy aspects for consideration. Labor costs deflated by consumer prices have not increased ahead of productivity, for instance, in Argentina, Brazil, Mexico or Peru and, hence, were not constraints to increased access to international markets. However, when expressed in US dollars rather than local currency, or when observed in relation to producer prices, the situation shows decreased gains and, in most cases, a loss of competitiveness (see again Table 1). This is due to the effects of macroeconomic policy during the period, which in most countries was based on overvalued national currencies, because of the need to reduce inflation and because of the liberalization of capital flows. Part of the loss is explained by the delay in adjusting the exchange rate.

Table 1

Labor costs and international competitiveness [1/]

	Wages Per hour In US$	Non-wage labor costs As % of wages	Labor costs per hour In US$	Labor costs per unit of output (US level = 100)	Annual changes 1990-1995					
					Labor costs		Productivity	Competitiveness [2/]		
					A	B		A	B	C
Argentina	4.6	42.5	6.5	55	-2.0	13.1	7.0	9.2	-6.1	3.7
Brazil	3.7	58.2	5.9	60	2.9	8.5	7.5	4.5	-0.9	4.3
Chile	2.5	38.0	3.5	43	4.3	9.4	3.2	-1.1	-5.7	5.9
Mexico	1.9	42.0	2.8	47	1.2	1.5	5.2	4.0	3.6	na
Peru	1.3	64.3	2.1	43	5.1	11.6	6.6	1.4	-4.5	0.3
United Sates	12.6	40.3	17.7	100		2.6	3.8		-1.2	na
Germany	16.1	78.5	28.7	150		2.1	1.8		-0.3	na
Korea	6.8	21.9	8.2	60		3.6	11.9		8.0	50.0

Sources: Martínez and Tokman (1997), ILO (1998), and updating by authors.

1/ Refers to manufacturing industry circa 1997. Competitiveness is defined as the difference between changes in productivity and labor costs.

2/ A. Refers to changes in local currency at constant prices, deflated by consumer price index (1990-95)

B. Refers to changes in US dollars (1990-95).

C. Refers to changes in US dollars between July 1997 and June 1998.

On the other hand, internal prices adapt at differing speeds to the more competitive economic environment; prices of traded goods, generally included in producer prices, adjust more rapidly, while consumer goods, more influenced by non-traded goods and services, tend to be slower in adjusting. The result is that, while labor costs expressed in consumer prices did not grow, they in fact grew very fast when denominated in relation to producer prices. This outcome of changes in relative prices, while beyond labor markets, does influence the dynamics of wage determination, because it generates different perspectives for workers (based on acquisition power of wages) and entrepreneurs (based on profit margins).

Furthermore, as illustrated clearly after mid-1997, competitiveness is also dependent on changes in other countries. In spite of an increase in competitiveness in Latin American countries of 0.4-10%, their capacity to compete with goods from Asian countries deteriorated. Competitiveness gains in those countries were around 50%—varying from 20% in Thailand to 60% in Malaysia—compared to the largest Latin American increase, around 10%, registered in Colombia.

To sum up, as expected, productivity grew as a consequence of the reform process, but some adjustments are still needed. First, to maintain international competitiveness, non-wage labor costs should be examined. Second, macroeconomic policies, particularly overvalued exchange rates and relative prices, should be reviewed. Finally, productivity gains were insufficient to close the gap with competitors.

b) Employment creation

A second effect of globalization is insufficient employment creation relative to the rapidly increasing economically active population (EAP). On average, the non-agricultural EAP has grown above 3% per year, partly because of increasing female participation in the wage economy. Job creation lagged due to slow and erratic economic growth. The result has been increasing unemployment.

The rate of unemployment on average for Latin America increased from 6% in 1980 to 8.7% 1983, i.e., during the first phase of adjustment. Unemployment decreased from 1983 to 1992, but never fell to the 1980 level. After 1992, unemployment grew continuously, reaching 8.4% in 1998, and is expected to reach 9.5% in 1999. This behavior shows not only the limited capacity to reduce unemployment but also increased vulnerability, since continuous adjustments imply returning to previous higher levels of unemployment. By 1998, Latin American unemployment had returned to the high levels of the mid-1980s. If the forecasted rate for 1999 comes about, it will be even higher than the maximum unemployment level of "the lost decade."

Four aspects should be taken into account to evaluate the way in which unemployment affects the people of Latin America. The first is that the level by itself can be misleading when compared, for instance, with rates above 10% prevailing in some OECD countries. Most countries lack unemployment insurance and protection is generally linked to occupation. Being without a job means no income and unprotected people. This is a main source of social exclusion. Secondly, unemployment affects more women and young people. While the rate of unemployment of women is around 30% higher than the average, the young people register rates that are usually double the national level. Unsurprisingly, a large share of the excluded is made up of women and young people. Third, there are also large regional variations within countries. Adjustment tends to affect in a biased manner where key sectors in need of restructuring are located. These activities generally constitute the main source of employment and production, and restructuring affects the whole region.

The situation also differs from country to country. Size, modernization level and stage of the reform process are determining factors in relation to unemployment. Small and open economies are more vulnerable to external fluctuations and unemployment rates tend to be higher and more erratic than in larger and more closed economies (where internal demand plays the major role and provides more autonomy). On the other hand, in countries that are at an advanced stage of urbanization and modernization, unemployment becomes the main source of adjustment in labor markets, while for those with a large agricultural population or small formal sector, underemployment constitute the main variable of adjustment. Finally, the stage in the reform process also matters. Early reformers have been more successful in reducing unemployment, while latecomers—particularly those today in the first phases of adjustment—tend to register larger and increasing rises in unemployment.

c) Changes in the employment structure

In addition to a higher unemployment rate, reform has produced profound changes in the structure of employment. Four main interrelated processes can be identified: *privatization, "tertiarization," "informalization" and "precarization."* These processes can be observed in the 1990s, when most countries were already beyond or well advanced in the adjustment process.

Privatization introduced a major behavioral change in employment creation in Latin America, given the historical role played by the public sector as employer of last resort (as will be discussed in the next section) and an important contributor to the development of the middle classes. Government did not directly contribute to employment creation in the 1990s. On the contrary, its share of non-agricultural employment fell for the region as a whole, from 15.5% in 1990 to 13.0% in 1997. This decrease does not include public employment reduction that took place in earlier periods, for instance, in Chile. This move from public to private employment was registered in all countries, while in some—including Panama, Argentina and Costa Rica—the decline reached levels of between five and ten percentage points.

Table 2

Growth, employment and wages: 1980-1998

	1980	1985	1990	1995	1998
Economic activity 1/					
GNP	-	0.6	1.9	2.9	3.8
GNP per capita	-	-1.6	-0.1	-1.0	2.3
Inflation	-	134.8	487.5	287.5	13.2
Population and employment					
Population 1/	-	2.1	1.9	1.8	1.8
EAP total 1/	-	3.5	3.1	2.6	2.6
EAP urban 2/	66.9	70.0	72.8	75.3	76.6
Non-agricultural employment 1/	-	3.5	4.4	3.0	2.8
Unemployment rate	6.7	8.3	5.7	7.2	8.4
Informal employment 3/	40.2	47.0	51.8	56.2	57.7
Public employment 3/	15.7	16.6	15.5	13.4	13.0 5/
Wages 4/					
Manufacturing wages	100.0	93.1	87.7	93.9	97.1
Minimum wages	100.0	86.4	68.9	70.8	72.9

Source: ILO, based on national statistics.

1/ Annual rates of growth during the period.
2/ Percentage of total EAP.
3/ Percentage of non-agricultural employment.
4/ Index 1980 = 100.
5/ Refers to 1997.

This employment shift from the public to the private sector was a direct consequence of the processes of privatization and deregulation accompanying globalization. State enterprises were transferred and government functions were reduced. It was also a main result of fiscal discipline, which is an important component of the stabilization policy. A reduction in the fiscal deficit was generally achieved by cutting public expenditure, mostly the payroll, in a sequence of wage *cum* employment reduction (see Table 3).

The transfer of jobs was not, however, on average made to medium and large private enterprises. They also declined in their share of total employment during the same period, although at a slower pace than government. Between 1990 and 1997, the share of employment in medium and large private enterprises fell from 33% to 29%. This was mainly concentrated in countries like Brazil, Peru and Venezuela, while in Mexico and Chile, the corresponding figures remained constant. Large enterprises were the most affected by economic opening and the need to increase productivity (mostly through employment reduction). Only 15 of each 100 new jobs created during the 1990s was contributed by these enterprises. In addition, increased labor flexibility facilitated adjustment, but at the cost of a more erratic employment level. This is clearly illustrated by the 1% reduction in employment in large and medium enterprises in 1998, when these firms had to adjust to increased competition from Asian products (see Figure 1).

Table 3

LATIN AMERICA: STRUCTURE OF NON-AGRICULTURAL EMPLOYMENT, 1990 - 1997							
Countries/ Years	Informal sector				Formal Sector		
	Total	Self-employed workers a/	Domestic service	Small business b/	Total	Public sector	Large private Enterprises
Latin America							
1990	51.8	24.7	7.0	20.1	48.2	15.5	32.7
1991	52.5	25.1	6.9	20.6	47.5	15.2	32.3
1992	53.2	25.6	6.9	20.7	46.8	14.8	32.0
1993	54.1	25.4	7.3	21.4	45.9	13.9	32.0
1994	55.1	25.9	7.3	21.8	44.9	13.5	31.4
1995	56.2	26.7	7.4	22.2	43.8	13.4	30.4
1996	57.4	27.3	7.4	22.7	42.6	13.2	29.4
1997	57.7	27.1	7.6	23.0	42.3	13.0	29.3
Argentina							
1990	47.5	24.7	7.9	14.9	52.5	19.3	33.2
1991	48.6	25.3	7.9	15.4	51.4	18.5	32.9
1992	49.6	25.9	7.8	15.9	50.4	17.7	32.7
1993	50.8	26.6	7.9	16.3	49.2	16.8	32.4
1994	52.5	27.0	7.4	18.1	47.5	14.3	33.2
1995	53.3	27.2	7.6	18.5	46.7	13.8	32.9
1996	53.6	27.1	7.8	18.7	46.4	13.2	33.2
1997	53.8	26.5	8.1	19.2	46.2	12.7	33.5
Bolivia							
1990	56.9	37.7	6.4	12.8	43.1	16.5	26.6
1991	56.1	37.8	6.8	11.5	43.9	17.1	26.8
1992	56.6	38.2	5.9	12.5	43.4	15.5	27.9
1993	61.2	36.4	6.5	18.3	38.8	12.7	26.1
1994	61.3	37.1	5.2	19.0	38.7	11.4	27.3
1995	63.6	39.6	5.4	18.6	36.4	11.4	25.0
1996	63.1	37.7	5.5	19.9	36.9	11.1	25.8
1997	56.6	35.4	4.0	17.2	43.4	11.1	32.3
Brazil							
1990	52.0	21.0	7.7	23.3	48.0	11.0	36.9
1991	53.2	21.7	7.7	23.8	46.8	10.7	36.1
1992	54.3	22.5	7.8	24.0	45.7	10.4	35.2
1993	55.5	21.9	8.9	24.7	44.5	9.7	34.8
1994	56.5	22.4	9.2	25.0	43.5	9.7	33.8
1995	57.6	23.0	9.4	25.2	42.4	9.6	32.8
1996	59.3	23.8	9.5	26.0	40.7	9.6	31.1
1997	60.4	24.3	9.8	26.3	39.6	9.3	30.3
Chile							
1990	49.9	23.6	8.1	18.3	50.1	7.0	43.0
1991	49.9	23.1	7.8	19.1	50.1	7.8	42.3
1992	49.7	22.7	7.3	19.6	50.3	8.0	42.3
1993	49.9	22.6	6.6	20.6	50.1	7.9	42.3
1994	51.6	24.2	6.7	20.6	48.4	7.7	40.8
1995	51.2	23.9	6.5	20.8	48.8	7.7	41.1
1996	50.9	22.7	6.8	21.4	49.1	7.6	41.5
1997	51.3	23.0	6.6	21.7	48.7	7.2	41.5
Colombia							
1990	55.2	23.5	5.4	26.3	44.8	9.6	35.2
1991	55.7	23.7	5.3	26.7	44.3	9.3	35.0
1992	55.8	23.6	5.2	27.0	44.2	9.0	35.2
1993	55.4	23.8	4.9	26.7	44.6	8.6	36.0
1994	54.8	23.9	4.4	26.5	45.2	8.3	36.9
1995	54.8	24.7	4.1	26.0	45.2	8.2	37.0
1996	54.6	25.6	3.8	25.2	45.4	8.2	37.2
1997	54.7	24.8	4.0	25.9	45.3	8.2	37.1

Table 3 cont'd

Countries/ Years	Informal sector				Formal Sector		
	Total	Self-employed workers a/	Domestic service	Small business b/	Total	Public sector	Large private Enterprises
Costa Rica							
1990	42.3	18.1	5.8	18.4	57.7	22.0	35.7
1991	44.6	19.0	5.6	20.0	55.4	20.3	35.1
1992	41.4	17.6	5.2	18.6	58.6	20.5	38.1
1993	43.7	18.6	5.0	20.1	56.3	20.1	36.2
1994	46.2	17.8	5.3	23.1	53.8	18.4	35.4
1995	44.6	18.1	5.0	21.5	55.4	17.9	37.6
1996	47.3	17.4	5.2	24.7	52.7	17.2	35.5
1997	46.8	18.8	5.4	22.6	53.2	17.0	36.2
Ecuador							
1990	53.4	33.5	4.8	15.0	46.6	18.7	27.9
1991	57.8	32.5	5.2	20.1	42.2	17.5	24.7
1992	58.3	34.3	4.5	19.5	41.7	15.7	26.0
1993	57.3	33.2	4.8	19.3	42.7	14.9	27.8
1994	56.1	31.5	5.1	19.5	43.9	14.7	29.1
1995	56.7	32.9	5.1	18.7	43.3	14.2	29.1
1996	57.0	33.0	5.1	18.9	43.0	14.8	28.1
1997	53.2	30.4	5.4	17.4	46.8	14.8	32.0
Honduras							
1990	54.1	36.3	6.9	10.8	45.9	14.9	31.0
1991	50.7	35.0	6.7	9.0	49.3	16.6	32.7
1992	50.7	35.1	6.7	8.9	49.3	16.4	32.9
1993	45.3	27.5	6.2	11.6	54.7	14.6	40.0
1994	51.8	32.5	5.9	13.4	48.2	12.4	35.9
1995	54.4	34.0	5.4	15.1	45.6	12.5	33.1
1996	56.3	36.5	6.0	13.8	43.7	11.4	32.3
1997	56.6	38.1	5.8	12.7	43.4	10.3	33.1
Mexico							
1990	55.5	30.3	5.6	19.6	44.5	25.0	19.6
1991	55.8	30.5	5.5	19.8	44.2	24.7	19.5
1992	56.0	30.5	5.5	20.0	44.0	24.5	19.5
1993	57.0	30.6	5.5	20.9	43.0	23.0	20.0
1994	57.0	30.7	5.4	20.9	43.0	22.9	20.1
1995	59.4	32.3	5.4	21.7	40.6	22.5	18.1
1996	60.2	32.5	5.4	22.3	39.8	22.0	17.8
1997	59.4	31.2	5.6	22.6	40.6	21.7	18.9
Panama							
1990	40.5	20.4	7.2	12.8	59.5	32.0	27.5
1991	41.2	19.7	7.9	13.6	58.8	27.5	31.3
1992	41.5	19.0	8.5	14.0	58.5	25.2	33.3
1993	39.9	18.2	8.0	13.7	60.1	24.6	35.5
1994	40.2	19.5	7.9	12.9	59.8	24.4	35.4
1995	41.3	20.5	7.6	13.2	58.7	23.4	35.4
1996	41.7	20.7	7.0	13.9	58.3	23.1	35.3
1997	41.5	21.5	7.1	13.0	58.5	21.8	36.6
Paraguay							
1990	61.4	21.2	10.7	29.4	38.6	12.2	26.4
1991	62.0	23.0	10.0	29.0	38.0	11.3	26.7
1992	62.2	22.2	11.0	29.0	37.8	14.6	23.2
1993	62.5	21.5	11.6	29.5	37.5	12.2	25.2
1994	68.9	22.3	11.7	34.9	31.1	11.8	19.3
1995	65.5	25.3	10.6	29.7	34.5	11.9	22.6
1996	67.9	26.9	10.0	31.0	32.1	13.1	19.0
Peru c/							
1990	51.8	35.3	5.1	11.4	48.2	11.6	36.6
1991	51.8	34.9	4.8	12.1	48.2	11.9	36.3
1992	54.5	37.2	4.9	12.4	45.5	10.0	35.5
1993	54.2	34.7	4.6	14.9	45.8	10.1	35.7
1994	53.8	35.1	4.6	14.1	46.2	7.9	38.3
1995	55.0	35.1	4.7	15.2	45.0	9.1	35.9
1996	57.9	37.4	4.2	16.3	42.1	8.2	33.9
1997	59.3	34.9	5.1	19.4	40.7	7.2	33.5

Table 3 cont'd

Countries/ Years	Informal sector				Formal Sector		
	Total	Self-employed workers a/	Domestic service	Small business b/	Total	Public sector	Large private Enterprises
Uruguay d/							
1990	36.3	19.3	6.0	11.0	63.7	20.1	43.6
1991	36.7	20.1	6.0	10.6	63.3	18.1	45.2
1992	36.6	20.1	6.3	10.2	63.4	17.5	45.9
1993	37.4	20.5	6.1	10.9	62.6	18.2	44.4
1994	37.9	20.9	6.3	10.7	62.1	16.9	45.2
1995	37.7	21.0	5.9	10.8	62.3	17.7	44.6
1996	37.9	21.3	6.3	10.3	62.1	17.0	45.1
1997	37.1	20.1	6.1	10.9	62.9	16.8	46.1
Venezuela							
1990	38.8	22.1	4.1	12.6	61.2	22.3	38.9
1991	38.3	22.2	3.9	12.2	61.7	21.6	40.1
1992	37.4	22.2	3.4	11.8	62.6	20.2	42.4
1993	38.4	24.1	3.2	11.1	61.6	18.8	42.8
1994	44.8	27.3	3.0	14.5	55.2	19.3	35.9
1995	46.9	27.0	2.3	17.6	53.1	19.5	33.6
1996	47.7	28.1	2.4	17.2	52.3	19.1	33.2
1997	48.1	29.9	2.4	15.8	51.9	19.0	32.9

Source: ILO estimates, based on household surveys and other official sources.

a/ Includes self-employed workers (except administrative, professional and technical workers) and family-business workers.
b/ Corresponds to establishments with fewer than 5 or 10 workers, depending on the information available.
c/ Corresponds to metropolitan Lima.
d/ Corresponds to Montevideo.

"Tertiarization" refers to a shift in employment from goods-producing sectors to services. The shift was rapid in countries such as Argentina, Costa Rica, Mexico and Venezuela, where the share of manufacturing employment decreased between four and six percentage points during the 1990s.

In other countries, the process was slower given the maturity in their productive transformation (Chile), or the gradual approach followed (Colombia, Brazil and Peru) or, in cases like Panama, because of the small and already open economy.

Given the new structural conditions after adjustment, these sectors are more vulnerable to changes in competition. Manufacturing industry contracted in 1998 as a result of increased competition from Asian products. This contraction of output and employment was particularly large in food processing, textiles and clothing, shoes and machinery and equipment.

The shift of employment from manufacturing to services is partly the result of increased competition in a more open economy. Decreased employment was accompanied by increased productivity, which, particularly in the short run, can only be achieved by employment reduction. It is also a result that is mostly concentrated in urban employment, since agriculture, fishing and mining tend to contribute to employment expansion during the opening process.

The expansion of employment in the service sectors cannot be *a priori* read as a move towards low-productivity jobs. Some of the jobs created in the sector are in services integral to the modernization and globalization processes, such as finance, communications and trade. The productivity of these sectors is usually higher than that of manufacturing and can expand more rapidly. Unfortunately, this has not been the situation in Latin America in the recent past. Nine of ten new jobs created in the 1990s were in services, but 80% of these were in low-productivity services, mostly in the informal sector in personal, retail trade and transportation services. "*Tertiarization*" in this context means a deterioration of employment quality.

Figure 1

Latin America. Selected Countries
Tendency of employment in the nineties
(participation in employment increase)

Towards tertiary sector

Towards informality

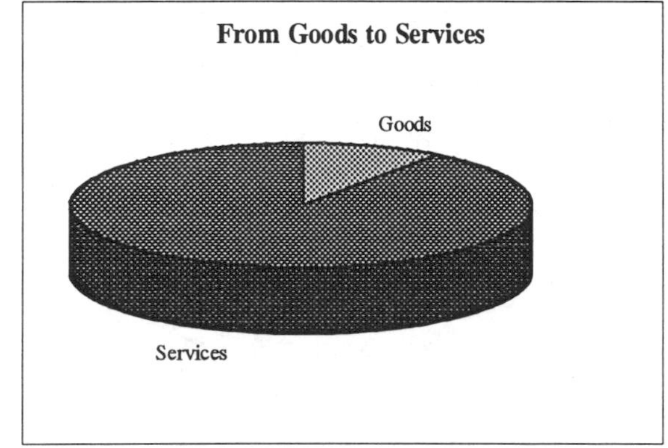

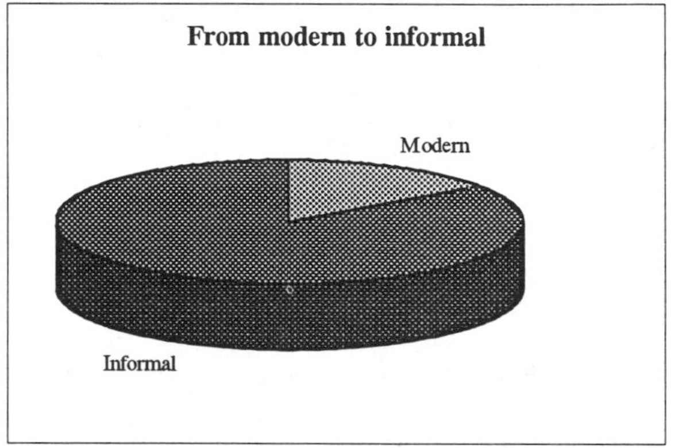

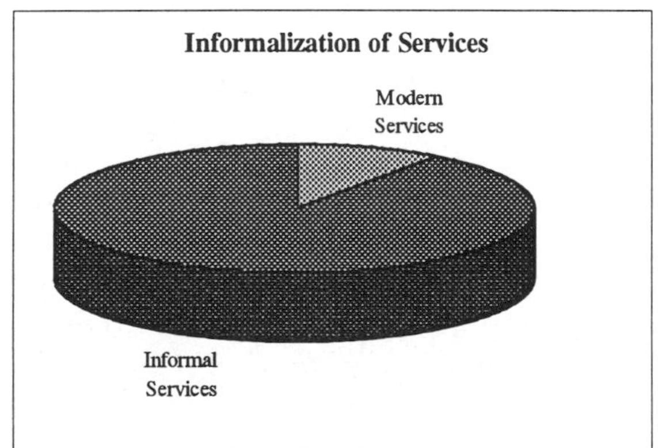

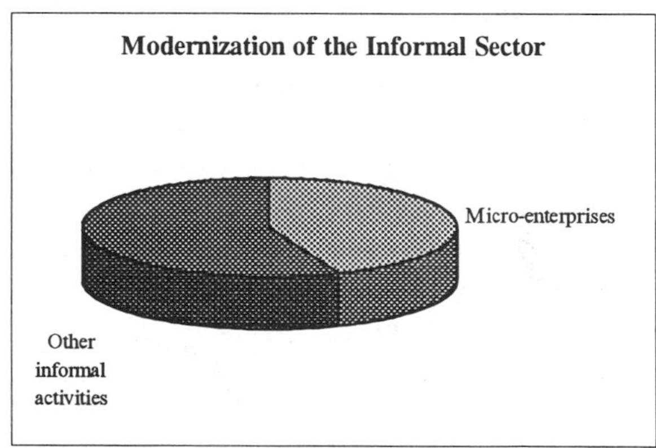

"*Informalization*", i.e., a shift from formal to informal employment, was the third major shift in the employment structure in the 1990s. As mentioned above, the limited capacity of the formal economy, both public and private, to absorb job seekers left increasing numbers of people with no alternative but to find or create their own occupations in the informal sector. Given the non-existence of insurance, unemployment is a luxury that very few can afford. Slow and erratic growth, as well as labor expulsion from the public sector during adjustment, conspired against the creation of jobs in modern activities.

As a result, informal employment expanded from 52% to 58% between 1990 and 1997. This includes self-employment, unpaid workers in family businesses, and domestic services and microenterprise occupations. Only Chile, Colombia Panama and Uruguay have managed to keep their share of informal employment constant, while in the rest, informal employment grew twice as fast as total non-agricultural employment.

For the region as a whole, 85 of 100 jobs created in the 1990s were informal. As mentioned above, a large majority of new jobs in services were informal; in addition, the most dynamic component of informal employment growth has been microenterprise occupations. Of each 10 new informal jobs, around four were contributed by microenterprises. This could suggest a positive change within informal employment, since microenterprises are more organized than most informal activities; average incomes from microenterprises are larger than those of the rest of the informal sector (although not as large as those of the formal sector). In fact, average income in microenterprises exceeds average income in the informal sector, and is around 90% of average income in modern activities. Averages, however, hide variations within the sector; for instance, wages in microenterprises are only 55% of those prevailing in medium and large enterprises. Only about one-fifth of total revenues received by microenterprise owners is passed on as wages to his or her employees.

Nevertheless, microenterprises are increasingly becoming valid employment options, being for instance in 1998, responsible for all new jobs created. This, however, has to be analyzed further since although income outcomes are better, working conditions, job stability and social protection are far from being acceptable. Between 65% and 95% of those working in microenterprises do not posses a written contract, and between 65% and 80% are uncovered of health risks or for old age. They tend to work more hours and are more subject to accidents at work. Violations of basic labor rights (child labor, freedom of association and collective bargaining and forced labor) are also more frequent in this size of establishments than in larger ones. Of course, precariousness is not a characteristic uniquely attributed to small enterprises; it also prevails in medium and large firms.

"Precarization" refers to the growing precariousness of work, resulting from increased competition in a more flexible labor environment. The search for cost reductions and flexibility to allow for improvements in competitiveness has led to labor law reforms introducing flexibility at the margin. "Atypical" contracts were introduced as a less costly and more flexible alternative in new hiring to the unlimited duration contract that had once prevailed in labor relations. The expected outcome of greater flexibility and lower labor costs was increased creation of salaried jobs.

The experience during the 1990s in fact registered an increase in waged employment that was faster than total employment growth, suggesting that the reform produced incentives to hiring. However, the social cost involved was the increasing precariousness of work. The introduction of "atypical" labor contracts was accompanied by an increase in the number of workers without any written employment contract. It must be noted that neither atypical contracts nor the lack of any written legal contract presumes that labor protection is lower than in the typical contract. Only the reform in Argentina allowed for reduced labor protection in the case of temporary contracts, and the terms of employment are subject to proof in the absence of a written contract. However, inspection and control become more difficult with temporary contracts. In the case of workers without contracts, many are underground workers receiving cash payments, whose conditions of employment are almost impossible to verify. This, in addition, happens in a situation where labor inspection is generally weak and as a result of the reform, has weakened its guidance by legally recognizing that the typical contract is rigid.

Workers without contract or with "atypical" contracts amounted to 30% of all workers in Chile in 1996, 40% in Argentina and Colombia, and 74% in Peru. The majority was in microenterprises: 50% in Chile, 65-70% in Colombia and Argentina, and 80% in Peru. However, medium and large enterprises registered the largest proportion of "atypical" contracts and significant percentages of workers without contracts: 6% in Argentina, 11% in Peru and 32% in Argentina and Colombia. In the case of microenterprises, there is a clear overlapping of informality and precariousness, since both are mainly the result of the inability to pay the cost of labor protection. For larger size enterprises, the numbers of unregistered workers is an indication of legal evasion.

The share of workers potentially or actually subject to precariousness is not only high but also accounts for all employment expansion in the 1990s in most countries. In addition, of four countries analyzed, only in Colombia was there an increase in employment of unlimited duration; in Chile, Argentina and Peru, there was a reduction in the absolute numbers of these contracts. The transition from permanent to temporary employment differed from country to country. In Argentina, the fall in unlimited contracts was entirely made up by the expansion of workers without contracts, mainly in larger enterprises. In Peru, the loss in employment of unlimited duration was made up half by workers with temporary contracts and half by workers without contracts, mostly in microenterprises. In Chile, the majority of the new jobs were under temporary contracts in larger enterprises.

The four processes described resulted in deterioration in the quality of labor protection in the 1990s. *Privatization*, potentially a positive shift, was not so because of insufficient job creation in modern private enterprises. *"Tertiarization,"* is also *a priori* neutral, since good jobs in services could make up for fewer jobs available in manufacturing. However, most of the new jobs in services were of low productivity. *"Informalization"* and *"precarization"* clearly downgraded job quality, somewhat offset by the rapid expansion of employment in microenterprises.

The changes in the employment structure can be more clearly identified in a longer-run perspective. As can be seen in Figure 2, during the three decades previous to adjustment (1950-1980), 60% on average of new jobs in Latin America were created by the formal sectors of the economy, with government responsible for 15% and medium and large private enterprises 45%. The informal sector contributed 40% of new jobs; of those, only 10% were in microenterprises.

Figure 2

Latin America: Sectoral contribution to employment creation, 1950 - 1996
(number of jobs contributed by each sector in each ten new jobs)

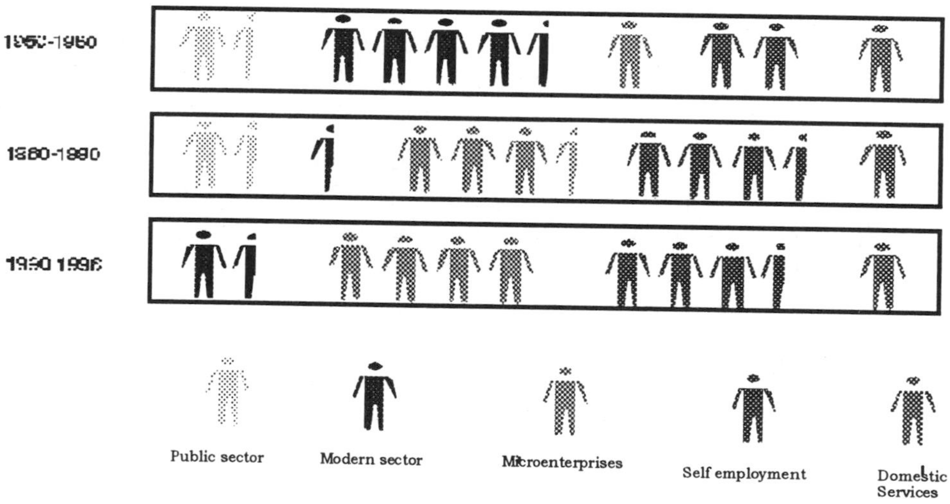

A substantial change in the structure occurred during the adjustment decade of the 1980s. The contribution of modern employment contribution decreased to two of ten new jobs, and the reduction was concentrated in private modern enterprises that had to adjust to a more open economy. The informal sector played a buffer function doubling its contribution to job creation, mostly in microenterprises, which more than tripled. The 1990s show a recovery in labor absorption in larger-size private enterprises and a continuous expansion of informal jobs.

To sum up, privatization has meant that public employment is no longer contributing to labor absorption. Larger enterprises, while recovering from the adjustment decade, are still well below the pre-adjustment level, and most likely will be unable to reach that level, given technological change and decentralization of production and employment. Indeed, enterprises independent of their size contribute the same 5.5 of every 10 new jobs as in the pre-adjustment period. The difference is that now the main contributors are the microenterprises. As it is, in this sector where informality and precariousness still prevail, the employment shift has resulted in deterioration of job quality.

d) Trends in wages and wage differentials

Two effects are expected on wages during the adjustment period. Wage levels should tend to increase as productivity expands, and wage differentials by skill levels should diminish, as the demand for unskilled labor increases because of the expansion of trade based on labor-intensive sectors.

As noted before, in 1998 both industrial and minimum wage levels in real terms were below the level of 1980. There has been, however, a recovery during the 1990s in both cases. This mainly as a result of the success in reducing inflation which declined from three digits to less than 10% on average across Latin America. Productivity expansion during the last period also contributed, particularly in the industrial sector (see Table 2).

Wage differentials have behaved in an unexpected manner. Differences between minimum and industrial wages and differences by skill or educational levels have tended to widen. Industrial wages grew by 1.4% per year between 1990 and 1997, while minimum wages only increased by 0.3%. Income differentials between professionals and technicians and workers in low- productivity sectors increased from 40% to 60% between 1990 and 1994 on average for Latin America. This resulted from a significant expansion of the real incomes of highly skilled workers in modern activities and a slow increase or even a reduction of wages of unskilled labor in low-productivity sectors. In eight out of ten countries for which data were available, the wage gap by skilled levels widened (CEPAL 1997). The same can also be seen when comparing wages of skilled workers with blue-collar workers since 1988 (IDB 1998).

It should also be noted that while wage gaps in Latin America widened during this period, the trend was exactly the opposite in Southeast Asian countries. In addition, Latin American wage gaps in 1980 were already the highest in the world. By 1997, the wage gap in Latin America was 1.9 times that prevailing in developed countries and Southeast Asian countries.

Several explanations can be given for this unexpected behavior. The effect of capital liberalization on capital goods prices could have induced an increase in investment and a complementary demand for skilled labor. The expansion of imports from countries like China, which are even more abundant in unskilled labor than Latin America, and the foreign exchange appreciation that favored an increase of non-tradable goods that are relative more skill-intensive (Lustig 1998).

In addition, studies made of Brazil, Chile and Peru (Meller and Tokman 1996; Páez de Barros et. al. 1996; Saavedra 1996) suggest that the maturity and the nature of the process of trade opening influence the evolution of wage differentials. In Chile, with a more mature opening process, large enterprises were able to expand employment after 1984; in Brazil and Peru (two late starters in the process), decreased employment occurred in large enterprises to increase productivity and competitiveness, while labor absorption concentrated in small and microenterprises. In the former case, there was an expansion of demand for skilled labor, while in the other two there was a shift of labor from higher- to lower-productivity enterprises and sectors. A net employment expansion in Peru, but a contraction in Brazil accompanied this. In both cases, however, wages of unskilled labor decreased either as a consequence of the occupational shift or because of the introduction of less protected labor relations. Workers in microenterprises earn on average 30-50% less than workers in larger establishments (ILO 1997) and still 20% less even when personal characteristics are homogenized (IDB 1998). On the other hand, large enterprises replacing workers under long-term contracts by temporary workers reduce wages by between 35-40% or by an additional 15-30% if no written contract is issued (see Table 4). This "precarization" of the labor contract is used mostly for unskilled workers and neutralizes any demand effect that could have originated as a result of trade opening (ILO 1998a).

Table 4

Precarious jobs

	Waged workers under: 1/			Labor costs per hour 2/			Decomposition of change in waged employment 3/			
	Temporary contracts	Without contracts	Total	Temporary contracts	Without contracts	Unlimited duration	Unlimited duration	Temporary	Without contracts	Total change in waged employment
Argentina	12.7	33.0	35.7	3.5	2.8	6.1	-652.7	25.7	726.9	100.0
Chile	14.7	15.6	30.3	1.4	1.0	2.1	-89.9	138.9	51.0	100.0
Colombia	8.3	31.0	39.3	1.9	1.6	3.3	81.9	13.3	4.8	100.0
Peru	32.6	41.1	73.7	1.4	1.1	2.1	-19.3	56.8	62.6	100.0

Sources: Martínez and Tokman (1999); ILO (1998).

1/ As percentages of total waged employment.
2/ In US dollars.
3/ As percentages of changes in waged employment between 1990 and 1996.

e) Poverty and equity

Poverty and inequality have increased during the process of reform. Today, on average, there are more poor people and income differences are larger in Latin America than before. The trend has not been a continuous one. During the 1990s, when several countries have already completed the stabilization and opening phases, poverty is diminishing in the majority of countries for which data is available. Only Argentina and Venezuela register an increased poverty level, and in Mexico, the level remains constant, but the 13 remaining countries that possess data show a reduction of poverty.

The present poverty level is still larger than in 1980 and has not been matched with increasing equity. On the contrary, income concentration has substantially increased since the early 1980s, reaching at present a Gini coefficient similar to that prevailing in 1970 (0.52). This is the result of a decreasing income share of the poorest quintile and a continuous increase of the upper quintile, an increase that was only interrupted between 1980 and 1983. The intermediate quintiles, while performing better than the poorest, still have not recovered their income share of the beginning of the 1980s. In fact, of the two countries (Chile and Uruguay) showing a significant decrease in poverty, only Uruguay was able simultaneously to register increased equity.

The concentration of income in Latin America has been historically the highest in the world. At present, the income share of the upper 5% is double that registered by the same group in industrialized countries, and it exceeds by more than 60% that of Southeast Asian countries. At the other extreme, the poorest 30% register the lowest income share in the world, which at 7.5% is only 60% of the level reached by the same group in industrialized and Asian countries (IDB 1998). Furthermore, when a successful performer like Chile is compared to the US, it can be observed that the income share of the bottom 20% are similar (around 4.5%). However, to find a comparable share for the upper 20%, it is necessary to go back as far as 1929. If the Gini coefficient is estimated for 90% of the Latin American population (excluding the upper 10%), its level would be on average of 0.36, similar to the US and in six of the countries it would be even lower than in the US (IDB 1998). This clearly indicates that higher concentration of income by the upper groups is a key explanatory factor.

Equally important is to explore why globalization and the adjustment package which accompanied it, did not help move Latin American levels of equity closer to the rest of the world. Conventional wisdom, based on the pioneering studies of Kuznets, leads one to expect that, after a period of increased income concentration in the early stage of development, equity would increase. This conventional wisdom does not seem to hold today, even for developed countries. The trend toward greater equity has been interrupted or, in the best cases, remained stable. Inequality has increased in the US since the end of the 1960s, in the UK, it increased from 1979 to 1989; and the same happened in Sweden after 1988 (Atkinson 1996 and Krugman 1995). This suggests that Latin American countries may be following a universal path as a result of policy homogenization, without having passed through the stage of increased equity as registered earlier in those countries.

Several factors can help explain why globalization has not improved equity in Latin America. They relate to *population dynamics, distribution of opportunities and the functioning of labor markets during the process of adjustment*.

Rapid population growth has resulted, particularly in poor households, in larger size (50% more members in the lowest quintile than in the highest), higher dependency rates (almost triple) and lower participation rates (60%) (CEPAL 1997a).

Access to opportunities, and particularly to education, also is unequal. Although, on average, the years of education have increased (albeit more slowly than in Southeast Asian countries), they tend to be unequally distributed. There is a high dropout rate in poor households. Ninety-four percent of poor children in educationally advanced countries are enrolled in the first year of school versus 76% in the less advanced countries. Enrollment rates decrease to 63% and 32% at the fifth year, and to 15% and 6% at the ninth year. Entry rates are similar for poor children and children from upper-income families, but the latter remained at school for longer periods. At the fifth year, the rates were 93% and 83%, while at the ninth year the rates were 58% and 49% (IDB 1998a). Unequal access is reinforced by higher rates of education to university level among upper-income families and by differences in quality of education. The academic achievements (math and science) in private schools, attended only by children from upper-income families, are on average 50% higher than those reached in public schools, where 90% of the children of the poor attend.

A significant part of income differences, more than 55%, is explained by labor market outcomes. As argued above, increased unemployment, employment shifts towards less productive, more unstable jobs and increased wage differentials, tend to widen income inequalities since they affect poor households in a biased manner. Unemployment rates are higher in poor households (in Chile, the rate of the poorest quintile was 2.7 times that of the richest quintile in 1996). In addition, job allocation is segmented. Good quality, well paid jobs are largely occupied by members of higher-income families, while low-quality, informal and unskilled jobs, tend to be covered by those coming from poor households. The poorest 40% in Chile registered an increase in employment between 1992 and 1994; while formal occupation decreased, informal jobs grew by more than 20%. The opposite happened for the upper quintile, which expanded formal employment by 13.5% and decreased informal employment by 2.7%. More than half of the new jobs requiring high educational levels went to the upper-income families, while the lower 40% only registered restricted upward mobility, by occupying jobs with secondary or technical requirements (Tokman 1998).

Labor market outcomes are determinants of the evolution of poverty and equity. This does not mean that other outcomes are unimportant, but they are not independent. Income concentration by households and labor income concentration by worker for 14 Latin American countries is presently similar (with Gini coefficients of 0.52 and 0.51, respectively) (IDB 1998). The analysis made above can then be translated into poverty and equity. This we have done for nine countries for the 1990s. The countries included were Argentina 1990-96, Brazil 1992-95, Chile 1990-96, Colombia 1992-96, Costa Rica 1990-95, Mexico 1990-95, Panama 1989-95, Peru 1991-95 and Venezuela 1990-96 (ILO 1997) (see Tables 5 and 6).

On average, for the nine countries included, both employment and income per worker increased in the 1990s, but the distribution of income favored the upper 20% of the families. Employment grew fastest in the poor households, followed by households in the upper 20% of income. Middle-income groups benefited the least. Average income, however, grew most rapidly in the higher income group, and less rapidly in the middle and most slowly among poor households. This is the consequence of the segmented access to jobs by different income groups. The poor with low human capital tend to get access to informal jobs, while the higher-income families tend to occupy better jobs. Around 70 of every 100 new jobs occupied by the poorest 40% was informal, while in the case of the middle 40%, the ratio was 52 out of every 100 new jobs. As a result, income concentration, as measured by the difference of income between the upper 20 and the bottom 40%, increased in all countries considered. Both the poor and the middle groups decreased their share of total income, with the upper 20% the only winner. Poverty however, most likely decreased. Expansion of employment and income per worker, plus an increase in the number of family members at work, resulted in higher income for the poor and a reduction of poverty in most countries during this period, except Mexico and Venezuela.

Table 5

Latin America. Selected countries

Indicators of employment transformation, informality and average income growth by income levels, 1990-1996 a/

(percentages and annual growth rates)

Country	Period	Employment b/				Informality c/				Average income of the employed d/			
		Total	Low	Medium	High	Total	Low	Medium	High	Total	Low	Medium	High
Argentina	(1990-96)	0.5	1.0	1.2	-1.3	66	79	77	—	4.5	3.5	4.2	6.4
Brazil	(1992-95)	3.5	5.8	2.2	3.5	81	66	85	95	1.3	1.3	1.2	1.5
Chile	(1990-96)	3.1	3.8	2.7	2.9	29	14	30	42	5.6	4.1	5.8	5.9
Colombia	(1992-96)	1.8	1.2	1.9	2.6	37	—	66	22	3.6	2.5	3.3	3.9
Costa Rica	(1990-95)	4.4	3.7	3.5	7.0	51	70	48	42	1.9	-0.6	1.4	2.7
Mexico	(1990-95)	6.4	7.8	6.0	5.5	58	87	54	18	-2.1	-3.8	-2.1	0.2
Panama	(1989-95)	6.8	6.3	7.2	6.8	38	45	35	31	1.4	2.6	0.6	2.2
Peru	(1991-95)	5.1	6.3	4.2	5.4	69	97	51	32	3.0	2.7	-0.2	3.0
Venezuela	(1990-96)	2.6	2.3	2.2	3.8	77	100	87	31	-10.3	-11.5	-9.8	-9.1

Source: ILO, based on household surveys in Argentina (Greater Buenos Aires), Brazil (urban area), Chile (urban area), Colombia (10 metropolitan areas), Costa Rica (urban area), Mexico (39 cities), Panama (metropolitan area), Peru (metropolitan Lima) and Venezuela (urban area).

a/ Data refers to those employed in the urban areas, excluding the agricultural and mining sectors. Workers have been grouped according to income levels determined by quintiles of per capita income of households. The income levels correspond to: low (quintile I + quintile II), medium (quintile III + quintile IV) and high (quintile V). All indicators refer to the indicated period in each country.

b/ Annual growth rate of employment (average of the period).

c/ Percentage of new jobs in informal activities during the period.

d/ Annual growth rate of average income of the employed measured in constant prices (average of the period).

Table 6:
Latin America. Selected countries
Distribution of income of the employed by income levels, 1990-1996 a/
(percentages)

Country and levels	Low	Medium	High	Ratio of Inequality b/
Argentina				
1990	7.9	34.6	57.5	7.0
1996	6.8	35.4	57.8	8.0
Variation	-1.1	0.8	0.3	
Brazil				
1992	5.1	29.2	65.7	19.2
1995	5.3	27.3	67.4	21.5
Variation	0.2	-1.9	1.7	
Chile				
1990	11.3	30.7	58.0	9.4
1996	10.8	30.6	58.6	10.4
Variation	-0.5	-0.1	0.6	
Colombia				
1992	16.8	33.5	49.7	4.3
1996	15.6	33.0	51.4	4.6
Variation	-1.2	-0.5	1.7	
Costa Rica				
1990	19.2	41.6	39.2	3.0
1995	15.8	38.7	45.5	3.4
Variation	-3.4	-2.9	6.3	
Mexico				
1990	15.0	37.5	47.5	6.0
1995	14.3	35.9	49.8	7.1
Variation	-0.7	-1.6	2.3	
Panama				
1989	14.3	37.7	48.0	4.7
1995	14.7	35.9	49.4	4.7
Variation	0.4	-1.8	1.4	
Peru				
1991	13.2	34.7	52.1	7.9
1995	14.2	30.9	54.9	8.5
Variation	1.0	-3.8	2.8	
Venezuela				
1990	18.4	38.5	43.1	4.7
1996	13.6	39.0	47.4	7.6
Variation	-4.8	0.5	4.3	

Source: ILO, based on household surveys in Argentina (Greater Buenos Aires), Brazil (urban area), Chile (urban area), Colombia (10 metropolitan areas), Costa Rica (urban area), Mexico (39 cities), Panama (metropolitan area), Peru (metropolitan Lima) and Venezuela (urban area).

a/ Constant prices.

b/ The rate of inequality measures the relation between the nominal average income of the high level (quintile V) and that corresponding to low income (quintile I and II).

Figure 3
Latin America – Selected Countries
Income and employment growth by levels, 1990-1996
(percentages)

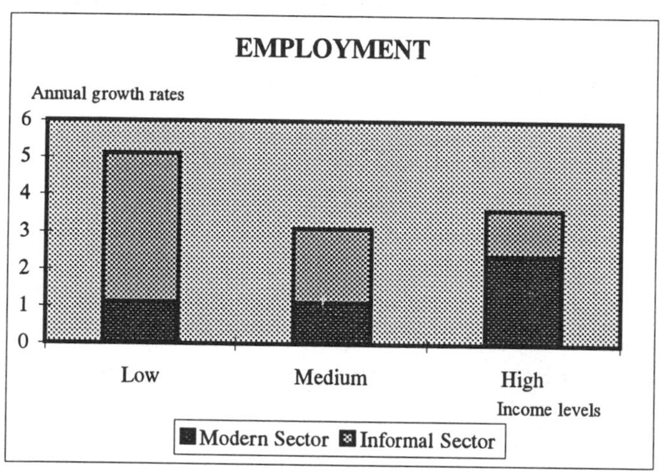

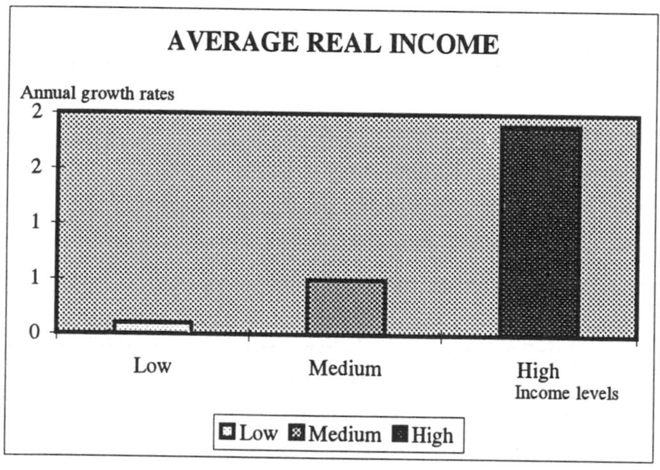

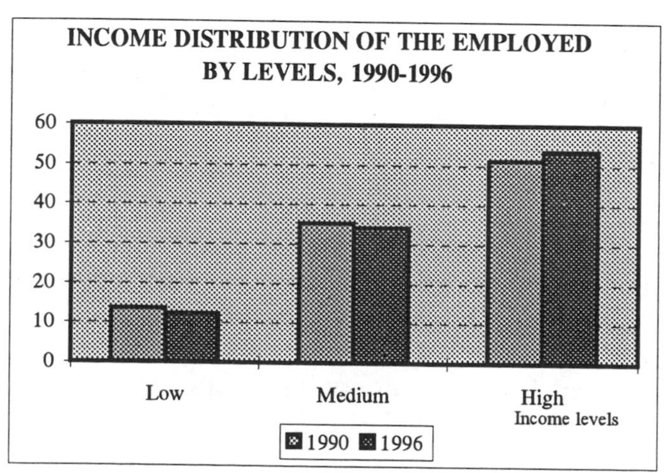

The situation is fairly homogeneous by country. Incomes per worker grew fastest in the upper-income group in all countries, and employment did so in six of nine countries considered. The situation becomes more diverse in relation to the evolution of the poor and middle groups. Employment grew more rapidly in most countries for the poorest 40% than for the middle 40%. However, income per worker grew faster for the middle-income group than the low-income group for six of nine countries studied. As noted earlier, this was the result of differentiated access to jobs. Income differentials between the upper 20% and the bottom 40% increased in all cases, with the cost being borne by the poor and the middle groups. In half the countries, the poor lost more ground than the middle class, while in the remainder, it was the reverse.

Adjustment, global economies and social stratification

Both the processes of adjustment of national economies and their subsequent economic integration into the international setting have had a significant impact on the social stratification system. This is because this system is mainly based on the occupational structure that in turn has changed, insofar as the labor market has been transformed by economic restructuring. Some of these changes and their sociological consequences will be analyzed below. In particular, we will examine four processes of change. The first is the relationship between public employment transformation and middle class impoverishment. The second is how privatization generates increased social heterogeneity, as a result of both involuntary labor mobility and expansion of outsourcing. The third is the influence of transnationalization on labor relation systems. Finally, we look at the increased differentiation emerging in expanding occupational areas, like microenterprises and agriculture.

1. Public employment and the middle class

The first important issue concerns the new role of the state, and its impact upon the labor market. This transformation has had two main effects. In the first instance, in practically all countries of the region, there has been a decrease in public employment. On average, as a proportion of the economically active population, public employment decreased from 16% at the beginning of the 1980s to 13% today, i.e., a fall of almost 20%. This average masks particularly steep drops in some countries. For example, between 1990 and 1997, public employment decreased by 32% in Argentina, in Bolivia by 33%, in Costa Rica by 22% and in Panama by 28%. This process has had an important influence on social stratification in Latin America. It is a well documented fact that the origins and development of the middle class in Latin America was closely associated with the role of the State in the promotion of social and economic development during this century. While in some countries it started during the early decades of the century, in others it took place after the Second World War, and in some it is still occurring. Nevertheless, it has been a generalized process. This role encompassed the creation of public employment and the hiring of civil servants to implement the development policies of the state, including health, education, public works, and housing. The state played a role in the creation of employment in public enterprises of all different sorts, but essentially in those sectors considered to be of national strategic importance (utilities, main natural resources and basic industries). One example of the importance of public employment to the development of the middle class is the observation (Echeverría 1985) that, during the decade of the 1970s, 60% of all Latin American professionals were civil servants.

The occupational status of public employees who lost their jobs as a result of decreasing public employment is unclear, and probably varies among countries. In some instances, former civil servants have been eligible to receive compensation payments, with which they have been able to start their own businesses—usually as independent contractors or as microentrepreneurs. In other cases, these redundancies have produced a downward mobility. In effect, in some countries, people expelled from public administration and enterprises have suffered a process of impoverishment and loss of status, especially in the case of civil servants who were not professionals and whose status was based not on their educational attainment but on the positions they held.

Likewise, those who stayed in public employment also lost status. With the economic adjustment measures that have been taken, the importance of state administration has been reduced. At the same time, the prevailing ideological standpoint undervalues the role of the state in society, and the public function does not have the same prestige as before. One indication of this is the reduced remuneration given today to those who work as civil servants; during the 1980s, average salaries of public employees decreased by 30% (ILO 1992).

Of course, civil servants still enjoy significant employment stability, coupled with a certain amount of social protection and safety nets that, even though they are far from satisfactory, provide some security from the most evident negative trends operating in today's labor market. In addition, not all remaining civil servants moved downwards. One group, albeit small, improved their incomes and status due to their increased responsibilities and high demand from the private sector for their type of specialization. This is particularly the case for those working in essential institutions in the new economic scheme, such as those in charge of fiscal revenues or custom duties control and collection. It is also the case for regulation of the financial system as in banking, insurance and stock markets, and in the institutions created to regulate the privatized activities in social security and utilities. As a result, wage and status differentials expanded in what used to be a very homogeneous sector.

2. Social heterogeneity and privatization of public enterprises

The second feature of the changed role of the state is the process of privatization of public enterprises that has occurred throughout Latin America. Privatization has had an important impact in the way in which the labor market works, particularly concerning certain of its institutional characteristics. Labor market flexibility has been achieved by various means. The first is a greater ability to dismiss workers. In almost all public enterprises that were privatized, a proportion of the labor force was made redundant, generating in the first instance an increase in unemployment. This process of course was similar to that taking place in the private sector. Some of these workers have not been able to find stable work and have become downwardly mobile, alternating between periods of underemployment and unemployment. Others have found employment similar to the jobs they had when working for public enterprises. Finally, the rest have transformed themselves in entrepreneurs, creating their own enterprises that oftentimes are functionally linked with the large enterprise in which they were formerly employed. Thus, when workers and employees in general are dismissed from the newly privatized enterprises, some of their previous functions, maybe even essential ones, are outsourced, and enterprises subcontract with smaller firms to fulfill these roles. In this way, a chain of subcontracting is established. These institutional arrangements have been traditionally quite common in some economic sectors, for example in the construction sector. Today, they are also present in the primary sectors, basic utilities, telecommunications, commerce and financial services.

Outsourcing introduces greater flexibility for enterprises, allowing them to respond adequately to fluctuations in the economic setting. Although there has been no thorough macroevaluation in terms of income and employment, national case studies show that the impact is heterogeneous. For example, in the Chilean public mining sector, where extensive redundancies have been made to reduce production costs, many workers have been re-hired under subcontracts. While they have indeed lost employment stability and significant non-wage benefits, they have improved in terms of working conditions and rate of accidents (ILO 1998b). On the other hand, in many other cases the conditions of income and employment have deteriorated. Precarious jobs abound in different sectors and countries, where subcontracting is becoming a common feature of the labor market. In these cases, temporary jobs, lack of social security coverage, absence of unions, collective bargaining, and training mechanisms may well be the norm, although they may go together with higher salaries.

3. Transnational enterprises and their social effects

Privatization of public enterprises has also increased the presence of transnational corporations. This has generated a new managerial stratum, characterized by very high incomes, an international outlook (as opposed to national interests), and a corporate ideology based on the idea that globalization redefines national boundaries and local interests. This stratum is present not only in privatized public enterprises but also in private enterprises, particularly concentrated in commerce, financial services and industry. One of the effects of the transnational status of these managers is that they tend to apply an international standard to labor relations in their management style, not recognizing national and local characteristics. On many occasions, they are also shareholders in the company, thus in practice being pragmatically concerned with the interests of the enterprise. But at a macro level they are also involved in making the whole economic system work, insofar as the results of the capital and financial markets are directly linked with their own total incomes. (In those countries where privatized pension funds have been allowed to invest in shares, this is also the case for all those workers and employees who participate in the system.)

One specific form of transnational presence is the so-called *maquila*, which refers to the transfer of certain parts of the production process of a company to another country, usually justified in terms of lower labor costs that have an important direct effect on total production costs. (Labor costs represent 54% of total costs in the typical *maquila* of Central America, where the labor costs are 3.5 times lower than in the US). In some areas of Latin America, this form of production is increasingly important. In Central America, *maquilas* now account for 250,000 jobs (400,000 if the Dominican Republic is included), representing 30% of employment in the formal industrial sector, 20% of the export value added, and around 10% of industrial GNP (ILO 1997b). Therefore, the impact of *maquilas* has been significant, and in some cases particularly disadvantaged groups in the labor market, mainly women, have benefited from the presence of *maquilas* in their respective countries. It has become a means of increasing their labor force participation, and this labor force is a social stratum clearly dependent on the transnational activities of firms from the developed world, favored by the globalization of national economies.

However, the same study shows that labor standards and even human rights are not always respected. The existence of sweatshops is widespread, although there is increasing pressure for foreign firms to comply with minimum standards in their host countries. The question that remains to be answered is whether this is at all possible when low labor costs are the driving force behind the very existence of the *maquilas*.

4. Microenterprises and the informal sector

Microenterprises, many of them informal, have been by and large the principal sources of employment in Latin America during the last decade. The social effects of this trend have been important. To begin with, it has weakened the salaried workforce that traditionally was the source of the labor movement. The blue-collar permanent worker of medium and large industrial companies has been increasingly outnumbered by wage earners in microenterprises. Others have been transformed into independent contractors, mainly in the commercial and services sectors.

The evolution of microenterprises has, in many cases, reflected their relationship to the international economy. While a large majority of microenterprises caters for national markets, a proportion is now linked, through exports, to the world economy. Some authors have argued that this "neo-informality" characterizes present labor markets, particularly when enterprises form part of subcontracting chains with foreign companies, *maquilas*, and when they have found defined niches in specific external markets (Pérez-Sáinz 1996). However, in all of them there is no important division between labor and capital.

At this stage, it seems important to recall that the evolution of social stratification in Latin America had been, up until the 1970s, a relatively straightforward process in which the labor force had experienced a clear social structural mobility. Indeed, the research carried out by Germani and Medina Echeverría, among others, suggested that there was a secular trend of upward mobility from low-productivity occupations to higher-productivity ones. This was mostly envisaged as a shift between sectors (from agriculture to manufacture and services) and between occupational categories (from blue collar to non-manual) (see Filgueira y Gianeletti, 1981).

This seems to be no longer the case. This paper argues that one of the results of adjustment policies and the globalization of national economies has been the development of heterogeneous characteristics inside segments of the labor market, and this phenomena is best seen when the microenterprises sector is analyzed. "Small scale" means many different things both in economic and social terms. Some microenterprises are highly capitalized, linked to dynamic markets, inserted in leading sectors, with an increasingly qualified labor force, while others still are conventional in terms of capital and labor use. Hence, heterogeneity is increasing as a result of present economic trends: those employed in enterprises that are linked to the developed strata have benefited in income and employment opportunities (although not necessarily in quality of employment), and those who remain disconnected from the main thrust of the economy have lagged behind. They continue to work in low-productivity occupations, with low skills and little job security.

Sectorial analysis

Heterogeneous trends in the labor market and their social impact can also be observed at the sectorial level. Depending of the way in which enterprises are linked with the rest of the economy (national and international), social strata will vary. The case of the development of agriculture clearly illustrates this point. Those agro-industrial sectors that have grown because of external markets have required a different type of labor force and have generated a set of new occupations than those previously present in traditional agriculture. First, they require a relatively trained and skilled labor force. Second, they generate mostly temporary jobs. Third, they have opened up new alternatives of wage employment for people that previously were unemployed and/or not economically active, particularly women. Their increased participation in the labor market has brought forward changes in the organization of the family and the distribution of roles inside it. Finally, most of these jobs are remunerated according to the productivity of labor. Compare these characteristics with those of the salaried permanent male worker occupied in an agriculture dedicated to traditional crops, with low skills and, if lucky, earning a minimum wage. Therefore, in the same economic sector, the variety of occupations has increased in terms of the required supply of labor, its personal characteristics, productivity standards, and permanence in the labor market.

Final remarks

Globalization cannot be isolated from the other policies that accompanied it during the last two decades. They constitute a policy compact that analytically and factually is very difficult to decompose. Three processes have been scrutinized: *globalization, privatization and deregulation.* The effects on social stratification, mainly through labor market outcomes, have been the focus of our analysis, because the occupational structure is the basis of the system of stratification.

The main conclusion is that the social structure in Latin America has been under tension during the reform period. This tension has affected social coherence and introduced increased heterogeneity. As in all processes, there are winners and losers. The difference this time is that changes are substantial and structurally affect not only the present but also the future of people, society and nations.

The change has not been, particularly during the 1990s, all for the worst. Poverty is showing a declining trend, and the poor are better off in terms of income. However, equity has deteriorated. The winners are a minority, while the rest, not only the poor but also the middle-income groups, increasingly lag behind in relative terms. The effects of the policy compact on employment and labor incomes, as well as unequal opportunities, have proven to be an important determinant of this result. In a region where inequality is the highest of the world, this constitutes an unwelcome trend.

There seems to be enough evidence to sustain the proposition that the policy compact has had concentrated effects. Most of the positive impacts benefited sectors that already were located in the upper echelons of the income distribution: the policy compact has favored the relatively rich. Those negative effects that have taken place in the labor market as a result of the policy impact—"precarization" of working conditions (lack of contracts, of social protection, etc.), "tertiarization" and "informalization" as well as unemployment—have been mostly concentrated among the sectors that were already relatively poor. Thus, differences have increased. Wage earners may even have higher salaries than in the recent past, but their jobs are in many instances more precarious and informal. In these cases, workers' status has changed for the worst.

The middle stratum has also experienced decreased levels of welfare. The paper described the negative impacts of the compact on public employment, and its consequent effect on social stratification. There is also a need to add that the benefits of social policies have diminished, insofar as these policies have become more focused on the poor at the expense of the middle-income groups. Consequently, the middle classes are less protected against unemployment and bad working conditions, public transfers (via subsidies) have diminished and many occupations that hitherto provided them with status have either lost their social significance or disappeared altogether.

This unequal distribution of gains and losses seems to be even more regrettable since high hopes are placed on the positive effects of globalization— a path to which all Latin American countries adhered from the early stages— on growth, equity and social integration. The issue however, is how far globalization has added additional distortions to an already unbalanced social situation. To place it in the right perspective, it should be recalled that the point of departure did not facilitate the process of social adjustment under globalization, since high income concentration and severe macroeconomic unbalances restricted any positive effects that could have emerged from closer integration to the world economy. The analysis should be then focused more on the post-adjustment situation.

As shown, there were fundamental changes in the employment structure as well as in incomes and job quality. Most of them constituted a downward move for people. Unemployment, a new feature in the scenario, also contributed to social exclusion. Volatility, associated with the functioning of a more open economy, also added instability in jobs and incomes. Unsurprisingly, the main worry of people in the region today is jobs and the main fears are instability and loss of labor protection. Demands for increased labor protection during times of adjustment were stymied by the need to save resources, and particularly for government to correct fiscal imbalances.

Globalization adds new dimensions to economic analysis of labor markets, given the increased link to trade, finance and communications at international level. The old center-periphery analysis, which strongly influenced Latin American intellectual tradition, is giving way to dependency and marginality analysis. Linkages today are not only closer but also of a different nature. Heterogeneity has increased.

A direct way to look at this relationship is by identifying those population groups that are more closely related to the global economy than they are to the country in which they live. An interesting case to illustrate the situation is Mexico, one of the countries in the region with perhaps more exposure to globalization in the recent past. Castañeda (1996) identifies four groups directly dependent on US economic behavior, amounting to 20-25% of the Mexican population. The first group is Mexican migrants living in the US. They constitute a source of income for an estimated 10 million Mexicans residents. Income remittances constitute an important and exponentially growing contribution for poor families (it is estimated that remittances in 1998 were US$5.5 billion and have tripled since 1990). A second group is related to exports, including *maquilas*, which include 2,500 establishments and benefit an additional two million people. It also includes other export-related activities in agriculture and manufacturing industry. Several examples serve as illustrations. General Motors of Mexico, the main private exporter of the country, is selling 40% more cars abroad than internally. Corona, the main beer producer, sell one bottle abroad for each bottle for the internal market, and Cementos Mexicanos exported 90% of its production in 1993.

A third group whose livelihood is dependent on foreigners is the tourist sector. It is estimated that 600,000 Mexicans are employed in this activity and hence isolated from internal fluctuations. Finally, there is a large number of people that are linked to foreign countries, as legal or illegal property owners, or simply because they save, own assets, use financial instruments (like credit cards) or study or temporarily work abroad in professional and technical jobs.

Castañeda's analysis can be extended to the rest of Latin America, with different proportions involved but with similar types of relations. Our own analysis also shows that not all sectors and occupations within sectors have become global. The effects have not been homogeneous. Not all sectors have been equally affected, and *intra* sectors, the impact has been differentiated. Parts of industry have integrated into the world economy, while others lagged behind; e.g., agro-industry has established strong links with international markets, while traditional peasant agriculture has remained autonomous. Occupations have become more heterogeneous, both *inter and intra* sectors. This is particularly the case in *maquilas,* in tourism and in subcontracting in manufacturing industry. Enterprises and hence, owners, managers, technicians and skilled labor are incorporated in the global economy; unskilled laborers, while better off than before, are in a precarious situation, characterized by poor incomes, instability and lack of protection. Unemployment has added to social exclusion, particularly of young people and women.

Changes in the social structure have resulted from the effects on labor markets; the diverse degree of global economic integration of different population groups goes beyond jobs and incomes and permeates social habits. Cultural and economic differences are translated into diverse social behavior. Urban life sees increasing segregation with *ghettos* for the rich on top of the traditional ones for the poor. Closed areas, private security, exclusive malls, clubs, and even schools, conspire against social integration. Public spaces, like parks and entertainment, which encouraged social interaction in the past, are less available. Separate schools divide children by social groups (Tokman and O'Donnell 1998). As O'Donnell (1988) puts it,

> *The sharp, and deepening, dualism of our countries severely hinders the emergence of broad and effective solidarity. Social distances have increased, and the rich tend to isolate themselves from the strange and disquieting world of the dispossessed. The fortified ghettos of the rich and the secluded schools of their children bear witness of their incorporation into the transnationalized networks of modernity, as well as to the gulf that separates them from large segments of the national population.*

Social categories—as key instruments to analyze social stratification and social inclusion—are under fundamental conceptual change. The issue today is not of class, or ideology, or regions (as correctly argued by Castañeda 1996). It is not class, because the family of the migrants or the workers in some export sectors benefit as do owners and managers. It is not ideology, because ideas are today increasingly exposed and nurtured by transnational events in a communications revolution. Nor it is a question of North against the South, since the new economic scenario and world ideological change blur divisions of the past. It goes beyond all this. Social groups are structured by occupations as in the past, but sectors tend to lose meaning when heterogeneity prevails, and more important, when people are culturally and economically related in a different manner to national and international interests.■

References

Atkinson, A.B., 1996. Income distribution in Europe and the United States. *Oxford Review of Economic Policy.*

Castañeda, J, 1996. *The Estados Unidos affair.* Cinco ensayos sobre un "amor" oblicuo (México).

Comisión Económica para América Latina y el Caribe (CEPAL), 1997a. *La brecha de la equidad. América Latina, el Caribe y la Cumbre Social.*

Comisión Económica para América Latina y el Caribe, 1997b. Rasgos estilizados de la distribución del ingreso en cinco países de América Latina y lineamientos generales para una política redistributiva. Proyecto Gobierno Holanda/CEPAL: "Distribución del ingreso y pobreza en políticas recientes de estabilizacón y ajuste en países de América Latina y el Caribe" (Serie Financiamiento del Desarrollo N° 72).

Echeverría, R, 1985. Empleo público en América Latina. Serie Investigaciones sobre Empleo (Santiago: Programa Regional del Empleo para América Latina y el Caribe).

Filgueira, C. & Gianeletti, C., 1981. Estratificación y movilidad ocupacional en América Latina. Cuadernos de la CEPAL N° 39 (Santiago: CEPAL).

Germani, G., 1969. Sociología de la modernización. (Buenos Aires: Paídos).

Inter-American Development Bank, 1998. América Latina frente a la desigualdad. Progreso económico y social en América Latina. (Washington D.C.: IDB)

International Labor Organization, 1992. Memoria del Director General. Decimotercera Conferencia de los Estados de América Miembros de la Organización Internacional del Trabajo (Geneva: ILO).

International Labor Organization, 1996. World employment report: National policies in a global context. (Geneva: ILO).

International Labor Organization, 1997a. Labor Overview '97 (Lima: ILO Regional Office).

International Labor Organization, 1997b. La industria de la maquila en Centroamérica (San Jose: ILO).

International Labor Organization, 1998a. Labor Overview '98 (Lima: ILO Regional Office).

International Labor Organization, 1998b. Chile: crecimiento, empleo y el desafío de la justicia social (Santiago: ILO).

Krugman, P, 1995. The age of diminished expectation. (Cambridge: MIT Press).

Lustig, N, 1998. Pobreza y desigualdad: un desafío que perdura. Revista de la CEPAL. Número extraordinario (Reflexiones sobre América Latina) (Santiago: CEPAL).

Martínez, D. & Tokman, V.E., 1997. Costo laboral y competitividad en el sector manufacturero de América Latina in Costos laborales y competitividad industrial en América Latina., ed. E. Amadeo et.al. (Lima: ILO Regional Office).

Martínez, D. & Tokman, V.E, 1999. Flexibilización en el margen (Lima: ILO) (in publication).

Medina Echeverría, J., 1973. Aspectos sociales del desarrollo económico. (Santiago de Chile:CEPAL).

Meller, P. & Tokman, A, 1996. Chile: Apertura comercial, empleo y salarios. Documento de Trabajo N° 38 (Lima: ILO Regional Office).

O'Donnell, G., 1998. Poverty and inequality in Latin America: some political reflections in Poverty and inequality in Latin America: Issues and new challenges, ed. V.E. Tokman & G. O'Donnell (University of Notre Dame).

Organization for Economic Cooperation and Development, 1994. Perspectivas del empleo. The OECD Jobs study. Facts, analysis, strategies (Paris: OECD).

Páez de Barros, R. y otros, 1996. Brasil: Apertura comercial e mercado de trabalho. Documento de Trabajo N° 39 (Lima: ILO Regional Office).

Pérez Sáinz, J.P, 1996. De la finca a la maquila (San Jose: Facultad Latinoamericana de Ciencias Sociales).

Saavedra, J, 1996. Perú: Apertura comercial, empleo y salarios. Documento de Trabajo N° 40 (Lima: ILO Regional Office).

Tokman, V.E, 1997. Jobs and solidarity: challenges for post-adjustment in Latin America in Economic and social development into the XXI Century, ed. L. Emmerij (Washington, DC: Inter-American Development Bank).

Tokman, V.E, 1998. Jobs and welfare: searching for new answers in Poverty and inequality in Latin America. Issues and new challenges, ed. V.E. Tokman & G. O'Donnell (University of Notre Dame).

Tokman, V.E. & O'Donnell, G, eds., 1998. Poverty and inequality in Latin America. Issues and new challenges (University of Notre Dame, 1998).

Williamson, J. 1990. Latin American adjustment: how much has happened? Institute for International Economics (Washington D.C., IDB).

Developing Countries In The Global Economy: A Forward-Looking View

John Whalley

This paper discusses what the next few decades could bring for the developing countries in terms of the size and composition of their trade and inward investment flows, as well as a possibly changing policy framework within the global economy in which they have to operate. Both the prospects and implications are clearly different from country to country, but given the breadth of the paper the focus is more on impacts on groups of countries rather than on specific countries.

In the shorter term, the influence of the current financial crises on previous strong trade performance is a concern, especially in Asia, although the positive exchange rate effects on the export side should eventually lead to even more elevated trade performance, assuming no major recession in the countries of the Organization for Economic Cooperation and Development (OECD). On the other hand, countries concerned by the large adjustments costs they face when excess volatility in global financial markets also affects their own economy,[1] and typified by Malaysia, are tightening their foreign exchange and investment regimes. This may limit their capital inflows and slow trade growth, which, for several key countries over the last decade, has been closely linked to direct inward foreign investment.

Assuming a recovery from the current financial turbulence over a period of three to five years, however, questions will still remain about how developing country participation in the global economy in the decade beyond will evolve. Can developing country involvement in the global economy accelerate further? Can their trade shares in developed country markets grow yet more, and for each exporter? Is there a fallacy of composition involved, that with initially only a few countries being able to successfully pursue an outward-oriented strategy (as against the 100 or some countries now that are attempting to do so), the increases in aggregate import volumes into the OECD markets cannot support success for all these countries? Can the growth of their trade perhaps be fuelled by more rapidly growing South-South trade as more and more developing countries achieve higher levels of income in a recovery phase, or for now does this remain too small? Equally, while investment flows into developing country markets have accelerated in the pre-crisis period, they remain concentrated, particularly in Asia and heavily in China. Is breaking away from this concentration is a further key element in a strategy for broadening trade and income growth in the developing world?

Independently of whether this accelerating trade performance can continue, the unevenness of impact of global developments on individual developing countries and the marginalization which has affected the lower income countries, particularly the poorer and smaller countries in sub-Saharan Africa, is an issue.[2] These countries remain almost exclusively commodity exporters; some have export revenues equal to only a small fraction of import costs, with the balance financed by aid flows (Mozambique is such an example). While many of these countries have been affected by political problems, civil unrest, and macroeconomic mismanagement, as commodity prices have fallen they have experienced sharp declines in their trade shares as a fraction of overall world trade, with in some cases, absolute declines in trade in value terms. To these countries, the outward-oriented strategies pursued in Korea and Taiwan since the 1960's seem to be so far removed from their current situation as to be irrelevant. Diversification of trade is sometimes held out as the way forward, but how is this to be achieved? Is it really as simple as establishing a stable pro-investment policy regime, and foreign investment will flow into these countries and trade will grow? At present, the core development strategy being offered by the World Bank and the International Monetary Fund (IMF) to such countries is policy reform, linked to opening of the external sector. But for the least developed countries, to place such a large bet on trade as the engine of their future growth seems extreme given their current situation. How to deal with the performance of the lowest-income countries within the global framework of the next two decades is thus also a central concern.

The policy environment that developing countries are likely to face in the global economy may also see sharp change over the next twenty or thirty years. A potential new round of World Trade Organization (WTO) trade negotiations, the Millennium Round, is widely mooted. Regional trade agreements may continue their spread across the globe, but regional conflict (as presently between the US and the European Union (EU) over bananas) may grow. Particularly critical is that the reductions in trade barriers on manufactured products which have taken place in the OECD countries over the post-war years have, in the tariff area, reached levels for which significant further reductions are to all intents and purposes inconsequential, except for a few product concentrated tariffs, such as in textiles and apparel. The odds seem to be that trade barriers on manufactured goods against developing countries, with little further downside potential, may begin to go up rather than down, while barriers on agricultural products, long thought poor prospects for developing country exports, may fall.

Key also are proposals linking increased trade barriers (sanctions) to developing country compliance with developed country policy objectives (including in environment and labour standards), and anti-dumping actions. The threat of increased trade barriers if compliance does not occur may increasingly be used to force countries to modify their domestic policies as Mexico experienced in their 1990 tuna dispute with the US. Thus, after fifty years of ever falling tariff barriers in developed country markets, the next thirty to forty years may well see pressures to raise barriers, fuelled in part by developed-country political interests wanting protection against competing imports. These could be likely key issues that developing countries will have to deal with in a future round of trade negotiations.

In addition to possible barrier increases, the developing countries may also face ever broadening WTO negotiations within the global trade policy framework. These will likely come on top of WTO Uruguay Round negotiations, which have only just concluded, and will involve complex issues on which few countries are fully informed. Developing countries have been somewhat passive in their approach to the prospect of such negotiations, usually attempting to resist broadening, and trying to mitigate potential negative effects of any broadening that might occur. Broadening of this type occurred in the 1990's in the WTO on intellectual property, and threatens to grow even further over the next ten years in a new Millennium Trade Round, into such areas as competition policy, environment, labour standards and investment.

But this changing policy framework is one that also offers opportunities for many countries. For instance, broadening the discussion of intellectual property rights negotiations to cover all forms of property rights, including those involved with environmental concerns (such as rights to emit carbon) could yield significant gains for developing countries. If the argument were accepted that developed countries had largely used up their emission rights cumulatively over their period of industrialization, and hence had to buy rights from individual developing countries, significant new flows of development assistance could result. In the area of environment, one in which developing countries have long resisted trade linkage, it seems clear that countries with significant environmental assets (Indonesia, Malaysia, Thailand, the Democratic Republic of the Congo, Cameroon, Brazil, and countries with significant forest cover, for instance) have the capability to make significant concessions in order to achieve benefits in other areas, such as trade and investment, if they choose to use it. This is because they are the custodians of major environmental assets and have significant global leverage in this area. Broadened negotiations thus offer countries opportunities as well as threats. And countries without the environmental endowments to make larger concessions, if they are to be beneficiaries of a trade and environment bargain, may want to support such a bargain by making concessions to other developing countries. Increased South-South trade could even flow from such arrangements.

Finally, there are the finance-related issues of a global exchange rate regime in turmoil following the onset of financial crises, and the clear weakening of the position of the IMF on these matters. Formulating a developing country strategy for international financial arrangements over the next two decades would seem to be paramount. And more broadly, the Bretton Woods institutions themselves, which were designed to deal with the problems of the 1940's, are now coming under increasing stress and even re-examination as discussion of new global arrangements into the next century gets under way. Developing country participation in these discussions will be central, and prior to that a clear sense of what the developing country interests are in different options needs to be formulated.

The bottom line of the paper, however, is a cautious one. Three nagging questions are repeatedly re-emphasized. Can trade growth really be high enough on the import side in the OECD, if now 100 or more developing countries see globalization and increased exports as their primary route to growth, industrialization, and development? Can barrier reductions in OECD markets and future WTO negotiations be relied on to fuel this, as in the past, or is there a more sinister scenario, in which increased barriers could choke off some trade growth? And what is to happen to development strategies if this course fails, as it seemingly already has done for the low-income countries? Having posed these questions, there are bright spots: the more rapid growth of South-South trade, especially of least-developed to mid-developed country trade; higher growth rates of foreign direct investment (FDI) than trade, and more and more developing country trade being investment-driven. The paper's overriding message is perhaps that the world is not static, and country strategies toward the global economy need to reflect this.

The paper first discusses developing country trade performance in recent years, highlighting its rapidly changing size and composition. It then moves to a discussion of the policy framework for future trade growth, including the prospects for a WTO Millennium Round. It concludes with a discussion of developmental strategies for developing countries that rely on their increasing integration into the global economy.

Developing country trade performance in the global economy

Trade-led development strategies

Over the last ten to fifteen years, more and more developing countries have placed a larger and larger bet on a development strategy of ever more integration by them into the global economy; a so-called outward-oriented strategy. In the 1950's, the countries that made this bet, Hong Kong and Taiwan (and a little later Korea), achieved spectacular results. Their very success was influential from the mid-1980's on, persuading perhaps a hundred or more other developing countries around the world that their future also lay in opening up their economies to trade, and exploiting the opportunities which they saw as emanating from more involvement with the global economy. The late 1980's and early 1990's saw the most extensive and far reaching trade liberalization ever achieved globally, and it was undertaken unilaterally (not negotiated multilaterally) and by the developing countries.

The financial crises of the last year have raised the obvious question as to whether this strategy has proved to be a little naïve, in terms of the excess weight which it places on global involvement as the main development strategy. Compounding such concerns is the bifurcated record of success (until last year) by the high-growth, larger and middle-income developing countries (in Asia and Latin America) and the poor trade and growth record and even marginalization of many low-income countries. In the 1930's, there was an active debate on whether trade was the engine or handmaiden of growth, a debate which in the 1990's has seemingly been lost in the assertion that it clearly is the engine. The experience of financial turbulence and negative growth in marginalized low-income countries revives that debate.

In reality, the developing countries are a heterogeneous group, and they have gone through many twists and turns over the last forty years in deciding upon their approach to trade-related issues. Besides sub-Saharan Africa and a small number of lower-income, non-African countries, developing countries have, in the main, been successful in raising the level of their participation in the global economy. Their exports of industrial products (especially from Asia) have soared, the higher-GDP-growth countries have been the rapidly growing exporters, and over thirty years, the more successful of those adopting this strategy have seen a five-fold increase in real income per capita.

In the 1950's, developing countries argued that their balance-of-payments problems made it impossible for them to liberalize their trade regimes. Facing ever declining terms of trade, they argued that they should jointly seek preferential access to developed country markets without liberalizing in their own markets. This strategy, which was initially pursued as a common approach by all developing countries with the exceptions of Hong Kong and Taiwan (and later Korea), became identified with the slogan of "special and differential treatment".[3] Through the middle of the 1980's, most countries supported a blocwide trade and development negotiating strategy, jointly emphasizing their need both to protect their own domestic markets and for preferential access to developed country markets. In essence, the argument was that to grow developing countries needed both special treatment and insulation from the forces of globalization. In the 1970's, coincident with these lines of argumentation, developing country exports began to surge.

Beginning in the mid-1980's, and reflecting growth generally in manufactured exports from Latin America and Asia, a number of developing countries began to change course and adopt a more open trade approach, focussing now on the need to liberalize to harness gains from trade and the long-run welfare benefits from unilateral trade liberalization. These developments were driven by North America-trained meritocrats, first in Latin American countries and subsequently elsewhere, and were strongly supported by the World Bank and the IMF. Country after country in the mid- to late 1980's moved to deep unilateral liberalization, not only in trade, but also in policies towards foreign investment. The result was a dramatic reduction in barriers to trade and inward capital flows in developing countries. Accompanying these changes were also clear movements away from a common developing-country negotiating position on global trade issues, and towards pursuit of individual country interest, even where this conflicted with other developing countries. Argentina, for instance, argued for global liberalization in grains and beef, and Thailand in rice, even if net food-importing countries, such as Egypt, were opposed on the grounds of wanting to remain beneficiaries of agricultural export subsidies from Europe.

The idea that a common blocwide position of special and differential treatment should be pursued as the pivotal developing country trade and development strategy has continued to weaken since the mid-1980's, and the strength of trade performance of developing countries has if anything, accelerated, at least until the onset of the current financial crises. Thus, putting on one side the marginalized lower income countries, developing country trade on the whole has showed remarkable gains over the last forty years, even though the developing countries have vacillated in their approach to both trade negotiations and their own trade policies.

Trade Performance

Table 1 sets out the 1995 export, import, and FDI performance of developing countries—as classified by the United Nations Conference on Trade and Development (UNCTAD)—reporting imports and exports in 1995 dollars and as a percentage of all trade.

Table 1: Trade and Investment Flows of the Developing Countries

	Billions of $US (1995)	% of Worldwide Flow
Imports	1,493	29.1
Exports	1,406	27.7
FDI	96.3	30.4
FDI (least developed countries)	1.02	0.3

Sources: UNCTAD (1997a) Tables 1.1, 1.2; UNCTAD (1997b) Table B.1.

The term 'developing country' implies a uniformity across countries, which in practice can be a little misleading. Per capita income ranges from highs of $20,000 in Singapore, to about $100 in Somalia and some of the lower-income African economies. And as emphasized in Whalley (1989), these differences in income levels are also accompanied by diversity in growth performance, trade patterns, degrees of industrialization, patterns of capital formation, and social welfare systems. The developing countries are in reality heterogeneous, and it is often difficult to discuss them as if they were a single, monolithic group.

The data in Table 1, despite this heterogeneity, indicate that developing countries now play a large and (until recently) growing role in the global economy, accounting for a little under 30% of world trade on both the import and export sides. Since exports of affiliated companies of foreign parents account for nearly 50% of developing country exports[4], it follows that inward foreign investment flows to these countries are now a key factor underlying this trade. Foreign direct investment flows into the developing countries were perhaps $100 billion in 1995, around 30% of worldwide direct foreign investment. However, only a small (if non-negligible) fraction of these flows ($1 billion) went to the least developed countries.

Trade in industrial products

Table 2 indicates developing country trade in industrial products only. In 1994, flows totaled around $400 billion on the export side, and a little over $200 billion on the import side. Unlike two decades earlier, developing countries are now significant net exporters of industrial products, and it is these exports which have surged in recent years. Key to this performance have been low tariff barriers in OECD export markets, which now average around 2½% (with higher rates on some products such as textiles and apparel). Barriers remain on the import side in developing countries, although there has been substantial unilateral liberalization in these regions in the last few years. Average developing country trade barriers on industrial products post-Uruguay Round average 13-14%; barriers of 20-25% apply to textiles and apparel, and around 20% to imports of transportation equipment.

Table 2: Developing Country Trade in and Tariffs on Industrial Products

	Billions of $US (1994)	
Developing country exports of industrial products (1994)	433.2	
Developing country imports of industrial products (1994)	229.4	
	Applied	**Bound**
Average developing country tariff barriers (post Uruguay Round) on industrial products: of which	13.3%	13.3%
Textiles/apparel	21.2%	25.5%
Transport equipment	19.9%	13.2%
Average OECD tariff barriers (post-Uruguay Round) on industrial products of which	2.5%	3.5%
Textiles/apparel	8.4%	11.0%
Transport equipment	4.6%	5.6%

Sources: UNCTAD (1997a) Tables 3-1, A, 13; Laird (1998)

Commodity trade

In contrast to trade in industrial products, commodity-based exports have been falling sharply as a share of overall developing country trade. In the 1950's, developing countries' exports were largely commodities such as rubber, coffee, cocoa, metallic ores and other products for which there was no immediate competitor in developed country markets. As Table 3 indicates, as a fraction of all developing country exports, these accounted for perhaps 30% of the total in the 1990's, whereas in the 1960's, the figure was closer to 80%.

Most commodity exports also continue to enter developed country markets free of barriers, because of the absence of immediately competing products. This is one reason lower-income countries often see themselves as having little to gain from WTO trade negotiations. A central issue repeatedly raised by them in this area over the last thirty years is that of tariff escalation. This reflects the concern in exporting countries that, as attempts are made by them to upgrade their production through higher levels of fabrication, they have faced ever higher tariff barriers on final products. Even if there are low barriers against raw commodity exports, they argue that any attempt to export products produced from them encounters higher barriers.

Table 3 reports WTO estimates of tariff escalation in OECD markets against developing country commodity exports, showing effective barriers as high as 6% for higher stages of production, but also showing that Uruguay Round tariff barrier reductions have considerably reduced their quantitative impact. As a working hypothesis, the assumption that developing country exports of both commodities and their immediate fabricated products are restrained more by supply factors and bottlenecks than by trade barriers thus seems appropriate. If this is the case, domestic infrastructure and global prices are more important issues for exporting countries than global negotiations on trade barriers.

Commodity exports is also an area where there has been profound pessimism as to the pricing prospects for developing countries, which continues until today. The original Singer/Prebisch thesis of the 1950's argued that developing countries would always face a secular decline in their terms of trade for their commodity-based exports. The argument was that commodities are basic items with low income elasticities in trade (necessities), while developing countries tend to import equipment and machinery (luxuries) based on high income elasticities. As a result, growth in the world economy with both rich and poor countries trying to simultaneously grow would depress the prices of commodities. In recent years, particularly in the post-crisis environment and also emphasized in the recent UNCTAD *Trade and Development Report*, the pricing prospects for commodities are widely regarded as poorer than ever; again elevating concerns over marginalization of low-income, commodity-exporting countries in the global economy.

Table 3: Commodity-Based Trade of Developing Countries

	Billions of $US (1994)	% of All Developing Country Exports
Developing country commodity exports (including fuel) (1994)	$383.5	27.3
	Pre-Uruguay Round	Post-Uruguay Round
Tariff rates for commodity exports		
Raw materials	0.1	0.0
Semi-finished	6.3	3.5
Finished Goods	6.6	2.6

Sources: UNCTAD (1997a) Table A.12; GATT (1994).

Agricultural trade

A further component of developing country trade is agricultural products for which data are set out in Table 4. Agricultural products are generally regarded as being the closest to autarchy in trade (a situation where countries consume largely what they produce), in part because of the barrier structure in global agricultural trade which precludes significant amounts of trade. As a result, potential exports of agricultural products by developing countries are large, particularly for countries such as Argentina and Brazil. But as Table 4 indicates, actual exports are extremely small, around 2½% of developing country exports. The potential gains for both developing country exporters and for consumers in developed countries from a significant opening to agricultural trade in the OECD are probably larger than for another trade category, suggesting high priority in this area from the point of view of global trade negotiations.

There is, however, a divide between the developing countries in this area, since along with (actual or potential) exporters of agricultural commodities, there are large net food importers, some of which are indicated in Table 4 and most of which are least-developed poor economies. These net food importers were concerned during the Uruguay Round over the potential implications of liberalization in agriculture, since they thought that with restraints on agricultural export subsidies agricultural world prices would rise; this would affect their low-income populations, and slow their development.

Table 4: Agricultural trade of developing countries

A. Agricultural Exports of Developing Countries, 1994 (billions of US$)	As % of all developing country exports	As % of all country agricultural exports
34.9	2.5	30.9
B. Agricultural Imports, 1994 (billions of $US)		
32.9		
C. Some Examples of Net Food-Importing Countries: (% of import bill spent on food items)	Egypt (28.4), Mauritania (29.6) Equatorial Guinea (36.9) Congo (26.5) Algeria (29.5) Benin (26.3) Grenada (28.0) Jordan (20.8) Samoa (27.1) Senegal (28.7) Somalia (32.5)	

Source: UNCTAD (1997a) Table 4.2.

Trade in textiles and apparel

A further key important component of developing country trade involves trade in textiles and apparel, discussed in Table 5. Accounting for only 12% of all developing country exports, textiles and apparel typically provide the first labour-intensive manufactured produced by developing countries as they surge in their trade and move ever more heavily into production of low-wage industrial products. Thus, countries such as Korea, in the early stages of industrialization in the 1960's, had 50% or more of their exports in textiles and apparel. Even today, as Table 5 indicates, countries such as Pakistan have over 60% of their exports in textiles and apparel, with similarly high numbers for Bangladesh. Hence, textiles and apparel are an important trade item for a number of developing countries. Some have noted that they also represented the first stage of successful industrialization that OECD countries such as the UK went through in the 1850's.

Textiles and apparel exports, however, have been restricted as a result of the General Agreement on Tariffs and Trade (GATT) Multifibre Arrangement (MFA), a system of bilateral quotas between developed and developing countries designed to slow adjustments in importing countries because of the low wage and regionally concentrated use of labour involved. As a result, global liberalization in textiles and apparel has become a central issue for the developing countries, especially since this system of bilateral quotas has made it more difficult for new entrants (or potential new entrants) to textiles and apparel trade to obtain market share. Some have even suggested that the presence of the Multifibre Arrangement has been a major impediment to the integration of African countries into the global economy, because these countries know that any significant surge of textiles and apparel by them (included that generated by inward foreign investment) would eventually provoke new trade quotas.

Table 5: Developing country trade in textiles and apparel

A. Value of Developing Country Exports of Textiles and Apparel, 1994 (billions of $US)	As % of all developing country exports	As % of all developing country exports of industrial products
173.5	12.3	40.1
B. Key countries with trade dependence on textiles and apparel (share of textiles and apparel in total exports)	Pakistan, Mauritius, India (66%) (53%) (28%)	

Source: UNCTAD (1997a) Table A.11.

Outsourcing and trade

Outsourcing exports, a further important feature of developing country trade, are highlighted in Table 6.[5] These data indicate that over 40% of developing country exports are produced by domestic affiliates of foreign parent companies. Outsourcing, the more extreme form of this activity, refers to the relocation of production from developed to developing countries, to take advantage of low wage labour, improving infrastructure, and increased openness within the developing world. In the case of the United States, over a period of twenty years significant amounts of outsourcing have gone to Mexico, concentrated in the *maquiladora* zone twenty miles south of the US border. In this zone, components initially produced in the US are assembled using designs from parent establishments, before being re-exported to the US. In some cases, complete assembly occurs (as in the case of autos).

Outsourcing has been strongly promoted by a number of developing countries through export processing zones. Outsourcing activity is often claimed to account for nearly 80% of China's manufactured exports.

As outsourcing has grown, so has the importance of this trade to the developing countries. Both its form and treatment in any future global trade strategy are key to many developing countries. However, in this area of trade, the commercial interest of large OECD companies in keeping export markets open and barrier-free is a key asset to the developing countries. This form of trade is not only growing rapidly, but is virtually barrier-free and will likely stay so given the policy influence in OECD countries of parent companies. In such cases, the policy issue for host countries may be more their terms for receiving FDI (tax and regulatory treatment) than the trade treatment of exports.

Table 6: Outsourcing Exports and Developing Country Trade Performance

Foreign Affiliate exports originating in developing countries, 1994 (billions of $US)	585
As % of total exports	41.6
Key outsourcing countries	China, Indonesia, Mexico

Source: UNCTAD (1997b) Table A.5.

Services

Table 7 summarizes the developing country situation in a further key and growing element of global trade, namely trade in services. The service sector of the economy includes banking, insurance, transportation, telecommunications, tourism and other trade in non-tangible items. These non-tangible items are thought to account for around 30% of global trade. Table 7 indicates that services are a relatively small percentage of overall trade by developing countries, and that the developing countries are net importers of services.

The developing countries often see themselves as having significant export opportunities in key segments of service trade. One example is the success enjoyed by India in exports of software. However, there are still many service areas where significant impediments to trade remain in both the developed and the developing world, through domestic regulation, such as in financial institutions, transportation and other areas. There is also concern in the developing world that full global liberalization in these areas could eliminate domestic capacity for some of these service related items (such as banking). For the lower-income countries, tourism is the most significant component of this trade. Generally, services are growing more rapidly than other areas of trade and are more heavily restricted. Barrier removal began in a small way in the Uruguay Round, but will be a major issue in a new Millennium Round and beyond.

Table 7: Growth of services trade and the developing countries

	Billions of $US	As % of merchandise trade
Service Exports (1996)[1]	227	15.2
Service Imports (1996)[1]	282	20.1
Value of tourism (in absolute terms and as a % of service exports)	94	33

[1] of Latin America, Africa, and now Japan, Asia

Sources: WTO (1998a), Table III.4; World Tourism Organization (1996).

South-South trade

Finally, Table 8 reports data on South-South trade, i.e., trade between the developing countries. This was at low levels in the 1970's, but in recent years has been more rapidly growing than developed-developing country trade. It now accounts for around 11% of world trade, but importantly around 40% of developing country exports. As Table 8 indicates, both these trade shares have increased substantially over the five-year period 1990-1995. Least developed countries now source over one half of their imports from other developing countries.

Over the years, it has often been suggested that increased South-South trade could ultimately represent a major opportunity for the developing countries in the trading system, but because of its seeming small size, this source has been frequently discounted. The issue is, therefore, at what point does South-South trade represent a large enough trading opportunity for the developing countries to become a motor for growth, and how important could it be over the next two decades. Given the current share of developing country exports that go to other developing countries, and the significantly higher growth rate of South-South trade compared to world trade in recent years, the indication is that this is an important source of opportunity for developing countries in their trade.

Table 8: South-South trade

South-South Trade, 1994 (billions of $US)	539.8
As a % of World Trade	7.7 (1990) 11.1 (1995)
As a % of Developing Country Exports	33.5 (1990) 39.6 (1995)

Source: UNCTAD (1997b).

The policy framework for globally based economic development

A future WTO millennium round?

A central global trade policy issue for individual developing countries is their stance towards a future round of trade negotiations under the WTO. This is now widely believed to be likely to be initiated in the year 2000 to coincide with the millennium (hence, the title, the Millennium Round), although there are still major issues to be resolved before such a round can be launched. A central unresolved issue concerns negotiating authority in the United States, and the lack of appetite for new trade negotiations within the US Congress. Nonetheless, in many parts of the world, particularly Europe, there is now a substantial gearing up underway for a new round.[6]

Since the creation of the GATT in 1947 (subsumed into the WTO in 1994), there have been eight negotiating rounds,[7] even though there is no inevitability which leads from one round to the next. These rounds, through negotiated exchanges and concessions reducing tariff barriers on manufactured products, are widely thought to have lowered tariff barriers between OECD countries to the point that they are now relatively insignificant barriers to trade. Other trade barriers are now thought to be more important, including (for developing country exporters) textiles and apparel restrictions as well as anti-dumping duties and actions, and restrictions in agriculture.

Understanding what a Millennium Round might involve requires prior understanding of the trade policy problem it is designed to solve. One feature of the Uruguay Round decisions was that they specified substantial detail as to their implementation over a long period of time (as long as twenty years). The Uruguay Round mandated a mini-negotiation in agriculture within five years of the conclusion of the Round, and granted special delays to developing countries (and especially the least developed) for implementation in such areas as intellectual property and agriculture. The Round also saw agreement by developed countries to terminate trade restrictions against textiles and apparel under the Multifibre Arrangement by 2004, although the initial phase-in of these arrangements has caused disquiet among developing countries as to what may replace the MFA. Thus some have suggested that the core of a new Millennium Round could be to concentrate on implementation issues stemming from the Uruguay Round. As such this would be a distinct departure from previous WTO Rounds, which have had a strong focus initially on tariff reduction and then on other barrier reduction. Moreover, the decisions from the Round also created a new permanent forum of biannual ministerial meetings, which some argued at the time could serve to replace Rounds through ongoing permanent negotiation, and so the rationale for a separate and new Round is even questioned in some circles.

Others have suggested that a Millennium Round could instead be dominated by discussion of so-called new-new issues (issues going beyond the new issues discussed in the Uruguay Round, which were services, investment, and intellectual property). These include trade and the environment, competition policy (with its trade implications), trade and investment, and trade and labour standards. Developing countries have been concerned about these developments in global policy discussion, because they see them as issues on which developing countries will likely be pressured to undertake measures which could slow their growth and development (such as in environment and labour standards) under a threat of increased trade barriers if they do not comply. Their fear is that a new Millennium Round, rather than focussing on further reductions in trade barriers, as in the past, may become embroiled in discussion of conditional increases in trade barriers which could close export markets.

A third view of the Millennium Round focuses on it as an opportunity, created in large part by the Uruguay Round, for large new market opening globally through yet more bargaining of reciprocal exchanges and concessions in similar vein to previous rounds. The argument is that, following the Uruguay Round, in a number of areas, there are now negotiable trade instruments that were not there before. In agriculture, for instance, tariffication of existing agricultural trade restrictions, including the recent tariffication of rice restrictions in Japan (at levels of over 1000%), has created transparent negotiable tariff instruments which can now be the subject of an exchange of concessions. The elimination of quota restrictions under the Multifibre

Arrangement in 2004 will leave in place tariff barriers in the OECD countries, which are the highest on manufactured products, and once again represent a negotiable instrument for reciprocal exchange. Developing countries greatly expanded the coverage of their tariff bindings in the Uruguay Round to cover nearly 80% of their imports (as against a little over 20% previously). Reciprocal exchange possibilities also arise here. There are also arguments that many more restrictions in services could also become negotiable in a wide-ranging reciprocal exchange in such a framework, and in both developed and developing countries.

This third view of the architecture of a Millennium Round is thus as an opportunity for a major expansion of the reciprocal exchanges and concessions beyond manufactures that have characterized previous tariff-cutting negotiations in the WTO (GATT) on agriculture and services, and also into key residual manufacturing items such as textiles. In this case, the opportunities for the developing countries to generate fresh market opening become significant because of the chance to reduce key trade barriers they face, particularly in textiles and apparel, but also in agriculture and some service items.

A future Millennium Round, if it comes to pass, may well contain all of these elements, and as such present both opportunities and threats to the developing countries.[8] The threats are that they could be subject to increases in trade barriers unless they move towards compliance with various forms of OECD-driven domestic policy changes, such as in environment and labour standards. On the other hand, major opportunities may be present for market-opening reciprocal exchange in which the developing countries, continually increasing in relative size compared to the developed countries, have significant leverage.

Regionalism

Another key element affecting the future position of the developing countries in the global trading system is regional trade agreements.[9] Regional agreements have been an ever present feature of the postwar trading system, but in the last ten years they have grown substantially in profile. The first round of postwar regional trade agreements came into the system in the 1960's, particularly with the creation of the European Community (later the EU), and also with regional trade agreements in many parts of the developing world. These agreements, and especially the 1957 Treaty of Rome, created the precedent for coexistence of regional agreements with the GATT, even though regional agreements were a clear violation of the spirit of non-discrimination central to the GATT. Indeed, in the 1960's, the Kennedy Round of GATT trade negotiations were in large part a result of the creation of the European Economic Community, and the perceived need of the United States to deal with their access problems to European markets through trade bargaining in the GATT system.

In the late 1980's, however, frustration over seemingly slow progress in multilateral negotiation and the exploitation of tactical linkage between multilateral and regional negotiation by some countries produced a ratcheting-up in regional trading agreements, especially with the 1987 Canada-US Agreement. Subsequently trilateralized to include Mexico in the North American Free Trade Agreement (NAFTA), the creation of a regional entity in North America set off a series of further concerns. Smaller countries strongly wanted to be part of one trade agreement or the other, and these regional entities in turn began to pursue new options to expand their network of trade agreements before their rival did so. This was particularly the case with the EU, which in recent years had been either negotiating or discussing regional trade agreements with South Africa, India, and others, as well as association or accession agreements with Eastern European countries and former Soviet Republics.

These developments have generated a series of further responses. Some developing countries have responded by forming their own regional entities, as a precursor to eventual negotiation with larger OECD groups; this, for instance, has been true of MERCOSUR (Argentina, Brazil, Paraguay, and Uruguay). Others have hung back, trying to avoid entanglements with developing-country regional trade agreements, so as to make their potential accession to developed-world regional trade agreements cleaner. This was the Chilean approach, but the Chileans in turn found that concerns in the US Congress have made it difficult for them to pursue this negotiation route, and as a result have subsequently joined MERCOSUR. In Asia, there has been new regional activity in the Association of South East Asian Nations (ASEAN), which has moved towards a regional trade agreement (the ASEAN Free Trade Area, or AFTA), in contrast to the framework for regional cooperation and the defence alliance which it was at its creation. Even in Africa, there have been new attempts to revive regional trade agreements, based on the argument that regional trade grows more rapidly than global trade.

Some of these new regional arrangements have also taken the form of smaller countries approaching larger countries seeking safe-haven trade arrangements. In these, the smaller country often pays what is akin to an insurance premium in the form of domestic policy restraints of various kinds beneficial to the large country, in return for firmer guarantees of access to the larger market. This characterization of the Canada-US Trade Agreement, for instance, has recently been offered by Perroni and Whalley (1998). From the point of view of smaller developing countries, the concern is that they will increasingly need to pay such premiums in order to join regional trade agreements, and that later entrants will be called on to pay larger premiums, a redistributive element in these arrangements adverse to smaller countries. As a result, a continued spread of regional arrangements is generally seen in the developing world as hostile to the interests of the developing countries.

Out into the next decade, the continued speed of regionalism therefore presents dilemmas for the developing countries. On the one hand, there is a fear that, with the OECD countries moving towards more clearly defined regional blocs, unless individual developing countries become part of one of these blocs, they will eventually suffer, particularly if there is eventually trade retaliation between these regional entities. On the other hand, these entities may finish up retaliating against each other in ways that could yield preferential access for developing countries to their markets, and if they any way generate growth and trade, developing countries will share in this to some degree.

Access problems

A further set of issues for the developing countries are future access problems that they are likely to encounter in OECD markets, independently of a WTO negotiating round or developments on the regional front. As mentioned above, tariffs in OECD countries on manufactured products, to all intents and purposes, have been eliminated as a result of exchanges of concessions in the Uruguay Round, with the notable exceptions of textiles and apparel and agriculture. Access problems remaining for developing countries tend to be product- and instrument-specific, but these will still pose problems for the developing countries in the decades ahead.

In the instrument area, developing countries have increasingly found themselves to be subject to anti-dumping duties.[10] Anti-dumping actions are initiated where countries are deemed to be dumping or selling below cost. They are a widely used protective device in the OECD countries, but one which more recently has spread to the developing countries as part of the safeguards offered to domestic producers when trade liberalization occurs. As part of the political consensus underpinning trade liberalization in the OECD countries, if imports surge into domestic markets, there are various mechanisms allowing for controls over the flow of imports; anti-dumping is one of the more important of these.

OECD anti-dumping practices over the last twenty years have slowly tightened in the ways they are applied, particularly against smaller countries. There are rules such as cumulation, which allow for the exports of one country to be added to those of another in determining injury; one of the key criteria for the imposition of an anti-dumping duty. There are also rules allowing for the construction of a cost basis for the dumping margin to be determined in the absence of data supplied by individual countries, and repeatedly anti-dumping cases, successful in the initial petitioning process, have resulted in high duties through the use of constructed cost.

In the product-specific areas, there are also potential access difficulties to be faced. As noted above, textiles and apparel is the most prominent of these. While there is a commitment to phase out MFA trade restrictions by the year 2004, it is also widely agreed that the three-part phaseout procedure instituted in the Uruguay Round has to all intents and purposes been tokenesque thus far.[11] The commitment in the year 2004 to eliminate all MFA restrictions on textiles and apparel in OECD countries has been compared by some developing country trade negotiators as akin to walking off a cliff, which they assume is not going to happen. In another area, agriculture, while the decisions in the Uruguay Round have included agriculture for the first time since the signing of the GATT, they have not substantially liberalized trade. Developing countries remain subject to high tariffs on key agricultural exports (including rice and sugar), and the issue for them is how to negotiate these tariffs down so as to improve access.

Non-Trade trade issues

A further set of key trade issues for the developing countries out into the early decades of the next century will be the so-called non-trade trade issues. These are issues in which a non-trade objective, such as improving environmental quality or raising so-called labour standards, is tied to possible use of trade sanctions, and they are likely to be part of a future WTO negotiation (including a Millennium Round). The broad structure of the proposals made thus far for these areas follows the agreement on intellectual property, which emanated from the Uruguay Round. In the intellectual property area, there was a negotiation on a common international standard, such that if countries fail to meet the standard, they are subject to dispute settlement and ultimately to trade sanctions.

The trade and environment area has been particularly contentious, especially in the early 1990's.[12] In this area, the activities of environmental non-governmental organizations (NGOs), trying to establish the principle that the use of trade-restricting measures to improve environmental compliance in exporting countries is legitimate under the GATT, have led to a series of precedent- setting trade conflicts. The 1990 dispute over tuna exported by Mexico to the US and incidental dolphin kills was especially high profile. Environmental groups in the United States were successful in using the courts to implement trade restrictions, appealing to the US Marine Mammal Protection Act of 1988. These trade restrictions were, however, subsequently found to be incompatible with the GATT in a preliminary ruling by a dispute settlement panel. This never went beyond its preliminary stages, but its report crystallized the issues and focussed the subsequent debate. To OECD environmental groups, the GATT was widely seen as environmentally unfriendly, and even incapable of allowing trade restraints in the name of what was viewed as sensible environmental policy. But from the developing-country point of view, trade restraints of this form were seen as potentially harmful to their growth and environmental prospects, and inconsistent with the general principles embodied in the GATT of helping developing countries speed their growth and development through increased trade.

Conflicts over trade measures for environmental management continued through the 1990's. Thus far, the developing countries have remained cautious of any proposals to negotiate a trade and environment agreement, and in the 1996 Singapore WTO Ministerial Meeting were successful in keeping further negotiation off the agenda. But the issue remains, and will likely surface again in the Millennium Round agenda-setting process.

Another related issue is labour standards.[13] Labour standards involve restraints on various production practices using labour in ways that are seen in the OECD countries as infringing either labour or human rights. These particularly involve the use of child labour, especially young children working for long periods of time, with allegations made of adverse labour practices in carpet factories in such countries as Pakistan. They also cover the use of prison labour and (in some versions of labour standards advocacy) nonunion labour.

The proposal strongly advanced by the United States is to agree on a series of core standards, not dissimilar to those already in the International Labour Organization (ILO), with violations of labour standards being subject to dispute settlement, and eventually, to retaliation. As with trade and environment, the developing countries have been steadfast in resisting attempts to engage them in negotiation on these matters, on the grounds, again, of the potential impairment of their growth and developmental prospects, but as with trade and environment, the issues remain.

There are also concerns that this approach of using trade sanctions as a form of policemen over domestic policies could spread beyond environment and labour standards. The developing country fear is that other issues could enter into this category, such as trade and human rights, and trade and political rights. Concerns over trade and environment and labour standards, therefore, also embody worries over the precedents involved. The effect of these developments could ultimately be to raise trade barriers against developing countries, especially if fears of domestic protectionist interests exploiting these opportunities for protective rather than genuinely held environmental or other concerns, were to be realized. The contrast relative to the earlier post-war years where trade barriers generally came down is especially marked; the concern is now that there may be circumstances under which trade barriers against developing countries go up.

New-New issues

Beyond the non-trade trade issues discussed above, there is a series of further issues only now becoming central to the trade policy agenda, but which also form part of a new potential trade round.

One is the issue of electronic commerce, so-called e-commerce. In electronic commerce, the issues reflect the rapid growth of the Internet as a vehicle for the conduct of trade. The value of trade conducted on the Internet seems likely to explode in the next few years, but most of it poses no immediate issues for trade policy, since if goods are ordered on the Internet but are physically shipped, they are dealt with at the border like any other shipped commodity.

The immediate focal point of the e-commerce debate has been more on the impact of transactions executed on the Internet. This type of e-commerce includes financial services and various kinds of professional and other services (including entertainment materials) that are wholly delivered over the Internet. There are proposals from the United States that all such transactions should remain free of all tariffs (indeed how to collect tariffs in such cases is unclear), and further discussion has been devoted to the tax treatment of these items.

More generally, with e-commerce there are debates as to how it affects the position of the developing countries. A recent WTO (1998b) report has suggested that developing countries would benefit substantially from a general spread of e-commerce, because the Internet represents a significant reduction in the transaction costs of conducting trade. As the developing countries face higher costs than other countries at present, they would benefit more than proportionally from this new format for the conduct of trade. If this is correct, e-commerce may offer new opportunities to the developing countries for their trade growth.

In the competition policy area, the issues are even more complex, and it is less clear what the interests of the developing countries are. On the one hand, there is talk of partial harmonization of competition policy, but at the same time many developing countries have no competition policy statutes. Some countries are fearful of the costs and complexity of instituting such regimes, remembering the obligations they incurred to install intellectual property regimes in the Uruguay Round. On the other hand, there are opportunities within a potential competition policy negotiation that developing countries may wish to explore. One involves questions of price fixing and collusive behaviour by firms from large countries supplying small markets, where the national government in the smaller market has no extraterritorial reach. Here the issue is the potential use of tariffs as a vehicle for offsetting the collusive practices involved. Another is whether the institution of competition policies in the developing countries could lead to significant gains because of the concentrated nature of their domestic markets, and a general opening up of their markets through changes in competition policy.

Developing country interests in a new post-Bretton Woods Architecture

Besides the issues falling under the general orbit of the WTO and the new Millennium Round, there is also a set of issues concerning developing country participation in the trading system which is part of the emerging debate on a new post-Bretton Woods architecture. The Bretton Woods system, as is well known, emerged from the 1940's with the tripartite structure of the World Bank, the GATT (now the WTO), and the IMF.

This structure is increasingly viewed as ineffective, given the operation of the contemporary global economy and the problems it faces. This has been made evident to many by the events surrounding the recent financial turbulence. For example, this financial turbulence took place within a regime of domestic banking regulation but no international regulation of banks, and many of the practices of OECD banks in developing countries (such as in Indonesia) would probably not have been acceptable to an overarching international regulatory body. There is also no set of global competition statutes operating antitrust policies on a global basis rather than a country basis, and neither will one result from a WTO negotiation on competition policy. In area after area, it is clear that the arrangements inherited from the 1940's are designed to deal with the problems of the 1940's rather than the problems of the 1990's. The Bretton Woods system, for instance, only treats interactions between countries as being based on trade and finance; there is no recognition of physical interaction, and recent calls for the formation of the World Environmental Organization reflect these concerns.

On a broader plane then, there are and will continue to be ongoing discussions about new global arrangements, with a reconfiguration of and restructuring in global institutional forms, involving particularly the World Bank, the IMF and the WTO. The developing country interest in these needs to be clearly articulated. On the one hand, developing countries have come to rely on the World Bank and the IMF, as much needed shorter (or longer-term) sources of cheaper developmental finance. On the other hand, these bodies are seen in some circles in these countries as being driven by an OECD-inspired policy agenda that does not mesh with local concerns. Strengthened agencies with even more powers will be viewed with caution and even alarm in some countries, while more financing and strengthened rule regimes to deal with country problems (as in the competition area) could prove beneficial.

Non-trading system trade issues

Another set of issues beyond the WTO, and of great potential relevance to the developing countries, reflects ways in which non-trading system issues have implications for the evolution of developing country trade. The trade implications of arrangements to reduce carbon emissions are a central element in this category.

These have been discussed recently as part of the debate on the Kyoto Protocol negotiated 18 months ago. Any attempt to reduce carbon emissions to meet the Kyoto target of a 7% reduction in 1990 emissions by 2012 will have associated with it a substantial increase in energy prices. Some modeling calculations suggest that induced increases in energy prices could have large impacts on world trade; trade in energy-intensive manufactured products could fall sharply, perhaps by 20- 50%.[14] In addition, the revenue implications of emissions reductions mechanisms could themselves also be substantial. Non-WTO issues affecting trade may thus prove important for the developing countries in deciding whether to focus on exports of manufactured products or remain in commodity-based exports. An environment of shrinking global trade in manufactures obviously has substantial implications for outward-oriented developmental strategies.

Negotiability

Within this discussion of a global policy framework, it is also important for negotiating strategies to emerge that build on the leverage of developing countries, recognizing how much they actually have and how they can best use it. It has generally been believed that developing countries are small in trade terms, and therefore have limited amounts of leverage they can use in global trade negotiation. This, of course, is not true in terms of international trade volumes, since developing countries account for over 30% of global trade. Developing countries are, however, a fractured group of countries (more than 100), even though within that group there are certain countries that are large and significant. Brazil for instance, is the tenth largest economy in the world.

In the past, the developing countries have pursued a negotiating strategy under which they have claimed to have problems that are similar across all developing countries but unique to developing country status. This approach, identified by the phrase "special and differential treatment" (S & D), defined their global negotiating strategy in the 1960's and the 1970's. The argument is that they have common problems and they should negotiate globally as a group to achieve improvements in their position, and jointly seek ways to first implement and then improve their special and differential treatment. This was manifest in the generalized system of preferences of the 1970's, which granted them special lower tariffs for their exports to OECD.

In the 1980's, however, it became widely believed that developing countries had not in fact received much in the way of substantive benefits from special and differential treatment. Their individual country interests were such that they crisscrossed one another, and pursuit of country interest made more sense than pursuit of common interests. In the Uruguay Round, therefore, we saw developing countries on different sides of the same issue. Countries such as Argentina were strongly arguing for liberalization in agriculture, while net importers of agricultural products, such as Jamaica and Egypt, were arguing strongly against such liberalization. We also had examples of coalitions being formed between developed and developing countries; in agriculture the example was of the Cairns Group, a coalition involving both Argentina and Australia and others, trying to pressure the European Community for more liberalization in agriculture.

The issue, then, of global negotiability for the developing countries in the Millennium Round and beyond is how far they should act jointly to form negotiating coalitions, and how far they should pursue individual country interest. In practice, they did both in the Uruguay Round, and will likely continue to do both, and so issues such as labour standards and trade and environment will tend to move the developing countries to a common position, while other issues such as agriculture will again fragment them.

In the longer term, their more rapid growth also means that they will have ever more leverage and hence their ability to negotiate will become stronger. Crucial to this is the position of China. China's trade has been growing rapidly, and now accounts for more than 60% of developing country exports of textiles and apparel. China's leverage in trade negotiations is potentially large, and the issue of Chinese accession to the WTO is therefore one that is central to other developing countries. Some developing countries see Chinese WTO accession as positive, allowing into the WTO an ally who will be part of a wider developing country coalition and add to its clout. Others see benefits in continued Chinese exclusion from the WTO, since trade restraints against China on textiles and apparel could continue beyond 2004 (MFA elimination) and be beneficial for them.

Implementation and policy making capacity

A final issue for the developing countries in assessing the impact of the emerging global framework for the conduct of policy is how to develop the capacity they need to negotiate, and even how to implement the trade decisions agreed to in the Uruguay Round. In the implementation area, one of the central concerns is intellectual property, where there is a ten-year lag for the least developed countries, following implementation in ten years. Issues of trade sanctions in this area will thus not impinge on these countries for a twenty-year period following the adoption of the decisions in 1994. But, in many countries, costly new intellectual property regimes will need to be instituted, which will require a capability and capacity beyond that of many developing countries.

In turn, many developing countries also have problems with their negotiating capacity. In the Uruguay Round negotiations, several countries participated only to a limited extent, partly fuelled by their belief that they had no negotiating leverage, and partly by the costs of maintaining delegations in Geneva. With upcoming WTO negotiations in store, the questions are how to enhance their negotiating capability; what forms of pooling can take place across countries to maintain common representations in a more cost-effective manner; how to identify the most important issues for them to negotiate on; and how these negotiations are to be concluded.

The future for the developing countries in the trading system

Given the discussion of country trade performance and where the trading system finds itself as we approach the new Millennium Round, what could the future hold for the developing countries? How will global trade volumes and product composition evolve over the next decade, and with what implications for the developing countries? As Hamilton and Whalley (1996) discuss, the decades since the 1940's have been remarkable for ever increasing interdependence within the global economy. Since the mid-1940's, global income growth has been perhaps 2-2½% per year in real terms, with higher growth rates in the 1960's and 1970's, some slippage in the 1980's, and a further acceleration in the 1990's. In contrast, trade growth has occurred at approximately double these rates, somewhere in the region of 5 to 6% over the forty-year period. In the mid-1990's, trade growth was approximately three times the rate of income growth at around 10-11% per year. It is this dramatic trade growth which as much as anything else has facilitated the rapid integration of the manufactured product-exporting developing countries in Asia and Latin America into the global economy.

The future for the developing countries in the trading system will be to a large degree determined by whether or not these trade growth figures continue. It should be remembered that long swings in trade performance in the global economy have been very uneven. From 1870 to 1913, there were large increases in international trade as a fraction of national income; from 1913 to the outbreak of the Second World War, there were declines, accelerated by the depression of the 1930's, but also brought about by increases in trade barriers over the whole of the 1920's and inconvertible currencies in the 1930's. Kindleberger (1973) estimates that, in the depression of the 1930's, world trade fell by 75-80% over a two-year period.

The strongly held belief in the likely continued success of outward-oriented trade strategies is based on the premise that there will be a continuation of the strong global trade performance of the last 50 years. It presumes no significant barrier increases; no unwinding of the direct foreign investment that has fuelled trade growth; in short a continuation and even acceleration of present trends of globalization.[15] The rate of growth of foreign direct investment has been even more rapid than that of trade. Throughout the 1980's, and with a drop only in the recession of the early 1990's, foreign direct investment globally had been growing at approximately 25% per year until the onset of current financial crises. This builds from a small base in the1970's, but these growth rates are in excess even of those for trade, and reflect ever more interdependence in the global economy and a progressive reduction in barriers to investment as well as to trade. And as this has happened, interaffiliate trade as a fraction of total trade has grown, to the point that FDI in recent years has itself become a major engine of growth for trade.

Factors underlying trade growth

There are clearly a variety of reasons why trade has grown so rapidly over this period, even if there is disagreement in the literature as to which is the most important. Some point to sharp reductions in transportation costs, with changes in the type of trade. Older trade in bulky items has been replaced by trade in light items such as computer chips, and now trade in intangible items over the Internet. Barriers to trade posed by transportation systems, which were substantial, are now much lower because the form of trade has changed.

Another factor is technical change, and particularly the growth of communications devices— first phones, then faxes, the Internet, and global media. There is now awareness in all countries of global products. It has become profitable to produce and market for the global marketplace, and to develop products establishing global brand identity to be traded on a global basis. Again, global trade growth inevitably accompanies these technological developments.

Finally, there is the global policy framework. The policy direction within the global economy since the 1940's has been one of progressive reductions in trade barriers, driven in part by a global determination not to repeat the 1930's and to keep markets as open as possible. This occurred first under the General Agreement on Tariffs and Trade (GATT), and since 1994 in the World Trade Organization (WTO), with global trade rules applied and trade negotiations completed. The Uruguay Round,[16] concluded in 1994, was the most recent of these and covered a wide range of issues, from agriculture to intellectual property, and textiles to dispute settlement. This process has established a general presumption of an ever more open global economy with declining trade barriers. Developing countries, while not significantly affecting the outcomes of these negotiations, have nonetheless been able to base policy strategies on the hypothesis that they would tend to face an ever more open global economy with lower barriers.

A fallacy of composition?

The system has, however, moved from one in which a small number of countries were focussed on an outward-oriented trade-driven strategy to growth and development in the 1960's, to a situation where today the vast majority of countries are pursuing such strategies. Meanwhile, the growth rate of the OECD markets absorbing these imports remains largely the same. The issue is whether there is a fallacy of composition involved: can developing countries continue to generate trade growth of the type that would be sufficient to meet the development objectives of all of these countries if OECD growth rates do not accelerate? As more countries follow these strategies, the initial experience can be high export growth rates from an initial low-trade, low-wage base, but can sustained trade growth occur for all or most of these countries over a period of decades sufficient to replicate the experiences of Korea and Taiwan? In turn, foreign direct investment flowing into these countries, while linked to strong trade performance, remains heavily concentrated, raising further questions about the sustainability of the process for the majority of countries.

Low-income (and typically smaller) countries, in Africa and elsewhere, who have generally not participated in this growth process, pose problems. Some have suggested that these countries now have low wage rates, and even with poor infrastructure offer large opportunities for inward foreign investors. This may be the case in such areas as textiles and apparel, since with the impending elimination of the Multifibre Arrangement and the removal of country-specific quotas (to follow in 2004),[17] a major blockage to trade growth for these countries. But for now, most of the low-income countries that have been encouraged by donor agencies and others to think in terms of an outward-oriented trade strategy have yet to see fruits for their endeavours.

The direction of Barrier Change

A further key element in a strategy for participation in the global trading system is whether there will be changes in the global policy framework of a type not seen before. As noted above, the scenarios for such change focus on a number of elements.

One such element concerns the level and type of trade barriers that the developing countries are likely to face in the next two decades. For the last fifty years, developing countries have proceeded with their trade strategy under the general expectation that trade barriers around the world would continue to come down. This reflected the process of ongoing negotiation both in the GATT and the WTO. The developing countries have been key to this process both through ever improved access to developed country markets, and also through large unilateral reductions in their own trade barriers made later on in the process (late 1980's/early 1990's). They were, however, able to liberalize unilaterally, reasonably secure in the belief that export markets for them were open, and barriers against them were, if anything, going to fall further.

The question is whether, after all these reductions, there is still scope for even further reductions in barriers that will significantly affect trade on the upside. The scope is there in key sectoral areas, such as services, agriculture, and textiles, but for the developing countries to rely on further generalized barrier reductions fuelling their trade growth for the next twenty years seems myopic.[18]

At a technical level, efforts by domestic interests within OECD countries, and also now increasingly in developing countries, to offset the effects of tariff reductions by other protective barriers, such as anti-dumping, seem to be a factor. For now, the trade coverage of these measures is relatively small, but the levels at which barriers which have been implemented are high; concerns have been expressed by many that the elimination of the Multifibre Arrangement could ultimately lead to an increase in anti-dumping measures applied against textiles and apparel.

A broader concern is that trade barriers will increasingly be linked to non-trade objectives through the use of trade threats. This direction for policy has already entered the trading system through the agreements on intellectual property in the Uruguay Round, but there have been more wide-ranging proposals made by the developed countries to link the use of trade sanctions to compliance with environmental policy objectives in the developing world,[19] and also to use trade sanctions to uphold labour standards. In all these cases, standards are to be set for the non-trade objective, and these are to be enforced through the use of WTO-approved trade sanctions if non-compliance takes place. Hence, having participated in a trading system in which trade barriers were generally coming down for the last fifty years, and are now so low that further declines are unlikely, these developments suggest a risk of trade barriers going back up. Export markets will not close, but exports may grow at a slower rate, and they may experience selective closing.

Broadening negotiations

A further element in this changing policy framework is a trend towards broadening of negotiations beyond trade, so as to inject other non-trade matters into trading system debates. There are pressures for broadening beyond the Uruguay Round into the new Millennium Round, to include environment, competition policy, investment and other matters.

Generally speaking, the developing countries have been resistant to attempts to broaden the agenda of trade-related negotiations, on the grounds that most of these are disadvantageous to them. Their concern has been to push for a negotiating framework that will limit the damage. This containment approach has been relatively successful in certain areas, such as in slowing the pace on environmental-trade negotiations and on labour standard negotiations in the 1996 Singapore WTO Ministerial Meeting, but they were unsuccessful with intellectual property in the Uruguay Round. This was, in part, because many developing countries had complied bilaterally with developed country pressures on the intellectual property front exerted in parallel regional negotiations to the Uruguay Round.

In this broadening process, however, there will also be opportunities to pursue new directions that could be advantageous, and even to do so aggressively. By way of example, there is no logical reason why future negotiations should be limited only to intellectual property rights; they could also be expanded to include other forms of property rights. In the Kyoto process, for instance, the developing countries have thus far taken a passive approach of arguing that carbon emission problems are fundamentally problems of the developed world. They have withdrawn from the negotiations in the hope that they would have neither disciplines nor obligations imposed on them, and, so far, have largely achieved this outcome. However, an activist developing country approach to a property rights negotiation could use the argument that all countries have only limited rights to emit carbon into the upper atmosphere, and that the developed countries have already overused their rights to do so through past emissions. The argument is that they should compensate the developing countries if they now continue to emit carbon. An aggressive pursuit of property rights in this and other areas could yield the developing countries both potential economic benefits and negotiating leverage.

Trade and environment is, again, an area where developing countries have largely taken an approach of withdrawing from negotiations and arguing that linked negotiations should not take place. Developing countries have tried to avoid WTO legitimized environmental trade sanctions being used against them, because they are seen as a mechanism through which pressure could be placed on the developing countries to undertake various kinds of domestic environmental policy initiatives which they see as potentially growth-retarding. However, developing countries are custodians of key global environmental assets, such as forests, and with existence value placed on these assets by the environmental groups in the OECD countries, there is negotiating leverage for the developing countries in linked trade and environment negotiations. Environmental concessions might be one way in which developing countries could get improvements in trade access in key areas of interest, and so increase their economic performance. The point, put simply, is that broadened negotiations represent both a source of both opportunity and risk for the developing countries, but the approach taken by them thus far has been to emphasize the risks and the downside, without aggressively exploring positive upside opportunities. This could be an area to reconsider.

Post-Bretton Woods Institutions

A clear shift in global attitudes towards the role and operation of international institutions has taken place following the recent crises. Things are in flux both intellectually and politically, and here the developing countries have a major opportunity to help shape the post-crisis global institutional framework out into the early decades of the next century.[20] Our present day global institutions, for want of a better description, are caught in a time warp of the 1940's. The IMF, the World Bank and the GATT (now the WTO) were institutions designed in the 1940's to deal with particular problems of the 1940's, connected to the events of the 1930's [21] and the subsequent military conflict. They are not institutional arrangements designed to deal with the problems of today's globalized economy, in which there are no clear global entities to redefine the authority leaking away from national governments. Our present global entities have only weakly defined powers. For instance, in the global area, we have no global regulation of financial institutions comparable to that which exists within nation states. There is no global antitrust policy comparable to that which operates within nation states. The institutions of the 1940's were designed on the premise that the only interactions between nation states were in trade and finance, with no physical interaction as in the environmental area, clearly a major omission in terms of global institutional design as seen from today. On top of this, pressures both for new regional arrangements and fragmentation of global arrangements seem to be growing, as in the late 1980's and 1990's.[22]

Given what has happened in recent financial crises, the next few years could witness a re-evaluation of our global institutions, and developing countries should be forthright in stating their needs in such institutions. A global competition policy agency, for instance, could be of major advantage to the developing countries. A global environmental agency facilitating some of the linked negotiations mentioned above could also be of great use. A new global financial authority, moving towards a global central bank, could even be mooted. All of these developments may well provide opportunities for the developing countries to aggressively explore.

Concluding remarks

This paper flags concerns over both the performance of the global economy, and the institution arrangements underpinning it, which may affect the developing countries in a major way for the next few decades. If trade growth over the next two decades does not continue at the levels we have seen in the last two decades (which could happen), developing countries may be forced to shift some of the focus of their developmental strategy away from global aspirations, and toward improved performance of their own domestic economies. The potential fallacy of composition of a hundred or more developing countries all pursuing outward-oriented, trade-led growth, compared to the small number of countries that successfully did so in the 1950's and 1960's, seems striking, and especially so in the current global environment.

In addition, clear challenges remain for an overall strategy that does not deal with the uneven performance and participation of countries in the system, particularly the African countries, which have achieved such low rates of trade growth in recent years. It may be the case that these countries will witness a resurgence of performance over the next 10 to 15 years, and activist intervention to promote their trade will not be necessary, but efforts thus far through regional and other incentives have been largely unsuccessful. Some new direction will likely be needed.

Finally, the policy framework underlying the global economy is undergoing change and will continue to do so. A new round of WTO trade negotiations seems imminent. Less can probably be expected of barrier reductions, and more emphasis may need to be placed on avoiding barrier increases. The linkage of trade to other areas through broadened negotiations, as well as attempts to redefine and refocus global institutions could all be major elements of debate. Developing countries need to understand these events, be ahead and not behind them, identify areas of key interest and help shape, more forcefully than has been the case in the past, the global trade structure emerging for the decades ahead.

It is fashionable in trade policy circles to argue that the developing-country global strategy of the 1970's, represented by special and differential treatment, broke down in the 1990's, as countries began to pursue individual country interest and adopted outward-oriented, trade-driven developmental strategies. Hence, it is argued now that country interest has now superceded blocwide interest in trade and economic matters more broadly. This may be to a large degree true of the global economy of the mid-1990's, and to some degree will remain so over the next two decades. But, this paper also highlights some key underpinnings of developing country pursuit of individual country interest, and in particular the assumption that both the structure of the global economy and its policy framework will both accommodate such a pursuit and will remain largely unchanged. This paper suggests that these assumptions may need to be challenged to some degree by the developing countries.■

Notes

---

1 [1]Rodrick (1998) also emphasizes the adjustment consequences more broadly from globalization.

[2] See the discussion of an African country's interests (Kenya) in the trading system in Mwega and Muga (1998). Also Armstrong and Read (1998) provide a recent discussion of the performance of smaller countries in the trading system.

[3] See the discussion in Whalley (1990).

[4]This estimate is discussed in more detail later.

[5]The significance of outsourcing for US trade is explored in Feenstra and Hanson (1996).

[6]See the discussion of the possible content of a new round of trade negotiations in the recent Institute of International Economics volume edited by Jeffrey Schott (1998).

[7]Although the Uruguay Round concluded in 1994, WTO Director General Renato Ruggiero has suggested (see his speech in Schott (1998)) that WTO negotiations on information technology, financial services, and telecommunications are of sufficient importance that they should be grouped together and be considered a Ninth Round, even though such a round was not formally declared.

[8]See the discussion of these alternative architectures for a new Round in Whalley (1998).

[9]Winters in Schott (1998) provides an alternative discussion of this issue and does not come to strong conclusions on the challenges posed by regionalism in the multilateral system for developing countries, although he does see threats.

[10]See the discussion in Spinager (1998b).

[11]The experience thus far is discussed by Trela (in Thomas and Whalley (1998)), and also by Spinager (1998a).

[12]The recent evolution of the trade and environment debate is discussed in Uimonen In Schott (1998), as well as in Uimonen and Whalley (1997).

[13]See Elliott's paper in Schott (1998).

[14]See Piggott, Whalley, and Wigle (1993).

[15]Although Tussie's (1998) recent analysis of the situation in Argentina argues that a more cautious approach to trade is now evolving there, focussed on regional rather than global trade growth, and reinstating some of the protection for the domestic market, in part through anti-dumping measures.

[16]Yeats (1994) and the papers in Martin and Winters (1995) provide quantitative assessments of the impacts of the Uruguay Round on developing countries.

[17]See Spinager's (1998a) recent discussion of the situation on the phase out of the MFA.

[18]And new regional agreements seem unlikely to give much added benefit on the access side to OECD markets (since barriers are low), and may serve to fragment global markets.

[19]See Whalley (1996) and Uimonen and Whalley (1997), both of which discuss the WTO and trade and environmental linkage.

[20]A recent piece by Richard Blackhurst (1998), a former director of research at the WTO, provides a useful summary of views on the role of the WTO in the global economy. See also Anne Kreuger's (1998) thoughts on the future of the IMF and the World Bank.

[21]The parallels to the present day situation are assessed in Perroni and Whalley (1996).

[22]There has been an active debate on regionalism in the trading system, and its implications both good and bad. See Bergsten (1997), Perroni and Whalley (1998), and Frankel (1998).

References

Armstrong, H.W. and R. Read (1998). "Trade and Growth in Small States: The Impact of Global Trade Liberalization", *The World Economy*, Vol. 21, No. 4, June 1998, pp. 563-585.

Bergsten, F. (1997). "Open Regionalism", *The World Economy*, Vol. 20, No. 5, August 1997, pp. 545-566.

Blackhurst, R. (1997). "The WTO and The Global Economy", *The World Economy*, Vol.20, No. 5, August 1997, pp. 527-544.

Feenstra, R. and G. Hanson (1996). "Globalization, Outsourcing, and Wage Inequality", *American Economic Review*, May, Vol. 86, No. 2, pp. 240-245.

Frankel, J.A.(ed) (1998). *The Regionalization of the World Economy*, University of Chicago Press, for the National Bureau of Economic Research, Chicago.

GATT (1994). "News of the Uruguay Round of Multilateral Trade Negotiations", Information and Media Relations Division of GATT, April 12th.

Hamilton, C. and J. Whalley (1996). *The Trading System After the Uruguay Round*, The Institute of International Economics, Washington, D.C.

Kindleberger, C.P. (1975). *The World in Depression, 1929-1939*, London: Allen Lane Penguin Press.

Kreuger, A.O. (1998) "Whither the World Bank and the IMF?" *Journal of Economic Literature*, December, Vol. 36, pp.1983-2020.

Laird, S. (1998). "Multilateral Approaches to Market Access Negotiations", paper prepared for a conference on Multilateral and Regional Trade Agreements: An Analysis of Current Trade Policy Issues, organized by the Organization of American States, WTO, and Georgetown University, and held in Washington, D.C. May 26-27, 1998.

Martin, W. and A. Winters (ed) (1995). *The Uruguay Round and The Developing Countries*, World Bank Discussion Paper No. 307, World Bank, Washington, D.C.

Michaelopoulos, C. (1998). "The Developing Countries in the WTO" (mimeo) and forthcoming in *The World Economy*.

Mwega, F.M. and K.L. Muga (1998). "Africa and the World Trading System: A Case Study of Kenya", paper presented to an African Economic Research Consortium workshop, Mombasa, Kenya, April 26-29, 1998.

Perroni, C. and J. Whalley (1996). "How Severe is Global Retaliation Risk Under Increasing Regionalism?", *American Economic Reviews (Papers and Proceedings)*, May 1996, Vol. 86, No. 2, pp. 57-61.

Perroni, C. and J. Whalley (1998). "The New Regionalism: Trade Liberalization or Insurance?", *Canadian Journal of Economics*, to appear.

Piggott, J.R., J. Whalley, and R.M. Wigle (1992). "International Linkages and Carbon Reduction Initiatives" in K. Anderson and R. Blackhurst (eds.), *The Greening of World Trade Issues*.

Rodrick, D. (1998). "Globalization, Social Conflict and Economic Growth", *The World Economy*, Vol. 21, No. 2, March 1998, pp. 143-158.

Schott, J.J. (Ed) (1998). *Launching New Global Trade Talks: An Action Agenda*, Institute for International Economics, Washington, D.C. Special Report No. 112.

Spinager, D. (1998a). "Textiles Beyond the MFA Phase Out", paper presented to a conference in honour of the 50th Anniversary of GATT/WTO, Warwick University, UK, July 7-10th, 1996.

Spinager, D. (1998b). "Background Statistics of Anti Dumping Measures", paper presented at a meeting of an Ad Hoc Expert Group of the Secretary General of UNCTAD on Preparing for Future Multilateral Negotiations, Geneva, September 21-22, 1998.

Thomas, H. and J. Whalley (1998). *Uruguay Round Results and the Emerging Trade Agenda*, UNCTAD.

Tussie, D. (1998). "Argentina and the WTO: As Good As It Gets", paper presented at a meeting of an Ad Hoc Expert Group of the Secretary General of UNCTAD on Preparing for Future Multilateral Negotiations, Geneva, September 21-22, 1998.

Uimonen, P. and J. Whalley (1997). *Environmental Issues in the New World Trading System*, Macmillan, London.

UNCTAD (1997a). *Handbook of International Trade and Development Statistics*, 1995, New York and Geneva.

UNCTAD (1997b). *World Investment Report*, 1997, Transnational Corporations, Market Structure, and Competition Policy.

Whalley, J. (1989). *The Uruguay Round and Beyond: Developing Countries in the Global Trading System*, Macmillan, London.

Whalley, J. (1990). "Special and Differential Treatment for Developing Countries in the Uruguay Round", *Economic Journal*, Vol.100, No.403, pp.1318-1328.

Whalley, J. (1996). "Trade and Environment Beyond Singapore", National Bureau of Economic Research Working Paper No. 5768, September 1996.

Whalley, J. (1998). "The Architecture of a New Millennium Round", paper presented to a conference on the 50th Anniversary of the GATT/WTO at Warwick University, July, 1998, and to appear in *The World Economy*.

WTO (1998a). *World Trade Organization Annual Report*, 1997, Geneva.

WTO (1998b). *Electronic Commerce and the Role of the WTO*, 1998, Geneva.

World Tourism Organization (1996). *Compendium of Tourism Statistics, 1990-94, Sixteenth Edition*, Madrid.

Yeats, A. (1994). "A Quantitative Assessment of the Uruguay Round's Effects and Their Implications for Developing Countries", Washington, D.C., World Bank PRE Working Papers Series, processed.

HUMAN DEVELOPMENT REPORT *CD-ROM: Ten Years of People-Centred Development, 1990-1999*

This 10-year Anniversary CD-ROM includes the full texts of Human Development Reports 1990-1999, the complete statistical data set for HDR 1999 and a full reference section on key human development terms, methods and resources. A comprehensive, user-friendly research tool, and an exciting introduction for the novice to human development. *Available in English only.*

HUMAN DEVELOPMENT REPORT *Statistical Databases*

Presents all the statistics in the 1998 and 1997 Human Development Reports in a user-friendly format for rapid retrieval on several diskettes. For use on personal computers. *Available in English only.*

- Human Development Report 1998 Statistical Database and User's Guide
  ISBN 92-1-126103-1 $24.95

- Human Development Report 1997 Statistical Database and User's Guide
  ISBN 92-1-126089-2 $24.95

HUMAN DEVELOPMENT REPORT *Background Papers*

Includes the best Background Papers commissioned for each Human Development Report. The collections provide detailed examination of the measurement tools, policies and issues discussed in each annual Report. *Available in English only.*

- Background Papers '99 Vols. 1 and II: Human Development Report
  Globalization with a Human Face
  450 pages for Vol. I and 220 pages for Vol. II
  ISBN 92-1-126116-3 $29.95

- Background Papers '98: Human Development Report
  Consumption for Human Development
  296 pages. ISBN 92-1-126102-3 $19.95

- Background Papers '97: Human Development Report
  Human Development to Eradicate Poverty
  240 pages. ISBN 92-1-126081-7 $19.95

Visit us in cyberspace!

Selections of past Human Development Reports and background studies prepared for the reports are now on the worldwide web: http://www.undp.org/hdro

To order the *Human Development Report CD-ROM, Statistical Databases or Background Papers*:

Mail oder: UN Publications
Room DC2-853, Dept. 1004
New York, NY 10017 USA
Tel: (800) 253-9646
Fax: (212) 963-3489
http://www.un.org/Pubs/catalog.htm

United Nations Publications, Sales Office and Bookshop, CH-1211, Geneva 10
Switzerland
Tel: (41-1) 917-2614
E-mail: unpublic@unog.ch

The Human Development Report is published in 10 languages. To order copies, please contact:

English:

Oxford University Press
2001 Evans Road, Cary, NC 27513, USA
Tel: (800) 451-7556 http://www.oup-usa.org
Fax orders from the US or Canada to: (919) 677-1303
Fax orders from other countries to: (212) 726-6453

Oxford University Press, Great Clarendon St., Oxford, OX2 6DP UK
Tel: (44 1865) 556-767; Fax: (44 1865) 556-646 http://www1.oup.co.uk

---

Catalan:

UNESCO de Catalunya
Mallorca, 285
08037 Barcelona, Spain
Tel: (34-93) 458 9595; Fax: (34-93) 457 5851

French:

Groupe De Boeck
Fond Jean-Pâques, 4
B-1348, Louvain-la-Neuve, Belgium
Tel: (32-10) 48 25 11; Fax: (32-10) 48 26 50

German:

UNO-Verlag GmbH
Dag-Hammarskjöld-Haus
Poppelsdorfer Allee 55
D-53115 Bonn, Germany
Tel: (49-228) 21 36 46; Fax: (49-228) 21 74 92

Italian:

Rosenberg & Sellier
Editori in Torino, Via Andrea Doria 14
10123 Torino, Italy
Tel: (39-11) 812 7820; Fax: (39-11) 812 7808

Japanese:

UNDP Liaison Office/Japan
UNU Building,
53-70 Jingumae, 8th Floor
5-chome, Shibuya-ku, Tokyo 150, Japan
Tel: (81-35) 467 4751; Fax: (81-35) 467 4753

Portuguese:

Trinova Editora, Ida.
Rua das Salgadeiras, 36-20 Esq0
1200 Lisboa, Portugal
Tel: (351-1) 347 5715; Fax: (351-1) 342 0751

Russian:

Forssan Kirjapaino Oy
Box 38, Esko Aaltosen katu 2
FIN-30100 Forssa, Finland
Tel: (358-3) 4155 703; Fax: (358-3) 4155 737

Spanish:

Ediciones Mundi-Prensa, s.a.
Castelló, 37
28001 Madrid, Spain
Tel: (34-91) 436 3700; Fax: (34-91) 575-3998

or:

Ediciones Mundi-Prensa, s.a.
Rio Pánuco 141
Col. Cuauhtémoc 06500
México, DF, Mexico
Tel: (52-4) 533 5658; Fax: (52-2) 514 6799

Arabic:

Please contact your local UNDP office.